AF797911

A Half-Century with the Internal Revenue Code

CAROLINA ACADEMIC PRESS
Legal History Series
H. Jefferson Powell, Series Editor

AMERICAN CONSTITUTIONAL LAW
Selected Essays
Henry Paul Monaghan

THE BIRTH OF AMERICAN LAW
An Italian Philosopher and the American Revolution
John D. Bessler

FEDERAL JUSTICE IN THE MID-ATLANTIC SOUTH
United States Courts from Maryland to the Carolinas 1836–1861
Peter Graham Fish

THE FETHA NAGAST
The Law of the Kings
Abba Paulos Tzadua, translator, and Peter L. Strauss

GENTLEMEN OF THE GRAND JURY
The Surviving Grand Jury Charges from Colonial, State, and Lower Federal Courts Before 1801
Stanton D. Krauss, editor

A HALF-CENTURY WITH THE INTERNAL REVENUE CODE
The Memoirs of Stanley S. Surrey
Lawrence Zelenak & Ajay K. Mehrotra, editors

JIM CROW IN NORTH CAROLINA
The Legislative Program from 1865 to 1920
Richard A. Paschal

LAW IN WAR, WAR AS LAW
Brigadier General Joseph Holt and the Judge Advocate General's Department in the Civil War and Early Reconstruction, 1861–1865
Joshua E. Kastenberg

LOST IN TRANSLATIONS
Roman Law Scholarship and Translation in Early Twentieth-Century America
Timothy G. Kearley

LOUIS D. BRANDEIS'S MIT LECTURES ON LAW (1892–1894)
Robert F. Cochran, Jr., editor

NEWSPAPER REPORTS OF DECISIONS IN COLONIAL, STATE,
AND LOWER FEDERAL COURTS BEFORE 1801
Stanton D. Krauss, editor

OUR CHIEF MAGISTRATE AND HIS POWERS
William Howard Taft
with Foreword, Introduction, and Notes by
H. Jefferson Powell

THE QUOTABLE BRANDEIS
Peter Scott Campbell, editor

THREE NEGLECTED PIECES OF THE DOCUMENTARY HISTORY
OF THE CONSTITUTION AND BILL OF RIGHTS
Remarks on the Amendments to the Constitution by a Foreign Spectator,
Essays of the Centinel, Revived, and Extracts from the Virginia Senate Journal
Stanton D. Krauss, editor

A VIEW OF THE CONSTITUTION OF THE UNITED STATES OF AMERICA
Second Edition
William Rawle
with Foreword, Introduction, and Notes by
H. Jefferson Powell

A Half-Century with the Internal Revenue Code

The Memoirs of Stanley S. Surrey

EDITED BY

Lawrence Zelenak

Ajay K. Mehrotra

Carolina Academic Press

Durham, North Carolina

LIBRARY OF CONGRESS CATALOGING-IN-PUBLICATION DATA

Names: Surrey, Stanley S. | Zelenak, Lawrence, editor. | Mehrotra, Ajay K., 1969- editor.
Title: A half-century with the Internal Revenue Code : the memoirs of Stanley S. Surrey / edited by Lawrence Zelenak, Ajay Mehrotra.
Description: Durham, North Carolina : Carolina Academic Press, LLC, 2021. | Series: Legal history series
Identifiers: LCCN 2021045131 (print) | LCCN 2021045132 (ebook) | ISBN 9781531021184 (paperback) | ISBN 9781531021191 (ebook)
Subjects: LCSH: Surrey, Stanley S. | Law teachers--United States--Biography. | United States--Officials and employees--Biography. | Tax expenditures--Law and legislation--United States. | Tax administration and procedure--United States. | Internal revenue law--United States.
Classification: LCC KF373.S86 S86 2021 (print) | LCC KF373.S86 (ebook) | DDC 340.092 [B]--dc23/eng/20211105
LC record available at https://lccn.loc.gov/2021045131
LC ebook record available at https://lccn.loc.gov/2021045132

Carolina Academic Press, LLC
700 Kent Street
Durham, North Carolina 27701
(919) 489-7486
www.cap-press.com

Printed in the United States of America

Editors' Table of Contents

Editors' Notes and Acknowledgments

This book is the formal publication of the typescript memoirs drafted by Stanley S. Surrey in the 1980s, before his death in 1984. The editors have attempted to keep nearly all aspects of the original, unpublished memoir manuscript intact, with a few editorial revisions. First, we have annotated the memoirs by adding numbered, editorial footnotes in places where greater context and background, especially regarding key individuals and events, seemed most appropriate. In the process, we have maintained Surrey's original sequenced endnotes at the end of each of the chapters (we have transformed Surrey's numerical endnotes into alphabetical endnotes to distinguish them from our editorial footnotes). Second, we have deleted or condensed long quotations in the memoirs that Surrey reproduced from published reports or books that can be easily found elsewhere. In these cases, we have noted the omission or condensation in the text or in an editorial footnote. We have also left intact many of Surrey's draft notes to himself in the manuscript (usually expressed by Surrey in brackets), except in those cases where any uncertainty about Surrey's notes could be easily resolved. Third, the original, unpublished memoirs did not include Surrey's anticipated final "Chapter 11: Tax Expenditure Analysis – A New Fiscal Concept, 1968 to date," though Surrey's annotated table of contents provides insights into his organization for the chapter. Finally, we have drafted an original introductory essay to help place Surrey and his ideas into a broader historical context and to provide our own assessment of his scholarship and his contributions to twentieth-century tax policy. Our introductory essay, "Stanley S. Surrey: A Life in Taxes," follows these notes and acknowledgements.

Many individuals and institutions supported this project and our introductory essay. We are particularly grateful to Edwin Moloy, Curator of Modern Manuscripts, and the Harvard Law School Archives for their overall assistance and permission to publish the Surrey memoirs. We would also like to thank the American Bar Foundation, Duke Law School, and Northwestern University Pritzker School of Law for their support. Others who assisted us with this project include: Dan Halperin for his explanation of how the typescript memoirs reached the archives; Peter Murray for directing us to articles co-authored by Murray and Surrey about their sailing adventures in Canada; H.A. Kogels and Peter Barnes for their assistance in identifying Surrey's predecessors (or lack thereof) as U.S. representatives to the Permanent Scientific Committee of the International Fiscal Association; Theresa Boyce for her tireless efforts in converting Surrey's twentieth-century typescript into a twenty-first century word processing document; Assaf Harpaz for his equally tireless work and valuable feedback on the editorial footnotes; Ryland Bowman and Steve Oliva at Carolina Academic Press for their editorial assistance; and Jeff Powell, the academic series editor, who first encouraged us to pursue this project.

Earlier versions of our introductory essay were presented at academic workshops and shared with colleagues and friends. We are thankful for the feedback we received from participants at Duke University School of Law, Florida State University School of Law, University of Miami School of Law, and the University of Southern California School of Law. Many individuals provided outstanding comments and assistance on our essay including, Reuven Avi-Yonah, Mirit Eyal-Cohen, Dan Ernst, Dan Halperin, Assaf Harpaz, Ed McCaffery, Mike Simkovic, Joe Thorndike, and George Yin. Colleagues and students at Northwestern University Pritzker School of Law and the American Bar Foundation provided excellent research assistance: many thanks to Matt Childers, Oren Depp, Jay Kaganoff, Ebenezer Ng, Jeff Svehla, and especially Clare Gaynor Willis and Brittany Nicole Adams for their research assistance on the early life of Stanley Surrey.

Editors' Introduction

Stanley S. Surrey: A Life in Taxes

Stanley S. Surrey's professional life with the federal tax system spanned half a century, starting with his co-authored publication of an article on the estate tax in the *Columbia Law Review* in 1932,[1] and ending only with his death in 1984 when he was still at work on his memoirs. As he writes in his introduction to these memoirs, Surrey had good reason to "doubt that any person alive today has had as close and as varied a relationship with the Internal Revenue Code as I have had."[2] Not seeking the financial rewards that could surely have been his from the private practice of tax law (although he took on private consulting work on occasion), Surrey divided the five decades of his professional life between academia and government service. His academic career spanned three early years at the University of California, Berkeley, School of Law, followed by three decades at Harvard Law School. Meanwhile, his time in government consisted of two lengthy tours of duty in the service of the U.S. Treasury Department. First, from 1937 to 1947, he served initially as a temporary advisor and then as Tax Legislative Counsel for the last five of those years. And from 1961 to 1969, as the Assistant Secretary of the Treasury for Tax Policy, Surrey occupied the highest position in the executive branch exclusively focused on tax policy.[3]

As an academic Surrey was remarkably prolific and influential. In a memorial tribute published in the *Harvard Law Review* shortly after Surrey's death, Erwin N. Griswold described Surrey as "[b]y common consent the greatest tax scholar of his generation."[4] Along with its collection of tributes to Surrey, the law review included

---

1. Jacob P. Aronson and Stanley S. Surrey, *Inter Vivos Transfers and the Federal Estate Tax*, 32 Colum. L. Rev. 1332 (1932).

2. *See* Introduction, at p. liii.

3. Although the memoirs have remained an unpublished part of the Stanley S. Surrey personal papers at the Historical and Special Collections division of the Harvard Law School Library, several scholars have relied on the memoirs to explore Surrey's career and his influence over tax policy. *See, e.g.*, Reuven S Avi-Yonah, Nir Fishbien, and Gianluca Mazzoni, *Stanley Surrey, the Code and the Regime, Available at* SSRN 3414965 (2019); George K Yin, *Who Speaks for Tax Equity and Tax Fairness: Stanley Surrey and the Tax Legislative Process* Va. Tax. Rev. 39 (2019); Dennis J. Ventry, Jr. *The Collision of Tax and Welfare Politics: The Political History of the Earned Income Tax Credit, 1969–99*, Nat. Tax J. 53:4 (2000), 983–1026.

4. Erwin N. Griswold, *A True Public Servant*, 98 Harv. L. Rev. 329, 331 (1984). Griswold was himself a tax law scholar and lawyer whose distinguished career in the academy and government service overlapped with Surrey's. Dennis Hevesi, *Erwin Griswold Is Dead at 90; Served as a Solicitor General*, New York Times, Nov. 21, 1994, at B10.

a bibliography of Surrey's published books and articles, listing eighteen books and well over one hundred articles, papers, and essays.[5] These publications shaped generations of tax scholarship. A recent study found that, as of 1970, Surrey was the most cited tax law scholar, with more than twice the citations of his closest contemporary and occasional rival, Boris I. Bittker.[6] (More on his rivalry with Bittker later in this essay.)

Surrey's impact as an academic, however, went well beyond citation counts. As a tax law teacher for over three decades and a founding member of the Harvard Law School International Tax Program, Surrey also left a lasting legacy as a mentor and academic institution builder. Through his teaching and mentorship, he influenced several tax policymakers who would go on to occupy pivotal government positions, including Donald C. Lubick and Jerome Kurtz.[7] Surrey also included among his former students and Treasury Department proteges Thomas F. Field, the founder of Tax Analysts, the publisher of *Tax Notes*.[8] Surrey even inspired a few of his students, such as Daniel I. Halperin, to follow his lead in traversing between the academy and the Treasury. In 1952, he helped establish the Harvard Law School International Tax Program, which published numerous reports about taxation in foreign jurisdictions, and brought international tax officials and professors to Harvard for an intensive educational training program. Through this initiative, Surrey had a hand in the many World Tax Series publications, and he assisted in providing training to more than 700 tax officials and teachers from all over the world, including many from developing countries.[9]

Yet Surrey's impact on tax law and policy extended well beyond his teaching and scholarship. If anything, Surrey was even more influential as a government official than as an academic. For better or worse (or better and worse), the income tax provisions of the Internal Revenue Code roughly doubled in length during Surrey's stint as the leading tax policy official in the executive branch.[10] No less an authority than Erwin Griswold attributed that change to Surrey's influence.[11] No other Assistant Secretary for Tax Policy has had nearly so high a congressional and public profile as Surrey; an edited collection of Surrey's "Selected Speeches and Testimony" while in office ran to well over 700 pages (and, to repeat, these were only his *selected* speeches).[12]

---

5. *The Writings of Stanley S. Surrey*, 98 HARV. L. REV. 346 (1984).

6. Terrance O'Reilly, *Tax Legal Scholarship to 1970*, 34 VA. TAX REV. 269, 273, tbl. 1 (2014) (showing 819 citations to Bittker and 1918 citations to Surrey).

7. *Biographical Sketch of Donald C. Lubick*, in *Hearing Before the Committee on Finance*, U.S. Senate, 94th Cong. (April 17, 1978); Emily Steel, *Jerome Kurtz, Leader of I.R.S. During Carter Era, Dies at 83*, NEW YORK TIMES, Mar. 3, 2015.

8. Joseph J. Thorndike, *The Battle For Transparency In Tax*, FORBES, Aug. 5, 2020.

9. James Vorenberg in STANLEY S. SURREY, 1910–1984: PROGRAM OF MEMORIAL SERVICE HELD OCT. 3 1984 AT MEMORIAL CHURCH, HARVARD UNIVERSITY (1984) (copy on file with the authors).

10. For details, *see* Part VII of this essay.

11. Erwin N. Griswold, *Is the Tax Law Going to Seed?* 11 AM. J. TAX POL'Y 1, 5–6 (1994).

12. STANLEY S. SURREY, TAX POLICY AND TAX REFORM: 1961–1969 (William F. Hellmuth & Oliver Oldman, eds.) (1973).

Summing up Surrey's accomplishments in office, Donald C. Lubick (who himself served as Assistant Secretary for Tax Policy some years after Surrey) wrote simply that Surrey "dominated tax policy both in the United States and internationally" in the 1960s.[13] Although Surrey was not to serve a third time in Washington, in 1976 he co-chaired a task force to provide tax background material for Jimmy Carter's presidential campaign, and after Carter took office Surrey served as an official advisor to the White House and to Assistant Secretary for Tax Policy Donald Lubick.

For Surrey, the academic and policymaking aspects of his career were part and parcel of his overall professional identity. As William D. Andrews wrote in his memorial tribute to Surrey, "The remarkable thing about Stanley Surrey's career is that neither public service nor teaching represented time out from the other; they were integrally intertwined aspects of a single enterprise. His life represented a nearly perfect unity of thought and action."[14] This introductory essay attempts to provide some historical context for the arc of an exceptional career that was built on this unity of thought and action. The outstanding example of that unity was Surrey's decades-long campaign to educate both Congress and the public about the existence, scope, and often pernicious effects of what he termed "tax expenditures." He defined tax expenditures as "a system ... under which Governmental financial assistance programs are carried out through special tax provisions rather than through direct Government expenditures."[15] We explore and assess Surrey's view of tax expenditures in greater detail later in this introduction.[16] For present purposes the crucial point is that Surrey's successful efforts at Treasury to institutionalize his vision of a tax expenditure budget, and his scholarly writings on tax expenditures (culminating in his 1974 publication of a monograph on tax expenditures[17]) were closely integrated aspects of a single massive anti-tax expenditure campaign.

Standing alone, either his law school career or his Treasury career would have been more than enough accomplishment for one lifetime, but even taken together they were far from the entirety of Surrey's professional achievements. In the late 1940s and early 1950s, Surrey served as the Chief Reporter for the American Law Institute's Income Tax Project, which in early 1954 produced a draft statute (accompanied by lengthy explanatory notes) "cover[ing] most of the substantive provisions ... relating to the income taxation of individuals, corporations, partnerships, and trusts."[18] The ALI's model income tax statute appeared just in time for consideration by Congress in its drafting of what became the Internal Revenue Code

13. Donald C. Lubick, *A View from Washington*, 98 HARV. L. REV. 338, 338 (1984).

14. William D. Andrews, *A Source of Inspiration*, 98 HARV. L. REV. 332, 332 (1984).

15. Stanley S. Surrey, excerpts from remarks before the Money Marketeers on *The U.S. Income Tax System: The Need for a Full Accounting*, Nov. 15, 1967, in U.S. Department of Treasury, *Annual Report of the Secretary of the Treasury on the State of the Finances for the Fiscal Year Ended June 30, 1968* (1969), at 322.

16. *See* part II.B of this essay.

17. STANLEY S. SURREY, PATHWAYS TO TAX REFORM (1973).

18. American Law Institute, Federal Income Tax Statute, Vol. 1, xxxi (February 1954 draft).

of 1954, and Congress borrowed substantial portions of the 1954 Code from the ALI model.[19]

Nor was it enough for Surrey to put his stamp on the tax system of only the United States. He was an influential member of the post-war Shoup tax mission to Japan (1949–1950), the recommendations of which continue to shape Japanese tax law even today. In the decades following his efforts in Japan, Surrey crossed the globe providing tax system design advice to the governments of numerous countries, including Venezuela, Argentina, Japan (again), India, Indonesia, North Yemen, Saudi Arabia, Syria, Israel, and China.[20]

I. The Making of an "Activist Scholar"

That Stanley Surrey would one day become a globe-trotting tax advisor would not have been obvious to young Surrey himself or to any of his early friends and colleagues. Yet, by the end of his career, Surrey would be well-known and highly respected, in the words of Griswold again, as "an activist scholar who wanted to see his scholarship put to work."[21] To understand how Surrey became an "activist scholar" and an international tax advisor, one must understand the long intellectual odyssey that marked his life.

Stanley Sterling Surrey was born in New York City on October 3, 1910, the first son of a relatively affluent Russian Jewish family. His father Samuel was born in Russia and immigrated to the United States with his parents when he was a child. Samuel worked for the Continental Oil Company for most of his adult life, and he apparently changed the family name from "Serhey" to "Surrey" sometime in the 1920s, perhaps in an effort to assimilate to American culture. Stanley Surrey's mother Pauline (Sterling) Surrey was also the child of Russian Jewish immigrants who settled in New York City. She was a schoolteacher for much of her career and eventually retired as head of the mental hygiene program at Abraham Lincoln High School in Brooklyn.[22] Together, Surrey's parents seemed to provide a supportive family environment that nurtured Stanley's interests and those of his youngest brother Walter, who would go on to become a leading international business lawyer. The Surreys

19. For more on the ALI's Income Tax Project and its influence on the 1954 Code, *see generally*, Lawrence Zelenak, *The Almost-Restatement of Income Tax of 1954: When Tax Giants Roamed the Earth*, 79 Brooklyn L. Rev. 709 (2014).

20. For more on the Shoup-led tax missions, *see generally*, the essays contained in The Political Economy of Transnational Tax Reform: The Shoup Mission to Japan in Historical Context (eds. W. Elliot Brownlee, Eisaku Ide, and Yasunori Fukagai, 2013).

21. Griswold, A True Public Servant, supra note 4.

22. Much of Surrey's family history was constructed from census data and other public documents. *Mrs. Pauline S. Surrey*, New York Times, Mar. 2, 1964; *Stanley S. Surrey Oral History* (interview with Judith H. Byne, April 13, 1970) Kheel Center for Labor-Management Documentation and Archives, Cornell University Library. *See also*, Avi-Yonah, *supra* note 3. Special thanks to reference librarians Clare Gaynor Willis and Brittany Nichole Adams of the Pritzker Legal Research Center at Northwestern Pritzker School of Law for their assistance, including the genealogical research that helped create a Surrey family tree (copy on file with the authors).

lived for a time in western Canada and Denver, Colorado, probably because of Samuel's job with Continental Oil, but the family returned to New York when Stanley was a teenager. Both sons remained in the United States to continue their formal education and legal careers.[23]

Young Stanley, or "Stan" to his friends, was an excellent student. At the age of 19, he graduated *magna cum laude* and Phi Beta Kappa from the City College of New York (CCNY) with a degree in history. At the time, CCNY was known for its open admissions policy and its progressive politics. While the country's leading colleges and universities catered mainly to the children of the native Protestant elite, CCNY became the city's preeminent institution of higher learning for generations of brilliant individuals from immigrant and working-class backgrounds.[24] Surrey capitalized on his educational opportunities. After excelling in college, he initially sought to continue his interests in history by enrolling in Columbia University's graduate history program. But because he was uncertain about his future career goals, he also applied and was admitted to Harvard Law School. Upon deeper self-reflection, Surrey was unsure whether he wanted to be a historian, and thus before starting graduate school, he decided "as a matter of default," as he explained, "to go to law school."[25] By this late date, it was not possible for him to matriculate at Harvard, but he was able to enroll at Columbia Law School.

When Surrey began law school in 1929, Columbia was not only one of the country's leading law schools, it was also a hotbed of American legal realism—a factor that was not lost on Surrey. American legal realism was an early twentieth century jurisprudential movement that challenged the prevailing orthodoxy that law was a closed and autonomous system of abstract rules that could be studied logically and verified deductively from an *a priori* understanding of law "on the books." By contrast, many legal realists, including those at Columbia who would influence Surrey, contended that law was integrated with society and that to understand how law operated "in action," one needed to study empirically how legal actors actually behaved, and how everyday people shaped and responded to law, legal institutions, and legal processes.[26] This would be a lesson that Surrey took to heart, especially during his

---

23. Apparently, Stanley was born in New York City at a time when his parents were already living in Canada. In a 1961 address before the Canadian Tax Foundation, Surrey mentioned his "strong claim to a Canadian character." As he explained: "My parents, originally from New York, were living in Western Canada at the time. They rushed back to New York at about the last minute impelled by some unreasoning desire that I should be able to claim that as my birthplace—and then at once returned to Canada." Stanley S. Surrey, *Aspects of Tax Policy in the United States*, in TAX POLICY AND TAX REFORM: 1961–1969 (ed. Hellmuth and Oldman, 1973) at 24.

24. JAMES TAUB, CITY ON A HILL: TESTING THE AMERICAN DREAM AT CITY COLLEGE (1994); THOMAS BENDER, NEW YORK INTELLECT: A HISTORY OF INTELLECTUAL LIFE IN NEW YORK CITY FROM 1750 TO THE BEGINNINGS OF OUR OWN TIME (1998).

25. *See* chapter 1, Surrey's note a.

26. Roscoe Pound, *Law in Books and Law in Action*, AM. L. REV. 44(1): 12–36 (1910); Karl N. Llewellyn, *Some Realism about Realism—Responding to Dean Pound*, HARV. L. REV. 44 (1931). For more on realism at Columbia Law School, *see generally*, JOHN H. SCHLEGEL, AMERICAN LEGAL REALISM

many international tax missions when he interviewed everyday taxpayers about their interaction with tax authorities.

During Surrey's time at Columbia, the law school boasted several leading realists, including Karl Llewellyn, Milton Handler, and Robert Hale. Surrey did not explicitly identify himself as a student of realism, though Handler did become an important influence on his life. As an antitrust scholar and teacher, Handler typified legal realism's focus on interdisciplinary approaches to the study of law; he worked closely, for example, with economists at Columbia and elsewhere in analyzing U.S. antitrust law and policy.[27] Surrey apparently disliked Llewellyn, whom he described as a "flashy" teacher who "dramatically shouted complex nonsense to frighten or hypnotize the first-year Contracts class."[28] Nevertheless, Surrey's lifelong commitment to merging academic ideas with practical policymaking and his affinity for working with public finance economists suggests that he absorbed many of the lessons of realism, especially Handler's interest in working with scholars outside of the law school. Indeed, law school seemed to stir in Surrey the start of what William Andrews referred to as "a nearly perfect unity of thought and action."[29] Reflecting back on his legal education, Surrey noted that "Columbia then was an exciting, vibrant school pursuing untraditional legal approaches and teaching, which did force those who met its challenge to think about the world rather than to accept matters just because they were around."[30] No realist could have put it more plainly.

While Surrey may have been repelled by Llewellyn's flamboyant teaching style, he seemed more suited to the "dry, taciturn" approach of Roswell Magill, who along with the junior professor Handler, became one of Surrey's early mentors.[31] Magill was Surrey's first-year Civil Procedure professor. Although Surrey found the course "dull and uninspiring," his class paper — on "a most dismal case" about the notice requirements necessary to call a valid shareholders meeting — caught Magill's attention and apparent admiration. As a result, Surrey developed a fondness for "this astringent teacher." Because Magill taught Taxation as an elective in the second year, Surrey took the course. At the time, law school tax courses dealt mainly with constitutional issues related to the tax jurisdiction of state governments, with only minor attention to federal taxation. With this one class, Surrey exhausted Columbia's tax curriculum. In his final law school year, he devoted most of his energies to the *Columbia Law Review* where he began as Book Review Editor and later became Managing Editor. He graduated second in his class as a three-year James Kent Scholar, the law school's highest honor for academic achievement. He was just 22.[32]

AND EMPIRICAL SOCIAL SCIENCE (1995); NATALIE E. HULL, ROSCOE POUND AND KARL LLEWELLYN: SEARCHING FOR AN AMERICAN JURISPRUDENCE (1997); LAURA KALMAN, LEGAL REALISM AT YALE, 1927–1960 (1986), Ch. 3; WILLIAM TWINING, KARL LLEWELLYN AND THE REALIST MOVEMENT (1973).

27. Milton Handler, *Unfair Competition*, 21 IOWA L. REV. 175 (1935).

28. *See* chapter 1, at p. 4.

29. Andrews, *A Source of Inspiration*, 98 HARV. L. REV. 332, 332 (1984).

30. *See* chapter 1, at Surrey's note a.

31. *Id.* at p. 3–4.

32. *Id.* at p. 6.

By the time Surrey graduated in 1932, the Great Depression had intensified and jobs with New York's leading law firms were scarce. With unemployment soaring, banks failing at a breakneck pace, and top Wall Street law firms still clinging to a covert anti-Semitism, Surrey likely faced significant challenges in securing a position with a prestigious law firm to match his outstanding academic credentials. Moreover, Surrey was deeply ambivalent about leaving "the interesting world of the Law School and the fascination [he had] found in the Law Review work."[33] Fortunately, he was able to defer his career decisions when Magill hired Surrey as a fulltime, one-year research assistant—a highly formative experience that would mold the young law graduate's thinking about taxation.

Magill was part of a team of Columbia University faculty which had secured a major grant from the Twentieth Century Fund—a New York-based nonpartisan research foundation—to study the country's current tax problems. The project, which focused initially on the federal income tax, was led by Carl Shoup, a young Columbia University economist who would go on to work closely with Surrey in the Treasury Department and on many international tax missions.[34] As part of the Twentieth Century Fund project, Shoup and other economists, including Shoup's Columbia mentor Robert Murray Haig, were responsible for analyzing the economic concepts of income. Meanwhile, Magill, with Surrey's assistance, focused on the legal aspects. Surrey was called upon, as he recounted, to survey "almost the entire structure of the income tax." Reflecting on this experience, Surrey proudly noted that he worked autonomously from Magill on a project that "was the first of its kind since no one had yet attempted a coordinated structural analysis of the federal income tax that covered both theory and substantive rules, in statute and cases." He found the research both "challenging and difficult." Most importantly, the experience left him with a broad-based conceptual map, an intellectual lodestar, that would guide his career as an "activist scholar." As he explained in his memoirs:

> I was forced to find the theoretical strands that held the structure together. As a result, I had the rare opportunity early on to obtain a sense of that structure as a whole and to understand that the structure could be analyzed and dealt with in logical terms. A rational framework could be devised for the structure and in turn structural errors could be perceived. I saw the income tax not as a random body of rules and edicts but as an internally consistent framework. All of my later work has been dominated by that approach.[35]

---

33. *Id.* at p. 6.

34. For more on the broader Twentieth Century Fund project and the interdisciplinary environment of Columbia University at the time, *see generally*, Ajay K. Mehrotra, *From Seligman to Shoup: The Early Columbia School of Taxation and Development*, in THE POLITICAL ECONOMY OF TRANSNATIONAL TAX REFORM: THE SHOUP MISSION TO JAPAN IN HISTORICAL CONTEXT 30–60 (eds. W. Elliot Brownlee, Eisaku Ide, and Yasunori Fukagai, 2013), at 44–5.

35. *See* chapter 1, at p. 7. Eventually, the larger Twentieth Century Fund project resulted in Magill's 1936 book and a Shoup-led 1937 publication. ROSWELL MAGILL, TAXABLE INCOME (1936); CARL S. SHOUP, ET AL. FACING THE TAX PROBLEM: A SURVEY OF TAXATION IN THE UNITED STATES AND PROGRAM FOR THE FUTURE (1937).

The explicit references to a "rational framework" and "structural errors" would become, as we shall see, the foundation for Surrey's life-long crusade against "tax expenditures."

Surrey did not elaborate in the memoirs on what he meant by the "internally consistent framework" that held together the income tax. A review of the publications from Magill and Shoup, and Surrey's own subsequent scholarship and policymaking, however, suggest that Surrey had in mind, as a starting point, a broad-based economic definition of income—a definition that Haig had developed in 1921, and that Shoup and Magill subscribed to.[36] Haig's definition of income would be refined famously by Henry Simons in the 1930s,[37] but the beginnings of the economic conception of income rested firmly with Haig and his cohort of public finance economists. Indeed, as economist Richard Musgrave noted in his 1984 memorial remarks, Surrey's "view of taxable income was rooted in the Schanz-Haig-Simons concept of income. Income was to be defined as total accretion to wealth or stated differently, as the sum of consumption and increase in net worth."[38]

Yet Surrey was too much of a realist and pragmatist to adhere rigidly to an abstract, conceptual definition of economic income. An effective and workable income tax, Surrey contended in his seminal 1973 book *Pathways to Tax Reform*, needed to be administratively feasible and thus had to accommodate the "generally accepted structure of the income tax" and "widely accepted definitions of income."[39] As Musgrave noted, "Surrey, ever the pragmatist, stopped short of going the whole way" toward an economic definition of income. Instead, Surrey "tolerated the omission of certain components of income even if inclusion would be required by the Schanz-Haig-Simons scheme."[40]

What Surrey did not tolerate, however, were other departures from a broad-based, comprehensive income tax base, or what he referred to as "structural errors." The deductions for mortgage interest and charitable contributions, for example, and the exclusion of interest from state and municipal bonds were the types of "tax expenditures" that Surrey singled out for elimination from the Internal Revenue Code.[41] In subsequent writings, Surrey would elaborate on the tax expenditure concept (with his co-author Paul R. McDaniel) by distinguishing between the "structural provisions necessary to implement a normal income tax, such as the definition of net income" and those "special preferences found in every income tax." The "special provisions" were "departures from the normative tax structure." And "whatever their form" they

---

36. Robert Murray Haig, *The Concept of Income—Economic and Legal Aspects*, in The Federal Income Tax 1, 7 (Robert Murray Haig ed., 1921).

37. Henry C. Simons, Personal Income Taxation: The Definition of Income as a Problem of Fiscal Policy (1938).

38. Richard A. Musgrave, *Pathways to Tax Reform*, 98 Harv. L. Rev. 335, 335 (1984). For more on the origins and historical development of this line of thinking about the economic definition of income, *see* W. Elliot Brownlee, Federal Taxation in America 129–31(2004).

39. Surrey, *supra* note 17.

40. Musgrave, *supra* note 38, at 335.

41. Stanley S. Surrey, *The Federal Income Tax Base for Individuals*, 58 Colum. L. Rev. 815 (1958).

represented "government spending for favored activities or groups, effected through the tax system rather than through direct grants, loans, or other forms of government assistance."[42] As we shall see, Surrey's reliance on this normative baseline to identify and measure "tax expenditures" was scrutinized and criticized by other academics and intellectuals—often to great effect.[43]

It would, of course, be implausible to suggest that Surrey had worked out his entire conception of tax expenditures and the importance of maintaining the integrity of a comprehensive income tax base back in 1932 when he assisted Magill with his influential book. Nonetheless, the seeds of one of Surrey's major contributions to tax scholarship and policymaking were clearly being planted early in his career, as he noted in his memoirs. And there was more during these early years. While he worked for Magill, Surrey began researching and writing about other aspects of tax law. In 1932, he co-authored his first law review article with his law school classmate, Jack Aronson, on the constitutionality of applying the federal estate tax to donative lifetime transfers.[44] He followed that publication with a second law review article about the doctrine of assignment of income.[45] Surrey's profile as an aspiring tax law academic seemed to be taking shape.

If working as Magill's research assistant was a formative experience for Surrey, the next chapter of his life would take his legal career in a dramatically different direction. After his year with Magill, Surrey ambivalently became a junior associate at the law firm of Proskauer, Rose, and Paskus, a position secured through his law school friend and co-author Jack Aronson. At the time, Proskauer was known as one of the "traditional" New York City Jewish law firms, with a practice area catering mainly to the personal, family, and real estate matters of prominent Jewish families.[46] Surrey's time in private practice was short lived, however. Within months, he grew restless with the "deadly dull" assignments he received, which did not appear to include any tax matters. Looking for his next challenge, Surrey turned to government service at a time when many law graduates and faculty members from schools like Columbia and Yale, including many legal realists, were attracted to the energy and vitality of President Franklin D. Roosevelt's New Deal. Indeed, the New Deal became a professional sanctuary for many talented Jewish lawyers during the Depression.[47]

---

42. Stanley S. Surrey and Paul R. McDaniel, Tax Expenditures (1985), at 3.

43. *See* sections V. B. and VI below.

44. Aronson and Surrey, *supra* note 1.

45. Stanley S. Surrey, *Assignment of Income and Related Devices: Choice of the Taxable Person*, 33 Colum. L. Rev. 791 (1933). Surrey later reflected on how this publication was read by Erwin Griswold, who at the time was a lawyer in the Solicitor General's office, and would as Dean of the Harvard Law School later recruit Surrey to teach at Harvard. *See* chapter 1, p. 8–9.

46. Eli Wald, *The Rise of the Jewish Law Firm or Is the Jewish Law Firm Generic*, 76 UMKC L. Rev. 885 (2008). International Directory of Company Histories, Vol. 47 (ed. Thomas Derdak, 1988), at 308.

47. Ronen Shamir, Managing Legal Uncertainty: Elite Lawyers in the New Deal (1995). Surrey does not reflect on his assimilated Jewish heritage in his memoir. But given his background, he was likely part of an entire generation of accomplished Jewish lawyers who during the Great Depression gravitated to the professional and social appeal of the New Deal. As historian Jerold Auerbach

Surrey's former law school professor, Milton Handler, who was working at the newly created National Recovery Administration (NRA), hired Surrey to assist him with reviewing and enforcing the legal aspects of the new industry codes. Thus, Surrey began his first tour as a government lawyer not as a legal advisor to the Treasury Department, but as a lawyer for the NRA.[48]

During his two years in the NRA's Legal Division, Surrey supervised compliance with different industry codes and learned many lessons that would shape his subsequent views on law and politics. He frequently advised lawyers in the field about their litigation tactics. The irony that a young lawyer with no trial experience was managing and counseling experienced litigators "way above [him] in status" was not lost on Surrey. Still, as a young lawyer working on labor issues, Surrey learned important lessons about the precision of legal language in codes and statutes, the importance of compliance and enforcement, and how sound policy often came into tension with patronage politics. He clearly identified himself with the wing of "young, mostly liberal leaning, lawyers scarcely out of eastern law schools attracted by the excitement of the New Deal." But he learned that New Deal lawyers "were a mixed lot." And he often disapproved of the "older, mostly conservative leaning, southern attorneys needing jobs and finding them via the Congressional patronage route."[49]

While Surrey seemed to enjoy his initial government experience, the May 1935 U.S. Supreme Court ruling in *Schechter* brought the NRA to an end.[50] Surrey was forced to reevaluate his career options. He considered a return to tax law and a position with the Bureau of Internal Revenue (BIR), the forerunner of today's Internal Revenue Service (IRS). When a personal acquaintance, however, advised him against the BIR, Surrey leveraged his NRA and law school contacts to obtain a position with the newly created National Labor Relations Board (NLRB). Hence, his early career as a liberal labor lawyer continued. In his two years with the NLRB, Surrey drafted several of the board's key opinions adjudicating allegedly unfair labor practices. He was also active in the field, managing union elections. In his memoirs and NLRB oral history, he boasted that he was the "Board's expert on large plant elections."[51]

At this time, Surrey also solidified his credentials as a politically moderate, liberal New Deal lawyer. He became an active member of the Washington, D.C. chapter of the National Lawyers Guild (NLG) — an organization created to counter the conservative, anti-New Deal posture of the American Bar Association (ABA) and the Liberty

---

has noted, "The Depression generation of talented Jewish law students were saved from professional extinction, insofar as it was saved at all, only by the New Deal alphabet agencies." JEROLD S. AUERBACH, UNEQUAL JUSTICE: LAWYERS AND SOCIAL CHANGE IN MODERN AMERICA 185 (1977); *see also*, Auerbach, *From Rags to Robes: The Legal Profession, Social Mobility, and the American Jewish Experience*, AMERICAN JEWISH HISTORICAL QUARTERLY 65 (1976).

48. For a brief introduction to the NRA and its industry codes, *see generally*, JASON SCOTT, A CONCISE HISTORY OF THE NEW DEAL (2014), 45–8.

49. *See* chapter 1, at p. 14.

50. Schechter Poultry Corporation v. United States, 295 U.S. 495 (1935).

51. *See* chapter 1, at p. 17; Surrey Oral History, *supra* note 22.

League. While he was the Washington representative to the NLG's national board, Surrey recounted that "the radical, often Communist, members," of the NLG were pushing the organization "the way the Communist Party was moving at the time." Surrey wanted no part of that and consequently resigned from the NLG.[52]

After roughly five years in the trenches of New Deal labor law, Surrey grew restless once again. And once again his law school contacts helped him secure a new position — this time with the U.S Treasury Department's General Counsel Office. Herman Oliphant, a former Columbia law professor and ardent legal realist who left Columbia before Surrey began law school, was Treasury General Counsel and Magill was, at this time, a Treasury Department undersecretary. In 1937, Surrey took a temporary leave from the NLRB to assist Oliphant, first, in trying to improve the procedures of the Board of Tax Appeals, the precursor to today's U.S. Tax Court. His second assignment brought him into contact with Roger Traynor, the University of California, Berkeley Law Professor who would go on to become a distinguished justice on the California Supreme Court and a lifelong Surrey friend who would eventually recruit Surrey into law teaching.[53]

Working with Traynor on such seemingly banal tasks as codifying the administrative provisions of federal tax laws and correcting defects in statutes of limitations led to "a major change in the direction" of Surrey's career.[54] He began to see how his work could have a lasting impact on U.S. tax law. Together with Traynor and Harvard law professor John Maguire, Surrey helped establish significant tax changes such as the eventual creation of IRS (at the time BIR) private letter rulings and the process of allowing Tax Court judges to travel throughout the country to hear cases. He also developed a plan — ultimately unsuccessful — for the creation of a single Court of Tax Appeals. Most importantly, Surrey's experience with Traynor opened the door for his permanent transition from the NLRB to the Treasury Department and his lifelong commitment to tax law. In 1938, Surrey joined the newly established Office of Legislative Counsel in the Treasury Department.

Surrey's first official tenure in Treasury (1938–47) solidified his professional profile as a New Deal liberal and as a voice for the department's focus on fiscal reform and tax equity. It was during this time that he assisted Oliphant and Magill in building the tax expertise of the Treasury Department, which since the 1920s had been gradually eclipsing Congress as the central source of new tax policy ideas. As *Time* magazine noted, "The Ways & Means Committee of the House, which normally would be busy drafting [tax reform] plans, has practically surrendered the job to the Treasury."[55] To help craft these tax reform plans, Surrey helped recruit many tax law experts

---

52. *See* chapter 1, at p. 19. *See also*, Surrey Oral History, *supra* note 22.

53. For more on the Traynor and Surrey collaboration, *see generally*, Mirit Eyal-Cohen, *Preventive Tax Policy: Chief Justice Roger J. Traynor's Tax Philosophy*, 59 HASTINGS L.J. 877 (2007).

54. *See* chapter 2, at p. 26.

55. *Atlas & His Burden*, TIME, Sep. 17, 1934. For more on Magill's role in early New Deal tax reform, *see generally*, Joseph J. Thorndike, *Profiles in Tax History: Roswell Magill*, TAX NOTES, Jan. 25, 2008.

to the department. He also worked closely with some of the country's top young "liberal leaning" public finance economists who were hired into the Office of Tax Analysis by Roy Blough — economists such as Walter Heller, Joseph Pechman, and Carl Shoup.[56] Surrey shared with these economists "a strong preference for a progressive income tax, and a strong regard for 'tax equity,' for treating people with equal incomes equally in the tax laws."[57] They also seemed to share "a distaste for tax preferences, and 'loopholes,'" as well as a disdain for the lobbyists and members of the specialized tax bar who advocated for such preferences and devised tax avoidance plans.[58] In this sense, these lawyers and economists were following the lead of Treasury Secretary Henry Morgenthau, Jr. and President Roosevelt, both of whom were publicly scornful of the tax bar and "their clever little schemes."[59]

From these experiences, Surrey developed a firm belief that the Treasury Department played a pivotal role — perhaps even *the* pivotal role — in guarding and maintaining the integrity of the tax system. As a key soldier in Oliphant and Magill's tax army, Surrey saw himself as part of the cohort of New Deal tax experts who favored using a broad-based income tax to generate sufficient revenue for Roosevelt's many experiments to combat the Great Depression. In contrast to other New Deal policymakers who favored "soak-the-rich" taxation, Surrey followed the more moderate path of ensuring that tax laws could raise revenue in a fair and effective manner.[60] The Treasury Department, from Surrey's perspective, was the key gatekeeper of this moderate path. "Conscientious work in the Treasury pushes a person very hard in the direction of tax equity," he noted, "for one quickly perceives the responsibility that rests upon the Treasury to safeguard the fairness of the tax system."[61] This sense of the Treasury Department's duty to defend the national fisc would become a central part of Surrey's professional character.

The Treasury Department's responsibilities and Surrey's own duties to safeguard the national treasury intensified when the United States entered World War II. At the start of the war, the New York lawyer, Randolph Paul, became a key figure in the formation of New Deal tax policy. Surrey continued to have a "front row center seat" in tax policy matters.[62] In fact, Surrey assisted Paul in drafting some of the most important wartime revenue laws — including the Revenue Act of 1942, which profoundly transformed the modern income tax from a class tax to a mass tax, as the number

---

56. *See* chapter 2, at p. 43–44. On the historical development of tax expertise in Congress and the Treasury Department, *see* Brownlee, Federal Taxation in America, *supra* note 38, at 73–77.

57. See Chapter 2, at p. 44. For more on Surrey's sense of tax equity as treating equals alike and how subsequent scholars challenged this notion of "horizontal equity," *see* section V. A. below.

58. *See* chapter 2, at p. 44.

59. Joseph J. Thorndike, Their Fair Share: Taxing the Rich in the Age of FDR (2013).

60. In this sense, Surrey can be seen as part of the cohort of New Deal tax experts who favored what Joseph Thorndike has referred to as "low-end" progressivity. *Id.*

61. *See* chapter 2, at p. 44.

62. *See id.*, at p. 65.

of individual taxpayers increased over ten fold.[63] With the 1942 Act, as Surrey later described in his tax law casebook, the federal income tax had "changed its morning coat for overalls," as it "spread from the country club group district down to the railroad tracks and then over to the other side of the tracks."[64] Spreading the burden of funding a global war was apparently one way to ensure the fairness of the tax system and defend the fisc.

Toward the end of the war, Surrey took a leave of absence from Treasury to become a Lieutenant (junior grade) in the U.S. Navy. Although Surrey "could not clearly articulate" in his memoirs why he decided to join the Navy in the midst of the war, he seemed to enjoy his two years of military service.[65] He moved initially from legal work on Navy contracts, to training on small ships, to radar school, to a trip finally to the Pacific theater at the tail end of the war. The Navy experience led to his life-long personal love for sailing and his first visit to Japan—an experience which would prove useful when he returned to that country as part of the post-WWII Shoup tax mission.

When Surrey returned to Treasury after the war, the novelty and initial excitement of his earlier experiences seemed to have faded. He took on several complex matters, including the tax treatment of employee stock options and the taxation of the family unit. But when Republicans took control of Congress in 1947, Surrey lamented that Treasury officials had lost their influence over tax policy; he thus began to consider other career options. Teaching law appealed to Surrey for several reasons, including that "[t]eaching seemed clearly closer to" the goals of a government official, namely, to determine "the correct overall answer to problem solving."[66] Surrey confidently believed that, during his first decade in Treasury, he and his colleagues solved many thorny tax problems. Reflecting on this period in his memoirs, Surrey was proud that he played a role in the adoption of such "relief provisions" as deductions for medical expenses, childcare costs, and expenditures related to investment activities. In a rare moment of candid self-reflection, Surrey also noted that the Treasury Department in these early years unwittingly played a part in increasing the complexity of tax laws and undermining certain aspects of tax equity and fairness. In its zeal to provide "relief for hardship," Treasury often recommended solutions that created "structural errors," such as the skewing of the benefits of the medical expense deduction in favor of high-income taxpayers.[67] Alas, Surrey's many accomplishments also came with some costs.

---

63. More specifically, the number of taxpayers went from roughly 3.9 million in 1939 to over 42 million in 1945. Brownlee, Federal Taxation in America, *supra* note 38, at 146. *See also*, Carolyn C. Jones, *Class Tax to Mass Tax: The Rise of Propaganda in the Expansion of the Income Tax during World War II*, BUFF. L. REV. 37 (1989), 685–737.

64. STANLY S. SURREY AND WILLIAM WARREN, FEDERAL INCOME TAXATION: CASES AND MATERIALS (1950).

65. *See* chapter 2, at p. 68.

66. *See id.*, at p. 77.

67. *See id.*, at p. 78.

II. From the Treasury to the Academy and Back

Surrey began his teaching career in 1947 when he took a position at the University of California, Berkeley, Law School, where his old Treasury colleague and friend Roger Traynor had taught before ascending to the bench. The life of a full-time academic suited Surrey. In addition to teaching tax and a seminar on administrative law, he became active with the Tax Advisory Committee of the American Law Institute (ALI), and he reconnected with economist Carl Shoup to accompany him on his first tax mission to Japan in the summer of 1949. Although Surrey appeared to miss the excitement of tax policymaking and interacting more regularly with economists, he continued to pursue the "correct overall answer" to tax problems through his academic writings and teachings. In 1948, he published a seminal article on the taxation of the family unit, building on his Treasury expertise. He also co-taught with Bay Area tax practitioners an "Advanced Taxation" seminar — an exercise that kept him on the frontier of innovative tax topics. He would repeat this teaching exercise in the future.[68]

Still, Surrey seemed to long for greater prestige and access to the corridors of power. In 1950, he had the opportunity to move to Harvard University when then dean Erwin Griswold — whom Surrey met in the 1930s when he first started at Treasury — recruited him to the law school. Surrey welcomed the opportunity to decamp to Harvard, which he described as "the pre-eminent law school," and as "a better — and closer — base of operations for one interested in tax policy."[69] For the next ten years, Surrey solidified his credentials as an "activist scholar," making significant contributions to both the academy and the practicing bar. He continued to publish regularly in law reviews, for specialized tax publications, and occasionally for the popular press. He co-authored (with William C. Warren) one of the leading casebooks on Federal Income Taxation. He elevated his involvement with the ALI and with the ABA Tax Section. Surrey helped establish the law school's new international tax program. In the process, he helped recruit Elizabeth A. Owens, who began as his research assistant and subsequently became a leading international tax law expert. In 1972, Owens became the first women granted tenure at Harvard Law School.[70]

While mainly an academic, Surrey remained involved in government work during the 1950s. He consistently participated in congressional hearings, including advising the U.S House Ways & Means Committee on an investigation of the BIR.[71] And he accompanied Shoup on several more international tax missions. Throughout this

---

68. Stanley S. Surrey, *Federal Taxation of the Family — The Revenue Act of 1948*, 61 HARV. L. REV. 1097 (1948).

69. *See* chapter 2, at p. 87.

70. William H. Honan, *Elisabeth Owens, 79, Pioneer at Harvard Law*, NEW YORK TIMES, Nov. 20, 1998, at B11. BRUCE A. KIMBALL AND DANIEL R. COQUILLETTE, THE INTELLECTUAL SWORD: HARVARD LAW SCHOOL, THE SECOND CENTURY (2020).

71. For more on the 1952 congressional investigation of the BIR and how it led to renaming the agency the IRS, *see generally*, Joseph J. Thorndike, *Reforming the Internal Revenue Service: A Comparative History*, 53 ADMIN. L. REV. 717, 755–80.

hectic period and for the rest of his career, Harvard University and the life of a teacher and scholar provided Surrey with a stable and secure anchorage. He and his wife, Dorothy, lived in Cambridge, not far from the university, where they raised their son, Scott.

In the 1950s, Surrey also expanded his interests in tax policy and began to develop a reputation as a "tax reformer." The post-WWII environment provided him and many other "activist scholars" with an opportunity to meld the world of ideas with policymaking. The war had ushered in a new, resilient tax regime for the United States, with a progressive income tax at its core.[72] Although a new Cold War led to several hot spots around the globe, a post-war peacetime economic boom and stable inflation provided lawmakers and analysts, like Surrey, with a chance to reevaluate and improve the existing fiscal system. His ALI work, for example, allowed Surrey to think broadly about new areas of tax law. At a time when individual marginal tax rates skyrocketed beyond 90% and tax preferences proliferated, Surrey had much fodder for academic writing and teaching. He began writing about corporate taxation, capital gains, and the taxation of foreign income, often adapting congressional testimony and his ALI work on these topics into published articles.[73] He taught a new class on Legislation. And he resumed his interdisciplinary engagement with public finance economists, co-teaching classes on "Current Tax Policy" with colleagues from other parts of the university, including economist Richard Musgrave.

At this time, Surrey also cemented his vision of what constituted fundamental tax reform. He had long been an advocate of taxing a broad base of income by removing tax preferences or "loopholes." Since his time as Magill's research assistant, as we have seen, Surrey had believed in using a modified economic definition of income as the conceptual ideal for taxable income. This is what he referred to as "the basic structural aspects of the tax system." He continued to believe that "the tax structure could possess a rational, integrated character and that a goal of tax policy was to work always in that direction." A modified, more pragmatic Haig-Simons definition of income remained his intellectual lodestar.[74]

By the late 1950s, Surrey combined his commitment to a broad income tax base with an aspiration for lower statutory tax rates. In his 1958 congressional testimony and a subsequent law review article about tax reform, Surrey analyzed the "tax differentials" between the high statutory marginal tax rates, which then topped out at 91%, and effective tax rates on the wealthy, which hovered closer to 48%. Reflecting on the origins of these "tax differentials," he explained that because a growing number of tax preferences had eroded the tax base, Congress had little choice

---

72. Brownlee, Federal Taxation in America, *supra* note 38, at 119–29.

73. *See, e.g.*, Surrey et al., *A Technical Revision of the Federal Income Tax Treatment of Corporate Distributions to Shareholders*, 52 COLUM. L. REV. 1 (1952); Surrey, *Definitional Problems in Capital Gains Taxation*, 69 HARV. L. REV. 986 (1956); Surrey, *The Pakistan Tax Treaty and 'Tax Sparing,'* 11 NAT'L TAX J. 156 (1958). For more on Surrey's views on international taxation, *see* Avi-Yonah et al, *supra* note 3.

74. *See* chapter 3, at p. 103–04.

but to increase tax rates over time to maintain revenue. These perniciously high "paper" rates, Surrey contended, not only masked the true tax rates paid by the rich; they also provided many high-income taxpayers and their lobbyists with an excuse to request new and increased tax preferences from lawmakers — an excuse that was often accepted by Congress.[75]

A system of high rates and a narrow base also offended Surrey's inherent sense of tax equity and fairness. Not all upper-income taxpayers could benefit from many of the existing tax preferences. For those who could not, "the high tax rates are very real," Surrey noted. "As a consequence, the high rate scale is severely discriminatory." To combat such discrimination and the general problem of tax differentials, Surrey recommended cutting top marginal rates. The combination of lower rates and a broader base, Surrey concluded, "would materially improve our income tax and would not necessitate a revenue loss."[76] Over time, the mantra of "a broad base and low rates" became the defining hallmark of modern fundamental tax reform and arguably culminated in the late twentieth century with the Tax Reform Act of 1986. Its origins, though, could be traced back to Surrey and his group of like-minded tax experts, if not earlier.[77]

In addition to outlining his vision of tax reform, Surrey also used his prominent perch at the Harvard Law School to scrutinize the tax legislative process. In a pivotal 1957 article, Surrey unleashed a torrent of criticism against Congress and its inability to maintain a broad-based income tax and defend the national treasury.[78] This article depicted most national lawmakers as either ignorant of the ways that special interests smuggled tax benefits into legislation, or worse yet complicit in littering the code with tax preferences for pressure groups. After nearly a decade of being on the sidelines of the actual tax legislative process, Surrey seemed liberated by his academic position to speak his mind. Such freedom, however, came at a significant price during Surrey's 1961 confirmation process, as we discuss below.[79]

Like many other Harvard professors, Surrey's connections with the university brought him to the attention of leading members of John F. Kennedy's inner circle. When Kennedy was elected president, his administration was eager to bring the country's best and brightest to Washington to craft new laws and policies.[80] As a result, Surrey began his second and arguably more influential tenure in the Treasury Department in 1961 when he became Assistant Secretary for Tax Policy in the Kennedy administration. Despite a rocky confirmation hearing that we describe below,[81] Surrey returned to the Treasury Department at a pivotal moment in American economic

75. Surrey, The Federal Income Tax Base for Individuals, *supra* note 41, at 815–830, 829–830.

76. *Id.*

77. Joel Slemrod, *Is this Tax Reform, or Just Confusion?* 32 J. of Econ. Perspectives 73 (2018); Avi-Yonah et al, *supra* note 3; Federal Taxation in America, *supra* note 38, 130–132.

78. Stanley S. Surrey, *Congress and the Tax Lobbyist — How Special Tax Provisions Get Enacted*, 70 Harv. L. Rev. 1145 (1957).

79. *See* section IV below.

80. David Halberstam, The Best and the Brightest (2002).

81. *See* section IV.

and political history. The 1960s witnessed the height of post-WWII U.S. economic prosperity, mild inflation, and the heyday of Keynesian economic policymaking. The explosive postwar growth in consumer demand fueled a booming economy with only periodic, albeit modest, downturns. The war experience convinced many policymakers that the state had an important role to play in managing the broader economy. Fiscal policy could be used as a countercyclical measure, and thus tax legislation was now seen not simply as a source of revenue, but as an essential macroeconomic tool.[82]

In his eight years (1961–69) as a key member of the Kennedy/Johnson Treasury Department, Surrey became increasingly open to using the tax system to manage the economy. As an academic, Surrey had developed a reputation as a tax reformer dedicated to revenue-neutral reform focused on low rates and a broad tax base. During his Treasury years, however, he was also willing to work with leading administration economists to use tax as a vital instrument of fiscal policy. In classic Keynesian fashion, Surrey approved of significant tax cuts in 1964 and 1965 to spur economic growth, despite budget deficits. And in 1968 he supported a temporary tax surcharge when the economy appeared to be overheating from government spending on the Great Society and the Vietnam War. From a structural perspective, Surrey did not give up on aspiring toward a comprehensive income tax base and improving tax compliance. During his tenure, Treasury led the charge in curtailing the deductibility of entertainment expenses and eliminating certain dividend credits and exclusions. Moreover, Surrey helped establish many improvements in information reporting.[83]

Ironically, however, one of the most significant contributions that Surrey made during this time was his championing of an innovative tax preference: the investment tax credit (ITC). Enacted as part of the Revenue Act of 1962, the ITC provided a seven percent tax credit for business investments in depreciable machinery and equipment.[84] The ITC quickly developed from concept to law, according to Surrey's account. The credit began as a creative idea in a 1960 Kennedy campaign report that Surrey drafted with Musgrave and MIT economist E. Cary Brown. It soon became a central part of a Surrey-led task force report on taxation once Kennedy was elected. Finally, Surrey brought the idea with him to his new Treasury post, where he eventually became one of the key figures in its enactment.[85]

Why did Surrey, the longstanding foe of tax preferences, favor this new tax benefit for big business? In chapter 6 of his memoirs, Surrey explains that the ITC was intended to be an experimental and temporary measure to encourage business investment in new capital at a time when the American economy was struggling through a moderate recession. Yet, in the memoirs, Surrey refrains from any serious or detailed introspection about how he reconciled support for the new ITC with his enduring

---

82. Brownlee, Federal Taxation in America, *supra* note 38, at 123–124.; C. Eugene Steuerle, Contemporary U.S. Tax Policy 68–69 (2004).

83. Stanley S. Surrey, *Past and Prologue in Tax Policy*, 17 Can. Tax J. 88 (1969).

84. The Revenue Act of 1962, Section 2.

85. *See* chapter 6.

opposition to tax preferences.[86] Perhaps he was just following orders. President Kennedy, as part of his Cold War rhetoric, was eager to use fiscal policy to encourage capital investments; Kennedy sought to improve and modernize American plant and equipment to keep up with the Soviet Union. Surrey acquiesced to the president's request. Most importantly, Surrey backed the ITC as an alternative to using "accelerated tax depreciation" as an incentive for business investments. The task force report stressed the difference between the two types of tax benefits. As Surrey recounted, the report "emphasized the greater effectiveness of the credit and the desirability of not turning the depreciation deduction, which had a proper place in the measurement of taxable income, into an incentive device since that course could lead only to confusion as to what was incentive and what was appropriate tax depreciation."[87] Maintaining the line between deductions necessary for the proper definition of net income and those tax benefits that were intended to be temporary subsidies — or "structural" departures from an ideal tax base — remained vital for Surrey. In short, the ITC appeared to be a lesser evil.[88]

The ITC may have been an important, albeit ephemeral, exception to Surrey's focus on preserving a comprehensive income tax base. But the new investment credit did not prevent Surrey from continuing his crusade to expose and perhaps eliminate tax preferences. Toward the end of his second Treasury tenure, Surrey began formulating a coherent and cogent rationale for identifying, measuring, and uncovering the many "hidden" tax preferences in the Internal Revenue Code. Although a planned chapter on tax expenditures is missing from the unfinished memoirs, Surrey's monograph, *Pathways to Tax Reform: The Concept of Tax Expenditures*, and the posthumously published follow-up, *Tax Expenditures* (coauthored with Paul McDaniel), provide insights into the aims and objectives of the tax expenditure concept.[89]

As we have seen, Surrey defined "tax expenditures" as tax preferences in the form of "permanent exclusions from income, deductions, deferrals of tax liabilities, credits against tax, or special rates" that were deemed "departures from the normative tax structure." They represented, for Surrey, "government spending for favored activities or groups, effected through the tax system rather than through direct grants, loans, or other forms of government assistance." In other words, tax expenditures were a form of indirect government spending disguised as tax benefits. Surrey's goal in labeling these benefits as "tax expenditures" and in creating a "tax expenditure budget" was to bring greater transparency and accountability to the fiscal policymaking process. He wanted to "include in the budget and the budget-making process the cost of special tax provisions." By doing so, he hoped to show that these tax expen-

86. For more on Surrey's lack of introspection or display of self-doubt in the memoirs, *see* section IX below.

87. *See* chapter 6, at p. 181.

88. For more on the ITC and Surrey's subsequent critique of this tax preference, *see generally*, Mirit Eyal-Cohen, *Lessons in Fiscal Activism*, 48 Conn. L. Rev. 873, 900, 917 (2016).

89. Surrey, *supra* note 17; Surrey and McDaniel, *supra* note 42.

ditures "can be considered as alternatives to direct expenditures and loan programs, so as to allow decisions which make the most effective use of all budgetary resources." The goal was to provide a "complete accounting" of national fiscal policy.[90]

Although Surrey was not the first tax expert to recognize that tax benefits were a form of indirect government spending, his tireless efforts to popularize the concept led to the institutionalization of a "tax expenditure budget" in the United States and subsequently in many other nations.[91] We assess in greater detail below the official creation of tax expenditure budgets, how Surrey attempted to stigmatize such stealth spending, and how other tax experts critiqued the concept. For present purposes, Surrey's preoccupation with tax expenditures demonstrates not only his melding of ideas and actions as an "activist scholar," but also his desire to reveal the many ways in which the modern fiscal state was distributing the fruits of post-WWII American capitalism. Ever the New Deal and Great Society liberal, Surrey wanted to ensure that lawmakers and the public alike were aware of such government spending. As he explained in one of his last speeches as Assistant Secretary for Tax Policy, "the appropriateness, equity, and vitality of a tax system depend upon constant attention."[92]

In 1969 Surrey left the Treasury and returned to Harvard after the Nixon administration swept into power. But Surrey's zeal for tax reform and exposing the potential inequities of tax expenditures continued unabated. He persisted in writing about and advocating for a more complete accounting of fiscal policy. By 1974, Congress had come to agree with Surrey and adopted a "tax expenditure budget" as part of the annual budget process.[93] Free of political constraints, Surrey's return to academic life also allowed him to speak his mind about other ways to improve the tax system. He wrote about possible revisions to federal estate and gift taxation, the integration of the corporate and individual income tax, comparative and international tax issues especially in developing countries, and his opposition to a national sales or value-added tax. All the while, Surrey remained loosely connected to liberal Democratic political leaders. In fact, throughout the 1970s, he was a tax advisor to Senators George McGovern and Ted Kennedy. A severe heart attack in March 1972 sidelined Surrey for several months, but it did not diminish his efforts in working with the McGovern presidential campaign later that summer and fall. Similarly, when Jimmy Carter became president, Surrey was a regular consultant to both the Treasury Department and the White House.

While Surrey was not an official member of the Carter administration, many of his proteges, whom he had recruited to Treasury in the 1960s, had accepted senior appointments in the new administration. Initially, the return of liberal Democrats

90. Surrey and McDaniel, *supra* note 42, at 3.

91. Harry A. Shannon II, *The Tax Expenditure Concept in the United States and Germany: A Comparison*, 33 Tax Notes 201 (Oct. 13, 1986); Daniel N. Shaviro, *Rethinking Tax Expenditures and Fiscal Language* 57 Tax L. Rev. 187 (2004).

92. Surrey, Tax Policy and Tax Reform: Selected Speeches, at 173.

93. Congressional Budget and Impoundment Control Act of 1974, Pub. L. No. 93-344, 88 Stat. 297 (1974) (codified at 2 U.S.C. §§ 681–688 (1982)).

to key tax positions signaled the promise of significant tax reform aimed at a comprehensive income tax. But the optimism was quickly dashed. To be sure, the political and economic conditions of the mid-1970s were dramatically different than what tax policymakers confronted during Kennedy's New Frontier and Johnson's Great Society. A combination of stagnant economic growth and high inflation, dubbed "stagflation" by experts, forced the Carter administration to focus on fiscal stimulus with individual tax rebates and small business tax cuts. Fundamental tax reform, of the type championed by Surrey and others, seemed unlikely. Indeed, when energy policy became the cornerstone of the Carter adminstration's early years, Surrey and other tax experts were disappointed that the White House turned to new tax preferences to solve nearly every energy problem, frequently without input from Treasury officials. Similarly, attempts at comprehensive tax reform were defeated in 1978 when Carter signed a bill that, as Surrey put it, "resembled only the palest reflection" of earlier tax reform blueprints. Among the most significant would-be reforms that were neutralized then was the reduction or possible elimination of the capital gains tax preference. Surrey attributed that particular failure to the powerful lobbying efforts of the business community and their shibboleth for "capital formation." Reflecting back on this period, Surrey concluded that the tax legislative process "was almost out of control by 1978."[94]

If Surrey and other liberal tax experts were disappointed by the Carter administration, that disappointment would soon turn to disdain. When Ronald Reagan first entered the White House, any hopes for comprehensive tax reform seemed highly unlikely. Indeed, Surrey considered the 1981 tax act "the most dismal measure in tax history, replete with new tax expenditures, individual rate reductions that favored the upper brackets and went too far in general, [and] corporate tax changes that in effect eliminated the income tax on new investment in structures and machines."[95] Of course, Surrey did not live to see the Tax Reform Act of 1986, which was more in keeping with traditional notions of revenue-neutral, broad-base, low-rates tax reform. Still, when Surrey was penning his memoirs in the early 1980s, he had little patience for what was passing at the time as tax reform.

In one of his last public speeches, delivered just weeks after Reagan's election, Surrey candidly took stock of the troubled state of American tax policy. We discuss below in greater detail the highlights of that speech, but the critical point is Surrey's enduring commitment to a progressive income and wealth-transfer tax system—one that could tolerate lower rates, but only if a more rational and equitable legislative process identified unnecessary tax expenditures and ensured that "effective rates ap-

94. *See* chapter 10, at p. 335. For more on the Carter administration and its economic policies, *see* Robert M. Collins, More: The Politics of Economic Growth in Postwar America 157–60 (2000).

95. *See* chapter 10, at p. 335–36.

proximate the scheduled rates."[96] In many ways, this speech recapitulated the lessons that Surrey had learned throughout his half-century with the income tax, from his formative experience working with Magill and Oliphant during his first tenure in Treasury to his final professional days as a consultant to the Carter White House and Treasury.

In many ways, the arc of Surrey's career mirrored twentieth century American political history. His "half century with the income tax," as he put it, reflected what historians have referred to as "the rise and fall of the New Deal order."[97] The five decades between the elections of Franklin Roosevelt and Ronald Reagan marked a unique era in American history—an era when the federal government, working closely with a fraught political coalition of business interests and labor organizations, greatly expanded its presence in the American economy and society. As a self-proclaimed "good Democrat,"[98] Surrey was both a product of New Deal and Great Society liberalism, and a bystander in the waning days of the modern activist state. From his early days as a law graduate in the 1930s when he first become Magill's research assistant and soon thereafter a New Deal labor lawyer, to his two tours of duty in the U.S. Treasury Department, to a decades-long teaching career, Surrey encapsulated the life of an "activist scholar." Traversing between the Treasury and the academy and back, he remained dedicated to improving the tax system and in the process American society.

III. The Memoirs

By the time of his death in 1984 at the age of 73, Surrey had completed drafts of most of the planned chapters of his memoirs. Based on Surrey's outline of planned chapters, it appears that the manuscript he left is incomplete in only two significant respects. First, Chapter 6 ("A Government Tax Career, Part II, 1961–1969") describes in detail the events leading to President Kennedy's nomination of Surrey to the Assistant Secretary post but includes nothing relating to the subsequent confirmation hearing or to Surrey's eight years in office. Second, there is not even a partial draft of a planned Chapter 11 on tax expenditures ("Tax Expenditure Analysis—A New Fiscal Concept, 1968 to date"). To be sure, the two unwritten portions are greatly missed. But to borrow from Tennyson's "Ulysses," though much is missing, much abides. The completed portions cover a large majority of Surrey's half century with the income tax in fascinating detail, and feature a cast of characters—from law professors to presidents—constituting a Who's Who of American and international tax policy in the middle half of the twentieth century.

---

96. The speech was published by *Tax Notes* a few months later. Stanley S. Surrey, *Our Troubled Tax Policy: False Routes and Proper Paths to Change*, 12 TAX NOTES 179, 195 (1981).

97. *See generally*, Steve Fraser and Gary Gerstle, eds., THE RISE AND FALL OF THE NEW DEAL ORDER, 1930–1980 (1989); LEWIS L. GOULD, THE RISE AND FALL OF THE NEW DEAL ORDER, 1930–1980 (1989).

98. *See* chapter 7, at p. 19.

These published memoirs are based on the typescript draft of more than 600 pages in the collection of the Harvard Law School Library. The typescript was transferred to the Library by Harvard Law Professor (now Emeritus) Daniel Halperin, who described the circumstances of his discovery of the manuscript in an email to one of the editors of the memoirs:

> I "found" a loose-leaf binder when I was cleaning my office to move quarters on my retirement. I had no recollection of obtaining it but I am assuming [Harvard Law Professor] Ollie Oldman gave it to me when he retired. I guess I put it aside to read it when I had the time and promptly forgot about it. I was surprised that the library knew nothing about the memoir, nor did they find a copy. I talked to Surrey's former secretary who was still around at that point and she had no remembrance of any missing chapters in preparation or otherwise.[99]

What is published here is not the complete manuscript left by Surrey. We have omitted material that will be of limited interest to most readers. Many of the omissions are of long — sometimes very long — quotations from various reports and the like. Significant omissions are indicated in the text and briefly described in the notes. Where Surrey makes references or observations that are likely to be obscure to twenty-first-century readers, we have provided what we hope will be helpful annotations. Throughout the manuscript, Surrey left numerous indications that it was a draft — leaving a blank, a question mark, or a note to himself, indicating where he needed to check on some piece of information. We have dealt with those indications in an ad hoc manner — in the more straightforward situations we have supplied or checked the information without noting the uncertainty Surrey expressed in the draft. In more difficult situations, we note the uncertainty in the draft and describe possible resolutions of it. And in the most difficult situations where we were unable to resolve the uncertainty, or where resolution might have been possible but only with an effort not justified by the limited significance of the matter, we have simply left the indication of the uncertainty as Surrey expressed it in his draft. The remainder of this introductory essay revisits selected aspects of Surrey's career and of his tax policy views, beginning with his 1961 confirmation hearing.

IV. Mr. Surrey Goes to Washington

The crisis moment in the tension between Surrey's roles in academia and in government arrived at Surrey's March 1961 confirmation hearing before the Senate Finance Committee. There was some predictable generalized concern about academics and their ivory towers, as exemplified by Senator Wallace F. Bennett's inquiry: "In your study [of possible new tax incentives for business investment in plant and equipment] are you discussing this with people who are actually going to have to live with the problem, men in business, or are you discussing it with

99. Email from Daniel Halperin to Lawrence Zelenak, August 14, 2019.

the, pardon the phrase, theorists who are trying to develop tax laws under which the rest of us will have to operate?"[100]

But the real problems for Surrey in the hearing came not from senatorial stereotypes of out-of-touch academics, but from senatorial objections to particular things this academic had written. Like many tax law academics, then and now, Surrey had written law review articles criticizing the products of Congress's tax legislative efforts, sometimes in harsher terms than might have been used by a writer anticipating having to defend his scholarship in a confirmation hearing before a tax-writing committee. For example, in his 1958 article regarding tax reform, discussed above, Surrey had flatly declared that the exclusion for interest on municipal bonds was "indefensible."[101] However, by far the most incendiary of Surrey's publications, from the perspective of a member of Congress, was his 1957 *Harvard Law Review* article, "The Congress and the Tax Lobbyist—How Special Provisions Get Enacted."[102] In that article Surrey claimed that only the Treasury Department "speaks for tax equity and tax fairness,"[103] and that Congress routinely enacts special provisions lobbied for by private interests. The article is most unflattering to Congress, suggesting (among other things) that Congress regularly sneaks special interest tax legislation past an unsuspecting public,[104] and comparing "the congressman" to a "small boy inwardly seeking parental bounds for his conduct while outwardly declaiming against them."[105] As harsh as the article is toward Congress, its tone would not have been remarkable for a law review article, then or now—but the author of this article had to answer for it to Congress four years after publication.

In Chapter 6 of his memoirs, Surrey writes at length about the shadowy opposition to his nomination, and his efforts to discover who opposed him and why.[106] He claims that the opposition resulted from his advocating the closing of various tax loopholes, and came from the industries benefitting from those loopholes (especially the oil industry) and from members of Congress friendly to those industries. He does not mention, however, that he had written about Congress in less than flattering terms, nor does he seem to consider that his perceived disrespect of Congress might have turned some members against him (and might also have been cited as a reason to oppose his nomination by members actually more concerned about Surrey's hostility to their favorite loopholes). Although Surrey devotes about thirteen typescript pages of Chapter 6 to recounting his efforts prior to the confirmation hearing to uncover

100. *Hearings before the Senate Committee on Finance on Nominations*, 87 Cong., 1st Sess., at 58 (1961).

101. Surrey, The Federal Income Tax Base for Individuals, *supra* note 41, at 817.

102. Surrey, Congress and the Tax Lobbyist—How Special Tax Provisions Get Enacted, *supra* note 78.

103. *Id.* at 1164.

104. "Perhaps the most significant aspect of the consideration of special tax provisions by the Congress is that it usually takes place without any awareness of these events by the general public." *Id.* at 1175.

105. *Id.* at 1164.

106. *See* chapter 6, at p. 191–200.

the opposition to his nomination, Chapter 6 says nothing about the hearing itself. The memoirs make only one passing reference to the hearing: in Chapter 3 Surrey notes that the 1957 *Harvard Law Review* "caused me much of the pain and anguish in confirmation Hearings."[107]

Surrey ends the story of his nomination with the White House sending his nomination to Congress, wryly noting that the *Congressional Record* reported the nomination as that of "Stanley S. Sorrey".[108] It is unclear whether Surrey planned to write about the hearing. The existing end of Chapter 6 reads as if Surrey intended it to be the end of the nomination story. It would be understandable if Surrey decided not to revisit in his memoirs so unpleasant an experience. The memoirs, however, are clearly unfinished. Elsewhere in the memoirs Surrey does not shrink from describing unpleasant events, so he may well have intended to write about the hearing. Surrey's summary of the planned Chapter 6, in his outline for the memoirs, does not shed much light on this question.[109]

Whatever Surrey intended for the memoirs, the hearing serves as an object lesson for any academic who may at some point be interested in a position in the federal government requiring Senate confirmation. Surrey was obviously not thinking about a possible future confirmation hearing when he chose the content and tone of his 1957 article, and to all appearances he was not prepared in 1961 for the utterly predictable senatorial grilling on the article.[110] Two passages from the hearing show how poorly Surrey responded when asked to explain the low opinion of Congress expressed in his 1957 article. Early in the hearing, Committee Chair Harry F. Byrd asked Surrey to explain what he meant by his statement that a member of Congress "will invariably interpret a Treasury statement that the matter is one for his own policy decision as a victory for the seeker of the special provision."[111] Bearing no resemblance to the spirited Surrey in the pages of the *Harvard Law Review*, the Surrey of the hearing hemmed and hawed,

> Well, I think what I meant by that was this, and I may be completely wrong in the analysis of the situation, because obviously that was based upon prior experience in representing the Treasury, and the officials in the administrative branch are not privy to the decisions of the committee itself. But my general impression at the time was that the committees did desire to hear the view

---

107. *See* chapter 3, at p. 98.

108. *See* chapter 6, at p. 200.

109. The chapter summary from the annotated table of contents reads: "Assistant Secretary for Tax Policy in Treasury Department under Presidents Kennedy and Johnson—presumably a summary chapter since activities very extensive in both domestic and international areas—legislative and administrative results—describe scene, 1961–1969, use of complete diary."

110. For details, we encourage the interested reader to consult both the transcript of the hearing and George K. Yin's excellent discussion of the hearing in a recent article. *See, generally*, George K. Yin, *Who Speaks for Tax Equity and Tax Fairness?": Stanley Surrey and the Tax Legislative Process*, 39 VA. TAX REV. 39 (2019).

111. *Hearings before the Senate Committee on Finance on Nominations*, *supra* note 100, at 11 (quoting Surrey, *supra* note 19, at 1164–65).

> of the Treasury with respect to policies on these matters, and if the Treasury had no policy formulation one way or another, it seemed to me — I may be wrong on that — that was understood by the committee to indicate that there was no basic objection by the Treasury Department to the proposal. Now, if I am wrong in that, and in the past misunderstood the reactions of the committee, then it is simply a misunderstanding as to the reactions of the committee.

When Byrd followed up by stating that the quoted passage from the 1957 article indicated that "selfish interests are controlling the Congressman," and that Surrey did "not have a very high opinion of the Congress," Surrey unconvincingly replied, "I did not mean that at all, sir," to the former, and "Sir, that is, I think, an implication which is wrong" to the latter.[112]

A bit later in the hearing, Byrd read to Surrey the passage from the 1957 article (quoted above) relating to the general public's unawareness of special tax provisions. When Byrd commented, "The inference there seems clear to me that you think that some of these things are sneaked through without the knowledge of the members of Congress or anyone else," the best Surrey could offer was an appeal to "the difficulties of expression in this area."[113]

Although Surrey certainly did not cover himself with glory at the hearing, he survived, was confirmed, and served eight years in office. During those eight years — as Donald Lubick aptly put it — "he dominated tax policy both in the United States and internationally."[114] Lubick also described Surrey as "calm in the face of adversity and completely resilient in the face of defeat."[115] Indeed, there is no better demonstration of those qualities than Surrey's accomplishing so much in the Kennedy and Johnson administrations after so inauspicious a beginning.

V. Tax Scholarship for the Real World

Just as Surrey the professor could make life difficult for Surrey the would-be Treasury official, sometimes the official created difficulties for the academic. Perhaps the two ideas most closely associated with Surrey the tax theorist are the overriding importance of horizontal equity in the imposition of tax burdens, and the concept of tax expenditures as hidden subsidies embedded in the income tax. Although both ideas were worthy of elaboration at great length — for example, Surrey wrote two books (one published posthumously) and numerous articles on tax expenditures — at their cores the ideas were sufficiently simple and intuitively appealing that Surrey could reasonably hope that his theoretical ideas would lead to tax reform in the real world. Yet the very simplicity and intuitive appeal of his ideas left them vulnerable to academic attack.

---

112. *Id.* at 11.
113. *Id.* at 12.
114. Lubick, *supra* note 13, at 338.
115. *Id.* at 339.

A. HORIZONTAL EQUITY

Consider first Surrey's championing of horizontal equity in numerous law review articles. In 1957, for example, he wrote that "the criterion of equity or fairness ... demands that the income-tax burden should as far as possible apply equally to persons with the same dollar income."[116] In 1966 he defined "horizontal tax equity" as "essentially the concept of elementary fairness in taxation — why should this taxpayer be treated better — or worse — than the rest of the public. It is the first and basic barrier that proposals for tax preferences face when pressed on the Congress, and it is the barrier which most cannot surmount."[117] Beyond such general statements, he also offered numerous examples of what he viewed as glaring violations of horizontal equity in the existing income tax laws. In 1958, he noted that "a married couple each over the age of sixty-five and each qualifying for the retirement and dividend credits may receive $6,100 free of tax.... Yet a young married couple with a salary of $6,100 would pay a tax of $863.80. Such a distinction seems impossible of justification."[118]

Surrey also presented the case for horizontal equity directly to the American public. Writing in *Collier's* in 1956, he declared, "An income tax is not the kind of tax that can tolerate many distinctions among persons of the same income group. Its basic principle is that a person with so many dollars of income is treated the same as any other person with the same amount of income. Arguments which seek to make distinctions among dollars that are earned from oil or dividends or salaries or interest are not — and should not be — sufficiently persuasive to produce a different tax for each."[119] Sixteen years later, in *Saturday Review*, Surrey urged the same point again on a general readership: "An income tax remains fair ... only if it reaches all income, only if there are no preferences or loopholes through which some people can escape."[120]

There are all kinds of problems with Surrey's invocation of horizontal equity — ranging from the fairly obvious to the very subtle — and academics have not hesitated to point them out, both during Surrey's day and more recently. Perhaps the most basic objection is, as Louis Kaplow has put it, "By definition, horizontal equity cannot tell us which groupings of individuals are 'equals' who are supposed to be treated equally, for that begs the very question at issue."[121] In 1979 Boris Bittker, Surrey's contemporary rival, published a witty essay noting that equity theorists such as Surrey implicitly or explicitly assume — often wrongly — that market forces do not counteract tax law violations of horizontal equity.[122] For example, the exclusion of municipal

---

116. *Congress and the Tax Lobbyist — How Special Tax Provisions Get Enacted, supra* note 78, at 1146.

117. Stanley S. Surrey, *Federal Tax Policy in the 1960's*, BUFF. L. REV. 477, 488–89 (1966).

118. Surrey, The Federal Income Tax Base for Individuals, *supra* note 41, at 823–24.

119. Stanley S. Surrey, *Do Income Tax Exemptions Make Sense*, COLLIER'S, Mar. 1956, at 26.

120. Stanley S. Surrey, *Taxes are a Moral Issue*, SAT. REV., Oct. 21, 1972, at 51.

121. LOUIS KAPLOW, THE THEORY OF TAXATION AND PUBLIC ECONOMICS 400 (2008).

122. Boris I. Bittker, *Equity, Efficiency, and Income Tax Theory: Do Misallocations Drive Out Inequities?* 16 SAN DIEGO L. REV. 735 (1979).

bond interest income does not produce inequity between investors in taxable and tax-exempt bonds if the market equalizes the tax-exempt interest rate and the after-tax interest rate on taxable bonds. In that case, efficiency theorists would object to the exclusion on the grounds of resource misallocation, but Surrey and his fellow equity theorists would have no grounds for complaint. Bittker went on to argue, more subtly but still convincingly, that there would be no horizontal inequity between recipients of tax-exempt interest and earners of taxable salaries, if market forces sufficiently reduced tax-exempt interest rates. Although Bittker did not claim that market adjustments always and everywhere drove out all inequities—and could not reasonably have made such a claim—his essay exposed a major weakness in Surrey's horizontal equity analysis.

Surrey's analysis was also vulnerable to the objection that it depended on artificially isolating the income tax from all other activities of the federal government. In his 1956 *Collier's* article, Surrey conceded that there might be some legitimate reason for the government to subsidize one taxpayer while not subsidizing another taxpayer of equal income—thus resulting in unequal treatment of equal-income taxpayers. In that case, however, Surrey contended that "the need for fairness—for treating equal incomes equally—is so vital under our tax system that if a particular industry is really in need of governmental aid, a direct grant or subsidy, wholly apart from the income tax, is the more appropriate method of financing that aid."[123] Surrey's insistence on analyzing the horizontal equity of the income tax in isolation was and is an easy target for academic criticism. Ironically, in the same years in which Surrey was arguing for a self-contained view of the income tax, economist James Mirrlees was developing his tremendously influential optimal tax analysis, which assumes that government tax and nontax programs must be evaluated together.[124]

In the post-Surrey era, Louis Kaplow has been the most prominent critic of Surrey-style horizontal equity analysis of tax systems.[125] It is not possible to do justice here to Kaplow's critique, but his basic point is that the concept of horizontal equity has no role to play in tax system design, if the goal is to produce the tax-and-transfer system that will maximize a chosen social welfare function.

And yet. However theoretically dubious Surrey's obsession with horizontal equity may have been, perhaps he was practically correct. As Kaplow acknowledges, "the maxim that equals should be treated equally has intuitive appeal," and "we often have moral intuitions that arise in contexts distinct from the setting of optimal tax design but that nevertheless seem compelling and may have a proxy role even though they are not independent moral principles."[126] For example, Kaplow suggests that some instances of unequal tax treatment may result from welfare-reducing "government favors to political allies," and that it may be politically easier to challenge such favors

---

123. Surrey, Do Income Tax Exemptions Make Sense, *supra* note 119, at 27.

124. J. A. Mirrlees, *An Exploration in the Theory of Optimum Income Taxation*, 38 Rev. of Econ. Studies 175 (1971).

125. Kaplow, The Theory of Taxation and Public Economics, *supra* note 121, at 396–401.

126. *Id.* at 398.

by appeals to horizontal equity than by appeals to a social welfare function.[127] And so, while a theorist of greater sophistication than Surrey might think in terms of social welfare functions rather than horizontal equity, in many cases horizontal equity analysis and social welfare function analysis will produce similar policy recommendations, with the horizontal equity approach having an immense advantage in terms of potential to influence the public and Congress. No one understood that advantage better than Stanley Surrey.

B. TAX EXPENDITURES

Even more than his commitment to horizontal equity, Surrey was and is identified with the tax expenditure concept and the regular production by the federal government of tax expenditure budgets. As we have seen, Surrey claimed to have conceptualized the notion of "structural errors" in the income tax as early as the 1930s, and he singled out several "unwarranted tax preferences" in his 1958 article on tax reform. But his clearest articulation of these "structural errors" as "tax expenditures" did not occur until a 1967 speech. According to Surrey, the federal income tax features "a series of tax expenditures under which Governmental financial assistance programs are carried out through special tax provisions rather than through direct Government expenditures. This second system is grafted onto the structure of the income tax proper; it has no basic relation to that structure and is not necessary to its operation."[128] As Surrey explained, a tax expenditure could take the form of a tax exemption for a particular type of income, a deduction for an expenditure that would not be deductible if the goal of the tax system were simply to measure a taxpayer's economic net income, or a credit reducing tax liability by the amount of the credit.

Well before Surrey's speech, others had made similar observations. As Surrey himself noted, German tax experts in the 1950s had identified the conceptual equivalence of indirect spending via tax benefits and direct government expenditures.[129] Similarly, in 1955, University of Chicago law professor Walter J. Blum had both described tax expenditures (although not by that name) and offered a catalogue of policy objections to them: "[I]f it be decided to subsidize a certain activity, we should be hesitant about administering the subsidy by way of a tax preference. Subsidies in this form vary directly in amount with the tax brackets of the recipients; they are invariably hidden in technicalities of the tax law; they do not show up in the budget; their cost is frequently difficult to calculate; and their accomplishments are even more difficult to assess."[130]

---

127. *Id.* at 399.

128. Surrey, *supra* note 15, at 322.

129. Surrey, Pathways to Tax Reform, *supra* note 17.

130. Walter J. Blum, *The Effects of Special Provisions in the Income Tax on Taxpayer Morale*, in Jt. Comm. on the Economic Report, Federal Tax Policy for Economic Growth and Stability, 84th Cong., 1st Sess., 252, 252 (1955).

Thus, Surrey's contribution was not a new theoretical insight, but rather his relentless proselytizing efforts to persuade legislators and other tax policymakers to think in terms of tax expenditures — and, having thought in those terms, to cleanse the federal income tax of most or all existing expenditures. Responding to Surrey's plea that "[w]e need a much higher degree of accounting for the dollars that the tax expenditure programs that grew up in the past are now absorbing,"[131] the Treasury Department issued the first set of federal tax expenditure estimates, for fiscal year 1968.[132] Surrey was tremendously successful in institutionalizing the concept of tax expenditures and the annual publication of official tax expenditure budgets (TEBs). Despite the absence of a legislative mandate for the preparation of TEBs in the early years, in 1970 Treasury produced a second TEB,[133] and in 1972 and 1973 Treasury and the Joint Committee on Taxation cooperated in the production of updated TEBs.[134] In 1974 Congress enacted legislation requiring the annual production of TEBs by both the executive branch and the legislative branch.[135] Pursuant to that legislation, for almost half a century (and counting) there have been two annual TEBs, one from the Joint Committee on Taxation and one from Treasury.[136]

In addition to institutionalizing tax expenditure budgets within the federal government, Surrey wrote frequently and at length on the topic, expounding on the many defects of tax expenditures. In Surrey's view, to identify a provision as a tax expenditure was to stigmatize it. His hope was that focusing congressional attention on tax expenditures by means of mandated annual reports would make this type of indirect spending more transparent, thus leading Congress to conclude that many tax expenditures were indefensible and should either be repealed outright or replaced with better-designed direct spending programs. A glance at any recent TEB will confirm the intuition that, despite Surrey's impressive success in institutionalizing the tax expenditure concept, the annual publication of TEBs has not produced the results for which Surrey had hoped.

From the beginning, Surrey faced criticisms from tax theorists that the project of identifying tax expenditures was hopeless. Surrey defined tax expenditures as provi-

131. *Surrey*, supra note 15, at 326.

132. U.S. Department of Treasury, *The Tax Expenditure Budget: A Conceptual Analysis*, in U.S. Department of Treasury, Annual Report of the Secretary of the Treasury on the State of the Finances for the Fiscal Year Ended June 30, 1968 (1969), at 326, 339–40.

133. *Murray Weidenbaum, Statement,* June 2, 1970, before the Subcommittee on Economy in Government of the Joint Economic Committee, in U.S. Department of Treasury, Annual Report of the Secretary of the Treasury on the State of the Finances for the Fiscal Year Ending June 30, 1970 (1971), at 296–308.

134. Staffs of the Treasury Department and the Joint Committee on Taxation, Estimates of Federal Tax Expenditures (October 4, 1972, JCS-28-72); Staffs of the Treasury Department and the Joint Committee on Taxation, Estimates of Federal Tax Expenditures (June 1, 1973, JCS-20-73).

135. Congressional Budget and Impoundment Control Act of 1974, Pub. L. No. 93-344, secs. 301(d)(6) (congressional TEB), 601 (executive branch TEB), 88 Stat. 297, 308, 323.

136. For recent TEBs, *see* U.S. Department of the Treasury Office of Tax Analysis, Tax Expenditures (February 26, 2020); Staff of the Joint Committee on Taxation, Estimates of Federal Tax Expenditures for Fiscal Years 2020–2024 (November 5, 2020, JCX-23-20).

sions "grafted onto the structure of the income tax proper." The problem, according to the critics, was that there was not and never could be agreement on "the structure of the income tax proper," and without the ability to identify that structure it was impossible to identify provisions "grafted onto" that structure.

As with Surrey's championing of horizontal equity, so too with tax expenditures; the most trenchant early criticism of Surrey-on-tax-expenditures came from Boris Bittker. Writing in 1969, Bittker noted that the production of a tax expenditure budget "requires an agreed starting point, departures from which can be identified. What is needed is not an ad hoc list of tax provisions, but a generally acceptable model, or set of principles, enabling us to decide with reasonable assurance which income tax provisions are departures from the model, whose costs are to be reported as 'tax expenditures.'"[137] As Bittker also noted, neither Surrey nor the Treasury in their tax expenditure analyses had defined the necessary "agreed starting point." To supply that omission, Bittker suggested the most obvious candidate was the Haig-Simons definition of income as "the algebraic sum of (1) the market value of rights exercised in consumption and (2) the change in the value of the store of property rights between the beginning and the end of the period in question."[138] But, Bittker continued, if all deviations from Haig-Simons are to be classified as tax expenditures, then the list of tax expenditures should include (among other things) the cash method of accounting, the deferral of tax on unrealized appreciation, the exclusion of gifts from gross income, and the failure to tax imputed rental income from owner-occupied housing — none of which were included in the Treasury's TEBs.[139] Bittker added that any actual income tax "is an aggregation of decisions about a host of structural issues the Haig-Simons definition does not even purport to settle" — relating, for example, to definitions of the taxable unit (individual, married couple, or entire nuclear family), the tax accounting period, and the tax rate structure.[140] "As to these," Bittker concluded, "one could lock forty tax experts in a room for forty days and get no agreement — except as a surrender to hunger or boredom — even if they all could recite the complete works of Henry Simons by heart. For such issues, every man can create his own set of 'tax expenditures,' but it will be no more than his collection of disparities between the income tax law as it is, and as he thinks it ought to be."[141]

Surrey published a response to Bittker (co-authored with William Hellmuth), arguing that neither Surrey nor Treasury had ever identified Haig-Simons as the starting point for tax expenditure analysis, and that by invoking Haig-Simons as the starting point "Bittker puts up a straw man which he proceeds to beat without mercy — and a Bittker beating is indeed an awesome sight."[142] According to Surrey

---

137. Boris I. Bittker, *Accounting for Federal "Tax Subsidies" in the National Budget*, 22 Nat. Tax J. 244, 247 (1969).

138. *Id.* at 247–48, n. 8, quoting Henry Simons, Personal Income Taxation 61–61, 206 (1938).

139. *Id.* at 249–50.

140. *Id.* at 260.

141. *Id.*

142. Stanley S. Surrey & William F. Hellmuth, *The Tax Expenditure Budget — Response to Professor Bittker*, 22 Nat. Tax J. 528, 531 (1969).

and Hellmuth, the selection of items for inclusion in the TEB was based not on deviations from Haig-Simons, but rather on whether a tax provision "was in essence operating to produce an expenditure system that would produce meaningful comparison with the direct expenditure approach."[143] So, for example, the deduction for charitable contributions is included in the TEB because replacing the deduction with a system of non-tax government matching grants for contributions to charity seems plausible, whereas the deferral of tax on unrealized appreciation is not included because replacing the deferral with non-tax subsidies for owners of appreciated property does not. Surrey and Hellmuth went on to argue that doubts about, for example, whether the non-taxation of imputed income should be included in the TEB should not stand in the way of including in the TEB oil depletion allowances in excess of basis: "The frontier may be uncharted and hazardous, but behind the frontier the area can be charted.... [W]e find a lack of perspective in Professor Bittker's article that may cause readers to believe all is confusion and no guidelines are available. This we do not see."[144]

A fair-minded reader of the Bittker-Surrey (and Hellmuth) debate might conclude that each side was right, on its own terms. Bittker was right that any effort to come up with a comprehensive accounting of tax expenditures is doomed by the impossibility of fully specifying "the structure of the income tax proper." But Surrey was also right, in insisting that we can confidently conclude that *some* tax provisions would have no place in that structure, though the "frontier" be "uncharted and hazardous." Perhaps the analogy is too grand for a mere tax policy dispute, but Surrey's position bears some resemblance to the common-sense notion that airplane designers can and should rely on Newtonian physics, despite the limitations of Newtonian physics exposed by Einstein's theory of relativity.

Whereas Bittker suggested that the inability to produce a perfect TEB was reason enough to abandon the enterprise, Surrey believed that even an imperfect TEB would "assist the legislators in developing the image of a proper tax structure and in analyzing the problems of structure and theory at the borderline."[145] As in other areas of tax policy, so too with tax expenditures — Surrey never allowed theoretical difficulties to interfere with his ability to advocate for his vision of good tax policy. If that required him to endure the occasional "Bittker beating," he was willing to pay that price.

VI. Surrey on *Firing Line*

In January of 1974 Surrey — whose book, *Pathways to Tax Reform,* had recently been published by Harvard University Press — was the sole guest on a one-hour episode of the public policy talk show *Firing Line*, hosted by the conservative pundit

143. *Id.* at 530.
144. *Id.* at 533.
145. *Id.* at 537.

William F. Buckley, Jr.[146] The episode is must viewing for anyone interested in Surrey. Buckley was well-prepared. He had clearly read *Pathways* very carefully; with a debater's instincts he had noted tensions between Surrey's theoretical positions and policies Surrey had advocated during his Kennedy/Johnson years, as well as vulnerabilities in the theoretical positions themselves. Surrey was taken by surprise by Buckley's first question, which posited an inconsistency between Surrey's attack on tax expenditures in *Pathways* and Surrey's support of the investment tax credit, the enactment of which during the Kennedy administration owed much to Surrey's efforts, as we have discussed above.[147] In response to Buckley's hybrid question-comment, "But isn't it your general proposition that to encourage a particular form of activity, economic or social, by the device of tax incentives is to be avoided and it interests me that you should make an exception here," Surrey weakly offered, "Well, I don't think that one can be an absolutist about these things." When Buckley pressed, Surrey added, "Everybody knows it [the ITC] has nothing to do with the tax system."

Turning to fundamental theoretical issues later in the show, Buckley raised the standard conservative objection to the tax expenditure concept: "You more or less start out with the assumption that what you're dealing with is the government's money, whereas I start out with the assumption that what you're dealing with is the individual's money or the corporation's money. So that what you insist on calling tax subsidies, or tax expenditures, I would simply view as a form of remission." Surrey replied, "People often say that when they want to attack me. I don't really think it's an accurate way of expressing the matter. I would put it this way. We have decided to have an income tax. Then the question is, what does it mean to have an income tax. [Having decided on an income tax] any exclusion from our concept of income becomes a particular preference for that individual as compared with other individuals who are differently treated." Using the example of municipal bonds, Buckley cited the reduced pre-tax interest rate on municipal bonds as undercutting Surrey's fairness complaint, and Surrey responded that the implicit tax is significantly lower than the top marginal tax rate. It is an impressively sophisticated tax policy discussion by television standards, then or now.

Still later, Buckley put his finger on a tension at the heart of Surrey's tax policy philosophy: "On the one hand you are a moralist, a tax moralist, and on the other hand you feign that scientific detachment by the very simple expedient of saying the fact of the matter is the American people voted a progressive rate.... You really aren't a scientist ... but you insist that your observations are scientific in nature whereas in fact I think that they are based on a highly articulated set of personal value principles."

In his recounting of the show in his memoirs, Surrey writes, "I believe I held my own and was not overpowered as are many of his participants," and that "after it was over Buckley said I handled the program very well." We urge readers to watch the

146. The episode is available for streaming online at digitalcollections.hoover.org/objects/6301.
147. Revenue Act of 1962, Pub. L. No. 87-834, sec. 2, 76 Stat. 960, 962.

show and judge for themselves. In our view, although Surrey is right that he remained metaphorically standing throughout the entire episode (and also right that many of Buckley's guests did not), it was not a particularly impressive performance. In a manner reminiscent of his confirmation hearing more than a decade earlier, he seemed unprepared for lines of attack which he should have anticipated.

VII. Surrey and the Complexity of the Tax Laws

In a speech provocatively titled, "Is the Tax Law Going to Seed?," delivered almost a decade after Surrey's death, Surrey's one-time Harvard Law School colleague Erwin Griswold described Surrey's "remarkable mind, which could penetrate deeply, divide thoughts into channels, and then subdivide, and organize, and reorganize and expand in precisely thought-out details."[148] Although on first hearing that would seem to be a compliment (especially from one tax lawyer to another), on this occasion Griswold had not come to praise Surrey. Griswold continued:

> Until Stanley became Assistant Secretary of the Treasury for Tax Policy, the tax law remained relatively simple.... But Stanley could see all the problems, and, having seen them, he felt that it was his duty to spell them out. Under his aegis, we began to have sections of the statute with large numbers of sub-sections, and sub-sub-sections. Sometimes a single section runs in length to several pages. Many of these provisions I find baffling.... Many of those who practice in the tax field have long since been overwhelmed by all this detail.[149]

Griswold was correct that the Internal Revenue Code had lengthened substantially during Surrey's years in Treasury's top tax policy position. A new official version of the United States Code appears every six years. In 1958, a few years before Surrey's tour of duty began, Subtitle A, Chapter 1 ("Normal Taxes and Surtaxes," including the substantive provisions of the individual and corporate income taxes) of Title 26 occupied 248 pages of the United States Code. There was no major tax legislation between 1958 and the beginning of the Kennedy presidency, so the page count would have remained close to 248 when Surrey took office. By 1970, shortly after Surrey's return to Harvard, the same portion of Title 26 had expanded to 521 pages—an impressive 110 percent increase in just a dozen years. Griswold was also correct that this was not merely the continuation of a trend that predated Surrey's time in office. In fact, the equivalent portion of the 1952 Code was 291 pages; the statute had actually shrunk between 1952 and 1958.

Whether Surrey was responsible for the increase in statutory length and complexity, and whether the increase was a bad thing, are harder questions to answer. Certainly,

148. Griswold, Is the Tax Law Going to Seed?, *supra* note 11, at 5–6.
149. *Id.* at 6.

Congress during the 1960s did not obediently enact whatever Surrey told it to enact. The ultimate blame (if blame there be) for the statutory hyperlexis of the 1960s belongs to Congress, not Surrey. Moreover, there is evidence that Surrey was not as fond of sub-sub-sections as Griswold suggests. In his memorial tribute to Surrey, Andrews offered a more nuanced view: "Some of the most intricate parts of the present tax code, *as well as some of the most general*, are said to have sprung from Surrey's mind and pen."[150] Surrey was not philosophically committed to sub-sub-sections in all circumstances. In 1953, as the Chief Reporter of the ALI's Income Tax Project, Surrey wrote that there was no all-purpose answer to the question of how detailed an income tax statute should be:

> [S]ome may urge that an income tax statute should contain a large amount of detail and that consequently we need a larger, more complex Code than the present one. Others may stress the desirability of a statute with little detail, limited to general propositions as far as possible, so that in their view we need a shorter and less complex Code.... It has been found that no one view can be adopted and rigidly adhered to throughout. Instead, one view will be more persuasive in one situation, and the other view will be more attractive in the next.[151]

In 1969 newly-returned-to-Harvard Professor Surrey proposed not an increase in statutory complexity but the opposite, "a gradual shift from a highly detailed statute to more generalized provisions which would furnish the basic structure for the income tax."[152] Surrey's recommendation grew out of his belief that, as of 1969, the Treasury Department's institutional capacity to manage tax detail exceeded that of Congress.[153] The recommendation was not so much for less detailed tax rules as for a shifting of the detail from statutes to regulations. Nevertheless, Surrey's 1969 article provides a counterpoint to Griswold's description of Surrey as unreservedly in favor of statutory complexity.

And then there is the question of whether any Surrey-inspired increase in statutory detail was necessarily a bad thing. As Griswold acknowledges in the midst of complaining, Surrey-driven statutory elaboration would have been a response to Surrey's ability to "see all the problems" and his determination to deal with those problems in the statute. The problems predated the statutory complexity, and in any particular instance an increase in statutory detail might have been the least bad of all possible responses to a problem. As Surrey wrote in his 1953 musings on the optimal level of statutory detail, it all depends. An elegantly simple statute may be defenseless against

150. Andrews, A Source of Inspiration, *supra* note 14, at 334 (emphasis added).

151. Stanley S. Surrey & William C. Warren, *The Income Tax Project of the American Law Institute: Gross Income, Deductions, Accounting, Gains and Losses, Cancellation of Indebtedness*, 66 HARV. L. REV. 761, 768–69 (1953).

152. Stanley S. Surrey, *Complexity and the Internal Revenue Code: The Problem of the Management of Statutory Detail*, 34 LAW & CONT. PROB. 673, 703 (1969).

153. *Id.* at 703 (asserting that Treasury "is in reality the agency best suited to provide the needed effective control over tax details").

tax-avoidance schemes; complex provisions may be necessary to protect the integrity of the tax.[154] Nor is protection of the tax base the only good reason for a detailed statute. A more elaborate statute may actually be simpler than a short and vague statute, if simplicity is thought of from the perspective of those who must deal with the tax laws, rather than in terms of a mere statutory page count. In many cases, the lived complexity — for both tax practitioners and taxpayers themselves — of a detailed statute may be less than that of a shorter statute. It may be simpler to find a definite answer in a detailed statute, than to have to consult dozens of judicial opinions interpreting a short vague statute. And, of course, detailed rules are not made more (or less) complex by being located in a statute rather than in a regulation.

In short, Griswold's speech both overstates Surrey's responsibility for the length and complexity of the Internal Revenue Code and fails to appreciate the virtues (in some situations) of statutory detail. It may well be that today's Internal Revenue Code would be somewhat shorter if Stanley Surrey had never existed (one imagines a movie, "It's a Wonderful Tax Life," in which Angel Clarence shows Stanley Surrey a vision of how differently the Internal Revenue Code might have developed in Surrey's absence), but *pace* Griswold, a longer Surrey-influenced Code may be a good thing.

VIII. All Tax, All the Time

In reviewing Surrey's thousands of pages of tax scholarship and his immense record of public service, it is hard to understand how anyone could have accomplished so much in a single professional lifetime — even one spanning "Fifty Years (A Half Century?)," as the memoirs' subtitle puts it. Part of the explanation is suggested by Erwin Griswold's observation that Surrey's "energy was boundless,"[155] and by Donald Lubick's recollection that Surrey's "capacity for work seemed limitless."[156] Another part of the answer to the puzzle is suggested by Richard Musgrave's remark, in his memorial tribute to Surrey, that "after working with Stanley for decades, I cannot recall our ever having talked at length about anything but taxation."[157]

Surrey's single-minded devotion to the Internal Revenue Code is also reflected in these memoirs. To be sure, the memoirs' title indicates that the subject is not Surrey's personal life, but his life "with the Internal Revenue Code." And the second sentence of Surrey's introduction to the memoirs announces that the subject is Surrey's "close and ... varied ... relationship with the Internal Revenue Code." Still, the paucity of information about Surrey's non-tax life is striking, even given the professional focus

---

154. Although they were enacted two years after Surrey's death, the passive loss rules (IRC sec. 469) are arguably the classic example of tax complexity in service of the protection of the tax base. Tax Reform Act of 1986, Pub. L. No. 99-514, sec. 501, 100 Stat. 2085, 2233.

155. Griswold, A True Public Servant, *supra* note 4, at 331.

156. Lubick, A View from Washington, *supra* note 13, at 339.

157. Musgrave, Pathways to Tax Reform, *supra* note 38, at 337.

of the memoirs. The reader never learns, for example, that Surrey and his wife had a child (Scott Stanley Surrey). The reader does learn that Surrey was married, but the memoirs never mention Mrs. Surrey (Dorothy Mooklar Surrey) by name, and she features prominently in only two passages.

In one instance, Surrey describes (in a footnote, despite the fact that it is one of the better stories in the memoirs) the visit of Senator Edward Kennedy to the Surreys' Cambridge home in 1976 to discuss tax policy (of course). When Kennedy lit a cigar, Surrey was in a quandary. He explains that cigars were "high on my wife's negative list," but that after greeting Kennedy upon his arrival she had gone upstairs. Surrey "decided that this time the Nation's interests came first and if the Senator concentrated best when he was smoking, so be it." After Kennedy left, Surrey learned that "[t]here was not full agreement on my wife's part, putting it mildly."[158]

The setting of the other story was the 1972 visit to Japan of a group of American tax experts and their wives, at the invitation of the Ministry of Finance. Surrey recounts that at a reception, "while our wives and Japanese women were talking, the Japanese officials decided to leave, and took us along. It was only when one Japanese woman told my wife 'Your husband is leaving' did she get the word."[159] Surrey gives no indication that she ever would have gotten the word from him.

Surrey's vacations also took second place to his tax work. In his memoirs Surrey describes how he was "able to keep a schedule of thirty-day cruises each summer" and that "[t]ax talk was not allowed on these cruises."[160] Later, however, the reader learns that in 1975 Surrey wrote an article on corporate tax integration "while on a cruise and waiting for a crew change in the little harbor of Cutler, Maine," which he accomplished despite the fact that his boat (like so many boats) "did not have a tax library."[161] On another vacation, this one in 1976, Surrey co-chaired a tax task force for the Carter presidential campaign while sailing in Canada and Maine. To receive material from Joseph Pechman, his co-chair, Surrey enlisted members of his crew as couriers:

> [A]s a new member came on board for his leg of the sail he had with him a packet of papers from Pechman. I read these, made my changes, and then whenever we came to a port where I could make a phone call I discussed the changes with Pechman. I remember with embarrassment using for an hour the only pay phone on a dock in East Boothbay Harbor with a number of tourists obviously fretting and wrathful.... Over twenty memoranda were prepared.[162]

Perhaps tax *talk* was not allowed on Surrey's *boat*, but the story makes clear that Surrey allowed himself tax *work* on the boat, and tax talk on the *docks*. These anecdotes

---

158. *See* chapter 7, at Surrey's note h.
159. *See* chapter 9, at p. 194.
160. *See* chapter 7, at p. 236.
161. *See* chapter 8, at Surrey's note o.
162. *See* chapter 10, at p. 308.

paint a picture of a Surrey completely devoted to tax and only tax — to the point that tax law took precedence over familial relationships and even cherished vacations.

IX. The Certainty of Surrey

At least since Augustine's *Confessions*, one of the great attractions of memoirs for readers has been the opportunity to enter into the mind of the memoirist — to be privy to the memoirist's introspection and self-doubts. But Surrey was no Augustine. In his memoirs he rarely second guesses himself even on matters of tactics and strategy, and never on his fundamental tax policy commitments. If, for example, William Andrews' argument for the superiority of a consumption tax to an income tax,[163] or Boris Bittker's withering critique of the foundations of tax expenditure analysis,[164] forced Surrey to reconsider his tax policy premises, Surrey does not say so.

Similarly, although Surrey devotes several pages of Chapter 6 to a discussion of his support for the investment tax credit during the Kennedy years, he does not note the irony that, once in power, Surrey-the-foe-of-tax-preferences began by championing a massive new tax preference. If this involved any soul-searching on Surrey's part, he does not reveal that to the reader. Even at a merely tactical level, the Surrey of the memoirs rarely admits to a mistake. To take one glaring example, although he concedes that his 1957 *Harvard Law Review* article excoriating the performance of Congress in the tax legislative arena came back to haunt him in his confirmation hearing,[165] he does *not* suggest that with the benefit of hindsight he might have written the article any differently.[166]

There is also no introspection about Surrey's basic life choices. The memoirs leave the reader with the impression that Surrey devoted almost his entire waking existence to his professional life, leaving very little time for family or leisure (except for the annual sailing trips). Did Surrey ever question his own time allocation? If so, he does not discuss it in the memoirs — not even in connection with his 1972 heart attack, which might well have served as a catalyst for such questioning.

The open question is whether Surrey was truly immune to introspection and self-doubt, or whether he simply considered such topics outside the scope of the memoirs of his professional life. The editors leave answering that question to the reader, although Donald Lubick's memorial description of Surrey as "completely resilient in defeat" and "always press[ing] forward undaunted" may hint at an answer.[167]

---

163. William D. Andrews, *A Consumption-Type or Cash Flow Personal Income Tax*, 87 HARV. L. REV. 1113 (1974).

164. *Accounting for Federal "Tax Subsidies" in the National Budget*, *supra* note 137.

165. *See* chapter 3, at p. 26.

166. It is possible that Surrey intended to write about his confirmation hearing in a subsequent draft of his memoirs, as the annotations to his draft table of contents suggest.

167. Lubick, A View from Washington, *supra* note 13, at 339.

X. The Surprising Surrey

Despite the near absence of Surrey's personal life from his memoirs, the memoirs contain a few aspects of Surrey's professional life that may come as a surprise even to readers well acquainted with Surrey's myriad tax accomplishments. We highlight three of those aspects here.

First, as we describe above and as Surrey recounts in Chapter One, he had a most impressive early career as a New Deal labor lawyer with the NRA and the NLRB. He drafted many of the early opinions of the NLRB, including the very first opinion,[168] and another opinion so remarkable — for its holding, extreme length, rhetorical flourishes, and novelistic detail — as to merit front page stories in the *New York Times* and *Washington Post*, as well as an editorial cartoon in the *Post*, and an exasperated (but affirming) opinion by Judge Learned Hand.[169] If Surrey had remained in labor law, he almost certainly would have risen to a prominence in that field comparable to his actual prominence in tax. On the other hand, tax arguably provided greater scope for Surrey's talents and boundless energy than labor law could have furnished.

Second, although Surrey is remembered for his work in government and his scholarship, rather than for his teaching, the memoirs reveal that he was a truly innovative educator. He pioneered the modern policy-oriented tax casebook.[170] Perhaps even more notably, as we observed above, at the beginning of his teaching career in 1947, Surrey created at UC Berkeley Law School a seminar in advanced taxation, in which each week a different tax practitioner presented a tax problem on which he was currently working, and the students prepared suggested solutions for discussion with the practitioners.[171] When he later moved to Harvard, Surrey took that seminar design with him. It is our impression that legal educators generally assume that the history of seminars resembling Surrey's (whether in tax or some other legal field) goes back only two or three decades. It is remarkable that a young Stanley Surrey, new to law school teaching, came up with this approach almost seventy-five years ago.[172]

Finally, Surrey's honesty and commitment to fairness led to two important assignments — neither having anything to do with tax — during the unrest of the late 1960s and early 1970s. In 1969, Surrey was chosen to chair a tense meeting between Harvard Law students and faculty relating to student grievances. As Bernard Wolfman later noted in a memorial tribute to Surrey, "Despite the age gap and the availability of younger professors, it was Stanley Surrey whom both students and faculty trusted

---

168. In the Matter of Pennsylvania Greyhound Lines, Inc., 1 NLRB 1 (1935).

169. In the Matter of Remington Rand, Inc., 2 NLRB 626 (1937); National Labor Relations Board v. Remington Rand, Inc., 94 F2d 862 (2d Cir., 1938), *cert. denied*, 304 U.S. 576 (1938).

170. Stanley S. Surrey & William C. Warren, Federal Income Taxation: Cases and Materials (1950).

171. *See* chapter 3, at p. 10.

172. Former students have also noted that Surrey was a dedicated and enthusiastic teacher who pursued justice with "intellectual integrity and enjoyment." Victoria A. Judson, *An Exemplary Teacher*, 36 Harvard Law School Bulletin 56 (Winter/Spring 1985).

to mediate."[173] A few years later (1973) Harvard University President Derek Bok, well aware of Surrey's reputation as an honest broker, appointed Surrey to chair a newly-formed high-profile Advisory Committee on Shareholder Resolutions, tasked with advising Harvard how to vote on corporate shareholder resolutions put forward by public interest groups.

XI. "Our Troubled Tax Policy"

In late 1980, two weeks after the election of Ronald Reagan, Surrey delivered a major speech, "Our Troubled Tax Policy: False Routes and Proper Paths to Change," as his Presidential Address at the Annual Meeting of the National Tax Association.[174] Although Surrey published a later book and several articles relating to tax expenditures, the speech was to be the last comprehensive survey of his views on the state of United States tax policy in the early 1980s, around the time he was writing his memoirs. In the speech Surrey is sometimes funny, often angry, unshaken in his long-standing tax policy convictions, and (in striking contrast to the Surrey of the 1961 confirmation hearing, but perhaps consistent with his earlier writings) utterly unafraid to say exactly what he thinks regardless of whom he may offend. We review here a few highlights from the speech.

Surrey, the lifelong champion of income taxation, begins by noting the then-fashionable view among "a number of economists and legal academics ... that we should replace our present income tax with a [graduated rate] tax on consumption," because a consumption tax is said to be more efficient than an income tax.[175] Surrey is having none of it. Invoking "the effects that would result for our society from the large untaxed accumulations of wealth," he bemoans "[t]he energy wasted on academic thinking about a consumption tax."[176] He next addresses academic support for the integration of the corporate and individual income taxes, and concludes that "academic thinking has led to a political approach that ... has yielded only a candidate for regressivity."[177] Turning to the political ascendancy of supply-side economics (which was soon to result in the massive tax cuts of the Economic Recovery Tax Act of 1981), Surrey calls out "supply-side economics, capital formation, and like slogans" as "cliches for tax reductions for upper-bracket persons," and opines that enactment of the tax legislation then being considered in Congress would be "destructive of the equity and fairness of the income tax."[178] (For Surrey "equity and fairness" functions as a single term, in a manner comparable to "cease and desist.") He laments the "dis-

---

173. Bernard Wolfman, *Statesman, Scholar, Mentor*, 98 HARV. L. REV. 343, 344 (1984). For more on the 1960s student protests, *see generally*, TODD GITLIN, THE SIXTIES: YEARS OF HOPE, DAYS OF RAGE (1993).

174. Surrey, Our Troubled Tax Policy: False Routes and Proper Paths to Change, *supra* note 96.

175. *Id.* at 179.

176. *Id.* at 180.

177. *Id.* at 182.

178. *Id.* at 184.

integration of the legislative process," to which business lobbyists have responded "with skill and vigor to make the most of the legislative chaos," with the result that—to Surrey's dismay—"[m]ore tax expenditures have been added in the last four years than in any prior period."[179] Surrey reserves perhaps his sharpest scorn for econometric models: "If... computer printouts are to carry a credence comparable to the religious sanctions behind the ancient oracles, then legislative action is a hostage to the testimony of economists with econometric models."[180]

Having scorched the earth with his denunciation of "False Routes to Change," Surrey offers a vision of "Proper Paths for Change." His vision includes an increased emphasis on tax expenditure analysis (of course),[181] and a "concerted attack" on tax shelters.[182] Surrey concedes it "may be appropriate to reduce our top individual rate [from 70 percent] to 50 percent," but only "when the effective rates approximate the scheduled rates."[183]

Given that Surrey's tone through most of the speech resembles that of an Old Testament prophet, one might not expect him to reach an optimistic conclusion. And yet, as Donald Lubick noted in his memorial tribute, Surrey was "completely resilient in responding to defeat," viewed all setbacks as temporary, and would always "press forward undaunted."[184] And so he ends his valedictory tax policy speech:

> [I]f one has a firm belief in the social desirability of income and transfer taxes and if one in turn thinks our society basically has the same belief, then one has to be optimistic.... How long and how difficult will be the paths to that goal remain unknown but the goal is still there.[185]

---

179. *Id.* at 185.
180. *Id.* at 187.
181. *Id.* at 190–92.
182. *Id.* at 192.
183. *Id.* at 195.
184. Lubick, A View from Washington, *supra* note 13, at 339.
185. Surrey, Our Troubled Tax Policy: False Routes and Proper Paths to Change, *supra* note 96.

Annotated Contents

by Stanley S. Surrey

Introduction.

Draft written — to be checked.

Chapter One: The Beginnings, 1929–1937.

Draft written — to be checked.

Chapter Two: A Government Tax Career — Part I, 1937–1947.

Draft written — to be checked.

Chapter Three: A Law School Professor — Part I, 1947–1961.

Draft written — to be checked.

Chapter Four: American Law Institute Tax Project — Part I, 1947–1960.

Commencement of Project in 1947 with Surrey as Chief Reporter and Warren as Associate — governing policy board of Darrell, Griswold, Rudick, Miller, etc. — Associates used, many now prominent lawyers — method of work — cross country trips — drafts and annual meetings — prominent consultants added — articles describing the work — final 1954 Volumes covering entire income tax — maneuvering to include much of 1954 Volume into 1954 Code — later work.

Chapter Five: International Tax Activities — Part I, 1938–1960.

Some earlier international tax legislation in Treasury such as Western Hemisphere Corporations, "in lieu of" foreign tax credits — general ignorance in Treasury — first major U.S. tax treaty trip to Europe in 1946 — visit to General Clay in Berlin in 1946 — Stam and Senator George — treaty work shifted to Treasury from IRS — member of Shoup Tax Mission to Japan, 1949 and 1950, first major international tax mission — starting in 1952 organization, with United Nations, and directorship of Harvard International Program in Taxation to train officials from developing countries, publish books on foreign tax systems and on international tax subjects — first such program and still successful — international tax bar saw this as beginning of end to their stranglehold on policy in this area — important foreign tax officials who went through this training program — development of an International Tax course at Harvard and articles in the field — drafting and enactment of Puerto Rico Excise Tax — member of Shoup Mission to Venezuela, 1956–1957 — member of International Institute of Public Finance and Brazil talk — writing of book for U.N. on U.S. Taxation of foreign income — testimony opposing H.R. 5 — Boggs reaction — 1959 testimony at Senate Foreign Relations Committee which single-handedly defeated government policy of adopting "tax-sparing" treaties — 1960 Argentina tax mission of Surrey and Oldman.

Chapter Six: A Government Tax Career — Part II, 1961–1969.

Assistant Secretary for Tax Policy in Treasury Department under Presidents Kennedy and Johnson — presumably a summary chapter since activities very extensive in both domestic and international areas — legislative and administrative results — describe scene, 1961–1969, use of complete diary.

Chapter Seven: A Law School Professor — Part II, 1969 to date.

Back at Harvard Law School — revised casebooks and new courses — participation in annual Brookings Institution Tax Conferences — articles and their translation into foreign periodicals — organization of May Annual Symposia of National Tax Association, and President 1979–1980 — consultant to Filer Commission on Philanthropy — member of Board of Trustees of Teachers Insurance and Annuity Association — member of Visiting Committee, Brandeis Heller School of Social Welfare — leading role in tax group providing McGovern Presidential candidacy with tax program — numerous Law School and University activities assigned to me because of government experience, e.g., chairing crucial meeting on discipline of students, committee to form Law School Student Council, Chairman of first University committee to vote Harvard stock proxies, Chairman of Harvard Institute of Politics Fellowship Selection panel, committee to establish Law School summer research program, committee on outside compensation, Chairman of Committee to oversee Law School Legal Services Institute, Chairman, Institute of Politics Panel on Fellowships.

Chapter Eight: American Law Institute Tax Project — Part III, 1973 to date.

My organization of project and raising the funds — work as Project Supervisor in charge of the various separate income tax programs, i.e., Taxation of Corporations, Taxation of Partnerships, Taxation of Trusts and Estates, and International Taxation — choice of Reporters and Consultants — methods of operation and results to date.

Chapter Nine: International Tax Activities — Part II, 1969 to date.

U.S. Member of Permanent Scientific Committee of International Fiscal Association (committee to plan the substantive work of the Association) 1969 to date — General Reporter and Panel Chairman for several Association meetings and recipient of first Gold Medal Award — initial U.S. Member (1968) and then Special Advisor to U.N. Ad Hoc Group of Experts on Treaties Between Developed and Developing Countries and as such responsible for drafting Model U.N. Treaty concluded in 1969 — continued work with this U.N. Group — several trips to Japan and decorated by Japanese Prime Minister — seminars in India and Indonesia for government officials — speeches and seminars for CIAT (organization of Latin American tax administrators) — tax mission in Spring 1980 in Middle East Arabic countries for U.N. — Lady Davis Visiting Professor Spring 1980 at Hebrew University Law School in Jerusalem — work with German Foundation for Economic Development on various tax conferences.

Chapter Ten: A Government Tax Career — Part III, 1969–1980.

Testimony in support of 1969 Act reform proposals — activity in opposition to some of President Nixon's 1971 Act proposals — Co-chairman of tax group advising on tax policy in Carter Presidential campaign and later a participant in planning initial program — participation in briefing Senator Mondale in his campaign debate with Dole — appointed Consultant on tax matters to Treasury Department and White House during entire Carter Administration — continuous discussion with all top ranking Treasury tax officials since they had worked with or for me in 1961–1969 period — participation with Professor McDaniel as advisor on tax matters for Senator Kennedy in Senate and in his Presidential campaign — continued work for Senator Kennedy — articles on pending tax matters.

Chapter Eleven: Tax Expenditure Analysis — A New Fiscal Concept, 1968 to date.*

My initial development while in Treasury of tax expenditure analysis concept — publication of first U.S. tax expenditure budget in 1968 — maneuvering with Woodworth, Chief of Staff of Joint Committee, first to institutionalize preparation of budget by Joint Committee Staff, Senator Javits Amendment, and then to secure Congressional legislative sanction of tax expenditure budget in Budget Reform Act of 1974 — initial Harvard Law Review articles and later publication of book "Pathways to Tax Reform" describing tax expenditure analysis — talks on this analysis at meetings of International Institute of Public Finance and International Fiscal Association conference on the subject — consultation with foreign officials (Canada and France) on use of tax expenditure analysis — adoption of analysis and budgets in Canada, France, Spain, U.K., etc. — McDaniel and Surrey current research project with Erasmus University (Rotterdam) on international guidelines for comparative tax expenditure budgets in seven countries and OECD — articles being currently written on the subject and book underway.

* Although Surrey clearly had planned a chapter on tax expenditures, no such chapter appears in the typescript of his memoirs. — Eds.

Introduction

by Stanley S. Surrey

Why this volume? As one reason, I doubt that any person alive today has had as close and as varied a relationship with the Internal Revenue Code as I have had. This is not a boast but merely a statement of the result of age — "seniority" is perhaps more dignified or at least more soothing. I confess this sounds as if I was a Senate page boy when the Sixteenth Amendment was adopted,[1] the tax version of the Civil War veteran who was a drummer boy of ten during the War! My long and very concentrated connection with our federal tax system does provide a vantage point to describe and reflect upon the fifty years of development that has occurred in that system. This volume has made me think about this development in a way that I would not otherwise have done. Indeed, as I write this Introduction I am not at all clear what conclusions will emerge. The very writing itself does become a mystery whose clues or insights will only be revealed as the writing moves along. I am interested in finding what will eventuate.

Another reason is that the volume is necessarily autobiographical, as well as an historical survey of much of the tax system. The volume thus gives a retrospective survey of how fifty years of professional life were spent. Does an intense relationship with the tax system confine the horizon of a lifetime to a narrow focus? Surely some must think this so — what can be more narrowing than the tax field, and fifty years of that! But I have thought otherwise, and this survey will — hopefully — support this belief. Perhaps also the survey will indicate to others that taxation is a field in which the width of the horizon depends only on one's interests and energies, for the opportunities are there. It must be remembered that this view is confined to a field of the law. Obviously I cannot compare a career shaped by a decision to be a lawyer with careers in other fields of life. It is only within that choice — which, again, some

1. The Sixteenth Amendment was ratified on February 3, 1913, when Surrey was merely three years old, not quite old enough to be a U.S. Senate page. The amendment provides that "Congress shall have the power to lay and collect taxes on incomes from whatever source derived, without apportionment among the several States, and without regard to any census or enumeration." Its purpose was to overrule the Supreme Court's decision in Pollock v. Farmers' Loan & Trust Co., 157 U.S. 429 (1895), *aff'd on reh'g*, 158 U.S. 601 (1895) (which had held the 1894 federal income tax unconstitutional for want of apportionment). Congress wasted little time in taking advantage of the Sixteenth Amendment; in October it included a new individual income tax in the Revenue Act of 1913, Pub. L. No. 63-16, 38 Stat. 114.

will surely see as much too narrow a confinement to begin with — that this volume has its purpose.

Fifty years is a long period, even though it seems to have moved so rapidly. Was it not only yesterday that I graduated from Columbia Law School — surely "Class of 1932" must be a typographical error. But research discloses the year is truly stated. It must then be obvious that memories dim, events are forgotten, for no diary was kept except for the period 1961–1969.[2] But some events and impressions do remain and even others will probably be dredged up as writing proceeds. Resort to histories of the tax system — for example, Randolph Paul's Taxation in the United States (1954)[3] and Sidney Ratner's Taxation and Democracy in America (1967)[4] — will help this process. Perhaps a review of my own writings will spur recollection of the situations and interests that prompted them.[5] This disclosure is intended to disclaim that the volume is a full, detailed history of the tax system over the past half century. It is instead only a remembrance of a particular journey through that history.

I must add that a quick glance at Randolph Paul's index discloses the main difference in what he and I observed and are describing in our writings. Paul wrote mainly of the very large events, the forces that moved the Congress and the Administration, principally those of Roosevelt and Truman, in their struggles over the broad shape of the tax system and the level of tax rates. He has related these struggles to the social and political movements of the years he examined. But much of the nuts and bolts of the formulation of the technical structure of our tax system is not described. As one example — perhaps the best — the index contains no reference to the names of Middleton Beaman, House Legislative Counsel, or his successors, John O'Brien and Gerald Morgan;[6] Colin Stam, Chief of Staff of the Joint Congressional

---

2. Surrey kept detailed notes of his daily experiences at the Treasury Department from 1961 to 1969. Photocopies of Surrey's journals from that period are in the Surrey archives at the Harvard Law School Library. Stanley Surrey archives, HOLLIS000601595, Boxes 400-2, 400-3, 400-4, 400-5, 401-1, 401-2, 401-3, and 401 (on file with Harvard Law School Library).

3. Randolph E. Paul, Taxation in the United States (1954). Paul had a long and very distinguished career as a tax lawyer, in both government service and private practice. He was the leading name partner in the law firm of Paul, Weiss, Rifkind, Wharton & Garrison. Surrey worked for Paul, during the New Deal and World War II, when the latter was General Counsel to Robert Morgenthau's Treasury Department. *Randolph Paul, 65, Dies; War II Treasury Counsel*, The Washington Post, Feb. 7, 1956, at 26.

4. Sidney Ratner, Taxation and Democracy in America (1967). Ratner was a Columbia University trained economic historian who served as an economist in the U.S. Board of Economic Warfare and the U.S. State Department during WWII, and who taught for many years at Rutgers University until his retirement in 1978. There is no evidence of any relationship or correspondence between Surrey and Ratner. Reed Abelson, *Sidney Ratner, 87; Scholar Specialized in Economic History*, New York Times, Jan. 17, 1996, at A17.

5. A complete bibliography of Surrey's writings can be found at *In Memoriam: Stanley S. Surrey*, 98 Harv. L. Rev. 329, 346–350 (1984).

6. Middleton Beamon, John O'Brien, and Gerald Morgan were key staffers in the U.S. House of Representatives during Surrey's early government career. Surrey recounts his professional relationships with these men in Chapter 2.

Committee on Taxation;[7] only one mention of Thomas Tarleau,[8] the first Legislative Counsel in the Treasury and of his successor Stanley Surrey; and only one mention during the period he was in the Treasury of Roy Blough, the Director of the Division of Tax Research.[9] Yet these individuals, and those who worked with them, were responsible for the rapidly developing structure of the tax law. Paul and I are thus describing different parts of the elephant.

The attempt to cover a half century presents a problem of organization. Should I proceed year by year, thereby covering disparate events connected only by chronology. Or should I attempt to group events by subject matter, letting each group cover a span of years. The solution chosen is a compromise — as is the outcome of the events themselves, for fifty years teaches the necessity if not the wisdom of compromise if one desires to continue a career in a particular field. I have chosen a substantive grouping of events, chronologically described within each group and with the groups themselves presented in a somewhat chronological order. This may cause some confusion. But again, fifty years in the tax field has not been without an element of confusion.

One last point. Many of the persons mentioned are now dead, another consequence of seniority. Thus I must proceed without the availability of a check in many situations. I have done my best to recollect correctly. If I have erred anywhere, all I can do is here express my regret.

---

7. Colin F. Stam was the Chief of Staff of the Joint Committee on Taxation for more than a quarter century, from 1937–1964. As Surrey recounts at length in later chapters, Surrey and Stam were rather bitter adversaries for much of that time. *Colin F. Stam Dies at 69; Tax Expert in Congress*, The Washington Post, Jan. 7, 1966, at C5.

8. Thomas N. Tarleau served in the Treasury Department from 1933 to 1947, becoming the first official Tax Legislative Counsel. He later became a partner in the law firm of Willkie, Farr & Gallagher and president of the Tax Section of the American Bar Association. *Thomas N. Tarleau*, New York Times, Dec. 31, 1985, at B10.

9. Economist Roy Blough was the Treasury Department's Director of Tax Research from 1938 to 1946. He was a member of the president's Council of Economic Advisors from 1950–1952, and later in the 1950s served as director of the economic affairs department of the United Nations. He was also a long-time academic, first at the University of Chicago, and later at Columbia University. *Roy Blough, 98, Official at the Treasury*, New York Times, Mar. 2, 2000, at C25.

A Half-Century with the Internal Revenue Code

ONE

The Beginnings
1929–1945

Strangely enough, my relationship to the Internal Revenue Code had its beginning in a classroom on Civil Procedure I in the Columbia Law School in the fall of 1929.[a, 1] The Professor was Roswell Magill — a dry, taciturn person who moved through the course in a most methodical fashion.[2] His sobriquet was "four cases a day Magill," and it was correctly applied for that was the pace, no more or no less than the magic number four. We students thought we did perceive an intelligence within the dryness and habitualness, and even flashes of wit. But the course and the cases were dull and uninspiring, just days to be spent in a subject prescribed by the curriculum. Magill, besides class recitation, required each student to write a short paper on the particular case assigned to the student. The assignments were mechanically made — move along the class list and assign the cases in order. My lot was the assignment of a most dismal case, involving the extent of the notice that must be given to shareholders to enable a validly called corporate meeting of shareholders. The case concerned only a particular statute in a particular state and the court naturally said the statute must be followed. There was no more to the case than that — no intriguing point of jurisprudence, no subtle reconciliation of precedents, no new doctrine. How does one write five to ten pages on a non-starter? The solution I found was that of statistical description. I would classify the shareholder notice rules of each state, as to time required, manner of notice, specificity of subject matter, and so on. Nearly all of the material was statutory and readily to be found. So the paper was written — an orderly, fully documented classification of the factors required by state law to produce satisfactory notice of shareholder meetings.

The important matter is that the paper caught Magill's eye. Indeed, he commented in class that naturally the papers varied but one was quite elegant, a detailed, extensive coverage of the subject matter. No name was mentioned but I correctly suspected

1. Joseph Wisan (mentioned in Surrey's note a) received his doctorate in history from Columbia in 1934. He chaired City College's history department from 1949 to 1965. He also coached the City College tennis team from 1929 to 1936. *Joseph E. Wisan, Professor, 89*, NEW YORK TIMES, Jul. 12, 1990, at D20.

2. In the mid-1920s Magill was the chief attorney for Andrew Mellon's Treasury Department. After joining the Columbia Law School faculty in 1927 (where he taught the first course in federal income tax ever offered at that school), he divided the remainder of his distinguished career among Columbia, additional high-level service at Treasury in the late 1930s, and private practice with Cravath, Swain & Moore. *Roswell Magill Dead; Once Treasury Expert*, THE WASHINGTON POST, Dec. 19, 1963, at B4.

that my paper was the example. So much for Civil Procedure I and my first contact with Professor Magill, and so far no connection at all with tax law. But Professor Magill, as I discovered in reading the course catalogue, taught Taxation in the second year. This was not a prescribed course and the choice was up to the student. Somehow or other, I had come to like this astringent teacher—was it the reference to the elegant paper?—indeed to prefer him over some of the flashy types, such as Professor Llewellyn[3] whom I often thought dramatically shouted complex nonsense to frighten or hypnotize the first-year Contracts class. Some other students had just the opposite opinion. One thing a law school teacher learns, often painfully, is that you cannot reach or appeal to every student in the class. Some students will consider you the very best professor they had in school while others will see you as the embodiment of the evils of the tenure system.

So I chose to register for Magill's Taxation course. It was the same Magill—dry and methodical. Yet there was a difference. I noticed that if a student showed an interest in a case, pushed a somewhat hard or reasonable question to him, his interest quickly perked up and the discussion immediately deepened. As I had suspected there was a deep intelligence in this person. Also, his interest in the Taxation course was far greater than in Civil Procedure. Why not, for the tax field was really interesting. At that period in tax history much of the subject matter was constitutional law regarding the jurisdiction of taxation by the states and the substantive coverage of state tax systems. But there was material on federal taxation also, though my recollection is that the latter was a distinctly subordinate aspect of the course. I liked the course and as a result Magill told me I had written the best examination paper. Still it received only an A, for he said, somewhat apologetically, he did not use A plus.

Here really ended my law school student connection with taxation. [check—did I do a Law Review piece?[4]] There were no more courses in the field. Today a law school curriculum is dotted with tax courses covering a variety of facets, but in 1931–2 Taxation was a subordinate course, just one of many electives. I took a variety of

3. Karl Llewellyn, a leader of the legal realist school, was among the most influential of mid-twentieth-century American legal academics. He taught briefly at Yale Law School, at Columbia Law School from 1924 to 1951, and at the University of Chicago Law School from 1951 until his death in 1962. Llewellyn published several notable books on commercial law and legal theory, including CASES AND MATERIALS ON THE LAW OF SALES (1930), and THE COMMON LAW TRADITION (1930). William Twining, *Llewellyn, Karl N.*, YALE BIOGRAPHICAL DICTIONARY OF AMERICAN LAW 346–348 (Roger K. Newman ed., 2009) [hereinafter YALE BIOGRAPHICAL DICTIONARY OF AMERICAN LAW].

4. Issues of *Columbia Law Review* from Surrey's student years contain a number of one- and two-page student-written notes on recent tax cases. Unfortunately, the notes are anonymous, so any attributions to Surrey would be purely speculative. Two longer tax-related student notes also appeared in the *Review* in the Surrey years: *Unlawful Expenditures and the Income Tax*, 31 COLUM. L. REV. 1344, 1344–48 (1931), and *The Revenue Act of 1932*, 32 COLUM. L. REV. 1205, 1205–24 (1932). If the former were written by Surrey, it would be of interest, as Surrey's first published musings on the pros and cons of using the income tax to serve non-tax purposes (in particular, denying business expense deductions relating to illegal activities in order to penalize or deter illegal conduct). And whoever may have written the latter, it is a remarkably sophisticated effort for a law student. It seems unlikely, however, that Surrey would have forgotten his authorship of either, even decades later as he was writing his memoirs.

subjects, avoiding those where I thought the subject matter or teachers were dull. I did take all of Professor Milton Handler's courses—three in all, Sales, Anti-Trust, and Vendor and Purchaser [check]—since I regarded him as an excellent teacher.[5] The last course was, however, dull and although I did some research for his casebook I found the work most uninspiring.[6] Handler did notice this, for he once said he had to "build a fire" under me and I responded that he just didn't have the necessary firewood. As I recall, I received an A in Anti-Trust and Sales (not an A plus because several years ago he had not given an A plus to another fine exam paper written by Wilbur Friedman, later an outstanding New York tax lawyer, and the precedent was set),[7] but only an A minus in Vendor and Purchaser. This grade surprised Handler, but I countered by pointing out that one of his questions—"Give the history of the Statute of Frauds" (a close approximation to the wording) was a terrible non-starter. I mention these relationships with Handler because in a surprising way they later became one of the links that brought about my connection with taxation.

Most of my third year was fascinating, partly because of the interesting, though perhaps impractical from a bar examination standpoint, courses I had selected, but mainly as a result of Law Review work. I had started the third year as Book Review Editor and Assistant Note Editor, a position held in the previous year by an outstanding legal scholar, Felix Cohen, the son of Professor Morris Raphael Cohen of City College.[8] Through a change in personnel I also became Managing Editor (a new title, to cover the superseding of the second in command—the Secretary of the Law Review), a position held the previous year by Walter Gellhorn, who went on to be a

---

5. Milton Handler was a long-time member of the faculty of Columbia Law School. During the 1930s he served as President Roosevelt's chief advisor on antitrust matters. Handler participated in drafting the National Labor Relations Act, Pub. L. No. 74-198, 49 Stat. 449 (1935) [hereinafter the National Labor Relations Act] and was the first general counsel to the National Labor Relations Board. Later he practiced law as a name partner with the firm of Kaye, Scholer, Fierman, Hays & Handler. David Klingsberg and Peter A. Barile III, *Handler, Milton*, YALE BIOGRAPHICAL DICTIONARY OF AMERICAN LAW, *supra* note 3, at 250–251.

6. The Handler casebook that Surrey mentions doing "some research for" was likely Milton Handler, *Cases and Materials on the Law of Vendor and Purchaser* (St. Paul, West Publishing Co., 1933).

7. Wilbur H. Friedman chaired the tax department of the Proskauer Rose law firm for a remarkable fifty years and lived to the age of 103. He is memorialized by the Wilbur H. Friedman Chair in Tax Law at Columbia Law School. *Wilbur H. Friedman*, NEW YORK TIMES, Dec. 23, 2010, at B19.

8. Between 1933 and 1947 Felix S. Cohen worked as an attorney at the Interior Department and became the leading expert on American Indian law. His HANDBOOK OF FEDERAL INDIAN LAW (1942) is perhaps *the* classic in the field. He was instrumental in drafting the Indian Reorganization Act, Pub. L. No. 73-383, 48 Stat. 984 (1934), which aimed to reestablish tribal governments in Indian reservations. After resigning from the Interior Department, Cohen opened a Washington office of a New York law firm and continued working with American Indian tribes. In addition, Cohen was a visiting professor at Yale Law School and City College from 1948 through 1953. Dalia Tsuk Mitchell, *Cohen, Felix S.*, YALE BIOGRAPHICAL DICTIONARY OF AMERICAN LAW, *supra* note 3, at 120–122. Felix Cohen's father, Morris Raphael Cohen, was a professor of philosophy at City College of New York (CCNY) and a leading legal theorist and public intellectual. Although Surrey does not mention whether he had Morris Cohen as a teacher when he attended CCNY, he most certainly was aware of his influence on American jurisprudence. *Morris Raphael Cohen,* NEW YORK TIMES, Jan. 31, 1947, at 22.

noted Columbia Law Professor.[9] Then our Editor-in-Chief, Arthur Krim,[10] a remarkable student whose promise was realized in a remarkable career, became ill for several months and I also took on his position. The previous year the position had been held by Herbert Wechsler, who also became a noted Columbia Law School professor and the Director of the American Law Institute.[11] Performing simultaneously the tasks separately done the previous year by Cohen, Gellhorn, and Wechsler was hard work but also fun. I survived, though my class attendance, while faithful, consisted only of taking copious notes on the discussion of cases which I had barely glanced at. An F, fairly awarded, in the examination on the first half of Advanced Civil Procedure, taught by Professor (later Judge) Harold Medina,[12] a consummate class performer with anecdotes galore but no real jurisprudential depth, jarred me a bit so that I was stirred to turn it into a final A. I managed, because of the notes and a most concentrated review of the courses just before the final examinations, to graduate as a Kent Scholar[13] (for all three years) and second in the class.

Law School was thus interesting, rewarding and enjoyable. But what next? The economic depression was still deep, and downtown law firm jobs hard to find. Still, a Law Review editor at least could secure an offer. I hesitated, however, doubtful about being forced to leave the interesting world of the Law School and the fascination I had found in the Law Review work. At this point Professor Magill reentered my life. I had not seen him since the second year Taxation course. But suddenly he offered me a year's position as his research assistant. He had been given a grant to write a book on federal taxation as part of a larger tax study being undertaken at Columbia University. Professors Robert Murray Haig[14] and also

---

9. Walter Gellhorn was on the faculty of Columbia Law School for more than four decades, from 1933 to 1975. He was a leading expert in both administrative law and civil rights law. Robert McG. Thomas Jr., *Walter Gellhorn, Law Scholar and Professor, Dies at 89,* New York Times, Dec. 11, 1995, at D10.

10. Arthur B. Krim was an entertainment lawyer and movie studio executive. He was the chairman of both United Artists (1951–1978) and Orion Pictures (1978–1992). *Arthur B. Krim,* The Washington Post, Sep. 23, 1994, at B6.

11. Herbert Wechsler was a leading expert on both constitutional law and criminal law. He was the chief reporter for the American Law Institute's influential Model Penal Code (1962). Norman I. Silber, *Wechsler, Herbert,* Yale Biographical Dictionary of American Law, *supra* note 3, at 577–578.

12. Harold R. Medina was a U.S. district court judge in the Southern District of New York from 1947 to 1951, a judge of the U.S. Court of Appeals for the Second Circuit from 1951 to 1958, and a senior judge of the same court from 1958 to 1980. J. Y. Smith, *Harold R. Medina, 102, Dies; Ran 1949 Conspiracy Trial,* The Washington Post, Mar. 17, 1990, at B5.

13. Since 1923, Columbia Law School has recognized students as James Kent Scholars, based on exceptional academic performance. Recognition is for a particular academic year; thus, a student can be recognized up to three times in his or her time at Columbia.

14. Public finance economist Robert Murray Haig is best remembered for his contribution to the formulation of the famous Haig-Simons definition of income (under which a person's income in a particular period equals consumption during the period plus or minus change in net worth from the beginning to the end of the period). *See* Robert Murray Haig, *The Concept of Income—Economic and Legal Aspects* 1, 27 in Robert M. Haig, Thomas R. Powell, and Thomas S. Adams, The Federal Income Tax (1921).

Carl Shoup[15] — whom I did not then meet but who later became a major influence in my work — were to study the economic concepts of income.[16] Magill was to work on the legal concepts. I at once accepted the position. I liked Magill and the offer postponed a career choice that I did not want nor know how to make.

Now I was really being connected with tax law. The classroom in Civil Procedure I had brought me, all unsuspecting and all unplanned, to this connection. The research work was both challenging and difficult. The project was the first of its kind since no one had yet attempted a coordinated structural analysis of the federal income tax that covered both theory and substantive rules, in statute and cases. There really were no precedents to guide my research. Moreover, Magill left me a completely free hand. He would simply say, "How about a chapter on this?" I would then see him a month or two later to turn over a complete draft on the topic — both text and footnotes. Then there would be the next request: "How about a chapter on this topic?" The chance to work on Magill's book and this method of working served me well. With only my own reading and my own plan of internal organization to guide me, I surveyed almost the entire structure of the income tax. The background I thus gained was far more thorough than that obtained by many a skilled practitioner. While they did possess the day-to-day technical handling of the tax tools, I was forced to find the theoretical strands that held the structure together. As a result I had the rare opportunity early on to obtain a sense of that structure as a whole and to understand that the structure could be analyzed and dealt with in logical terms. A rational framework could be devised for the structure and in turn structural errors could be perceived. I saw the income tax not as a random body of rules and edicts but as an internally consistent framework. All of my later work has been dominated by that approach.[17]

---

15. Public finance economist Carl Shoup had a lengthy and distinguished career in both academia (at Columbia) and in public service. Shortly after World War II, he led the so-called Shoup Mission to advise the Japanese government on the design of its post-war tax system. Surrey, who was also a major contributor to the Shoup Mission, discusses the Mission in some detail later in Chapter 5. For more on the Shoup Mission, *see generally* the essays contained in THE POLITICAL ECONOMY OF TRANSNATIONAL TAX REFORM: THE SHOUP MISSION TO JAPAN IN HISTORICAL CONTEXT (W. Elliot Brownlee, Eisaku Ide and Yasumori Fukagai eds., 2013).

16. Haig was Shoup's Columbia University mentor and thesis advisor. They had been working for many years on a collaborative project about the economic concepts of income, but apparently did not publish their research, perhaps because University of Chicago economist Henry Simons published a similar book in 1938. HENRY C. SIMONS, PERSONAL INCOME TAXATION (1938).

17. Boris I. Bittker, Surrey's only rival for the title of the most influential American tax law scholar of the mid-twentieth century, expressed a strikingly similar belief in the rationality of the federal income tax:

> I am convinced that the Code is more than a laundry list of discrete items, that almost all provisions can be understood in light of their antecedents and relationships to the rest of the Code, and that routes through the bog can be picked out. After devoting five years to this project, I am more convinced than when I started that the proportion of senseless detail to pervasive structural principles is relatively low, and that the Code, while not the most majestic attainment of human thought, is much less rickety than is commonly believed.

BORIS BITTKER, FEDERAL TAXATION OF INCOME, ESTATES AND GIFTS, at vii (1st ed., vol. 1, 1981).

Magill in the meantime was also served well. All of my material was used, some of it verbatim, in the final work, "Taxable Income," published in 1936 and viewed as a classic in the field.[18] Magill somewhat apologetically said that in the nature of things he could not name me as a co-author, but later he usually jocularly referred to me as the author of "Taxable Income." I was satisfied, for I had spent an interesting year, learning much. During this year, other connections with taxation developed. A law school classmate, Jack Aronson (later Allison) employed downtown in New York in Proskauer, Rose and Paskus, had been given a federal estate tax problem to work on.[19] The problem intrigued him and he asked me to join in writing a law review article on the federal estate tax. One would think I would have had my fill of taxation during the day, solitarily pursuing my research in my small office and the school library. But the request intrigued and excited me—writing a law review article just after I had graduated. So every night for over two months Jack and I worked in my office, each doing his assigned share of research and writing and then discussing our conclusions. Here also there were really no earlier materials to guide us, for the subject we chose had not been comprehensively treated. We persevered—correcting each other's ignorance—and the article was accepted by the Columbia Law Review. It appeared as "Inter Vivos Transfers and the Federal Estate Tax," 32 Columbia Law Review 1332 (1932).[20] The article took a strong position on the constitutionality and desirability of applying the estate tax to donative life-time transfers that had a connection—through donor control or a change of interests at the donor's death—with that death. Other writers—and many practitioners—had taken the opposite view, pushing a narrow application of the estate tax. Time proved we were on the right track and the article reads well even fifty years later.

The publication of this article prompted a further thought. Here I was writing away day after day but only turning over the drafts to a drawer in Magill's office since his schedule called for his proceeding at a later date. I decided to counter this anonymity, coming as it did alongside the estate tax article, by publishing one of

18. Roswell Magill, Taxable Income (1936). The book's acknowledgment of Surrey's contribution does not suggest it remotely approached that of a co-author:

> Stanley Surrey, of the New York Bar, and George E. Ray, of the Massachusetts Bar, assisted me materially in prosecuting the study as a whole: Surrey at the beginning of the work, in collecting, organizing and analyzing a great many of the federal decisions, Ray, in similar work in the last stages, in picking up loose ends of English, federal and state decisions, in checking citations, and in reading proof.

Id. at v. If Surrey was miffed that his contributions were described as similar to those of a cite-checker and proofreader, he gives no indication of that here.

19. Jacob (Jack) P. Aronson did not rise to the level of prominence of most of the lawyers whom Surrey mentions in this chapter. He did join Wilbur H. Friedman on the brief for the taxpayer in a 1940 Supreme Court case, Neuberger v. Commissioner, 311 U.S. 83 (1940). He likely changed his name from Aronson to Allison to combat the anti-Semitism that existed among elite circles of the New York Bar at the time. Jerold S. Auerbach, *Unequal Justice: Lawyers and Social Change in Modern America* (1977), 159.

20. Although adherence to alphabetical order would have suggested otherwise, the article's authors are listed as "Stanley S. Surrey and Jacob P. Aronson."

my research chapters as an article under my name. Magill kindly consented, and in the spring of 1933 the Columbia Law Review once again accepted an article, published as "Assignments of Income and Related Devices: Choice of the Taxable Person," 33 Columbia Law Review 791 (1933). As a side note, when the article was in galley, I had not yet settled on a title. I was told a galley title was absolutely necessary or else the galley would be misplaced at the printer. So I suggested "Life and Love in the Board of Tax Appeals." The Review office's prim secretary frowned on this, so we settled on "Life in the Board of Tax Appeals." Those on the Law Review staff not aware of this situation wondered what kind of material was being accepted by the Review.

This article also explored new areas, for there was little prior writing on the subject and none that attempted to offer an integrated theory to explain the rapidly growing case law. The article was thus the first attempt to develop a structural theory to determine who should be chosen as the individual liable to tax when one person earned a salary or owned property producing interest or dividends but had assigned the receipt of the funds to another.[21] The discussion necessarily developed into the choice of the proper unit for income taxation and how a family should be treated under that tax. This article also still reads well fifty years later. I knew that the organization and analysis were sound, but the style, while clear, was only straightforward. But style was added, since the then Editor-in-Chief of the Review, Benjamin Kaplan, a superb writer, personally edited the article.[22] Ben was later to become a colleague at the Harvard Law School and then an eminent member of the Massachusetts Supreme Court. He was — and is — a kindly person, willing to accept in his year of editorship two articles by the same author. Naturally their publication pleased me. What I could not foretell was their being read by a young lawyer — Erwin Griswold — then handling tax cases in the Office of the Solicitor General.[23] His reading of the articles was almost twenty years later to lead me to a teaching career at the Harvard Law School.

---

21. The topic was timely in the early 1930s. The Supreme Court had decided the leading case on this topic, Lucas v. Earl, 288 U.S. 111 (1930), in which Justice Holmes famously pronounced that "fruits" must not be "attributed to a different tree from that on which they grew," at the beginning of the decade.

22. Benjamin Kaplan spent most of his lengthy career on the faculty of Harvard Law School, specializing in copyright and civil procedure. As Surrey notes, he also served on the Massachusetts Supreme Judicial Court (1972–81). Bryan Marquard, *Benjamin Kaplan, 99, Esteemed Jurist, Law Professor*, BOSTON GLOBE, Aug. 20, 2010, at B12.

23. Early in his legal career, from 1929 to 1934, Erwin Griswold was an attorney in the Office of the Solicitor General. Although Griswold had a remarkable career — including serving as U.S. Solicitor General from 1967 to 1973 and as dean of Harvard Law School from 1946–1967, while also finding time to be a leading tax scholar — he may be best known today for his long-standing decanal practice of asking each woman matriculating at Harvard Law School (including future Supreme Court Justice Ruth Bader Ginsburg) to justify taking a place in his class that otherwise could have been occupied by a man. *See, e.g.*, Ira E. Stoll, *Ginsburg Blasts Harvard Law*, HARVARD CRIMSON, July 23, 1993; Roger K. Newman, *Griswold, Erwin N.*, YALE BIOGRAPHICAL DICTIONARY OF AMERICAN LAW, *supra* note 3, at 239–240.

The research year with Magill ended in the summer of 1933. What next? I had obtained a broad background in taxation but at that time the field was not the organized specialty in law firm practice that it is today. My friend Jack finally persuaded me to join him downtown as a beginning associate in the law firm.[24] After an interesting research and writing year at Columbia and the prior Law Review experience, I at once found the law firm assignments deadly dull. A divorce case in which I had no interest. An assignment to appear in court—my first and only act as a courtroom litigator—and answer, "Ready for the defendant" when our case was reached on the call of the calendar. I did not have the faintest idea what would next befall our client—a street railway—if anything else had happened. My orders were only to answer with that legal sounding sentence. After two months of this Frank Shea, who was hiring young lawyers for the legal staff of the Department of Agriculture, asked me to meet with him.[25] The result was an offer to join his staff. A classmate of mine, George Bronz, had done this some months before.[26] George, incidentally, had fascinated me by spending most of his classroom time in the first year practicing a distinctive and attractive handwriting. This effort apparently was quite useful, for his grades were good and he became Note Editor of the Review. I suspect an acute, perceptive mind also helped. More of George later. The offer was tempting compared to the work at the firm. But at the same time I learned Shea was making similar offers to two graduates of the year after me, for whom I had little respect for their ability and judgment. This bothered me, and I finally declined.

Then came a turning point. Professor Handler had taken the job of Counsel to the Wagner Labor Board created under the National Recovery Act.[27] He asked me to work with him and that offer was a different one—I knew him and the work appeared fascinating. I accepted at once. I then learned something about New York senior law firm partners. One of the two partners with whom I had worked wished me well. The other was outraged. How could I leave his firm! No beginning associate had ever done that, the term was for three years! I explained in vain that law firm

24. Surrey's friend Jack was Jacob P. Aronson (*see* annotation number 19 above), and the law firm was Proskauer, Rose and Paskus.

25. After a varied career in public service during the 1930s and World War II, including assisting in the preparation for the Nuremberg trials, in 1947 Francis M. Shea became a co-founder of the Washington, D.C., law firm of Shea & Gardner; he continued as a partner there until his death in 1989. *Francis M. Shea, 74, Legal Firm Founder*, NEW YORK TIMES, Aug. 10, 1989, at B8.

26. Following World War II, George Bronz served as Special Assistant to the General Counsel to the Department of the Treasury. *George Bronz Dies, Lawyer, International Trade Expert*, THE WASHINGTON POST, Apr. 25, 1976, at B7.

27. The Wagner Labor Board (officially, the National Labor Board), created under the National Industrial Recovery Act, Pub. L. No. 73-67, 48 Stat. 195 (1933) [hereinafter the National Industrial Recovery Act of 1933], was a predecessor to the National Labor Relations Board created in 1935 under the National Labor Relations Act, *supra* note 5. The Wagner Labor Board lacked any real power; the only stick available to it was to deny offending employers the right to display the NRA Blue Eagle (which the Board did on only four occasions). National Labor Relations Board, *1933 the NLB and "the Old NLRB,"* https://www.nlrb.gov/about-nlrb/who-we-are/our-history/1933-the-nlb-and-the-old-nlrb.

associates were a dime a dozen and he could readily replace me, while on the contrary it was my career—not his firm's future—that was involved. He would not listen to this viewpoint but ordered me out of the room, with the parting words of never, never seek to return. I must say I left surprised, but controlled, by this command.[28]

So I went to Washington and entered the legal life of President Roosevelt's New Deal. All connections with taxation appeared ended. I did renew a law school association for my classmate George Bronz, still in Agriculture, and we rented an apartment together. My initial assignment was to assist Professor Handler in preparing legal material for the cases he presented to the Wagner Board, presided over by Senator Wagner of New York. One case stands out in memory, both because I spent Thanksgiving Day in the old Department of Justice Library working on it and because it aroused my indignation. The Jones and Laughlin Steel Co. had ordered two investigators, sent by the Board to check a complaint of an NRA (National Recovery Administration) labor violation under the steel industry code, off the premises as trespassers. This high-handed and arrogant treatment of government employees typified much of the employer attitudes in that period, as my later experiences bore out.[29]

Work for Handler did not occupy all my time. Technically I had been placed in the Legal Division of the NRA and soon I was given a regular assignment there. The job was to go over the complaints, made generally by competitors, of NRA code violations and decide which should be prosecuted in the courts. I soon saw the job involved a dual task. I first had to ascertain from the file whether the facts really showed a violation and then, if so, whether the code provision was in accord with NRA policies. I stretched the latter inquiry into whether the provision made any economic or industry sense, or instead was the work of an overzealous attorney or code administrator, sometimes catering to a particular part of the industry. In a number of instances I sent the file back with the comment that the code provision asserted to be violated could not be defended as a rational policy, so that proceeding with the case was improper. Nearly always my decision closed the matter of litigation, and often the Code was amended. I thus came to occupy an interesting policy position, and dealt with government figures way above me in status. Thus, I worked with Charles Fahy,[30] Associate Interior Department Solicitor (later a Court of Appeals Judge) on

---

28. Thus, Surrey spent just a few months in private practice before he embarked on his lifelong career in government service and the legal academy, explaining perhaps his consistent skepticism of what he referred to as "client-driven" tax reform.

29. The National Recovery Administration was created by the National Industrial Recovery Act of 1933, *supra* note 27. A key aspect of early New Deal economic policy, the NRA was a federal agency created to stimulate business recovery by drafting and implementing industry-wide codes addressing such topics as unfair trade practices, minimum wages, maximum work hours and labor's right to bargain collectively, inter alia. DONALD R. BRAND, CORPORATISM AND THE RULE OF LAW: A STUDY OF THE NATIONAL RECOVERY ADMINISTRATION (1988).

30. Charles Fahy was U.S. Solicitor General from 1941 to 1945, a judge of the U.S. Court of Appeals for the District of Columbia Circuit from 1950 to 1967, and a senior judge of the same court from 1967 until his death in 1979. Representing the government, he successfully argued Korematsu v. United States, 323 U.S. 214 (1944) (upholding the constitutionality of the wartime internment of

what to do with the oil code cases. On one rather silly case involving a refusal by a small dry cleaning company to comply with the prices fixed in the Code for that industry, I was sent to the Office of the United States Attorney for New York City to handle the initial steps. (Here one should recall my "extensive" litigation experience earlier described—"Ready for the defendant.") I entered the office of this eminent and dignified member of the bar, Martin Conboy,[31] and told him I had been sent by Washington to oversee his handling of the case. Then I added "Let us forget such nonsense, and please tell me if there is any way I can be helpful." He took this approach in good humor and I worked together with his staff. The case itself went nowhere and properly so.

Soon the volume of litigation over NRA violations grew so rapidly that a Litigation Division was established. It was headed by A. G. McKnight,[32] an elderly, cheerful, kindly, midwestern, old style lawyer who did not have the faintest idea what the NRA or the litigation was all about. Since I had been working on compliance and litigation matters, I was assigned as his assistant. Soon I found myself constantly on the telephone as calls came from the Litigation Division attorneys in the field trying cases: "The defense has just filed this motion—what do we do next?"; "What affidavits should we use to obtain an indictment?"; "How shall we handle the cross-examination?". (Again, remember my extensive experience as a litigation lawyer!) At another level, when McKnight was given the assignment of making several speeches in Kentucky, I was told to go with him and make sure his talks were on safe ground. On this trip we met Governor Ruby Laffoon who appointed both of us Kentucky Colonels.[33] At our meeting someone asked the Governor whether the people in Kentucky stood behind the President: "Yes, most of them do. But there are some sons of bitches in this state who won't stand behind anybody."

I soon realized that McKnight's lack of leadership and my inexperience were not the best combination, so that the appointment of a knowledgeable assistant director was needed. I visited the Associate Chief Counsel of NRA, Larry Bernard, and suggested this.[34] He said he fully agreed and asked me for a suggestion. I suggested Irving

Japanese Americans). Long after Fahy's death, evidence came to light that in *Korematsu* and related cases Fahy deliberately suppressed evidence that Japanese Americans did not pose a threat to national security. *See, e.g.*, Peter Irons, *How Solicitor General Charles Fahy Misled the Supreme Court in the Japanese-American Exclusion Cases: A Reply to Charles Sheehan*, 55 Am. J. Legal Hist. 206 (2015). In 2011 Acting Solicitor General Neal Katyal publicly described and denounced Fahy's misconduct. David G. Savage, *U.S. Official Cites Deceit in WWII Internments*, Los Angeles Times, May 25, 2011, at A1.

31. Martin Thomas Conboy, Jr., served as United States District Attorney for the Southern District of New York from 1933 to 1935.

32. A. G. McKnight served as the litigation division chief of the NRA during the NRA's brief existence.

33. Ruby Laffoon, a Democrat, was governor of Kentucky from 1931 to 1935. McKnight and Surrey were in good company in being appointed Kentucky Colonels by Laffoon; Harland Sanders of Kentucky Fried Chicken fame was also so honored.

34. Lawrence J. Bernard appears in a rather remarkable document—a listing of all the employees of the NRA, including their NRA positions and salaries, and pre-NRA employment, submitted by

Levy, an experienced, able New York attorney who later became Counsel to the UAW.[35] He replied he appreciated the suggestion but he had decided to appoint a Florida attorney, also in the Division. My response was that this attorney was about the most helpless, inept and untrustworthy lawyer on the whole staff. Incidentally, my judgment was correct for later on others agreed on his incompetence. But the deed was done and so I requested a new assignment. I thereupon became Assistant to the Counsel for the Compliance Division, involved in deciding whether to move a case to prosecution and whether to deny the Code violator the right to display the "Blue Eagle" emblem. Removal of that emblem did have some bite, both in lessened patronage by the public and, more importantly for some companies, the inability to bid on government contracts.[36]

In one such case I met Dean Acheson, then a Washington attorney again after a falling out with Roosevelt.[37] Acheson represented the Colt Firearms Company in a case symbolic of the labor relations of that period. A union had been organized at Colt and under the applicable industry code the company had to bargain with the union. This they did and a contract was agreed to and signed. But then the rub — Colt insisted the union negotiators could sign only their names and could not place beneath those names words signifying their representation of the union. I was handling the case and thought the company position a clear violation. Acheson appeared for a conference, and I had great difficulty focusing on the issue because I was dazzled by the attractiveness of his attire. His suit, shirt, tie, pocket handkerchief, socks and shoes were a perfect, subtle matching of shades of brown. But neither the attire nor his arguments persuaded me and, with government contracts at stake, the company yielded.

Another task was to work out detailed rules to govern proceedings for the removal of the Blue Eagle — initial steps, administrative appeals, etc. In charge of this task was Frank Pollak, an older New York lawyer.[38] He was a hard taskmaster but intelligent

---

the NRA to the Senate at the Senate's request, EMPLOYEES OF THE NATIONAL RECOVERY ADMINISTRATION, S. DOC. NO. 73-164 (Mar. 20, 1934) [hereinafter EMPLOYEES OF THE NATIONAL RECOVERY ADMINISTRATION]. The document indicates Bernard was an "examiner" at the NRA and had previously been engaged in the private practice of law in Florida. Incidentally, the same document indicates that Stanley S. Surrey was an NRA "assistant counsel," at a salary of $4,000, and had previously been employed as a lawyer at Proskauer Rose and as a research assistant at Columbia.

35. Before becoming general counsel of the United Auto Workers, Irving Levy practiced law in partnership with the high-profile civil rights lawyer Joe Rauh. *See* MICHAEL E. PARRISH, CITIZEN RAUH: AN AMERICAN LIBERAL'S LIFE IN LAW AND POLITICS 123 (2011).

36. The "Blue Eagle" emblem signified that a business was compliant with NRA industry codes. Its display not only assisted with increased customer patronage, it also signified eligibility for government contracts. CHARLES J. MORRIS, THE BLUE EAGLE AT WORK: RECLAIMING DEMOCRATIC RIGHTS IN THE AMERICAN WORKPLACE (2005).

37. Dean Acheson was U.S. Secretary of State from 1949 to 1953. His account of those years was awarded the Pulitzer Prize in history in 1970. DEAN ACHESON, PRESENT AT THE CREATION: MY YEARS IN THE STATE DEPARTMENT (1969).

38. Franklin S. Pollak was an NRA Assistant Counsel. Prior to that, he had practiced law in New York with Sullivan & Cromwell (according to EMPLOYEES OF THE NATIONAL RECOVERY ADMINISTRATION, *supra* note 34). Almost two decades later, as a lawyer in private practice in Washington, D.C., Pollak had his fifteen minutes of fame as the plaintiff in the Supreme Court case of Public Utility Commission

and above all a persistent stickler for using precise terminology — the right word in the right place and consistency throughout. From him I really learned much about legal drafting and the disciplined patience it required, an experience which later was to prove very helpful.

One day all this suddenly ended. On May 27, 1935, the Supreme Court in one of its 5–4 [check] anti-New Deal decisions, Schechter v. United States (the "sick chicken" case), declared the NRA unconstitutional for lack of a proper standard to govern the statutory delegation of authority.[39] The scene in the NRA Legal Division was both gloomy and weird. About fifty attorneys sat along the walls of a large room reading the opinion, by handing one page after another down the line. We were a mixed lot — young, mostly liberal leaning, lawyers scarcely out of eastern law schools attracted by the excitement of the New Deal, and older, mostly conservative leaning, southern attorneys needing jobs and finding them via the Congressional patronage route. But young or old, liberal or conservative, we were all out of a job. The NRA arranged to keep most of us on the payroll for a time, writing a history of the NRA, but our essential occupation was in finding a new payroll.

Remembering now my background in taxation I decided to try the Bureau of Internal Revenue (today the Internal Revenue Service). The initial contacts were promising. Then one evening I met in our elevator a resident of the same apartment house, Herman (Hy) Biegel, with whom I was casually acquainted.[40] I did know that Hy, a recent Yale Law School graduate, worked in the Bureau and so I asked him about the place. His response — it took only the elevator ride — was quick: "Avoid that place by all means. I can tell you it is deadly and I am just waiting to get out." So ended what was nearly a renewed connection with the tax system.

The National Labor Relations Act had just been passed by Congress and the Board created by it was hiring lawyers.[41] Its General Counsel was Charles Fahy, an acquaintance from NRA days, and one of its principal attorneys was Phillip Levy, a law school friend from the 1933 class who had drafted much of the Act as a staff member for

---

of the District of Columbia v. Pollak, 343 U.S. 451 (1952). When Capital Transit began playing commercial radio broadcasts — mostly music but including some advertisements — on its busses and streetcars, for which it was paid a considerable sum by the favored radio station, Pollak sued. He claimed being subjected to the broadcasts violated his First Amendment rights (by interfering with his freedom of conversation) and Fifth Amendment rights (by invading his privacy). Although the Supreme Court ruled against Pollak, the opinion produced a stirring dissent by Justice Douglas and an even more stirring recusal by Justice Frankfurter: "My feelings are so strongly engaged as a victim of the practice in controversy that I had better not participate in judicial judgment upon it." For an interesting recent essay inspired by the case, *see* Louis Menand, *Nowhere To Hide: Why Do We Care About Privacy?,* The New Yorker, Jun. 18, 2018, at 24.

39. A. L. A. Schechter Poultry Corp. v. United States, 295 U.S. 495 (1935). Surrey was right to remind himself to check on the votes in *Schechter*; in fact, the decision was unanimous, rather than one of the five-to-four splits typical of that era. Surrey's recollection in his memoirs of events in the public record is generally quite good; for him to be off by this much is unusual.

40. Later in his career, Herman C. Biegel was a partner in the Washington law firm of Lee, Toomey & Kent, and the author of a treatise on pensions and profit sharing.

41. The National Labor Relations Act, *supra* note 5.

Senator Wagner.[42] The work — a new act and a new agency plus people I respected — appeared attractive and I obtained an appointment. My initial orders were to proceed to one of the field hearing offices being organized throughout the country, but at the last minute, as I was packing, this order was changed to a Washington assignment in the Review Division. The attorneys in the Division went over the written record developed in the field hearing and then wrote a draft opinion for the three Board Members. The Members, however, were so busy that the draft nearly always became the final decision without a change. And so I wrote the Board's opinion in 1 NLRB 1 (1935) "In the Matter of Pennsylvania Greyhound Lines, Inc.," involving the dismissal of union members in a manner constituting an unfair labor practice under the Act.[43] I later wrote the majority and dissenting opinions in ________.[44] Another case involved the Radio Corporation of America Co. in Camden across the river from Philadelphia.[45] Here the newly formed United Electrical and Radio Workers of America, with James Matles as its young President, had organized the plant and was seeking an election to become the representative of the employees under the Act.[46] I handled the case for the Board, visited the plant, and wrote an opinion ordering an election. It was the first large election — about 5,000 employees — that the Board had ordered. Because I had written the opinion the Board asked me to go to Philadelphia and conduct the election with the assistance of the Director of the Philadelphia field office. My knowledge of election procedures was even less — zero — than my litigation knowledge. I asked a Board Member, John Carmody,[47] who had in an earlier status handled some railroad elections, to give me a half-hour briefing on elections, and off I went with this knowledge. The election opponents were the local branch of the UERWA and a company-wide organization composed of employees who had not joined the UERWA.[48] The election was to be held on a Saturday in a polling place set up in Camden. Suddenly, several days before the election the company organization said it would boycott the election. This meant that employees going to vote could readily be identified as union members. I could see this could mean trouble. In addition, tension ran high. I called in the Camden Chief of Police and said I wanted

42. In 1937 Philip Levy left the NLRB to become Legislative Counsel to Senator Robert F. Wagner (Dem., N.Y.). After wartime military service Levy entered private practice in 1947 (with Charles Fahy until Fahy's judicial appointment).

43. In the Matter of Pennsylvania Greyhound Lines, Inc., 1 NLRB 1 (Dec. 7, 1935). The published opinion indicates the participation of "Mr. Stanley S. Surrey, of counsel to the Board."

44. Probably In the Matter of M. H. Birge & Sons Co., 1 NLRB 731 (May 14, 1936). The employer refused to reinstate workers following a strike; the board ordered reinstatement (Chairman Madden dissenting).

45. In the Matter of R.C.A. Manufacturing Co., Inc., 2 NLRB 159 (1936).

46. James J. Matles was the "young President" of the United Electrical and Radio Workers of America. Alden Whitman, *James J. Matles, A Top Official Of Electrical Workers, 66, Dies*, New York Times, Sep. 17, 1975, at 48.

47. President Roosevelt appointed John Carmody administrator of the Rural Electrification Administration in 1937, and head of the Federal Works Agency in 1939.

48. Surrey has "company-wide" here, but it probably should be "company-controlled," or something to similar effect.

his force to see that no pictures were taken of those voting and his men were to keep as far away as possible any observers seeking to identify voters. I also said in case any fights started no arrests were to be made until I was first notified—I did not want newspaper reports going out to the effect that violence and arrests marked the efforts of the Board to hold an election. All went well on election day, and of course the UERWA won, ____ to nothing.[49] [check] I returned to Washington with a case of the grippe.[50]

When I reported to the office a few days later, Chairman Charles Madden[51] (later a Court of Claims Judge but earlier a labor law professor) congratulated me on a job well done but then said the Board could not certify the UERWA as a bargaining agent. Amazed I asked why, since it had won the election. He said that while it did win, it had not secured a majority of all the employees in the plant. Moreover, the labor consultant to RCA, General Hugh Johnson,[52] formerly head of the NRA, had telephoned Madden before the election to inquire what rule governed the election and specifically did an organization have to obtain a majority of the total plant employees entitled to vote. Madden had said yes to that. The boycott suddenly became clear—Johnson, knowing the company organization could not win but realizing the intimidating effect of a boycott on undecided employees, had ordered the boycott, indicating incidentally that the organization was a company-guided union. I asked Madden why he had so informed Johnson and he said he thought it was the correct statutory interpretation. I replied that his position was just not sensible, as demonstrated by the situation in this case, and offered to check whatever law there was on the matter of elections. My research soon disclosed that the governing rule in other situations was that a majority of those actually *voting*—not of those *eligible to vote*—sufficed. When I reported this to Madden he agreed he was wrong and had answered Johnson too hastily. But he had given his answer to Johnson and could not see how he could alter it. I pointed out that Johnson would never publicly reveal that conversation, for it would mean disclosure that the organization was a company-controlled union and that Johnson had manipulated both it and the election. Madden quickly but somewhat ruefully agreed and I wrote an opinion certifying the UERWA. The opinion thus interpreted the NLRA that a "majority" meant

49. For news coverage of these events, *see United Radio and Electrical Workers Union vs. Employes [sic] Committee Union R.C.A. Vote is Ordered*, NEW YORK TIMES, Aug. 5, 1936, at 10; and *Strike Union Wins in R.C.A. Ballotting: Gets All but 147 of 3,163 Votes Cast in Selection of Bargaining Agency*, NEW YORK TIMES, Aug. 16, at 23. Surrey was correct that the election was held on a Saturday (August 15). As the *Times* headline indicates, the vote, although lopsided, was not quite as lopsided as Surrey described it.

50. Influenza.

51. J. Warren Madden was the first chairman of the NLRB (1935–1940). Later he was a judge of the U.S. Court of Claims (from 1941 until 1961), and still later a senior judge of the same court (from 1961 until his death in 1972). *Judge J. Warren Madden Dead; First Head of N.L.R.B. Was 82*, NEW YORK TIMES, Feb. 19, 1972, at 34.

52. For his efforts with the NRA, *Time Magazine* recognized Johnson as its Man of the Year for 1933 (over Roosevelt!). After the demise of the NRA in 1935 Johnson became a syndicated newspaper columnist. He died in 1942.

a majority of those voting in an election, and ended any view that it meant a majority of the eligible voters.[53]

After this I became the Board's expert on large plant elections, and held a number of them such as Studebaker, Sun Oil Co., and General Electric. At Studebaker, which was my next election, the company kept complaining that an election would disrupt its production schedule. I countered this by deciding to hold the election in the plant itself and the schedule of voting worked out so well that the assembly line did not drop even by one car. I remember one poignant moment going through a section of the plant where men were working at a tough job and saying it was their turn to vote in the election. One elderly worker, his years of hard work evident, asked who was running the election:

I replied "The United States Government."

"Would it be fairly run?"

"Yes, you have my word on that."

In amazement, he shook my hand and said he had never expected to see this day. The realization what it meant to represent the *United States Government* and the faith these workers had in *their Government* and a *Government*-run election was gratifying but sobering. The union did win the election. [check][54]

In 1936 a field office had held a hearing on a complaint against the Remington-Rand Corp. When the voluminous record arrived in Washington, Chairman Madden asked me to write the Board's opinion. He added: "I am pretty sure we and the NLRA will be declared unconstitutional. At least we should leave a record that all can understand on the tactics that an employer uses to break a union strike. So be sure to go all out in writing that opinion." For that was the situation in the case. Remington-Rand had used ruthless tactics: goons imported as strikebreakers, threats of closing to intimidate the cities in which its plants were located, alliances with police forces, and so on to break the strike. It had called its tactics the "Mohawk Valley Formula" and urged that approach on other employers.

I decided to write the opinion — 121 pages long — in dramatic narrative form, telling the story of a strikebreaking.[55] It was indeed unlike any opinion by an ad-

---

53. *Radio Union Made R.C.A. Bargainers: Federal Labor Board Certifies Group Which Voted at Camden Plant*, NEW YORK TIMES, Nov. 10, 1936, at 13.

54. The editors have not found any record of a union-certifying election in a Studebaker plant during Surrey's time at the NLRB. On May 21, 1937, a two-day wildcat strike at a Studebaker plant in South Bend, Indiana, ended with workers voting by acclamation to return to work and accept a proposed contract. *Studebaker to Resume Work*, CHICAGO TRIBUNE, May 22, 1937, at 9. But this does not match with Surrey's description, both because the vote was by acclamation and because it was held when the plant was shut down by the strike.

55. In the Matter of Remington Rand, Inc., 2 NLRB 626 (1937). As officially published, the opinion spans 121 pages. The opinion describes in great detail "the respondent's grim determination not to bargain collectively with its employees but to settle the issue by force" (*id.* at 648). The opinion also notes Remington Rand's labeling of its tactics as the "Mohawk Valley Formula," and its recommending the Formula to representatives of the National Association of Manufacturers (*id.* at 659).

ministrative agency that I had ever seen. But I was careful at the necessary places to insert the legal findings of fact and conclusions that were customary in the Board's decisions. The Remington-Rand opinion received considerable publicity[56] and was the subject of a political cartoon in the Washington Post,[57] just as Madden had desired. But then the Board and the NLRA were held constitutional as Justice Roberts shifted from the majority in the 5–4 initial decisions against New Deal legislation to the majority in the subsequent 5–4 decisions upholding such legislation.[58] This was the pragmatic victory that President Roosevelt's plan to "pack" the Supreme Court had achieved. The Remington-Rand case was appealed to the Second Circuit Court of Appeals. Faced with this completely unorthodox opinion by an administrative agency, I fully believe Judge Learned Hand, who decided the case, was considerably annoyed by so manifest a departure from the traditional style. But he recognized that the requisite legal findings and conclusions were there to be read, and the decision was upheld.[59]

[Quote][60]

I spent the better part of two years writing Board opinions and holding elections. The opinion writing was a confining task, sitting in an office day after day reading the record and then writing the opinion.[61] This anonymity of the work bothered me. So I checked the decisions of other administrative agencies and found they did give recognition to the lawyers who had assisted in the decisional function. Asking my fellow lawyers to join with me, I requested similar recognition by our Board. The

56. *See, e.g.*, William V. Nessly, *NLRB Demands Remington Rand Reinstate 4,000: "Ruthless, Callous Disregard" of Men Cited in Bitter Attack*, The Washington Post, Mar. 15, 1937, at 1; Louis Stark, *U.S. Board Orders Remington Rand to Re-employ 4,000: Labor Relations Decision Assails Company for "Medieval Ruthlessness" in Strike*, New York Times, Mar. 15, 1937, at 1. Both stories quote extensively from the very quotable Surrey-drafted opinion.

57. Gene Elderman, *The Mohawk Valley Formula*, The Washington Post, Mar. 16, 1937, at 8 (editorial cartoon). In a boxing ring, referee Uncle Sam (with "Labor Relations Board" on his pants) empties one of the gloves of boxer "Remington Rand Co.," and a horseshoe, a brick, and brass knuckles (labeled "terrorism," "provocation," and "espionage") fall out. The other boxer, labeled "union labor" and sporting a black eye, woozily looks on. The cartoon is captioned, "The Mohawk Valley Formula."

58. National Labor Relations Board v. Jones & Laughlin Steel Corp., 301 U.S. 1 (1937). The Court had decided the case generally considered "the switch in time that saved nine" two weeks earlier. West Coast Hotel v. Parrish, 300 U.S. 379 (1937) (upholding a Washington State minimum wage law).

59. National Labor Relations Board v. Remington Rand, Inc., 94 F.2d 862 (2d. 1938), *cert. denied*, 304 U.S. 576 (1938).

60. Presumably Surrey intended to insert here a quotation from Learned Hand's *Remington Rand* opinion. Perhaps he had in mind one or both of the following, suggestive of Hand's annoyance. "The decision on which the order was issued is extremely voluminous ... ; it is rather in the nature of a discursive opinion than of specific findings of fact...." *Id.* at 865. "The underlying tone and the style of the decision may not indeed have evinced that judicial detachment which is the surest guarantee of even justice; but the respondent does not apparently complain of that...." *Id.* at 873.

61. In each NLRB opinion Surrey mentions in his memoirs, as well as in a number of other opinions he does not mention, Surrey is credited at the beginning of the opinion as "Mr. Stanley S. Surrey, of counsel to the Board."

Board agreed and when Volume 1 appeared it had the phrase "Stanley S. Surrey, of counsel to the Board," in the cases I had worked on, with similar recognition for the other attorneys.

During this period the Review Division head was Nathan Witt, who rather openly supported the Communist Party point of view and later admitted membership in the Party.[62] Such membership in that period did not mean the loss of a government job and probably some other Board lawyers had the same attachment. When Witt was away I was in charge of the Division. I remember, as I went over the drafts of some radical lawyers, that I had to strike out phrases such as "We are glad and proud to announce that we are granting recognition to the complainant union in this case." Clearly there was a difference of opinion on how to reach the end result. I doubt that Witt would ever hold against a union. Also, in this period the Board attorneys, I included, were active in the formation of the National Lawyers Guild,[63] a legal organization to rival the American Bar Association. Our action was obvious, since that association along with the Liberty League was actively supporting attacks on the constitutionality of the Board and other New Deal legislation. The formation of the Washington Chapter became a power struggle between the radical, including Communist attorneys, and the liberal attorney group. As part of the latter I was elected the Washington representative on the National Board of the organization. At its meetings I soon observed the radical, often Communist, members gradually gain control of the Board, forcing it to vote the way the Communist Party was moving at the time. In consequence, I resigned from the Board and then from the organization.

Was I in this period on my way to becoming a leading member of the labor law bar? I doubt it, for as I have described above, the work was confining. The Board offered only two lines of work—hearings in the field, which did not interest me, and writing opinions in Washington which was becoming repetitious. In my restlessness I considered a position in the Anti-Trust Division of the Department of Justice but then rescued myself in time.

I had forgotten I had once been a tax person. Suddenly without warning, in the spring of 1937 I was reminded of that learning. Herman Oliphant, General Counsel

---

62. Nathan Witt was promoted to Secretary of the NLRB in the fall of 1937. He resigned from the position in late 1940 following allegations that he was a communist or communist sympathizer (although he denied the allegations at the time). Contrary to Surrey's statement, Witt never admitted to membership in the Communist Party, although he did invoke his Fifth Amendment privilege in refusing to answer questions posed by the House Un-American Activities Committee (actually, by Richard M. Nixon as a one-person subcommittee). C. P. Trussell, *Pressman, Abt, Witt Refuse to Answer Spy Ring Questions: Former New Deal Lawyers Will Not Say if They Are or Were Reds*, New York Times, Aug. 21, 1948, at 1.

63. The National Lawyers Guild (NLG) was founded in 1937 as a broad and inclusive association of legal workers and as the progressive alternative to the then more exclusive and conservative American Bar Association. In subsequent years, the NLG was accused of having ties to the American Communist Party. The National Lawyers Guild: From Roosevelt Through Reagan (Ann Fagan Ginger and Eugene M. Tobin eds., 1988).

of the Treasury Department, asked me to see him.[64] We had never met before, but there I was in his office listening to a request to undertake a special assignment for him. He desired a lawyer to review the procedures of the Board of Tax Appeals to see if its work could be speeded up. Also, he wanted a look taken at the entire judicial process in the tax field. But why Surrey, who was unknown to Oliphant? Professor Roswell Magill, my mentor from law school days, was now Under Secretary in the Treasury Department but he was not aware of Oliphant's action. As best as I could determine a New York lawyer and Columbia graduate, George Jaffin, whom I could not recall ever meeting, had suggested my name to Oliphant.[65] I did see if Jaffin had ever written an article and found one in the Columbia Law Review (______________) with the wonderful quotation from ________ at the start: "When there are clouds on Mt. Olympus, there is darkness in the valleys below," [check] a sentence that should be on the desk of every government official—and law professor![66] With a leave of absence from the Labor Board, I immediately found myself sitting at a desk in the Bureau of Internal Revenue, as a special representative of the Treasury General Counsel. My connection with the tax system was renewed. This time that connection was to remain unbroken for a lifetime.

Note

a. Why was I in Columbia Law School? City College gave me almost a rote education, with little pushing in the direction of inquiring about the world. But it did shape, because of its serious examinations, an ability to memorize and organize material, and to comprehend how to take examinations, especially of the true-false type. In college I had specialized in history for reasons I know not why. History, especially in the person of Professor Joseph Wisan, was an exception to the rote education and he did his best in the term papers he guided me through to open my mind. As a result I had done well in the field, receiving the Ward Medal in this subject, and graduating in 1929 magna cum laude and Phi Beta Kappa.

The history concentration prompted me to register for graduate work at Columbia University. I also had, because my career choice was so uncertain, applied to and was granted admission by Harvard

---

64. Although Surrey does not mention the fact, Herman Oliphant spent a good portion of his career on the faculty of Columbia Law School, before Surrey arrived at Columbia as a student. Oliphant served as Treasury Department General Counsel from 1934 until his early death (from heart disease, at the age of 54) in 1939. Wilfrid E. Rumble, *Oliphant, Herman*, YALE BIOGRAPHICAL DICTIONARY OF AMERICAN LAW, *supra* note 3, at 407–408.

65. George H. Jaffin earned both his bachelor's degree and his law degree from Columbia University. He had a long career as a real estate investor, philanthropist, and lawyer (founding the law firm of Jaffin, Conrad & Finkelstein). Eric Lipton, *George Jaffin, 94, Lawyer and Arts Benefactor, Is Dead*, NEW YORK TIMES, Dec. 26, 1999, at 43.

66. As of 1937, Jaffin had published two articles in the *Columbia Law Review*: *Theorems in Anglo-American Labor Law*, 31 COLUM. L. REV. 1104 (1931), and *Prologue to Nomostatistics*, 35 COLUM. L. REV. 1 (1935). He had also published two articles in other law reviews: *Preliminary Analysis of Concurrent Jurisdiction*, 79 U. PA. L. REV. 869 (1931) (with Hessel E. Yntema), and *Federal Procedural Revision*, 21 VA. L. REV. 504 (1935). Each of the four articles begins with one or more quotations, but no quotation remotely resembles the Olympus quotation remembered by Surrey. In fact, the editors have been unable to locate anything close to the quotation—memorable though it is—anywhere, even with the assistance of Google and other twenty-first-century wonders. A mystery indeed.

Law School. But the choice had been definite for the graduate history field. Then, during the summer, someone asked me just why did I want to be a history scholar and go on to teach history. I suddenly found myself without a convincing answer. So I decided, as a matter of default, to go to law school. This was late in the summer and somehow it seemed impractical to go to Harvard. I hastily took the late entrance examination for Columbia—a sort of legal aptitude task—and was admitted. So there I was in Columbia Law School.

Although I did not know it at the time, the choice between the two schools was indeed a wise one. Columbia then was an exciting, vibrant school pursuing untraditional legal approaches and teaching, which did force those who met its challenge to think about the world rather than to accept matters just because they were around. The Law School in this respect was far ahead of Harvard, which was still following its long-structured traditional path. The choice of Columbia was a sheer unsuspected windfall.

TWO

A Government Tax Career

Part I, 1937–1947

The Board of Tax Appeals was the body that heard taxpayer appeals from adverse Bureau of Internal Revenue administrative assertions of deficiencies in tax cases. It was not a court—later it did become the United States Tax Court—but it functioned much as did a court, with its appointees called Members.[1] It appeared to Herman Oliphant, the Treasury General Counsel who had hired me, that its procedures were too slow moving. My earlier research had not extended to the administrative or judicial aspects of income tax procedures, and I was a complete novice in this field. Oliphant, a very smart former law professor but with no experience of his own in the tax field, though the lawyers in the Bureau were under his jurisdiction, personally believed lack of experience was an excellent qualification for my assignment. I interviewed some of the Bureau's trial attorneys, some Washington tax lawyers and some Board Members. Here my friend, Hy Biegel, who had warned me about the Bureau, was a valuable guide.[2] Incidentally, I came to understand his previous warning. The Bureau's pace was ponderous and slow, without any of the tension and liveliness of the New Deal agencies. The hours were a steady nine to five, far from my reading in bed at 6:00 a.m. my NRA files or the late evenings writing Board opinions. The New Deal could never have existed as far as the Bureau was concerned—but there was Surrey, sort of smuggled into the Bureau by New Dealer Oliphant to look at its pace. To underline the contrast I shared an office with a much older attorney, on his way to retirement, who regularly slept at his desk for three hours after lunch. When awake he managed to methodically and slowly shuffle the papers in the few files assigned to him, so that rarely did any case on his desk reach a conclusion.

---

1. Congress established the Board of Tax Appeals in 1924 and renamed it the Tax Court in 1942. It is a so-called Article I court (created by Congress under the general legislative power conferred on it by Article I of the Constitution), rather than a so-called Article III court (the Supreme Court and lower courts created by Congress pursuant to its power to "ordain and establish" courts inferior to the Supreme Court). *See, generally*, HAROLD DUBROFF & BRENT J. HELLWIG, THE UNITED STATES TAX COURT: AN HISTORICAL ANALYSIS (2014).

2. Herman (Hy) C. Biegel, a lawyer in the office of the chief counsel of the Bureau of Internal Revenue from 1934 to 1937, went on to practice law in Washington D.C. at the firm of Alvord and Alvord. He became a pensions and profit sharing expert and founded the firm of Lee, Toomey & Kent in 1946, where he worked until his retirement. *Herman C. Biegel: Lawyer*, THE WASHINGTON POST, Apr. 19, 1993, at B4.

I concluded that the hearings of the Board were too centralized in Washington, with only a few scattered appearances of a Member in other cities. My recommendation to alter this was a regularly announced and orderly schedule of hearings throughout the country, so that lawyers outside of Washington would not have to travel there and would know when and where their cases would be heard. The Presiding Member at the time was Judge J. Edgar Murdock,[3] a gracious, somewhat extroverted, not overburdened, but decidedly a dignified lawyer. I remember once meeting with him while I was walking in Rock Creek Park and he was on horseback. I am not sure why the sight impressed me — a judge on horseback — but it did, though I frequently went riding myself. He was willing to institute the calendar change. I also made some recommendations to the Bureau itself, to speed up the administrative appeals within the agency and to attempt to see that cases were really ready for trial when their turn came on the calendar. But these efforts did not achieve very much.

My assignment came to an end in the late summer of 1937. I was still on leave from the Labor Board. In fact, on the assumption I was going to return I had joined the Bureau chapter of a fledgling union seeking to organize government employees. My purpose was to gain some knowledge from the inside on how unions operated. The experience was sad and enlightening. Most of the few members were clerical employees, really lost souls but desirous in a sincere way of seeking better employment conditions. Only one besides myself was a lawyer — he later left the Bureau and now heads one of Washington's largest tax firms. I recall several members meeting with the Director of the Bureau of Printing and Engraving to discuss grievances of employees there, with no success. After a few meetings of the group I ceased attending. Years later this union was to grow and become a force as (name).[4]

Instead of a return to the Labor Board, I again suddenly was offered a new assignment by the Treasury. Under Secretary Magill had asked Roger Traynor, a tax professor at the University of California School of Law at Berkeley, to spend a year in Washington working on special research projects for the Treasury.[5] It was Magill I believe — or Magill and Oliphant — who suggested I join Traynor in the research. After meeting Traynor, I immediately accepted. He was an impressive person, who, besides his teaching, had worked for the tax administration in California. There he had devised what we called a "use tax," to be levied by California on goods purchased

3. J. Edgar Murdock was appointed to the Board of Tax Appeals in 1926 and remained on the Board and its Tax Court successor until he retired in 1961. He was chief judge of the Tax Court from 1955 to 1961. *J. Edgar Murdock Dies, Retired Tax Court Judge*, The Washington Post, May 6, 1937, at B6.

4. The National Treasury Employees Union (NTEU) grew out of the early efforts Surrey describes. For a brief history, *see* National Treasury Employees Union, *Our History*, https://www.nteu.org/who-we-are/history.

5. Roger J. Traynor later served for thirty years on the California Supreme Court (as an associate justice from 1940 to 1964, and as chief justice from 1964 to 1970). His *New York Times* obituary accurately noted that he was (and still is) widely considered "one of the greatest judicial talents never to have sat on the United States Supreme Court." Les Ledbetter, *Roger J. Traynor, California Justice*, New York Times, May 17, 1983, at B6.

from outside California by Californians hoping thereby to escape the California sales tax. But Traynor's "use tax," a tax on the use in California of such goods at a rate equal to the California sales tax rate, had closed this escape route. The use tax thereafter spread to other states.[6]

Traynor's overall assignment was to work on the administration of the federal tax system. One phase of this assignment was to update and codify the administrative provisions of the federal tax laws, e.g., procedures for the collection of the tax, levy and distraint for non-payment, civil penalties, etc. The task was a large one and several Bureau attorneys were made available to work for Traynor. Fortunately Traynor treated me as an equal, so supervision rather than legwork marked my days. This assignment was largely a matter of updating outmoded provisions, many of which had been enacted decades earlier, to make the procedures rational and efficient in the current world. The revision was done with insight and comprehensiveness, a suggested codification published (Internal Revenue Administrative Code, United States Government Printing Office, Washington, 1941), but nothing else came of it.[7] Neither the Treasury nor the Congressional tax technicians desired to expend the time and manpower, in hearings and technical changes, to respond to the inevitable criticisms, some of which would probably be justified, of the tax bar.

However, two other assignments did find their way into the law. On these Traynor and I were joined by Professor John (Jack) M. Maguire of Harvard Law School, who came to Washington periodically for a few days at a time.[8] Maguire was a friend of Magill's—the casebook I had used in Taxation at Columbia was Magill and Maguire, Cases on the Law of Taxation (1931), really the first taxation casebook with some pages allocated to federal taxation.[9] Traynor and Maguire were both similar and contrasts. They were intelligent and careful, methodical thinkers, easy to work with, no pride of authorship and no stand on their seniority over me. But Maguire, though born in the West (Colorado) was the embodiment of the conservative, New England gentlemen. Traynor, on the other hand, born in Utah, was a person with more rough and ready ways. His father had been a miner and he had grown up in relative poverty in Utah. He was a thorough liberal, but with the liberal instincts at the very core of his being rather than merely worn conspicuously on

---

6. Traynor helped draft the Use Tax Act of 1935, 1935 Cal. Stat. 1297, which became the model for many other states. *See generally*, Mirit Eyal-Cohen, *Preventive Tax Policy: Chief Justice Roger J. Traynor's Tax Philosophy*, 59 HASTINGS L.J. 877 (2007).

7. Although Surrey, from time to time, overstates his role with certain projects, in this case, Surrey did play a critical supervisory role along with Traynor, as confirmed by IRS Commissioner Guy T. Helvering in the introduction to the publication cited by Surrey. *See*, "Introduction," Internal Revenue Administrative Code, at v (1941).

8. John MacArthur Maguire was on the Harvard Law faculty from 1923 until his retirement in 1957, specializing in evidence and taxation. *John M. Maguire*, NEW YORK TIMES, Jan. 28, 1978, at 24.

9. ROSWELL MAGILL & JOHN M. MAGUIRE, CASES ON THE LAW OF TAXATION (1931). For a contemporary review, *see* Henry Rottschaefer, *Book Review*, 41 YALE L. J. 787 (1932) (commenting that the income tax portion of the book "includes sufficient material to form the basis for a sound exposition of this tax").

his sleeve. He was given to stretches of quiet contemplation. On coming to the office I would often find him there brooding, with his thoughts summarized in such statements as "Doesn't the South give you one big bellyache?" or "Aren't bankers a terrible bunch of people?" Traynor went on in life, as I will later relate, to become Chief Justice of the California Supreme Court and on that bench to be regarded as one of our most distinguished — and liberal — state court judges. Of more significance in my world, this year with Traynor later meant a major change in the direction of my work.

One of the two interesting assignments was to devise a solution for the current statute of limitations maneuvering. The federal tax law had a provision — the statute of limitations — which prevented the Bureau from pursuing a taxpayer for failure to disclose the taxpayer's full income or for claiming improper deductions after three years had run from the filing of the taxpayer's return. On the other side, there was also a three-year limitation period in which a taxpayer could file a claim for refund if the return involved an overpayment. After three years had run, the books were closed. These two statutes of limitations were not unusual in themselves, for such measure with varying time periods exist in all branches of civil or criminal law. At some point, some witnesses die, memories fade, facts recede into vague recollections, so the law declares there must be repose and an end to liability. The problem in the tax law was that these statutes of limitations had led to extensive and intricate maneuvering by both taxpayers and Government. For example, a taxpayer would wait to file a refund claim until just before the end of the three-year period, so that the Government could not check the return and discover a larger underpayment of tax. Both Government attorneys and taxpayers took positions inconsistent with their prior actions just as the statute was to bar the other side from countering with an otherwise available defense.[10] [check this] The Treasury desired to end this opportunistic use of the statute of limitations, whether the use was by its attorneys or the taxpayers' attorneys. The tax stakes were too high to be decided by this trickery.

The goal was thus clear but reaching it was far from easy. The basic problem was to separate the situations in which the statute of limitations had a proper role, for there must be repose and mistakes forgotten at some point, from the situations in which the statute of limitations was being misused in clever manipulation. After many months of deliberation and trial and error, the three of us worked out a complex set of rules which we thought satisfactorily steered the correct path between the two sides of the problem. Our work was finished at the time when the Senate Finance Committee was considering the Revenue Act of 1938. The Treasury was satisfied

---

10. "The [judicial] decisions [under the pre-1938 law] often permit taxpayers or the Commissioner to obtain a twofold advantage by assuming in one year a position different from that taken in another year, with respect to which the period of limitations has expired, so that adjustment of the tax liability for the earlier year is impossible." REP. OF A SUBCOMM. OF THE COMM. ON WAYS AND MEANS ON A PROPOSED REVISION OF THE REVENUE LAWS, 75th Cong., 3rd Sess., at 54–55 (1938). Although the quotation supports Surrey's general claim that both taxpayers and the government attempted to exploit the statute of limitations, it does not address Surrey's particular claim about actions taken just before the expiration of the limitations period.

with our solution and presented it to the Committee, which accepted it, pretty much on faith, since the purpose was clearly desirable.

At this point I was introduced to the process by which tax legislation was drafted once a policy had a committee's approval. The person in charge was Middleton [Mid] Beaman, the House Legislative Counsel.[11] The Office of the House Legislative Counsel had been formed in 1918, apparently as a result of the legislative drafting research project conducted at Columbia Law School.[12] This project was guided by Professor Thomas Parkinson, who taught, not too profoundly, a course in Legislation at Columbia Law School.[13] But Parkinson was a practical fellow and had established the legislative drafting bureau at Columbia. Beaman had come to head the Office from a post as law librarian at the Library of Congress and earlier had been in charge of the Law School research staff. His Office was in charge of drafting all House legislation for committees that desired assistance. The Office from the start was—and still is—by agreement between the party leaders a completely non-political, non-partisan office. No one knew Beaman's political persuasion, and he had a free hand in choosing his staff. The obvious result was a staff of high caliber. Beaman, though responsible for the entire staff of the office, assigned to himself the tax field. He was a remarkable person, rather along in years, with a superb analytical mind and a way with words that no one has since matched. His was a crusty disposition and one that did not suffer fools or foolish talk, and he made this very evident. His assistant, and later successor, was John O'Brien, also an able draftsman with a more affable disposition and less rigorous in his handling of people.[14] While Mid and John argued with each other as equals, the final decisions were Beaman's. There was also an Office of Senate Legislative Counsel headed by Steve Rice, later a Board of Tax Appeals Member.[15]

---

11. Middleton Goldsmith Beaman was House Legislative Counsel from 1919 to 1949. He was the first person to serve in that position. (More precisely, Beaman was appointed House Legislative Draftsman in 1919; in 1924 his title was revised to House Legislative Counsel.) As Surrey notes, earlier in his career Beaman had been a law librarian at the Library of Congress, and on the faculty of Columbia Law School. *Beaman, Long A Legislative Counsel, Dies*, The Washington Post, Sep. 17, 1951, at B2.

12. In 1918 Congress created the Legislative Drafting Service. Revenue Act of 1918, Pub. L. No. 65-254, § 1303, 40 Stat. 1057, 1141. The 1918 legislation was an outgrowth of an experiment begun in 1916, under which the Legislative Drafting Research Fund at Columbia University—directed by Beaman, then on the Columbia Law faculty—assisted the Ways and Means Committee in legislative drafting. *See* Office of the Legislative Counsel of the U.S. House of Representatives, *History and Charter*, https://legcounsel.house.gov/about/history-and-charter.

13. Thomas I. Parkinson preceded Beaman as director of the Columbia Legislative Drafting Research Fund. Later he served briefly as dean of Columbia Law School (1923–1925), and much longer as president of the Equitable Life Assurance Society (1927–1953). *Thomas I. Parkinson is Dead; Ex-Head of Equitable Life, 77*, New York Times, Jun. 18, 1959, at 31 (describing Parkinson as a "pioneer" for his work with the Drafting Research Fund).

14. Although John O'Brien was indeed Beaman's long-time assistant, he never became Legislative Counsel. For a list of all House Legislative Counsels (there have been only eight), *see* United States House of Representatives: History, Art & Archives, *Office of House Legislative Council*, https://history.house.gov/People/Appointed-Officials/Legislative-Counsel/.

15. Stephen Rice headed the Office of Senate Legislative Counsel from 1933 to 1950 and was a judge of the Tax Court from 1952 to 1958. *Tax Judge Rice Dies Here at 52*, The Washington Post, Feb. 11, 1958, at B2.

While able and practical Rice was no match for Beaman. But they did not conflict. Since tax legislation had, under the Constitution, to originate in the House, Beaman's Office necessarily drafted the first—the House—version of a tax bill. Then, by tradition based on good sense, Beaman and his staff followed the bill through the Senate and the Conference Committee. While occasionally a member of the Senate Office would sit in, Beaman was thus in full charge of tax legislation in its entire journey through Congress.

With the policy approval of the Senate Finance Committee in hand, Traynor and I presented our draft to Beaman. Time was running short, for the bill that became the Revenue Act of 1938 was long and Congress was impatient. Beaman, after a quick look at the draft, said, with his customary high standards of drafting in mind, that it was too complicated for him to work on in the time available, and it would have to go over. But I persuaded Beaman that the draft, though complicated, really did fit together and deserved at least a few days. Beaman reluctantly agreed, but then became annoyed with Traynor. Traynor's working method was to proceed at a careful, slow, methodical pace. Beaman however was an impatient person, and wanted quick responses keyed directly to his questions. Since the two personalities thus clashed, Traynor decided to leave the job to me of satisfying Beaman. The other Treasury staff people provided encouragement but, not having worked on the draft, were not familiar with its intricacies. I was able to persuade Beaman that the draft was technically in satisfactory shape. He then presented it to the Committee, who again simply took it on faith. It thus became law, as section 820 of the Revenue Act of 1938.[16] The provision still survives, largely unchanged, as sections 1311–1315 of the Internal Revenue Code.[17] Thus my first legislative effort achieved immortality, or least a life that has lasted for over 45 years.

The provision almost immediately ended most of the senseless and unfair statute of limitations maneuvering, and thus achieved a marked improvement in tax administration. Admittedly the tax bar found it very complicated, for so it was, and some objected on this ground. I remember Robert Miller, a friendly, dignified Southerner who was the leader of the Washington tax bar,[18] saying to me that the provision "Was just like a remarkable Swiss clock. It had bells that chimed on the hour, cuckoos that appeared at certain times, then dwarfs, all elegance and intricately designed. But he did not need a Swiss clock! A plain American watch would tell time just as well." But while right about watches, Miller was wrong about the provision, for complexity and not simplicity was a necessary attribute. I decided, on hearing Miller's views, that the provision demanded a full explanation so that the bar would understand its op-

16. Revenue Act of 1938, Pub. L. No. 75-553, § 820, 52 Stat. 447, 581.

17. Although Congress repealed section 1315 in 1976 (in time for Surrey to have noted the repeal in his memoirs), Surrey was correct that sections 1311 through 1314 had survived largely unchanged. In fact, they continue to survive largely unchanged to this day.

18. In 1920 Robert Netherland Miller co-founded Miller & Chevalier, the first Washington D.C. law firm specializing in federal taxation. Prior to that he had served as solicitor of the Bureau of Internal Revenue. *Robert N. Miller Dies, District Tax Attorney*, THE WASHINGTON POST, Jan. 2, 1968, at B3.

erations, what it did and did not do. I wrote a long article describing the provision in complete detail. Traynor and Maguire signed it, with me, and it was published as Maguire, Surrey and Traynor, "Section 820 of the Revenue Act of 1938," 48 Yale Law Journal 509, 719 (1939).[19]

Our second assignment that ended in legislation grew out of Oliphant's desire to develop a system of declaratory judicial judgments through which a taxpayer, before entering into a transaction, could have the courts decide what the tax consequences would be. Oliphant asked the three of us to work out this judicial procedure. After considerable study we decided such a process of judicial declaratory judgment would be far too cumbersome to work efficiently. We then discovered section 606 of the Revenue Act of 1928 which provided:

> "(a) Authorization. — The Commissioner (or any officer or employee of the Bureau of Internal Revenue, including the field service, authorized in writing by the Commissioner) is authorized to enter into an agreement in writing with any person relating to the liability of such person (or of the person or estate for whom he acts) in respect of any internal revenue tax for any taxable period ending prior to the date of the agreement.
>
> (b) Finality of agreements. — If such agreement is approved by the Secretary, or the Undersecretary, within such time as may be stated in such agreement, or later agreed to, such agreement shall be final and conclusive, and, except upon a showing of fraud or malfeasance, or misrepresentation of a material fact —
>
> > (1) the case shall not be reopened as to the matters agreed upon or the agreement modified, by any officer, employee, or agent of the United States, and
> >
> > (2) in any suit, action, or proceeding, such agreement, or any determination, assessment, collection, payment, abatement, refund, or credit made in accordance therewith, shall not be annulled, modified, set aside, or disregarded."[20]

The predecessor statue providing for this closing agreement procedure had been adopted in 1921 to enable a taxpayer to close a case with finality even before the statute of limitations (then four years) had run. The 1928 version had eliminated some of the restrictive aspects of the earlier provision. It quickly became the method used by the government in almost every case in which the tax return liability was altered. But this widespread use soon backfired, for many cases were closed much too early as either taxpayer or government learned after the agreement had been signed

---

19. The article was published in two parts in successive issues of the *Yale Law Journal*. John M. Maguire, Stanley S. Surrey & Roger John Traynor, *Section 820 of the Revenue Act of 1938*, 48 Yale L. J. 509 (1939), and 48 Yale L. J. 719 (1939).

20. Revenue Act of 1928, Pub. L. No. 70-562, § 606, 45 Stat. 791, 874.

that errors in the determination of the tax liability remained. So by 1938 the use of the closing agreement was restricted to situations when the taxpayer requested it or for some special reason the government desired finality. The number of agreements signed in 1937 was 161.[a]

As matters thus stood in 1938 the closing agreement applied only to completed tax years and past transactions. The agreement served to impart finality to completed transactions, so that its function did not differ in purpose from that of the statute of limitations or the judicial doctrine of res adjudicata. The closing agreement was an administrative device to advance the time of finality. As to prospective transactions the Bureau policy was not to provide any guidance whatsoever on the position it would take. But taxpayers contemplating important transactions desired some certainty on the tax consequences, and hence our research project.

Our thinking, while rejecting judicial declaratory rulings as the answer, seized quickly on the closing agreement device. The only statutory change that would be required would be to remove the words "ending prior to the date of the agreement" that then came at the end of subsection (a) quoted above. With this change an agreement could be entered into "for any taxable period." But this very slight change would, however, make the closing agreement available to give Bureau guidance that possessed finality as regards prospective contemplated taxpayer transactions. The agreement could relate both to fact determinations and, more important, questions of law. Our suggestion for this simple statutory change, and the policy motive behind it, was accepted by the Treasury and the Congress, and the change was made in the Revenue Act of 1938.[21]

This simple statutory change and the cautious use that followed of the closing agreement to guide contemplated transactions has gradually developed into the now widely applied private letter ruling policy of the IRS today.[22] Taxpayers began to dispense with the securing of a closing agreement, but instead had a clause inserted in their rulings that on request such an agreement would be signed by the Government. Soon even that clause was dropped, for as the private letter ruling process expanded a practice firmed up under which the Bureau would stand behind a ruling it had issued to a taxpayer even though it later changed its mind as to the applicable law.[23] Today, no one, in or out of Government, would take the view that a tax law so complicated as our present Code could be successfully administered without this procedure of IRS private rulings on future transactions. There were, for example, ________ rulings issued in ________.[24] This vital part of our tax machinery, the rules governing

21. Revenue Act of 1938, Pub. L. No. 75-553, § 801, 45 Stat. 447, 573.

22. For a brief history of IRS private letter rulings, *see generally,* Donald E Osteen, Lori J. Jones, and Howard S. Fisher, *The Private Letter Ruling Program at the Half Century Mark*, 42 MAJOR TAX PLAN. 12, 1 (1990).

23. For the current statement that the Internal Revenue Service will stand behind a taxpayer-favorable letter ruling issued to a particular taxpayer even if the Service later changes its mind on the legal issue, *see* 26 CFR § 601.201(l)(5).

24. For fiscal year 2015, to take one recent year, the IRS Office of the Chief Counsel processed user fees associated with 866 private letter ruling "lead cases." Treasury Inspector General for Tax

its procedures and its widespread use by taxpayers, traces back to the elimination of eight words suggested by the Traynor-Surrey-Maguire project in 1938.

These two assignments — the statute of limitations maneuvering and finality for Bureau determinations as to taxpayers' future transactions — were thus successfully completed by our group. But our proposal under the final assignment still remains a controversial topic today, though more than forty years have passed. Oliphant had initially asked me to consider the peculiar processes of judicial review of tax cases. Under that process the initial consideration of most tax controversies created by Bureau issuance of deficiency letters (meaning an asserted increase in tax liability) at that time was made by the Board of Tax Appeals. While not a court, the Board was an independent agency located within the Bureau and did function as a court. It issued opinions, and applied them as precedents. Centralized in Washington, though as earlier described with a field hearing calendar as well, its decisions were the law binding on taxpayers and government alike — unless an appeal were taken. Here came the problem that concerned Oliphant. Appeals from the Board were heard by the federal Circuit Court of Appeals within whose jurisdiction a taxpayer resided. There were then eleven circuits, so that appeals from the Board fanned out to eleven different courts. Obviously this made for some uncertainty, since the decision of one Circuit Court, while an interesting factor, did not control any other Circuit Court. Under this process judicial finality could come only through decision by the Supreme Court in cases it accepted under its certiorari procedure. But the Court under that procedure, except for a few cases it regarded as highly important largely because of the revenue involved in the issue, granted certiorari only when a conflict existed within the Circuit Courts. This practice thus made for extended litigation in the Circuit Courts, as taxpayers' attorneys and government attorneys sought to create a conflict when the first Circuit Court opinion went against their position. It sometimes required three or four Circuit Court decisions before a conflict developed that produced the grant of certiorari. The inevitable result was excessive litigation, a disparity among Circuits and often a decade before judicial uniformity and certainty were established by a Supreme Court decision (assuming of course that its decision was sufficiently clear, not always a safe assumption).

In addition to this pattern of judicial decision for most tax cases — original decision by one body, the Board of Tax Appeals (about 80% to 85% of the decided cases passed through that Board), appeals fanning out to eleven Circuit Courts, then generally only after a conflict developed in those courts, the cases flowing again to a single court — the Supreme Court — the process was made more complicated by the existence of other courts having original jurisdiction in tax cases. These were the then 85 federal district courts and the single Court of Claims (in Washington) which would hear refund suits brought by a taxpayer under any federal tax (the Board's jurisdiction was restricted to income, estate and gift tax deficiency cases and did not

Administration, Ref. No. 2017-10-012, The Office of Chief Counsel Accurately Administered User Fees but Could Improve Its User Fee Refund Process, 3 (Jan. 12, 2017).

cover excise taxes). The choice of the original forum was thus the taxpayer's—either contest the asserted deficiency or pay the tax claimed and sue in the local District Courts, where a jury trial was available on request, or in the Washington Court of Claims. A decision of a District Court could be appealed to a Circuit Court; a decision of the Court of Claims could be appealed to the Supreme Court if certiorari were granted.

It was these complex methods of tax litigation that Oliphant wanted studied. I carried over the task to the Traynor-Maguire group and we worked on the problem for a year. The solution we suggested was along these lines:

> Original jurisdiction in all income, estate, and gift tax cases would be confined to one tribunal, the Board of Tax Appeals, which would be given jurisdiction over refunds as well as deficiencies. To expedite consideration of the cases and to compensate for the elimination of the localized district courts, the Board would be decentralized into five boards, each composed of three members and having exclusive jurisdiction in a defined geographical area. Appeals from these five boards would be taken as a matter of right to a single Court of Tax Appeals, whose decisions in turn would be subject to review on certiorari by the Supreme Court. Denial of certiorari to a decision of this court would mean that a final answer had been obtained to the issue involved, for there would be no opportunity to compel later Supreme Court review as at present exists through the device of producing a conflict. It is suggested that a new Court of Tax Appeals be created, or that the jurisdiction of the Court of Appeals for the District of Columbia or the Court of Claims be enlarged for this purpose.[25]

Obviously such a far-reaching series of changes was neither to be accomplished overnight nor accepted with unanimity. Traynor and I saw the need to explain the plan for the tax bar and I therefore wrote an article describing the proposal for the Columbia Law Review. It appeared as Roger John Traynor, "Administrative and Judicial Procedure for Federal Income, Estate and Gift Taxes—A Criticism and a Proposal," 38 Columbia Law Review 1393 (1938). The title had this somewhat cryptic footnote: "At his own request the name of Stanley S. Surrey does not appear as co-author, although this article could not have been written without his unselfish interest and cooperation." It was not that I was modest. The fact is that, as later to be related, I had by then commenced working as an attorney directly in the Treasury Department. Herman Oliphant, on hearing of the article—all articles by Treasury attorneys required a clearance, generally a formality—requested me not to co-sign the article because he thought the recommendations on judicial review would not be viewed favorably by the Justice Department and he wanted no trouble with that Department. While he was probably correct as to the Justice Department reaction I said that the recommendations were Traynor's and mine, and not any official position of the

25. Stanley S. Surrey, *Some Suggested Topics in the Field of Tax Administration*, 25 Wash. U. L. Q. 399, 417 (1940).

Treasury. He did not accept this argument. I then asked if he was ordering me not to sign the article and, politely but firmly, he said he was. I replied that ended the matter and I would not sign the article.

But this solution of a non-signature to the article was futile. Traynor on his own, being free to do so, inserted the quoted footnote. The Washington Kiplinger Tax Letter of January 14, 1939 started off with "A stir has been created within certain Washington tax circles by an article in the December issue of the Columbia Law Review" and then referring to me as co-author stated I was a Treasury employee.[26] It said the Justice Department officials opposed the "Traynor plan," as it had become styled, and predicted a deluge of tax bar opposition. The Letter was correct on the latter score, for the Washington tax bar, then the vocal group on tax legislation, was adamantly opposed to the plan.

I recall a meeting of the American Bar Association Section of Taxation, then a small group of tax lawyers completely controlled by Washington tax practitioners. A part of the meeting was a debate on the "Traynor Plan," and I defended the plan. An opponent of the proposal, carried away by the vehemence and emotion of his opposition, ended with the remark that Traynor was a professor and everyone knew that all matters coming from a professor end in the ash can. Fortunately, at the time, Felix Frankfurter, a Harvard law professor, had just been appointed to the Supreme Court, so that I was able to respond "Not everything a professor does ends in the ash can. Sometimes it ends up on the Supreme Court"—and the good-natured applause of the group indicated this round was mine. After this public defense of the Traynor plan I then later just went ahead and indicated my connection with and approval of the recommendation. See Stanley S. Surrey, "The Traynor Plan—What It Is," 17 Taxes 393 (1939)[27] and Roger John Traynor and Stanley S. "Surrey, New Roads Toward the Settlement of Federal Income, Estate, and Gift Tax Controversies," 7 Law and Contemporary Problems 336 (1940).[28] Others later made similar recommendations but the tax bar never strongly pushed the idea, though its first violent opposition changed to a willingness on the whole to consider the question of the judicial tax structure in a far less emotional way and even in some cases to endorse such a court, e.g., Report of the Executive Committee of the Tax Section of the New York State Bar Association, May 1973, to the Commission on Revision for the Federal Court Appellate System Regarding the Need for a Court of Tax Appeals.

---

26. The editors have been unable to locate the quoted issue of the Washington Kiplinger Tax Letter.

27. Surrey's essay in support of the Traynor plan was followed immediately, in the same issue of *Taxes*, by an essay in opposition. E. Barrett Prettyman, *The Traynor Proposals—Some Considerations*, 17 Taxes 397 (1939).

28. Again, Surrey's effort was followed immediately by the expression of an opposing view. William A. Sutherland, *New Roads to the Settlement of Tax Controversies: A Critical Commentary*, 7 Law & Contemp. Probs. 359 (1940) (describing the views of Traynor and Surrey as "as unsound as they are radical").

In 1979 Senator Edward Kennedy, as then Chairman of the Senate Judiciary Committee, revived the proposal for a single Court of Tax Appeals.[29] The issue proved still to be controversial, with the bar thoroughly divided.[30] One part of the controversy was how the judges on such a court would be selected. I had come to favor the assignment, by the Chief Justice, of judges already sitting on the Circuit Courts, who would serve on the Court of Tax Appeals for several years, a process similar to that used to staff the Emergency Court of Price Appeals in World War II and the Korean War.[31] This, I and others thought, would offset the specialization of the Tax Court judges who were generally selected from the tax profession. Other lawyers, however, favored specially selected judges even for the Court of Tax Appeals. Given this division of opinion, plus other divided viewpoints not materially different from those involved in the discussion on the original Traynor plan proposal, and also Senator Kennedy's loss of the Judiciary Committee chairmanship, thus ended this latest consideration of a single Court of Tax Appeals.

My work with Traynor concluded when he returned to Berkeley in 1938, though the friendship that was established later altered my career and continued over the years.[32] But the end of this second special assignment did not mean a return to the Labor Board. This work with Traynor led to an offer later in 1938 to join the newly established Office of Legislative Counsel in the Treasury Department.[33] Undersecretary Magill had made important changes in Treasury organization and operations designed to strengthen the consideration of tax policy and legislative issues in the Treasury. The purpose behind these changes was his decision to move the focus of work on

---

29. Warren Weaver, Jr., *Kennedy Proposes to End Tax-Law Conflicts*, NEW YORK TIMES, Mar. 18, 1979, at 27.

30. For the range of views, *see Tax Court Improvement Act of 1979: Hearing Before the Subcomm. on Taxation and Debt Management Generally of the Comm. on Finance*, U.S. Sen., 96th Cong., 1st Sess. (1979).

31. The temporary Emergency Court of Price Appeals was established by the Emergency Price Control Act of 1942, Pub. L. No. 77-421, 56 Stat. 23. The court consisted of judges designated by the Chief Justice of the Supreme Court, chosen from the judges of the United States district courts and courts of appeals.

32. In 1947, when Surrey left the Treasury Department, Traynor was instrumental in assisting Surrey to secure his first law school teaching position at the University of California Berkeley Law School. *See* chapter 3.

33. Surrey's 1938 decision to remain at the Treasury Department and not return to the Labor Board was a momentous one for his professional life. It also coincided with a key marker in the development of New Deal economic policy. The years 1937–38 marked a pivotal period in the history of the New Deal. This was the time when President Franklin D. Roosevelt proposed his "court-packing" plan as a way to neutralize obstructionist conservative members of the U.S. Supreme Court. With the economy rebounding slightly during this time, the federal government also began cutting spending, leading to a "Roosevelt Recession." And perhaps most importantly, 1937–38 marked the period when New Deal policy pivoted away from a bold and ambitious attempt to transform American capitalism towards a more cautious and restrained effort to regulate economic life and provide greater individual social-welfare benefits. In many ways, Surrey's transition from the Labor Board to the Treasury Department mirrored the structural changes in the New Deal. For more on this shift in New Deal policy, *see generally*, ALAN BRINKLEY, THE END OF REFORM: NEW DEAL LIBERALISM IN RECESSION AND WAR (1995) [hereinafter THE END OF REFORM].

those issues from the Bureau of Internal Revenue to the Headquarters of the Treasury Department. Magill believed that the tax policy judgements being made by the Bureau officials were often faulty, partly because of the influence of worries over any consequent changes that any new legislation would produce in the tax administration procedures of the Bureau, partly because of lack of time to consider issues deeply, and partly because of his lack of confidence in the abilities and judgments of a number of the Bureau officials working on tax legislation. Also, over the years the preparation of Administration tax legislative proposals had been a haphazard affair. Thus the 1936 proposal for a corporate tax on undistributed profits had apparently been suggested by Oliphant, a former professor with no tax background.[34] The 1937 act closing several loopholes was participated in by a number of Washington attorneys, many without tax experience, hastily called upon to assist on various aspects of the Treasury proposals.[35] Another concern of Magill's was the inadequacy of the economic input into the formulations of tax legislative proposals. While the Treasury economists were able, they did not specialize in the tax field and also were spread thin. In addition, there was little coordination on tax legislation between the lawyers and the economists. One strand of Magill's reorganization plan was the creation in the main Treasury of a Division of Tax Research composed of fiscal economists chosen to work exclusively on tax policy matters, rather than having those matters, as before, considered by persons in the Division of Research and Statistics who handled the general run of Treasury economic problems. The other strand was the creation, also in the main Treasury, of the Office of Legislative Counsel, to consist of lawyers to work exclusively on legislative tax proposals. The two offices would have the basic responsibility for developing legislative tax proposals, though they were to work closely with the Bureau of Internal Revenue. The offices were to operate together as an overall unit under whatever Treasury top official was charged with the final supervision of tax matters. This official could be an Undersecretary, a General Counsel, or an Assistant Secretary, and tax matters would be only one of his areas of responsibility. Moreover, it was not considered that he needed to have, and usually he did not have, expertise in the tax field. Obviously, since this top official often lacked tax expertise, the heads of these two new offices and their staffs at once assumed considerable responsibilities and were immediately recognized as possessing an important influence.[36]

These two offices, though with enlarged staffs, still exist today, with the same overall functions. They are known as the Office of Tax Legislative Counsel and the

---

34. The tax on undistributed corporate profits was not merely *proposed* by Treasury in 1936; it was *enacted* by Congress (in watered-down form) in that same year. Revenue Act of 1936, Pub. L. No. 74-740, § 14, 49 Stat. 1648, 1655–57. The tax, which was the subject of widespread and withering criticism, survived only through 1939. For a detailed history of the tax, *see* STEVEN A. BANK, FROM SWORD TO SHIELD: THE TRANSFORMATION OF THE CORPORATE INCOME TAX, 1861 TO PRESENT 155–186 (2010).

35. Revenue Act of 1937, Pub. L. No. 75-377, 50 Stat. 813.

36. For more on Magill's attempts to increase the influence of tax experts in Treasury and his complicated relationship with New Deal tax policy, see generally, Joseph J. Thorndike, "Profiles in Tax History: Roswell Magill," Tax History Project, January 25, 2008.

Office of Tax Analysis. The only basic changes have been to separate the international tax work, which was non-existent in 1938, in the Office of International Tax Counsel, and, commencing in 1961, to place in charge of the three offices an Assistant Secretary for Tax Policy, chosen for his experience in the tax field.[37]

Let me insert here an occurrence that bore no special significance for me at the time. On an occasion when I was in Under Secretary Magill's office to discuss a matter, just before he left the Treasury, a lawyer from the Solicitor Ceneral's office came in to see the Under Secretary. Magill introduced the lawyer — Erwin Griswold — to me and Griswold remarked "Oh yes, so you are the fellow who wrote those two Columbia Law Review articles that I liked." Just these few words, but again they were destined years later to alter my life.[38]

Fortunately for the new organizational structure created by Magill the two Offices were headed by able persons. The first Legislative Counsel was Thomas Tarleau, a City College and Columbia Law graduate and New York tax attorney who had worked for Magill in the law firm for which Magill was a consultant while at Columbia.[39] Tarleau had come to Washington to assist in the legal work on the Revenue Act of 1938. He was a very able attorney with an informed and integrated view of the tax system. However, he was a nervous, worrisome person who disliked both running an office and confrontations. The first Director of the Bureau of Tax Research was Roy Blough, then in his late thirties, a former professor of public finance at the University of Cincinnati. Blough was a well-grounded, steady person, not brilliant but with sound judgment.[40] Both Tarleau and Blough, moreover, understood quality and desired their offices to be staffed with able persons. Luckily for the then Treasury and future developments the two Offices thus started under auspicious circumstances.

I joined Tarleau as Assistant Legislative Counsel. My leave of absence from the Labor Board became permanent and a promising career as a labor lawyer had ended! The initial staff of the Office consisted, besides Tarleau and me, of Lucien Shaw, a California attorney with some tax experience, a good mind, conservatively inclined

37. The precise official titles are the "Office of the Tax Legislative Counsel", the "Office of Tax Analysis", and the "Office of the International Tax Counsel". Although Surrey does not mention the fact at this point in his memoirs, when the position of Assistant Secretary of Tax Policy was created in 1961 President Kennedy appointed Surrey to the new position. For much more, *see* chapter Six.

38. Griswold would later become Dean of the Harvard Law School and was instrumental in hiring Surrey in 1950 onto the Harvard faculty.

39. Thomas N. Tarleau, a graduate of City College of New York and Columbia Law School, served in the Treasury Department from 1937 to 1943, after which he had a long career as a partner in the New York law firm of Willkie, Farr & Gallagher. *Thomas N. Tarleau*, NEW YORK TIMES, Dec. 31, 1985, at B10.

40. Blough, who was born in 1901, was on the faculty of the University of Cincinnati immediately before his years at Treasury. After Treasury, he taught at the University of Chicago and then became a member of President Harry Truman's Council of Economic Advisors in 1950. He taught at Columbia University from 1955 to 1970 when he retired. *Roy Blough, 98, Official at the Treasury*, NEW YORK TIMES, Mar. 2, 2000, at C25.

and a stickler for detail;[41] Robert Eichholz, with a fine mind, perceptive sharp insights, little tax background, and in a sense, as we saw it, plagued by too large inherited wealth, so he was not forced fully to use his remarkable talents;[42] Fred Lusk, a veteran Bureau attorney, somewhat inarticulate, but with a fully coordinated and intelligent view of the tax system in his head and years of experience behind him;[43] and Seymour Mintz, a young lawyer just starting out in the tax field.[44]

The harassed and overworked staff of the present Office of Tax Legislative Counsel can only marvel at our working days in late 1938 and early 1939. The two principal technical problems on which we worked were the treatment of assumption of liabilities in corporate reorganizations and of cancellation of indebtedness. The pattern of the work involved many long group discussions at which all of us fully explored every aspect of these problems. The pace, while not leisurely, was steady and unpressured, permitting stimulating exchanges of views and a poring over of detail. The assumption of liabilities problem had developed from a Supreme Court decision in *United States v. Hendler*, 303 U.S. 564 (1938), a pyrrhic victory won by the Government at the urging of the Bureau.[45] After winning in the Supreme Court the Bureau then found that the decision, by considering an assumption of liabilities as money received by the transferor in a corporate reorganization, permitted the transferee to increase the tax basis of the assets received in the transaction. Since the entire Bureau and taxpayer practice had been just the opposite, transferee taxpayers were now in a position to claim an increased basis while transferor taxpayers were protected by the statute of limitations from any assertion of an increased tax liability through the assumption of their liabilities. The Bureau was threatened with the possible loss of a very large amount of revenue through the operation of the basis provisions. The situation was caused, as often was the case, by a Government attitude on litigation that sought victory in a particular case without regard for the overall effect on the tax system. The task of our Office was to design a retroactive reversal of the Supreme Court's statutory

41. Later in his career Lucien W. Shaw served as executive vice-president and general counsel for Bekins Van and Storage Co. *Lucien W. Shaw, Bekins Vice President, Counsel*, LOS ANGELES TIMES, Mar. 5, 1993, at A26.

42. In 1963 Robert B. Eichholz married Mercedes Hester, who had previously been married to Supreme Court Justice William O. Douglas. In addition to his career as a tax attorney, Eichholz was a noted art collector and philanthropist. Barney Brantingham, *Philanthropist Mercedes Eichholz Talks about Life and Politics*, SANTA BARBARA INDEPENDENT, Aug. 2, 2007.

43. Although Surrey describes Lusk as already a veteran Bureau attorney in 1938, Lusk was still at Treasury in 1956, as "Assistant Head, Legal Advising Staff" in the Office of the General Counsel of the Treasury. ANNUAL REPORT OF THE SECRETARY OF THE TREASURY ON THE STATE OF THE FINANCES FOR THE FISCAL YEAR ENDED JUNE 30, 1956, xiii (1957).

44. Later in his career Seymour S. Mintz joined the Washington law firm of Hogan & Hartson and became a prominent tax attorney. He was reported to have played a leading role in transferring most of the assets of Howard Hughes to a charitable foundation (the Howard Hughes Medical Institute) in 1953. Wallace Turner, *Fight Reported Lost by Hughes Institute*, NEW YORK TIMES, Feb. 20, 1977, at 21.

45. In the *Hendler* case, the Supreme Court ruled that the assumption of debt by an acquiring corporation in a formal reorganization was not excluded from the gross income of the indebted corporation.

interpretation and provide acceptable guidelines for the treatment of liabilities in corporate reorganizations.

The cancellation of indebtedness problem was caused by another Supreme Court decision, *United States v. Kirby Lumber Co.*, 284 U. S. 1 (1931). Correctly decided and following Treasury Regulations, the Court had held that a corporate obligor realized taxable income when it purchased its bonds in the open market at a figure less than par. But, as a result of the depression, many financially embarrassed corporations, seeking to adjust their liabilities to reduce current interest obligations and avert bankruptcy, found themselves faced with a large tax liability if they purchased their bonds, which were then selling far below par. As a consequence, corporations strongly urged that relief from this dilemma be given to them by Congress. In addition, there were no real guidelines, apart from cryptic sentences in the *Kirby* opinion, as to just how the various circumstances under which a cancellation of indebtedness could occur should be treated under the income tax. The entire situation, just as in *Hendler*, called for a complete statutory change.

The work of our Office produced the technical proposals which the Treasury presented to the Congress in the course of its consideration of the Revenue Act of 1939. The House Ways and Means Committee tentatively approved the proposals and they were then turned over to Beaman. In this period Beaman was the chief technical expert for the tax committees. He did not, however, initiate proposals. His task instead, was to take the Treasury proposals, or those made by the bar, representatives of business, Committee members, etc., after their initial acceptance by the Committee and draft the necessary statutory language. Then he would present the drafts to the Committee and explain the details. It was first in 1939 that I was really exposed to the Beaman drafting process, for the hurried 1938 acceptance of our statute of limitations draft was a distinct exception. Beaman took our 1939 drafts on assumption of liabilities and cancellation of indebtedness, grumpily examined them for a few minutes, and then put them aside. He then commenced his "seminars" on these subjects. The group attending these seminars, besides Beaman and his assistant John O'Brien, were the Treasury representatives — Tarleau, Shaw, Eicholz, Lusk and I; several attorneys from the Legislation and Regulations Division of the Chief Counsel's Office in the Bureau — so that the Bureau could keep itself informed of the provisions it would later have to administer — and a representative of the Staff of the Joint Congressional Committee on Taxation. At that time this was a small group, first headed by Lovell Parker until 1937 and then by Colin Stam, whose main function on that staff until that time had been passing on large refund claims granted by the Bureau.[46]

The seminar proceeded by Beaman's asking question after question, probing the points of analysis, immersing himself in the subject, holding up words or phrases to the light and exposing their defects, exploring alternative methods of organizing the

46. Lovell H. Parker was the first chief of staff of the Joint Committee on Taxation, serving from 1926 until his retirement in 1937, after which he worked for a time as a tax consultant. *Lovell H. Parker, Revenue Specialist*, THE WASHINGTON POST, Jan. 18, 1961, at B8.

material. The intellectual rigor of these discussions was high. Day after day we sat in his office, as he indefatigably pursued his inquires. Obviously, we became impatient—when would he actually begin to draft! All of a sudden he would reach for pencil and paper and start to put down some phrases. We then could relax for we knew the actual drafting had commenced. Soon he would call in his male secretary and dictate an initial draft. But the process was not yet ended. As the typed pages came back, sometimes with a sentence or two, sometimes a subsection or paragraph, they were passed around to the group to be pored over as with a microscope. Finally Beaman would be satisfied and the material sent to the printer to be part of the draft bill presented to the Committee.

Only once did I see Beaman become flustered in his seminar. Late one evening as the group was working on a difficult drafting problem, Assistant Secretary Sullivan, who was in charge of the Treasury tax offices, wandered into the room.[47] I do not know what prompted this visit but there he was. Beaman was at a loss as to how to proceed. He knew, as did the rest of the group, that Sullivan had no knowledge of technical tax law and no expertise in drafting. Yet he could not be ignored, nor treated as was Stam who was often abruptly told by Beaman to shut up, since Sullivan was an important administration official. Beaman decided to filibuster, gearing down the technical discussion and politely asking Sullivan some simple questions. Sullivan soon saw he was out of his element and good naturedly left. Beaman, much relieved, resumed his seminar. This was the only time a Treasury official higher than the Tax Legislative Counsel attended the drafting sessions.

I sat in this office, for many hours and days, repeating this procedure, for almost eight years, first with Beaman, then after he retired with John O'Brien, and when he retired, his assistant Gerald Morgan.[48] Often we worked until late at night, eating dinner at a restaurant near the capital. Tarleau, and later I, would have the responsibility of signing off for the Treasury and accepting the drafts. The entire process was as rigorous an intellectual task as any I have observed in my teaching career. I learned how words should be used in a statutory draft—words held up to as intense an examination as would a jeweler searching a precious stone. I saw how a section could be structured, how technical phrases could be formed, how various sections of the law could be tied together by those phrases. It was an elegant process producing a finely tuned structure. But it did have one weakness. For this approach always to be successful everyone else construing the statute would have to play the game by the rules Beaman and his successors devised, would have to recognize the function

47. Within three months of John L. Sullivan's arrival in Washington in 1939 as an assistant to the Commissioner of Internal Revenue, President Roosevelt appointed Sullivan Assistant Secretary of the Treasury. Sullivan later served as Secretary of the Navy, from 1947 to 1949. Edward A. Gargan, *John L. Sullivan Dies at 83: Navy Secretary for Truman*, New York Times, Aug. 11, 1982, at A20.

48. Gerald D. Morgan had a varied career in government service and the private practice of law. He worked in the Office of House Legislative Counsel from 1939 to 1945, and later served as special counsel to President Eisenhower. *Gerald D. Morgan Dead at 67, Helped Draft Taft-Hartley Act*, New York Times, Jun. 16, 1976, at 34.

he had decided a word or phrase should perform. The rest of the world was not up to this assignment, and as a consequence courts would sometimes fail to perceive the meaning inherent in the intricate phrasing or interlocking of sections that Beaman produced [check — where have I said this — in complexity article?][49] Today, of course, the style of drafting is far different. While the congressional tax draftsmen are skilled and experienced, they do not have the time necessary for a "Beaman seminar." The pace of legislation, the greatly increased complexity of the code with so many sections and concepts compared with Beaman's days, make the process of drafting one of doing the best one can do in a short time, with the understanding that mistakes will be corrected in a Technical Changes Act to follow the initial legislation.

It was Beaman's assignment to explain the draft bill to the Committees. This was a difficult assignment. He had to assure them, by some examples and references to the language, that he had carried out the policy they had adopted. Yet he had to avoid overwhelming the Committees with details they could not follow nor desired to in the time available. The Committees realized they had tentatively adopted a proposal only in the large, with Mid to work out the details. The entire process depended on trust, the Committees' trust for Beaman and Beaman's trust in the Treasury staff. On one occasion Beaman told the House Committee that a provision was so complicated that the Committee would have to accept on faith Beaman's assertion it was properly drafted. But it was not, and Beaman made important changes when the bill reached the Senate Committee. Once again he said this draft would have to be accepted on faith, explaining while he had so informed the House and nevertheless had made changes, still faith must be granted to him. The Committee agreed. Then, still pursuing his goal of perfection, Beaman made additional changes, explaining to the Conference Committee, composed of Senators and Representatives who had heard his previous explanations, that this final draft — for the legislative process on the bill was ending — had also to be accepted on faith. Both he and the Members were good-humored about this, recognizing the position he was in, and faith was once more granted.

At each stage of the legislative process a Committee Report had to be written stating in one part the major policy decisions of the Committees and in a second part providing technical explanations of the provisions. The first part was then written largely by Beaman's office, though the Treasury sometimes participated. [check] The technical part was written by our Treasury group and only quickly checked by Beaman. We were in effect placed on our honor to present an objective, technical explanation that could not be slanted to support a later Treasury interpretation not in accordance with the drafting discussions. Often in our deliberations

49. Perhaps Surrey was thinking of the following passage: "If one is willing to play by the draftsman's rules — to accept a highly technical, highly stratified arrangement under which a series of arbitrary definitions and terms are intricately interwoven — then the content of complex provisions can be pieced together and the answers to many, many questions will be found. It is not an easy game to play. It requires long practice, familiarity with the drafting techniques, and close and hard reading." Stanley S. Surrey, *Complexity and the Internal Revenue Code: The Problem of the Management of Tax Detail*, 34 LAW & CONTEMP. PROBS. 673, 697 (1969).

on a draft, when either Beaman or someone else would wonder whether a phrase was perhaps ambiguous or did not fully spell out the concept, Beaman would end the discussion by saying "Leave this to the Committee Report," and it was our task to cover the point in the technical part of the Report. The Committee, though some Members did read the first part, did not read the technical explanation. But the tax bar did read that explanation with a fine eye, for they fully understood that "law" was being made there as well in the statutory words. It was then our job to hear their questions or complaints and deal with them objectively in the later Senate Committee or Conference Committee Report, even though it would often mean a result contrary to an interpretation favorable to the Treasury. But we trusted Beaman and Beaman trusted us.

Much of our proposals on these two subjects in 1939, despite the changes in business practices and new insights on the tax structure that inevitably occur over the years, still remain in the tax code.[b, 50] Our group had done its work well and the outside tax bar was impressed with the capability shown by our Office. I then described the details of this 1939 legislation and its entire statutory and legal background in two articles in the Yale Law Journal.[c] I wrote the articles in the strong belief that government attorneys who worked on important legislation had an obligation, time permitting, to inform the tax bar of the details and background of the legislation and the drafting nuances involved. Also, having spent so much time in preparation of the legislation, I had obtained ample material for the articles.

The 1939 Act, besides these two major technical changes, introduced a two-year carryover of net operating losses and ended the remnants of the tax on undistributed corporate profits. At this time, John Hanes, a southern businessman, was Treasury Under Secretary,[51] succeeding Magill who had resigned, and also then left teaching for a New York tax practice.[52] Incidentally, Magill, who had been somewhat liberal in his approach to tax policy, or at least centrist, in later years grew conservative—perhaps the influence of a Wall Street practice and the absence of a professorial tug. Hanes was distinctly conservative, seeing only the business point of view. It was to him the two tax Offices now reported. The other significant 1939 legislation was the

50. For the provisions governing assumptions of liabilities in certain corporate transactions, *see* Revenue Act of 1939, Pub. L. No. 76-155, § 213(a), 53 Stat. 862, 870 (codified at former IRC § 112(k)). It survives today—modified, but readily recognizable—as IRC § 357. For the provision governing cancellations of indebtedness of corporations in financial distress, *see* Revenue Act of 1939, § 215, 53 Stat. at 875 (codified at former IRC § 22(b)(9) and 113(b)(3)). Much of the substance survives today in IRC § 108(a) and (b), albeit in significantly different form. The "recent bankruptcy legislation" mentioned in Surrey's note b is the Bankruptcy Tax Act of 1980, Pub. L. No. 96-589, § 2, 94 Stat. 3389, 3389 (putting § 108(a) and (b) in essentially the form that has endured to this day).

51. John Wesley Hanes II served as Assistant Secretary of the Treasury and as Undersecretary of the Treasury in 1938 and 1939. He had a long and successful career as a corporate turnaround specialist and was also deeply involved in thoroughbred horse racing. George James, *John Wesley Hanes Sr., 95, Aide to Roosevelt and Corporate Chief*, New York Times, Dec. 31, 1987, at A24.

52. From Treasury, Magill returned to teaching at Columbia Law School. In 1943 he left Columbia to become a partner with the New York law firm of Cravath, Swaine & Moore. *Roswell Magill Dead; Once Treasury Expert*, The Washington Post, Dec. 19, 1963, at B4.

Public Salary Tax Act.[53] This Act, following Supreme Court decisions upholding the Bureau view that the salaries of state and local government officials and employees were subject to the federal income tax, thus overriding the constitutional objections of the states, adopted statutory provisions taxing those salaries on a non-retroactive basis from January 1, 1939.[54] The Act also finessed the question whether state income taxes could reach federal salaries by "consenting" to nondiscriminatory state taxation of those salaries.[55] At this time the federal income taxation of federal bond interest, and more important as a political issue, the federal taxation of the interest on state and local bond interest, were starting to emerge as major issues. But though recommended by the President in 1938,[56] the matter was not dealt with in 1939.

A major tax event in 1939 was the adoption of the Internal Revenue Code of 1939.[57] Up to that year each major revenue act—e.g., 1932, 1934, 1936, 1938—had embodied in full the income, estate, and gift tax substantive provisions [check—also the administrative provisions?].[58] One act thus did not amend another but simply repeated old language along with the new changes. Colin Stam, who had become [check] the Chief of Staff of the Congressional Joint Committee on Taxation,[59] had his staff for several years working on a Code that would contain the entire federal tax law. It was a lengthy and tedious exercise finished in 1939. The question was whether Congress should adopt it. Here Beaman made a tactical error, inevitable in his penchant for scrupulous examination of detail. He was against adoption of this Code, since, not having been examined by his Office or others, how could there be any assurance mistakes had not been made? Moreover, Beaman detested Stam. The dislike did not stem from pettiness but from their different perspectives. Stam, who had come from a minor position in the Bureau, to be Lovell Parker's assistant, nowhere approached Beaman's level. Stam's mind was rather ordinary and he did not have a really detailed knowledge of tax law. His talent instead was shrewd and wily perception of where

---

53. Public Salary Tax Act of 1939, Pub. L. No. 76-32, 53 Stat. 574.

54. The effective date rules in the Act were highly elaborate, but Surrey was correct that January 1, 1939, was generally the effective date.

55. Public Salary Tax Act of 1939, Pub. L. No. 76-32, § 4, 53 Stat. 574, 575.

56. Franklin D. Roosevelt, *Text of the President's Tax Message*, NEW YORK TIMES, Apr. 26, 1938, at 2 ("a fair and effective progressive income tax and a huge perpetual reserve of tax-exempt bonds cannot exist side by side").

57. Internal Revenue Code of 1939, Pub. L. No. 76-1, 53 Stat. 1.

58. In addition to the acts listed by Surrey, the Revenue Act of 1935, Pub. L. No. 74-407, 49 Stat. 1014, arguably qualifies as a major revenue act. Surrey was correct that the revenue acts contained not only the substantive tax provisions, but administrative provisions as well. *See, e.g.*, Revenue Act of 1938, Pub. L. No. 75-554, Part V and Supplements L through O, 52 Stat. 447, 476–80, 534–45.

59. Stam became chief of staff of the Joint Committee on Taxation in 1937. George Yin has offered a detailed and insightful analysis of Surrey's antagonism toward Stam, as expressed in this paragraph of Surrey's memoirs (and elsewhere in the memoirs as well). George K. Yin, '*Who Speaks for Tax Equity and Tax Fairness?' Stanley Surrey and the Tax Legislative Process,* 39 VA. TAX REV. 39, 49–66 (2019). As Yin explains in depth, "Surrey and Stam seem to have had very different policy views and conceptions of the role of a staff person advising Congress." *Id.* at 61. *See* also, John L. Connolly, "Colin F. Stam—The Individual" in Essays on Taxation Contributed in Memory of Colin F. Stam, 1–8 (1974).

the influential Committee Members — and the influential lobbyists — desired to move. Decidedly pro-taxpayer, he considered his role to be that of providing the technical bridge to their goals. He also had a skill in explaining proposals in outrageously simple terms, which covered up major problems and led as a result to committee acceptance without any understanding of the issues. But he had no patience or talent for deep analysis or the subtleties of drafting. Indeed, seeing this attitude so foreign to Beaman's sense of craftsmanship, at several drafting sessions which Stam attended, Beaman hastily told Stam to shut up and not offer comments. Stam decided in turn not to attend drafting sessions.

The Treasury staff, though growing to dislike Stam, who would become over the years an antagonist and a nemesis, and having a loyalty to Beaman, nevertheless saw that Stam was right on the question of adopting his Code. While there might here and there be mistakes — who really knew if this were so — still a Code compilation of the statutory tax law would be a major structural achievement, making easier the drafting of future legislation. Beaman, we thought, had both let his perfectionism color his position and also overplayed his hand, since we could easily see the Committee liked the idea of a Code. The Treasury therefore endorsed the Code and its adoption was assured.[60] With this, Beaman's star began to dim and give way to Stam's ascendancy to importance as the Congress' technical man.

The years beginning in 1940 found a steadily increased pace of tax legislation as the defense program and then war produced great demands for more revenues. The maneuvering between Democrats and Republicans in Congress on the amounts of revenue to be raised and the types of taxes to be used is fully described in Randolph Paul's book. "Taxation in the United States" (1954). This phase of the Treasury work need not be repeated here. Let me instead describe some events of this period as seen by the workers in the tax vineyards. The two tax offices expanded their personnel. Since Tarleau, as I have said, disliked supervision or confrontation, increasingly I found myself dealing with the Bureau officials; meeting more and more with the tax bar, lawyers and accountants seeking Treasury approval for their proposals; and keeping the work of the Office on schedule. I was careful to check policy conclusions with Tarleau, both to keep him informed and because of his good judgment. But much of the technical detail became my responsibility.

Also, I had more interest than Tarleau in talking with the economists on Blough's staff. Blough had an amazing ability to seek out young economists in the early stages of their careers and persuade them to come to the Treasury for a stint of a year or two. Among those so attracted were Carl Shoup, Walter Heller, Milton Friedman, Cary Brown, Richard Goode, Louis Shere, Joseph Pechman, William Vickery, and Lowell Harriss. [check][61] It was a tribute to Roy Blough's ability to appreciate talent

60. According to George Yin, Surrey understates Treasury's resistance to codification: "[T]here is ample evidence both on and off the public record to contradict Surrey's assertion and show that the Treasury resisted the codification effort until the very end." *Id.* at 59.

61. In this list of extremely distinguished public finance economists, all except Richard Goode did indeed work for the Treasury Department at some point in their careers (and Goode spent time

and use it wisely that so many of the outstanding public finance figures of later years were in the Treasury during this period. I worked closely with them, partly because our responsibilities brought us together and partly because of a desire to understand how they approached problems. In turn, I learned how to put questions to them and to have them focus on the issues I saw as of importance to molding Treasury proposals or fending off the proposals of others. I gained from this experience a high respect for the contributions an able tax economist could make and also some background for judging which economists could lead a lawyer down some intellectually dazzling but impractical path, which economists only pushed their own prescriptions for the world, and which economists — fortunately for the lawyer — could give objective advice and fairly describe where that advice stood in the spectrum of views that could be obtained. Most of the Treasury economists of this period had liberal leaning fiscal views, a strong preference for a progressive income tax, and a strong regard for "tax equity," for treating people with equal incomes equally in the tax laws. This stress on tax equity led naturally to a distaste for tax preferences and "loopholes."[62] Moreover, conscientious work in the Treasury pushes a person very hard in the direction of tax equity, for one quickly perceives the responsibility that rests upon the Treasury to safeguard the fairness of the tax system.

It was during this period that Stam became a major force in the formulation of Congressional tax policy. Given the political divisions in the Tax Committee — conservative Republicans and some conservative Democrats versus liberal Democrats and straight Democratic party liners — the field was ripe for Stam's talent for maneuverability. His adeptness at advancing simple explanations that, deliberately, kept the problems hidden gave him a built-in advantage over the Treasury representatives in appearances in the closed executive sessions of the Committees. The Treasury staff regarded it as an obligation to be objective in their explanations. But objectivity can quickly lead, unless one is extremely skilled, into complexity and the Congressional mind in general is not tuned to complexity, oral or written. Add to this the generally conservative leanings of a majority of the tax committees, and the result was that on major policy issues the Treasury representatives were usually either not a match for Stam, or the struggle between Stam and Treasury produced an unsatisfactory compromise. On technical issues, especially where Stam had no interest, the Treasury did better. But if there was important lobbying pressure for a particular proposal, opposed by the Treasury, especially when some committee Members favored the proposal, the Treasury had a rough time and often lost in their opposition.

---

with the Bureau of the Budget). Two members of the group were later awarded the Nobel Memorial Prize in Economic Sciences — Friedman in 1976, and Vickrey in 1996. For more on the interactions between lawyers and economists in the Treasury Department at this time, *see generally*, JOSEPH J. THORNDIKE, THEIR FAIR SHARE: TAXING THE RICH IN THE AGE OF FDR (2013).

62. Surrey would, of course, famously become one of the leading advocates of exposing such "tax preferences" and "loopholes," as "tax expenditures," though it is unclear whether all of the "liberal" economists he worked with agreed with his views of "tax equity."

As for tax legislation, the year 1940 saw the First Revenue Act of 1940, with a "defense" supertax of 10%, increased excise tax rates, and a start in the lowering of the income tax personal exemption levels.[63] But the major technical work in 1940, as well as a policy change, was the adoption of an excess profits tax in the Second Revenue Act of 1940.[64] At the time the Vinson-Trammell Act, limiting profits on the construction of naval aircraft and vessels, was on the books. In June, 1940, following large Navy contracts let without competitive bidding, there was hasty legislation enacted to lower the allowed rate of profit on Navy contracts. This legislation was a Treasury responsibility and I performed the technical work. The policy was set by Senator David Walsh of Massachusetts, Chairman of the Senate Committee on Naval Affairs. Walsh, who had a large imposing physical presence and a true Senatorial image, several times received me in his office much as an oriental potentate issuing orders to his vizier.[65] The orders once given, my task was to produce the drafts which the Senator accepted without a glance on the assurance they carried out his imperial command. But because of the rapid growth of government defense contracts generally pressure was building in 1940 for a broad excess profits tax. In July, 1940, President Roosevelt called on Congress to enact such a tax.[66] Our two Treasury Offices were plunged into the task of formulating such a tax on corporations. As I will discuss later, I had been teaching a summer session in California, but was at once called back to participate. The technical work was speedily accomplished. A policy struggle then ensued in Congress over the measure of what was "excess"—should it be an increase in earnings over prior years or a rate of return on capital that was higher than that considered normal. In the end both approaches were adopted by Congress, with the choice left to the corporation.[67]

When I think of this legislative activity and then look back at my writing at that time I now wonder how it was done. I must have spent my evenings in 1939 and 1940, when not working in Beaman's office, on constant writing. In addition to the two Yale Law Review articles and the Washington University Law Quarterly article earlier mentioned, with 1940 publication dates, I wrote an article, with Traynor, on "New Roads Toward the Settlement of Federal, Income Estate and Gift Tax Controversies," 7 Law and Contemporary Problems 336 (1940), and an article, also with a

63. Revenue Act of 1940, Pub. L. No. 76-656, 54 Stat. 516. Surrey's description is accurate.

64. Second Revenue Act of 1940, Pub. L. No. 76-801, 54 Stat. 974.

65. David I. Walsh (D., Mass.) was a United States senator from 1919 to 1925, and again from 1926 to 1947.

66. By July 1940, the war in Europe was intensifying. Although the United States would not enter the conflict officially until December 1941 after the bombing of Pearl Harbor, by the summer of 1940 the U.S began war preparedness, thus leading to an increased demand for government defense contracts. DAVID M. KENNEDY, FREEDOM FROM FEAR: THE AMERICAN PEOPLE IN DEPRESSION AND WAR, 1929–1945 (1999); MARK WILSON, DESTRUCTIVE CREATION: AMERICAN BUSINESS AND THE WINNING OF WWII (2016).

67. The dual method excess profits tax that Surrey discusses was modeled after a similar tax enacted during World War I. *See, generally*, AJAY K. MEHROTRA, MAKING THE MODERN AMERICAN FISCAL STATE: LAW, POLITICS, AND THE RISE OF PROGRESSIVE TAXATION, 1877–1929 Ch. 6. (2013).

1940 date, in 88 University of Pennsylvania Law Review 556 on "The Scope and Effect of Treasury Regulations Under the Income, Estate, and Gift Taxes." This article was one of the first on the subject of Treasury Regulations to distinguish between interpretative Regulations, issued under a general statutory authority, and legislative Regulations, issued under those sections of the Code which specially authorized Treasury Regulations. The article commented on several Supreme Court decisions dealing with the Treasury's regulatory powers, one of the decisions, Helvering v. Hallock,[68] having been written by Justice Frankfurter. I must say my ego was considerably increased on receiving, out of the blue for I had not even considered sending him a copy of the article, a note from the Justice.

I should mention one other article, started in this period but published in 1941, "The Supreme Court and the Federal Income Tax: Some Implications of the Recent Decisions," 35 Illinois Law Review 779 (1941). Having had articles published in the Columbia, Yale and Pennsylvania Law Reviews, I sent this article to the Harvard Law Review. It was promptly rejected. My disappointment was mixed with a distinctly lowered opinion of whoever, student editors or faculty, made decisions on articles for the Harvard Law Review.[69] In my judgment—and I really was objective—this was clearly one of the best articles I had written. The article was prompted by a rather silly comment by two New Dealers that for the first time as a result of several recent Supreme Court decisions the federal tax law had become a clear-cut body of judicial utterances:

> "The lines of the new attack stand out even in a highly technical field such as income taxation. Here the cases come along in never ending parade; and, at every opportunity, the Court has erased fine distinctions, demolished esoteric dialectic, torn away corporate veils, looked to the realities of transactions. As a result an ingenious mosaic of theology is being swept into the discard; and for the first time in its history, the law of the income tax begins to stand out as a simple, clear-cut, consistent body of judicial utterances."

Walton Hamilton and George Braden, "The Supreme Court Today" 103(6) New Republic 178, 179 (August 5, 1940).

Obviously anyone working in the Treasury knew that the federal income tax was basically a statutory system and not a judicial structure. But these recent Supreme Court decisions were significant in their acceptance of serious Bureau interpretations

68. 309 U.S. 106 (1940).

69. At least by twenty-first century standards, the sense of entitlement Surrey here expresses—that if one submits an excellent tax article to the Harvard Law Review, of course the Review should accept it for publication—is almost incomprehensible. If Surrey ever had the opposite reaction—that a top student-edited journal had foolishly accepted one of his minor efforts, better suited to publication in a lesser journal—he does not mention it anywhere in these memoirs. Incidentally, lest the reader think that being relegated to the Illinois Law Review was a stunning fall from grace for an article that belonged in the Harvard Law Review, it should be noted that this was the Illinois Law Review of Northwestern University, later to become simply the Northwestern University Law Review.

of the statutory law and in the freedom they gave to the Bureau to strike down tax avoidance devices. One decision, going far in this direction, was *Helvering v. Clifford*,[70] written by Justice Douglas at the point in his judicial career when he was very pro-Government in his tax opinions—and correctly so on the issues involved—and before he turned bitterly anti-Government, never holding against a taxpayer.[d, 71] No one had attempted a detailed analysis of these decisions against a background of how the Treasury and Congress worked, so that their effects on the legislative process in the tax field could be realistically assessed. I have used this article in my casebooks and remain convinced the Illinois Law Review editors who accepted the article for publication far outdid Harvard in their discernment of what was an important tax article! Finally, as I will describe later, in this period I was preparing the cases and syllabus for a summer session at Berkeley. It must have been a busy year!

During this time I was made aware—and shocked as a result—of how careers are made in Government. I had worked with the Members of the Board of Tax Appeals but never thought of their backgrounds or how they had achieved their positions. They were "Members" and while I recognized they differed in ability, I simply assumed they belonged on the Board. But then a vacancy occurred. The Treasury had the jurisdiction to recommend to the President persons for appointment to the Board. It was suddenly announced that Marion Harron would be named. This was a person I knew! She was an assistant to General Counsel Oliphant, totally lacking any tax experience and in no way different from the average bureaucrat. Just an average intelligence and no particular quality of judgment. The realization that such a person, only because she was a protege of Oliphant's, could become a Board Member—a position I did understand—shocked my sense of how Government should operate. Miss Harron turned out to be an undistinguished Board Member, disliked by the lawyers who appeared before her because of her erratic petulance and harshly critical attitudes on how *she* thought attorneys should present cases.[72] [check Herwitz and time]

---

70. 309 U.S. 331 (1940).

71. Later in his years on the Court, Justice Douglas routinely dissented without opinion in tax cases in which the majority ruled in favor of the government. For a scathing critique of this practice, *see* Bernard Wolfman, Jonathan L. F. Silver & Marjorie A. Silver, Dissent without Opinion: The Behavior of Justice William O. Douglas in Federal Tax Cases (1975).

72. Marion Janet Harron served on the Board of Tax Appeals, and the successor Tax Court, from 1936 to 1960. For some, Harron's main claim to fame is that she reputedly had a romantic relationship with Lorena Hickok shortly after the end of Hickok's romantic involvement with Eleanor Roosevelt; Harron was a frequent visitor at the White House during this period. Doris Kearns Goodwin, No Ordinary Time: Franklin and Eleanor Roosevelt: The Home Front in World War II 339 (1994). Surrey's note to himself to "check Herwitz and time" is a mystery. Perhaps he thought that his Harvard Law School colleague David R. Herwitz (whose academic interests included taxation) had some information about Harron. Although a reader might be understandably suspicious that, when Surrey in these memoirs finally encounters a female tax professional, he has for her nothing but scorn, Surrey's view was not without foundation. At the time of her appointment to the Board of Tax Appeals Harron lacked substantial tax experience. The appointment may have been due to Harron's friendship at that time with Eleanor Roosevelt. Sheryll Stratton, *Tax Court Judges May Not Be Back, Even by*

In the Treasury late in 1939 John Hanes resigned as Under Secretary to be succeeded by Daniel Bell, an able, balanced career official with a background in Government financial and budgetary matters but not the tax field.[73] At that time John L. Sullivan, a genial, New Hampshire lawyer, average ability, but very good Democratic connections was appointed an Assistant Secretary. Our two Tax Offices, along with some other Treasury offices, were now to report to him. While emotional — he once had his whole office turned upside down because he had misplaced a paper but thought his office was subject to theft — he had a reasonable judgment, at least sensible enough to listen to us most of the time, but did not exercise leadership in the tax field. He later, in 1947, was Secretary of the Navy.

Under the pressure for additional revenues the year 1941 saw the enactment of still another revenue act, the Revenue Act of 1941.[74] This Act increased the individual and corporate surtaxes, made changes in the excess profits tax, lowered personal exemptions and several other changes. The main structural battle was fought on the issue of mandatory joint returns for husband and wife. With rising individual income tax rates the community property states, ( ) in number and in the West ____ California, Washington, Oregon, Texas, Nevada, Louisiana, (?) [check] under their state property laws, inherited from the Spanish, treated husband and wife as each owning one-half of the income earned by either and from property obtained by either during marriage.[75] This ability to "split income," with each spouse filing a separate tax return to be taxed under the progressive rate structure at lower tax rates than would a couple elsewhere with the same amount of income but earned by or belonging only to one spouse, gave these community property couples a distinctly lower federal income tax liability. Also, even in non-community property states one wealthy spouse could through a variety of legal devices shift some of the tax liability on income from property to the other spouse, also producing a lower tax bill for the family. But this could not be done with earned income, so that inequalities in non-community property states existed between families with earned income, and families with unearned income depending on how that income was divided. The Treasury had recommended that these serious inequalities be ended by requiring all married couples to file a joint

---

Popular Demand, TAX NOTES, Jan. 12, 2004, at 176, 180. Stratton also notes that Harron's "legendary lack of judicial temperament has made for many colorful anecdotes in Tax Court lore." *Id.*

73. Prior to his appointment as Undersecretary of the Treasury, Daniel W. Bell directed the Bureau of the Budget from 1934 to 1939. He later became president of the American Security and Trust Company. *Daniel Bell, Retired Banker,* NEW YORK TIMES, Oct. 5, 1971, at 44.

74. Revenue Act of 1941, Pub. L. No. 77-250, 55 Stat. 687.

75. Surrey's list is not quite accurate. Prior to the community property incentive created by the income-splitting tax advantage of community property, the eight community property states were Arizona, California, Idaho, Louisiana, Nevada, New Mexico, Texas and Washington. In the aftermath of two 1930 Supreme Court federal income tax opinions permitting income splitting by spouses in community property states (Poe v. Seaborn, 282 U.S. 101 (1930)), but not by spouses in separate property states (Lucas v. Earl, 281 U.S. 111 (1930)), five other states (Michigan, Nebraska, Oklahoma, Oregon and Pennsylvania) enacted community property statutes between 1939 and 1947. *See* Jennifer E. Sturiale, *The Passage of Community Property Laws, 1939–1947: Was More than Money Involved?*, 11 MICH. J. GENDER & L. 213, 215 (2005).

tax return. This mandatory tax return, combining the incomes of the two spouses, would lift community property couples and also non-community property couples with divided income into a higher tax bracket and thus meant an increase in tax liabilities. While the House Ways and Means Committee, by a divided vote, supported the proposal, it was stricken on the House floor after a stormy debate attacking the change. The attack was led by the community property states, and by clergymen who argued it would encourage living in sin.[76] [check state and local securities, federal securities, sales tax]

In this period the Chairman of the House Ways and Means Committee was Robert L. Doughton of North Carolina, Chairman since 1933. He was a crusty, rugged, individual with stubbornly held views—hence, I believe, the nickname "Muley"—but on the whole a loyal Democrat who did have the respect of the Committee.[77] Next in line was Jere Cooper of Tennessee, a person of some asperity with a rigorous down-the-line Democratic party loyalty. He succeeded Doughton as Chairman in 1955.[78] The Republican ranking minority member was first Allen T. Treadway of Massachusetts, a kindly gentleman who was a thorough Republican but without any bitterness.[79] (He was succeeded in 1945 by Harold Knutson of Minnesota, hard-nosed, solidly Republican, who had no love for the Treasury.)[80] We were on good terms with all of the first three, and indeed most of the other Committee members. In this Committee party lines were often very important, and the Democrats on the Committee would frequently caucus, often with the Treasury present, to determine their position. I believe Doughton and Treadway had respect for Stam, but Cooper had none. Other members when they disagreed with the Treasury knew they could rely on Stam to present their viewpoints, cloaked usually with a veneer of technical language that often made differences with the Treasury sound like a complex dispute between technicians. In this posture it was

---

76. For a brief history of the failed 1941 attempt to reform the federal income tax treatment of marriage, *see* LAWRENCE ZELENAK, FIGURING OUT THE TAX: CONGRESS, TREASURY AND THE DESIGN OF THE EARLY MODERN INCOME TAX 195–197 (2018) [hereinafter FIGURING OUT THE TAX]. The proposed reform would have eliminated the separate taxation of married couples in the most marriage-unfavorable manner possible—by requiring spouses to combine their incomes on a joint return and to pay tax on that combined income under the same rate schedule (including the same bracket widths) applicable to single taxpayers.

77. Robert Lee Doughton (D., N.C.) was a member of the House of Representatives from 1911 to 1953, and chairman of the Ways and Means Committee from 1933 to 1947, and from 1949 to 1953. He was indeed sometimes known as "Muley Bob." *Robert Lee Doughton*, NEW YORK TIMES, Oct. 2, 1954, at 16.

78. Jere Cooper (D., Tenn.) was a member of the House of Representatives from 1929 to 1957, and chairman of the Ways and Means Committee from 1955 to 1957. *Jere Cooper Rites Set For Tomorrow*, NEW YORK TIMES, Dec. 20, 1957, at 27. Daniel A. Reed (R., N.Y.) was chairman from 1953 to 1955, between Doughton and Cooper.

79. Allen T. Treadway (R., Mass.) was a member of the House of Representatives from 1913 to 1945. *A.T. Treadway, Former House Member, Dead*, CHICAGO TRIBUNE, Feb. 17, 1947, at 18.

80. Harold Knutson (R., Minn.) was a member of the House of Representatives from 1917 to 1949, and chairman of the Ways and Means Committee from 1947 to 1949. *H. Knutson is Dead; 32 Years in House*, NEW YORK TIMES, August 22, 1953, at 15.

relatively easy on the conscience of a Member, who disliked the Treasury proposal for whatever his reason, to say he was guided in his vote by the Committee's own technician.

On the Senate side, the Chairman of the Finance Committee was Walter George of Georgia.[81] [check when succeeded Pat Harrison] A gracious Southern gentleman, with a high intelligence and important influence in the Senate, he was quite conservative and not at all worried—as Doughton could be—about disagreeing with the Treasury and the President. He also, I believe, fully recognized Stam's plusses and minuses and used him adroitly, with Stam ever willing to be led by the Chairman. Next in line was _________,[82] [check] On the Republican side the senior member was ___________. [check]

The Committee on the whole was more conservative than the House Committee and while the relationship of our staff was cordial, it was not as close as in the House. Perhaps the most loyal Democrat was Senator Tom Connally of Texas. [check][83]

Late in 1941 Randolph E. Paul, a well-known New York tax lawyer who had at times advised President Roosevelt and had friendships with important New Dealers in government, became a Special Advisor to the Treasury Secretary and then General Counsel.[84] Paul, besides his tax practice, had scholarly interest in tax matters and had published in 1934, both tax texts and several studies in Federal Taxation, each book containing essays on different topics. I had reviewed—favorably—the second volume in 48 Yale Law Journal 1111 (1939).[85] Paul was deeply interested in tax policy and held liberal views. He was impatient with those tax practitioners who constantly sought devices to reduce the taxes of their wealthy clients, and also of those practitioners, usually the same persons, who constantly berated the Treasury and never

81. Walter F. George (D., Ga.) served in the Senate from 1922 to 1957, and as chairman of the Finance Committee from 1941 to 1946. *Walter F. George, 79, Dies; Georgia Senator 34 Years*, New York Times, Aug. 5, 1957, at 1. He followed Pat Harrison (D., Ga.), who was chair of the Finance Committee from 1933 until his death in 1941. *Pat Harrison, New Deal Leader, Dies*, The Washington Post, Jun. 23, 1941, at 1.

82. As of 1941, David I. Walsh (D., Mass.) was next in line to George among Democrats, and Robert M. ("Young Bob") La Follette, Jr. (Prog., Wisc.) was the ranking minority member.

83. It is not clear how Surrey hoped to check Connally's loyalty, or whether the note to "check" related to something else. In any event, Tom Connally (D., Tex.) served in the Senate from 1929 to 1953 and was indeed a member of the Finance Committee as Surrey writes. *Tom Connally, Former Texas Senator, Dies*, Los Angeles Times, Oct. 29, 1962, at 1.

84. In 1938 Paul declined the opportunity to become Assistant Secretary of Tax Policy and remained in private practice and an unofficial Treasury Department advisor. After Pearl Harbor, he became one of Morgenthau's special assistants, and in August 1942 he became the department's general counsel. Joseph J. Thorndike, *Profiles in Tax History Randolph E. Paul, available at* http://www.taxhistory.org/thp/readings.nsf/ArtWeb/AFD2A67073F6B87085256F8600681F74? [hereinafter *Profiles in Tax History Randolph E. Paul*].

85. Stanley S. Surrey, *Book Review*, 48 Yale L. J. 1111 (1939) (reviewing Randolph E. Paul, Selected Studies in Federal Taxation Second Series (1938)). In the review Surrey notes that, aside from the work of Roswell Magill, Paul's efforts "represent practically the entire body of legal literature offering a critical analysis of Federal income tax law," and that consequently "our tax law is woefully in need of searching examination." *Id.* at 1114.

aided in efforts to improve the tax system.[e, 86] With a really qualified tax person now in a top Treasury position, our two Offices naturally reported to Paul. We also continued to report to Sullivan, who had a loose general oversight over the Bureau of Internal Revenue. While Paul and Sullivan strove to cooperate with each other, Secretary Morgenthau looked to Paul to determine tax policy.[87]

Paul exercised a rather curious supervision over us. He had a casual, often at times seemingly vague, manner of discussing issues. He would say in a general way that we should recommend this or that and then leave it to Tarleau and Blough to work out the details and shape the recommendation. He had full confidence in these two and their staffs and simply assumed a good job would be done. It usually was. Though mild in appearance and talk, and unassuming, Paul had his ambitions, which were concentrated on producing a major revenue act in 1942 that would cover a wide variety of corrective structural measures, both affording relief from certain tax hardships or other situations where the tax system operated unfairly and also closing loopholes. This goal meant high pressure, continuous work by the tax staffs.

In this period I along with the staffs worked on a large number of new substantive provisions. For example, a deduction for medical expenses whose origin is none too clear but I believe was suggested by Paul; taxation of alimony to the wife and deduction of the payment by the husband — this was suggested by Paul who understood a husband's existing problem of no deduction but tax rates reaching over 80%,[88] since he was paying alimony; a deduction for child care, which barely got through the Ways and Means Committee who believed mothers should stay at home; a section allowing a deduction for expenses incurred in investment activities, the then current law having limited the deduction to business expenses; permission to a corporate group to file a consolidated return; a carryback of business losses in addition to the existing carry forward; a change in the treatment of capital gains to provide a 50% exclusion after a holding period reduced to six months which produced a higher tax than before (this was more generous tax treatment than the Treasury had sought); removal of the corporate tax from mutual investment companies who distributed almost all their income — I had worked this latter aspect out with the industry and the SEC over many a conference; a backward averaging of compensation received in one year for work done over a number of years; a rule limiting inclusion in income of recovered items previously deducted — such as bad debts or refunded tax — to situations in which the earlier deduction had produced a tax benefit; a provision straightening out the rules governing income earned by decedents before their death but received later by their estates; and a number of

86. In his note e, Surrey has in mind Randolph E. Paul, *The Responsibilities of the Tax Advisor*, 63 Harv. L. Rev. 377 (1950).

87. Henry Morgenthau, Jr., was Treasury Secretary for most of the Roosevelt administration, and for the early part of the Truman administration, from 1934 to 1945. He did not have a background in taxation. *Henry Morgenthau Jr., 75, Dies; Secretary of Treasury, 1934–45*, New York Times, Feb. 7, 1967, at 1.

88. The top marginal tax rate was 81% in 1941 and 88% in 1942.

other relief provisions.[89] These provisions, dealing essentially with situations in which the structural part of the income tax needed repair or change, were made more important by the increase in tax rates in the Act.

There were also loophole closing measures in the Act on which I and the staffs worked. The entire treatment of pension plans was revised, to allow businesses to deduct contributions to those plans but only when the coverage and contributions were non-discriminatory and thus did not favor only executives and higher-paid employees, for until then many of the plans being adopted with their costs offset by high corporate taxes were open only to the latter group.[90] (We made one mistake here. To relieve the bunching of income that would occur when a plan paid a retiring employee the pension in a lump sum — the Sears Roebuck plan — we provided that the payment would be treated as a capital gain.[91] While this treatment was rather close to an averaging result for the employees under that plan and was simpler, it later became a windfall for executives under other plans and even today has not been fully corrected). The estate tax was strengthened with elimination of the special exclusion for insurance, the taxation of decedents possessing powers of appointment covered, and community property taxed more heavily than before.[92] But many suggested tightenings were not accepted — elimination of the exemption of interest on state and local securities — here the Treasury unwisely pushed to include both outstanding and new securities, when a recommendation to cover only the latter might have succeeded; the elimination of the percentage depletion deduction for oil and minerals; the requirement of joint returns.[93] [check]

All of these matters were presented to the Ways and Means Committee in a long, detailed statement by Paul on which I had the principal drafting role.[94] Nearly all the new provisions that did survive in the act, principally the relief provisions, remain in the Code today in much the basic way they were drafted in 1942. That legislation, the Revenue Act of 1942, was the largest bill in tax history. Paul, in the book earlier referred to, described that Act in these words:

---

89. Revenue Act of 1942, Pub. L. No. 77-753, 56 Stat. 798. For the provisions mentioned by Surrey, *see* §§ 127 (medical expense deduction), 120 (alimony), 121 (investment expenses), 159 (consolidated returns), 153 (net operating loss carrybacks), 150 (capital gains), 170 (regulated investment companies), 139 (backwards income averaging), 116 (exclusionary tax benefit rule), and 134 (income in respect of a decedent). Surrey's recollection was faulty in only one respect; Congress did not enact a (very limited) deduction for childcare expenses until 1954.

90. Revenue Act of 1942, Pub. L. No. 77-753, § 162, 56 Stat. 798, 862 (codified at former IRC § 23(p)(1) and 165(a)(4)).

91. Revenue Act of 1942, § 162, 56 Stat. at 862 (codified at former IRC § 165(b)). For an example of the Sears Roebuck plan, *see* Knapp v. Commissioner, 41 B.T.A. 23 (1940) (retiring employee taxed at ordinary income rates on lump sum withdrawn upon retirement, despite the resulting bunching of income and high marginal tax rates).

92. For the estate tax revisions, *see* Revenue Act of 1942, § 401-415, 56 Stat. at 941-951.

93. Surrey was correct that the 1942 Act included none of these proposed reforms, although § 145 of the Act revised the percentage depletion rules for some minerals (not including oil or gas).

94. For Paul's statement, *see Hearings Before the Comm. on Ways and Means, House of Representatives*, 77th Cong., 2nd Sess., on Revenue Revision of 1942, 80–95 (vol. 1, 1942).

"In the official copy the Revenue Act of 1942 ran to 208 pages, as compared with 8 pages in the 1894 Act. It contained more relief provisions than any other revenue measure in American history. One hundred and twenty pages, or more than half of its total, were devoted to the relief of inequities. The principal loopholes of the revenue system were not closed, but several loopholes which for years had offered opportunities for avoiding taxes disappeared from the statute. The act devoted 42 pages to the clarification and definition of existing provisions to enable more equitable enforcement. Out of its 173 sections, 104 were corrective. In pages, this was nearly 78 percent of the act, 162 pages out of 208. In this sense, if not in a fiscal sense, the bill performed an outstanding service. The rate structure had reached the point where loopholes resulted in drastic loss of revenue, and where inequities and discrepancies threatened to be not only troublesome, but even disastrous, to taxpayers.

The income tax was now a mass tax. It had, in the estimate of Professors Surrey and Warren, 'changed its morning coat for overalls.' Membership in the country's taxpaying group had 'spread from the country club group district down to the railroad tracks and then over to the other side of the tracks.' The Senate Finance Committee report on the 1941 act noted an increase in the number of annual returns to over 22 million, of which over 13 million would be taxable returns. This seemed a long jump from 2 million taxable returns in 1932. But the 1942 act carried the total number of returns to nearly 37 million of which almost 28 million would reflect tax liability. There would be more than 50 million taxpayers when Victory taxpayers were counted."[95]

While these structural changes were working their way through the legislative process, major policy battles swirled around the bill. These are fully described in Paul. Here, while our two Offices did the staff work, fleshing out proposals which the Secretary and Paul, or the Democrats in Congress desired, and producing the debating points and describing weaknesses to counter Republican, and some Democratic proposals, the decision lay with the political forces on the Hill. Stam, as in all this period, was a foe of the Treasury, both because of his own thinking and as the technical front-runner for the legislators opposing the Treasury. The major issues revolved on the ways to increase revenues, for some increase was seen as necessary. In this struggle over revenues, Congressmen and some business representatives, determined to introduce a national sales tax as one method of financing the war, lost that bitter fight. But Stam won a round with his "Victory Tax," a 5% tax

95. RANDOLPH E. PAUL, TAXATION IN THE UNITED STATES 318–319 (1954) [hereinafter TAXATION IN THE UNITED STATES]. The "morning coat ... overalls" quotation is from STANLEY S. SURREY & WILLIAM C. WARREN, FEDERAL INCOME TAXATION, CASES AND MATERIALS 15 (1950) [hereinafter FEDERAL INCOME TAXATION].

on all income above a yearly $624, part of which tax was to be refunded postwar.[96] This tax was a complicating measure, but it had the seeds of future important developments. It reached far down in income levels and also, for wages, was to be withheld at the source by employers. The Treasury had recommended withholding at the source on all salaries wages, dividends and bond interest.[97] But this overall proposal lost when Commissioner of Internal Revenue Guy Helvering, without warning to the Treasury, testified personally that such withholding could not be handled by either the Bureau or employers.[98] This conflict between the Bureau and the Treasury was really the last display of an independent position on tax policy openly to be taken by the Bureau against a Treasury position. Thereafter, the pros and cons of administrative aspects of substantive policy proposals were debated within the Treasury and not in public. Generally in those discussions it was the Treasury's task to distinguish between real administrative problems presented by Bureau executives and those objections that were based only on the conservative and limited vision that a large bureaucracy often presents.

Also, at this time, a major controversy arose in Congress over what to do about the "Ruml plan." At that time, tax payments were made once a year, on March 15, for the preceding year. Taxpayers thus had to save funds in order to meet their March 15 bills. Many did not plan carefully, or could not as taxes increased, and serious problems of collection developed. Beardsley Ruml, Treasurer of Macy's (a New York department store) conceived the idea of making taxpayers pay in a current year the taxes on the income of that year, not on the income of a prior year.[99] The plan had merit but its details were sketchy. The Treasury was sympathetic and had also been thinking about current payment, as witness an earlier 1941 proposal and its 1942 recommendation for withholding. The major issue presented by the Ruml plan was that he wanted to obtain currency in tax payments, to go from "here to there," through

---

96. Revenue Act of 1942, Pub. L. No. 77-753, § 450, 56 Stat. 798, 884 (1942). As Surrey states, the rate of the tax was a flat five percent, imposed on "victory net income" above an exemption amount of $624.

97. Statement of Randolph E. Paul, *Hearings Before the Comm. on Ways and Means, House of Representatives*, 77th Cong., 2nd Sess., on Revenue Revision of 1942, 81–82 (vol. 1, 1942) (proposing withholding on wages, salaries, dividends, and bond interest).

98. Guy T. Helvering was a U.S. Representative from Kansas from 1913–1919. He was Commissioner of Internal Revenue from 1933–1943, and later a federal judge for the District of Kansas. "Guy T. Helvering," Biographical Dictionary of the United States Congress. For more on Helvering's position with regard to withholding, see Statement of Guy T. Helvering, Commissioner of Internal Revenue, *Hearing Before a Subcomm. of the Comm. on Finance*, U.S Sen., 77th Cong., 2nd Sess., on Data Relative to the Withholding Provisions of the 1942 Revenue Act, 75 (Aug.19, 1942). Helvering noted that he had previously told the Ways and Means Committee that the Bureau "could not satisfactorily administer the withholding plans unless adequate personnel, equipment, and space are made available to it," and that in the time since Helvering appeared before Ways and Means the equipment situation had worsened and the personnel situation had not improved.

99. In addition to being Treasurer of R. H. Macy & Co., Beardsley Ruml was chairman of the Federal Reserve Bank of New York. Randolph Paul had briefly worked for Ruml at the NY Fed. *See Profiles in Tax History Randolph E. Paul, supra* note 84.

forgiving a year's taxes. This problem of transition defeated the plan in 1942, but 1943 was to see a solution.[100]

One really bizarre event occurred in the consideration of the 1942 bill. The Treasury staff had been working on a tax on "spending" as a counter to sales tax proposals and to raise additional revenue. This was to be a tax, additional to the income tax, on moneys spent on consumption items. The proposal, without any warning, was presented one day by the Secretary to the Senate Finance Committee. The tax was novel and had its complications. The Treasury presentation was simply terrible, putting forth the suggestion for the tax and its basic structure along with a full recital of its complex details. Disorganized Committee questioning, followed by disorganized answers, sank the plan in one morning without a trace. I wondered at the time whether a Stam, with a simple explanation forgetting all complications, could have sold the proposal if he had conceived it. The Treasury certainly did not sell it. This debut of a spendings tax, now the favorite of many an economist, was a miserable failure of exposition.[101]

At this time, I had delivered a long speech before the National Retail Dry Goods Association on both the sales tax and the Ruml plan.[102]

Incidentally, in ____ [check] I chose a clerk of the Ways and Means Committee (now called the Chief Counsel) for Chairman Doughton. One morning, in my office early at 8 a.m., I received a call from the Chairman saying the present Clerk was leaving and could I suggest a replacement. Our Office had recently hired a young lawyer, Charles Davis, in part to handle correspondence. He was performing quite well and, in addition, I thought it would be nice to have a friendly voice on the Committee staff. I suggested Davis and started to discuss his abilities. Doughton interrupted to say he wanted to know two things: "Can he type and will he come in at 8 a.m.?" I checked and fortunately Davis met these rigid "qualifications" and so he obtained the position. He also had the brains and negotiating skills to accompany the attributes Doughton emphasized. Because of the former—and not those attributes—he per-

---

100. For more on the Ruml Plan in Ruml's own words, *see generally*, Beardsley Ruml, *The Pay-As-You-Go Income Tax Plan*, 28 THE BULLETIN OF THE NATIONAL TAX ASSOCIATION 166 (1943). *See* also, W. ELLIOT BROWNLEE, FEDERAL TAXATION IN AMERICA: A SHORT HISTORY (1996), 95–7 [hereinafter W. ELLIOT BROWNLEE].

101. For a fuller account of the fiasco that was Treasury's 1942 spendings tax proposal, *see* JOSEPH THORNDIKE, THEIR FAIR SHARE: TAXING THE RICH IN THE AGE OF FDR 240–244 (2013); Lawrence A. Zelenak, *The Federal Retail Sales Tax That Wasn't: An Actual History and an Alternate History*, 73(1) LAW & CONTEMP. PROBS. 149, 149–205 (2010).

102. *Victory Tax Held Just a Beginning: Treasury Aide Calls It Basis for Big Increase Facing Citizens in Future*, NEW YORK TIMES, Jan. 14, 1943, at 11. The story quotes extensively from Surrey's speech to the National Retail Dry Goods Association. Among many other things, Surrey referred to a federal retail sales tax as "Miss Spending Tax," and described it (or her) as "out of the question." Throughout his career, Surrey was a staunch opponent of a national consumption tax. As for the Ruml plan and withholding, Surrey observed that "[m]ost everyone favors placing the income tax on a current basis," and that in Treasury's view "the best method of placing the income tax on a current basis is through collection at the source."

formed extremely well, and he became a force in the Committee work. Later he went on to be a leading tax lawyer in Chicago.[103]

Tarleau left the Treasury after the 1942 Act was concluded to return to tax practice in New York. Paul appointed me in his place as Legislative Counsel. Since Blough stayed on, he and I were the top "technical-policy" persons in the Treasury, reporting primarily to Paul as General Counsel but also working with Assistant Secretary Sullivan from time to time. The year 1943 continued the steady pace of tax legislation. The work in the first part of the year was concentrated on the development and enactment of the Current Tax Payment Act of 1943. Everyone—the President, Treasury, Congress, and the prime private proponent, Ruml, now favored current payment. It was also recognized that current payment for salary and wage earners required withholding by employers. For non-withheld income, and salaries above the tax liability level satisfied by withholding, the Treasury devised a system of declarations of estimated current tax, filed four times a year. Then for everyone there was a final reconciliation on the March 15 return with the actual tax liability. The only real debate was over transition—was the 1942 tax liability to be completely forgiven as Ruml advocated, collected in full over a period of years as the Treasury proposed, or a compromise adopted. The legislative debate and maneuvering are described by Paul [here quote my talk].[104] In the end, as to be expected, a compromise prevailed, with 75% of the 1942 tax forgiven. But the important aspect of that Act was the start of our present collection system for the income tax.

The second legislation in 1943 was the Revenue Act of 1943.[105] It started with a call for more revenue by the President. But the measure as it went through Congress produced little in the way of increased revenues. Instead it accumulated a large number of relief provisions, hardly any of which had substantive merit. Examples were capital gain treatment on the cutting of timber; exemption of "Western Hemisphere corporations" from wartime tax increase [check and add Mitchell Carroll & "regime"];[106] additions to the minerals granted percentage depletion; certain exemptions from the excess profit tax, e.g., natural gas pipelines; and an additional personal exemption for the blind. (The additional exemption had suddenly been proposed by Congressman Reed of New York in an Executive Session of the House Committee

103. Charles W. Davis was appointed chief counsel to the Ways and Means Committee in 1949, and chief counsel of the Bureau of Internal Revenue in 1952. He spent most of his career practicing tax law as a partner in the Chicago firm of Hopkins & Sutter. Kenan Heise, *Charles W. Davis, 69, Prominent Tax Lawyer*, CHICAGO TRIBUNE, Feb. 19, 1987, at 10.

104. TAXATION IN THE UNITED STATES, *supra* note 95, at 326–49. For a more recent account of the Ruml plan and the Current Tax Payment Act, *see* FIGURING OUT THE TAX, *supra* note 76, at 54–60. It is not clear what talk of his Surrey planned to quote here.

105. Revenue Act of 1943, Pub. L. No. 78-235, 58 Stat. 21. Congress passed the legislation over President Roosevelt's veto.

106. For the favorable tax rules for Western Hemisphere Trade Corporations (WHTCs), *see* Revenue Act of 1943, § 108, 58 Stat. at 32 (codified at former IRC § 108(c)). Surrey has more to say about both WHTCs and international tax lawyer Mitchell B. Carroll in chapter 5.

on the ground of the handicaps presented by blindness.[107] Representing the Treasury, I had no warning of the proposal.[108] I started to argue against it, along the line that Reed's proposal would really require an additional exemption for all handicapped persons and then started to explain the problems with such a measure. Reed interrupted me with the cold statement: "The trouble with you Surrey is that you have no sympathy for the blind!" That statement ended discussion and Reed's amendment was adopted unanimously. When the meeting was over I spoke to Reed, saying I thought his statement was uncalled for. He readily agreed, saying he knew it was wrong but then added: "You were making a good strong argument and I had to say something to stop you." The provision remains in the law today—limited to only those handicapped by blindness.)[109]

Another provision was the result of a comedy of errors on the Senate floor. Republican Senator Danaher[110] asked us to draft an amendment that would hit Marshall Field, a wealthy Chicago publisher whose newspaper, which was losing a large amount of money, was outspokenly liberal.[111] Danaher said that, since Field deducted the newspaper losses from his other income, here was the tax law subsidizing this outrageous liberal paper. We did draft a provision, which would have prevented continued losses in a trade or business over a period of years from being deductible. The amendment was dubbed the "hobby loss" provision. After considerable debate—would it affect cattle breeders, oil operators and other losing ventures or hobbies?—the amendment survived in rather moderate form, being triggered only by losses of an individual of $50,000 a year for five years.[112] The farce in this legislative venture against hobbies was that it did not affect Marshall Field, who it turned out operated his newspaper through a corporation which had sufficient income to absorb the losses. But the provision survived in the tax law until 1969, when it was revised as section 183.[113]

One provision of this 1943 Act was an operation I had carefully planned. It had come to my attention, partly through advertisements in the Wall Street Journal and

107. Daniel A. Reed (R., N.Y.) was a member of the House of Representatives from 1919 until his death in 1959, and chairman of Ways and Means from 1953 to 1955. *Rep. Daniel Reed, 83, Dies in Capital,* New York Times, Feb. 20, 1959, at 25.

108. For the proposal as enacted, *see* Revenue Act of 1943, § 115, 58 Stat. at 36 (codified at former IRC § 23(y)).

109. Current IRC § 63(f)(2) provides a larger standard deduction amount for blind taxpayers. There is no comparable tax relief for taxpayers with other disabilities.

110. John A. Danaher (R., Conn.) was a member of the Senate for a single term, from 1939 to 1945. He later served as a judge of the United States Court of Appeals for the District of Columbia Circuit. *John A. Danaher; Ex-U.S. Senator,* Los Angeles Times, Sep. 27, 1990, at A26.

111. Marshall Field III founded the *Chicago Sun* (later the *Sun-Times*) in 1941. *Chicago Publisher Marshall Field Dies,* Los Angeles Times, Sep. 19, 1964, at D1.

112. Revenue Act of 1943, § 129, 58 Stat. at 48 (codified at former IRC § 130). Under the provision, if an individual's losses from a particular business exceeded $50,000 per year for five consecutive years, annual losses in excess of $50,000 were disallowed. The provision was the predecessor of current IRC § 183, although the current provision takes a quite different approach to the hobby loss problem.

113. Congress enacted current IRC § 183 in 1969.

other papers, that corporations no longer operating because their activities had failed were being purchased by corporations possessing large profits and desiring to use these defunct corporations in various ways to reduce the taxes on those profits. One way was, since the excess profits tax allowed a credit for invested capital, to take over as a part of the acquiring corporation's capital the original but later lost capital of the defunct corporation. Another method was to utilize the operating losses incurred by the loss corporation. These ads—"Corporation for Sale"—or "Corporation Wanted"—meant that these defunct corporations—now but corporate shells—were being pulled off the shelves of law firms and investment houses as safe refuges for corporations with profits. Obviously, these practices could not be tolerated. I turned the problem over to the veteran in our office, Fred Lusk, with instructions to write the toughest and most comprehensive provision he could, together with a proposed Committee Report that would explain, and with examples amplify, the technical language. With this work in hand, I then in Executive Session read some of the ads to the Committee, said this blatant tax avoidance had to be ended, and offered our suggestion. The ads easily convinced the Committee and with a few changes the provision became law.[114] It still survives, as section 269, which prevents a corporation from acquiring another corporation for tax avoidance purposes. But it is the inevitable fate of tax technicians that they cannot think of everything. In that same 1943 Act [check] Congress granted tax reductions to U.S. corporations whose income came almost exclusively from operations in the Western Hemisphere but outside the United States.[115] The provision—intended to cover three corporations—was through error poorly drafted by the House draftsmen. While intended to cover these three companies all of whose operations were in Latin America, its wording raised the question whether major U.S. manufacturers exporting world-wide could form—"acquire"—a separate subsidiary to handle exports to Latin America and thus reduce taxes on these exports. Was this "acquisition" a tax avoidance operation barred by section 269? Neither Lusk nor I nor anyone else had thought of the connection, though the two provisions entered the law in the same bill.[116] Reluctantly I concluded that section 269 could not be extended to these Western Hemisphere subsidiaries. The provision covering those subsidiaries, because of the poor drafting, nevertheless could be read as so favoring that activity as to permit corporate structures to be rearranged in order to qualify. With that ruling, the clearly erroneous tax policy embodied by the Western Hemi-

---

114. Revenue Act of 1943, § 128, 58 Stat. at 47 (codified at former IRC § 129). Under the provision, if a profitable corporation acquired a loss corporation for the principal purpose of "evasion or avoidance of a Federal income or excess profits tax" through the use of deductions of the loss corporation, the deductions were disallowed. As Surrey states, the provision was the predecessor of current IRC § 269.

115. Surrey's recollection is inaccurate. In fact, Congress created the special tax treatment for Western Hemisphere Trade Corporations (WHTCs) the previous year. Revenue Act of 1942, Pub. L. No. 77-753, § 141, 56 Stat. 798, 838 (codified at former IRC § 109). Surrey has additional comments on WHTCs in chapter 5.

116. Actually, as described in the preceding note, the two provisions were enacted in consecutive years, rather than as part of the same bill.

sphere provision took off, with perhaps thousands of such subsidiaries being formed. It was not until 1976 that this provision was eliminated.[117]

The 1943 Act was vetoed by President Roosevelt in a stinging message calling it "not a tax bill but a tax relief bill providing relief not for the needy but for the greedy."[118] As described by Paul, apparently this action was the President's own judgment. Congress resented both the veto — the first tax measure ever to be vetoed — and the message, and the veto was easily overridden.

During this period I worked closely and on friendly terms with the Bureau officials, who brought their important policy rulings — such as the Western Hemisphere ruling — to me for discussion. Another troublesome problem involved the pension plans of motion picture companies. Though these plans complied with the non-discrimination rules of the 1942 Act, their generosity combined with the high salaries of executives meant over $50,000 a year pensions for some executives on retirement — a figure unheard of under any other pension plans and very large in those times. Should the Bureau approve these plans? I could see no way not to approve, the plans being non-discriminatory, and took the responsibility for their approval.

That particular pension situation was being handled for the industry by Ellsworth Alvord, of Alvord and Alvord, then the leading tax firm in Washington. The lawyers in the firm — my friends Arthur Kent, Hy Biegel and Rudolph Peterson among them — were highly competent persons.[119] But the power in the firm was Alvord, a driving buccaneer lobbyist with excellent Hill contacts. He had worked briefly before my time in the Treasury and in Beaman's Office. He was personable and could turn on his charm — and also his largesse, such as the present of a fur coat to an important woman Senate committee staff member. Alvord and I liked each other, and I believe his regard for me went beyond the needs of a Washington lobbyist to be on good terms with Treasury officials. I admired his skill and shrewdness, which often defeated the Treasury in a tussle over one of his lobbying proposals. They usually involved a provision designed to give a tax reduction to only one, or a few beneficiaries. Sometimes he was even on the right track. I recall a 1938 special provision which allowed

---

117. Congress repealed the WHTC provision in 1976. Tax Reform Act of 1976, Pub. L. No. 94-455, § 1052(b), 90 Stat. 1520, 1648.

118. Franklin D. Roosevelt, *Tax Bill Veto Message*, NEW YORK TIMES, Feb. 23, 1944, at 14 (full text of veto message). Roosevelt's defeat at the hands of Congress with the Revenue Act of 1943 signaled the end of a conflict between progressives and big business that had begun in World War I over attempts to adopt a highly progressive, "soak the rich" tax system. W. ELLIOT BROWNLEE, *supra* note 100.

119. Prior to cofounding the Alvord & Alvord law firm in 1932, Ellsworth C. Alvord had served as a special assistant to Treasury Secretary Andrew W. Mellon. *Ellsworth C. Alvord, 68; Tax and Fiscal Expert*, THE WASHINGTON POST, Jan. 18, 1964, at B2. Arthur Kent was likely a law partner with Hy Biegel when they founded the law firm of Lee, Toomey & Kent in 1946. Rudolph Peterson was also a partner in that law firm. He was a year ahead of Surrey at Columbia Law School, and was a tax lawyer for 60 years, including as IRS Chief Counsel and as a member of the American Law Institute. *Carl Rudolf Peterson, '28* Princeton Alumni Weekly, October 25, 1995.

three industries he represented to use an inventory method common in those industries called "last-in first-out," under which the latest products were considered by a manufacturer as the first to be sold.[120] The Bureau had followed a "first-in, first-out" practice under which the earliest products were deemed to be those first sold. In these three industries with fluctuating or rising prices Alvord had claimed, and Congress agreed, that the last-in, first-out method made more sense. Once this method was approved for only the three named industries, I suggested the Treasury consider whether it really was a sensible inventory approach. I formed a three-man advisory committee of accountants—one of the group being Carman Blough, Roy's brother, to advise us.[121] Though the Bureau technicians frowned on the method, this advisory group said "last-in first out" was a respectable inventory method for a company in any industry, provided—and this was the key—the company considered the method appropriate for its business and thus used the method in its financial statements. I followed the advice of this group and the Treasury suggested the extension of the method to all industries, on the condition it be used consistently for tax and financial purposes.[122] Later I had the Bureau work out a mechanism by which retailers, who faced certain problems in using this inventory method, could apply it. The basic provision, and its retail use, remain in the law today. It has a special significance in an inflationary period, since it has the effect of reducing profits, as price levels rise, compared to the profits that would exist under first-in-first-out. But—as long as the original condition of consistency remains—a firm seeking to use last-in, first-out to lower its taxable profits in an inflationary period must also show lower financial profits to its shareholders and bankers.

My relationship with the Alvord firm had an odd result during the 1943 Act. [check Act] A highly technical amendment in the depletion section had been adopted as a Senate floor amendment. It seemed to me to be far too generous, to the extent we understood it in the time available, and I objected to it at the Conference Committee. But the House conferees quickly accepted it. Obviously, its proponents had lobbied quietly and successfully. I checked around that same day and found that Alvord's firm had proposed the amendment. The next day, before the Conference Committee met, I called Alvord's firm and reached Arthur Kent. In strong terms I said I thought their procedure in lobbying through that amendment without talking with the Treasury was outrageous. We had always dealt fairly with the situations they

---

120. Revenue Act of 1938, Pub. L. No. 75-554, § 22(d), 52 Stat. 447, 459. The provision permitted LIFO inventory accounting for smelters and refiners of non-ferrous metals, producers of certain brass and copper products, and tanners.

121. Carman George Blough was the first chief accountant of the Securities and Exchange Commission. Later in his career he was a partner with the accounting firm of Arthur Andersen & Co., and still later the research director of the American Institute of Certified Public Accountants. *Memorial: Carman George Blough*, 57 THE ACCOUNTING REV. 147 (1982).

122. Congress made LIFO accounting available to all industries in 1939. Revenue Act of 1939, Pub. L. No. 76-155, § 219, 53 Stat. 862, 877 (codified at former IRC § 22(d)). The provision was the predecessor of current IRC § 472.

had frequently brought to us, either agreeing or fully stating our objections. This particular operation was, I said, directly contrary to what I considered the "rules of the lobbying game." Kent, somewhat taken aback, asked me what I wanted done. I said he should talk at once to the Senators, tell them to reverse the position of the Conference, and withdraw the amendment — which was, I had to admit, a rather unusual procedure. Kent agreed, and at the Conference that day the Senate conferees solemnly said that on second thought they believed the provision required more study and would the House Conferees therefore please change their acceptance to permit the Senators to withdraw the provision. A bit puzzled at this unprecedented action of the Senate conferees, the House conferees agreed.[123] Later, as I had promised Kent, we had full discussions with him on the problem which had troubled his client, Alvord and Kent agreed his legislative solution was far too broad, and worked out an appropriate administrative solution. The situation proved to me two things — first, a Treasury official must get to know Washington lobbyists and then be fair and tough with them as the situation really demanded that attitude, and second, a decent lobbyist, like Alvord and Kent, will understand this approach and reciprocate in turn. It simply happened here that Alvord's firm had made a mistake and, when called, had the decency — and good sense — to correct the mistake.

One episode in particular in this period influenced my view of how *not* to deal with Congress. After the pension plan legislation of 1942, which required pension plans to be non-discriminatory, we faced the issue in preparing regulations of how to handle plans, rather widely used, that covered only that portion of an employee's wage or salary that was above the level subject to the Social Security tax. Was it sufficient to meet the non-discriminatory test by just covering the wages above the social security level or did the plans have to be "integrated" with the amounts being contributed under Social Security? The first view would permit a sharp jump in the level of employer contributions, considering the Social Security tax as a contribution, when the Social Security ceiling was reached, a jump favorable to higher paid employees. The second view required a relatively smooth schedule of contributions, with the employer either continuing to contribute for the salaries above the Social Security level on a formula amount determined by the Social Security tax and benefit figures, or, if a higher contribution was desired, making additional contributions for the wages below the Social Security level so as to keep the combination of contributions on a smooth scale. I decided the latter approach was correct and should be adopted in Treasury Regulations. But Paul was uncertain and suggested that because the question involved statutory interpretation and the "intent of Congress," why not ascertain that intent. He therefore decided to present the problem to an Executive Session of the Senate Finance Committee, since the legislation on pension plans had been more fully developed in the Senate. At this Committee session, I explained the problem

---

123. For the resolutions of several depletion-related House-Senate disagreements in the 1943 legislation, *see* H.R. Rep. No. 1079, at 20–21 (1944) (Conf. Rep.). It is not readily apparent which of the several disagreements is the one Surrey describes.

and then the position contemplated for the regulations. After a while, Republican Senator Robert Taft,[124] a proponent of the contrary "non-integration" view being urged by some companies, stated with full Senatorial assuredness and asperity that my argument and position were about the most foolish he had ever heard. At that point as silence prevailed our solution and proposed Regulation were clearly dead. Finally, Senator Arthur Vandenberg,[125] the ranking Republican minority member of the Committee, quietly said he thought I had persuasively stated what seemed to him a reasonable position on the issue. We were alive once more. No other Senator spoke and the session ended. We issued the Regulation adopting the integration solution.[126] This was the origin of the important rule that pension plans could not exclude persons receiving Social Security benefits but instead to avoid discrimination in favor of upper bracket employees would have to integrate the two forms of benefits if Social Security benefits were an offset to the plan benefits. The rule still prevails. But I had learned never to seek a declaratory judgment from a Committee where the answer can turn on the attitude of a powerful Senator and there is no responsibility for a vote on actual legislation. Far better to take the step administratively and force objecting legislators to have to use the regular processes to overturn the action.

Senator Vandenberg was similarly helpful on another occasion in the Finance Committee. The "reorganization" provisions of the Code for many years had permitted tax-free mergers or other stock acquisitions if the acquiring company ended with 80% control. One company, after going through an acquisition, found that its control fell just short of 80%. Stam, pushed by a lobbyist and perhaps a Senator, brought the problem up in an Executive Session of the Finance Committee and suggested an amendment to change "80%" to "more than 79%." Opposing the change I merely said 80% had always been 80%. Senator Vandenberg, and also Chairman George, turned Stam down in short order, saying the change would make the Committee look silly, and, as Surrey had said, if the company's lawyers couldn't count that was their problem. Stam sheepishly withdrew the proposal. I was never clear how strongly Stam felt about presenting such silly proposals. But I am sure if the Committee had accepted the proposal, Stam would not in the least have been troubled by such a ridiculous change in the Code's technical provisions, for the performance was a typical Stam suggestion. Only once—and I forget the occasion—did I hear him seriously say a lobbyist's proposal just wasn't "right".

Other unrelated episodes come to mind. For several years I checked Mrs. Roosevelt's income tax returns. The White House had requested that the returns be ex-

124. Robert A. Taft (R., Ohio), son of President William Howard Taft, and commonly known as "Mr. Republican," was a member of the Senate from 1939 to 1953. Russell Porter, *Sen. Taft is Dead at 63; Eisenhower Leads Tributes; Republicans' Unity Shaken*, New York Times, Aug. 1, 1953.

125. Arthur H. Vandenberg (R., Mich.) was a member of the Senate from 1928 to 1951. *Arthur H. Vandenberg*, New York Times, Apr. 19, 1951, at 30.

126. Treas. Dec. 5278 (1943), amending Treas. Reg. § 19.165(a)(3)-1, 1943 C.B. 478. For the legal analysis in support of the regulatory amendment, *see* Mimeo. 5539, 1943 C.B. 500 (1943).

amined carefully before being filed, especially the deductions for charitable contributions, and Paul asked me to do the job. A Bureau ruling—later a Regulation—in 1934 by Chief Counsel Robert Jackson, later a Supreme Court Justice, had held that services performed directly for a charity which resulted in funds received by the charity—for example, an evening's entertainment where admission was charged and star performers appeared voluntarily—did not result in income constructively received by the performers and then contributed to charity.[127] This approach kept the performers from running up against the barrier that their total yearly charitable deductions could not exceed 15% of income, the limit at that time. Mrs. Roosevelt's assistance to charity covered both arrangements, those that fell within the Ruling and direct contributions. I had to be sure all activities were properly reported on her returns. The other aspects of the return did not involve any problems.

In a different task, we were faced in the excess profits tax of providing a constructive credit under the average earnings method for a growing firm, generally a relatively new firm, whose growth was not due to war profits but whose base period average would not, because of the inherent growth, represent a fair picture of what its earnings would have been absent the war. I recognized this was not a job for a lawyer. So I asked one of Blough's economists, Carl Shoup, to develop a formula for the situation. Carl did so, and it was incorporated in the law. The incident in a sense is trivial but it had two interesting facets. It demonstrated the close day-to-day working relationship I encouraged between my lawyers and Blough's economists. Also, working jointly with Shoup on an interesting and important technical problem allowed us to become acquainted, and this Treasury acquaintance later resulted in many joint projects with Shoup throughout the years.[128]

President Roosevelt, whose earlier legislative recommendation that in wartime no individual should have more than $25,000 in net income after taxes did not receive Congressional approval, in October of 1942 decided to issue an executive order applying that principle to salary income.[129] I developed the mechanics and an Executive

127. In 1934, the legal office of the Bureau of Internal Revenue, then headed by future Nuremberg prosecutor and future Supreme Court Justice Robert H. Jackson, advised Mrs. Roosevelt as described by Surrey. In 1937, when questioned about that advice by Congress, Jackson (by that time Assistant Attorney General Jackson) responded that Mrs. Roosevelt "was in the position of an artist or actor who aids a charity by a benefit performance," and that "[t]here is no tax on such a kindness and whatever spiritual enrichment comes of good works is not estimated as taxable income." *Hearings Before the Joint Comm. on Tax Evasion and Avoidance*, 75th Cong., 1st Sess., 418 (1937). The later regulation Surrey mentions is Treas. Reg. § 1.61-2(c), added by Treas. Dec. 6272, 1957-2 C.B. 18, 21 (1957), and still on the books today ("The value of services is not includible in gross income when such services are rendered directly and gratuitously to an organization described in § 170(c)").

128. In the post-WWII years, Surrey would take part in several of Carl Shoup's tax missions to other countries to help them "reform" their fiscal systems, as Surrey relates in chapter 5. *See, also*, The Political Economy of Transnational Tax Reform: The Shoup Mission to Japan in Historical Context, (W. Elliot Brownlee, Eisaku Ide and Yasumori Fukagai eds., 2013).

129. *President's Order Limits His Own Pay: But Experts Explain $25,000 Limit as Net After Taxes, Insurances, Fixed Charges,* New York Times, Oct. 4, 1942, at 44.

Order embodying my draft was issued. Secretary Morgenthau had me explain the mechanics in a press conference in his office.[130] The Order did not meet with public approval and after a short life was retroactively rescinded.

These years when I was carrying a heavy load in 1942 as Tarleau's almost alter ego and then as Legislative Counsel required day and night work. Vacations were non-existent, for the legislative pace was steady. Along with the legislation came administrative activity. Treasury Regulations were being issued in increasing numbers to buttress the legislation by providing the Treasury's descriptive and interpretative analyses of the legislation. These regulations were initially prepared in the Bureau by the "Legislation and Regulations" lawyers who had sat in on the drafting sessions. But since, besides being signed by the Commissioner, they also had to be signed by a Treasury official who was a presidential appointee, my Office had to carefully check the regulations sent over by the Bureau. Formerly the Treasury signature was rather a pro forma action. But I insisted on a careful examination, and this greatly increased the work of my office.

The legislative work continued in 1944. The principal measure was the Individual Income Tax Act of 1944, whose purpose was to simplify the application of that tax.[131] The great expansion of the coverage of the income tax, its increased rates, the initial shift to current payment somewhat hastily designed under the political warfare surrounding the Ruml plan, the mixture of a regular tax and a victory tax in the return due March 15, 1944, all added to a confused system. This confusion was intolerable given the wide coverage of the tax. Hence early in 1944 the Treasury, with the Bureau, worked on methods of simplifying the procedure. This work culminated in a plan which quickly was enacted by the Congress. The simplification involved a number of elements: (1) the application of a graduated withholding through the second surtax bracket with the withholding tables having narrower brackets and thus greater accuracy; (2) the introduction of tables to which taxpayers could go directly from their gross income to determine their final tax liability, thereby dispensing with the need to make actual tax computations; (3) the introduction of the "standard deduction," an allowance (10%) equal to the average of the personal deductions then being taken by individuals — for property tax and mortgage interest on residences, medical expenses, charitable contribution, casualty losses — so that these deductions no longer had to be itemized if the standard deduction was used.[132] The elimination of this itemization for nearly 90% of individuals made the widespread use of the tables feasible; (4) elimination of the appendage of the victory tax and the adoption of a single, graduated rate schedule; (5) a change in the filing of the December 15 declaration of estimated tax to January 15, permitting it to be combined with the final return if the taxpayer desired. This structure which our Offices developed in 1944 — graduated

130. For news coverage of Surrey's performance at Morgenthau's press conference, *see* John H. Crider, *Supertax Request is Shunted Aside*, New York Times, Feb. 19, 1943, at 26.

131. Individual Income Tax Act of 1944, Pub. L. No. 78-315, 58 Stat. 231.

132. The standard deduction amount was the lesser of $500 or 10 percent of a taxpayer's adjusted gross income. Individual Income Tax Act of 1944, § 9, 58 Stat. at 236 (codified at former IRC § 23(aa)).

withholding on wages and salaries, with the graduation later increased; declarations of estimated tax; the standard deduction which evolved through a minimum standard deduction and allowance into the zero tax bracket; and tax tables — survives today as the basic techniques determining taxpayers' payment of the annual tax.

With the signing of this Act, my participation in principal Treasury legislative activity temporarily ended, for reasons I will shortly relate. I might therefore here summarize some overall aspects of my experiences during this period, as I then saw them.

(1) I had the combination of a front row center seat and important member of the cast for all of the tax drama from 1939 through 1944. As a member of the cast I saw how a major Department — the Treasury — operated, and moreover perceived this on a level at which I worked with the top Treasury officials. I also observed the whole legislative process — from Treasury presentation and public hearings to committee executive sessions, in which I participated and at times was the Treasury spokesman, to drafting the legislation and then floor debate, a process that occurred in both House and Senate and then culminated in the Conference Committee. Thus I had the opportunity to watch at close hand legislators at work, and obtain some understanding of the legislative process and the legislative mind. I used the word "some" because I became convinced that only a member of Congress could really understand the process and the reasons for the decisions, and perhaps here also I should qualify this conclusion by saying that only "some" members reached this level of understanding.

During these years, it was customary for a Treasury tax technician to be on the Senate floor to provide information to Senators on tax legislation under debate, and for a period, I performed this role. There was one uncomfortable occasion when the Senate solemnly debated whether it was proper for me to remain, while I sat at the rear of the Chamber awaiting the outcome. The debate ended favorable to my staying. On other occasions I would sit alongside a senator, say Tom Connally, and provide him with arguments during the debate, often whispering words of advice which he smoothly worked into his flow of words without a pause. I just had to remember to duck my head to avoid the oratorical gestures.

In this period I came to a basic conclusion: "Never underestimate a Member of Congress." The Member to be sure may not know any tax law. This was true for even those on the Tax Committees. They were generally on the Committee because they considered the ability to influence tax legislation an important part of their career and not because they understood, or desired carefully to learn, the intricacies of the tax system. Also the Ways and Means Committee was the House Committee on Committees and thus chose the members of all the other House Committees, so that positions on the Ways and Means Committee were based by the House leadership on geographical areas and the political power of a representative in his area. Many Members of the Tax Committee, moreover, may not have been bright or quick to see an issue. But — and this was crucial — they each possessed a quality that enabled them to be elected to Congress. Good judgment, common sense, a command of language, an ideology, experience in state or local government, whatever the quality was it had meant success in the electoral process. Also they came from varied backgrounds and there was always the chance when a particular issue was presented that some Member had worked in the industrial, commercial, agricultural or business area involved. Naturally his judgment, and not that of a Treasury official, would be persuasive to the other Committee Members. It also never paid to try to upstage a Member, to meet his asperity or even rudeness with a reply in kind, to dismiss a question as irrelevant or silly. They had the votes and the Treasury did not. Also, they did on the whole understand and appreciate helpful, informative, objective and uncomplicated answers. Their votes may not be based on the answers, for their ideology, predilections, a view expressed by a friendly constituent whom they trusted, or a lobbyist's request could be the controlling factor. But they did not want a government official to play games with them and they readily knew when and when not this was being tried by an official.

A Treasury official appearing before a committee had to watch every word he spoke carefully, so as not to rub the sensibilities of a member the wrong way. This self-censorship was not always easy to achieve, given the range of backgrounds and views of the members, and also the desire of the official to get a point across. One time Roy Blough was urging a proposal relating to automobiles. He said that a problem faced by the Treasury was the sale of used cars and in describing the issue used as an example cars from New York that were sold second hand in North Carolina. Roy had used North Carolina offhand just as an example but what he momentarily forgot was that Chairman Doughton came from that State. The Chairman was outraged at the implication that every North Carolinian was driving a second hand car. As a result Roy lost the issue.

The Tax Committees were quite capable of quickly sizing up the Treasury officials who appeared before them. The Treasury technical staff — Office of the Tax Legislative Counsel (as its new name) and the Office of Tax Analysis — were accepted for what they largely were, technicians to give reasonably objective presentations to the Committee and answers to its questions. But the top policy officials in the Treasury were viewed quite differently, for they were there to present the administration's major tax policy recommendations and to defend them in partisan fashion. They were advocates whose views were either to be accepted by members supporting the Administration or rejected by those opposed to it. Even here however the members perceived differences and acted upon the perceptions. Thus a Randolph Paul, a non-political appointment with a professional tax background, was listened to more carefully and sympathetically by the committees than was a John Sullivan, a political appointment without a tax background and therefore viewed as only a politician, just as the members were.

(2) I learned to work with a large bureaucracy — the Bureau of Internal Revenue — and to appreciate its strong side and its weak sides. Its strength lay in those hard working and experienced officials and employees who earnestly attempted to do a good job and to cooperate with the Treasury. Its weakness lay in the lethargy and conservativism of thought and operation, and both an unwillingness to change and a difficulty in achieving change itself.

(3) I also learned to work with and respect a breed of professionals largely new to me—the economists. Fortunately, as I have described, the Treasury economists were an extremely able group, and I saw how much they could contribute. I also saw the limits of their contributions, just as they saw the limits of a legal background. But by pushing hard for real cooperation between our two offices and professions I discovered how well lawyers and economists can work together.

(4) Another part of my tax education was the opportunity to meet with a wide range of non-Government people working in the tax field—lawyers, accountants, businessmen, labor officials, lobbyists, and so on. They came to the Treasury to present their views, to urge adoption or defeat of tax proposals, whether broad policy measures or narrow technical issues, whether involving tax benefits in general or special client-oriented legislation. One learned to sort them out—who was really knowledgeable; who could be trusted to be both objective in a presentation of the facts and discussion and yet be candid about pushing for a conclusion helpful to the interests being represented; who could perceive the Government's doubts and problems and, respecting them, seek to resolve them; and who were of the opposite type and relied instead on wielding levers of power and influence.

(5) The Treasury position naturally resulted in many opportunities to speak before professional and business groups on current tax issues and I took liberal advantage of invitations. My purposes were to explain and advocate the Treasury's views and to get feedback on those views and hence of the difficulties and problems for the Treasury. I also hoped to gain in experience as a speaker under circumstances where I had some advantages, in that because of where I sat I possessed information the audience wanted—what was current Treasury thinking on this or that subject—but where also I had to be careful not to arouse opposition or to say anything that produced media consequences my superiors or the Administration would not appreciate.

The Treasury Secretary throughout this period was Henry Morgenthau, Jr., a friend of the President. The Secretary, neither financial expert, lawyer nor economist, was not familiar with the tax field. He was often regarded in the press and in Congress as not very competent but just a misguided liberal protege of Roosevelt. I did not meet with him often, since I reported directly to the layer of officials just below him. But whenever I saw him perform at first hand in his office at a staff conference on a tax matter, I found him very sensitive to issues and their nuances, and often to show a sharper perception and better overall judgment than his advisors. The persons in direct charge of the two technical tax offices changed from time to time. Assistant Secretary Sullivan had oversight of the offices commencing in 1940. He was succeeded in 1942 by Randolph Paul, the General Counsel.[133] Paul resigned in 1944 to enter private practice, with the firm of Paul, Weiss, Wharton and Garrison. His reputation in the tax field was considerably enhanced by his work in Washington, and he became known as the outstanding advocate of tax reform. He testified frequently on major

133. Although Paul succeeded Sullivan in 1942, Sullivan remained at Treasury until 1944.

tax policy issues, and was stricken with a heart attack in 1956 while appearing before the Joint Committee on the Economic Report.[134] Paul was followed by Joseph O'Connell, a pleasant, capable lawyer but with no background in taxation.[135] The supervision of the tax offices was largely assigned to O'Connell, though from time to time the Under Secretary, Edward Foley, Jr., a genial Democratic politician, shared the task though he also had no tax background.[136]

In late 1943 I had decided temporarily to leave the Treasury and join the military. As an important Treasury official I had a deferment from the draft and military service. But, for reasons I certainly could not clearly articulate, I thought I should give up that deferment. While still holding on to my deferment, I therefore applied for an officer's commission in the Navy, believing that branch would be the most interesting. But here a problem arose. The head of the local Navy recruiting office, a really conservative officer, did not like the appearance in my application of memberships in the National Lawyers Guild or, of all things, the American Civil Liberties Union. These, in his mind, disqualified me for a commission, even though I pointed out that as an important Treasury official I had been entrusted with many a government secret. Obviously not willing to accept this officer's decision, I embarked on a campaign within the Navy to change it. I found that the judgment of a local recruiting officer was not lightly to be overruled. Finally Paul called the matter to the attention of Thomas (Tommy) Corcoran, a friend of Paul.[137] Later, at a luncheon with Navy Secretary Forrestal, Corcoran presented my case to him.[138] Forrestal quickly decided in my favor and I was commissioned a Lieutenant (j.g.) in _____ 1944.[139]

---

134. Not surprisingly, Paul's sudden death while testifying before the Joint Committee on the Economic Report was widely covered by the nation's newspapers. *See, e.g.*, *Randolph E. Paul Dies at Hearing*, NEW YORK TIMES, Feb. 7, 1956, at 19. Paul is frequently remembered today for being one of the New Deal Treasury lawyers who vigorously defended Keynesian ideas of using the tax system to stimulate and manage the national economy. *See* W. ELLIOT BROWNLEE, *supra* note 100.

135. Joseph J. O'Connell, Jr., was Treasury General Counsel from 1944 to 1947. He was later the first chairman of the National Transportation Safety Board. *J. J. O'Connell Dies; Ex-Chief of Safety Board*, THE WASHINGTON POST, Jul. 15, 1983, at B11.

136. Edward H. Foley, Jr., was Assistant Secretary of the Treasury from 1946 to 1948, and Undersecretary from 1948 to 1953. J.Y. Smith, *Edward H. Foley Dies, Lawyer Appointed to Treasury by Truman*, THE WASHINGTON POST, Mar. 19, 1982, at B14.

137. Thomas (Tommy) Gardiner Corcoran was a prominent member of President Roosevelt's "brain trust." He later had a lucrative (and controversial) career as a high-powered lobbyist. *Thomas G. Corcoran, Aide to Roosevelt, Dies*, NEW YORK TIMES, Dec. 7, 1981, at D18. For more on Corcoran's role in shaping New Deal economic policy, *see generally*, THE END OF REFORM, *supra* note 33.

138. James V. Forrestal was Secretary of the Navy (1944–1947), then a cabinet level position, and later the first Secretary of Defense (1947–1949). Shortly after President Truman forced Forrestal's resignation as Secretary of Defense, Forrestal committed suicide (apparently) by jumping from a sixteenth-floor hospital window. *Forrestal's Suicide Leap Brings Inquiry by Navy: Ex-Defense Chief Left Unattended in Hospital*, LOS ANGELES TIMES, May 23, 1949, at 1; Alexander Wooley, *The Fall of James Forrestal*, THE WASHINGTON POST, May 23, 1999, at F01.

139. By the time Surrey entered the Navy, Allied Forces in Europe were turning the tide. In September 1944, Italy had accepted Allied surrender terms, though German troops still occupied key posts in Italy.

Then the humorous side of a change from civilian life to military life developed. Clothed now in a uniform rather than a civilian suit I was assigned by the Navy to legal work — in Washington! I shifted my workplace from the Treasury to the nearby building housing the Bureau of Supplies and Accounts, where I was put in the legal department working on Navy contracts. After an important role in the Treasury, I was a cog in a large legal machine staffed by other reservists. Hy Biegel was one, Martin Norr (later to work for me at Harvard)[140] and Dick Salant (later Richard Salant of CBS)[141] others. Ironically, my first task was to work out an agreement with Bureau of Internal Revenue officials on the tax aspects of certain Navy contracts. I found the work of this office exceedingly dull. So one day I met with the head, a civilian New York lawyer, Struve Hansel, and said I thought my experience was really being wasted and I would be more useful overseas in a military government job.[142] Struve, who had a hard-boiled and blunt approach to matters, at once said "So you don't like it there!" I replied that was obviously not the point, but rather the Navy could better use me elsewhere. The meeting ended with Struve merely saying that he would handle the situation.

He did handle it, but not in the way I had suggested. For the next day I received orders transferring me at once to Small Ships Training School in Miami! This School prepared junior officers for assignments on just what its name indicated — small ships, such as destroyers, destroyer escorts, landing craft, etc. The course was for two months and covered the basic subjects of navigation, maneuvering, signaling, damage control, and so on. All the officers in my class had been to a Navy indoctrination school and many had served on ships. I was completely inexperienced and moreover the oldest in the class. But I found the courses interesting, the instructors able, and the examinations understandable to one who had law school and legal training. I did well — first in the class — and was therefore given my choice of the next assignment. I asked to go to radar school, also in Florida, to be trained as a radar officer. Here also I was the oldest in the class. This was likewise a good school and I did well. After a few weeks as an instructor at the Miami school, I sought as my next assignment a large ship which would make extensive use of radar training. Then I discovered one of the many "catches" the Navy possessed. Since I had first gone to "Small Ships School" I had to be assigned to a "small ship." The extensive radar training did not count.

So in the summer of 1945 I found myself as a deck officer on the Stockdale, Destroyer Escort 399. The ship was steaming out of New York on a calm day headed

140. Martin Norr later became the editor of the World Tax Series of Surrey's international tax program at Harvard Law School. *Martin Norr*, New York Times, Nov. 21, 1972, at 46.

141. Richard S. Salant was president of the CBS News Division for most of the 1960s and 1970s. Bruce Lambert, *Richard Salant, 78, Who Headed CBS News in Expansion, Is Dead*, New York Times, February 17, 1993, at B8.

142. H. Struve Hensel had several high-level positions in the Department of the Navy and the Department of Defense in the 1940s and 1950s. He also practiced law as a partner with Simpson Thacher & Bartlett, and later with Coudert Brothers. In 1954 he was a target of unsubstantiated, but widely publicized, accusations by Senator Joseph McCarthy. Glenn Fowler, *H. Struve Hensel is Dead at 89, Ex-Assistant Secretary of Defense*, New York Times, May 30, 1991, at D20.

for Panama and I was at once thoroughly seasick. This seasickness lasted a week, abruptly ended and never returned. Again I was the oldest but most inexperienced officer on the ship. All the ensigns knew more than I did. But one learns the routines and I stood my regular deck officer watch, handled the simple radar equipment, and also was Assistant Communications Officer. We travelled to Hawaii and there, while I was attending for a few days a LORAN school on this just introduced method of navigation, the war ended.[143] Our orders before this had been to join the fleet off Japan. The orders were changed to escort a medium size carrier to northern Japan where there was a prisoner of war camp. The larger ships in the area gathered these prisoners for return to the States. Later I received a clipping from my local Virginia paper headed "Lt. Surrey's Ship Rescues Neighbor." Indeed, a neighbor was in that camp. Clearly the Navy's Public Relations Office thought "exceeding small," for I had known nothing about this.

Our ship went on through a typhoon and seas still spotted with floating, unexploded mines to Tokyo Bay. There, just after the surrender, I went ashore to see my brother-in-law, an artist-correspondent with a Marine Air Wing, who secured a jeep in which we travelled in the area. With a fellow officer, Lt. Wiley Mayne our Supply Officer and former F.B.I. lawyer, and later a Congressman from Iowa and a leader of the Iowa bar,[144] I also traveled by train from Yokohama to Tokyo. We were the only Americans on the train, which was heavily peopled with Japanese army members. To our consternation the train started to go through one dark tunnel after another and we wondered just when someone was going to hit us on the road. But the Japanese had indeed surrendered and nothing happened. We saw the devastation in Tokyo, and walked to the famous Imperial Hotel which was now an Army housing unit.[145] But it was reserved for higher ranking officers and we were not allowed in the lobby. Four years later, as a civilian with the simulated rank of Brigadier General [check] I had a room in this hotel.[146] Life-and rank-change!

Our ship then travelled around the Pacific Islands, carrying Australian government officials to reclaim jurisdiction over the small islands that had been occupied by the Japanese. On a trip to Guam I suddenly received orders requiring my going to San Francisco for assignment to another DE.[147] So I travelled by army transport to San Francisco and lined up for the new orders. To my astonishment the orders were now to go to Washington and report to the Treasury Department. That same night, seated

143. LORAN (short for long-range navigation) was a hyperbolic radio navigation system used by the Navy during World War II.

144. Wiley Mayne (R., Iowa) was a member of the House of Representatives from 1967 to 1975. *Wiley Mayne, 90; House GOP Member Who Voted not to Impeach Nixon*, Los Angeles Times, Jun. 6, 2007, at B9.

145. The Imperial Hotel, Tokyo, designed by Frank Lloyd Wright, opened in 1923 and was closed for demolition in 1967.

146. The reference is to Surrey's visit to Japan as a member of the Shoup Tax Mission, described by Surrey in chapter Five. *See also*, The Political Economy of Transnational Tax Reform, *supra* note 128.

147. Destroyer escort.

three to a coach seat, I was on a train for Chicago. When I finally arrived in Washington, I learned that Joseph O'Connell, now the General Counsel, had requested the Navy to assign me to the Treasury. So there I was, still in uniform back in my former job. My assistant previously and successor, Robert Wales,[148] a New York lawyer, had decided to return to practice and O'Connell therefore wanted me back. A few months later I was mustered out of the Navy, still a Lt. (j.g.).

There had been one tax measure enacted in 1945 while I was on leave from the Treasury. This was the Tax Adjustment Act of 1945, providing for a number of corporate "relief" provisions under the excess profits tax.[149] Also in this period Morgenthau had resigned and Fred Vinson, a former Congressman, Court of Appeals Judge and then Director of Economic Stabilization (later a Chief Justice of the Supreme Court) had succeeded him.[150] Vinson did not really have a sharp intellectual mind but was politically astute. He had neither a knowledge of taxation nor any real interest in the subject. The top policy officials were Joseph O'Connell, a genial, able General Counsel with no tax background and Under Secretary Edward Foley, a Democratic, easy going politician also with no tax background. Sullivan had left to be Navy Secretary, leaving O'Connell and Foley in divided command of the tax field. Blough and I were still the two experienced Treasury tax officials. Louis Shere, Blough's assistant, an able economist but with less prestige than Blough, succeeded him as Director of the Office of Tax Research in 1946.[151] My relations with Shere were friendly and the two Offices still worked well together.

On my return I found on my desk three troublesome problems. The first concerned employee stock options. These were options granted to top executives to buy stock in their company at a price equal to, sometimes lower than the then market price. The assumption behind the option grant was that the stock would rise in value so that on exercise of the option the executive would have a large profit. The tax issue was how to treat these options: should there be taxable compensation found at the time of the grant of the option, since presumably the option could be said to have a value. But it was really impossible to measure that value with any reasonable degree of accuracy. Another course was to say that compensation existed at the time of the exercise of the option, in the amount of the spread between the exercise price and the value of the stock. This was the position being taken, somewhat halfheartedly,

---

148. Following World War II Robert W. Wales served at the Treasury Department from 1946 to 1952. Still later he was a partner in the New York law firm of Cleary, Gottlieb, Steen & Hamilton. *Robert W. Wales, 76, Lawyer and Treasury Department Counsel*, NEW YORK TIMES, Apr. 20, 1983, at B5.

149. Tax Adjustment Act of 1945, Pub. L. No. 79-214, 59 Stat. 556.

150. Fred M. Vinson was a member of the House of Representatives (D., Ky.) from 1931 to 1937, a judge of the Court of Appeals for the District of Columbia Circuit from 1937 to 1943, Director of the Office of Economic Stabilization from 1943 to 1945, Secretary of the Treasury from 1945 to 1946, and Chief Justice of the United States from 1946 to 1953. James Reston, *U.S. Mourns Vinson; Delicate Balance of Court at Stake*, NEW YORK TIMES, Sep. 9, 1953, at 1.

151. Louis Shere joined the faculty of Indiana University in 1948 and spent the rest of his career there. *Louis Shere, Tax Researcher*, NEW YORK TIMES, Aug. 26, 1988, at D15.

by the Bureau. Corporate executives disliked this result since it left the spread taxable at the high rates applicable to ordinary income. Instead, they clearly preferred a rule that considered the exercise of the option as a "purchase" of the stock, which could be held for six months and then sold, with the resulting profit treated as a capital gain taxable at a maximum 25% rate. The Board of Tax Appeals (check-when Tax Court and when decision) had ruled in favor of the executives,[152] as had a Court of Appeals in 1944.[153] Indeed, the Bureau was ready to give up and not appeal the Smith case, but I persuaded the Chief Counsel to ask the Justice Department to take the case to the Supreme Court. It did, and the case was won in 1945.[154] However, its facts were so favorable to the Bureau, although Bureau lawyers had never so appreciated the situation, that the decision did not resolve the litigation. In the meantime [check] I considered whether the Treasury should issue a Regulation on this subject. The issue turned on how to regard these stock options. The executives, and some courts, saw them as incentive devices to purchase company stock and induce the executive to work harder, with the incentive closed out and the effort rewarded on the *sale* of the stock. I was of the opinion that there was an incentive present but it consisted of the opportunity to buy the stock at a price lower than market, and that this opportunity given by the company to an executive, was when *exercised* compensation for his efforts. One day, trying to see if there was really any rational argument under the Code against this compensation characterization, I spoke again with my friend Hy Biegel, now in tax practice. He said: "Look, executives are never really happy unless they are always getting something new. First, it's a fine office, a title and so on. But once this becomes accustomed to, something more must be done. A swimming pool installed, a car always at the executives' disposal. This soon pales and another company gesture is needed. Just now the favored gesture is a stock option and it is obviously compensation. But don't tell my clients I said that!" This really settled it, for there was no rational legal argument against the compensation approach. The Treasury issued Regulations in 1946 stating that approach.[155] Later, after I had left the Treasury, these Regulations were overruled by statute in 1950 at the urging of executives encouraged by a rising stock market.[156] After many years of tax reform efforts chipping away at this statutory largesse for executives, the statutory stock option route was ended by Congress in 1976. But then, in the disgraceful surrenders to lobbyists in the 1981 Act, the stock option benefit was restored, up to $100,000 a year of options granted.[157]

---

152. Surrey's recollection is inaccurate; the decision was of the Tax Court (not the Board) and the decision was in favor of the government. John H. Smith v. Commissioner, 1 T.C.M. 672 (1943).

153. The Ninth Circuit, reversing the Tax Court, ruled that the taxpayer did not realize income upon the exercise of the option. Smith v. Commissioner, 142 F.2d 818 (9th Cir., 1944).

154. Commissioner v. Smith, 324 U.S. 177, *op. on reh'g*, 324 U.S. 695 (1945).

155. Treas. Dec. 5507, 1946-1 C.B. 18 (1946).

156. Revenue Act of 1950, Pub. L. No. 82-814, §218, 64 Stat. 906, 942 (codified at former IRC §130A; providing that a taxpayer did not realize gain upon the exercise of a "restricted stock option").

157. Economic Recovery Tax Act of 1981, Pub. L. No. 97-34, §251, 95 Stat. 172, 256 (now codified at IRC §422).

The second problem was harder. In 1940 the Supreme Court had decided *Helvering v. Clifford*, 309 U.S. 331, holding that where a husband created a five-year trust with the income going to his wife during the five-year period, the husband as trustee, and the property to return to him at the end of the five years, the trust income remained taxable to the husband under the general language of the Code defining "income" and did not shift to the wife. Obviously the Court was correct in turning down a scheme the taxpayer's lawyer had regarded as clever in its goal of shifting the income from the husband's higher tax bracket to the wife's lower bracket. The Court in its decision stressed three aspects — the short term of the trust, the husband's control as trustee, and the wife as the beneficiary of the trust income. But lawyers, still seeking to shift the tax, pondered which aspect was really crucial — would ten years suffice, would a bank as trustee suffice, could a child be a beneficiary? Even lawyers in situations far fewer in number where the trust had a non-tax motivation were uncertain on the tax consequences. In the wake of the *Clifford* decision, almost a hundred [check] lower court cases followed, with only a pattern of confusion resulting.[158]

The Supreme Court in *Clifford* had inserted the phrase "In the absence of a Treasury Regulation on the Subject."[159] [check] I therefore wondered whether we should draft a Regulation covering all of the *Clifford* issues and describing with definiteness just which trusts the Treasury would, as in *Clifford*, seek to tax the trust grantor and which it would not tax the grantor but look instead to the beneficiary. This meant drawing many a fine line, arbitrary in that sense, over the entire range of trust attributes. No prior Treasury Regulation had really gone down such a path, which essentially resembled a legislative enactment. But I considered it a Treasury responsibility to set its litigation standards in order and saw no reason why we should not use our regulatory power for that purpose and to provide reliable guidance in this area. I sought the informal advice of friendly New York lawyers whom I regarded as neither pro-taxpayer nor pro-government, and certainly not just protecting their clients. With them as advisors I developed what we considered appropriate guidelines and they were adopted in a Treasury Regulation in 1946.[160] Some members of the bar grumbled at this use of Treasury authority, but on the whole the regulation was accepted as giving sensible guidance on the use of the trust device. Later the Regulation was enacted into statutory law in 1954, with the provisions largely unchanged and so they stand today.[161] I may observe that at present I am engaged in an American Law Institute Project examining — and proposing to tighten — these provisions toward more taxation of grantors.[162]

---

158. It is not clear what time frame Surrey had in mind in his "almost a hundred" statement. In any event, by 2020 Helvering v. Clifford had been cited in over 1,300 judicial opinions.

159. "In the absence of more precise standards or guides supplied by statute or appropriate regulations, the answer to that question must depend on an analysis of the terms of the trust and all the circumstances attendant on its creation and operation." Helvering v. Clifford, 309 U.S. at 334–335.

160. Treas. Dec. 5488, 1946-1 C.B. 19 (1946).

161. Internal Revenue Code of 1954, Pub. L. No. 83-591, § 671-678, 68A Stat. 1, 226-232.

162. Surrey recounts his late-career work with the ALI in chapter 8.

The third problem was the income taxation of married couples. I have already described the problem — couples living in community property states, couples in non-community property states where the wealthier spouse through trust arrangements, gifts or other methods sought to shift income to the other spouse, the formation of "family partnerships" for that purpose, even the situation of two spouses having earned or unearned incomes of their own, all meant that couples with the same amount of total income had far different tax liabilities. This result followed from the then prevailing principle that the income tax applied to individuals as individuals, whether single or married. The effort to achieve tax equality among married couples at the same total family income level had earlier failed when the approach advanced by the Treasury was that of mandatory joint returns. I saw the problem essentially whether we should continue with the principle of taxing individuals as individuals or instead should seek tax equality among couples with the same total income. If Congress would not approve joint returns, was there another way?

I had been asked to talk in a program on taxation of family income in a 1946 meeting of the National Tax Association. I decided to use this talk to suggest an alternative to joint returns. This alternative was, as I called it, a "split income" approach under which a husband and wife would total their income, divide the total by two, compute the tax on each half under the regular rate scale, and then add the two tax liabilities to find the total tax. The couple would, voluntarily, file a joint return using this method of computation. Since a split income approach meant lower taxes for nearly every married couple and not higher tax unlike the "mandatory" joint return, it would be expected that the "split-income" joint return would be used by married couples. This approach meant, of course, a higher tax level for a single individual with, say $20,000 of income than a married couple with a total $20,000 income.[163] But I thought equality among married couples outweighed this aspect, and certainly there were far more married couples than single individuals at the point where the tax differential would be significant. I then carefully checked the talk with Roy Blough and he approved.

In the talk itself I said either approach — mandatory joint returns or this new split income approach — was satisfactory. The talk was issued as a Treasury press release and then published as Surrey, "Family Income and Federal Taxation," 24 Taxes 980 (1946). The Washington tax letters and some newspapers quickly saw its importance, for it indicated that the split-income solution, called by some the "Surrey Plan," was acceptable to the Treasury as a solution to the taxation of family income. The plan was pushed in the Senate in 1947 and finally enacted as law in the Revenue Act of 1948.[164] A similar split approach, the marital deduction, was also adopted for the gift and estate taxes.[165] Incidentally, the tax reduction provided by the split-income device

---

163. For journalistic acknowledgment of Surrey's pathbreaking effort, see John D. Morris, "*Community Property" is Big Tax Bill Item*, NEW YORK TIMES, Feb. 1, 1948, at E7 (noting that the income-splitting approach adopted in a pending bill — which became law later in 1948 — "was first proposed in 1946 by Stanley S. Surrey, then tax legislative counsel of the Treasury Department").

164. Revenue Act of 1948, Pub. L. No. 80-471, § 301, 62 Stat. 110, 114.

165. Revenue Act of 1948, § 361, 62 Stat. at 117.

proved the lever that enabled Congress to override President Truman's third veto of a tax reduction bill in 1947–1948, since the tax reduction in the upper brackets came not through a decrease in the rate schedule that had prompted two previous successful vetoes arguing against rate reduction, but through the split-income device itself. Probably a third rate reduction bill would have passed anyway, but split-income changed the lowered tax liabilities in the upper brackets into a sensible approach to the taxation of family income. This split-income approach exists in its basic form today. The changes grafted on to it have been a separate rate schedule for individuals enacted in 1969 through lobbying by mainly well-paid single women, which schedule somewhat narrowed the difference between single individuals and married couples,[166] and a special deduction enacted in 1981 for two-earner married couples, which to the extent of that deduction does depart from the concept of family equality that underlies the 1948 split-income solution.[167]

A fourth matter — but not a problem requiring immediate solution — stemmed from my view that the structure of the estate and gift taxes was defective. To begin with, these two taxes were essentially separate levies, with the gift tax rates lower than estate tax rates and with the estate tax possessing a rate schedule that started at the bottom bracket regardless of prior gifts. Also, some lifetime gifts were subject to the estate tax, with a credit for gift tax paid, if the donor-decedent still possessed an interest in the property subject to the gift, an interest such as a power to revoke the gift or a life-interest in the property. But the overlap was characterized by rules not following a consistent pattern. Further, there was no consistent correlation between the income tax and the gift tax. A donor could on a gift be subject to the gift tax, indicating the transfer was *complete* for gift tax purposes, but remain subject to the income tax on the income from the donated property, indicating that the transfer was *incomplete* for income tax purposes. With the objective of seeing if a better tax structure could be devised for lifetime and death transfers, I formed an advisory group of lawyers. Among them were[168] [check]. After months of study, the Treasury published the Report of this group.[169] The Report suggested sweeping changes, such as a unification of the gift and estate taxes into a single tax and a complete set of rules to produce correlation between the income tax and this unified transfer tax. The Report — which was printed with a salmon pink cover and was referred to as that "Salmon Pink Report" when the reference was intended to be derogatory, an illustration of how a government official must think of every detail — was ahead of its times and far more progressive than the probate and tax lawyers could even con-

166. Tax Reform Act of 1969, Pub. L. No. 91-172, § 803, 83 Stat. 487, 678.

167. Economic Recovery Tax Act of 1981, Pub. L. No. 97-34, § 103, 95 Stat. 172, 187. Congress repealed the two-earner deduction in 1986. Tax Reform Act of 1986, Pub. L. No. 99-514, § 131, 100 Stat. 2085, 2113.

168. The five members of the Advisory Committee were George K. Bowden, Jesse R. Fillman, Lawrence E. Green, Erwin Griswold, and Harry J. Rudick.

169. Advisory Committee to the Treasury Department and the Office of the Tax Legislative Counsel, Federal Estate and Gift Taxes: A Proposal for Integration and for Correlation with the Income Tax (1948).

template. Indeed it was not until 1976 that a partial unification of the gift and estate taxes was adopted, and correlation with the income tax still remains as an unmet problem. But the study furthered, or brought about, my acquaintance with the outside lawyers, and this relationship was renewed several years later when I started to work on an American Law Institute tax project.

There was no major tax legislation in 1946. But everything was changing. Tom Lynch, again not a tax person, had succeeded O'Connell and John Snyder, then Director of War Mobilization and Reconversion, had become Treasury Secretary in June of 1946, when Vinson went to the Supreme Court.[170] Snyder, a Truman friend, had no tax background and seemed an amiable, rather ordinary person with no particular quality of leadership. On the Hill the world was upside down, as the Congress turned Republican in 1947, Chairman Harold Knutson succeeded Doughton on the House Ways and Means Committee and Chairman Eugene Milliken, of Colorado, succeeded George on the Senate Finance Committee.[171] Neither change was a plus for either the Treasury staff or tax work in general.

The 1947 legislation was thus formulated by the Republicans in the Congress. That party was interested in large tax reductions, and the amount and structure of the reduction were being devised on the Hill. The Treasury did not count for much in that process. But Truman was President and he vetoed two tax reduction bills in rapid succession in June and July 1947 on the grounds that reduction was in itself inadvisable and moreover the method of reduction was skewed to benefit higher incomes. As earlier described, the third Republican bill was passed over Truman's veto with the reduction in upper-bracket tax liabilities coming not through a reduction in the tax rates but through the adoption of the family split-income device.

In the spring of 1947 I decided to leave the Treasury. Working with a Republican Congress was not very interesting or congenial on policy issues. But the basic reason was I increasingly felt that under Snyder as Secretary the top level decisions on technical issues were being made on the basis of what business or political pressures, or both, were involved rather than what was the right answer under a proper tax structure. The latter approach was the atmosphere I had always worked under until then, and the change was not pleasing. I realized this vividly in a conference one day in Snyder's office with railroad representatives, some of whom may have been his friends but all had good business and political connections, who presented their request for an important technical change. I argued against the change. In a previous period the Secretary or the official responsible for Treasury tax policy would have followed my advice on such a technical point. Snyder decided otherwise. The railroad's proposal came up for a hearing before the House Ways and Means Com-

---

170. John Wesley Snyder was appointed Treasury Secretary in June of 1946 and served until 1953. *John Snyder, Treasury Chief under Truman*, CHICAGO TRIBUNE, Oct. 9, 1985, at A6.

171. Eugene D. Millikin (R., Colo.) was a member of the Senate from 1941 to 1957, and chairman of the Senate Finance Committee from 1947 to 1949 and from 1953–1955. *Eugene Millikin, Ex-Senator, Dies*, NEW YORK TIMES, Jul. 27, 1958, at 61.

mittee. Representing the Treasury I explained the proposal and discussed, rather lengthily, the pros and cons. Chairman Knutson, in on the play, was impatient and kept saying "Get on to the conclusion." I finally did conclude with the statement the Treasury was leaving the matter to the Committee to decide. The Members well knew this was code language for "Go ahead and adopt the proposal," which the committee proceeded to do.[172]

So I decided to leave. But to where? As for career tax positions elsewhere in government I had already declined Assistant House Legislative Counsel as too confining a position since it was not policy oriented and Assistant Commissioner in the Bureau because I knew from experience that the real action was in the Treasury and not the Bureau. Private tax practice was a clear possibility as far as offers were concerned. Indeed, my Navy leader, Struve Hensel, had earlier asked me to come to his firm as a partner, an offer I declined not because of his Navy action but I was then still interested in government. Alvord and other Washington firms made offers at attractive salaries. But I held back. Then I had lunch with a New Deal lawyer friend, Tom Emerson, who was leaving government to teach at Yale Law School.[173] Why did he want to teach? His reply was that he was still interested in government and he thought a law school was an excellent base of operations from which to continue his interest. This viewpoint seemed sound. In addition I had learned how difficult it was for a tax lawyer, even a skilled lawyer, to move rapidly into the top tax circles of his city since there were simply too many good tax lawyers. But, I reasoned, there are few tax professors in any city and a respected tax professor could immediately join the top circle. Finally, I was not so sure I wanted to change roles—from problem solving as a government official where the goal was the correct overall answer to problem solving as a practitioner where the goal was the best answer for a client. Teaching seemed clearly closer to the first goal. While teaching salaries were low compared to private practice, they were comparable, perhaps a bit higher, than government salaries.

So teaching became the answer. The remaining question was where to teach.

I thus left the Treasury after ten years of work in the tax field. Those ten years covered major changes in both tax law and the Treasury itself. The income tax had greatly expanded in scope and technical detail, with the inevitable increase in complexity. As I wrote in my casebook, the tax law had under wartime pressures become a factor in the life of most Americans:

---

172. Reorganized Railroad, *Hearings Before the Comm. on Ways and Means, House of Representatives*, 80th Cong., 1st Sess., on H.R. 3369 Superseded by H.R. 3861, 28–37 (1947). For a fairly typical exchange between Knutson and Surrey, *see id.* at 33 (Knutson: "Why do you not come before us and say the Treasury has no recommendation? You have been arguing against the bill." Surrey: "No; I have been trying to bring the facts out which were not brought out.").

173. Thomas I. Emerson, among the greatest civil liberties scholars of his generation, joined the Yale Law School faculty in 1946 and remained there for more than three decades. Glenn Fowler, *Thomas I. Emerson, 83, Scholar Who Molded Civil Liberties Law*, New York Times, Jun. 22, 1991, at 21.

> "Almost overnight it changed its morning coat for overalls. Its membership spread from the country club district down to the railroad tracks and then over to the other side of the tracks. The exemption for a single person dropped to $500. The surtax commenced at the first dollar of taxable income and, with the normal tax, came to an initial rate of 23 percent. A 50 percent combined rate was reached at the $14,000 bracket. Forty-three million individuals were filing taxable returns by 1945—about 50 million in all were required to file a return."[174]

Also, in this period the tax law was slowly but increasingly being used to meet social problems that were not tax oriented but instead lay outside a proper technical structure for an income tax. Examples of this departure were the deduction for medical expenses and for child care, the Western Hemisphere rate reduction, [add others]. Some of these departures were suggested by the Treasury and others by the tax bar. What we did not realize was that gradually there was being developed two strands of statutory tax law. One strand represented the constant shaping of a proper technical structure necessary to an income tax based on an accepted definition of "income". The second strand involved using the income tax either to achieve desirable social goals or to provide incentives for activities that the Treasury or Congress decided should obtain government financial assistance through tax reduction. Gradually in subsequent years this second strand grew larger and today we find it responsible for the numerous and costly "tax expenditures" present in the tax system. But in that period and later the difference between the two strands and the problem thereby created were not perceived by the Treasury. Indeed, when relief for hardship was recommended, as for medical expenses, there was no clear realization that the deduction came at the top marginal rates and in this sense had an upside-down effect that would not be followed in any direct program of alleviation.

Another development, as the Code expanded in coverage and detail, saw the participation of lobbyists from the tax bar rapidly grow more significant. Until this period the structural changes in tax law were largely recommended by the Treasury and on the whole accepted by Congress. But with the rapid and controversial changes under wartime conditions the Treasury and the Congress became less cooperative partners in the development of the tax system.[175] Instead, the Treasury became only one of the forces contending for Congressional decisions, with the other forces being the tax bar representing their clients and trade associations acting for their members. In part the presence of Stam as the chief congressional technical expert assisted in this development through his willingness to support committee members urging the proposals advanced by lobbyists. But the development was inevitable as the tax bar expanded and more lawyers became acquainted with congressional procedures and realized that solutions to their clients' tax problems could be achieved through statu-

---

174. FEDERAL INCOME TAXATION, *supra* note 95, at 15.

175. For more on the relationship between Congress and the Treasury Department in the making of post-World War II tax policy, *see generally*, JULIAN ZELIZER, TAXING AMERICA: WILBUR MILLS, CONGRESS, AND THE STATE, 1945–1975 (2000).

tory changes. Also in this period the Tax Section of the American Bar Association expanded its membership and activity. The Section, still led by the Washington tax bar, was nearly always an advocate for client causes and special benefits.[176]

The Treasury underwent changes during this ten year period. On the plus side the two technical staffs expanded and gained prestige and influence. They were recognized both within the administration and by the tax bar as focal points where Treasury policy was developed. The offices were staffed by able persons who came to them with a background in tax law and fiscal policy. Unlike the personnel in the NLRB who learned on the job the knowledge evolving in the new specialty of labor law, the Treasury personnel already had a strong technical base. What they lacked was an understanding of tax policy issues. The law firms really had no awareness of tax policy and the law schools did not teach that phase of taxation but only history and current nuts and bolts. The economics departments taught rather abstract fiscal policy and were not aware of the institutional aspects of taxation. But jobs in the Treasury were ideal for a quick education in the formation of tax policy and an approach to the many issues constantly arising in the daily work.

The Office of Tax Legislative Counsel was not a career service and its lawyers rarely stayed for more than two or three years — in fact, I had the longest period of service in that Office. As members of that Office went back to private practice or on to teaching they formed a segment of the tax bar that was now aware of tax policy issues. As a consequence they were more balanced in how they viewed the tax system and thus not so client oriented in the public positions they took. This Office in subsequent years continued to serve that function and, along with an increased emphasis on tax policy in law school courses — often taught by Treasury graduates — was a major force in producing an increasing number of tax lawyers who would understand tax policy issues and in articles and bar association work see both sides, Treasury and client. The economists tended to be career people, for the Treasury provided interesting work in pivotal positions and outside positions were neither plentiful nor as attractive. The Treasury here also developed the side of fiscal policy that concerned itself with structural issues and not just fiscal theory.

The ascendency of these Offices within the Treasury marked the recognition by the Bureau of Internal Revenue — later the Internal Revenue Service — that policy formulation had been yielded by it to the Treasury. The Treasury Offices in turn worked closely with the Bureau in shaping the administration's tax views, for there was a sensible recognition of the Bureau's practical experience and the ability of many who served there, usually as career officials. But it was clear, both in and out of government, that the determination and public articulation of the administration's tax views rested with the Treasury.

---

176. For more on the history of tax policy advocacy by the Tax Section of the American Bar Association, *see* Joseph J. Thorndike & Ajay K. Mehrotra, "*Who Speaks for Tax Equity and Tax Fairness?" The Emergence of the Organized Bar and the Dilemmas of Professional Responsibility,* 81 LAW & CONTEMP. PROBS. 203 (2018). The quotation in the title of the article is from Surrey.

As the Treasury technical staffs grew in strength and stature there was on the other hand a weakening of leadership at the political level. The successors to Secretary Morgenthau were not as able nor had the public vision he possessed. Randolph Paul was not matched by those who followed him in charge of the technical offices. The leadership in the Bureau also weakened. Both the Treasury and the Bureau were moving slowly toward involvement in a major scandal in tax administration. But at the time this development was not foreseen and only sharply emerged four years later through a Congressional investigation.[177]

Notes

a. For this history of closing agreements and the development up to 1940 see Stanley S. Surrey, *Some Suggested Topics in the Field of Tax Administration*, 25 WASHINGTON U. L.Q. 399 (1940).

b. Insert a reference to recent bankruptcy legislation.

c. Stanley S. Surrey, *The Revenue Act of 1939 and the Income Tax Treatment of Cancellation of Indebtedness*, 49 YALE L. J. 1153 (1940); Stanley S. Surrey, *Assumption of Indebtedness in Tax-Free Exchanges*, 50 YALE L. J. 1 (1940).

d. The reason for this complete reversal has never been explained. [Cite Wolfman]

e. Paul's attitude on this point is summed up in his *Taxation in the United States* (1954) at page 771 in the conclusion entitled "The Responsibilities of Tax Experts," and his earlier [check] article. [check]

177. Surrey describes "the major scandal in tax administration" and its investigation in chapter 3.

THREE

A Law School Professor

Part I, 1947–1961

In 1947 I had decided to move from an important government tax position in the Treasury Department to the teaching of tax law. Earlier I had in 1940 taught one summer at the University of California School of Law at Berkeley. This summer session teaching was at the request of Roger Traynor, back in his position as the tax law professor at Berkeley. I finished my legislative work on the Vinson-Walsh Act with Senator Walsh in time for my wife and I to drive to California, where I met my class just as the session commenced.[1] There were about twenty students in this summer course in Income Taxation. I did not use a casebook but instead assigned cases, statutory sections, Regulations and Rulings for the students to read and then somewhat informally discuss.[2] The class was going well when it was interrupted by an imperative call to return to Washington to work on the first draft of an excess profits tax. President Roosevelt had suddenly requested such a tax and because of my Vinson-Walsh experience and a shortage of experienced hands, I was needed in Washington. Edwin Dickinson, the Law School Dean, was dismayed but I told him not to worry.[3] I prepared a schedule of reading for a week or so for the class. Then I drafted a letter for Dickinson to send to Treasury Assistant Secretary Sullivan saying how serious my absence would be and how necessary it was that Surrey return as soon as possible, yet also recognizing the needs of the Treasury for his services. I then flew to Washington. In true bureaucratic fashion, as I expected from experience, the letter was sent pro forma by Sullivan's office to our office with a sheet to prepare a reply for

1. Surrey's manuscript has "Vinson-Trammell" here. In fact, however, Surrey's work was not on the Vinson-Trammell Act of 1934, but on the Vinson-Walsh Act of 1940, Pub. L. No. 76-757, 54 Stat. 779. The 1940 Act, also known as the Two-Ocean Navy Act, was the largest naval procurement bill in U.S. history, increasing the size of the Navy by 70 percent. David I. Walsh (D., Mass.) chaired the Senate Naval Affairs Committee.

2. Federal tax casebooks which Surrey could have used existed in 1940, including a book co-authored by Surrey's mentor Roswell Magill. JOHN M. MAGUIRE & ROSWELL MAGILL, CASES ON THE LAW OF TAXATION (2nd ed., 1936). For much more on the federal taxation casebooks of that era, see Terrance O'Reilly, *Tax Legal Scholarship to 1970*, 34 VA. TAX REV. 269, 285–89 (2014). The first edition of Erwin Griswold's CASES AND MATERIALS ON FEDERAL TAXATION was published in September of 1940, a few months too late for Surrey's summer teaching.

3. Edwin DeWitt Dickinson was dean of the UC Berkeley School of Law from 1936 to 1948. He later joined the faculty of the University of Pennsylvania School of Law, specializing in international law. *Edwin Dickinson, A Law Professor: Ex-Dean at U. of California Dies—Served Permanent Court of Arbitration*, NEW YORK TIMES, Mar. 27, 1961, at 31.

Sullivan's signature. So in Washington I drafted Sullivan's reply, stating the vital need to the Treasury of Surrey's presence, but recognizing the serious inconvenience caused the Law School. The two principals very clearly agreed on the importance of Surrey! The drafting was quickly finished and less than two weeks later I was back teaching in California.

While I was in Berkeley, Traynor was appointed an Associate Justice of the California Supreme Court. A vacancy had first been filled by the Governor, a liberal, in appointing Max Radin, an outspoken, very liberal Berkeley law professor whose field was Jurisprudence.[4] In California, appointees to the Court had to be approved by a three-person committee, the Attorney General, the Chief Justice of the California Supreme Court, and a state appellate judge.[5] They did not approve Radin, probably because of his liberal views and perhaps because of inexperience. The Governor at once selected another professor, this time Traynor. Traynor's liberalism was deep but not widely known. Also, he had served for a number of years as an advisor on California state tax matters. He was quickly approved. The choice, the disappointment to Radin aside, was a wise one. Traynor was better qualified, by temperament and background, than was Radin. He was able to persuade his fellow judges to a liberal conclusion where Radin would have failed. Later Traynor became Chief justice and over the years was recognized as an outstanding, probably the foremost, state court Chief Justice.

A typical Traynor episode occurred when he was appointed. He did not then own a hat but for his interview with the three-man committee he thought it was prudent to have a hat. He bought one, wore it to the meeting, and hung it in the outside office. When he left, the secretary said "Professor Traynor, you have forgotten your hat." "Oh no," he replied "I never wear a hat!"

In 1947, in seeking where to teach I turned, rather naturally, to the law school I had attended, Columbia. I had a conference with the Dean, Young B. Smith, which was decidedly unsatisfactory.[6] The Dean had not bothered to read my resume carefully or check my writings. He said, politely, that I could start as an Assistant Professor and after I had written some articles and become known in the tax field, I could move to a full professorship. I declined the offer in a letter which pointed out I had already written more articles than most full professors, implying Dean Smith included. Many times later, when a number of Columbia professors asked me to join their faculty, they ruefully apologized for Dean Smith's lack of judgement. At this point Dean

---

4. Max Radin, a scholar of jurisprudence and ancient Greek and Roman law, was on the faculty of the UC Berkeley School of Law from 1919 to 1948. Richard Hyland, *Radin, Max*, YALE BIOGRAPHICAL DICTIONARY OF AMERICAN LAW, *supra* Chapter 1 note 3, at 444–445.

5. The three members of the State Qualifications Committee were California Attorney General Earl Warren, California Supreme Court Chief Justice Phil S. Gibson, and Judge John T. Nourse of the First District Court of Appeal. *Max Radin Rejected as State Justice: Appointee of Olson, Criticized as Leftist, Disqualified by Board*, LOS ANGELES TIMES, Jul. 23, 1940, at 1.

6. Young Berryman Smith served as dean of Columbia Law School from 1927 to 1952. *Young Smith, 70, of Columbia Dies*, NEW YORK TIMES, Jun. 25, 1960, at 21.

Arthur Vanderbilt of New York University Law School made a personal appeal at a breakfast to join his faculty as a full professor.[7] However, when Traynor learned of my decision to teach, he spoke to Dean Dickinson at Berkeley. Dickinson immediately telephoned to offer me a full professorship position. Berkeley appeared more attractive than New York City, especially after the pleasant 1940 experience, and I accepted at once. I had not given any thought to Harvard or Yale, or any other school.

While still at Treasury, I spent the 1947 summer commuting to New York two days a week to teach a large summer session tax class at Columbia. The regular tax professor there, William C. Warren, whom I knew casually, had asked me to teach his course.[8] Then it was a drive across the county to the house my wife had purchased and to start a new career as law school professor.[9]

The choice of Berkeley was sound. The law school was housed in a pleasant band-box building. The classes were rather on the small side and the students able and cooperative. The faculty had its distinguished members — such as Radin in Jurisprudence, Kidd in Criminal Law, Ballentine in Corporations, Dickinson in international law, Prosser, who later succeeded Dickinson as Dean, in Torts, and so on.[10] The younger faculty were able persons, to go on later to recognized positions — Dick Jennings in corporate law, Frank Newman in administrative law and later California Supreme Court judge, Ed Barrett, later founding dean at UC Davis Law School.[11] This younger group, of which I was a member, would play handball at the nearby university gym, then have lunch at the swimming pool, and talk over school policy.

My principal teaching naturally was in the field of taxation — individual income tax, corporate income tax, and gift and estate taxes, all in one course. I also taught

7. Arthur T. Vanderbilt was dean of New York University Law School from 1943 to 1948, and chief justice of the New Jersey Supreme Court from 1948 until his death in 1957. *Vanderbilt, 68, Dead: Jersey Chief Justice*, NEW YORK TIMES, June 16, 1957. Vanderbilt Hall, the main building of NYU Law School, bears his name.

8. Warren was later dean of Columbia Law School, from 1952 to 1970. Surrey and Warren later worked closely together, especially in connection with the American Law Institute's income tax project of the late 1940s and early 1950s (the subject of Chapter Four), and the Surrey and Warren income tax casebook (discussed by Surrey later in this Chapter).

9. This is the first mention of Mrs. Surrey — Dorothy Mooklar Surrey (1905–1997) — in these memoirs. Surrey mentions her only a handful of times in his entire manuscript, never by name and largely in footnotes.

10. Alexander Marsden Kidd (affectionately known as Captain Kidd) was on the UC Berkeley Law School faculty from 1909 to 1949. Henry Winthrop Ballantine was on the same faculty from 1924 to 1951. William Lloyd Prosser, arguably the greatest American torts scholar of his generation, was dean of UC Berkeley Law School from 1948 to 1961.

11. Richard W. Jennings was a member of the UC Berkeley Law School from 1947 to 1975. Frank C. Newman was on the same faculty from 1946 to 1966, serving as dean from 1961 to 1966. He was later a justice of the California Supreme Court, from 1977 to 1982. In addition to his work on administrative law, Newman did pioneering work on international human rights. Edward L. Barrett (constitutional law and criminal procedure) was a member of the UC Berkeley Law School faculty from 1946 to 1964, and later the founding dean of the UC Davis Law School, in office from 1964 to 1971.

first a seminar on Administrative Law and then one on Legislation. In the tax course, as would be expected, I emphasized what I had learned in the Treasury—the importance of the structure of the tax system, the essential legislative character of the law, and the importance of policy issues. Since existing casebooks and courses did not stress these facets, but largely only used court opinions, I prepared my own casebooks. In this I was joined by Professor Warren of Columbia. I prepared mimeographed material on the income tax and he worked on the estate and gift taxes. At this time, as related later, we were working on the American Law Institute income tax project and this activity helped in the casebook preparation.[12] The two casebooks were published in 1950 by Foundation Press: "Surrey and Warren, Federal Income Taxation, Cases and Materials" and "Warren and Surrey, Federal Estate and Gift Taxation, Cases and Materials."[13] These were the first casebooks to cover separately these two facets of the federal tax system. Also they were the first casebooks to emphasize both the statutory structure of the taxes, along with the administrative material, and the policy decisions and struggles that lay behind the Tax Code and administrative action. Warren and I were fortunate in combining with Commerce Clearing House to have it publish a loose-leaf annual student edition of the Code and Regulations, together with our preparation of monthly material containing recent important cases and legislation and our comments on them plus a page-by-page reference to our and other casebooks of these current tax events. This enabled us, and other casebook editors, to use the Commerce Clearing House publication to keep the casebooks up to date. Thirty years later these casebooks, now prepared with me by Professors Paul McDaniel and Hugh Ault of Boston College Law School and Harry Gutman of Virginia Law School, contain more policy materials than any of the other casebooks, though gradually some policy discussion has crept into some of the other casebooks.[14]

I started a seminar on Advanced Taxation [check] in which each week a different tax practitioner from San Francisco presented to the students a combined tax and business problem on which he was currently working. Organized in groups, the students were to prepare their suggested solutions, which the practitioner could read

---

12. Surrey describes his work on the ALI income tax project in some detail in Chapter Four.

13. Stanley S. Surrey & William C. Warren, Federal Income Taxation, Cases and Materials 15 (1950); Stanley S. Surrey & William C. Warren, Federal Estate and Gift Taxation: Cases and Materials (1950). For a perceptive contemporaneous review of both books, see Leo A. Diamond, *Book Review*, 19 U. Chi. L. Rev. 147 (1951). Diamond comments, "The student who utilizes either or both of these casebooks will definitely realize that court opinions are but only a small part of the stuff of which law is made." *Id.* at 149.

14. For the editions current around the time Surrey was writing these memoirs, *see* William C. Warren, Paul R. McDaniel & Hugh J. Ault, Federal Income Taxation: Cases and Materials (2nd ed., 1980); Stanley S. Surrey, William C. Warren, Paul R. McDaniel & Harry L. Gutman, Federal Wealth Transfer Taxation: Cases and Materials (2nd ed., 1982). Although the lists of authors are completely different from the lists of the early 1980s, successors to the Surrey and Warren casebooks remain in use today. Daniel L. Simmons, Martin J. McMahon, Jr., Bradley T. Borden & Dennis J. Ventry Jr., Federal Income Taxation (7th ed., 2017); Paul R. McDaniel, James R. Repetti & Paul L. Caron, Federal Wealth Transfer Taxation: Cases and Materials (7th ed., 2015).

in advance. The practitioner, assisted by me, then led the students through the problem, their solutions, and his course of action. In this fashion the students—and far more important I as an academic—were able to learn at first-hand what was going on in the day-to-day application of tax law. In taxation, the problems faced by law firms and their solutions are the frontier, ahead of the cases and generally the statute. The seminar provided a very simple way by which I could see this frontier. The practitioners were quite willing to participate. After all, it is nice for a San Francisco lawyer to say, "Just the other day, as I was telling a class at Berkeley." But they were genuinely interested in the process. Though I found them to be experienced practitioners, Washington was a remote place. So with the help of a few lawyers, we organized monthly lunch meetings—the "Surrey club"—at which we discussed current legislative and administrative developments, as well as current tax practice situations. I soon found I had judged correctly how rapidly a law professor can join the tax bar elite of the locality. But at the same time I saw that tax law can only really be taught well in a law school located near a large city with a strong tax bar.

I also attempted to keep up my contacts with economists. This was hard for the local public finance teacher, Earl Rolph, while able, had no basic tax policy experience.[15] I soon learned this in sitting through his seminar on Public Finance. Later, I persuaded him to spend a year in Washington.

Shortly after I came to Berkeley, Rowan Gaither, a San Francisco lawyer, asked me to prepare material for a committee he headed which was formed to suggest a structure and program for the newly-established Ford Foundation.[16] My assignment was straightforward—how to organize the foundation so that it could stay out of tax trouble over the years if government ever showed an interest in how foundations operated. This was pure crystal ball gazing. I wrote several memoranda, the main suggestions being (1) the selection of a rather sizeable and independent board of trustees—while Henry Ford could be Chairman, the Board was not to consist only of Ford, his wife, his lawyer and a Ford executive, which was the pattern of many a foundation; (2) while the Foundation had been created through the gift of non-voting stock in the Ford Motor Company, the Foundation should as feasibly as possible diversify its portfolio; and (3) while its programs could enter any field of activity, they should be objectively oriented and balanced, without any ideological bent. These recommendations were followed by Gaither and the Foundation.[17] They proved sound, for despite the inevitable attacks on it because of its size, the Foundation remained

---

15. Earl Robert Rolph taught economics at UC Berkeley from 1937 to 1977, with several breaks for government service.

16. Horace Rowan Gaither, Jr., was hired by Henry Ford II to assist in setting the priorities of the new Ford Foundation; the study committee he chaired produced THE REPORT OF THE STUDY FOR THE FORD FOUNDATION ON POLICY AND PROGRAM (1949) [hereinafter REPORT OF THE STUDY], informally known as the Gaither Report. *H. Rowan Gaither Jr. Dies at 51; Led '57 Study of U.S. Defense; Former President of Ford Foundation was Lawyer and Financier on Coast*, NEW YORK TIMES, Apr. 8, 1961, at 19.

17. For the Gaither Report's discussion of administrative design issues, *see* REPORT OF THE STUDY, *supra* note 16, at 100–137.

unscathed. Years later, when I was once again in the Treasury, and foundations were really examined, Ford stood up very well. It was only in 1968–1969 when its then President, George McBundy,[18] made the political mistake of subsidizing for a while a number of Senator Robert Kennedy's staff after his death that the Foundation found itself in trouble in Washington[19] and helped to bring about tax legislation affecting foundation operations.[20]

In the Treasury, my assistant Adrian DeWind had succeeded me as Legislative counsel.[21] He soon left to join Randolph Paul's law firm, Paul, Weiss, Wharton and Garrison, in New York, and his assistant, whom I had earlier employed, Vance Kirby, succeeded him.[22] Though able, they had their problems with the Congress. Another skilled lawyer and scholar I had employed, Louis Eisenstein, also joined that firm and assisted Paul in writing his book.[23] While I kept in touch with DeWind and Kirby I was not regularly involved in Treasury work. I did find the time, despite the casebooks, to write an article that the Harvard Law Review *did* accept: "Surrey, Federal Taxation of the Family—the Revenue Act of 1948, 61 Harvard Law Review 1097 (1948)." This article was appropriate, since the 1948 Act had adopted the split-income method of taxing the family unit which I had suggested in 1946.[24] I

---

18. Of course, "George McBundy" should be "McGeorge Bundy," but Surrey's spoonerism is too charming to correct in the text. McGeorge Bundy was president of the Ford Foundation from 1966 to 1979. He had previously served as National Security Adviser to Presidents Kennedy and Johnson, in which capacity he played a significant role in the escalation of the Vietnam War. *McGeorge Bundy Dies at 77; Top Adviser in Vietnam Era*, NEW YORK TIMES, Sep. 17, 1996, at 1.

19. On Bundy's "political mistake," *see* Eileen Shanahan, *Bundy Backs Ford Grants as Within Limits of Law*, NEW YORK TIMES, Feb. 21, 1969, at 1 ("Under questioning by members of the House Ways and Means Committee, [Bundy] defended grants for travel and study to eight members of the staff of the late Senator Robert F. Kennedy as 'educational,' within the meaning of the foundation's charter and the laws granting tax-exempt status to the group").

20. Tax Reform Act of 1969, Pub. L. No. 91-172, § 101, 83 Stat. 487, 492–536 (distinguishing for the first time between private foundations and public charities, and using the tax laws to impose a comprehensive regulatory regime on private foundations).

21. Adrian William DeWind, Sr., served as tax legislative counsel from 1947 to 1948, after which he joined the New York law firm of Paul, Weiss, Rifkind, Wharton & Garrison, where he remained for thirty-five years. He was deeply involved in public interest activities, including chairing the Natural Resources Defense Council and founding Human Rights Watch. Dennis Hevesi, *Adrian DeWind, Tax Expert and Human Rights Watch Founder, Dies at 95*, NEW YORK TIMES, Aug. 19, 2009, at 26N.

22. Vance N. Kirby served as tax legislative counsel from 1948 to 1957. In 1957 he both joined the faculty of the Northwestern University School of Law and became a partner with the Chicago law firm of Ross and O'Keefe. He remained on the Northwestern Law faculty until his retirement in 1980.

23. Louis Eisenstein practiced tax law as a partner in Paul, Weiss, Rifkind, Wharton & Garrison, before moving his practice to the Washington firm of Arnold and Porter. He died at the age of 50. *Louis Eisenstein, Tax Attorney, 50*, NEW YORK TIMES, Jan. 8, 1966, at 26. His witty, insightful, and provocative book, THE IDEOLOGIES OF TAXATION (1961), a classic analysis of tax policy and politics, was reissued by Harvard University Press in 2010.

24. The split-income method, as enacted in the 1948 Revenue Act, provided that when a married couple filed a joint return, their net incomes and exemptions would be divided by two, an initial tax would be computed, and the result multiplied by two to obtain the final tax. Revenue Act of 1948, Pub. L. no. 8–471, tit. III, pt I, 62 Stat. 110, 114–116.

also persuaded the California Law Review to devote an issue to policy considerations relating to the federal estate and gift taxes, for which issue I obtained articles from prominent practitioners and wrote, with guidance from James Lewis,[25] a Bureau acquaintance and then with Paul's firm, the introduction: "Surrey, An Introduction to Revision of the Federal Estate and Gift Taxes," 38 California Law Review 1 (1950).

During these years in California along with teaching I had commenced work as Chief Reporter for the American Law Institute Income Tax Project and also in the summer of 1949 and 1950 went to Japan with Carl Shoup as a member of his Shoup Tax Mission. These assignments, however, are major matters in themselves to be discussed later.[26] But these, and the other activities, including the new career of teaching, made the Berkeley years interesting and active. Once more, however, events from the past combined to change this life.

In the summer of 1949 the Erwin Griswold of Chapter Two—now Dean Griswold of Harvard Law School—asked me to visit Harvard for a year to teach Administrative Law, substituting for a person on leave. I did not like the idea, since Administrative Law was not really my field though I had a seminar on the subject at Berkeley which Griswold had noted. Besides I was about to go to Japan for the summer on the Shoup Mission and would not have time to prepare. Also, we had just settled in California. So I declined. Then late in 1949 Dean Griswold offered me a permanent full professorship at Harvard in the tax field. This was a totally different matter! While the California Law School was a fine place, Harvard was then—and still is—the preeminent law school.[27] I had been flying east each month for the American Law Institute, and these monthly flights would continue if I stayed in California. Also, I realized that Harvard was a better—and closer—base of operations for one interested in tax policy than was California. Much as we liked Berkeley these factors pointed to the change and I informally accepted the offer. I say "informally" because my California colleagues asked me to wait until President Sproul[28] of the University of California had the chance to persuade me to remain by offering a higher salary than I was then paid, even though this required breaking the law school salary ceiling. The higher salary was offered, the ceiling broken, but I decided to leave. My Berkeley colleagues then gratefully were in a position to have their salaries increased!

---

25. James B. Lewis was a partner with Paul, Weiss, Rifkind, Wharton & Garrison from 1955 until his retirement in 1982. Kenneth L. Gilpin, *James B. Lewis, 84, Tax Lawyer, Professor and Founder of Clinic*, New York Times, Jun. 16, 1996, at B16.

26. Surrey describes the ALI project in Chapter Four, and the Shoup Tax Mission to Japan in Chapter Five.

27. The strangely influential *US News* annual law school rankings, which consistently rank Yale Law School as the nation's best (for the current rankings, *see* www.usnews.com/best-graduate-schools/top-law-schools) originated in 1987, so at the time he was writing his memoirs Surrey could make his claim without fear of contradiction by a news magazine. Of course, more than a few lawyers (not all of them graduates of Harvard Law School) would agree with Surrey even today.

28. Robert Gordon Sproul was president of UC Berkeley from 1930 to 1952, and of the University of California system from 1952 to 1958. *Dr. Robert Gordon Sproul, Ex-President of UC, Dies*, Los Angeles Times, Sep. 11, 1975, at A1.

Harvard was, of course, a far different place to teach. Its graduates quite naturally could not perceive of any other institution as being worthy of the name law school. I recall John O'Brien of House Legislative Counsel days writing to say "now you are in the big league. So step up to the plate and hit away!" Harvard had four tax law teachers while Berkeley had only one. The faculty was larger and one passed many famous names walking in the halls. Some faculty members I already knew—Griswold, Ben Kaplan, my fellow Columbia graduate, Jack Maguire of the 1938 Traynor year. Others I had met at American Law Institute meetings. Incidentally, there was a Harvard rule that only Harvard graduates could teach at Harvard. I was brought within the rule, as had the other very few non-Harvard members of the Law School Faculty, by receiving in the mail an honorary M.A. degree! The student body was far larger. But Berkeley was a fine school so that my teaching techniques remained the same and the class performances did not appreciably change. Berkeley students did not wear suits or ties while Harvard students did—then. There were more women in the Berkeley classes since Harvard had only recently commenced to admit women.[29] The earlier historic Harvard refusal was strange to a 1932 Columbia graduate who assumed the women present in that class just naturally belonged there. But otherwise the sea of faces before one in a classroom was pretty much the same.

My main course was Taxation, two hours a week for a year covering income, estate and gift taxes, and I used the two Surrey-Warren casebooks. In my first year at Harvard I had joined with professors from the Economics Department and Business School in a statement relating to fiscal policy—"Tax Program for Sustained Mobilization," with J. Keith Butters, Willian Fellner, John Lintner, Dan Throop and Arthur Smithies, 29 Harvard Business Review 119 (1951). As I became acquainted with these professors from other disciplines I decided to institute a Law School seminar on "Current Tax Policy" to be taught with an Economics professor and at times with a Business School professor. The purpose was two-fold: to give the students in the seminar a feeling for tax policy from both the legal and economic aspects and, far more important, to enable me to keep up with the current trends in economic and fiscal policy so that I could use this learning in my basic tax course. Not having an academic background in economics and not seeing the time to obtain that background, and more important to maintain it, this seminar device seemed, shall I say, the most economical approach. Ever since this start I continued the seminar, always with a Harvard economics professor. It was, I believe, the first interdisciplinary

---

29. Very recently indeed. Harvard Law School first admitted women in the fall of 1950, in the same semester that Surrey moved from Berkeley to Harvard. *Harvard Law Will Admit Women First Time in School's 132 Years*, NEW YORK TIMES, Oct. 10, 1949, at 1 (explaining that the first women were to matriculate in the fall of 1950). Dean Griswold did not exactly fling the door wide open, however. He commented, "Opportunities for women in the law are still limited, and the faculty is well aware that many able men are turned away from our doors every year. It is our expectation that we will admit only a small number of unusually qualified women students for the present, at least." *Id.*

seminar in the Law School. I was, of course, fortunate in having available highly qualified fiscal economists who enjoyed meeting law school students.

I also rapidly became acquainted, through Dean Griswold's assistance, with the Boston tax bar and joined the group of top tax lawyers who met monthly to discuss current issues. In Boston, as in San Francisco, my theory on the mobility of a professor to move in tax bar circles—if the professor so desired—was verified with this knowledge of the Boston tax bar. I continued my seminar on Current Problems in taxation, with a different Boston practitioner each week. I was equally successful—just substituting Harvard for Berkeley in the phrase casually dropped "As I was telling the Harvard class the other day." (See Surrey, Seminar in Current Problems in Taxation, 3 Harvard Law School Bulletin No 4, at page 7 (1952), describing the seminar.[30]) I believe this seminar was the only one at the time which involved the Law School in a close relationship with the outside bar. As in Berkeley the value to me was of great importance since I could bring to my basic tax course the current thinking in the frontier of the law firms. The seminar continued until the late 1950's. Then Professor Dave Herwitz, a corporation lawyer, and I jointly taught a class in "Business Planning" covering the interaction of corporate and tax aspects of business transactions.[31] Dave went on to become a business tax expert in his own right and the course under his teaching remains today in the curriculum.

Finally I taught a course in Legislation, concentrating on the Congress. Here I found the existing casebooks rather antiquated and unreal, focusing on the canons of statutory interpretation, state constitutions and local authority, and the like. All this was far removed from the legislative world I had known in Washington. So with my Berkeley colleague, Frank Newman, who spent a year visiting Harvard, I prepared a casebook in Legislation.[32] It was indeed a modern casebook, concentrating on what a lawyer should know in dealing with the Congressional world—the rules of the Committees, how to represent a client hauled before an investigating Committee. Most of the text consisted of excerpts from Congressional sources,.unlike the cases that were the main materials in the other books. We even introduced each chapter with a political cartoon capturing the essence of the material. For this purpose I had

30. In the short article in the *Bulletin*, Surrey noted that many students survived the "ordeal" of the basic tax course "with an Oliver Twist hunger for more, including a number who had originally approached taxation with attitudes varying from resignation to antipathy." He also observed that in the seminar "the high quality of the students' answers often comes as a pleasant surprise to the practitioner, as he realizes he will be able to conduct the discussion at quite a sophisticated level and still be understood."

31. David Richard Herwitz is the Royall Professor of Law, Emeritus, at Harvard Law School. His scholarly interests are in corporate law, accounting, and the legal profession. He joined the Harvard Law faculty in 1954 and retired in 2006.

32. Frank C. Newman & Stanley S. Surrey, Legislation: Cases and Materials (1955). A reviewer described the book as "a superb teaching instrument, an invaluably thoughtful guide and reference for the practitioner, and a notable contribution to the scholarly literature." Winston M. Fick, *Book Review*, 45 Cal. L. Rev. 570, 571 (1957).

spent two days in the Washington Post newspaper office going through the files of its eminent political cartoonist, Herbert Block. Also, I was able to draw on my own experience with a Congressional investigating committee, the King Subcommittee of the House Ways and Means Committee.[33]

This experience came about when early in 1951 Charles Davis, clerk of the House Ways and Means Committee (the Charles Davis of Chapter Two who could type!) called to say the Committee was about to appoint a subcommittee to investigate the administration of the tax laws. Would I take the position of Chief Counsel for this Subcommittee? Acceptance would mean a leave of absence from Harvard after I had just started there and also a leave from the American Law Institute Project. Both these leaves were out of the question in fairness to the two institutions. So I declined, suggesting Adrian DeWind from New York and saying I would participate on a part-time basis as Special Counsel. The Subcommittee was formed and DeWind was named the Chief Counsel. The Subcommittee consisted of Cecil King of California,[34] Democrat, a friendly, easy-going Chairman with no tax experience but with backbone and courage when both were needed—much, I believe, to the surprise of many, on the main Committee, Wilbur Mills, Democrat from Arkansas.[35] [Check]

The principal initial staff members were young New York lawyers—Charles Lyon, later a New York University professor,[36] Donald Schapiro, later a leading New York practitioner,[37] Jim ____________, later a high executive in Mobil Oil, and ____________, an investigator.

I spent the 1951 summer in Washington as the Subcommittee organized its work. Since I had taught Legislation, I prepared the Subcommittee Rules of Procedure. We

---

33. Reviewer Winston M. Fick noted that the book's chapters on legislative investigations "occupy three hundred pages in a book of seven hundred; this seems too much." *Id.* at 571.

34. Cecil Rhodes King (D., Cal.) was a member of the House of Representatives from 1942 to 1969. *Ex-Rep Cecil King of California Dies*, New York Times, Mar. 21, 1974, at 44.

35. Wilbur Daigh Mills (D., Ark.) was a member of the House of Representatives from 1939 to 1977, and chairman of the Ways and Means Committee from 1958 to 1974. He arguably had more influence on the mid-century development of federal income tax law than any other politician. His career came to an ignominious end; he resigned his chairmanship and decided not to seek reelection to Congress following two incidents of his public intoxication in the company of Fanne Foxe, an Argentinian stripper. For a thorough examination of Mills' tax legislative accomplishments, see Julian E. Zelizer, Taxing America: Wilbur D. Mills, Congress, and the State, 1945–1975 (2000). It is not clear what Surrey intended to say about Mills in the material following the dash. Perhaps "including" should precede "Wilbur Mills" in the text. In any event, as noted above, Mills did not become chairman of Ways and Means until 1958. He was a member of the Ways and Means Committee in 1951, but he was not a member of the King subcommittee. The chairman of Ways and Means in 1951 was Robert L. Doughton (D., N.C.).

36. In 1951 Charles S. Lyon resigned as a partner in the Skadden Arps law firm to become counsel for the Ways and Means Committee. He later had a long career teaching tax law on the faculty of NYU Law School. *Charles S. Lyon, Retired Law Professor, 72*, New York Times, Aug. 13, 1989, at 36.

37. Following his service with the Ways and Means Committee, Donald Schapiro practiced tax law in New York, first with Barrett, Smith, Schapiro, Simon & Armstrong, and later with Chadbourne & Park. He taught legal accounting at Yale Law School for many years as an adjunct professor. *Deaths: Schapiro, Donald*, New York Times, Jul. 6, 2014, at A18.

met with the House Speaker, Sam Rayburn,[38] who said he would back King all the way no matter what was uncovered, with the one command that he should run a responsible investigation and not a circus.

DeWind was an able, imaginative and energetic investigator. Shortly after the Subcommittee was formed, we heard rumors of corruption in the top Bureau circles. We were all neophytes and really wondered whether there was any truth to the rumors. Our investigator, who had some experience, said he had heard a recording implicating the Deputy Commissioner, Carroll E. Mealey.[39] We discussed whether the recording was for real. Amateurs all, we suggested to Dewind that he talk with Mealey in a friendly way, mention the recording, and observe the reaction. DeWind did so and came back with the impression that we had a real investigation ahead of us. What was intended largely as an investigation of the general efficiency and operations of the Bureau of Internal Revenue thus quickly turned into an investigation of corruption and misconduct at high levels throughout the Government tax world. Other stories and rumors began to find their way to us as news of the Subcommittee's presence spread and the word went around that it and the staff were honest and could be trusted. A schedule of Hearings was planned against a background of intensive preparations.[40] After I returned in the fall to Harvard I travelled frequently to Washington to participate in Staff planning and attend the important Hearings. My assignment at the Hearings was to suggest questions to DeWind and then each day prepare on the spot, from the developments at the Hearings, a sharp, concise statement that Chairman King could read, which summarized the Hearing highlights in a way calculated to make front page news.

There was plenty of front page news to be made, for the rumors were true far beyond what anyone had thought. The Commissioner, Joseph D. Nunan;[41] the

---

38. Samuel Taliaferro Rayburn (D., Tex.) was a member of the House of Representatives from 1913 to 1961, and the immensely powerful speaker of the House from 1940 to 1947, 1949 to 1953, and 1955 to 1961. For much more on Rayburn, *see* D. B. HARDEMAN & DONALD C. BACON, RAYBURN: A BIOGRAPHY (1989).

39. Carroll E. Mealey was deputy commissioner, heading the Alcohol Tax Unit, from 1946 until his resignation—purportedly on account of poor health—in 1951. In 1954 a grand jury indicted him for income tax evasion, but because of his ill health he was never tried. *Carroll E. Mealey, 69*, NEW YORK TIMES, Apr. 1, 1963, at 36; *Ex-Revenue Aide Indicted on Tax*, NEW YORK TIMES, May 4, 1954, at 26 (noting that in 1953 two Internal Revenue agents had testified before the Ways and Means investigative subcommittee that Mealey had accepted a fur coat and an automobile as bribes; the indictment, however, did not mention the car or the coat).

40. *Hearings Before a Subcomm. of the Comm. on Ways and Means, House of Representatives*, 82nd Cong., 1st Sess., on Administration of the Internal Revenue Laws, 1-5 (1951–1952). *See also* REPORT OF THE SUBCOMM. ON ADMINISTRATION OF THE INTERNAL REVENUE LAWS TO THE HOUSE COMM. ON WAYS AND MEANS, 82nd Cong. 2nd Sess. (1952).

41. Joseph D. Nunan, Jr., was commissioner of Internal Revenue from 1944 to 1947. In 1954 a jury convicted Nunan of income tax evasion (involving more than $91,000 of evaded income tax liability over a five-year period); he actually served two years of a five-year sentence. James P. McCaffrey, *Nunan is Guilty of Tax Evasion; Faces 25 Years in Jail, Big Fine*, NEW YORK TIMES, Jun. 30, 1954, at 1; *Joseph D. Nunan Jr. Dead at 70; Tax Official Jailed for Fraud*, NEW YORK TIMES, Feb. 23, 1968, at 33.

Deputy Commissioner, Mealey; the Assistant Attorney General in charge of the Tax Division in Justice, Tom Caudle;[42] the Massachusetts Collector of Internal Revenue, Denis W. Delaney (at that time the Collectors were Presidential political appointees and poor Delaney,[43] previously a State official who was accustomed to the bribe activity in Massachusetts, just didn't comprehend that a *federal* job might be a different matter); and several other collectors were investigated. They were revealed as participating in corrupt activities. Other top officials were shown to be grossly inefficient or unsuited for their positions. There were numerous resignations and removals as well as convictions. The revelations went far beyond what we had initially suspected. The then Treasury top officials, Secretary John Snyder, undersecretary Edward Foley and General Counsel Tom Lynch were themselves not really aware of how bad things were, though Snyder revealed an insensitivity to how tax matters should be handled at high levels which in turn contributed to worse conduct on the part of the Bureau's top officials.

I remember one meeting rather early between the Subcommittee and Secretary Snyder (the John Snyder of Chapter Two) and his Chief Counsel, Tom Lynch,[44] at which Snyder protested the attitude of the Subcommittee and said it was disrupting the work of the bureau. I thought the Subcommittee members were treating him too gently and therefore spoke up, saying that there was much more to come out and he really better be prepared for it. That rather ended the meeting. Tom Lynch, a friend, asked if I was serious and I indicated indeed I was. Soon after the Bureau Chief Counsel, Charles Oliphant (a son of Herman Oliphant of Chapter Two), in a position far beyond his abilities, was shown to have made important decisions on a political basis.[45] Oliphant was not really acting with criminal intent but stupidly. He assumed that every time Secretary Snyder sent a taxpayer or a group over to discuss a tax problem with Oliphant this meant Snyder desired a decision favorable to those persons. Perhaps Oliphant discerned correctly—but correct or not—he did not have the maturity or character to say no.

At another time I recall the Subcommittee debating in private whether, because of Tom Caudle's obvious criminal activities, the Subcommittee should call his superior

---

42. T. Lamar Caudle was convicted in 1956 of accepting bribes (in the form of oil royalties) for using his influence to hinder the income tax evasion prosecution of Irving Sachs, a shoe manufacturer. *Caudle, Connelly Get 2 Years Each*, New York Times, Mar. 6, 1957, at 1. President Johnson pardoned Caudle in 1965. *Lamar Caudle Gets Presidential Pardon*, New York Times, Aug. 21, 1965, at 1.

43. One-time Massachusetts Collector of Internal Revenue Denis W. Delaney was convicted in 1952 of accepting bribes of $7,500 while in office. John H. Fenton, *Delaney Convicted of Tax Bribery, Faces 18 Years and $37,500 Fine*, New York Times, Jan. 23, 1952, at 1.

44. Thomas J. Lynch, an Ohio attorney, was general counsel of the Treasury Department in the late 1940s and early 1950s. *Senate Confirms Lynch*, New York Times, Jun. 10, 1948, at 41.

45. In December of 1951 Charles A. Oliphant resigned as Bureau Chief Counsel and released copies of his tax returns in an effort to rebut shakedown allegations against him. Gershon Fishbein, *Bureau's Counsel Resigns 'to Protest Name;' Releases His Tax Reports*, The Washington Post, Dec. 6, 1951, at 1. He returned to private practice, and in 1952 received temporary permission to represent clients before the Treasury Department. He died of a heart attack in 1960, at the age of 51. *C. A. Oliphant, 51, Former Tax Aide*, New York Times, Mar. 30, 1960, at 37.

at the time, Attorney General Tom Clark.[46] There was no direct evidence one way or the other as to Clark's knowledge of what was going on in the Justice Department Tax Division. Clark was then a Justice of the Supreme Court. The Subcommittee decided not to call him — the evidence was not in hand and a public Hearing, even though who could tell what it might produce, would so adversely affect the Court as to be inadvisable. Both the Republican and Democratic members of the Subcommittee reached this unanimous conclusion and Clark was not called.[47] But the Subcommittee did not hesitate to call Senator Brewster of Maine, who spent an uncomfortable morning explaining at least poor judgement on his part.[48]

There was a certain sadness in this work for many of the individuals involved had been our friends and we had trusted them. DeWind and I were in the uncomfortable positions of learning of conduct on the part of former colleagues that we had been unaware of when we were in the Treasury. It was an unpleasant task to have to uncover all this, but obviously a necessary one. The corruption at the top was so clear and widespread that strong action was needed. As this became evident, President Truman suddenly, without discussion with the Subcommittee, issued an Executive Order reorganizing the Bureau.[49] This order eliminated the political Collectors of Internal Revenue and made other changes. On the morning the Order was made public DeWind telephoned me in a furious mood, stating Truman was simply stealing publicity from the Subcommittee. But here my teaching of Legislation was of real help. I explained to DeWind that under the Reorganization Act authorizing such a Presidential Order it could only be set aside by a vote of both [check] Houses of Congress.[50] I added that DeWind was certainly going to recommend the elimination of the Collectors, but obtaining affirmative legislation would be a political battle. The Executive Order achieved his goal and he should at once take credit for it. The real task was to be sure the order was upheld in Congress. DeWind saw the Order in this new light and at once agreed. He asked me to go with an honest Assistant Commis-

---

46. Tom C. Clark was the Attorney General of the United States from 1945 to 1949, and an associate justice of the Supreme Court from 1949 to 1967. *See generally* MIMI CLARK GRONLUND, SUPREME COURT JUSTICE TOM C. CLARK: A LIFE OF SERVICE (2010) (Gronlund is Clark's daughter).

47. Robert W. Kean (R., N.J.), the top Republican member of the King subcommittee (soon to become the chairman of the renamed Kean subcommittee) announced that the subcommittee had determined that former Attorney General Clark had not improperly intervened in any tax fraud cases, and that there was no need to call Justice Clark as a witness. Kean also noted, however, that Clark had been "undoubtedly negligent" in his supervision of Caudle. *Kean 'Clears' Clark in Tax Fraud Cases*, NEW YORK TIMES, Jan. 1, 1953, at 40.

48. Ralph Owen Brewster (R., Maine) was a senator from 1941 to 1952, and a close associate of Senator Joseph R. McCarthy (R., Wisc.). For the rather sordid facts that came to light during Brewster's "uncomfortable morning," *see* Clayton Knowles, *Brewster in Deal with Grunewald: Defends Exchange of $10,000 Checks as Cover-Up for Secret Primary Help*, NEW YORK TIMES, Mar. 21, 1952, at 1. One of the beneficiaries of the secret primary help was Richard Nixon of California, running (successfully) for the first time for the United States Senate.

49. W. H. Lawrence, *Truman Revamps Tax Set-Up to Eliminate 64 Collectors; Civil Service for New Heads*, NEW YORK TIMES, Jan. 3, 1952, at 1.

50. Actually, the order could have been overridden by a majority vote of either the House or the Senate. Reorganization Act of 1949, Pub. L. No. 81-109, § 6(a), 63 Stat. 203, 205.

sioner to persuade the Council of the American Bar Association Section of Taxation, then meeting in Chicago, to support the Executive Order. This request had its problems for at that time the way for a taxpayer to bring a refund suit in the Federal District Courts, and also to obtain a jury trial if desired, was through the old action of a suit against the Collector.[51] A number of the Council members were opposed to the Order. I argued they simply could not stand in the way of ending this avenue of corruption in tax administration, and they could seek separate legislation preserving the suit in the District Courts. After a long debate, a majority of the Council voted not to oppose the Order. With that vote, lobbying against the Order by the organized tax bar was stopped and the Order was accepted on a Senate vote.[52]

The Subcommittee accomplished, along with this Order it had made inevitable ending the system of politically appointed Collectors and substituting career Regional and District Commissioners, many other changes, the ending of automatic non-criminal action if a voluntary disclosure was made, this being an open avenue for corruption in fixing the date the disclosure.[53] Reorganization of many aspects of the enforcement work of the Bureau and the activities of the Department of Justice Tax Division took place. The King Subcommittee thus successfully ended a sordid downward plunge of these agencies and brought them to a revitalized and respected position. It was a needed and successful task of major surgery on Government Departments. DeWind left in the summer of 1952 and my direct participation greatly diminished. The Subcommittee continued for several years as the Kean (a New Jersey Republican) Subcommittee, and steadily made improvements in tax administration.[54] An honest and able Assistant Commissioner, George Schoeneman, was made Commissioner and the Bureau turned a real corner.[55] Ever since there have been no rumors

51. For background on the former treatment of a refund suit as a suit against the tax collector personally, *see* Flora v. United States, 357 U.S. 63 (1958), *aff'd on reh'g*, 362 U.S. 145 (1960).

52. *Collectors' Civil Service Move Won by Truman: 23 Republicans and 30 Democrats Override Adverse Committee Report*, The Washington Post, Mar. 14, 1952, at 1. The Truman reorganization plan had previously easily survived a House vote. George T. Draper, *Hoffman's Move to Reject Truman's Streamlining Plan is Disapproved: House Approves Truman Plan to Streamline Revenue Bureau*, The Washington Post, Jan. 31, 1952, at 1.

53. Although Surrey generally writes clearly, this sentence is a bit of a disaster. Being uncertain how Surrey might have fixed it, the editors have chosen to make no changes. In January of 1952, Treasury announced it was abandoning "its thirty-three-year-old policy of granting immunity to tax evaders who disclose their violations before an official investigation begins." *Tax Evaders Lose Another Loophole*, New York Times, Jan. 11, 1952, at 11. For a thoughtful analysis approving the policy shift, see Charles S. Lyon, *The Crime of Income Tax Fraud: Its Present Status and Future*, 53 Colum. L. Rev. 476, 491–96 (1953).

54. Robert Winthrop Kean (R., N.J.) was a member of the House of Representatives from 1939 to 1959. Joan Cook, *Robert W. Kean, 86; Formerly in House*, New York Times, Sep. 24, 1980, at D23.

55. George J. Schoeneman served as commissioner of Internal Revenue from 1947 to 1951, far too early for his appointment to have been in response to the findings of the King subcommittee. Surrey must have been thinking of John Bettes Dunlap, who was commissioner from August 1951 to November 1952. The *New York Times* described Dunlap as having "stepped out of a quiet, 18-year Civil Service career to lead an often hectic reorganization," and noted that when Dunlap resigned as commissioner "he could say that he had burnished the reputation of a Government agency that had

or evidence of corruption at the top levels or below in Washington or even in the field. There was — and is — some inevitable corruption among the agents in certain districts and in 1961, when I returned to the Treasury I worked with the Treasury General Counsel and the Commissioner to reduce this corruption.

The work with the King Subcommittee provided me with experience on a side of Congress I had not known. Now I could teach Legislation with the authority of the real world, and, as stated earlier, the work helped to shape a part of Legislation casebook. I also came to know Congressmen King, Mills, Byrnes,[56] and __________, [check] and our paths were to cross again in the future.

My work in Legislation and Taxation combined to allow me later to play a role in an important Supreme Court case that covered both aspects. A federal Circuit court had denied a beer distributor a tax deduction for contributions to a campaign to defeat a state referendum on instituting state liquor stores.[57] The taxpayer's local lawyer came to Harvard to seek someone to handle the case on appeal in the Supreme Court. Dean Griswold, who did argue occasionally in the Court, decided that a Dean and beer did not mix, especially this teetotaler Dean, and declined. Ernest Brown, another Harvard tax professor, also declined saying he did not prefer to appear in court. (Interestingly, Brown years later left Harvard for the Department of Justice where he became a master at arguments on the government's side.[58]) I was next in line but declined on the ground I thought the government should win the case on policy grounds! A Washington lawyer took the case. At that time the Assistant Attorney General for the Tax Division, Brian Holland of the Boston Bar, was a personal friend.[59] [check was Holland still there or did I write to Davis.] I had suggested his appointment, as a Republican, to Harry Rudick,[60] also a friend and law partner of

---

been spattered with charges of bribery and corruption." *John Dunlap, 61, Ex-Tax Chief, Dies*, New York Times, Dec. 8, 1964, at 45.

56. John William Byrnes (R., Wisc.) was a member of the House of Representatives from 1945 to 1973, and the ranking minority member of the Ways and Means Committee from 1963 to 1972. Richard Pearson, *Ex-Wisconsin Rep. John Byrnes, 71*, The Washington Post, Jan. 14, 1985, at B4.

57. Cammarano v. United States, 246 F.2d 751 (9th Cir., 1957) *aff'd* 358 U.S. 498 (1959) [hereinafter Cammarano].

58. Ernest J. Brown was a member of the Harvard Law School faculty from 1947 to 1971. After Brown left Harvard he worked for three decades for the Tax Division of the Department of Justice, finally retiring shortly before his death at the age of 95. *Ernest J. Brown, Emeritus Law Professor, Dies at 95*, Harvard Gazette, Jan. 24, 2002.

59. H. Brian Holland was the head of the Tax Division of the Department of Justice from 1953 to 1956. The Ninth Circuit did not issue its Cammarano opinion until 1957, so Surrey would not have written to Holland. Holland was followed in office by Charles K. Rice, who served as assistant attorney general from 1956 to 1960. However, Surrey's note to himself ("check ... or did I write to Davis") suggests that he wrote not to Rice, but to Oscar Hirsh Davis, first assistant to the Solicitor General from 1954 to 1962. Davis served as a judge of the United States Court of Claims from 1962 to 1982, and as a judge of the Court of Appeals for the Federal Circuit from 1982 to 1988. *Oscar H. Davis, 74, U.S. Appellate Judge*, New York Times, Jun. 20, 1988, at D11.

60. At his death Harry J. Rudick was both a tax professor at the New York University School of Law and a senior member of the New York law firm of Lord, Day & Lord. *Harry Rudick, 64, Tax Lawyer, Dies; A Lord, Day & Lord Senior Member Since 1940*, New York Times, Jun. 1, 1964, at 29.

the new Attorney General, Herbert Brownell,[61] in the Eisenhower administration, and he agreed Holland was the right person. Holland was soon appointed to the position. I wrote Holland, suggesting a line of argument and paragraphs to use in the Government's brief. The paragraphs were used and—shall I claim cause and effect—the case won by the Government, Cammarano v. United States, 358 U.S. 498 (1959), and a companion case, F. Strauss & Son, Inc., of Arkansas v. Commissioner. I had urged that the Government's case be argued in terms of "tax equilibrium"—that neither business nor private persons could lobby at the Government's expense through tax deductions for the lobbying expenditures. When the case was concluded, I received the following letter from Oscar Davis, Counsel for the Government, and now a Federal Judge on the Court of Claims:[62]

> Thank you for your note on the *Cammarano-Strauss* cases. We were all surprised that the decision was unanimous, since there had been considerable questioning at the argument—particularly from Justice Frankfurter. But in the end it turned out all right.
>
> As you probably gathered from the Law Week, I stressed the notion of "tax equilibrium" quite extensively. In the second case (the *Strauss* case), Justice Frankfurter wanted to know where did that phrase come from, who invented it (with some reference to its shorthand nature). I called it a portmanteau word and said that I was indebted to you for it. With a look of surprise and concern, F then indicated that you must have thought of the notion before you came to Harvard (evidently thinking of your earlier connection with the Treasury). I said that, no, I thought it was after you had come to Harvard (knowing that your testimony before the Senate Committee had taken place after you came east). The Justice—who, as I have mentioned, had not at all seemed favorable to our position, but really quite hostile—looked slightly disconcerted, and there was a burst of laughter in the courtroom, led by the Chief Justice [Earl Warren] (who was very decidedly on our side) who practically turned to F, sitting next to him, with a gesture which seemed to say, "Your own boys weren't with you on this one." The point of the episode, to those in the courtroom, revolved around F's connection with and love for the Harvard Law School—coupled with his seeming antagonism to the notion of tax equilibrium sponsored by the eminent Harvard professor of taxation....
>
> Again, let me express our thanks to you for articulating this central concept which played such a large role in the Court's disposition of the cases. Even

---

The Harry J. Rudick Memorial Award is given annually to the outstanding graduate of NYU's tax LLM program.

61. Herbert Brownell, Jr., was United States Attorney General from 1953 to 1957. As Attorney General he encouraged President Eisenhower to appoint judges in the South who would enforce the desegregation decisions of the Supreme Court. Eric Pace, *Herbert Brownell Jr., Eisenhower Attorney General, Dies at 92*, New York Times, May 3, 1996, at A29.

62. For Davis, *see supra* note 59.

though the term "tax equilibrium" does not appear in the opinion, the concept does; and I feel sure that the idea was one of the controlling factors."[63]

Work as a tax professor both enabled and prompted me to write a number of articles. One article dealt with the types of capital gains and discussed the large number of definitional problems that arose under the special treatment of those gains. My writing in this area developed from a paper in Federal Tax Policy for Economic Growth and Stability, Joint Committee on the Economic Report, 84th Cong., 1st Sess. 404 (1955) and Hearings thereon before the Subcommittee on Tax Policy, at 312. It then appeared as a Surrey, "Definitional Problems in Capital Gains Taxation," 69 Harvard Law Review 986 (1956). The material, revised, was also included in the significant Congressional tax reform document, published in 1959, Tax Revision Compendium, House Ways and Means Committee, 86th Cong., 1st Sess. 1203 (1969), and Panel Discussions thereon, at 675. This, incidentally, was the best collection of materials on where tax reform issues stood as the nineteen-fifties closed. I had worked on planning the subjects and Panel Members for this Compendium together with Norman Ture,[64] who under Chairman Mills' direction was the chief Congressional architect for the project.

Perhaps one of the important articles and also Congressional testimony in this period was a discussion of the contrast in our individual income tax between very high tax rates and the undercutting of the tax base through many tax preferences—"loopholes" in popular parlance—that made the actual effective rates of tax far lower than the high rate schedules would indicate, especially in the upper brackets. I suggested as a broad corrective approach the removal or lessening of the preferences and a reduction in top rates of tax. See Surrey, "The Federal Income Tax Base for Individuals," 58 Columbia Law Review 815 (1958), which developed from a statement in Hearings on General Revenue Revision, House Ways and Means Committee, 85th Cong., 2nd Sess. 2281 (1958), and was revised for inclusion as a paper presented in the 1959 Tax Revision Compendium, at which I appeared as the first witness in the Panel Discussions. The theme of this writing had been the subject of an article for Collier's Magazine, March 30, 1956, my first effort at "popular writing."[65] It had the assistance of a kind Collier's editor, Leonard Gross, who showed me the real skills required for that style of writing. I did have this to say about the article in the Ways and Means Committee Panel Discussions above: "[I] n about 1956 I wrote an article for Collier's Magazine on this subject. Unfortunately the magazine went out of busi-

63. Perhaps the closest approach to the "tax equilibrium" concept in the Court's opinion is the Court's approving quotation of Judge Learned Hand's remark in a 1930 opinion that "political agitation, as such, is outside the [business expense deduction] statute, however innocent the aim.... Controversies of that sort must be conducted without public subvention; the Treasury stands aside from them." After quoting Hand, the Court adds, "The Regulations here contested appear to us to be but a further expression of the same sharply defined policy." Cammarano v. United States, 358 U.S. 498, 512 (1959), quoting Slee v. Commissioner, 42 F.2d 184, 185 (2nd Cir., 1930).

64. Economist Norman B. Ture was on the staff of the Joint Economic Committee of Congress from 1955 to 1961. Decades later he played a leading role in designing the massive 1981 Reagan-era tax cuts. Irvin Molotsky, *Norman B. Ture, Architect of the 1981 Tax Cut, Dies at 74*, New York Times, Aug. 13, 1997, at A21.

65. Stanley S. Surrey, *Do Income-Tax Exemptions Make Sense?*, Colliers, Mar. 30, 1956, at 26.

ness shortly thereafter. Now this is not a fate that can befall this Committee, and therefore, I welcome these hearings."[66]

In this period I had also written a somewhat related article, which found its way into many political science materials, on "The Congress and the Tax Lobbyist — How Special Tax Provisions Get Enacted," 70 Harvard Law Review 1145 (1957). The title fully describes its contents and suggests the sensitivity of the topic. The article had the benefit of discussions with Charles W. Davis,[67] now a Chicago tax lawyer but earlier Clerk of the House Ways and Means Committee, and William M. Horne, Jr.,[68] a former staff member for the Joint Committee on Internal Revenue Taxation, so there was an effort to obtain insights from those who had been inside observers of the Congressional scene. When I briefly discussed the article a year or so later with Chairman Mills of the House Ways and Means Committee, he said, cryptically, that he generally agreed with what I had written but he might not have put it in the same way. When I wrote the article, I realized how difficult it really was to get at all facets of that subject. I learned much more later on. Also, it was this article in particular that caused me much of the pain and anguish in confirmation Hearings in 1961 by the Senate Finance Committee.[69]

During my Harvard teaching, I became increasingly active in testifying before Congressional Committees on tax policy issues as an invited witness and in writing on these subjects. This activity was in addition to many talks on policy issues and technical subjects before professional and business association audiences. A principal area considered in Congressional testimony covered, for example, the taxation of foreign income, where I argued against tax reduction for income from investment abroad, contrary to the efforts of most businesses with foreign investment activities and also the Treasury Department. See Hearings on General Revenue Revision before the Committee on Ways and Means, 85th Cong., 2nd Sess. 1143 (1958). This was a rough Hearing because the then proponent of preferences for foreign income, Representative Hale Boggs, was hostile and sarcastic (at 1166–1169).[70] (Quote). Conditions do change, and when I later joined the Treasury we were staunch allies on Admin-

---

66. *Income Tax Revision, Panel Discussions Before the Committee on Ways and Means, House of Representatives*, 86th Cong., 1st Sess., 6 (1959) [hereinafter *Income Tax Revision*].

67. Charles W. Davis was appointed chief counsel to the Ways and Means Committee in 1949, and general counsel to the Bureau of Internal Revenue in 1952. He spent the later portion of his career as a partner in the Chicago law firm of Hopkins and Sutter. Kenan Heise, *Charles W. Davis, 69, Prominent Tax Lawyer*, CHICAGO TRIBUNE, Feb. 19, 1987, at A10.

68. William M. Horne, Jr., later became senior vice-president and general counsel of Citibank. *William 'Bill' McHenry Horne*, ARIZONA DAILY STAR, Apr. 26, 2015, at C004.

69. Surrey may have planned to describe his 1961 confirmation hearing in Chapter Six, but what he wrote of Chapter Six ends before the hearing. For descriptions of the confirmation hearing, see the editors' introduction to this volume, and George K. Yin, *"Who Speaks for Tax Equity and Tax Fairness?": Stanley Surrey and the Tax Legislative Process*, 39 VA. TAX REV. 39 (2019).

70. Perhaps Surrey was thinking of the following exchange (among others):

Mr. Boggs: Well, it is not absolutely essential that all of us agree with you completely, is it?

Mr. Surrey: I would be surprised if everybody agreed with me.

General Revenue Revision, Hearings Before the Comm. on Ways and Means, House of Representatives, 85th Cong., 2nd Sess. (1958), at 1169.

istration tax matters. Past friendships do help, for the Hearings show the kind efforts of Representative King—remember the King Subcommittee—to place my appearance in the proper perspective (at 1171–1172).[71] (Quote)

I also testified on lobbying activities and tax benefits for political contributions. Hearings on Oil and Gas Lobby Investigation before the Senate Special Committee to Investigate Political Advertising, Lobbying, and Campaign Contributions, 84th Cong., 2nd Sess. 559, 1257 (1956).

These Congressional appearances and writings put me in the category of a "tax reformer," and in the special classification thereunder of a "base broadener." But I realized that an academic tax reformer carries little weight with the practicing tax bar. He is viewed—simply—as an academic and as such automatically unaware of the real world, so that the reform suggestions are regarded ipso facto as impractical, to say the least. It is only when the academic can meet the practitioners on the latters' own ground and talk with knowledge and understanding about their problems that the academic is really listened to. Understanding this, I attempted to build bridges between my teaching and the problems of the tax bar. One bridge was the seminar mentioned above on Current Tax Problems. Another bridge was some consultation work with a Boston law firm and some private clients to whom Griswold, too busy to handle their work, recommended me. Here I made it a rule, however, not to sign briefs, appear before the Congress, or appear before the Treasury and Bureau. Since I publicly in writings and testimony before Congress as a professor took positions which were, I assume, considered as representing the appropriate course from a legislative or public interest viewpoint—at least I intended the positions to be so regarded—I thought it would be confusing to be an advocate publicly at times for a particular client's position. Perhaps too self-importantly, I thought the audience—judicial, legislative, or administrative—in the latter situation might consider I was still professorially and objectively weighing the conflicting interests and really thought, so viewed, that the client's position was the proper national position. In any event, I thought the chance of this occurring was inappropriate. So my consulting work was limited to intra-firm and client discussions.

I undertook a particular consultation task that involved legislative change because it offered a chance to see how the machinery of obtaining a special Code amendment really operated. The client faced a necessary business organization transaction that would produce relative to its size a large and, his lawyer thought and I did also, unfair tax under the existing law. The only solution lay in obtaining a statutory amendment. The matter involved a narrow technical point and in absolute terms a minor sum. I

---

71. Mr. King: You are concerned enough to just point up the field that needs some looking into when and if we get along to that state of our Government's taxing methods and systems. Is that about it, Mr. Surrey?

Mr. Surrey: That is very nicely put.

Id. at 1172.

suggested the lawyer engage a particular Washington tax firm, which I selected for its basic competence, and the firm handled the matter in the House and Senate. I kept in close touch with all the steps, strategies, and drafting. The client had the appropriate connections in the House to obtain a not-to-be-ignored suggestion from Speaker John McCormack[72] to Colin Stam, Chief of the Congressional Tax Staff, to see that the proposed change, as worked out between Stam and the law firm, was presented to and accepted by the Ways and Means Committee. The Treasury, which did not really understand the technical issue, did not strongly object. In the Senate the law firm closely advised an effective Senator on the Senate Finance Committee, Senator Smathers,[73] who had been suggested by the client's own Senator who was not on the Committee. The statutory change was thus successfully accomplished and I knew a little more about "how special tax provisions get enacted."

Another bridge was active participation in the work of the Section of Taxation of the American Bar Association. When in Government I had been critical of their work for it often was only a forum utilized by a small group to advance the special interests of their clients. But Dean Erwin Griswold had argued that academics could help change this focus of the Section if they would present and defend the public point of view, as they saw it. I agreed with him and began my participation, while in Berkeley, by filing a dissenting opinion to a Committee Report favoring preferential treatment for professional earnings.[74] In 1954 I had the chance to appear on a Section of Taxation panel discussing a proposal, which was a current favorite of some Republican Congressmen and some tax lawyers, to separate the Bureau from the Treasury. The appearance permitted me also to write what I regarded as a forceful but humorous article against the proposal: Surrey, "A Comment on the Proposal to Separate the Bureau of Internal Revenue from the Treasury Department," 8 Tax Law Review 155 (1953). After the panel discussion the General Counsel of the Treasury, Elbert P.

---

72. John W. McCormack (D., Mass.) was a member of the House of Representatives from 1928 to 1971, and speaker of the House from 1962 to 1971. *See generally* GARRISON NELSON, JOHN WILLIAM MCCORMACK: A POLITICAL BIOGRAPHY (2017).

73. George Armistead Smathers (D., Fla.) was a United States senator from 1951 to 1969. His greatest claim to fame is that during his 1950 campaign he supposedly gave a stump speech accusing his opponent, Claude Pepper, of being a "shameless extrovert," of having "practiced nepotism with his sister-in-law," of having a sister "who was once a thespian," and of having "habitually practiced celibacy" before he was married. Despite *Time Magazine* having run a story to that effect, it is unlikely it ever happened. Howell Raines, *Legendary Campaign: Pepper vs. Smathers in '50*, NEW YORK TIMES, Feb. 24, 1983, at B8.

74. *See Tax Notes*, 34 A.B.A. J. 837 (1948). The article describes a recommendation of the Tax Section's Committee on Taxation of Earned Income that Congress provide several forms of tax relief for the earnings of high-income professionals (lawyers, for example). It also notes that "Stanley S. Surrey is opposed to the recommendations as 'upper-bracket proposals' designed primarily for the benefit of the group which has already benefitted greatly by the split income provisions of the Revenue Act of 1948." *Id.* at 838. For a review of the history of the ABA's taking positions on actual and proposed tax legislation, *see* Joseph J. Thorndike & Ajay K. Mehrotra, *"Who Speaks for Tax Equity and Tax Fairness?" The Emergence of the Organized Bar and the Dilemmas of Professional Responsibility*, 81 LAW & CONTEMP. PROBS. 203 (2018) (the quotation in the title of the article is from Surrey).

Tuttle,[75] later a Fifth Circuit Judge, said my talk was a good one and strengthened his view that the proposal was a fool idea.

In 1957 I was nominated to be a member of the governing Council of the Section, succeeding to the "professorial seat" being vacated by Dean Griswold as his term expired.[76] I think the Section was gradually changing over the years as a few academics and more importantly a wider and younger group of lawyers became involved. Here also was an opportunity to learn which members of the tax bar were capable of looking beyond the special concerns of their clients and accepting a responsibility for fairly weighing the concerns of the Government and the public against the problems they saw created for their clients.

Another bridge was the extensive work for the American Law Institute, which merits a separate chapter.[77] This work brought me into close contact with the ablest and most progressive practitioners of that period. The group I worked with was composed mostly of tax economists, and the work was largely on major fiscal policy issues. My contribution was essentially that of looking at the economists' ideas and considering whether the recommendations could be structured to operate effectively and how they would be viewed by legislators. I was a strong supporter of Democratic Presidential candidates, so working in this fashion fitted both my professional and political bents.

In this period I developed a relationship with a major Boston law firm, Bingham, Dana and Gould.[78] I came to regularly attend the weekly luncheons held by the tax department of the firm and through the discussion at lunch obtained an understanding of the tax cases passing through a law firm and the reactions of practicing tax lawyers. I also worked on several briefs for them, though did not sign the briefs since, as indicated earlier, I thought public use of my name could confuse the two statuses—law school professor and client advocate—and might because of the objectivity presumably associated with the first status provide an aura of correctness for the position in the brief. This cautious attitude probably overstates the influence of a professor. Nevertheless, I then and after did not appear before the Congress or the Treasury

75. Elbert P. Tuttle had been a tax litigator and name partner with the Atlanta law firm of Sutherland, Asbill & Tuttle, prior to serving as Treasury General Counsel from 1953 to 1954. He was a judge of the United States Court of Appeals for the Fifth Circuit from 1954 to 1968, and chief judge from 1960 to 1967. As chief judge Tuttle ordered the integration of the University of Georgia and played a crucial role more generally in enforcing the civil rights of African Americans in the South. President Jimmy Carter, in awarding Tuttle the Presidential Medal of Freedom in 1980, called Tuttle a "true judicial hero." Jack Bass, *Elbert P. Tuttle, Federal Appeals Judge Who Sought Racial Justice in South, Dies*, New York Times, Jun. 25, 1996, at B9.

76. Surrey was elected in 1957 to a three-year term on the Tax Section's governing Council. *Activities of Sections*, 43 A.B.A. J. 961 (1957).

77. Surrey's work for the American Law Institute in the late 1940s and early 1950s is the subject of Chapter Four.

78. In dire financial straits in 2014, the firm—by then named Bingham McCutchen—was taken over by the Philadelphia-based firm of Morgan Lewis. Deirdre Fernandes, *Some Lose Jobs as Law Firm Joins Another in Pa.*, Boston Globe, Nov. 25, 2014, at B5.

and Service in the posture of representing a client. I was not adverse to consulting on behalf of clients or advising clients directly, since such work broadened my insights into the practice of tax law and contributed to more effective law teaching.

My most important legislative appearance was in 1959 as the first witness in Hearings on Income Tax Revision conducted by Chairman Mills of the Ways and Means Committee, sitting however in his capacity as a member [chairman ?] of the Joint Economic Committee. [check] Mills had a sincere interest in improving the tax system, and this interest was responsible for the Hearings.[79] The Hearings really marked the emergence of Mills as a major figure in the tax scene.[80] [check—when did he become chairman, etc.] I was asked by Mills to work with one of his staff assistants, Norman Ture an economist, to plan the Hearings. Together in a harmonious cooperation we developed the topics to be covered and then selected the individuals to be called upon to speak. Our plan was ambitious and wide-ranging. It led to three volumes of testimony and represented the broadest survey of tax issues ever conducted by the Congress.[81] [Refer to topics I chose to testify on—also to articles that grew out of testimony.]

While a law professor I was introduced to the task of advising presidential candidates on tax matters. Randolph Paul was the chief tax advisor to Adlai Stevenson, the Democratic candidate in 1952 and 1956. Paul in turn asked several persons to work on special assignments for him. In this capacity I and the others jointly prepared memoranda for Paul to use.

I doubt that our work had any real effect but it did contribute to my reputation. Also, in this connection I became acquainted with Professor Richard Musgrave,[82] an economist rapidly coming to prominence as a fiscal policy theorist. This was the start of a close association with Musgrave that was especially important to my work, both in government and teaching. Musgrave was one of the small group of economists

79. There were no hearings of the Joint Economic Committee (JEC) matching Surrey's description, and Mills was not a member (let alone chairman) of the JEC. Surrey is almost certainly thinking of the Ways and Means Committee's 1959 Income Tax Revision hearings. Surrey was indeed the first speaker in those hearings. *Income Tax Revision*, *supra* note 66, at 6.

80. Mills had become chairman of Ways and Means one year earlier, in 1958, so the 1959 Income Tax Revision hearings did indeed mark "the emergence of Mills as a major figure in the tax scene."

81. Surrey contributed two papers to the three-volume TAX REVISION COMPENDIUM: COMPENDIUM OF PAPERS ON BROADENING THE TAX BASE, SUBMITTED TO THE COMMITTEE ON WAYS AND MEANS (1959). STANLEY S. SURREY, THE FEDERAL INCOME TAX BASE FOR INDIVIDUALS, *id.* (vol. 1) at 1; STANLEY S. SURREY, DEFINITIONAL PROBLEMS IN CAPITAL GAINS, *id.* (vol. 2) at 1203. For the law review versions of the two papers, *see* Stanley S. Surrey, *The Federal Income Tax Base for Individuals*, 58 COLUM. L. REV. 815 (1958); Stanley S. Surrey, *Definitional Problems in Capital Gains Taxation*, 69 HARV. L. REV. 985 (1956). Both of the articles were published before 1959, so Surrey's testimony grew out of the articles, rather than (as Surrey incorrectly remembered) the articles growing out of the testimony.

82. Richard Abel Musgrave was the author of THE THEORY OF PUBLIC FINANCE (1959), the first English-language treatise on public finance. In addition to working for the Federal Reserve Board during World War II and serving as an economic adviser to several developing countries later in his career, Musgrave taught at a number of universities, including Harvard, the University of Michigan, Johns Hopkins, and Princeton. Mary Williams Walsh, *Richard A. Musgrave, 96, Theoretician of Public Finance, Dies*, NEW YORK TIMES, Jan. 20, 2007, at C10.

who had outstanding reputations in their field of economics but who could also talk with lawyers in terms that the latter could understand. Carl Shoup and Roy Blough were others who had this ability and were thereby of great assistance to the lawyers who worked jointly with them. They also could communicate with Congressmen and Treasury officials and hence had a significant influence on the shaping of tax policy, for they were the link between the theoretical world of the fiscal policy economists and the government world of decision-making. Most economists could not bridge the two and instead knew only how to write and talk in economic jargon that only their peers could understand.

I have not here described my international activities during this period, because like my ALI work, they require separate discussion.

In 1961 my Harvard career as a law professor ended when President Kennedy appointed me Assistant Secretary for Tax Policy in the Treasury Department. Obviously that new career must be described in itself.[83] But it may be useful, as my academic career ended, to summarize both how I regarded my experience up to this point and how I thought others saw it. An attempt at summary would be along these lines:

A wide general acquaintance with the provisions of tax law, court decisions, and tax doctrines and a sense of how they fitted together. This acquaintance, though starting from the research in 1933, was largely the result of thirteen years of teaching tax law and the authorship of comprehensive and detailed casebooks. This acquaintance extended to international tax matters and to foreign tax systems, which on the whole was not characteristic of most academics or even most practicing lawyers. As an academic, I was on the faculty of the foremost law school in the country and in the top ranks of my field.

A participation in nearly every major tax act from 1938 to 1961. The participation varied, sometimes quite extensive as in the period from 1939 through 1947 when I was in the Treasury and also in 1954 through the ALI work, sometimes very direct with the legislative language being my words as in the period from 1938 through 1947, sometimes the consequences of views expressed in articles such as the "split-income" system for husbands and wives in 1948, the work in the King Subcommittee, or positions presented to Treasury officials or Congressional persons.

An interest, greater than that of most lawyers or even of academics, in the basic structural aspects of the tax system, especially the income tax. This interest derived from my Treasury work, the ALI project, and my writing and teaching. The interest was based on the belief that the tax structure could possess a rational, integrated character and that a goal of tax policy was to work always in that direction.

A deep concern for tax equity and fairness, and hence a dislike of tax preferences and "loopholes." This was coupled with a suspicion of the efficiency, let alone fairness, of tax incentives and tax subsidies, especially in the business area.

83. That is the topic of Surrey's Chapter Six, although sadly he was able to write only the beginning of the Chapter before his death.

The regard for tax structure and concern for equity naturally led to an interest in tax policy issues and decisions. They also led to an approach that sought to find the "right" answer to a policy issue in terms of structure and equity, and to the firm conviction that a "right" answer existed. The approach, of course, is one that academics can indulge in unlike practitioners, whose problem-solving and legislative advocacy lie in seeking the right answer to the *client's problem.* For the best practitioners, the right answer for the client does involve an assessment of the right policy answer for the problem in the sense I have used for the academic, thereby to enable the practitioner to weigh the relationships and the chances of the academic right answer occurring. But the practitioner's goals is still the right answer for the client. A good acquaintance with public finance economists, a feel for their activities and ways of thinking, and an ability to work with them. This acquaintance covered most of the liberal-leaning economists who took an interest in federal tax issues.

Some understanding of fiscal policy issues—probably as much as lawyers possessed—but a realization that the analysis and framing of those issues are not in the lawyers' domain.

Some familiarity, perhaps as much as most lawyers outside Government with the exception of some of the Washington tax bar who were acting as lobbyists or who otherwise maintained close contacts with the Government, with the processes of Government in the tax field, covering the legislative and executive branches, and an acquaintance though not close with a number of legislators and Congressional staff involved in tax matters.

A good acquaintance with the working bar and some feel for their problems, activities, and daily life, and an awareness in many particular cases of individual capabilities, knowledge, and attitudes.

No first-hand knowledge of how business concerns and business executives actually arrived at either business decisions or decisions on positions regarding Government proposals or legislative proposals of their own or their trade associations.

On the whole and viewed from the usefulness for Government service this was a broader and more rounded background than most tax academics or lawyers possessed. The interesting aspect is how significant were the many gaps in the background that I later discovered through painful experience. But given this background, how would I describe the attitudes toward me, trying to place myself in the summer of 1960:

The recognition by the tax bar that I had a competent technical background in tax law and hence could not be faulted for lack of technical knowledge in, say, a bar association debate on some policy issue. Some would say I was open-minded and could be educated on a matter in the sense I would listen to a logical argument and objective assessment of the facts—but it had to be logical and objective. Others would say I was an unrealistic fellow since I had never really practiced tax law, though the consulting I did was well received by those for whom it was done.

My work with the tax bar had generally cast me in the ranks of the opposition at meetings or in articles, since my views often conflicted with the positions being advocated by practicing lawyers on current issues in the technical field. The opposition was understandable in the sense that our vantage points necessarily differed because our professional work differed. But some—by no means all—lawyers saw the opposition in an unfavorable light that colored their view of me as an individual, so that I was regarded with suspicion by some and even worse by others. I thus feel relatively sure that a secret ballot on my election to the governing Council of the American Bar Association Section of Taxation in 1957 would have produced many negative votes though perhaps not a majority—but who knows? Further, though I had good personal but not close relationships with a number of tax executives, I was not well known in business circles.

All in all, to the extent persons thought about me at all, I was regarded as a "tax reformer," with whatever content people and groups read into that term. A "tax reformer's" role is not a popular one in legal and certainly business circles. I suppose that, again to the extent any business group heard or thought about me, the image would be that of a tax reformer and an academic and therefore—what shall I say—"unsound" or at least "unrealistic." I was better known, however, in legal tax circles than to the business community and I would suppose my standing with the lawyers was higher.

FOUR

American Law Institute Project

Part I, 1947–1961

The American Law institute is the elite organization of the legal profession.[1] Its membership—just under 2,000—is composed of judges, practicing lawyers and law professors. Ex officio members consist of the Chief Justice and Justices of the Supreme Court of the United States, the Chief Judge of each United States Court of Appeals, the Attorney General and the Solicitor General of the United States, the Chief Justice or Chief Judge of the highest court of each state, Deans of law schools and incumbent bar association officials. The Institute was organized in 1923, and its organizers represented the legal establishment at that time.[a] Its principal activity over a considerable period of time, and one continuing today, was the formulation of Restatements of various parts of the common law, e.g., Agency, Conflicts of Laws, Contracts, Property, etc., purporting to describe the state of the law in each area, and reducing the conflicts by setting forth the rule considered more appropriate.[2] These Restatements have had a profound effect on courts' decisions. The respect they commanded rested on the prestige, anchored in ability, of the Reporters and their Advisors who collaborated on the work. The Reporters were almost invariably the leading law school professors in the fields, and their advisors were respected professors, judges and lawyers.

In 1947 a Special Committee, chaired by Judge Learned Hand and selected to report on the future work of Institute, recommended an active program in the field

---

1. The mission of the American Law Institute (ALI) is "to promote the clarification and simplification of the law and its better adaptation to social needs, to secure the better administration of justice, and to encourage and carry on scholarly and scientific legal work." ALI, *How the Institute Works,* https://www.ali.org/about-ali/how-institute-works/. Today membership is limited to 3,000 elected members (judges, lawyers, and legal scholars). For a collection of essays and materials on the history of the organization, *see* AMERICAN LAW INSTITUTE, THE AMERICAN LAW INSTITUTE 75TH ANNIVERSARY (1998) [hereinafter ALI 75TH ANNIVERSARY]. For a more on the historical context that gave birth to the ALI and its early impact, see generally, G. Edward White, "The American Law Institute and the Triumph of Modernist Jurisprudence," *Law and History Review* 15:1 (1997): 1–47.

2. As of 2020, the ALI has produced restatements of twenty-six areas of law: agency, American Indian law, charitable nonprofit organizations, children and the law, conflict of laws, consumer contracts, contracts (generally), employment law, foreign relations law, international commercial and investor-state arbitration, judgments, the law governing lawyers, liability insurance, property (landlord-tenant), property (servitudes), property (wills), restitution, suretyship, torts (generally), torts (apportionment of liability), torts (physical harm), torts (economic harm), torts (products liability), torts (intentional), trusts, and unfair competition.

of legislation. From this recommendation, for example, there have developed the Uniform Commercial Code, the Model Penal Code and the Federal Securities Code. During the deliberations of the Committee, tax lawyers suggested that the Institute draft a Model Federal Income Tax Law. My understanding was that Norris Darrell,[3] the top tax partner in Sullivan and Cromwell, a leader in the New York tax bar, and son-in-law of Judge Hand, was the principal proponent of the suggestion.[4] The Committee agreed, in the following words:

> The suggestion has been made to the Institute by tax lawyers of experience and standing that it would be a public service for the Institute to draft what, in effect, would be a Model Federal Income Tax Law. The experience and prestige of such a body as the Institute, it is urged, would give the recommendations great weight. The field is one in which a fair and critical piece of work by a non-political body could provide the country with a set of rules that would protect the Government on the one hand and the taxpayer on the other.
>
> The Committee has given the matter considerable thought. The dangers are obvious. Of course, we dismiss at the start any question of settling rates. That is a matter for the Legislature to settle from time to time as needs vary. But aside from this, the questions presented are necessarily filled with controversy, although the controversy does not necessarily involve those ordinarily referred to as partisan political disputes. On these matters of controversy feeling sometimes runs high. Honest differences of opinion develop. Settlement of a question in accordance with one side's opinion or the other may make differences of millions of dollars.
>
> The proposal is a challenging one. It is based on the theory that the difficulty in the income tax law is not one of language alone, but in the concepts involved in the language used. How far should tax liability on corporate reorganization extend, for instance? Can one draw, in advance, a line which will protect the Government against the distribution of what, in fact, are dividends distributed under the guise of reorganization, without at the same time unnecessarily hampering the business concern in an attempt to put its house in order? Again, could an uninformed and intelligent body write a rule of law which would impose fair limits on the application to the doctrine of the Clifford case dealing with the tax upon the income of short term trusts? Many such questions would be encountered. They have been litigated; they

---

3. Norris Darrell was a partner of the New York law firm of Sullivan & Cromwell for 42 years, specializing in tax. He was president of the ALI from 1961 to 1976. *Norris Darrell, Lawyer and Tax Expert*, NEW YORK TIMES, Aug. 15, 1989, at B5.

4. According to then-ALI Director Herbert F. Goodrich, Colin Stam (chief of staff of the Joint Committee on Taxation and Surrey's long-time nemesis) informally suggested to Darrell in 1946 that an ALI-produced model income tax statute would be helpful to the Joint Committee and to Congress. *General Revenue Provision: Hearing Before the House Comm. on Ways and Means*, 83rd Cong., 1st Sess., 1812–13 (1953). It is unclear whether Surrey was unaware of Stam's role or aware but disinclined to give Stam credit.

> have been made the subject of treasury regulations. Some are still unanswered, others have been answered badly.
>
> Your committee, after considerable thought and discussion, recommends that we undertake the project. We quite realize its dangers. We also realize the public benefit which would be rendered in the performance of a good piece of work from a disinterested body. Care must be taken to see that the primary responsibility for the work, that is the draftsmen and their immediate advisers, represent more than one point of view. We believe that there is a sufficient wealth of good scholarship in the law schools to help maintain that balance. Care should be taken to consult, in advance, public authorities both in the executive and legislative departments. This would not be with a view to getting any commitment from them except that the work is one to be encouraged and that fair consideration will be given to its results. We think, however, that the carrying through of the project would be an exciting intellectual venture and would stand a fair chance of improving the law.
>
> It should be noted that this proposal is not necessarily an all or nothing matter. Of necessity, the major problems would have to be met one at a time and, quite likely, results could be submitted a piece at a time. For instance, if with as good a group as the Institute could command and the intelligent understanding which we could bring to the group's work, we worked out what we thought was a good solution to the problem of corporate reorganization, we could test the probable success of the effort as a whole by what such a fair sample showed. This method might well, in operation, prove to be the best one to follow, although in considering the feasibility of the project as something to undertake we should, your Committee thinks, envisage it in terms of a unified whole.[b, 5]

Darrell then wrote to the Treasury and Congressional Joint Committee on Internal Revenue Taxation asking whether they would in any way consider the project a usurpation of the Government's role in developing tax law and if the two bodies would provide appropriate cooperation. As Tax Legislative Counsel I replied for the Treasury that we would welcome the project and would fully cooperate. Colin Stam replied in the same vein for the Joint Committee. Incidentally—or perhaps not so incidentally—Darrell had been a consultant on several projects my Office had undertaken with the aid of outside lawyers.

Around this time I had decided to leave the Treasury and was considering law teaching positions on the East and West Coasts. I asked Darrell whether, if I decided to locate on the West Coast, that would bar me from consideration for a position in the ALI Income Tax Project, and he assured me the location would not be a barrier.

5. Learned Hand (chairman), REPORT OF SPECIAL COMMITTEE ON FUTURE PROGRAM (1947), *reprinted in* ALI 75TH ANNIVERSARY, *supra* note 1, at 306–308.

I proceeded to accept a position as Professor at the University of California Law School in Berkeley, starting September 1947.

Later in the fall I was asked to come east to discuss the ALI project. The group met in the summer house on Long Island of Harrison Tweed, President of the Institute.[6] Tweed was the "beau ideal" of the New York bar, a handsome, tall person of aristocratic bearing, possessed with a command of words and ideas that enabled him to speak gracefully and forcefully on any occasion. He had come to the Presidency of the Institute in that year. He was not a tax lawyer. In the Group also was Judge Herbert Goodrich, formerly a professor at the University of Pennsylvania Law School and, as of 1940, a judge on the Federal Court of Appeals for the Third Circuit.[7] Goodrich had been appointed Director in 1947, having become the Assistant Director in 1944. He also had no experience in the tax field, except for the few cases that had floated before his court. Darrell was also a member of the group. Another member was William C. Warren, a professor of tax law at Columbia Law School and formerly a lawyer in Tweed's firm, Milbank, Tweed, Hope & Webb.[8] The project was discussed at length, all being in favor.

Early in the next morning Tweed and Darrell met to decide on the personnel for the Project. They recognized that Warren had a reasonable amount of private practice and was possessed of good common sense. Darrell thought that my Treasury experience was an excellent asset and should be the determining factor. Tweed agreed, and so it was decided I would be the Chief Reporter. How do I know of this brief meeting? I had been given an alcove bed in the room in which they were meeting, and was awake in bed when they walked in. Should I leave or stay, once I heard what they were to discuss? Either course had its problems, and so, instead of exiting bleary-eyed from the alcove in my pajamas I decided to stay, a somewhat unwitting listener.

Later in the day the suggested appointments were announced and Warren and I agreed to serve. We then drove to New York to meet with Judge Learned Hand to

---

6. Harrison Tweed spent the bulk of his long career as a name partner in the New York law firm of Milbank, Tweed, Hadley & McCloy. His remarkable public service efforts included terms as president of the Legal Aid Society of New York, the National Legal Aid and Defender Association, the New York City Bar Association, and the ALI. *Harrison Tweed, Lawyer and Civic Leader, Dead*, NEW YORK TIMES, Jun. 17, 1969, at 47.

7. Herbert F. Goodrich was dean of the University of Pennsylvania Law School from 1929–1940, and later a lecturer from 1940–1948. He was a judge of the United States Court of Appeals for the Third Circuit from 1940 until his death in 1962. He was director of the ALI from 1947–1962. *Judge Goodrich of U.S. Bench Dies*, NEW YORK TIMES, Jun. 26, 1962, at 33.

8. In 1948 William C. Warren left his law practice with Milbank, Tweed, Hope & Webb to join the Columbia Law School faculty. He became dean of Columbia Law School in 1952 and served until 1970. After stepping down as dean he returned to the private practice of law with the New York firm of Roberts and Holland. Sheila K. Dewan, *William Warren, 91, Ex-Law Dean, Dies*, NEW YORK TIMES, Sep. 15, 2000, at C19. In addition to working closely together on the ALI tax project (including co-authoring several law review articles on the project), Surrey and Warren collaborated on an influential tax casebook. *See* STANLEY S. SURREY & WILLIAM C. WARREN, FEDERAL INCOME TAXATION, CASES AND MATERIALS 15 (1950) [hereinafter FEDERAL INCOME TAXATION].

secure approval of the appointments.[9] Though Judge Hand did not know me, I assume Darrell had briefed him ahead of time. The Judge welcomed us and said the Council approved the appointments. The Project would be financed by a grant from the Maurice and Laura Falk Foundation.

The next step was the formation of a Tax Policy Committee to guide the Reporters. In the Restatements the Reporter decided policy and other questions, subject to the approval of the Council of the Institute and then the membership at the Annual Meeting. Darrell, along with Tweed and Goodrich, thought that the Tax Project should be handled differently, with the final decisions on substance to be made by a Tax Policy Committee. I agreed at once, for I recognized that the personalization of the Project that would occur if I were to make the final policy decisions would be dangerous to the Project. I had the reputation of a strong government man and in some circles this extended to being regarded as a liberal reformer with an anti-tax practice bias. I, therefore, considered it important to the Project that I would work under the guidance of a Committee. A Tax Policy Committee of five members was chosen, all able and largely with different backgrounds. No chairman was named but Darrell acted as an informal chairman. The other members were, alphabetically:

Lawrence E. Green, a Boston tax lawyer not widely known in the tax bar. He was rather on the conservative side and often more forceful in discussion than other members of the group. But he also could listen well and could be persuaded to see the other side. He died in 1952.

Dean Erwin N. Griswold, Harvard Law School, recognized as the leading tax professor in the law schools, with experience in the Solicitor General's office and a consulting practice. He was probably regarded as a bit left of center on tax policy issues, in the sense of seeing the Government's side of an issue considerably more clearly than the average practitioner.

J. Paul Jackson, a Texas tax lawyer who came to the Committee later on.[10] Though a "country boy" in speech and manner, he had a keen practical mind that was open to discussion of any issues on the merits. His forte was partnership tax law.

Robert N. Miller,[11] a Washington D.C. tax lawyer well along in years but still regarded as the leading Washington tax lawyer and a prominent figure in the Section of Taxation, American Bar Association. Miller was an out-and-out conservative in his thinking on tax policy issues, generally concluding in favor of the taxpayer's side.

---

9. Learned Hand was a judge of the United States District Court for the Southern District of New York from 1909 to 1924, and a judge of the United States Court of Appeals for the Second Circuit from 1924 to 1951. He is widely considered one of the greatest—perhaps the greatest—federal appellate court judges in American history, well deserving of a scholarly biography of more than 700 pages. GERALD GUNTHER, LEARNED HAND: THE MAN AND THE JUDGE (2010). In 1947 Hand chaired the ALI's Special Committee on Future Projects, which recommended that the ALI undertake the Federal Income Tax Project.

10. John Paul Jackson was a founding partner of the Dallas law firm of Jackson Walker.

11. Robert N. Miller is discussed in Chapter Two, note 18.

But his graciousness and willingness to listen, plus a low keyed stance in pressing his views, made him a useful member.

Randolph E. Paul,[12] a New York lawyer who had a reputation as a strong believer in tax reform, based on his writings and career in the Treasury, where at the end he was General Counsel in charge of tax matters. Paul was known for his articles and books in the tax field.[c] He was often an ambiguous figure, given to somewhat inarticulate, rather cryptic words spoken in a low voice that at times made it difficult to decide what point he was making. In a deceptive way he had a keen mind, with his instincts for reform accompanied by a recognition of the realities of tax practice.

Paul G. Rodewald, a Pittsburgh tax lawyer not really known outside that city. I imagine he was a member at the suggestion of John Buchanan, a prominent ALI figure, and the senior partner of the law firm in which Rodewald was a partner.[13] Rodewald had a solid tax grounding, somewhat conservative in his thinking, but not to the extremes that his senior partner went.

Harry Rudick, a prominent New York lawyer who had been a consultant to the Treasury.[14] He was probably the most liberal of the group, and the one most interested in pushing reforms. But his mind was also aware of the pull of day-to-day tax practice.

Judge Goodrich and President Tweed were ex-officio members.

The group was remarkable in many ways. All the regular members had a solid grasp of tax law. More important, all approached each issue in as objective a fashion as humanly possible, clearly putting aside client interests or the often set thinking of the general tax bar. They all had a serious, intellectual interest in the work and carefully read the materials. They worked extremely well as a group, with no cliques or obdurate resistance to the thinking of others. Matters were decided by a consensus approach, without votes being taken. Each had the patience to reason with a minority viewpoint and a minority, always a shifting group, would not press too insistently for acceptance of their views. Fortunately also, the Reporters, who had known some of the members before, had full rapport with the group. We were free to press our viewpoints, argue as equals over an issue, but always recognizing when the decision did not go our way that the matter was settled. All in all, however, there were few disagreements. Rather, material prepared by the Reporters would be reshaped by the Reporters as the discussion brought forth better insights and a wider range of factors to be considered.

To secure a professional check on the conclusions, the Tax Policy Committee formed a Tax Advisory Group of about fifty tax lawyers, mostly practicing lawyers,

---

12. Randolph E. Paul is discussed in Chapter Two, note 84.

13. The Pittsburgh law firm of which Rodewald and Buchanan were partners was the predecessor of today's Buchanan Ingersoll & Rooney.

14. At his death Harry J. Rudick was both a tax professor at the New York University School of Law and a senior member of the New York law firm of Lord, Day & Lord. *Harry Rudick, 64, Tax Lawyer, Dies; A Lord, Day & Lord Senior Member Since 1940*, NEW YORK TIMES, Jun. 1, 1964, at 29. The Harry J. Rudick Memorial Award is given annually to the outstanding graduate of NYU's tax LLM program.

from various geographical locations to meet once a year. These members were chosen for the prestige and recognition they had achieved in the cities in which they practiced. They presented, as a Group, a complete range of viewpoints, from those customarily seeing at first glance the Treasury's side of an issue to those customarily at first glance seeing the client's or tax practitioner's side. But as far as possible they were also chosen for a willingness to debate issues openly and consider the arguments coming from their opposites. Government tax officials and members of the Board of Tax Appeals (now the Tax Court) were invited to attend. There also was an ABA Section of Taxation Subcommittee which maintained liaison in the corporate area. Disputed matters were generally put to a non-binding vote. However, the Reporters recognized that if this Tax Advisory Group could not be convinced to support a proposal it was very unlikely that the proposal would obtain the backing of the tax bar generally and, hence, be unlikely to succeed if suggested to the Congress. The Tax Advisory Group, on the whole, was composed of lawyers more used to thinking on issues of tax policy — what should the tax law be — than the general tax bar. The latter generally saw the provisions of the Tax Code as tools given to them to plan and structure transactions and did not question the wisdom of the provisions. Usually this approach tended to color any reaction to a tax policy issue by echoing the desires of their clients and by a resistance to change unfavorable to taxpayers in general. The Tax Advisory Group, to be sure in varying degree, was as a whole able to consider tax policy issues free from the strong tug of what a client would desire. The discussions with this Group, and the changes that often resulted, thus strengthened the proposals made under the Project.

All ALI projects, Restatements and legislative, had to secure the approval of the Council of the Institute. In this period the Council, with around forty members, composed of eminent practitioners, judges and a few law professors, was an elite group reflecting the "establishment," and rather on the elderly side. In many respects it was a social organization, with drinks preceding lunch and following the afternoon session, with somewhat of an "old boy" atmosphere. In many respects they partook of the attitudes of Tweed and Goodrich — this is good work, the ALI Reporters are a capable bunch who usually know what they are doing, let's keep our balance and don't become over-serious, end up having some fun by being with companionable people of some esteem. There was no snobbery in this, but rather a reflection of their way of life. Being with them was enjoyable — and fun, and they let the work proceed. On the whole, they were generalists with little knowledge of tax law and its technicalities. Hence, only a very few informed voices joined in the discussion, with their observations mixed with the efforts of the Reporters to explain in almost layman's language the meaning and complexities of a particular provision. On the whole, the Council as a result made few changes in the material. There was always Darrell on hand to lend a soothing, authoritative voice in support of our — his — work. The Council looked at the material once a year, in December.

Proposals approved by the Council then went before the Annual May meeting of the full membership of the Institute. Generally, close to about 750 to a thousand members attended. The voices of these members ranged in all directions. Some, a minority, were well versed in tax law since the project itself had induced them to join the Institute and thus the number of tax lawyer members had increased significantly. Others had a smattering of tax knowledge that came from a general law practice. Some wore their clients' hats, generally not out of a dictatorial obeisance but out of the convictions produced by a long association with their clients' problems and years of adversary contests with the Internal Revenue Service. Some, and generally always the professors, were partial to the Government's point of view. But taken as a whole, it was still a more open-minded group than would be the membership of the American Bar Association Section of Taxation and, even more so, than the corresponding organization of certified public accountants.

The proposals were explained by the Reporters, discussion ensued with support and objection voiced, the Reporters here and there agreed to changes though, on the whole, defended the proposals as presented, votes were taken and differences settled. Generally, even most frequently, the work of the Reporters was approved, either because the Reporters were persuasive or more likely because there was a sense of going along with those that had done the work—voting for the establishment.

And so the Project was launched. Warren and I, as well as the Policy Committee, recognized that tax policy issues had to be viewed at different levels. Some aspects were purely political, such as rates of tax, and not within the province of the Institute. Other issues were also political in the sense they raised fiscal policy questions that had been resolved over the years in an amalgam of the pressures produced by conflicts between Government and private interests, conflicts that could only be decided by Congressional votes and not technical memoranda. There was a clear need to keep the Institute from being drawn into these conflicts. The demarcation lines between those conflicts and the scope of our work was described in these terms:[15]

> The overall objective of the income Tax Project is an improvement of the technical provisions of the present income tax statute. This improvement is to be accomplished by a critical examination, overhauling and revision of those provisions. Consequently, the Project looks considerably beyond a mere codification of the present income tax rules. Its ancestry is not that of the famous Restatements of the American Law Institute. At the same time, the Project is not designed to produce a fully developed "model income tax" in the complete sense of the term. A fiscally complete model income tax would require exploration and decision respecting many issues of an economic, social, and fiscal policy nature, such as the level of rates and exemptions, the desirability of taxing capital gains, the treatment of tax-exempt securities, the function and character of the corporation income tax, the extent of the percentage depletion deduction, etc. Solutions to these problems

15. With a few small differences, the passage below can be found in Stanley S. Surrey & William C. Warren, *The Income Tax Project of the American Law Institute: Gross Income, Deductions, Accounting, Gains and Losses, Cancellation of Indebtedness*, 66 HARV. L. REV. 761, 764–66 (1953).

are not the special province of the members of the Institute. Moreover, for the most part, these issues and others like them are surrounded by the echoes of history and the overtones of responses which are almost emotional rather than analytical. Debate on these issues is therefore neither tranquil nor contemplative. More important, the tempers and passions aroused by that debate would inevitably carry over to the discussion on less combative issues and thereby make objective consideration impossible.

The ground to be covered by the Project thus extends far beyond the areas of codification and restatement but does not reach into the areas of political and fiscal policy. Most of our tax provisions fall within this broad middle ground, and are the provisions which we have come to refer to as the "technical" provisions of the income tax. The term "technical" is not applied to contrast a highly-complicated abstruse provision with a clear, simply worded statutory section. We have no shorthand phrase for the latter, perhaps because there is no need for the phrase—no tax provision is simple and non-technical in that sense! Rather the term "technical" is used to contrast the provisions which are largely shaped by tax technicians, representing both government and taxpayer, with the provisions whose content is determined by the political compromises embodying the resolution by the Congress and the Executive of the conflicting goals of the various pressure groups and forces in our nation. The proper development of the technical provisions is vital to an effective and equitable income tax structure. It is also the area in which the tax lawyer must bear the brunt of the analytical work and policy formulation, and the area in which he can make his greatest contribution to the achievement of a proper income tax structure.

The Project represents a major frontal attack on the technical shortcomings of our federal income tax. It is not intended to be a mere tinkering here and there, a tidying up of this provision and a smoothing out of another. It is sufficiently flexible to permit the scope of revision that is responsive to the problem. All of the major segments of the income tax—gross income, deductions, gains and losses, accounting provisions, partnerships, trusts, corporations, income from sources abroad—are within its scope. Clearly such a sweeping re-examination will raise questions of substantive policy. The necessary improvements cannot be accomplished without making some policy changes, either through adopting a different statutory treatment than exists at present or through rejection or alteration of an existing judicial rule or administrative interpretation. However, since the problems at the political and fiscal policy level are beyond the scope of the Project, the policy changes will exist only at the technical level. While in certain areas technical policy merges at some point into political or broad economic questions, an awareness of the difference between the two and a desire to stay within the confines of technical policy affords proper guidance. With respect to the policy changes at the technical level, the proposals adopted must necessarily be those thought

> defensible as proper tax policies. The changes must be within the boundaries of governmental and political realities.
>
> One final point as to the character of the Project. The Project does not seek a statute that need not be changed from year to year, except for changes relating to rates, exemptions and the like. An unchanging tax law is an impossible and undesirable goal. What is needed, instead, is a technically efficient statute which covers current problems and as much of their future ramifications as can reasonably be foreseen. It is proper, in considering a particular provision, to aim for a result less likely to be subject to patchwork amendment or drastic change in the immediate future. But essentially the task will always be one of periodic stocktaking and overhauling.[d]

We went to work early in 1948, Warren in New York at Columbia and I in Berkeley at California. It was a heady task, challenging, and somewhat awesome. No one had attempted such a task before, and indeed it seemed almost presumptuous to undertake. Yet it offered the promise of progress if logic, imagination and technical knowledge could be carefully applied. Both Warren and I had enough experience to guess at the limits of the range within we could make improvements and still avoid the derogatory term of "too theoretical—just what a couple of professors would do."

We prepared a tentative outline of our task and then began with the easier parts of the Code. These were the definition of gross item and the enumeration of items included in income and those excluded. An interesting question at once arose—should we define "income." Economists in various countries had wrestled for years and years, with disagreements and incompleteness. The economist's definition accepted in the United States, that of Haig-Simons: "Personal income is the algebraic sum of (1) the market value of rights exercised in consumption and (2) the change in the value of the store of property rights between the beginning and end of the period in question"[e] covered too much ground—for example, imputed income would be included—and this would put a strain on the exclusion sections. The Supreme Court's definition in *Eisner v Macomber*—"'Income may be defined as the gain derived from capital, from labor, or from both combined,' provided it be understood to include profit gained through a sale or conversion of capital assets"[f] was incomplete—would it cover cancellation of indebtedness?—and would in cases at the periphery force continued dissection of the terms "labor" and "capital." Moreover, the Supreme Court had in *United States v Kirby Lumber Company*[g] explicitly abandoned the search for a definition. We therefore decided to place the tax on "income" as a base, amplifying the term as far as possible through enumerated inclusions and exclusions designed to provide certainty for the problems raised by previous case law, and leaving future problems to be decided in a rational way through the combinations of flexibility and restraint that the term "income" afforded. So "gross income" was defined in terms of "income," with certain inclusions and exclusions set forth.[16] Then "net income" was defined through a set of specified

16. For a fuller discussion of the ALI's approach to the definition of gross income, *see id.* at 769–76.

deduction items and specified non-deductible items. The overall structure was not a major departure from the existing law, but the separate inclusions and exclusions from income and the deductions refined areas of existing uncertainty and here and there changed the existing rules, e.g. the treatment of prizes and awards, of annuities, of cancellation of indebtedness, transfers of property in marital settlements, elimination of the ordinary and necessary requirements for deductions, and explicit denial of expenditures contrary to public policy.

As Warren and I prepared drafts of proposals, we began to recognize that major improvement could be made in the mechanical way the substantive rules were set forth in the present law. While the drafting of the present law had been shaped by skilled hands, still there had been no overall reexamination of the results. We were not experts ourselves and so we consulted frequently with specialists in legislative and other forms of drafting.[h] It may be interesting to set forth the conclusions we reached on drafting, especially since, as will be explained later, this phase of the work was not adopted by Congress:

DRAFTING ASPECTS

It is difficult to describe the manner in which the statutory material proposed in the Draft is actually drafted. A reading of the Draft itself is obviously required. Mention might be made, however, of some of the goals that were sought, if not always kept in mind.

(1) Section Breakdown and Length. — The Draft follows the section subdivision designations used in the Internal Revenue Code: Section 100, subsection (a), paragraph (I), subparagraph (A), clause (i). An effort was made, however, to have as few subdivisions as possible within a section, and most sections stop at the paragraph level. The result is to produce more sections since the breakdown is avoided by dividing a section into several sections. But it is believed that a large number of sections is easier to handle than are fewer but more complicated ones. Moreover, the Draft attempts to make the paragraphs and subparagraphs as short as possible.

(2) Cross References. — Cross references are used in the text only when they will materially aid in the understanding of substantive content. While it is desirable to keep cross references at a minimum, the statute would lose in clarity if they were omitted entirely. The use of definitional cross references at the end of the sections, as indicated [below], makes it easier to achieve a balance in the use of cross references in the text.

(3) Title Headings. — Title headings are used for each section and as much as possible within each section in order to identify its theme. They are avoided within a section if they obviously duplicate the text and the text is brief.

(4) Drafting Style. — For many years the drafting of the federal revenue statutes has been on a high level in comparison with statutory drafting generally. Skilled draftsmen have molded our present tax provisions. Their work has been quite creditable, especially when one keeps in mind such pressures

as the need for hasty action and the demands often made by idiosyncrasies present in the legislative process. While recognizing the quality of revenue drafting, however, some urge that it is too inclined to present rules in terms of verbal formulae without an expression of the basic purposes to be served. The result is a somewhat artificial, stilted prose, renowned for the length of its sentences and the complexity of their structure.

Improvement is not easily achieved. It is believed, however, that the proposed Draft is on the whole less stilted and less artificial in style. An effort, by no means always fulfilled, has been made to keep the sentences less unwieldy in length and structure. In the more complex substantive sections the purpose of the section is often stated at the outset, preceded by a phrase such as "in order that." Some sections do no more than present a summary of the sections to follow, so as to indicate the substantive pattern to be developed. Transitions in layman's language, as "However, if" to cover provisos, are utilized. "Such" is avoided wherever possible and "the," "this," or "that," used instead. Superfluous verbiage has been dropped, when the superfluity is seen. For example, "income" replaces "the amount of income," "less" is used instead of "reduced by," and "described in Section oo" in place of "in situations to which Section 00 is applicable."[17]

DEFINITIONS

The income tax statute, being highly technical, is bound to transform a great many words into tax words of art. The process by which everyday words become technical tax terms is that of statutory definition, and the income tax is thus necessarily replete with definitions. Statutory definition has its drafting problems — the definitions in each instance must be precise; a word once defined must thereafter be used in the same sense throughout the statute or the reader must be told that it is not so used. The latter can be accomplished by using a different term or a qualifying adjective with the basic term. But the process of definition also has its mechanical problems. Basic among these is the task of informing the reader, as he reads along in a provision, when an ordinary English word is a word of tax art. The reader who reads "gift" must be alerted that the word is used in a special tax sense, that is has an artificial meaning not conveyed by its everyday usage. And so with "person," "dividend," "capital asset," and hundreds of other words. How is this to be done?

(1) List of Definitions. — The Draft has in subchapter A a complete list of all defined terms, together with references to the sections where the terms are defined. This list is thus an index of definitions. The section references also indicate whether a word is specially defined for a particular section or group of sections, or whether its definition holds for the entire statute. Thus the taxpayer can easily ascertain

17. *Id.* at 828–30.

which are the defined terms used in the statute. Since the interpretation of undefined terms is often aided by the content of the defined terms, this complete index of the defined terms should facilitate application of statute.

(2) Definitional Cross References. — This index of definitions is not, however, sufficient to meet the entire problem since it does not by itself inform the taxpayer reading a substantive section whether a particular word is a defined term or not. True, if he suspects that the term "gift" is defined elsewhere he can then look in the index to confirm or refute his suspicion. But this trial and error method is far from adequate. Several possible solutions to this problem were considered. Each defined term could be accompanied by a cross reference every time it appeared in the text. But cross references in text are clumsy, break up the continuity, and should be kept at a minimum. The defined term could be identified everywhere it appeared by special print, for example, italics, quotation marks, underlining, black letter type, or small capitals. But this solution might complicate the task of reading and cause numerous printing errors.

The Draft adopts the solution of including definitional cross references at the end of each section. If a defined term is used in a section, at the end of that section the term is listed with a cross reference to the section in which it is defined. The reader is thus immediately informed whether tax words of art are being used in the section, without the text being cluttered with cross references. A few defined terms are used so often, however, that they are grouped in one section at the beginning (Section X12) and no further cross reference is made to them other than in the general index. The reader is, however, constantly made aware that a few defined terms are used in the text without definitional cross references because the cross reference heading at the end of every section reads "Cross References to Defined Terms Not Contained in section X12." There are about twenty-five very common tax terms in section X12, such as "gross income," "individual," "person," and "taxable year." Most of these terms are defined in Section X12 itself. A few are defined only in the substantive provisions to which they most immediately relate, so that the Section X12 listing is merely a cross reference. Thus "taxable year," while used often enough to warrant a listing in section X12, is so closely related to the accounting provisions that it is advisable to leave its definition to those provisions. For the same reason, it was also decided not to have the definitions themselves appear in the index of definitions. Rather, each term is defined in the section to which it most closely relates so that the definition is a part of the logical development of the section.[18]

18. *Id.* at 827–28.

In those years we were not aware of what later became tax expenditure analysis, an approach to the income tax that divides the law into two parts, the normative structure and the special provisions that are essentially a form of government spending—assistance—to accomplish certain non-tax objectives, such as incentives and relief from hardship. We therefore, in our ignorance, continued the present law process of mixing these two types of provisions without any identification of their different character. We could not eliminate the tax expenditure provisions—e.g. deductions for property tax, mortgage interest, consumer interest, charitable contributions, medical expenses, capital gain treatment, etc.—for that step would clearly contradict the policy constraints which guided us. We did, more as a matter of logical presentation, separate deductions between those related to gainful activity and those involving personal, family or living expenses (the latter being essentially the tax expenditure items). It would have been interesting to see an organization of a Code that was based on the normative provision-tax expenditure provision dichotomy.

As Warren and I worked through the spring of 1948, we saw more hands were needed. We therefore commenced the practice of hiring each year, for a year, two current law school graduates who had outstanding records and hopefully the temperament for the concentrated work. One research assistant worked in New York, one in California. Initially, they were selected by Warren and usually from Columbia Law School; later, when I moved east, I also did selecting, usually from Harvard. A large number of these Research Assistants, then only known within the circles of their class and school, have gone on to prominence in the tax bar. Warren and I immodestly but, I believe, not inaccurately credited their success to the training and then the recommendations they received from us.[i, 19]

As our work moved into the more difficult provisions involving taxable entities—corporations, partnerships, trusts, etc.—both the Reporters and the Policy Committee recognized the need for the specialized experience that could be obtained through high-level lawyers engaged in these fields in their daily practice. So we added the following special consultants to our group, who worked along with Reporters, Policy Committee and Research Assistants:

Accounting :	Maurice Austin, N.Y.
Corporations :	Edwin S. Cohen, N.Y. Thomas N. Tarleau, N.Y.
Partnerships :	J. Paul Jackson, Texas (also Member of Policy Committee) Mark H. Johnson, N.Y.
Trust and Estates :	H. Brian Holland, Boston Lloyd W. Kennedy, Chicago

19. Surrey is correct, in his note i, that Ruth Ellen Goldman later became Ruth Goldman Schapiro. After her apprenticeship with the ALI tax project, Schapiro became a prominent tax lawyer as a partner with the New York firm of Proskauer, Rose, Goetz & Mendelsohn. *Ruth G. Schapiro, 64, Leading Tax Lawyer*, New York Times, Aug. 28, 1991, at D21.

Gross Income and Deductions :	John M. Maguire, Cambridge
Gain and Loss in Respect of Property :	J. Rex Dibble, Los Angeles (June, 1949 to June, 1950)

At this time I was also preparing a casebook on the income tax.[20] The two tasks dovetailed nicely—the work on the casebook disclosed areas that required attention in the ALI Draft and the ALI work provided insights for the structure and contents of the casebook. The combination of tasks, though thus overlapping, meant steady work also. Practically every month I had to fly east for meetings with the Policy Committee, the Tax Advisory Group, the Council and the Annual Meeting. Indeed when I transferred to Harvard in 1950. Judge Goodrich was immensely relieved that the strain on the budget caused by my travel costs would end.[j]

Thus the work progressed from year to year and the drafts grew in number and purpose: Preliminary Memorandum No. __________ for the Policy Committee; Discussion Draft No. ____________ for the Advisory Committee; Council Draft No. _______________ for the Council; Tentative draft No. ____________ for the Annual meeting.[21] The drafts in each case set forth the proposed statutory material. There then followed comments providing explanatory material enumerating any changes from existing law and, where necessary, amplifying the statutory text. The work finally came together in 1953 and we published a series of law review articles designed to make the material known to a wider audience. Because of my greater familiarity with the material and a willingness to undertake the task, I would prepare the initial article draft for my co-authors to examine and improve.[k]

What should be done with these drafts? This question was answered by the political events of 1954. A Republican President had been elected and for the first time in years both the House and Senate were Republican. The Chairman of the House Ways and Means Committee, Harold Knutson, a stubborn, inflexible person with little knowledge of the tax system but great determination to achieve goals he formed, decided that in 1954 there should be a complete revision of the 1939 Code and subsequent laws—all to be done in one year. This was not to be a compilation as in 1939, but a complete substantive revision. However, the incoming policy people in the Treasury, as well as the career Internal Revenue Service (then Bureau of Internal Revenue), were completely unprepared for this task. The Institute, therefore, saw the demand for the quick drafting of a Code as the opening for consideration of its Draft. So the Reporters were asked quickly to put together as one Draft all of the work that had been done. This was entitled "Federal Income Tax Statute, February, 1954 Draft"

20. The casebook was, of course, Federal Income Taxation, *supra* note 8.

21. The editors share Surrey's apparent lack of enthusiasm for tracking down the precise numbers of the various types of memoranda and drafts, and so the blanks left by Surrey remain in these published memoirs. One number, however, is readily available. Surrey and Warren produced a total of eleven tentative drafts for presentation to the full membership of the ALI at its annual meetings. Herbert F. Goodrich & Paul A. Wolkin, The Story of the American Law Institute, 1923–1961, 29 (1961).

and was in two thick volumes. 960 pages in all.[22] The Institute prefaced the volumes with these words:

> February 15, 1954
>
> This volume (numbered February, 1954, Draft — Volume I) and its companion (numbered Volume II) represent the work which has been done on the American Law Institute Income Tax project up-to-date. The text and the comments thereto have never been promulgated by the Institute as were the Restatements, for example. Their publication has been authorized by the Executive Committee.
>
> What we have done in the course of the many months of hard work which has gone into this material is to act as an objective research and advisory body. The material in these volumes represents a composite of the views of the Tax Policy Committee and the Reporters assisted by the Special Consultants and guided by the consideration given to the material within the Institute framework by the very helpful Tax Advisory Group, the Council of the Institute and the Institute membership and by informal discussion with other organizations in the tax field. We think that it represents pretty accurately a consensus of the thought of tax specialists and others interested in tax matters.
>
> It is coming out to you now because a revision of the Internal Revenue Code is being worked upon by the Congress. If there ever was a time when an objective study would be helpful to a legislative group in considering problems, this seems to be the time. The Institute does not lobby for this Code or any other piece of legislation. But if its considered, objective view is helpful to those responsible for our tax structure, the project will be well worth all the hard work it has required from many people.
>
> Herbert F. Goodrich,
> Director
> The American Law Institute[23]

The Draft could obviously be of great utility to the Government tax personnel faced with the huge task thrust upon them by Chairman Knutson. But at this critical point, the personalities of the Government policy makers took an unfortunate turn.

Norris Darrell, a Republican, had been offered the position of Treasury Under Secretary (George M. Humphrey was the Secretary),[24] which would put him in charge of tax policy. An acceptance on his part would obviously guarantee a full consideration

22. AMERICAN LAW INSTITUTE, FEDERAL INCOME TAX STATUTE (drft., Feb. 1954) [hereinafter FEDERAL INCOME TAX STATUTE]. Of the 960 pages, 374 were proposed statutory language and 587 were explanatory comments.

23. *Id.* at iv.

24. George M. Humphrey served as Treasury Secretary from 1953 to 1957. Prior to his appointment he was president of M. A. Hanna Company, a steel manufacturer. Philip D. Carter, *George M. Humphrey Dies: Eisenhower Treasury Secretary*, THE WASHINGTON POST AND TIMES HERALD, Jan. 21, 1970, at C6.

of the usefulness of the ALI Draft in devising the new Code. But Darrell declined the offer for reasons never publicly articulated: was it because a senior partner of Sullivan and Cromwell, John Foster Dulles, had already left to be Secretary of State; was it because Darrell, who was an unchallenged, uncriticized leader of the New York tax bar, realized that as an important Government figure he would be necessarily the target of some criticism and often be embroiled in dispute with the Congress, some of which he would lose? Perhaps he had no taste for such a public life. The result was that with his declination of the appointment, the ALI Code lost the opportunity, albeit if unforeseen, for a full, sympathetic examination by the Government.

After Darrell declined, the top Treasury tax policy post was filled by Professor Dan Throop Smith of the Harvard Business School, appointed as Special Assistant to the Secretary.[25] Smith was clearly a conservative in his thinking and sympathetic to the general views of the business community. Democratic tax policy was anathema to him. He viewed the taxation of capital gains as almost immoral. But he had a streak that moved him to oppose what he called "shenanigans," such as any non-taxation of fringe benefits. Smith was an economist by training and taught a tax course in the Business School. He was not highly regarded as a fiscal policy expert by his fellow economists, but rather seen as a person with good knowledge of the effect of tax rules on business transactions. Not being a lawyer, he had not been involved in the ALI project. Smith and I, though of opposite political and tax views, had shared teaching a tax policy seminar at Harvard and were good friends. Smith, despite his dogmatic views, was a cheerful, friendly person. He had even asked me whether he should accept the position, and knowing his desires, I urged him to do so. The other Treasury position that had a bearing on tax policy was that of General Counsel, and this was filled by Kenneth Gemmill.[26] Gemmill was a tax lawyer in Philadelphia, with no experience in dealing with issues of tax policy and, alas, not a member of the ALI Tax Advisory Group—who can fully read the future?

---

25. Economist Dan Throop Smith was on the faculty of the Harvard Business School, and later a senior research fellow at the Hoover Institution. As Surrey notes, Smith was unmistakably a conservative. Upon his arrival at Treasury in 1953, Smith told an interviewer, "I'm a professor all right. But I was always violently anti-New Deal." Ronald Sullivan, *Dan T. Smith Dies, Tax Policy Expert*, NEW YORK TIMES, Jun. 2, 1982, at B5.

26. Kenneth W. Gemmill, a longtime partner in the Philadelphia law firm of Dechert Price & Rhoads, took a leave of absence to work at Treasury in 1953 and 1954. For most of his time at Treasury he was an assistant to the Treasury Secretary. He served as Treasury acting general counsel only from June to September of 1953, after which Elbert P. Tuttle became general counsel. Tuttle, who had been a tax litigator with the Atlanta firm of Sutherland, Tuttle & Brennan, remained at Treasury only until August of 1954, when the Senate confirmed his appointment to the Fifth Circuit Court of Appeals. Nevertheless, Tuttle, rather than Gemmill, was Treasury general counsel in the critical time frame for the 1954 Act. Apparently Gemmill, in his capacity as assistant to the Secretary, took on the legislative work that would more commonly be assigned to the general counsel—so much so that Surrey remembered him as having been general counsel in the crucial months. Gemmill's fifteen minutes of fame came two decades later, in 1974, when he defended President Nixon's tax returns (which Gemmill had not prepared) to the House Judiciary Committee. Gemmill retired from the practice of law in 1979 and died in 1998. *Husband and Wife Die Separately, Yet Together*, PHILADELPHIA INQUIRER, Dec. 15, 1998, at 107.

Thus, Smith and Gemmill, the two central Treasury officials, had little or no real knowledge of the contents of the ALI Draft. I suspect also that Smith, aware of my liberal views from our prior joint teaching, had an adverse reaction to the ALI work, without knowing its contents, because of my participation. Unlike Smith, Gemmill had no deeply felt views on tax policy and appeared to be willing to follow Smith's lead. Warren and I did invite ourselves to several conferences with Smith and Gemmill to explain the ALI work and offer both it and our personal assistance in connection with the 1954 revision that was underway. We were politely received and that was the end.

At the Capital, Colin Stam, the Chief of the Congressional Joint Committee on Internal Revenue Taxation and the accepted top Congressional expert on tax matters, desired to leave his imprint on the new 1954 code. He had his own ideas and held almost a veto power over Treasury proposals. But he and his staff had not done any prior work in preparation for the task. Stam, after giving in 1947 his perfunctory approval to the initiation of the ALI Project, had thereafter played no part in the work. Moreover, like Smith, he looked on Surrey as too liberal in tax policy matters.

Time was also a major factor militating against a full, unbiased consideration of the entire ALI Draft. The legislative tax draftsmen simply had no time to consider the format and drafting techniques utilized in the ALI Draft. The 1939 Code format had to be followed if a revision was to be done in one year. This lack of time also was a serious factor inhibiting consideration of the many substantive changes made by the Code in the determination of taxable income, though here and there some ALI material was used.[l]

The pressure of time, working against consideration of some of the ALI work, on the other hand, led to a favorable use of other ALI material. The persons in Internal Revenue working on Code revision were hard pressed to develop in time necessary revisions in a number of important fields, such as the taxation of partnerships and trusts. The 1939 Code was characterized by only a few sketchy provisions on how to treat these entities. The litigation since 1939 and the experience of the tax bar with those provisions showed that the Code left many questions unanswered. It was far from satisfactory to have the courts, slowly through decisions as litigation developed, struggle to find the answers. Coherent rules could not be developed through this process. Fortunately, in these two areas the ALI had spent considerable time and thought in formulating a full scale statutory treatment that provided the necessary answers to the problems then perceived. As a result, those Government lawyers working on the 1954 revision utilized practically all the ALI proposals in these areas.

The House bill in these two areas — trusts and partnerships — followed very closely the ALI Draft and the Senate accepted the result.[m] Thus, the basic Code provisions today that relate to trusts and partnerships represent a major ALI contribution to the present Code.[27]

27. Compare FEDERAL INCOME TAX STATUTE, *supra* note 22, at vol. 2, 21–46 (trusts) and 86–119 (partnerships), with Internal Revenue Code of 1954, Pub. L. No. 83-591, §641-92 (trusts) and §701-771 (partnerships), 68A Stat. 1, 215-38, 239-54. Most of the 1954 Code provisions relating to trusts and partnerships remain in the Code today (with the same section numbering).

The corporate provisions, such as the treatment of corporate distributions and reorganizations, proved difficult for both the ALI and the 1954 Code personnel: The ALI had suggested a number of changes from the present law, such as the nonrecognition of gain to shareholders on a corporate liquidation; rules differentiating shareholder debt from shareholder equity; the elimination of the "continuation of business" test in net loss carryovers on reorganization; an objective collapsible corporation test; uniform attribution rule; a more compact definition of "reorganization"; a brother-sister corporation limit for multiple corporations.[28] These suggestions did not find their way into the House or Senate bills.

However, the present Code rule on "section 306" stock—sale of preferred stock earlier distributed as a dividend to common stock shareholders—was adopted in the Senate Bill as a solution for the "preferred stock bailout." The House Bill had dealt with the problem in a different, and unsatisfactory manner. The tax bar, led by Tarleau and Cohen, warned Smith and Stam that their treatment was over-generous to taxpayers and wouldn't work, and then cooperatively developed the present treatment modelled on the ALI Draft.[29] Other Code corporate features traceable in part to the ALI Draft were the elimination of the proportionate interest test in section 351 situations, the transfer of attributes on a corporate reorganization, and a rule allowing tax-free corporate divisions.[30] The House bill had moved in the ALI direction on tax-free liquidations but the Senate returned to the earlier law. All in all, much greater progress was made in 1954 revision in the partnership and trust provisions than in the corporate area.[n]

The ALI tax work continued after the 1954 revision but at a somewhat slower pace. Some of the tasks undertaken were a review of the corporate tax rules adopted in 1954 and suggestions for revision undertaken with an American Bar Association Section of Tax Liaison Committee;[o] a preliminary consideration of the estate and gift taxes looking to their correlation with the income tax;[p] further consideration of the 1954 Code trust and partnership rules;[q] a proposal for revision of the capital gains area with the objective of providing a detailed statutory definition of capital gains that codified and clarified the court decisions in this troublesome field.[r] All of this provided interesting material for the ALI May Annual Meetings, and lively discussion of the proposals took place.[s] But the Government was not interested in pursuing these topics, and therefore they were not considered for legislative action.

In 1961, on my appointment as Treasury Assistant Secretary for tax policy, I ended my relationship with the ALI Project. I soon found myself involved in many matters that I initiated and which had a higher priority than the 1954–1960 ALI material. So

---

28. For the ALI's corporate tax proposals, *see* Federal Income Tax Statute, *supra* note 22, at vol. 2, 1–85.

29. Internal Revenue Code of 1954, § 306, 68A Stat. at 90–91. The provision survives today (with the same section number), albeit with modifications.

30. Respectively, Internal Revenue Code of 1954, § 351, 68A Stat. at 111–112; § 381, 68A Stat. at 124–129; and § 355, 68A Stat. at 113–114. All three provisions remain in the Code today (with the same section numbers), albeit with modifications.

I did not fit that material into the Treasury schedule for legislative action. The ALI continued its work in the tax field through study of a revision of the estate and gift taxes, drawing to some extent on the earlier ALI material. Professor A. James Casner of Harvard Law School was the Reporter, and the Project had its own set of consultants, Tax Advisory Group and liaison with the American Bar Association.[31] The Project was finished in 1969.[t] The Treasury also made its own study in this area, and kept aware of the ALI developments. The conclusions reached were only partially similar, but both studies were reinforcing in the view that serious revision was needed. These studies were utilized in 1976 when the Congress suddenly turned to a consideration of these taxes.

The venture of the ALI into the federal income tax, and later the estate and gift taxes, on the whole must be pronounced a success.[32] A considerable number of its recommendations found their way into the statute, sometimes almost verbatim, sometimes with the language changed by the Congressional draftsman but with the underlying substance unchanged. Other material provided ideas for discussion in law review articles and casebooks, ideas that increased an understanding of the structure of the tax law and the policy issues which were presented.

Twenty-four years later (?), the ALI would once more look at these taxes in a Project which I supervised — but that is another chapter.[33]

Notes

a. The history of the Institute is set forth in ALI, *The American Law Institute 50th Anniversary* (1973). Brief versions appear in Norris Darrell & Paul A. Wolkin, *American Law Institute*, 52 New York State Bar Journal 99 (February 1980) and Bernard G. Segal, *First Vice President's Letter*, 5 ALI Reporter 1 (October, 1982).

b. Report of Special Committee on Future Program, Submitted to the Council [of the Institute], March 18, 1947.

c. Randolph E. Paul, Studies in Federal Taxation (1937; Second Series, 1938; Third Series, 1940); Randolph E. Paul, Federal Estate and Gift Taxation (1942); Randolph E. Paul, Taxation in the United States (1954).

d. Stanley S. Surrey, *The Income Tax Project of the American Law Institute*, 11th Annual Institute on Federal Taxation, New York University 1049 (1953).

e. Henry C. Simons, *Personal Income Taxation* 50 (1938).

---

31. A. James Casner taught at Harvard Law from 1938 to the 1970s, serving as associate dean from 1961–1967 and acting dean from 1967–1968. In addition to federal income tax issues, Casner also advised the ALI on property, trusts, and estate taxes. *A. James Casner, 83, Harvard Law Professor*, New York Times, Sep. 4, 1990, at 11.

32. For a description and evaluation of the ALI's efforts in the federal tax arena from the late 1940s to the twenty-first century (with an emphasis on the Income Tax Project culminating in the 1954 draft Federal Income Tax Statute), in some respects more detailed than Surrey's account in this Chapter, *see* Lawrence Zelenak, *The Almost-Restatement of Income Tax of 1954: When Tax Giants Roamed the Earth*, 79 Brook L. Rev. 709 (2014).

33. Surrey describes his efforts in the 1970s and early 1980s as supervisor of the ALI's Federal Income Tax Project of that era in Chapter Eight.

f. 252 U.S. 189, 207 (1920).

g. 284 U.S. 1 (1931).

h. The drafting consultants were: Lincoln Arnold, Washington, formerly of the Office of the House Legislative Counsel, U.S. Congress; Fred Chait, Philadelphia; Professor Harry Jones, Columbia Law School; Professor John MacDonald, Executive Director, and Mrs. Laura Mulvaney, Assistant Director of Research, of the New York State Law Revision Commission; John O'Brien, New York, formerly of the Office of the House Legislative Counsel, U.S. Congress; James Craig Peacock, Washington; John Simms, Office of the Senate Legislative Counsel, U.S. Congress; Henry Wood, New York, formerly the Senate Legislative Counsel, U.S. Congress.

i. Some names that come to mind, largely because they have remained in contact with us in various ways, are: Robert Anthoine, Alan J.B. Aronsohn, Richard Barnet, Marvin Chirelstein, Moses G. Ehrlich, Arthur A. Feder, Frederick Gelberg, Ruth Ellen Goldman (now Schapiro (?)), Sherman Kamin, Arthur L. Kimmelfield, William D. McKee, Arthur Michaelson, Fred M. Ringel, Jesse G. Silverman, H. Peter Somers, Lawrence M. Stone, Marvin T. Tepperman, Robert M. Winokur. The complete list is in American Law Institute 50th Anniversary 1973, *supra* note a, at 192.

j. I recall a travel incident that reflected the influence of Judge Goodrich. The San Francisco airport is a good ways out and I reached it by bus from the center of the city, after a plane trip from Cambridge. However, one night the plane arrived quite late and the prospect of long bus travel was not enticing. Should I take a taxicab home? This question was answered by another "What would Judge Goodrich do in these circumstances?" I took the taxicab.

k. The principal articles are:

> *The Income Tax Project of the American Law Institute: Deductions, Accounting, Gains and Losses, Cancellation of Indebtedness* (with Warren), 66 HARV. L. REV. 761 (1953);
>
> *The Income Tax Project of the American Law Institute: Partnerships, Corporations, Sale of a Corporate Business, Trusts and Estates, Foreign Income and Foreign Taxpayers* (with Warren) 66 HARV. L. REV. 1161 (1953);
>
> *A Technical Revision of the Federal Income Tax Treatment of Corporate Distributions to Shareholders* (with Cohen, Tarleau and Warren) 52 Columbia Law Rev. 1 (1952);
>
> *A Proposed Revision of the Federal Income Tax Treatment of Trusts and Estates—American Law Institute Draft* (with Holland, Kennedy and Warren) 53 *Colum. L. Rev.* 316 (1953);
>
> *A proposed Revision of the Federal Income Tax Treatment of the Sale of a Business Enterprise—American Law Institute Draft* (with Cohen, Tarleau and Warren) 54 COLUM. L. REV. 157 (1954);
>
> *A Proposed Revision of the Federal Income Tax Treatment of Partnerships and Partners—American Law institute Draft* (with Jackson, Johnson and Warren) 9 TAX. L. REV. 109 (1954).
>
> *See also Surrey, The Income Tax Project of the American Law Institute, 31 Taxes 959 (1953); Surrey, The Income Tax Project of the American Law Institute*, 11 NYU TAX INSTITUTE OF FEDERAL TAXATION 1049 (1953); Miller, *The Law Institute's Income Tax Project: An Answer to a Challenge*, 37 AMER. BAR ASSOC. J. 191 (1951).

l. For example, the treatment of prizes and awards; the elimination of "surtax net taxable income" and "normal tax net income," replaced by "taxable income."

m. A concise enumeration of the House, Senate and Conference Committee Bills in relation to the 1939 Code appears in the Internal Revenue Code of 1954, Comparison of the Principal Changes Made in the 1939 Code by H.R. 8300 After Action By House, Senate, and Conference (August 13, 1954), compiled by the staffs of the Joint Committee on Internal Revenue Taxation and the Treasury Department.

n. Once the 1954 Code revision became law, the ALI personnel wrote a number of law review articles describing the rules in various areas. These articles, when compared with those cited in note k above, indicate the differences between the ALI Draft and the 1954 Code. The initial drafts of these articles were written by the Research Assistants who had worked in the area (my name appears as one of the authors in each article):

The Internal Revenue Code of 1954: Trusts, Estates and Beneficiaries (with Sherwin Kamin and William C. Warren), 54 COLUM. L. REV. 1237 (1954);

The Internal Revenue Code of 1954: Partnerships (with J. Paul Jackson, Mark H. Johnson, Carolyn K. Tenen and William C. Warren), 54 COLUM. L. REV. 1184 (1954);

The Internal Revenue Code of 1954: Corporate Liquidations (with Edwin S. Cohen, Frederick Gelberg, Thomas N. Tarleau, and William C. Warren), 55 COLUM. L. REV. 37 (1955);

The Internal Revenue Code of 1954: Corporate Distributions, Organizations, and Reorganizations (with Edwin S. Cohen, Jesse Silverman, Jr. Thomas N. Tarleau and William C. Warren), 68 HARV. L. REV. 393 (1955);

The Internal Revenue Code of 1954: Carry-overs and the Accumulated Earnings Tax (with Edwin S. Cohen, Paul A. Phillips, Thomas N. Tarleau, and William C. Warren), 10 TAX L. REV. 277 (1955);

The Internal Revenue Code of 1954: Tax Accounting (with Maurice Austin, William C. Warren, and Robert M. Winokur), 68 HARV. L. REV. 257 (1954).

o. ALI, Federal Income, State and Gift Tax Statute, Report for 1956–57 (May 14, 1957); ALI, Income Tax Problems of Corporations and Shareholders (October 31, 1958).

p. ALI, Federal Income, Estate and Gift Tax Statute, tentative Draft No. 9 (May 7, 1954); Tentative Draft No. 10 (April 30, 1955); Tentative Draft No. 11 (April 24, 1956).

q. ALI, Federal Income, Estate and Gift Tax Statute, Tentative Draft No. 11 (April 24, 1956).

r. ALI, Draft of a Study of Definitional Problems in Capital Gains Taxation (April 22, 1960); ALI, Discussion Draft of a Study of Definitional Problems in Capital Gains Taxation (October 20, 1960).

s. This material, although presented for discussion at the May Annual Meetings of the Institute, was not presented for a final vote of the Institute, following the practice adopted with the February 1954 Draft. Changes resulting from votes taken at the Meeting on particular topics were incorporated in the material.

t. American Law Institute, Federal Estate and Gift Taxation, Recommendations of the American Law Institute and Reporters' Studies (1969).

FIVE

International Tax Activities

Part I, 1938–1960

First Experiences[a]

International tax matters, both as to policy and legislative developments, played a minor role in the Treasury Department in the years I served in the Office of Tax Legislative Counsel. The lawyers in that office and the economists in the Office of Tax Analysis[1] [Check name] had no experience in the international tax field and only a smattering of knowledge. One piece of legislation in the World War II years, the preferential rate for Western Hemisphere Trade Corporations, highlighted the ignorance of the Treasury technicians, as well as that of the staffs in Congress.[2] A very minor special proposal, pushed by several lawyers to relieve a few corporations operating entirely in Latin America from the World War II increase in corporate tax rates, was drafted so poorly because of that ignorance that it opened a wide preferential tax rate for U.S. companies exporting to any country in North America. The drafting error was made in the Office of House Legislative Counsel, who used language whose effect was far broader than the proposal required. Yet none of the technicians comprehended the error. It was not until then that this preferential rate for Western Hemisphere Trade Corporations was ended.[3] The other World War II international tax legislation fared better. A lobbying effort had been made to extend the foreign tax credit provision, which granted a credit against the United States income tax as applied to foreign source income for foreign net income taxes on that income, to gross income or gross receipts taxes levied by some underdeveloped countries. These countries in general applied such taxes to certain activities, shipping, for example, which the countries found difficult to tax on a net income basis. Unless care were taken, this proposal would, unwisely and erroneously as a matter of tax policy, make all foreign gross sales taxes available for credit, which some tax lawyers also desired.

1. Surrey correctly notes that the relatively new "Office of Tax Analysis" housed the public finance economists led by Roy Blough. *See* Chapter Two for more on the origins of this office.

2. Surrey's work with the Western Hemisphere Trade Corporation provision is discussed in greater detail in Chapter Two. *See* Chapter Two, note 106.

3. The referent of "then" in Surrey's sentence is obscure. In any event, Congress did not repeal the Western Hemisphere Trade Corporation provision until 1976. Tax Reform Act of 1976, Pub. L. No. 94-455, § 1052(b), 90 Stat. 1520, 1648.

The Treasury replied with a carefully and narrowly drafted provision to credit only a tax levied "in lieu of" a net income tax otherwise applicable to the activity. This language persists today as Section 903 of the Code and has achieved the narrowing result intended by the Treasury.[4]

When World War II ended, I was introduced to the world of international tax treaties. Commencing with work in the League of Nations, efforts had been made prior to the War to develop bilateral "double taxation" treaties designed to reduce or eliminate the taxation of the same item of income by two countries.[b, 5] The efforts had resulted in the United States in only two such treaties adopted before World War II, those with France and Sweden.[6] The Bureau of Internal Revenue, through Eldon P. King, an Assistant Commissioner, was in charge of negotiating these treaties.[7] While the actual negotiations were handled in this fashion, the treaties were formal documents signed within the State Department and subject to approval by the Senate Committee on Foreign Relations, not the Senate Committee on Finance.

In 1946 King renewed the negotiations of these treaties. He invited Roy Blough, Director of the Office of Tax Analysis (?) and myself as Tax Legislative Counsel to participate in a trip to Europe, with an assistant from each office.[8] Blough's assistant was Henry Bloch, a young economist born in Alsace-Lorraine (?).[9] We travelled in treaty talks to France, Belgium and the United Kingdom [Check] and the trip resulted

---

4. Internal Revenue Code of 1954, Pub L. No. 83-591, § 903, 68 Stat. 730, 287.

5. Although it is unclear which scholarly articles Surrey had in mind (in his note b) regarding the historical origins of these treaties, possibilities include Stanley S. Surrey, *The United States Taxation of Foreign Income*, 1 J. L. & ECON. 72 (1958) and H. David Rosenbloom & Stanley Langbein, *United States Tax Treaty Policy: An Overview*, 19 COLUM. J. TRANSNAT'L L. 359 (1981) [hereinafter *United States Tax Treaty Policy: An Overview*].

6. The United States had two bilateral double tax treaties before World War II. They were with France (1932) and Sweden (1939). *See generally, United States Tax Treaty Policy: An Overview, supra* n. 5, at 374. For more on bilateral double tax treaties, *see generally*, Reuven S. Avi-Yonah, *Double Tax Treaties: An Introduction*, in THE EFFECT OF TREATIES ON FOREIGN DIRECT INVESTMENT: BILATERAL INVESTMENT TREATIES, DOUBLE TAXATION TREATIES AND INVESTMENT FLOWS 99–106 (K. P. Sauvant and L. E. Sachs ed., 2009).

7. In the 1930s and '40s, Eldon P. King was officially special deputy Commissioner of Internal Revenue. *Eldon P. King, Expert for IRS*, THE WASHINGTON POST, Nov. 13, 1962, at B3.

8. Roy Blough was, indeed, director of the Office of Tax Analysis from 1938–1946. This was the office containing the many public finance economists that Surrey references throughout his memoirs. In the 1950s, Blough continued his engagement with international tax matters, when he became principal director of the economic affairs department at the United Nations from 1952–55. *Roy Blough, 98, Official at the Treasury*, NEW YORK TIMES, Mar. 2, 2000, at C25. Roy Blough's personal papers are housed at the Harry S. Truman Presidential Library in Independence, Missouri.

9. Henry Simon Bloch was originally from Kehl, Germany which was then part of Alsace-Lorraine. He earned a doctorate in economics from the University of Nancy and emigrated to the United States in 1937 and taught at the University of Chicago. After WWII, he joined the U.S. Treasury Department and then the United Nations. He subsequently went on to become an investment banker at Zinder International and then E. M. Warburg Pincus & Company. From 1953–1986, he taught at the law school and the school of International Affairs at Columbia University. *Henry S. Bloch, 72, An Investment Banker*, NEW YORK TIMES, Mar. 2, 1988, at A20; Henry S. Bloch & Cyril E. Heilemann, *International Tax Relations*, 55 YALE L. J. 1158 (1946).

in treaties with ____.[10] I must confess that while I thus received a superficial knowledge of the negotiating process and the substantive content of the treaties, I really had no integrated view of the basic policy objectives sought in these treaties and the content of the articles adopted in response. Roy and I made a two-day detour by train from the mission to Berlin to see General Lucius Clay, in charge for the United States of American activities for the Occupation. Roy at least had the excuse—and it was an excuse because the main idea was to see Berlin—of talking about the economic policies under the Occupation. I just tagged along.

This treaty trip gave Roy a desire to participate more directly in tax treaty policies. A dispute arose in _____[11] between Roy and King over certain policies involved in a negotiation with Canada. Roy then persuaded Secretary Morgenthau to place him in charge of treaty negotiations. As a result, the focus of treaty policy formulation shifted to the economists in Roy's office. My office then did not play a significant role. It was not until I became Assistant Secretary and restructured the Treasury work on international tax matters that the Treasury lawyers really participated in this area.

I did contribute to an important procedural aspect. Colin Stam, the Chief of the Joint Committee Staff (?) suggested to the Treasury that a member of his staff be a part of the treaty negotiating team.[12] I clearly thought this undesirable, since we would be led into compromising our policies to mesh with Stam's desires—and idiosyncrasies. I at once went to see Senator George, Chairman of the Senate Finance Committee and also a member of the Committee on Foreign Relations (?), to object to the suggestion.[13] I pitched my viewpoint on the ground that the negotiation of tax treaties was a function of the Executive Department, and the Congress participated after the negotiation through its constitutional prerogative to ratify treaties. I had no objection to Stam's presenting his views to the Foreign Relations Committee, either directly or through the Finance Committee, when the treaty was up for ratification. Senator George fully understood this division of power between the Executive and Legislative and told Stam to drop his request. This procedure has been followed

---

10. As of 1946, the U.S. had four tax treaties: the pre-WWII treaties with France and Sweden, Canada (1942), and the U.K. (1945). Surrey's blank in the memoirs seems to suggest that new treaties were negotiated with France, Belgium, and the U.K. But there is no historical record of signed treaties from the negotiations. The U.K. treaty already existed and was not revised until 1966; the Belgium treaty dates from 1952; and the French treaty already existed and wasn't revised until 1967. Moreover, it appears that Surrey's memory was imperfect: the 1946 negotiations were with Belgium, Luxembourg, and the Netherlands. 15 *Department of State Bulletin* 73, Vol XV., No. 366 (July 14, 1946) (listing Surrey, Blough, Bloch, and King among the members of the U.S. delegation). According to *United States Tax Treaty Policy: An Overview*, *supra* note 5, the Belgian treaty dates from 1952, Netherlands from 1948, with no Luxembourg treaty in the relevant time frame.

11. The dispute between Blough and King that led Morgenthau to give the economists authority over future treaty negotiations may have taken place in late 1946 or early 1947, before Surrey departed the Treasury Department for an academic career.

12. For more on Colin F. Stam, *see* Introduction, note 7.

13. Senator Walter F. George (D-GA) was chair of the Senate Finance Committee from 1941–46, and chair of the Foreign Relations Committee from 1940–41, and again from 1955–57. *Walter F. George*, THE WASHINGTON POST AND TIMES HERALD, Aug. 5, 1957, at A10.

through the years and the Congressional Staff does not participate in the negotiations. I did, however, as Assistant Secretary confer informally with Lawrence Woodworth, the then Chief of Staff, to obtain his insights on what might be the Senate's reaction to policies we were pursuing.[14]

I left the Treasury in 1947 obviously with a very limited knowledge of United States tax policies and legislative provisions in the international tax field. Law School tax courses then did not extend to that field and I saw no occasion therefore to extend my knowledge.[15] I did participate in a tax mission to Japan in 1949 and 1950 — more on this event later — but that mission was concerned solely with Japanese domestic tax policies.[16] All this changed when I came to Harvard in 1950 and international taxation became an important part of my life.

The Harvard Law School International Program in Taxation

William S. Barnes had been added to the staff of the Law School in 1950 to investigate research possibilities in the field of foreign law.[17] As part of this research he discussed the subject with Karl E. Lachmann, Chief of the International Tax Section of the Fiscal Division of the United Nations.[18] That Division was one of four divisions of the Department of Economic Affairs, which in turn was one of the four substantive departments of the Secretariat. The Barnes-Lachmann discussions were soon joined

14. Surrey and Woodworth had a productive and cordial professional relationship throughout their careers, especially after Woodworth came out from under the shadow of his longtime supervisor, Stam. For more on Woodworth's relationship with Surrey and the tax policy community, *see generally*, JULIAN E. ZELIZER, TAXING AMERICA: WILBUR D. MILLS, CONGRESS, AND THE STATE, 1945–1975 (1998). For a lengthier discussion of Woodworth, *see* Chapter Ten.

15. Although it is uncertain when international tax law was first taught in U.S. law schools, casebooks on the topic first began appearing in the 1970s and 1980s. *See, e.g.*, WILLIAM C. GIFFORD, INTERNATIONAL TAX PLANNING: MATERIALS ON THE PLANNING OF INTERNATIONAL TRANSACTIONS (1974); DAVID R. TILLINGHAST, TAX ASPECTS OF INTERNATIONAL TRANSACTIONS (1978); and ROBERT HELLAWELL & RICHARD PUGH, THE STUDY OF FEDERAL TAX LAW: TRANSNATIONAL TRANSACTIONS, 1981–1982 (1981). One of the first casebooks on federal income taxation of international transactions used at Harvard was ELISABETH A. OWENS, INTERNATIONAL ASPECTS OF U.S. INCOME TAXATION: CASES AND MATERIALS (1980). Surrey may not have predicted the rise of international tax law as a critical tax policy matter, but when he returned to the Treasury Department in the 1960s, he became one of the central players in the development of U.S. international tax policy. Reuven S. Avi-Yonah, *All of a Piece Throughout: The Four Ages of U.S. International Taxation*, 25 VA. TAX REV. 338 (2005).

16. For more on Surrey's role in the Shoup tax mission to Japan, *see generally*, THE POLITICAL ECONOMY OF TRANSNATIONAL TAX REFORM: THE SHOUP MISSION TO JAPAN IN HISTORICAL CONTEXT (W. Elliot Brownlee, Eisaku Ide, and Yasunori Fukagai, eds., 2013) [hereinafter THE SHOUP MISSION TO JAPAN].

17. William S. Barnes was a 1947 graduate of the Harvard Law School, who would go on to become a professor of international law at the Fletcher School of Law and Diplomacy at Tufts University. *In Memoriam — Spring 2003 Bulletin: William S. Barnes '47*, HARVARD LAW TODAY, Apr. 6, 2003. *Gallery: William S. Barnes*, 19(5) HARVARD LAW RECORD 2 (Oct. 28, 1954).

18. For more on Karl E. Lachmann, *see* Chapter 9, note 11.

by Henry S. Bloch,[19] Director of the Fiscal Division and Associate Dean David F. Cavers and myself.[20] In these talks we developed the idea of Harvard Law School to create an organization to provide a research and training program in cooperation with the United Nations.[21] When general agreement was reached, Mr. Bloch arranged for the following Resolution of the Fiscal Commission of the United Nations:

Text of Draft Resolution H* of the Fiscal Commission of the United Nations

PUBLICATION OF A WORLD TAX SERVICE

The Economic and Social Council,

Having in mind that the promotion of trade and investment between countries is of great importance in the economic development of Member countries;

Having in mind that the establishment of a modern tax structure constitutes an important factor in attracting foreign trade and investment and in promoting national development;

Having in mind that the availability of comprehensive and authentic information on the tax systems of Member countries serves these aims;

Having in mind that the United Nations is best suited to obtain the basic information on national tax systems from Member governments; and

Having in mind that Harvard University, through its Law School, maintains a center of International Law and conducts specialized research in the field of taxation,

Requests the Secretary-General to consider:

(a) The publication of a World Tax Service, providing a continuous service of information on national tax laws and administration;

(b) Keeping this service on a current basis by the publication of a looseleaf or booklet supplement;

(c) Inviting governments in each of the countries to be covered by the World Tax Service to cooperate in supplying the legislative documentation and other materials;

---

19. For more on Henry S. Bloch, see *supra* note 9.

20. David F. Cavers was a 1926 graduate of the Harvard Law School, where he was president of the law review. He taught at Duke Law School and served as associate general counsel of the Office of Price Administration during WWII. He also taught at the Harvard Law School from 1946–1969 and was the school's first associate dean. *David F. Cavers Dies; Legal Scholar Was 85*, NEW YORK TIMES, Mar, Mar. 12, 1988, at 10.

21. The Harvard Law School International Program in Taxation became the initial venture in the law school's development of an international legal studies program. With financial support from corporate donors and the Ford Foundation, the program quickly became a leading training ground for foreign tax officials and a central source for research on international taxation. For more on the origins and early development of the program, *see generally*, Oliver Oldman and Elisabeth A. Owens, *The Harvard Law School International Program in Taxation,* in 54 PROCEEDINGS OF THE ANNUAL CONFERENCE ON TAXATION UNDER THE AUSPICES OF THE NATIONAL TAX ASSOCIATION 570–585 (1961).

(d) The cooperation of Harvard University in this project by providing supplementary research and analysis, based on such materials, and in editing the above information for joint publication;

(e) The possible cooperation of the other universities in this undertaking; and further

Requests the Secretary-General to make a report on such project to the 13th session of the Economic and Social Council, if possible.

* Resolutions proposed by the Commission are designated as Draft Resolutions until approved by the Economic and Social Council.

This Resolution was followed by the following exchange of letters between the honorable Trygve Lie,[22] Secretary-General of the United Nations and Dr. James B. Conant,[23] President of Harvard University:[24]

The final formal step was the following United Nations Resolution:

Resolution of the United Nations Economic and Social Council—
13th Session

Adopted August 10, 1951, Geneva

G

PUBLICATION OF A WORLD TAX SERVICE

The Economic and Social Council,

Having in mind that the promotion of trade and investment between countries is of great importance in the economic development of Member countries;

Having in mind that the establishment of a modern tax structure constitutes an important factor in attracting foreign trade and investment and in promoting national development;

Having in mind that the availability of comprehensive and authentic information on the tax systems of Member countries serves these aims;

---

22. Trygve Lie was a long-serving Norwegian Labor Party politician and UN official. He received a law degree from the University of Oslo in 1919 before serving as Executive Secretary of the Norwegian Labor Party, Minister of Justice, Minister of Trade and Industries, Minister of Supply and Shipping, and ultimately acting Foreign Minister after the German invasion of Norway. After decades of service to his home country he was elected the first Secretary-General of the United Nations in 1952. *Trygve Halvdan Lie*, United Nations Secretary-General (Oct. 28, 2020), https://www.un.org/sg/en/content/trygve-halvdan-lie.

23. James Bryant Conant was a noted chemist and educator. He was a professor of chemistry at Harvard, helped develop the atomic bomb, and served as Harvard's president from 1933 to 1953. After resigning from his post at Harvard, Conant served first as High Commissioner for and later Ambassador to Germany. His series of studies on secondary education published after his return from Germany are credited as the blueprint for modern high school and collegiate curricula. J.Y. Smith, *James B. Conant Dies*, THE WASHINGTON POST, Feb. 13, 1979, at D9.

24. The June 1951 correspondence between Conant and Lie has been omitted from this published version of the memoirs. The full text of both letters can be found in the original manuscript of the memoirs.

Having in mind that the United Nations is best suited to obtain the basic information on national tax systems from Member governments; and

Requests the Secretary-General to consider:

(a) The publication of a world tax service, providing a continuous service of information on national tax laws and administration;

(b) Keeping this service on a current basis by the publication of looseleaf or booklet supplements;

(c) Inviting governments in each of the countries to be covered by the world tax service to cooperate in supplying the legislative documentation and other materials;

(d) The possible cooperation of universities in this undertaking.

As a result of the above discussions and documents the Law School then established the program as part of its newly organized International Legal Studies Program headed by Professor Milton Katz. The commencement of that Program was financed by a grant from the Ford Foundation. The School named me as Director and also appointed me to the Jeremiah Smith, Jr. chair in the international field, one of two new chairs financed under the Ford grant. My friendship with Bloch and immediate interest in the program were the basis of these appointments.

The United Nations and Harvard envisaged a year's program of training at Harvard in tax matters. The persons to be trained would mainly be tax officials from the less developed countries, though academics and interested non-officials were welcome, as well as a few officials from developed countries. The major part of the financing for this training came from the Ford Grant and United Nations funds, with a few trainees financed by their own governments or other funds and by the United States. The annual number of trainees was to be about twenty.

The Harvard program — ITP — commenced in 1952, entered an uncharted area for the Law School.[c] There was no precedent, either at Harvard or elsewhere, for the endeavor. We had to devise a training program, based on our limited experience with the degree of knowledge possessed by the trainees. My experience with the Shoup Japanese Tax Mission helped, and also invested me with a degree of prestige and authority that aided in my relations with the trainees. The first problem was that of language. We had made knowledge of English a qualification for selection — the selection was done by countries presenting names to the funding agencies — but soon found that such knowledge was interpreted in a very elastic way, so that some trainees came to Harvard with only a limited grasp of the language. To remedy this, we set up an English language course to be attended by those with that weakness. Moving on to technical subjects, we developed courses in income taxation, tax administration, public finance, tax policy, and accounting. Our aim was to provide a background running across the tax field that would qualify the trainees for high level positions in their countries. Some of the trainees were already in that posture; we hoped — and our hopes were largely realized — that others would progress to those positions. We also required the trainees to take the basic Law School course on United States tax law, not because we wanted them to develop a full expertise in our law but because we reasoned that on return to their own countries they would be automatically regarded as being experts in our law—they had studied in the United States—and we desired them to have some background in our law so they could handle the questions with confidence.

As the Program developed over the following years through experimentation, a full-fledged curriculum evolved. Staff members were added who had competence in the subjects taught, such as tax administration and public finance, at a level the trainees could absorb. These trainees often had only a limited general education background, supplemented by specialized tax training in their countries. Also, they had tended to work only in segmented parts of their tax system and did not possess a broad grasp of the substance or policy. Many had not seen the inside of a classroom for years nor studied material over an extended period. The work at Harvard was thus really new to them, almost bewildering at first, and arduous throughout the year. But the chance to study at Harvard, to be a part of the Law School, was highly valued by them and kept their efforts at a high level. As the Program developed it became an institution in itself and membership was a mark of prestige in tax circles in their countries.

The participants came from all over the less developed world—Latin America, Asia, the Middle and Near East, Africa. Several countries, Japan, for example, made it a practice to send one or two trainees each year. The success of the program was clearly evident in many ways. A relatively large number of trainees eventually came to occupy the top tax positions in their countries—Director of Taxation, Associate Director, Head of the International Division and so on. When I later became Assistant Secretary and negotiated tax treaties as part of my work, I often found that sitting across the table as the representative of the other country was an official who had earlier been an ITP trainee. As the negotiation progressed and the representative acted with skill and knowledge in advancing his countries' objectives I saw that the training had indeed left its mark. A negotiation with a country so represented was far more satisfactory than that with a country whose officials had no similar training.

A brochure[d] describes the nature of the training when I left in 1961:

THE INTERNATIONAL PROGRAM IN TAXATION

> The international Program in Taxation, established in 1952 as part of the Harvard Law School's broad program in International Legal Studies, provides facilities for research and instruction in the various fields of taxation. The Program's activities are an organic part of the teaching and research at the Harvard Law School. In general, the objectives toward which the Program seeks to contribute are: (1) an enrichment of the life of the Law School through increased and more fruitful participation by students, scholars, lawyers, public officials, and university teachers from other countries; and (2) an extensive and varied program of tax research and training to organize and increase the world's store of knowledge about taxation and to provide

materials and guidance for those involved in the development or improvement of tax systems throughout the world. The taxation curriculum, a one-year plan of study designed primarily for tax officials and other interested persons from abroad, is described in detail in this pamphlet.

THE CURRICULUM IN BRIEF

Summary of Subject Matter and Conduct of Courses.

The taxation curriculum of the International Program in Taxation attempts to integrate the related disciplines of law, economics, accounting, and public administration into a comprehensive one-year program of instruction in taxation. The income tax is discussed from many points of view and occupies a central place in the curriculum. This emphasis is justified by the growing importance of the income tax throughout the world and its suitability for pedagogical purposes in conveying an understanding of major current tax problems. As indicated below, however, attention is also given to other important forms of taxation such as sales taxes and taxes on land, and to newer taxes such as those on value added by businesses and on personal expenditures. Also considered are various problems of overlapping or conflicting tax jurisdiction, including those problems which arise among countries, states, and provinces which are economically integrated with each other in such varying arrangements as customs unions, common markets, or federated countries. [25]

The Program in addition to its training work, also had a research and publication program. Its general contours in 1961 were described as follows:[e]

BACKGROUND

Increased legal knowledge in private international relations involving domestic law, foreign law, and international law is needed to keep pace with America's emergence as a great trading and investing nation. Ever since World War II, the forward propulsion of world events has been reflected in the Harvard Law School curriculum, which is offering an increasing number of courses and seminars in international legal studies,—so much so, in fact, that a new International Legal Studies wing was added to the Law School to house faculty, classrooms, and a library devoted exclusively to continuing development in this area. With the recognition of the fundamental importance of law in the institutional framework for international trade, investment, and economic development, there came also the recognition that areas existed in which even the most basic knowledge was lacking and in which considerable research would be needed. The expansion of trade and investment opportunities abroad increased the demand for more information about for-

25. The editors have deleted the remaining portion of Surrey's block quotes from the 1961 International Tax Program brochure. The deleted quote describes the program's teaching structure and pedagogical goals. The full quote can be found in the original manuscript of the memoirs.

eign taxes. Although some information was available, the lack of comprehensive data made international tax planning difficult.

The United Nations had long hoped for a coordinated body of international tax literature. In its 1951 resolution seeking university aid for such a project, it pointed out that "availability of comprehensive and authentic information on the tax systems of Member States would serve in bringing about the establishment of modern tax structures; and that these, in turn, constitute an important factor in advancing foreign trade and investment and in promoting international development."

Thus, the conclusion by Harvard that research in tax law was highly important was directly parallel to the desires of the United Nations. The research facilities already existing at Harvard, plus the cooperation of the Fiscal and Financial Branch of the United Nations Department of Economic and Social Affairs, made it possible to set up the International Program in Taxation in response to the invitation of the United Nations.[26]

American companies to whom tax information affecting international business was essential had independently attempted the difficult process of developing research in this area. When the Program was conceived, they appreciated the importance of financial support for this center where research in international tax problems could be done economically, systematically, and with the help and cooperation of the various foreign countries themselves.

RESEARCH

The Program's research goals are twofold: to develop knowledge of taxation as it relates to international trade, investment, manufacturing, and to the problems involved in establishing and operating common markets or other regional arrangements; and to explore the significance of taxation in relation to the pace of economic development, particularly in less-developed countries. This research established a primary source of information useful to those who are aiding the economic development of foreign countries; it has given lawyers, accountants, scholars, and government officials an opportunity to learn how other countries are meeting their revenue needs and developing sound tax systems. It has also proved valuable to businessmen trading and investing in areas which are already economically developed.

The World Tax Series was a very ambitious and novel project. Early on Assistant Dean William S. Barnes became its Director. The goal was a comprehensive volume describing, in English, the entire substantive tax law of a given country. We started by preparing a comprehensive format which each volume had to utilize, chapter by

26. The editors have deleted the remaining portion of Surrey's block quote describing the subsequent World Tax Series publications that emerged from the International Tax Program's research goals.

chapter, and an organization and numbering of topics within each chapter. A glossary of common terms to be used throughout the volumes was devised. The goal of the format and glossary made possible the use of the Series for comparative purposes, since a reader reading the volume say on France could readily go from a particular tax aspect in that volume to the same subject matter discussed under a parallel place in the volumes for other countries. The method of preparation for a volume involved a research assistant, at Harvard, familiar with the language but not necessarily the tax law of the country, to prepare an initial draft. This draft was then sent to a correspondent in the particular country selected by Harvard on the basis of recognition in his country, broad knowledge of its tax system, and an ability to organize material. Generally the correspondent was a high tax official, a prominent academic, or a prominent practicing tax lawyer. The final draft was checked by the tax unit within the country and given a final editing at Harvard. The names of the Harvard research assistant and the foreign correspondent appeared as co-authors.[27] The work on the U.S. Volume was done by Marvin Chirelstein (later a professor at Yale Law School), Elisabeth A. Owens (later a professor at Harvard Law School) and Langdon Day.[28] I acted as the United States correspondent.[29]

These volumes, of course, were the first in the United States to present in one volume a careful, relatively deep, substantive description of the tax systems of the various countries. What was early—and surprisingly—discovered was that these countries did not in their own literature have a comparable volume. The United States itself was not an exception to this situation. The World Tax Series thus really had to start from scratch, and could not in any way just be English translations of a foreign study.

---

27. The first publication in the Harvard Law School World Tax Series was a series of papers presented at a 1954 conference. *Papers and Proceedings of the Conference on Agricultural Taxation and Economic Development, Held Under the Auspices of the International Program in Taxation*, Law School of Harvard University, January 28–February 3, 1954 (Haskell P. Wald ed., 1954).

28. Marvin Chirelstein was a member of the Yale Law School faculty from 1965–81. He was a graduate of the University of California, Berkeley, and the University of Chicago Law School, where he was editor-in-chief of the law review. He practiced tax law in Washington, D.C. and New York, before embarking on his academic career. In 1981, he left the academy to practice law briefly and then returned to teach at Columbia University until his retirement. *Chirelstein, Marvin A*, NEW YORK TIMES, Feb. 18, 2015, at A19. Elisabeth Ann Owens was a graduate of Smith College and Yale Law School, and she began her legal career as a research assistant to Surrey in 1951. Although she remained at Harvard for the rest of her career (except for a stint at Treasury with Surrey in the 1960s), she did not receive tenure until 1972, when she became the first women to be tenured in the history of Harvard Law School. Surrey was extremely supportive of tenure for Owens; it is possible she would have been tenured at some point in the 1960s if Surrey had not been at Treasury. Herma Hill Kay, *In Memoriam: Elisabeth A. Owens*, 112 HARV. L. REV. 1403, 1407 (1999) (describing Surrey as Owens' "chief advocate" and as "extremely supportive" of her tenure). Owens' first book, THE FOREIGN TAX CREDIT (1961) is a classic of international tax scholarship. William H. Honan, *Elisabeth Owens, 79, Pioneer at Harvard Law*, NEW YORK TIMES, Nov. 20, 1998, at B11. Langdon Day was a Harvard trained tax lawyer who practiced with Sullivan and Cromwell. *E. M. Langdon Day, Expert in Tax Law*, PHILADELPHIA INQUIRER, Mar. 21, 1973, at 52; *Langdon Day, Tax Law Expert*, BOSTON GLOBE, Mar. 21, 1973, at 39.

29. The U.S. study was published as MARVIN A. CHIRELSTEIN, LANGDON DAY, ELISABETH A. OWENS & STANLEY S. SURREY, TAXATION IN THE UNITED STATES (World Tax Series, 1963).

Indeed, the Series were seen by the countries covered as a valuable contribution to their tax literature.

It became clear that the goal of the Series—currently supplemented volumes on about 30 countries—was way beyond the resources of the Program. So after the initial volumes the work was altered to a few volumes over the years. The Commerce Clearing House publishing company was given the rights to publish loose-leaf periodically supplemented volumes and this has done been for ___.[30]

The second branch of the research activity was the publication of material on tax aspects of U.S. foreign investment and economic aspects of various public finance areas. The initial volume, requested by the United Nations, was United States' Income Taxation of Private United States Investment in Latin America, by Stanley S. Surrey, D. T. Smith (of the Harvard Business School) and Ira T. Wender (a New York Lawyer) (1953).[31] This was followed by an ambitious and innovative study by E. R. Barlow (of the Harvard Business School) and Wender on Foreign Investment and Taxation (1955).[32] The book analyzed United States policy on the taxation of foreign income, presented case histories of business decisions to invest abroad, and explored the extent to which taxation was a factor in influencing foreign investment. It was the first comprehensive attempt at this task and really marked a turning point in the study of U. S. international tax law and policies. Up to this point, the law and policy had largely been the terrain of about a handful of company tax executives and lawyers. At the time, one executive prophetically remarked that the Program and its research marked the end of their domination of the field. This volume was followed by Gibbons (a tax lawyer), Tax Factors in Basing International Business Abroad (1977),[33] a description of the tax treatment of corporations organized in "tax haven" countries which summarized the laws of thirteen such countries and analyzed U.S. tax law relevant to the use of "tax havens." It was, of course, a fine "how to do it" volume on these tax havens. But it had the other purpose, understood in the ITP, of focusing attention on the subject of tax havens and what should be the U.S. appropriate policy toward them.

I followed with a lengthy article, Current Issues in the Taxation of Corporate Foreign Investments, 56 Columbia L. Rev. 815 (1956). In this period corporations engaged

---

30. Presumably, Surrey is trying to list the number of volumes in the series. According to a 1972 article in the Harvard Law Record, at that time books on eleven countries had been published, with three more (Belgium, Japan, and the Netherlands) in the works, although it is unclear whether any of the pending works were ever published. Michelle Scott, *Tax Program Celebrates Years of International Research*, HARVARD LAW RECORD, Mar. 30, 1972. Worldcat lists World Tax Series books on 12 countries: Australia, Brazil, Colombia, France, India, Italy, Mexico, Sweden, Federal Republic of Germany, Switzerland, U.S., and the U.K.

31. STANLEY S. SURREY, D.T. SMITH, & IRA T. WENDER, UNITED STATES INCOME TAXATION OF PRIVATE UNITED STATES INVESTMENT IN LATIN AMERICA (UNITED NATIONS, DEPARTMENT OF ECONOMIC AFFAIRS, 1953).

32. E.R. BARLOW AND IRA T. WENDER, FOREIGN INVESTMENT AND TAXATION (1955).

33. WILLIAM J. GIBBONS, TAX FACTORS IN BASING INTERNATIONAL BUSINESS ABROAD: A STUDY OF THE LAW OF THE UNITED STATES AND OF SELECTED FOREIGN COUNTRIES (1957).

in foreign activities were pressuring Congress to reduce the scope of U.S. taxation on the income from those activities and both Congress and the Republican Administration wavered indecisively on the policies to adopt. The article was a strong attack on the proposals and their underlying thesis, that current tax policies hindered U.S. foreign investment. I pursued the same view in testimony before Congressional Committees (add Boggs).[f]

Other research covered path-breaking volumes on various technical but important aspects of U.S. tax law, such as Owens (a research assistant in the Program and later Professor of Law), The Foreign Tax Credit (1961), which was instantly recognized as the authority on the subject.[g] The Program thus in a variety of ways developed a growing literature in international taxation and public finance.[h]

The work with the ITP plus membership in several tax missions abroad, enabled me to obtain a considerable amount of information on tax administration in developing countries. This led to one of the first articles on the subject, Tax Administration in Underdeveloped Countries, 12 University of Miami Law Review 158 (1958). (The adjective kept shifting around in this period — underdeveloped, less developed, developing). This was a version of a paper delivered in 1954 in Rio de Janeiro, Brazil at a meeting of the International Institute of Public Finance, then a small annual gathering of public finance economists. The meeting was my introduction to the international non-governmental organizations working in taxation.

From the ITP work in this period, there developed the Law School course in International Trade and Investment. At first I gave a seminar in Comparative Taxation and then a seminar on Taxation of International Trade and Investment for the more advanced participants in the Program plus a few interested Law School students, especially graduate students. Among the early members of these seminars was Helmut Debatin,[34] then on the Staff of the West German Finance Ministry and later ______[35] in West Germany, followed by a career as an Under Secretary in the United Nations, and Pierre Kerlan, then in the International Tax Division of the French Ministry of Finance, and later its Chief and to become the senior tax official in the ranks of career international tax officials.[36] Later, in a two-part course on Legal Problems of Doing Business Abroad given jointly with Professor Kingman Brewster, I handled the tax part of the course. Brewster and Professor Milton Katz then decided to develop a

---

34. Helmut Felix Debatin was a German tax lawyer and later a tax law professor. He obtained his LLM in tax law at Harvard in 1956 and later became ministerial director in the Federal Ministry of Finance in the Federal Republic of Germany (FRG). When the FRG was admitted into the United Nations, he subsequently became Assistant Secretary General for Administration. 16 UN CHRONICLE 107 (Jul. 1979).

35. It is unclear what Surrey expected to add to the blank at the end of the description of Helmut Debatin's career. Perhaps it was a reference to Debatin becoming a tax law professor at the University of Hamburg or his subsequent role as the founding partner of a Cologne-based tax law firm.

36. Pierre Kerlan served in the French Ministry of Finance in high-level international tax positions in the 1960s and 1970s. He co-authored a volume as part of the World Tax Series of Harvard Law School's International Program in Taxation. MARTIN NOOR & PIERRE KERLAN, TAXATION IN FRANCE (1966).

non-tax course in ____.[37] In turn I introduced a new course, ____,[38] into the Law School curriculum for third-year and graduate students. It was among the first, perhaps the first continuous law school course on the subject. There being no adequate course materials, I prepared a lengthy xeroxed set of materials. I was on the verge of turning these into a published casebook when I left the Program in 1961.[i]

My position as Director of the Program ended when I entered the Treasury. For a brief period, Professor Milton Katz, Director of the International Legal Studies Program supervised the ITP.[39] He was followed by Oliver Oldman,[40] who had come to the staff in 1955 as ITP Director of Training, and was named a Professor on the Faculty in 1959. Under Professor Oldman's direction the Program continued on a steadily expanding course. Training continued, growing more sophisticated through the years as knowledge of tax and public finance in developing countries grew. The ITP developed links with government agencies here and abroad and continued its research and publication activities. It inaugurated a Visiting Scholars Program to bring one or two academics in the tax field annually to the ITP. It also established an International Tax Program Liaison Committee, composed of U.S. corporations interested in the Program's research work who contributed annual amounts to the Program. The Director met from time to time with this Committee to review the work of the Program and solicit ideas for its research activities. ITP remains today an important part of the Law School's activities and occupies a high level of prestige among the other countries, especially the developing countries. It was indeed one of the Law School's successful innovations.[j, 41]

---

37. The non-tax course developed by Katz and Brewster was likely a class based on their subsequently published casebook. MILTON KATZ & KINGMAN BREWSTER, JR., THE LAW OF INTERNATIONAL TRANSACTIONS AND RELATIONS: CASES AND MATERIALS (1960). For more on this new course, *see generally*, Milton Katz & Kingman Brewster, Jr., *New Course will be Offered in International Law Field,* HARVARD LAW RECORD, March 20, 1958, at 2. Milton Katz was a Harvard Law School professor, who administrated the Marshall Plan after World War II. Milton Katz; *Professor Administered Marshall Plan,* LOS ANGELES TIMES, Aug. 19, 1995, at A18. Kingman Brewster was a Harvard Law School Professor, the president of Yale University, and the United States Ambassador in London during the Carter Administration. Eric Pace, *Kingman Brewster Jr., 69, Ex-Yale President and U.S. Envoy, Dies,* NEW YORK TIMES, Nov. 9, 1988, at D29.

38. The course that Surrey taught was likely International Aspects of U.S. Income Taxation. While Surrey taught the course in the 1970s, Elisabeth Owens taught it from 1964–1969. Before he departed for Treasury in 1961, Surrey also taught a two-week course in the Harvard Law School Summer Program of Instruction for Lawyers on Taxation of International Trade and Investment. HARVARD LAW RECORD, Apr. 9, 1959, at 20.

39. Katz directed the Harvard Law School International Legal Studies Program from 1954 to 1974, confirming Surrey's account. Wolfgang Saxon, *Milton Katz, Teacher, Dies at 87; Was Law Expert and U.S. Envoy,* NEW YORK TIMES, Aug. 11, 1995.

40. Oliver Oldman joined the Harvard Law School faculty in 1955, as director of training for the International Tax Program. He went on the tenure track in 1959, and was promoted to full professor in 1961. He became director of the International Tax Program in 1964. *Minoru Nakazato & J. Mark Ramseyer, In Memoriam: Oliver Oldman,* 122 HARV. L. REV. 1296, 1296 (2009).

41. Despite the mention in Surrey's note j, there does not appear to be a Harvard University Bulletin. Moreover, the 25th anniversary of the International Tax Program would have been in 1977, not 1972 as Surrey cites.

International Tax Missions — Japan

The [following passage] is the Foreword to a Report in four volumes, with both an English and Japanese text, side by side for each page [describing the U.S. Tax Mission to Japan led by Carl Shoup]:[42]

> The present report on the Japanese tax systems is submitted to the Supreme Commander for the Allied Powers, at whose request the Tax Mission was formed.
>
> The chief aim of our mission has been to draw up a plan of a permanent tax system for Japan. Emphasis has therefore been placed on considerations that go beyond the financing problems of the present and the coming fiscal year. Nevertheless, we have found it necessary to specify in some detail how our recommendations affect the 1949–50 and 1950–51 budgets. The long-term program must be of a kind that can be put into force without endangering the stabilization recently achieved with the aid of the recommendations made in the spring of 1949 by the Dodge Mission.
>
> The long-term program itself could have been either of two kinds. We could have recommended a rather primitive type of tax system, one which would depend on external signs of income and wealth and business activity, not on carefully kept records and intelligent analysis of difficult problems. Such a system could raise the required revenue, but it would perpetuate the gross inequities among taxpayers, dull the sense of civic responsibility, keep the local governmental units in uneasy financial dependence on the national government, and give rise to undesired economic effects on production and distribution. Moreover, we soon became convinced that the current difficulties in obtaining fair and efficient administration of the tax laws, and a high degree of compliance by the taxpayer in Japan need not be taken as inevitable. Our aim therefore has been to recommend a modern system, which depends upon the willingness of business men and all taxpayers of substantial means to keep books and to reason carefully about some fairly complicated issues of equity. For the small taxpayer, at the same time, the task of filing returns and paying the tax should be kept a simple one. Under this approach, we see no reason why Japan may not within a few years, if she so desires, have what would be the best tax system in the world. In any event, the consistent aim of this report has been to keep open the road that may lead to that goal.
>
> What we are recommending here is a tax system, not a number of isolated measures having no connections with one another. All of the major recommendations, and many of the minor ones, are interconnected. If any of the major recommendations are eliminated, some of the others will thereby be-

42. The editors have inserted this opening sentence before the block quote to provide some context for Surrey's use of the block quote describing the U.S. tax mission to Japan,. In the original memoirs, this was Surrey's first sentence after the block quote from the Report.

come of less value, or even harmful. Consequently, we disclaim responsibility for the results that may follow the adoption of only part of our recommendations. For example, we have devised a tax system that avoids the double taxation of corporate income under the national income taxes, and at the same time blocks permanent tax avoidance. Among the essential parts of this system are the full inclusion of capital gains and the full deduction of capital losses, with permission to spread the gain over a series of years, and with the exemption of large capital gains that are due merely to a change in the value of money. If capital gains and losses were to be included not in full but under some percentage plan like that now in effect, our set of recommendations for corporation and individual income taxes would have to be revised extensively ...

The recommendations in this report are those of the tax mission, and no one in the GHQ or the Eighth Army, or in the Japanese Government, is in any way responsible for them. We have attempted to adapt the recommendations to the needs of the various sections and divisions in GHQ, the officials of each of which have their own set of difficult problems to face, and who have nevertheless gone to considerable lengths to find a solution acceptable from all points of view. But the responsibility for this report attaches to us alone.

... The members of the tax mission, and their professional connections, are as follows: Dean Howard R. Bowen, College of Commerce and Business Administration, University of Illinois; Professor Jerome A. Cohen, Department of Economics, College of the City of New York; Mr. Roland F. Hatfield, Director of Tax Research Department of Taxation, St. Paul, Minnesota; Professor Carl S. Shoup, School of Business and Graduate Faculty of Political Science, Columbia University, (Director of the Tax Mission); Professor Stanley S. Surrey, School of Jurisprudence, University of California, Berkeley, California; Professor William Vickrey, Graduate Faculty of Political Science, Columbia University; and Professor William C. Warren, School of Law, Columbia University.

The Report marked the climax of a really amazing U.S. tax mission, probably the most important made by United States tax experts.[43] It shaped to a major extent the post-war Japanese tax structure and contributed directly to the development of the high level technical skills in taxation now possessed by the Japanese. The Mission also made the Shoup name known to nearly all Japanese, a remarkable result for a technical mission. The Shoup Report passed into the annals of Japanese history and

43. The central charge of the Shoup mission was "to frame a tax system that both strengthened a democratic state and helped accelerate the pace of capital investment and economic development" in Japan. By referring to the U.S.-led investigation as a "mission," its American leaders gave it "an aura of public service." But in reality, the Japanese mission, like the other tax assistance provided before and after WWII, was often aimed at strengthening American economic and political interests. *Introduction: Global Tax Reform and an Iconic Mission*, THE SHOUP MISSION TO JAPAN, *supra* note 16, at 1–12.

more than 30 years later is still remembered with honor in the Japanese public finance profession.[44]

The Shoup mission was the result of an inspired thought of Harold Moss, the head of the Internal Revenue Division in the Economic Section in the General Headquarters of the American Occupation Organization, under General MacArthur, the Supreme Commander for the Allied Powers in Japan (SCAP).[45] Moss, an official of the United States Internal Revenue Service on leave, had the responsibility under the Occupation for supervising the operation of the then current Japanese tax system. He decided the task was highly important and demanded far more competence than his office possessed. With MacArthur's permission he came to the United States in 1949 and persuaded Professor Carl S. Shoup of the Columbia University Economics Department to organize a mission to work over the summer. This did not require much persuasion for Shoup, a respected public finance authority, had an adventurous streak which responded at once to the request. But, though he understood the general importance of the mission, he greatly underestimated the respect and significance it would have for the Japanese people. Shoup had worked briefly in the Treasury when I was there, so he had some acquaintance with me. Also, Professor Warren of the Columbia Law School, my collaborator on casebooks, told Shoup I would be useful as the other lawyer in the group. Shoup asked me to join them, to which, owing to a similar adventurous streak, I at once agree. This was clearly to be a working mission, and wives were left behind.

Because my Law School had a later closing date, I arrived two weeks after the others. With the simulated rank of a Brigadier General in the Army [Check],[46] I flew to Japan in an army plane. Because of rank, although I was in civilian clothes, all the officers on the plane had to wait until I entered or left—rather amusing for a person who in the Navy had been only a Lieutenant, junior grade. Even more amusing was our lodging in the Imperial Hotel in Tokyo, which because of my low rank I had been barred from entering in 1945.

While each member of the Mission kept current with overall developments and the knowledge gradually being acquired, each had a specific assignment. My assign-

---

44. For the continuing legacy of the Shoup mission in Japan, *see, generally*, Satoshi Sekiguchi, *Corporate Income Tax in Postwar Japan and the Shoup Recommendations*, in THE SHOUP MISSION TO JAPAN, *supra* note 16, at 365–396.

45. L. Harold Moss was a Bureau of Internal Revenue agent appointed by General MacArthur as head of SCAP's Internal Revenue Division. Moss began working at the BIR in 1932 and quickly rose up the ranks of collection agents. He gained MacArthur's trust and friendship through his collection efforts when Moss was stationed in Manila. By 1940, he was chief of the Far Eastern division of the BIR. During the war, he served as an intelligence officer and aviator in the Navy. After the war, he returned to the BIR and in 1947 he worked with the U.S. Army as tax advisor and acting budget advisor to the South Korean interim government. Following his efforts in post-war Japan, Moss had a lengthy career in high-level IRS international tax positions. W. Elliot Brownlee and Eisaku Ide, *Shoup and the Japan Mission*, in THE SHOUP MISSION TO JAPAN, *supra* note 16, at 195–198; *Tax Loss Feared on Yields Abroad*, NEW YORK TIMES, May 23, 1957, at 65.

46. The editors have been unable to verify Surrey's rank during the Japanese tax mission.

ment was to cover the administration of the Japanese tax system that we would recommend. The Mission had assigned to it some junior officials in the Ministry of Finance who spoke English. Those who worked most closely with us, were Sumio Hara and Keiichiro Hirata,[47] both highly intelligent, informed on the current Japanese tax system, and very friendly companions. In later life both rose to high positions in the Government. We also had assigned to us Shigeharu Takahashi,[48] a young American citizen of Japanese descent who had studied in the field of agricultural economics. He was to act as our full-time interpreter of both language and customs.

My first two weeks, starting June 4, 1949, were spent in Tokyo in a steady round of interviewing in as many ways as I could think of those persons whose work touched the tax system. The doors had already been opened for the interviews, both because we had the authority of SCAP and equally important because the Shoup Mission was so widely known. Shoup had made several appearances on Japanese television and his friendliness, obvious sincerity, and absence of any pomp and circumstance at once appealed to all the Japanese. He, and his group, were as a result regarded as friends of the Japanese people working to devise a system that would be in the best interest of all.

The flavor of my work can be gathered by listing some of the interviews I made, always making notes in a notebook that somehow still survives![49] Head of the National Tax Administration Agency and many of its officials, SCAP personnel in the tax office, Japanese and foreign accountants and the Japanese Institute of Public Accountants, the Agriculture Ministry, the Union of Tax Employees, the Tokyo Chamber of Commerce, officials of foreign corporations operating in Japan, academic economists and teachers of administrative law. So it went, with persistent but friendly questions, confirming these facts, finding difference as to others, gathering the varying views on the good and bad parts of the existing systems and on the changes to be made. The days were fully occupied with the interviews. In the evenings the group would meet to exchange opinions gradually being formed.

Then around June 20 the focus of our work shifted from Tokyo to the rest of Japan. Shoup was a firm believer in getting the views of the population in general

---

47. Sumio Hara was the head of the Tax Systems Department of the Japanese Ministry of Finance's Tax Bureau. His proficiency with English is explained largely by time he spent in England prior to the outbreak of World War II. Keiichiro Hirata was Director of Japan's Central Tax Office. He was an active author who later wrote a seminal paper describing the breakdown of the Japanese tax system in 1949 that precipitated the Shoup tax mission. *See*, W. Elliot Brownlee and Eisaku Ide, *Shoup in the "Social Laboratory,"* in THE SHOUP MISSION TO JAPAN, *supra* note 16, at 229; Ryo Muramatsu and W. Elliot Brownlee, *Tax Reform During the American Occupation in Japan: Who Killed Shoup?* in THE SHOUP MISSION TO JAPAN, *supra* note 16, at 263.

48. Shigeharu Takahashi was a University of Chicago trained economist who spent most of his career (26 years) as an agricultural economist for the World Bank. *Shigeharu Takahashi*, SAN FRANCISCO EXAMINER, Aug. 25, 2000, at 21.

49. It is unclear whether the notebook that Surrey is referring to has been preserved. If it exists, it might be part of the Stanley S. Surrey Papers at the Harvard Law School archives in "Tax Mission (1), 1949," "Tax Mission (1), 1950," and "Tax Mission (2), 1950," Identifiers 28-2, 28-3, and 28-4, respectively.

and not just those of the persons who worked in Tokyo. A railroad combined sleeping and dining car with a chef was placed at our disposal and with it we travelled throughout three (?) of the Japanese islands.[50] A train would let the car off at a station, and the car would stay there, perhaps for several days, until we were ready to leave. It would then be attached to a train going to our next destination. In each city we followed the same procedure — a visit to the Head of the Regional Tax Bureau or other senior tax official in the city and a dinner given by the top civilian officials in the city. But then we worked at different pursuits in the various cities. In Hiroshima we met with several unions of government officials, to obtain their views on exemption levels and other aspects of the system, and whether their negotiations centered on pre-tax or post-tax take home pay (it was the former but they understood the tax system). In Yahata we went through the steel works questioning employees at random on their wages and amount of tax withheld, which they all knew. We then donned miner's clothing and went through a coal mine at Omita. It was both an amusing and characteristic scene, reminding me of the Mrs. Roosevelt cartoons.[51] We crawled to the very end of the mine where Shoup stopped a Japanese using a pick axe to get at coal to ask him about the tax system. With no surprise on his face and complete self-control the worker gave Shoup the amount of his wages, the amounts of tax withheld and the exemptions to which he was entitled. We thus recognized that the Japanese people could readily grasp the essentials of a tax system. In Fukuoka, I questioned the Procurator's office on the tax and other cases he handled, what lawyers did, the court system and their operations. All of the group in many cities performed one rite together. Shoup was followed by newspaper reporters, cameramen, even television crews in many cities. In some cities we desired to talk with small shopkeepers. So an arrangement was made with the media that they could come with us to the first interview, get their news and pictures. Then we would be free to see other shops alone. The agreement was kept, and at random, in a group or several of us, we would walk into a shop to question the shopkeeper on whether he thought the tax system was fair, how it could be changed, and so on. Always we received direct answers and no refusals to talk.

At Kummamoto, we visited a Training School for lower tax officials, went through a factory to see its books and records, and I talked to the Bar Association Head. In Beppu, a minor resort, we relaxed for a couple of days but also talked with the local SCAP official in charge of tax matters. In Hamoda, a small fishing town, I talked with the Fishing Association and then with individual fishermen as they worked on their equipment or came ashore — what did they think of the tax system, was it fair or un-

---

50. In *Shoup in the "Social Laboratory"*, in THE SHOUP MISSION TO JAPAN, *supra* note 16, at 232, Brownlee and Ide describe as the group's "most ambitious journey" a two-week trip through much of Honshu and Kyushu. The description includes a nice episode in which Shoup, Surrey, and translator Takahashi arrive unannounced at Nagano Communist party headquarters.

51. A famous Robert J. Day *New Yorker* cartoon (published June 3, 1933) depicts two coal miners deep underground; one of the miners says to the other, "For gosh sakes, here comes Mrs. Roosevelt." Surrey's reference to "cartoons" rather than "cartoon" may have been a slip. Robert J. Day, *For gosh sakes, here comes Mrs. Roosevelt*, NEW YORKER, Jun. 3, 1933 (editorial cartoon).

fair, were they being taxed and on what basis. Generally Takahashi accompanied me on these trips and he and I knew the routine well by then. In Kamogawa, an agricultural area, we visited the markets and then Takahashi and I drove a few miles outside the city to question farmers hauling their crops in carts to the markets. At random we questioned some of them briefly — they had to get on to market — along the line of questioning we had worked out. In Nagano the group met with the local Communist Party Headquarters (the Party was legal).[52] After each city we would discuss our impressions and knowledge with Hara and Hirata, who themselves learned much from the trip.

We then came back to Tokyo for a round of final discussions. We obtained the suggestions of Moss, his staff and General Shavell, head of the Economic Section.[53] We also had many meetings with Hayoto Ikeda, the Finance Minister, and his staff and special discussions with Hara and Hirata for their detailed views on all aspects of the present system and, more important, their attitudes toward a potpourri of suggested changes we were thinking about.[54] The minister gave each of us a copy of one of his paintings. We took time to visit with the Japanese Labor unions and then the Trade Associations, and also newspaper editors and academics, such as Professor Tsuru, a noted economist.[55] My interviews ended around July 24.

Our group during this period was having intensive discussions on all of the suggestions we would make. The discussion was free flowing, each member's views being given and considered. The various parts of our recommendations were thus built and coordinated within an entire new system. On all matters a group consensus was reached, with no bitter dissents or serious splits occurring. The group had worked

---

52. Surrey likely inserted this parenthetic comment because in the U.S. at the time anti-communist sentiment was growing, and would eventually lead to the Communist Control Act of 1954, Pub. L. No. 83-637, 68 Stat. 775.

53. Henry Shavell was an economist and tax adviser during the American occupation of Japan from 1946–1951; later, he was in government service, mostly or entirely with the Agency for International Development, until 1973; still later, he was an economist and vice president with the Mosely-Hallgarten securities firm. *Henry Shavell*, Boston Globe, Dec. 17, 2007, at 33.

54. Hayato Ikeda was a career tax official, and prime minister of Japan from 1960–1964. Ikeda entered the Ministry of Finance in 1925, eventually heading the Tokyo District Tax Office in 1940. In 1945, he was appointed chief of the Ministry of Finance Tax Bureau, making him the country's highest tax official. In 1946, he was named administrative vice-minister of finance. Ikeda joined the Liberal Party in 1948 and was appointed minister of finance a year later. He became prime minster in 1960, concentrating on economic improvement, and eliminating trade barriers against Japanese products abroad. Laura Hein and Mark Metzler, *Raising Taxes for Democracy*, in The Shoup Mission to Japan, *supra* note 16, at 171–173; *Ex-Premier Ikeda Of Japan Is Dead: Former Premier Ikeda, 65, Dies; Led Japan to Postwar Recovery*, New York Times, Aug. 13, 1965, at 1.

55. Shigeto Tsuru was an American-trained, Japanese economist, who was educated at Lawrence College, the University of Wisconsin, and Harvard University where he received his doctorate. During the war, Tsuru was repatriated to Japan as an enemy alien. He served briefly in the Japanese military toward the end of the war and then joined the Foreign Office. After the war, Tsuru was an economic adviser to the Economic and Scientific Section of the Supreme Commander of the Allied Powers when Surrey first met him. Kotaro Suzumura, *Obituary — Shigeto Tsuru: life work and legacy*, 13 Euro. J. History of Economic Thought 613 (2006).

together so intensively in the prior weeks that we had considered judgements on the strengths and knowledge of each, and the type of judgement each possessed. Then we worked on the preparation of our parts of a Draft Report.

I wrote the draft of Volume IV, the Appendix dealing with the Administration of the Individual and Corporate Income Taxes. I then left for California, travelling this time as a civilian on Northwest Airlines. Most of the others left about the same time, except for Shoup, Vickrey, and Warren who worked on the final form of the Report at a resort on one of Japan's lakes. My Appendix went through as written. The English Report was translated into Japanese, and then as a check on the translation, to English. Shoup had undertaken the Mission on the understanding that the Report would be published as written, with wide dissemination to all who desired to see it. Hence there was no censoring of the contents and the Report did not end up in a filing cabinet. The Report covered 227 pages and 163 pages of appendices.[56]

I have written at this length on the mechanics of the Mission work, since I believe the method of operation was a good blueprint for the functioning of a tax mission, especially where little written material exists and where sweeping changes are to be suggested.

The recommendations themselves can be read in the Report and only the highlights need be mentioned.[k] The income tax was made the mainstay of the entire system and the level of individual tax rates and exemptions carefully presented. To balance lowered top rates of tax, from 85 percent to 55 percent, a strong accessions (inheritance) tax was suggested, along with an annual low rate net worth tax of 1 to 3 percent that would cover about 15,000 taxpayers. The corporation tax rate was set at 35 percent, but a system of integration with the income tax developed through a shareholder credit of 25 percent of a dividend and an annual 1 percent interest surcharge on non-distributed corporate earnings. In result there was not much difference whether a business was operated in corporate or non-corporate form. Capital gains and losses were to be fully taken into account, with taxation of appreciation in assets at death or on gift. The national transactions tax of one percent, essentially a turnover tax on sales, was to be eliminated since it raised little revenue at a one percent rate and any increase in the rate would make the tax, because of its turnover aspect, undesirable from an economic standpoint. There was an elaborate discussion of the relationships between the central government on the one hand and the prefectures and towns on the other, both as to allocation of the responsibilities for government services and allocation as to revenue sources. A value added tax was recommended for the prefectures. A system of equalization grants made according to formulae was suggested to help those prefectures that were not as well off and systematize revenue sharing, rather than requiring the prefecture governments "coming with their hats in their hands to beg funds from Tokyo." The "land and house" tax, based on estimated rental value, should be changed to a tax on land and depreciable assets, called in the Report, a real property tax, based on capital value assessed annually on a market basis, with

56. Carl S. Shoup, Report on Japanese Taxation by the Shoup Mission (1949).

the responsibility for the new tax to rest on the cities, towns and villages, and all the revenue to go to them.[57]

On the administrative side a modern system of self-assessment and withholding was recommended to replace the fixing of taxes on the basis of quotas from the local offices, with the quota then allocated among firms through negotiations with trade associations or some other device. While the quota system was perhaps necessary to prevent the total collapse of revenues in the somewhat chaotic and inflationary post-war period, it was obviously alien to a rational tax system. Investigation of returns was to be aided by the use of carefully prepared "standards." But the keeping of books and records was encouraged through models to be prepared by the tax offices and the allowance of special tax benefits, such as loss carryovers, if books and records were kept. A taxpayer who kept books and records would be entitled to re-assessment only on the basis of an actual investigation and not on standards. Those agreeing to keep books and records were to file on a special colored form, the "blue return." The blue color came from a question of Shoup to our Japanese driver: "What is a color that the Japanese like?"[1]

The Report was written in a relatively non-technical style with full exposition of the choices that had to be made and the reasons for the final decisions. Shoup intended the Report to be an educational document for the Japanese and also for other governments and peoples. In many respects it combines a textbook in public finance with specific recommendations to the Japanese on a wide variety of matters.

The Report, as can be gathered, focused on an equitable tax system without preferences and incentives. In some respects it was an ideal tax system—perhaps better overall than the United States then possessed under its income tax—and written for a liberal government. While nearly all of the recommendations were at once adopted, under SCAP influence, Japan came to be governed by a Conservative Party which made many changes in the proposed system. And as to be expected the passing of time itself, with new problems and increased knowledge, produced changes. The conservative turn of events and especially the importance given by political leaders to matters desired by the business community, such as capital formation, worked against the retention of a number of the recommendations. Some of the leaders in carrying out the changes of the Conservative Party were Finance Minister Hayoto Ikeda, who at the time of the Report was more sympathetic to it, and Keiichiro Hirata, Administrative Vice Minister of Finance, who in the earlier period, with a less prominent position, had worked closely with the Shoup Mission. The tax law was changed, contrary to the Report, to provide preferences for capital gains, and interest income, thus making the tax in part a schedular tax rather than a global tax. The foreign community secured a cutback in the taxation of foreign individuals who were residents of Japan. Some of the recommendations had involved aspects not really yet tested in a large scale in other countries, and their novelty led to rejection later on: the value

57. For more on the Shoup mission, *see generally* the essays collected in THE SHOUP MISSION TO JAPAN, *supra* note 16.

added tax (never adopted, but of course now a normal figure in European tax landscapes),[58] abandonment of the net worth tax (though used now in some European countries), change of the accessions tax to an estate tax (most countries use an estate tax though a few have an accessions tax). In these instances Shoup may have been moving too fast in making the Japanese tax system experiment with these taxes when it had so many other problems to be met and new paths to develop. Other advocates of changes argued that the Report was too American, not in harmony with Japanese tax or social traditions or Japanese needs. In some respects the contentions were correct simply because the recommendations were intended to produce departures from the poor ways of conducting the Japanese system. In other respects they were arguments used to cloak changes stemming from a desire to move from Shoup's stress on equity in a tax system to a stress on incentives for capital formation.[m]

As changes were made, some Japanese began to develop the theme that these changes were "the adjustment of theory to reality." But tax policy debating points are the same the world over, and one staple criticism of the recommendation being fought over is that it is "too theoretical."[n] This contention, however, generally marks a position that is being taken for different policy reasons. Thus a criticism of Shoup's recommendation to tax capital gains in full as theoretical is, as the argument unfolds, merely the result of the critic's belief that capital gains do differ from other forms of income, which though not fully proved, is the starting point of policies to reduce the tax on capital gains. Another criticism by some was that the tax reduction from the earlier SCAP-imposed high rates was not large enough. But Shoup had no jurisdiction over the size of the contemplated expenditure budget, and hence had to match his revenue figures to that budget.

No country is ever ready for an ideal tax system. But the blueprint for such a system must constantly be a part of tax policy. The blueprint is necessary to highlight departures from the ideal and to provide a force to measure the merits of the departures. Shoup was right in sticking to the ideal, rather than making the compromises he knew could occur in the customary battles over tax policies between equity and other goals, e.g., capital formation, incentives and in more modern terms, efficiency. To have made those compromises in the Report would have meant both losing the battles in advance and also not giving those policy makers involved in the battles and the public a way of judging the significance of the battles. Shoup was therefore right in aiming at the target he did. Considering the knowledge that existed thirty years ago on tax structures, he did a remarkable job. He suffered the misfortune that the political turn of the wheel produced a more conservative leadership in Japan, and in political leaders more sensitive to the claims of the business community, when he had hoped for a government and climate more sympathetic to fiscal equity.[59]

---

58. Japan now has a VAT (introduced at a rate of 3% in 1989, and currently at 8%). KATHRYN JAMES, THE RISE OF THE VALUE-ADDED TAX (2015).

59. For more on how changing Japanese politics shaped the implementation of the Shoup report, *see generally*, Martin Bronfenbrenner & Kiichiro Kogiku. *The Aftermath of the Shoup Tax Reforms: Part* I, 10 NAT. TAX J. 236 (1957).

While tax systems must of necessity continually change, and it was not to be expected that the various parts of the Report would survive through the decades, some suggestions of the Mission have become fixed in the Japanese structure. The income tax remains the mainstay of the tax system; a national sales tax is not used by Japan whereas if the abolition of the transactions tax had not occurred, that tax could have developed into a significant turnover tax or perhaps a value added tax; the real property tax remains with the changes recommended. Equally as important, if not more so, recommendations that went beyond the substantive tax law have been fully pursued. One such recommendation was the formation of the Japanese Tax Association, on the model of the National Tax Association in the United States, composed of academics, tax officials, and tax executives to hold meeting on tax matters, both policy and technical, and encourage publication in the tax field.[60] Another basic suggestion was the establishment of tax chairs in several Universities so that taxation as a subject itself could become a part of the law school curriculum. At the time of the Mission tax matters were covered in the courses on Administrative Law and teaching in substantive tax law was not done. Since then professors of taxation in the United States have become a part of Japanese law school faculties, and have international reputations such as Professor Hiroshi Kaneko in Tokyo University,[61] as well as economist tax specialists, such as _____, who heads the _____ Institute.[62] A very important result of the Mission was to strengthen the view that tax techniques and tax administration involved extremely important and often difficult questions which had to be analyzed with scientific care. This in turn means a highly skilled tax agency with expertise on the legal and economics aspects of tax policy generally and tax structures in particular, and also expertise on the methods and techniques of tax administration. The present Japanese Ministry of Finance today has a world-wide reputation for possessing such expertise.

The Shoup Report period has been described in books on Japanese history and specialized economic and legal texts. [Add Japanese books][63] It is generally treated with a mixture of respect and admiration for the diligence and care of the Mission, and also for the willingness to consult with all aspects of Japanese life before coming

60. On the importance of the Japanese Tax Association, *see generally* Laura Hein and Mark Metzler, *Raising Taxes for Democracy*, in THE SHOUP MISSION TO JAPAN, *supra* note 16, at 167–194.

61. Hiroshi Kaneko was a longtime tax law professor at the University of Tokyo. He graduated from the University in 1953 and was a research associate before he became an assistant professor of administrative law in 1956. Soon thereafter he moved to the tax chair established by the Shoup mission. J. Mark Ramseyer and Minoru Nakazato, *Tax Law, Hiroshi Kaneko, and the Transformation of Japanese Jurisprudence*, 58 AM. J. COMP. L. 721 (2010).

62. It is unclear which "economist tax specialist" or "Institute" Surrey had in mind, but it is possible that the public finance economist was Ishi Hiromitsu, who in the 1980s was chair of Japan's Tax Advisory Commission, and who helped capture the Japanese view of the implication of the Shoup Mission by leading a financial history project in Japan's Ministry of Finance. *See generally*, THE SHOUP MISSION TO JAPAN, *supra* note 16 at 279.

63. *See* S. SATO AND H. MIYAJIMA, SENGO ZEISEI SHI [History of the Post-war Tax System System] (1990), at 1–2; H. KANEKO, SOZEI HO [Tax Law] (2010) at 54–60. For more on the legacy of the Shoup mission for Japan, *see generally*, the essays contained in Part III of THE SHOUP MISSION TO JAPAN, *supra* note 16.

to conclusions. Shoup and I were later decorated by an award of the Order of the Sacred Treasure, with my award bestowed in person by the Prime Minister during a trip I made in 1972.[64]

The description of the Shoup Mission does read as if it were all work and no play. There indeed was a heavy work load, but the trip did have lighter moments. Thus, I was able through expert guidance to buy one of the then first round of Japanese 35mm. cameras plus gifts for my wife. One gift was a complete set of dishes, purchased by Takahashi and I looking at a manufacturer's models and then sketching the variations I wanted. But the purchases were not the only moments of play. We saw, on our train trip, fascinating scenery and vignettes of the countryside, on which I could use my new camera. We also went to Japanese plays, saw the July 4 U.S. celebration on the Palace Grounds, had two lunches of our group with MacArthur, who was impressive and appreciative of our being in Japan. Since everything was new to us—none having visited Japan—the entire trip in this sense was a sort of vacation, but one involving serious work and long hours.[65]

International Tax Missions—Puerto Rico

In 1954 I was asked by the Secretary of the Treasury of Puerto Rico, Sol Luis Descartes,[66] to advise on a revision of the Puerto Rican excise taxes. As in most countries[67] the excise tax had grown up without a consistent pattern and the law reflected that growth. Excise taxation was not one of my fields of expertise, since only a relatively small amount of time was devoted to it by the Treasury when I was there. The excise tax portions of the Code, and any revisions, were largely done by the Bureau and one career lawyer in the Treasury.

My first task therefore was carefully to study the structure of the U.S. excise taxes and especially the administrative aspects. Through such study I developed views on how to organize an excise tax law and on what administrative provisions were necessary. I then went to Puerto Rico to become familiar with the existing taxes and structure. My assignment was to draft the law and not decide what goods and transactions should be taxed or the rates. Therefore I had to question the Puerto Rican officials at length on what excises they desired to tax and the precise coverage of each

---

64. Surrey describes his 1972 visit to Japan in Chapter Nine.

65. For those interested in archival historical sources related to the Shoup mission to Japan, Carl Shoup's personal papers are available at the Yokohama National University Library. *See* THE SHOUP MISSION TO JAPAN, *supra* note 16, at ix.

66. Sol Luis Descartes was the Secretary of Treasury of Puerto Rico from 1949 to 1955. Paul P. Kennedy, *Puerto Rico Funds in Sound Condition*, NEW YORK TIMES, Nov. 16, 1950, at 12. Surrey seemed to believe that a U.S. tax mission to Puerto Rico qualified as an "international" tax mission, illustrating his rather idiosyncratic view of both what constituted "international" and the concept of Puerto Rican sovereignty.

67. Surrey's description of Puerto Rico as similar to other "countries" demonstrates Surrey's "world" view at the time.

tax. This was not an easy task since many of the problems under excise taxation arise from the indefiniteness with which the various objects of the tax are described.

As a result of my work for the American Law Institute, I had views on how the draft of a tax law should be structured, even though that work involved the income tax and not excise. Therefore, back in the United States, I worked out the organization of an Act to codify the excise taxes decided upon by the government.[68] The Act had the following outline; some descriptive content has been inserted:[69]

After I completed my draft, in 1955, I went over it with the Puerto Rican officials to check the language especially the scope and rates of the various taxes, to determine whether I had correctly described them. The format of the draft was fully acceptable to them. Finally, as I had drafted it, the draft was enacted into law on January 20, 1956 as the "Excise Act of Puerto Rico."

This project was interesting and provocative. It gave me an opportunity to present my views on the structural organization of a tax law, and to make the presentation of the material orderly and understandable.[70] [check—does Act survive?]

International Tax Missions—Venezuela[71]

THE FISCAL SYSTEM OF VENEZUELA

A REPORT

CARL S. SHOUP, Director of the Commission to Study The Fiscal System of Venezuela

JOHN F. DUE
LYLE C. FITCH
Sir DONALD MACDOUGALL
OLIVER S. OLDMAN
STANLEY S. SURREY

THE JOHNS HOPKINS PRESS: BALTIMORE, 1959

FORWARD

At the request of the Minister of Finance of the Republic of Venezuela, a Commission to Study the Fiscal System of Venezuela was formed by the Di-

68. Excise Act of Puerto Rico, Act. No. 2, Acts of the 5th, 6th, 7th and 8th Special Sessions of the Legislature of Puerto Rico 306 (January 20, 1956).

69. The editors have deleted Surrey's outline of the Act which is drawn directly from the law. See, Excise Act of Puerto Rico, Act. No. 2, Acts of the 5th, 6th, 7th and 8th Special Sessions of the Legislature of Puerto Rico 306 (January 20, 1956).

70. The Act was formally repealed by new excise tax legislation in 1987. 1987 Excise Act, Act No. 5, Acts and Resolutions of Puerto Rico, 1987, 3rd Regular Session, 9th, 10th and 11th Special Sessions 857 (October 8, 1987).

71. Once again, Surrey begins his description of this Shoup-led tax mission with the Foreword from the published report. The editors have deleted portions of this Foreword which can be found in the publication: Carl Shoup, The Fiscal System of Venezuela: A Report of the Commission to Study the Fiscal System of Venezuela (1959).

> rector of this project, with the approval of the Minister, in May, 1958. Research and writing occupied the summer months. The report was submitted on August 22, 1958, then mimeographed, translated into Spanish, and circulated within the Government. Additional information thus obtained led to some revision and explanation of the report in June, 1959, in the course of a three-week visit to Caracas by two members of the Commission (Professors Shoup and Surrey). Changes that have occurred in the Venezuelan tax law since August, 1958, are described in footnotes and, with respect to the income tax reform of December 19, 1958, in Appendix C. The text of the tax chapters therefore remains a description and analysis of the Venezuelan tax system as it was in August, 1958. Some minor administrative changes that have been made since that date, mostly along lines recommended in the report, are not specifically noted. A Spanish-language edition of the report is being printed by the Government of Venezuela.
>
> The study is focused on the tax system of Venezuela in the comprehensive sense of including national, state, and local taxes. Both tax policy and tax administration are covered. In the first two chapters, the Venezuelan economy is described and analyzed with respect to characteristics important for tax policy: distribution of income, rate of investment, and sources of its finance, and optimum uses of capital. Estimates of costs for certain goals are given for education and public health. The Government accounting system is analyzed with a view to changes that would provide data for national income accounts.

As the above format indicates, I again worked with Professor Shoup on a foreign tax mission. This mission was in one sense very different from that to Japan. In the Japanese Mission we faced the task of creating anew an entire tax system, in a country whose language, culture and history were unfamiliar to us.[72] The Venezuelan Mission on the other hand meant the examination of a tax system in place to determine where improvements could be made. Some members of the Mission understood Spanish and a number of the Venezuelans we worked with had studied in the United States. The techniques used, however, to gather material and insights were much the same as in Japan. Professor Oldman and I worked on the income tax and administrative structure. We persistently questioned a variety of Venezuelans, much like in Japan. To understand the problems of tax administration we physically traced the course followed by a tax return from taxpayer access to the return and instructions, its filing in a local tax office, the handling in the local tax office and in Caracas, through audit, re-assessment, collection, judicial procedures and many by-paths. Of course we brought our American background—plus my Japanese experience—to this task.

---

72. The Shoup Mission's assumption that they were working in Japan to create "anew an entire tax system" may say as much about post-WWII American hubris as it does about the realities of the Shoup Mission to Japan. But whatever the realities of the two situations, undoubtedly Shoup, Surrey, and their colleagues approached the Venezuelan project with a very different mindset from Japan. The Shoup Mission to Japan, *supra* note 16, at 281.

Since neither Oldman nor I knew Spanish, interpretation at our interviews for questioning was a major hurdle. Such a hurdle is often overcome by a mission using a member of the economic section of our embassy in the country. But, while fluent in the language, such a person generally does not have a background in taxation and interpretation is thus lengthy and probably does not always reflect the actual conversation due to the unfamiliarity with tax terminology. So, instead of the usual practice, we went to one of the top law firms specializing in taxation to obtain the services of an American fluent in Spanish and knowledgeable on tax terminology and the Venezuelan tax system in general. I have followed the same practice on other missions, as the most efficient way to make the understanding of both my questions and the responses as accurate as possible and not too time-consuming. Translation of documents was done by an office staff made available to us by the Government.

We made numerous suggestions on reforming the income taxes such as elimination of the individual schedular taxes and the complementary tax to be replaced by a single, overall tax, with suggested exemptions and rates; the institution of a separate corporate tax instead of the existing application to corporations of the same schedular and complementary tax, and a discussion of the dividend distribution deduction and shareholder credit methods of providing partial integration; a suggestion that Venezuela improve the structure of its territorial income tax approach and look forward to a world-wide income rule; full taxation of capital gains and taxation on gift or at death of the appreciation in value of assets; abolition of the turnover tax and a number of technical changes.

Of course, we followed the Shoup pattern of going outside of the capital city. One of the trips was to the Andes near the border. Another was to the U.S. Steel area in Orinoco. We stayed overnight at a cabin for visitors and awoke to learn that perhaps a revolution had occurred and the Caracas Airport could be closed. Since further news did not come through, we decided on the following course. We had arrived in a U.S. Steel plane, there being no other ready transportation. We would therefore return on that plane, following behind a regularly scheduled Venezuelan airline flight after it passed overhead. The rumor turned out to be false and we landed without a problem. We also visited a number of cities and rural areas.[73]

Again following his practice of having mission reports published and distributed, Shoup arranged for the Johns Hopkins Press to publish the report—"The Fiscal System of Venezuela (1959)." The Report was also published in Spanish. Besides our chapters on the income tax, there are chapters on the excise taxes, with a recommen-

---

73. Surrey's trip to Venezuela coincided with a significant near coup in the summer of 1958 when the Minister of Defense, Jesus Maria Castro Leon, ordered the arrest of key civilian political officials. In response, thousands of Venezuelans protested in the streets of Caracas and other urban areas, and Castro Leon soon fled Venezuela. *Caracas Upsets a Military Coup*, New York Times, Jul. 24, 1958, at 1 (the Venezuelan government completed a victory over a coup attempt by a group of military figures headed by the defense minister); *A Persistent Rebel; Jesus Maria Castro Leon*, New York Times, Apr. 23, 1960, at 8; *see, also*, William Arceneaux, *The Venezuelan Experience: 1958 and the Patriotic Junta*, LSU Historical Dissertations and Theses (1969) at 239–40.

dation for a general sales tax at the wholesale level, customs duties, state and municipal finance. A table was included of hypothetical budgets and tax burdens of twelve Venezuelan families drawn from diverse sectors of the economy. There was a remarkable chapter on the distribution of income in Venezuela, prepared by Sir Donald MacDougall, an Oxford economist.[74] It was truly an amazing feat of "detective work in economics," drawing a picture of the distribution from the few scraps of data that Venezuela then collected.

There was no SCAP in Venezuela to enact our Report into law, and no immediate action was taken on the recommendations. Over time, however, some of our advice was incorporated into the tax structure. But the Report, like that of most missions, did not have the major impact of the Japanese Report.

International Tax Missions — Argentina

REPORT OF A PRELIMINARY SURVEY OF THE TAX SYSTEM OF ARGENTINA°

by STANLEY S. SURREY and OLIVER OLDMAN

Introduction

This Report on Argentine tax problems is the result of about a two weeks stay in Buenos Aires, June 7–20, 1960. The trip was made at the request of Dr. Guillermo Walter Klein, Secretario de Estado de Hacienda, and its purpose was to provide advisor assistance to the Government of Argentina with respect to aspects of its tax systems. The assignment was undertaken through the auspices of the Ford Foundation, to whom Dr. Klein had made his request. We received the full cooperation of Dr. Klein and that of the officials in the Hacienda and in the Tax Office (Direction General Impositiva). Our work was essentially twofold in character: A considerable part of the time, six afternoons, was spent in first-hand examination of aspects of the organization and procedures of the Tax Office, through interviews with the head of the various operational divisions and through visual inspection of activities being performed. Several conferences were also held with the present Head of the Tax Office and his immediate staff. The Head of the Tax Office was appointed only a few weeks ago as an "Interventor" to reorganize the Tax Office. The second aspect involved interviews and conferences with persons in and out of Government who had a reasonably close relationship to the tax scene. Thus, meetings were held with accountants and lawyers practicing in the tax field; persons on the staff of the Faculty of Economic Sciences of the University of Buenos Aires and of the Faculty of Law and Social Sciences,

---

74. Donald MacDougall was an Oxford University trained economist who spent most of his professional career, like Surrey, traversing between the academy and public service. D.R. Thorpe, *Sir Donald MacDougall*, THE INDEPENDENT, Mar. 23, 2004, at 34.

> teaching in the field of Taxation, as well as the Deans of the two schools; persons in the Government (Hacienda and Banco Central) engaged in statistical work; the Minister of Agriculture, who was the Director of the Tax Office on its formation; and several experienced business executives. Meetings were also held with United States and United Nations Personnel, including the Ambassador and the Economic Counsellor at the United States Embassy, personnel of the International Cooperation Administration, and United Nations officials in the fields of public administration and technical assistance training. The work was concentrated on the aspect of taxation and no effort was made to explore to any significant extent conditions, the relation of revenues to expenditures, or the like. We understood that recent studies respecting the Government's economic program had been made by the International Bank and the International Monetary Fund. Also, the work was confined to Buenos Aires, so that no consideration was given to the administration of Federal taxes outside of Buenos Aires or to the taxes levied by the provinces and municipalities. With respect to the taxes we considered, attention was primarily concentrated on the income tax.
>
> It must be recognized that the information and generalizations contained in this Report are qualified necessarily by the infirmities implicit in the shortness of the trip and the lack of prior familiarity with the country. There undoubtedly will be errors of detail and perspective. But we have gained a number of impressions, some of a broad nature and some by way of detail. These are set forth not as the final word but as an introduction to some of the problems of the Argentine tax situation. While, as stated above, the purpose of the study was to provide advisory assistance to the Government of Argentina through the auspices of the Ford Foundation, this Report is to be considered as reflecting the views only of the Authors.

As the above Introduction indicates the Report was the result of a hurried two weeks stay in Buenos Aires. Considering the limited time available, Professor Oldman and I did well to get out a Report of 56 pages. Our Venezuelan experience was of considerable assistance. The procedure was the same as in Venezuela—talk to as many persons as possible who had a relationship to the tax structure. Here also we used as an interpreter a young American tax lawyer practising with an Argentine law firm. The objective of the visit and Report was not to make firm recommendations, as in Japan and Venezuela, but to survey the Argentine substantive tax law and tax administration and then point out areas for study and suggestions on the direction of the study. It was not difficult to find such areas, for the entire tax system was poorly organized and poorly administered. The tax situation was far below the level that we had experienced in Venezuela.

The recommendations were directed to future efforts. Thus, as to tax administration, it was suggested that Argentine officials visit the United States and Canada to observe tax administration in those countries; that personnel qualified in tax administration visit Argentina for three to six weeks, after the first visit; and two qualified

Argentine tax officials be sent annually to the Harvard Program (a number did attend in the following years). As to tax policy, it was suggested that several economists publish a study of present tax policy issues, along the line of the Venezuelan Report, and that assistance be given to developing adequate non-Governmental facilities in Argentina for study and research on tax policy matters.

It is interesting that from this visit we developed two broader ideas for Latin American taxation generally. One was improvement in university teaching and training in the field of taxation. A second was a conference for Latin Americans on tax administration problems, to be attended by high level personnel from Latin America and also personnel from the United States and Canada. We pointed out that the problems faced by Argentina in reorganizing its tax administration were similarly experienced in other Latin American countries, so there was common ground for the conference. Such a conference was held in October, 1961 in Buenos Aires, under the auspice of the Joint Tax Program of the Organization of American States, the Inter-American Development Bank, and the United Nations Economic Commission for Latin America. The Harvard International Program collaborated in its organization and was largely responsible for the entire effort.[p] Out of this recommendation and this conference there developed a permanent organization of Latin American tax administrators and their counterparts in the United States and Canada, called CIAT—Centro Interamericano de Administradores Tributarios (InterAmerican Center of Tax Administration) and headquartered in Panama. It was first organization of its kind and has proved to be highly successful in strengthening tax administration in Latin America.[75]

The Pakistan Double Taxation Treaty—and "Tax Sparing"

The United States and other countries have entered into bilateral tax treaties to reduce or eliminate possibilities of double taxation of income in situations when both of the two countries involved, one taxing on the basis of the source of income and the other taxing the world-wide income of its residents on a resident basis, or on a citizenship basis as in the United States, apply their taxes to the same income. Most countries by their unilateral statutory legislation go far in eliminating double taxation through either the foreign tax credit device e.g., a [*credit*][76] against the United States income tax on foreign source income for the income tax paid to the foreign country, or by an exemption device, e.g., exempting from domestic tax some items of foreign source income. But these devices are sometimes incomplete and still offer room for double taxation to exist. Bilateral tax treaties have been the

75. The Inter-American Center of Tax Administrations continues to thrive today, with an impressive range of activities. For details, *see* the website: www.ciat.org.

76. It is unclear why Surrey created this blank, which appears to be for the term "credit." It is possible that the blank was left by a typist who could not decipher Surrey's handwriting.

international device to narrow this double taxation. The treaties, which generally adhere to a rather set pattern, also are designed through exchanges of information between the tax administration of the two treaty countries and other devices, to counter fiscal evasion. Thus, the general title of these treaties is "Convention of the Government of America and the Government of (___) for the Avoidance of Double Taxation and the Prevention of Fiscal Evasion With Respect to Taxes on Income."

In December 1954 in the Harvard Law School course on Legal Problems of Doing Business Abroad, which I taught with Professor Brewster, I gave the following examination question:

> III
>
> (45 minutes)
>
> The following statement was made by Secretary of the Treasury Humphrey at the Meeting of Ministers of Finance and Economy of the United States and Latin America held at Rio de Janeiro on November 23, 1954:[77]
>
> "In the spirit of the resolution on private investment and taxation adopted at the Caracas Conference, the United States continues to explore feasible measures to remove tax impediments to increased foreign investments. The Administration and the Congress, as well as numerous private groups in the United States, have given the matter intensive study. This has disclosed the complexity of the problems involved. In the light of this experience, the Administration will again submit to the Congress proposals with respect to the reduction of taxation of foreign income along the general lines recommended by the President last year. We trust these proposals will find acceptance by the Congress.
>
> We desire to complement these unilateral legislative steps with bilateral tax treaties. To that end, we are prepared to explore with individual countries the possibilities of the tax treaty as a medium for creating a more favorable tax climate for international trade and investment. For example, one of the matters which might be considered in treaty discussions is how the United States might give recognition to tax concessions made to foreign capital by the country where the investment is to be made. Under proper safeguards, we would be prepared to recommend giving credit for general foreign income taxes which are waived for an initial limited period as we now grant credit for taxes which are imposed. Such a measure as this will give maximum effectiveness to your own laws designed to encourage new enterprises."

---

77. For Treasury Secretary George M. Humphrey, *see George M. Humphrey, 79, Dies, Former Secretary of Treasury*, and Carter B. Holseley, *A Power in the Capital*, NEW YORK TIMES, Jan. 21, 1970, at 47. For news coverage of Humphrey's speech in Brazil (actually delivered in November, rather than in winter as Surrey states), including his favorable comments on tax sparing, *see U.S. Offers Partner Role to Aid Latin Economy*, THE WASHINGTON POST, Nov. 24, 1954, at 1.

Assume you are an attorney on the staff of the Congressional Joint Committee on International Revenue Taxation. You are asked to prepare a memorandum on the second paragraph of the above statement, providing information for the Committee on the following points:

1. What is the "more favorable tax climate" which the Secretary is suggesting would result from the specific type of treaty provision stated in the next to last sentence of the statement?

2. In the light of the present provisions of the United States income tax and the various methods whereby American foreign investment may be conducted, what is your opinion as to the effectiveness of such a treaty provision if adopted?

3. Do you see any difficulties in the phrasing and implementation or administration of such a treaty provision if adopted?

Write the memorandum requested, giving your answers and reasons therefor.

The subject of the question had not been touched on in class, though treaties were discussed. This question marks the beginning of a long road in U.S. tax treaty policies, a road that continues to wind along even today.

The background of the question was this: Treasury Secretary Humphrey was to make a visit to Latin America and had told his tax assistants, principally Dan T. Smith, a Professor at the Harvard Business School with whom I had taught seminars on tax policy before he went to Washington in the Eisenhower period as Deputy to the Secretary of the Treasury in charge of tax policy, that he wanted to say something new on international tax policy.[78] Smith had read a recommendation of a British Royal Commission that the foreign tax credit extend not only to taxes actually paid to another government but also to tax amounts that would have been paid to that government but for reductions in tax resulting from tax incentive provisions adopted by that government. These incentives, enacted to encourage foreign investment in the country though also extending to domestic investors, were in the nature of full tax holidays (exemption from income tax during the initial years), partial tax holidays (exemption of profits below a certain rate of return), greatly accelerated depreciation, and other devices. Typically these incentives were only available to investments approved by that government, generally either in selected industries or selected areas. Smith advised the Secretary to make a proposal to Latin America governments along lines to the British recommendation.

The statement used in my examination was a literal quotation from Secretary Humphrey at a conference statement in Rio de Janeiro in the winter of 1954–1955. I was greatly surprised that the class answers were almost uniformly opposed to the proposals. Perhaps they sensed from my policy views on other matters that I would dislike the proposal — which I did — but on the whole I believe they were generally

78. For more on Dan Throop Smith *see* Chapter 4, note 25.

making an independent judgement. I let the matter rest there. But late in July, 1957, I read that the Senate Committee on Foreign Relations was to hold a hearing on the Pakistan Tax treaty, our second treaty with a developing country. The notice stated that the treaty contained a provision along the lines of the proposal made by Secretary Humphrey. In Article XV (I) there was the customary, though unimportant clause because of our unilateral tax credit, stating that the United States will grant a credit for Pakistan taxes. The following sentence then appeared in Article XV (I):

> For the purposes of this credit there shall be deemed to have been paid by a United States domestic corporation the amount by which such Pakistan taxes (other than the business profits tax) have been reduced under the provisions of section 15B of the Income Tax Act, 1922 (XI of 1922) as in effect on the date of the signature of the present Convention: Provided, That any extension made by law of the period within which an industrial undertaking may be set up or commenced in order to obtain the reduction provided in section 15B shall be deemed to be in effect on the date of the signature of the present convention.

The reduction referred to in the sentence resulted from a Pakistan exemption from income tax of profits up to 5 percent (computed after depreciation) of capital invested in Pakistan.

On reading of this Hearing I called my brother Walter, who headed a Washington law firm working in the international area, to say that the provision embodied an undesirable policy and could he pass this view on to any appropriate Senate staff person that he knew personally.[79] I heard nothing more and the Hearing was held on July 30, 1957, by the committee.[q] Senator John Kennedy, with whom I was not directly acquainted, was a member. The only witnesses were Government officials from the Treasury and State Departments and representatives of various private organizations. They discussed the treaty in the somewhat general terms typical of tax treaty hearings, but did mention in a low key the provision quoted above and pointed out that it was a new provision.

The essential reason advanced for the provision was its importance in not nullifying, through the operation of the regular foreign tax credit, concessions made by Pakistan to U.S. corporations. It was observed that it was a new provision and presumably would be a precedent to be followed in future negotiations with developing countries. There was no discussion relating to the basic problems inherent in this provision. Senator Kennedy did have the following dialogue with Dan Throop Smith, Deputy to the Secretary of the Treasury:

> SENATOR KENNEDY. A Prof. Stanley Surrey of Harvard with whom I am not acquainted. I understand there are some objections and I understand

---

79. At the time of his death in 1989, Walter Sterling Surrey was a senior partner in the Washington law firm of Jones, Day, Reavis & Pogue, specializing in international law. He was four years younger than Stanley. *Walter Sterling Surrey, Lawyer*, The Washington Post, Feb. 1, 1989, at B7.

he discussed them with Mr. Smith and I don't know if Mr. Smith can state them or not.

MR. SMITH. I am afraid I can't recite them very specifically. I know Professor Surrey very well. In fact when I had a little bit more time at Harvard than I now have he and I gave a joint seminar, and we have argued with each other and with students there as well as in other situations.

He told me some months ago that it was his impression that there was no need to make a concession of this sort, that we could get treaties otherwise.

SENATOR KENNEDY. You mean on the tax?

MR. SMITH. The income tax concession. I told him two things. I said in the first place I thought it was a fair and reasonable thing to have, because without it we were—and I can only repeat my phrase—nullifying the tax concessions that other countries did give, nullifying it only for American companies.

Secondly that in the give and take of negotiation, we were not able to get treaties. I don't want to put Professor Surrey in the position of being in the academic cloisters saying what ought to be done. But those of us who are trying to do things find that what he might theoretically like is not in fact practical. But I think I am inclined to do that in this instance and say also that this concept is one that has had very full and very high level discussion over many months in the executive branch.

We think it is a matter of mutual and reciprocal advantage. We think the concession is a reasonable one on our part.

We think that the treaty that comes out of it is a good treaty, good for both countries, and we think the principle is a desirable one to apply with other under-developed countries.

I don't know what his specific objections are other than he said he thought we could get the treaty without it and I said I thought it was a reasonable thing, and secondly I didn't think we could get the treaty without it, and I still stand on both of those points.

SENATOR KENNEDY. I think that in the case of Pakistan it may be worthwhile to do this, and it may be generally, but I think that we should proceed with a good deal of caution.

MR. SMITH. I assure you we have proceeded with a very great caution in the course of the negotiations.

SENATOR KENNEDY. We want to help Pakistan but we don't want to give a bonus to a lot of American companies who are doing this as a tax dodge. I understand that in some of these countries which have had this tax encouragement, after the period of time has passed they are liquidated and then they start all over again in a new corporate entity, so that I think we should certainly concern ourselves with how this is carried out.

MR. SMITH. I assure you that exactly that situation is one that we are concerned with.[r]

About five or six days later while I was vacationing in Martha's Vineyard I received a call from Carl Marcy, Chief of Staff of the Foreign Relations Committee and his assistant.[80] Marcy said he had heard from someone in Senator Kennedy's office that I had some objection to the treaty (the phone call from my brother) and he was calling as a result. He added, however, that I should know the treaty had been approved on July 30, 1957, by the full Committee. I could only reply that I was sorry to hear that since they had made a mistake. I then talked for an hour giving Marcy my objections to the provision. The emphasis was on the significant departure from previous United States treaty policy, and that an entirely new matter was involved. This was no perfunctory treaty. At the end, somewhat to my surprise, he said I had raised some interesting issues, which the Committee and he had not appreciated. They had not realized that a new treaty policy issue was presented, but rather assumed the treaty was just another treaty in the line of treaties they usually approved as a formality. Marcy added he would recommend holding up presentation of the treaty to the Senate and that a second Hearing should be held, this time by the full Committee. Could I attend as a witness if the Hearing were held August 9, 1957, and present a statement of my views? I answered I would.

Then the work began. I had only a few days to work out a statement, with no tax books at all in the house. The statement had to be typed and it turned out the only public typist available on the Island was a rather eccentric lady who lived, along with her animals, on a back road. But she proved to be an excellent typist and I could therefore arrive in Washington with a statement plus copies for the Committee, xeroxed I recall in my brother's office.

I was the first witness at this second hearing, and the only witness to oppose the treaty.[s] I summarized my objections in an oral statement, coming down hard on the point that this was the first treaty to reduce the United States tax on United States taxpayers. All other treaties only reduced the United States tax on foreigners receiving income from United States sources. Further, the reduction came in an almost fantastic manner. The foreign tax credit was designed to give a credit for foreign income taxes *paid*, and thereby to reduce the otherwise double taxation that would arise from application of both the United States and the foreign tax on the same income. But the Pakistan treaty would extend the foreign tax credit to a foreign tax *not paid* in a situation where no double taxation could exist. A U.S. corporation that could obtain a reduction of its U.S. tax on the foreign source income by showing a receipt for a foreign tax it had *paid*, could now also obtain the credit by showing a receipt for a foreign tax *not paid*. As a result neither the foreign country, here Pakistan, because

80. Carl M. Marcy was the longtime chief of staff to the U.S. Senate's Foreign Relations Committee. He served in that role from 1955–1974. He received his law degree and a Ph.D. in international law from Columbia University and spent nearly his entire career in public service, mainly on the Foreign Relations Committee. *Carl M. Marcy, 77, Long Chief of Staff of Key Senate Panel,* NEW YORK TIMES, Sep. 21, 1990, at B6.

of its tax incentive reduction, nor the United States, because of the grant of a credit for a non-tax reducing pro tanto the U.S. tax, would be taxing the income involved, and the corporation would be home free.

The issue was not a narrow one and just in the context of the Pakistan treaty. If the Committee and the Senate were to approve the provision, it would appear in the future in treaties with any developing countries using tax incentives. A concession of this significance once made by the United States becomes a precedent for future treaties, since the United States would not be in a position to differentiate. Nor would it be U.S. policy to differentiate, since in the Hearing the Treasury had said the Pakistan treaty would set a precedent. Hence, while U.S. investment in Pakistan was almost nil, there being an increase of only $20 million in the years since 1948 when the incentive was adopted, and the Treasury said it had heard from only one company, so that investment in Pakistan was not the real issue, the precedential value of the treaty would extend over a considerable range of investment.

The above was stated in as forceful a manner as I could. As the Senators drifted in for the Hearing, with about one-half the Committee there including the Chairman, Senator Green of Rhode Island, they increasingly become intrigued by the issue and all asked me a number of questions. It was clear they had not realized the importance of this one sentence in the treaty and had not seen the issue it presented. Some of the Senators tended to agree with me, others thought the issue should be considered and the treaty referred to the Senate Finance Committee. Senator Morse made the following statement which gave me considerable comfort:

> Professor Surrey, I want you to know that I appreciate very much the seminar I have attended this morning. It was not my good fortune to be at the meeting of the Senate Foreign Relations Committee when this matter was taken up because of a conflict with another committee of the Senate meeting, which is a practice we find ourselves in so frequently. So, this is all new to me. I shall reserve final judgement until I hear the representatives of the Treasury Department, but I have tried enough cases and sat in judgment enough to know when I have listened to a prima facie case, and you have made one and a strong one. (18)

Another colloquy also gave me comfort:

> SENATOR HICKENLOOPER. May I ask one question on the last answer?
>
> THE CHAIRMAN. Go ahead. He is a very good witness. (25)

There were, of course, many questions relating to our policies regarding private foreign investments in general, with some Senators stressing the need to do something to induce more investment by U.S. companies. I had to prevent the discussion from getting too involved in this matter and off the point I was interested in. So I would answer the questions on this phase in a general way by agreeing with the importance of such investment, mildly indicating that there were differences of opinion as to the effectiveness of tax incentives to achieve an investment increase, but then getting back to the point that as "a particular incentive device the treaty is one of the most unsound incentive devices that could have been thought of." (12) At another point Senator Long, who earlier had wondered whether we should be taxing foreign investment at all and that the foreign tax credit in itself may not be desirable since in his view it could induce some countries to raise their tax rates, went on to say,

> SENATOR LONG. Out of all the proposals I have seen to handle this problem, this present proposal seems to me at the moment — and my mind is open — to be the worst of all.
>
> MR. SURREY. I will rest there. (24)

All the other witnesses were in favor of the treaty. Mitchell B. Carroll,[81] counsel to the Tax Committee, National Foreign Trade Council, Inc., a witness generally found at hearings involving international tax matters, gave the Committee an example, based on his chosen facts to show that there could be no reduction in U.S. tax since the balance of the Pakistan tax, apart from the exempt portion, could be taxed at 62 percent, so the credit for the "tax spared" under the incentive merely reduced the excess credit over our 52 percent rate. Incidentally, I thus learned a new phrase, for the proponents of the Pakistan provision called it the allowance of a "tax sparing" credit. A rather high-sounding technical phrase that presumably was intended to create the presumption that it must be all right, just another technical matter in the foreign tax credit area. As Mr. Carroll finished his testimony, Senator Humphrey said:

> I realize the time factor. I see Dr. Surrey constantly shake his head in protestation. While we don't have the time, I would like to ask Dr. Surrey if he has some thoughts on this, to furnish a memorandum for insertion in the record.
>
> I am interested in this subject and I don't want to be prejudiced. I might have been in the beginning. I want to know what the facts say.
>
> THE CHAIRMAN. Professor Surrey will bear that in mind and can comply or not as he sees fit. (44)

I had indeed been shaking my head to catch attention, since much of Mr. Carroll's testimony consisted of half-truths and platitudes, but the Committee, not versed in tax matters, could not appreciate this situation.

The next witness was one of Washington's foremost tax lobbyists, Ellsworth C. Alvord, a lawyer.[82] Curiously, though he supported the treaty, his views did help my

---

81. Mitchell Benedict Carroll, international tax lawyer, was elected president of the International Fiscal Association (IFA) in 1950 and was named IFA's honorary president for life in 1971. For a discussion of Carroll's efforts in the 1930s and 1940s to bring about tax treaties between the United States and other Western Hemisphere nations (describing Carroll as "a charismatic figure [who] had the trust of many Latin American experts in the field of taxation"), *see* Jose Antonio Sanchez Roman, *The Challenge from the Periphery: Latin America's New Deals and the Shaping of Liberal Internationalism in FDR's Era*, 61(2) REV. BRAS. POLIT. INT. 1, 16–19 (2018).

82. For more on Ellsworth C. Alvord *see* Chapter Two, note 119.

argument. He said he did not want the Treasury, because of this tax-sparing device, to think it had solved the problems of inadequate U.S. investment in developing countries, nor did he want Pakistan to believe that this device would attract any serious capital from the U.S. But he said it would be unfortunate if the Committee refused to ratify the treaty, even though it would be virtually of no use. The psychological repercussions of non-approval would be bad.[t]

The first government witness was Dan T. Smith, from the Treasury. He stressed that the reduction resulting from a foreign tax incentive automatically served to lower the foreign tax credit and thereby increase the United States tax. The U.S. Treasury was thus the beneficiary of the foreign tax incentive. His point that the foreign incentive was negated by the operation of the credit was a half-truth since most U.S. corporations invest abroad through foreign subsidiaries and until they declare a dividend out of foreign profits, the U.S. tax is deferred and the only applicable tax is of the foreign country, so that to this extent the incentive is effective. Mr. Smith, later in his testimony, acknowledged this since in my oral statement testimony I pointed out that Smith had made the same point in an earlier speech. Smith said there was resentment on the part of the developing countries because of this result under the credit. Smith was fully correct in his assertion on the attitude of foreign countries, for they were hard put to accept that incentives designed to help U.S. taxpayers ended up by aiding the U.S. Treasury. In their resentment they overlooked the fact that the unilateral foreign tax credit for taxes *paid* was far more important, indeed a sine qua non for U.S. foreign investment, than the tax sparing credit. Moreover, in pushing for a tax-sparing credit they were distorting the very premise on which the foreign tax credit rested, i.e., relief from *double* taxation. He agreed the provision would not be a major item in attracting U.S. capital, but he stated "it has symbolic value." At one point this colloquy occurred:

> SENATOR HUMPHREY. Weren't you once a professor?
>
> MR. SMITH. I am still a professor.
>
> SENATOR HUMPHREY. There is another professor back here and he says you are wrong.
>
> MR. SMITH. I might say that these two professors, Senator Humphrey, Professor Surrey and Professor Smith, both of Harvard, have written joint articles and conducted joint seminars and we disagree so fundamentally on matters of tax policy sometimes it is a bit hard for the students to get in and argue with each other because the professors are arguing with each other. I had not ever expected that my colleague, Professor Surrey, and I would be arguing before this illustrious body but it seems we are. (57)

Smith concluded by saying:

> The final point I want to make. This provision has great symbolic value. That is, I think it has great emotional appeal to those countries which had chosen as a matter of their national policy to try to use differential tax treatment to develop their economies.

> All this does is to recognize, subject to what we regard as great limitations and safeguards, their right to do that without having the United States law, and the United States as a country, arrogate to itself the position that we are going to nullify whatever they do, and on that basis on behalf of the Treasury Department and the administration I strongly urge the ratification of this treaty.[83]

This was the opposite side of the coin. I saw the provision as allowing the foreign country, through its tax incentive approach and the allowance by the U.S. of a tax sparing credit, to determine the overall rate of tax to be paid by a U.S. corporation, whereas this should be a matter to be determined by the United States. The Treasury approach, by combining the incentive with the tax sparing credit, allowed U.S. investors abroad to pay an overall tax less than that paid by domestic investors, and thus discriminated against investment at home. Obviously, the two views of the foreign tax credit—that of its nullifying effect held by developing countries and my view that a tax-sparing credit was the very negation of the whole idea behind the foreign tax credit—avoidance of double taxation—could not be fully reconciled. There was only the partial reconciliation provided by our unilateral decision to grant deferral of tax on the profits of our foreign subsidiaries until the profits were repatriated.

The Assistant Secretary of State for Economic Affairs submitted a statement supporting the Treasury position as one in harmony with the tax philosophies of the developing countries.[84] He also stressed the overall value of a treaty with Pakistan:

> In conclusion, just a word about the Pakistan agreement as a whole. Our relations with Pakistan have long been friendly and close. We are allies under the South East Asia Treaty Organization and associated under the Baghdad Pact, and we are linked by a mutual security treaty. We view many of the great issues of the day in the same way. This fundamental accord can be supplemented and strengthened by a practical agreement in the sphere of business operations such as the double tax treaty before you. We have an investment guaranty agreement with Pakistan. We hope to have a treaty of friendship, commerce, and navigation as well. The double tax treaty with Pakistan is the first of its kind to be negotiated in this part of the world. It is a good, comprehensive treaty that should make a substantial contribution to a sound economic relationship between our two countries.

The final witness was Colin F. Stam, Chief of Staff for the Congressional Joint Committee on Internal Revenue Taxation and thus the principal tax advisor to the Congress. Mr. Stam downplayed the precedent value of the treaty, saying that the

---

83. Supplementary Memorandum on Executive N, Tax Convention with Pakistan, *Double Tax Convention with Pakistan: Hearing Before the Comm. on Foreign Relations*, U.S. Sen., 85th Cong., 1st Sess., on Income Tax Convention with Pakistan, 28 (1957).

84. Thorsten V. Kalijarvi was the Assistant Secretary of State. His testimony appears on page 63 of the hearing (written testimony only, as he had to leave before it was his turn to testify). Kalijarvi was ambassador to El Salvador from 1957 to 1961. *T.V. Kalijarvi, Ex-Ambassador, Official at State*, THE WASHINGTON POST, Jun. 7, 1980 at C6.

tax sparing device was only a small part of the whole treaty, and he saw no objection to its approval. Senator Long seemed, in a colloquoy with Stam, to have somewhat shifted his own view:

> SENATOR LONG. That's correct. I just wonder about the attitude of the members on the Finance Committee. My guess is—and I serve on that committee, as you know—that those members would feel that they were entitled to a look at particularly this first precedent before it was established. They might not feel that they are entitled to look at anything but this provision.
>
> THE CHAIRMAN. It seems to me the Finance Committee is as much interested as we are.
>
> SENATOR SMITH. Senator John Williams is on your committee. He has requested that that committee be permitted to look over this.
>
> SENATOR LONG. I think a very good case has been made for this particular situation here, not as a general proposition, but as a specific proposition.
>
> MR. STAM. That's right.
>
> SENATOR LONG. But I do feel that the members of the Finance Committee who pass on the subject of this foreign tax credit, the whole general field of it, would feel that before the Foreign Relations Committee might start offering executive agreements and treaties that deal with taxation of foreign corporations they would want to know what we are doing here.

The Hearing ended. I informally told Chairman Green I would submit an additional statement, which he said the Committee would include in the record of the Hearing and added that "I had been a very good witness," comforting words. I returned this time to Cambridge and prepared a Supplementary Memorandum which in considerable detail at length answered the arguments made at the Hearing on behalf of the treaty. I did point out that the Administration had earlier recommended a rate reduction by statute from 52 percent to 38 percent in the case of foreign income. This recommendation had not been adopted by the Congress, yet now the Treasury was seeking by treaty to provide a reduction that could go below a 38 percent rate and even to zero. I concluded:

> The Pakistan Treaty thus involves a very basic issue of tax policy in the field of foreign income—an issue as important and far reaching as any that Congress has faced on this subject. On the technical side, it involves a consideration of the foreign tax credit approach, already under examination by the tax committees of the Congress. It also involves a consideration of suggestions elsewhere advanced which would give effectiveness to foreign tax concessions in the limited areas in which they are not effective today.
>
> Then, there are all the broad and difficult policy issues presented to the committee in these hearings. Certainly a proposal as important and far reaching as this one merits extended study and discussion by the Congress. It is

> respectfully suggested that at the very least this course be taken with regard to the Pakistan Convention. This committee, together with the Senate Finance Committee and the House Ways and Means Committee, at the very least should give extended study to these basic problems in the taxation of foreign income before any decision is taken on this particular clause in the treaty. (34)

Silence then ensued. The Committee at its executive session of August 13, 1957, did not report out the treaty but gave no other indication of its position. I did talk with Nathan Gordon, a career economist in the Treasury who handled treaty negotiations at a level just below the top tax officials.[85] He said Smith really had to come up with something for the Secretary's 1954 Latin American trip and Smith thought the tax-sparing idea met that requirement and was also a good idea. I sensed that Gordon, though noncommittal, did not favor the approach.

It was Pakistan that resolved the immediate issue of the tax-sparing sentence. During 1958 it unilaterally terminated the tax incentive that was involved, not because of the doubts in the Senate Foreign Relations Committee but apparently because it did not consider the incentive of much use. This action by Pakistan enabled the Committee to proceed to report the treaty with this observation in its Committee Report:[u]

> The Committee on Foreign Relations has had under consideration the conventions listed below and recommends that the Senate give its advice and consent to their ratification:
>
> 1. Taxation convention with Pakistan, signed at Washington July 1, 1957 (Ex. N, 85th Cong., 1st sess.), with a reservation.
>
> Committee consideration of the Pakistan convention hinged around the tax-sparing provisions of article XV (1), and it is to this section that the reservation applies.
>
> The paragraph provides, in effect that the United States will allow as a foreign tax credit Pakistani taxes which are waived. Under Pakistan law at the time the treaty was negotiated, earnings up to 5 percent on certain types of invested capital were tax exempt for the first 5 years after the investment was made. Without a provision such as that in article XV (1), United States tax laws would have effectively nullified this concession on the part of Pakistan in an effort to attract foreign investment. This would have been so, because the United States tax would have been increased to the extent that the Pakistan tax was reduced.
>
> Tax sparing, as incorporated in article XV (1), is a new principle in United States tax treaties. Its application requires careful consideration on a country-by-country basis. During the period when the Pakistan convention was pending in the committee and before the committee came to any conclusions

85. For more on Nathan Gordon *see* Chapter Nine, Surrey's note c and accompanying text, and note 15.

> regarding the tax-sparing article, the Pakistan law providing a waiver of taxes expired. The question of tax sparing in this case, therefore, becomes moot. The committee accordingly recommends a reservation excepting the second sentence of the first paragraph of article XV from the resolution of advice and consent. This is the sentence which provides the United States credit for taxes waived by Pakistan. Because Pakistan has terminated its tax waiver, this provision would be inoperative for the present and future even without a reservation. If approved, it would operate to the retroactive benefit of two United States corporations. The principal argument for tax sparing is that it is a means of encouraging foreign investment and this argument loses validity when made retroactively.
>
> In recommending a reservation to article XV (1), the committee wants to make it perfectly clear that this is without prejudice to future consideration of the matter in the event the Pakistani tax-waiver law is reenacted and the question again comes before the committee. There is no occasion for the Senate at this time to decide the question. The committee reserves complete freedom of decision for the future.

I thought this method of ending the dispute was fully satisfactory. The Committee had not endorsed tax sparing and thus there was no ratified treaty containing this approach.

This Pakistan episode was, as I said earlier, just the beginning of a long winding road in tax treaty policy. The Eisenhower Treasury had sent three additional tax sparing treaties to the Senate — India, Israel and United Arab Republic — but no action was taken on them. Stam had earlier said he would advise the Treasury not to push these three treaties in the Senate. In a curious way, as I will later describe, at the start of my work in Treasury tax sparing helped me to cement my relations with Treasury Secretary Dillon,[86] who had been the State Department Under Secretary when that Department had supported the Pakistan Treaty. Dillon now saw it my way. Soon thereafter I was faced with a push by Kaiser Aluminum to work out a tax sparing agreement with Ghana as part of the financing for a major proposed project in that country. I informed the State Department Solicitor, Abe Chayes — another Harvard Law School Professor on leave! — that Treasury would not endorse tax sparing but would work with Chayes to develop alternative means of financing.[87] That exchange ended any push by the State Department for tax sparing treaties. The President on June 8, 1964, at the Treasury's request withdrew the three earlier tax sparing treaties still pending in the Senate.

---

86. Clarence Douglas Dillon served as Secretary of the Treasury from 1961 to 1965. Earlier he had been ambassador to France under President Eisenhower, and later he became president of the Metropolitan Museum of Art. Eric Pace, *C. Douglas Dillon Dies at 93, Was in Kennedy Cabinet*, New York Times, Jan. 12, 2003, at 32.

87. Abram Joseph Chayes was a longtime professor of international law at Harvard from 1955 to 1993, except for the four years when he served in the Kennedy Administration's State Department. *Abram Chayes, John Kennedy Aide, Dies at 77*, New York Times, Apr.18, 2000, at B8.

Since then and up to the present the United States has refused to enter into tax sparing treaties with developing countries, although those countries have consistently requested such a provision in negotiations with the United States and the other developed countries have agreed to various, rather mild on the whole, tax sparing clauses. Also, it became widely known throughout the international tax world, especially among developing countries, that Surrey was the evil genie preventing the United States from agreeing to tax sparing and that belief persists today. When I later became Special Advisor to the United Nations Ad Hoc Group of Experts on Tax Treaties Between Developed and Developing Countries, the issue of tax sparing was a very live one and again Surrey was the culprit in the eyes of the developing countries.

I suppose no other issue in the international tax area has been so identified the world over with a particular individual. I doubt that the matter will ever fully and finally be put at rest. But that innocent examination question in 1954 was the beginning for me of a determined effort to show the undesirability of the tax sparing approach.[88]

Notes

a. For the history of this episode and its consequences, see Stanley S. Surrey, *Current Issues in the Taxation of Corporate Foreign Investment*, 56 COLUM. L. REV. 815, 830–838 (1956).

b. For a historical review of the origins of these treaties, *see* _____.

c. For some descriptions of the Program's early years, see International Center for Taxes, 9 Harvard Law School Bulletin (1937) [check], Oldman & Owens, *The International Tax Program* — Canadian Tax Journal 444 (1968) (anything else).

d. The Taxation Curriculum of the Harvard Law School International Program in Taxation, prepared in February 1961.

e. The Harvard Law School International Program in Taxation (1961).

f. Hearings on General Revenue Revision, House Committee on Ways and Means, 85th Cong., 2d sess., (Jan. 20, 1958) 1143; Hearings on Private Foreign Investment, House Ways and Means Subcommittee on Foreign Trade Policy, 85th Cong., 2d sess., (December 4, 1958) 377.

g. Later Prof. Owens and Gerald Ball, an accountant on loan to the ITP, published the two volume Indirect Foreign Tax Credit. ELISABETH ANN OWENS & GERALD T. BALL, THE INDIRECT CREDIT (1975, 1979).

h. For a bibliography of Program Publications finished or commenced in the early years of the program, see the brochure, The International Program in Taxation (1964).

i. Prof. Owens continued the course in 1964 and I taught it again in some years in the 1970s and 1980s.

j. *See* Harvard Law Record, Tax Program Celebrates Years of International Research (March 30, 1972), Harvard University Bulletin Law School Tax Program Marks 25th Birthday ( ). For a partial list of publications through 1982, see the brochure ITP 82 Publications. (?) For a list of participants

88. Surrey's opposition to tax sparing provisions in U.S. tax treaties has prevailed to this day. *See, e.g.*, Tracey A. Kaye, *Taxation and Development Incentives in the United States*, AM. J. OF COMP. LAW 617, 619 (2014) (tracing the long-standing U.S. position back to Surrey's 1957 opposition to the tax sparing provision in the treaty with Pakistan).

in ITP, see Alumni Directory of Former Participants and Visiting Scholars, 1952–1982, 30th Anniversary Edition, Harvard Law School International Tax Program.

k. For a brief summary of the Report, written at the time by one of its members, *see* Cohen, Tax Reforms in Japan, 18 Far Eastern Survey 307 (1949).

For an English language bibliography on the Shoup Mission, see Ward and Shulman, The Allied Occupation of Japan, 1945–1952 (1974) 538.

l. Shoup, Warren, Vickrey and I made a follow-up trip in the summer of 1950. The Introduction to this "Second Report on Japanese Taxation by the Shoup Mission" states:

> Introduction
>
> This statement of conclusions and recommendations is based primarily on seven weeks of travel and study in Japan during August and September, 1950. It is a report to SCAP by the Shoup Tax Mission. Hence it does not necessarily represent the views of SCAP or the Japanese Government.
>
> When we arrived, the new national tax system had been in force for some months, but the new local tax system had been enacted by the Diet only the day before. Even under the national tax system, there had not been time for substantial experience. The first installment payment under the new reduced income tax, for instance, was just falling due.
>
> On the other hand, there had been a year of intensive debate throughout Japan over the recommendations submitted last year. Despite the limited amount of experience with the new system, therefore, we found no lack of issues to study.
>
> The present statement is consequently a compound of three things: an appraisal of such experience as has been gained under the new system; a statement of position on new issues that have developed in the public discussions of the past year; and an analysis of the chief problems that the coming year may bring. Unlike last year's report, it makes no attempt to be comprehensive; many segments or aspects of the tax system are not touched upon at all.
>
> The main conclusions and a considerable amount of supporting data and reasoning are presented in this statement, but many technical details have been deferred to a series of supplementary memoranda to be released within the next week or so.

Essentially this Second Report amplifies some of the prior recommendations and covers some new points. Perry, Beneath the Eagle's Wings, Americans in Occupied Japan (1980) contains a brief description of the Shoup Mission.

m. For a summary of the changes between the issuance of the Report and 1957, *see* Bronfenbrenner and Kogiku, *The Aftermath of the Shoup Tax Proposals*, 10 Nat. Tax J. 237, 339 (1957), also giving the authors' views of the reasons for the changes.

There were, naturally, some technical weaknesses in the Recommendations. Thus, the averaging system of the Report, in itself perhaps too complex, did not adequately handle the treatment of employee severance pay which typically is paid in a lump sum. The Report does not mention severance pay.

n. Uematsu, Computation of Income in Japanese Income Taxation: A Study in the Adjustment of Theory to Reality, in Law in Japan, The Legal Order in a Changing Society (von Mehren ed., 1963). The article, though making some valid criticisms, seems to be an overreaction to the Report in order to bolster its support of the changes. A more moderate criticism appears in Ito, Direct Taxes in Japan and the Shoup Report, 8 Public Finance 357 (1953).

o. 16 Public Finance, Finances Publiques, No. 3-4 (1961). There is a Spanish version published by the Government, Examen Preliminar del Sustema Impostivio de la Republica Argentina (1960).

p. The Proceedings of the Conference were published in Problems of Tax Administration in Latin America, Joint Tax Program, OAS/IDB/ECLA (Johns Hopkins Press (1965)). A Spanish version was published in 1964 by the Pan American Union. At the Conference I gave a paper on a newly developing aspect of tax administration, "Automatic Data Processing and Tax Administration: The Potentialities of ADP and Factors Involved in its Adoption," based on the experience of the United States Internal Revenue Service with ADP, and Prof. Oldman had a paper on "Controlling Income Tax Evasion."

q. Senate Foreign Relations Committee, Hearing on Income Tax Convention With Pakistan (Ex. N., 85th Cong., 1st sess.), July 30, 1957.

r. Hearings, *supra* note q, at 18–19. Dan Smith's put-down of Surrey by implying I lived in "academic cloisters" was a characteristic of his when he was called on to discuss my views; he was the "practical" person and I the ivory tower thinker. Smith, of course, did not mention I had worked in the Treasury for many years nor that he was likewise a professor at Harvard. Presumably he became "practical" when he went to Washington in 1952, though he may be said to have a dual personality, since he was returning to "academic cloisters" each week to teach a course at the Harvard Business School.

s. Double Taxation Convention with Pakistan, Hearing Before the Committee on Foreign Relations, United States Senate, Ex. N., 85th Cong., 1st sess., (August 9, 1957). The subsequent page references in the text are to this Hearing.

t. In a letter sent to the Committee on its first Hearing, Alvord had validly criticized the provision as not offering a solution in the case of underdeveloped countries which had adopted a general policy of low or moderate levels of taxation applicable to all businesses — a valid criticism, but one which showed why the provision was inherently wrong. His only solution, however, was to shift to an approach that recognized the country of source as having the exclusive right to tax the income involved.

u. Double Tax Conventions, Senate Executive Report No. 1, 85th Cong. 2nd Sess. (July 7, 1958), reprinted at 1960-2 C.B. 906, 907.

I did write two articles on the subject: Surrey, The Pakistan Tax Treaty and "Tax Sparing," 11 National Tax Journal 156 (1958), which summarized my statements at the Hearing, and Surrey, The United States Taxation of Foreign Income, 1 Journal of Law & Economics 72 (1958), describing the issues in the international tax area, including tax sparing.

Stanley Surrey, ca. 1970
HARVARD LAW SCHOOL LIBRARY, HISTORICAL AND SPECIAL COLLECTIONS

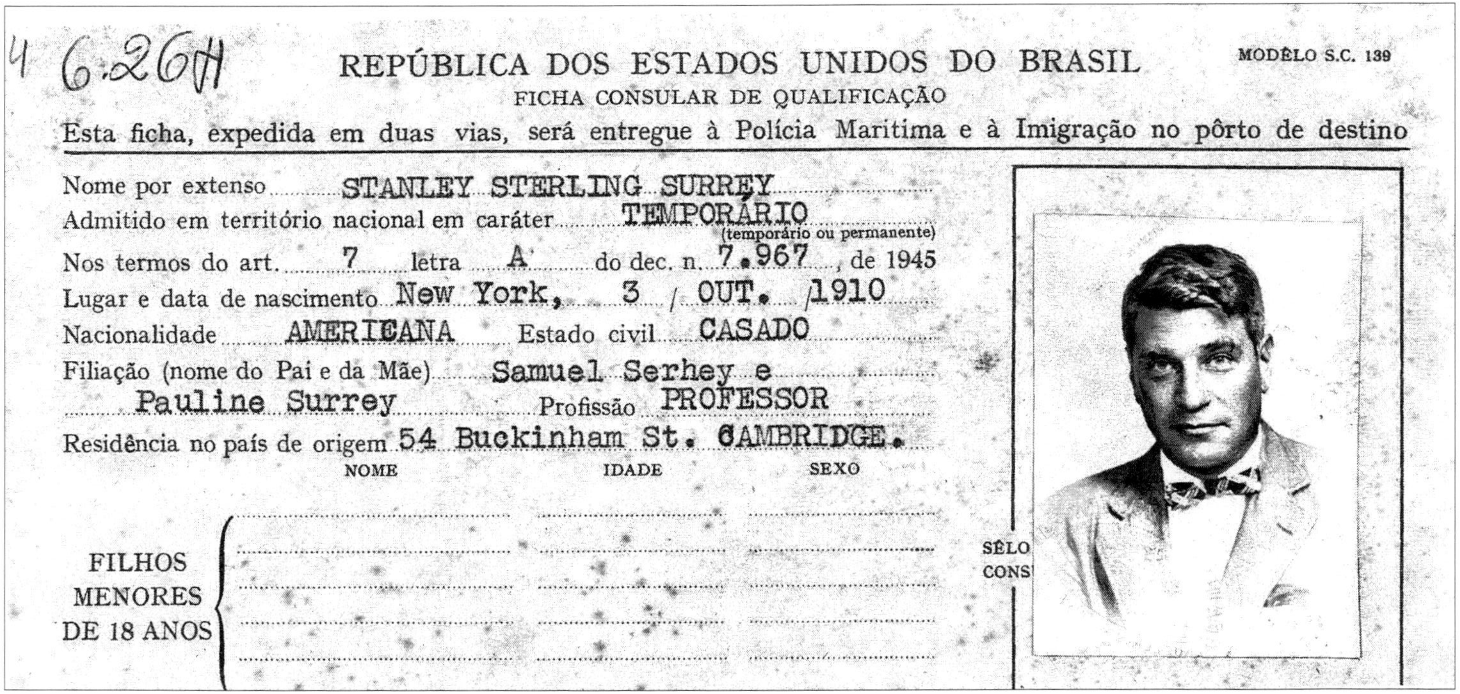

4 6.264

REPÚBLICA DOS ESTADOS UNIDOS DO BRASIL

MODÊLO S.C. 139

FICHA CONSULAR DE QUALIFICAÇÃO

Esta ficha, expedida em duas vias, será entregue à Polícia Maritima e à Imigração no pôrto de destino

Nome por extenso STANLEY STERLING SURREY

Admitido em território nacional em caráter TEMPORÁRIO (temporário ou permanente)

Nos termos do art. 7 letra A do dec. n. 7.967, de 1945

Lugar e data de nascimento New York, 3 / OUT. /1910

Nacionalidade AMERICANA Estado civil CASADO

Filiação (nome do Pai e da Mãe) Samuel Serhey e Pauline Surrey Profissão PROFESSOR

Residência no país de origem 54 Buckinham St. CAMBRIDGE.

FILHOS MENORES DE 18 ANOS — NOME / IDADE / SEXO

SÊLO CONS

Photograph from Surrey's 1947 Visa issued by the Brazilian government

Stanley Surrey in his Harvard Law School office, ca. 1972

HARVARD LAW SCHOOL LIBRARY, HISTORICAL AND SPECIAL COLLECTIONS

Stanley Surrey by Stephen Gersh, ca. 1977
HARVARD LAW SCHOOL LIBRARY, HISTORICAL AND SPECIAL COLLECTIONS

SIX

A Government Tax Career

Part II, 1961–1969

1960 — The Kennedy Campaign

Much of the tax policy of the Kennedy years, especially as that policy related to tax structure, had its beginning in the summer of 1960. This origin was a memorandum on "Tax Policy" prepared at Harvard University as a research resource for the Presidential campaign. At that time, however, no one recognized the significance of the paper or its position as the start of more important documents to develop from it. This was certainly true for those who prepared the memorandum.

In July, 1960 I was asked by Professor Archibald Cox,[1] Senator Kennedy's Research Director in the campaign, to prepare a paper on tax policy. Since we were both on the Harvard Law School faculty, we knew each other though we were not close friends. Cox also knew that of the several professors of tax law at the Law School, I was the one most interested in tax policy issues and tax legislation. Presumably he also knew I was a Democrat. But I doubt he knew much, if anything, about my views on particular tax issues, since we had not had occasion before to speak about such matters. Nor did he give me any guidance as to points to be covered.

I asked two public finance economists, Professor E. Cary Brown of M.I.T.[2] and Professor Richard Musgrave of Johns Hopkins University, to work with me. I knew both of them well, appreciated their ability, and had worked with them before in

1. During the 1960 presidential campaign, John F. Kennedy tapped Archibald Cox of Harvard Law School, a labor law specialist, to serve as the coordinator for "an astonishing galaxy of [Harvard] scholars [who] had made themselves an informal brain trust for Senator Kennedy." *Kennedy's Nomination Drive Aided by Mixture of Amateurs, Professionals, Eggheads and Hardheads*, NEW YORK TIMES, Jul. 15, 1960, at 18. Cox later served as Solicitor General (1961–65), and most famously in 1973 as the Watergate special prosecutor (ending with his firing in the infamous "Saturday night massacre"). On Cox generally, *see* KEN GORMLEY, ARCHIBALD COX: CONSCIENCE OF A NATION (1997).

2. E. Cary Brown joined the MIT faculty in 1947 and remained at MIT until his retirement in 1986. *E. Cary Brown, Fiscal Policy Expert, Dies at 91*, MIT NEWS, Jun. 27, 2007. He is perhaps best known for what has come to be called the Cary Brown theorem, holding that under certain conditions an immediate deduction for the cost of a long-lived business asset is equivalent to tax exemption of the income produced by the asset. E. Cary Brown, *Business Income Taxation and Interest Incentives* 300, 309–310 in INCOME, EMPLOYMENT AND PUBLIC POLICY: ESSAYS IN HONOR OF ALVIN H. HANSEN (1948).

preparing material for a Stevenson campaign. While I considered myself able to handle those tax policy issues that turned on broad policy concepts or legal aspects, I thought that the public finance issues should be dealt with in the first instance by experts. Moreover, since these two economists were used to working both with lawyers and lay audiences, I knew there would not be much required on my part to make their economic discussion and conclusions usable by non-experts.

We prepared a paper of over 70 pages covering a wide range of topics. Assuming the candidate's commitment to economic growth, we discussed various avenues of tax policy and then focused on increasing investment incentives. Here for individuals the paper stressed the importance of measures that would lead individuals to utilize their savings for productive investment. The program suggested elimination of the exemption of interest on state and local bonds, with direct federal grants substituted, since the exemption was inefficient and drew individual funds away from business investment, and also elimination of the 4% dividend credit and $50 dividend exclusion (1954 Republican innovations) as useless and inequitable incentives. The revenue so gained should be used to lower top income tax rates to 65% from the then 91%. The very large preference for capital gains was considered inequitable, largely wasteful and too unselective to be useful as an incentive to capital formation since the bulk of the benefit went to trading shares of established concerns. But it was recognized drastic change was not in order, so that instead various degrees of tightening were suggested, such as lengthening the six months required waiting period and eliminating the maximum 25% rate while keeping the exclusion of one-half the gain. For corporations, the goal was that of inducing firms to increase new investments. The device suggested was a tax credit of 10% for investment in new plants and equipment. As an alternative, to reduce revenue loss, the credit could be limited to increases in investment, thus focusing on the rapidly growing business firm. This credit device was suggested by Cary Brown who said Belgium had utilized it. The group without stressing the point preferred the credit to more rapid depreciation. This discussion on the investment credit — the first I believe in American writing — covered four paragraphs. The conclusion was in this form:

> The question remains whether private capital formation or public capital formation or both in varying degrees are to be utilized in achieving economic growth. The stress to be placed on private capital formation and the extent to which a budget surplus and an easy money policy alone [measures previously discussed in the memorandum] are not sufficient to achieve the desired degree of that formation, will thus determine whether such a tax incentive device should be adopted.

The paper then turned to a strongly urged recommendation for reform of the income tax through broadening the taxable base. This goal was to be achieved by eliminating or reducing many existing preferences that presently narrowed that base severely and thus made high statutory rates misleading. Items stressed, in addition to the previously mentioned elimination of the state and local bond interest exemption and of the dividend credit and exclusion and a lessening of the capital gain preference included: withholding on dividends and interest payments to end the non-compliance in reporting this income; reduction in percentage depletion for oil and other material resources; a cut-back in various personal deductions such as for state and local taxes and mortgage interest; and restrictions on expense accounts. Along with this base broadening went the suggestion, stated earlier, of reducing the rates in the upper brackets and the additional suggestion of reducing lower bracket rates through splitting the then 20% $0–$4000 first bracket into two brackets with a lower rate of 18% for the new first bracket.[a]

Other matters discussed were an examination of the estate and gift taxes to tighten their structure and perhaps increase the rates; retention of the existing excise taxes because of revenue needs but staying away from general sales taxation since the sales tax was relied on by state and local governments; and a strengthening of tax administration through application of modern date processing systems and electronic equipment.

The paper went to Cox in the latter part of August, and nothing more was heard about it. Like many a campaign document, it seemed just to vanish. This was, I thought, an appropriate result for I believed that the candidate could not make points by stressing issues in the tax field. Indeed, Professor Kenneth Galbraith[3] did call me once, saying somewhat desperately he had to write a speech on tax reform and asking what he should say. I replied that he should stress the need to eliminate tax abuses and if examples were needed he could mention withholding on dividends and interest and doing something about expense accounts since those two items would draw little flak. But he should stay away from other specifics because mentioning them—e.g. oil depletion—could only arouse opposition from those affected. He agreed. All in all, tax issues did not play a part in the general campaigning. The candidate did make several statements that later came to have considerable significance though at the time they presumably went largely unnoticed.[b]

1960–1961 — The Kennedy Pre-Presidential Task Force

I had no further contact with the campaign. And after the successful election I had no concrete thoughts of further activity. But on the Sunday after Thanksgiving, Theodore Sorensen,[4] Special Counsel to the President-Elect, called to ask me to head a Task Force on Taxation. This call was a complete surprise. I did not know

3. Harvard economist John Kenneth Galbraith had a long, varied, and high-profile career, including a stint with the Office of Price Administration during World War II, service as ambassador to India (1961 to 1963), and more than three decades on the Harvard faculty. He was a prolific writer, especially of books on economics aimed at a general readership. THE AFFLUENT SOCIETY (1968) was a bestseller. *See generally* Richard Parker, JOHN KENNETH GALBRAITH: HIS LIFE, HIS POLITICS, HIS ECONOMICS (2004) (an authorized biography).

4. Theodore Chaikin Sorensen was President Kennedy's special counsel and primary speechwriter. In later years he was of counsel with the law firm of Paul, Weiss, Rifkind, Wharton & Garrison. He wrote a number of books, including KENNEDY (1965) (a biography of JFK) and COUNSELOR: A LIFE AT THE EDGE OF HISTORY (2008) (an autobiography). He also drafted most of the chapters of PROFILES IN COURAGE (1957), officially authored by Kennedy. *Theodore Sorensen, 1928–2010; Kennedy Wordsmith and Muse,* NEW YORK TIMES, Nov. 11, 2010, at A1.

Sorensen and even now am not clear just how he heard of me or even decided to use me. I understand he did have a list of the people who had done work for Cox—my paper in this sense may not have vanished after all. Sorensen said the other members of the Task Force would be Professor Mortimer Caplin of Virginia Law School,[5] Richard Musgrave, and Norman Ture, a Washington economist who was Counsel to the Joint Economic Committee and close to Chairman Mills of the House Ways and Means Committee. I do not know how Sorensen chose these persons but I said I knew them, could work with them, and the selection was suitable. I did ask to add another lawyer and on the spur of the moment suggested Adrian DeWind, a New York tax lawyer who had earlier succeeded me for a brief period as Tax Legislative Counsel in the Treasury in 1947.[6] I knew him to be reform-minded and I especially wanted the benefit of his tax practice experience. Sorensen said there was to be no publicity (check) and the report was due the end of December—a month away!

Our general instruction was to prepare concrete recommendations for action in the year 1961. We had two specific instructions. Another task force under Professor Paul Samuelson was to make recommendations for dealing with the current recession and high unemployment rate of 6.6%.[7] Hence broad fiscal policy was outside the agenda of my group. However, we were to formulate the technique of a temporary tax reduction in the event such a course developed from the Samuelson report. The second instruction came in a meeting I had with Sorensen a few days later. He also called attention to a speech of Senator Kennedy before the Associated Business Publications Conference that stated:

> Fourth, we must make certain that there is proper encouragement to plant modernization. Post-war Europe has a new and modern industrial plant. So has the Soviet Union. We cannot compete if our plants are out of date or second rate. Wherever we can be certain that tax revision, including accelerated depreciation, will encourage the modernization of our capital plant—and not be a disguise for tax avoidance—we should proceed with such re-

5. Mortimer Caplin served as Commissioner of Internal Revenue from 1961 to 1964 (in which capacity he was featured on the February 1, 1963, cover of *Time Magazine*). He also taught at the University of Virginia Law School for more than three decades and co-founded the Washington tax law firm of Caplin & Drysdale. He died in 2019, a few days after his 103rd birthday. *Mortimer Caplin, 103, a Tactful but Tough Tax Collector*, NEW YORK TIMES, Jul. 19, 2019, at A23.

6. Adrian W. DeWind was a partner and longtime head of the tax law department at the New York law firm of Paul, Weiss, Rifkind, Wharton & Garrison. DeWind worked for Randolph Paul and alongside Surrey in the World War II Treasury Department. He was also a civic leader and advocate for international arms control and civil and human rights. Dennis Hevesi, *Adrian DeWind, Tax Expert and Human Rights Watch Founder, Dies at 95*, NEW YORK TIMES, Aug. 19, 2009.

7. Paul Samuelson, long-time professor of economics at MIT, was the first American to be awarded the Nobel Memorial Prize in Economic Sciences (1970), and among the most influential twentieth-century economists. His textbook, titled simply ECONOMICS (1st ed., 1948), now in its nineteenth edition, has sold millions of copies. Michael M. Weinstein, *Paul A. Samuelson, Economist, Dies at 94*, NEW YORK TIMES, Dec. 14, 2009, at A1.

vision. It is sound, liberal policy to see that our productive plant is the best and most modern in the world.[c]

Sorensen asked me to consider this matter, though he did not press for a specific proposal. At this meeting he did ask me if I were interested in appointment to a position in the Treasury involving taxation. I answered yes.

Our Task Force went to work, meeting as a group several times. The recommendation of the technique to follow if a temporary reduction in the individual income tax were to be Presidential policy took us into new ground. We emphasized that a temporary reduction should be as neutral as possible as respects the distribution of the tax load and thus not alter the present pattern of progression. We therefore suggested a uniform percentage point reduction in each tax bracket, favoring this approach over the other alternative of cutting all bracket rates by a constant percentage. Both approaches could be said to maintain present progressivity, but the preferred route concentrated more of the reduction in the lower brackets. We said that the termination of such a temporary reduction "should, if possible, be made flexible so as to introduce the concept of a flexible use of the tax system to meet economic conditions (for example, the reduction could be scheduled to end December 31, 1961, but with power in the President to extend the reduction for one or more six months periods, with final termination in any event on December 31, 1962)."

We then turned to recommendations for tax legislation which it would be desirable to enact in 1961. Here we had before us Sorensen's request on something to encourage business investment. We also knew that spokesmen for the business community had been recently urging more accelerated tax depreciation as the best approach. In 1954 the Republican Administration had introduced as an incentive to investment "accelerated depreciation," under which a business could write off (deduct) the cost of a plant or a machine for tax purposes at a rate considerably more rapid than the rate at which the cost was being reflected in the determination of profits in reports to shareholders.[d] This deduction for accelerated depreciation produced a reduction in income taxes, especially for large corporations with considerable investment in plant and equipment.[8] The business community had thus become quite familiar with accelerated tax depreciation and had started to push for more of the same—a faster acceleration.

Musgrave and I urged the investment credit approach—and thus the idea originating in the campaign paper started on a new journey. Caplin and DeWind were willing to accept the concept but Ture desired more accelerated depreciation. Musgrave and Ture debated the approaches at length. In the end, the group decided for the investment credit with Ture grudgingly going along. The Report thus contained a recommendation for an "investment tax credit" as an "incentive to increased private

8. Internal Revenue Code of 1954, Pub. L. No. 83-591, § 167, 68A Stat. 1, 51. For more on the origins of the 1954 calls for "accelerated depreciation," *see generally*, David W Brazell, Lowell Dworin, and Michael Walsh. *A History of Federal Tax Depreciation Policy*. Vol. 64. Office of Tax Analysis, US Treasury Department, 1989.

capital formation." "The credit would be 15% (a figure in the 10% to 20% range is acceptable) of the increase in business outlays for new plant and equipment [which result in a net increase in those assets]. The amount of the credit would be a direct off-set against the taxpayer's tax. The 'increase' in business outlays would be measured in terms of the excess of expenditures for new plant and equipment over current depreciation deductions."[9]

The argument for this credit repeated some of the points made in the campaign paper for focusing on increase on business investment as a spur to economic growth. It was stressed, however, that the credit was not an anti-recession measure.

> This investment tax credit is not recommended as an anti-recession measure in the same sense as, say, an individual income tax cut. With large under-employment, the emphasis should be on using present capacity and this target can be reached much more quickly by concentrating on an immediate increase in general consumer demand. Since the investment credit essentially is an expenditure program operating in the private sector, it has the same drawbacks considered as an anti-recession measure as does a public expenditure program. It is not capable of working at once at top effectiveness.
>
> The investment credit is instead aimed at giving greater strength to the business recovery when it sets in by providing a tax incentive for increased capital outlays and through offsetting the shrinkage in profit margins which ordinarily occurs when recovery is well along and which acts to check plant and equipment outlays. The goal is a more rapid rate of private capital formation through an emphasis, to the extent of the credit, on investment activity rather than consumption. The success of the credit, in this view, depends in part on there being available the resources (in addition to those released by the reduction in tax resulting from the credit) needed to make possible the investment which the credit is designed to stimulate. This in turn requires a shift from consumption to investment, which means a general tax policy that moves to some extent in the direction of cutting consumption. Thus, the individual income tax revenues must be higher than they would otherwise be, leaving the individual with less spending power. Since at full employment the credit presupposes a rearrangement of resources in the direction of more capital formation, the individual income tax must be at levels sufficient to restrain consumption and avoid inflationary pressures. These factors reinforce the view expressed earlier that any anti-recession individual income tax cut be clearly regarded as a temporary measure.

9. The quotations in this paragraph and the following pages are from Taxation Task Force, *Tax Policy for 1961: Contents, Listing of Matters Covered, Brief Summary of Recommendations, Detailed Discussion of Recommendations* (Dec. 31, 1960), in Taxation Task Force, Box 1072, Task Force Reports, Pre-presidential Papers, John F. Kennedy Presidential Library. For additional historical context on the Kennedy-Johnson tax policy, *see generally*, RONALD KING, MONEY, TIME, AND POLITICS: INVESTMENT TAX SUBSIDIES AND AMERICAN DEMOCRACY (1993); CATHIE JO MARTIN, SHIFTING THE BURDEN: THE STRUGGLE OVER GROWTH AND CORPORATE TAXATION (1991).

The report presented at length the comparison between the credit and accelerated depreciation, and here emphasized the greater effectiveness of the credit and the desirability of not turning the depreciation deduction, which had a proper place in the measurement of taxable income, into an incentive device since that course could lead only to confusion as to what was incentive and what was appropriate tax depreciation. It was pointed out, however, that adoption of the credit should not preclude a study of the proper useful guidelines to be allowed for tax depreciation. The Service had a study underway and this study and a survey of the entire depreciation deduction should be pursued:

> The subject of tax depreciation rules to measure net profits over time thus should be kept separate from the question of tax incentives to private capital formation. The adoption—or rejection—of an investment tax credit or other incentive device should not act as a barrier to the continued study of present depreciation rules and practices.

A relatively full technical blueprint for working out the details of the credit was presented. The termination of the credit was then discussed:

> The credit is not to be regarded as a permanent part of the tax law. For one, it is experimental, and we will have to see how it operates. For another, if it is effective and at some time we desire to slow down capital formation, the credit can be suspended. The fact that the credit is a subsidy in the sense that it operates as a reduction in tax in addition to the recovery through depreciation of the full cost of an asset makes its use fully flexible for these purposes. Indeed, this is a reason why the incentive device is designed as a credit rather than as a change in depreciation. The credit offers flexibility and the depreciation change does not.
>
> Since it will be desirable a few years later to reassess the investment tax credit, it is probably helpful to place an automatic termination date in the legislation. This will make it somewhat easier to withdraw the credit if the reassessment so warrants, since the automatic termination date will operate in the absence of affirmative legislation to continue the credit. (Is Presidential flexibility here desirable; a termination date with Presidential power to extend for yearly periods?) A termination date placed at less than two years in the future is undesirable since it is likely to encourage hasty planning (and the use of imports if bottlenecks develop in the United States). A three-year span would seem safer from the standpoint of efficient business planning and efficient use of existing productive capacity.

In all, 28 pages of the Report were devoted to the investment credit. Though Cary Brown was not a member of the Task Force, he helped prepare this part and checked all of the discussion.

The investment credit was estimated to involve a revenue loss somewhat under $2 billion. The Report recommended that this loss be offset by four revenue-raising reforms. The first related to withholding of tax by payors of dividends and interest to individuals. It was generally recognized that compliance in reporting dividends and interest on tax returns was quite poor and it was believed that a considerable amount of revenue — no one knew how much — escaped tax as a consequence. There had been previous discussion of introducing a withholding system to eliminate this non-compliance but the Republican Treasury opposed it, preferring increased taxpayer education.[e, 10] Our Report came down strongly for withholding of tax at the source at the first bracket rate of 20%. Here also we presented a detailed blueprint for such a withholding system which, as in the case of investment credit, plowed new ground. The Report — here covering 20 pages — developed the technique to use, the problems involved, and the areas where further study was required. What had been an item mentioned in the campaign paper thus here moved to a developed plan.

The second revenue raising item recommended was the repeal of the 4% dividend credit and $50 dividend exclusion. The case for repeal was succinctly presented, and it was stated that "a majority of those expert in the field" would agree. It was pointed out that the Senate had voted in 1959 and 1960 to repeal the credit, and indeed it was a favored target of Democratic Congressional tax reformers. This recommendation had also been stressed in the campaign paper.

The third revenue raising item recommended related to expense accounts. The Congress in 1960 had started to consider this area, reflecting a growing public concern over the "expense account racket." This concern was being fueled by sporadic articles on the wonders of expense account living. A Senate floor amendment denying deduction for entertainment expenses except food and drink had ended up as legislation requiring a report in 1961 on recent IRS efforts to strengthen audit enforcement.[11] Clearly the issue was moving to the forefront of tax reform, though here also the Treasury seemed philosophically inclined to stay away from legislative change and seek only strengthened enforcement. In contrast, we presented a strongly worded recommendation for extensive legislative correction, stating that administrative action would be inadequate but at the same time would mislead the public into thinking something had been done. The Report stressed the pervasive influence of the tax system itself in creating the expense account problem:

> It is very difficult to accept the view that the entertainment expense account and the generous business gift in the proportions to which they have grown

---

10. The ABA Tax Section committee mentioned by Surrey in Surrey's note e issued a report. REPORT OF THE SPECIAL COMM. ON EXTENSION OF WITHHOLDING TAXES, 1961 A.B.A. SEC. OF TAXATION PROGRAM AND COMM. REP., Vol. 1961, at 186–222 (1961). The conclusion was slightly less hostile to withholding than Surrey indicates: "The committee would favor a withholding tax on dividends and interest, if it were demonstrated to be a practicable way and the only practicable way to close the gap in reporting of dividends and interest within a reasonable time." *Id.* at 206.

11. Public Debt and Tax Relief Extension Act of 1960, Pub. L. No. 86-564, § 301, 74 Stat. 290, 291 (directing the Joint Committee on Internal Revenue Taxation to study the operation and effects of the existing tax rules governing entertainment expenses, and to report the results to Congress, along with any recommendations for changes in the law or in administrative practices). For a description of the events in Congress leading to this result, *see* Russell Baker, *500 Million Rise in Taxes Shelved*, NEW YORK TIMES, Jun. 25, 1960, at 46.

> are essential to the conduct of business. Rather, one has the feeling that here the tax system itself has set in motion a force which is steadily distorting the methods and patterns of business conduct. A way of life is being created whose origins are in large part traceable to the tax system and not to the real dictates of business.

Here also detailed guidelines for proposed legislation were set forth, covering denial of deductions for customer entertainment in restaurants, homes, nightclubs, yachts and the like except for necessary meals or other facilities furnished in the direct course of predominantly business discussions, meeting and conventions—it was here stated that "there is a difference between the meal that is incident to business activity on the one hand and the business activity that is incident to the meal or other entertainment on the other hand"; for expenses of executive apartments, country clubs, hunting lodges, yachts, etc. provided for executives where the use made was primarily for personal living, recreation or entertainment; for business gifts; and for travel expenses of personal travel joined with business travel. In addition, otherwise allowable deductions would have to be fully substantiated and not merely estimated, as was done under existing rules. Adrian DeWind had undertaken the initial writing on this part of the Report.

The fourth recommendation was to eliminate the treatment as capital gain of the excess of the sale price of machinery or buildings over its depreciated cost, to the extent the excess represented previously deducted depreciation. The 1954 allowance of accelerated depreciation had resulted in large depreciation deductions for tax purposes although the economic value of the asset had not declined as rapidly. This created a large tax gain on a sale of the asset but the gain was taxable only at preferred capital gain rates whereas the previous deduction, which the gain reflected, had been allowed at the higher ordinary income rates. We said the investment credit proposal should be made conditional on the elimination of this capital gain treatment.

These were the principal changes we recommended for 1961. They were deliberately limited in scope to what we thought feasible of legislative accomplishment in one year. We then proposed that:

> The President should announce that the Administration will develop in 1961 a program to achieve basic reform of the income tax structure through reconsideration of present preferences and inequalities, combined with reexamination of the rates in all brackets, upper brackets as well as lower brackets. The preparation of the legislation to implement this program is to be worked out by joint Executive branch-Congressional Committee and Staff efforts. The program should extend to estate and gift taxes as well as individual and corporate income taxes. This work is to be aimed towards the presentation of legislation in 1962. (Examples of topics involved in this program would be capital gains; personal expense deductions for interest and state and local taxes; employee fringe benefits; depletion; depreciation; tax-exempt securities; retirement income; tax treatment of the family; tax treatment of mutual organizations such as cooperative and mutual banks.)

The Report then sketched the background for this recommendation, here using almost verbatim the description developed for the campaign paper.[f] There then followed a strong statement on the need for Presidential leadership and dramatization of the issue of tax reform:

> Tax reform is difficult to achieve. An essential factor is strong Presidential and Executive Branch leadership, willing to present the case for reform in forcible fashion to the public. While another factor is cooperative Congressional support, such support is likely to be forthcoming only because of the Presidential leadership in urging the reform to the public. It must be remembered that the case for reform rests on an unassailable base — the concept of tax equity under which persons with equal incomes pay equal taxes. The argument that with each taxpayer paying his share, in relation to other taxpayers with the same income, the rates of tax can be reduced and the same revenue still obtained is a highly effective argument. This aspect of associating reform of the tax base with rate reductions in the upper and lower brackets significantly differentiates this approach from the usual "loophole closing" campaign. What is needed is strong leadership to bring this argument forcibly to the attention of the public, backed by a program to accomplish the objective.
>
> Along with this Presidential leadership, ways must be sought to dramatize the issues. Perhaps one way is a Congressional hearing which in a dramatic way could focus on the inequalities involved. Thus, cases of actual taxpayers — not named as individuals — could be presented to the Committee to show the effects of the existing preferences on actual tax liabilities. Ways must be sought of getting the public — and the Congress — really to appreciate the extent of the present inequalities.
>
> At the same time, the basic issues that lie at the core of each preference must be brought to the surface. One possible way is a series of private technical conferences — perhaps under the auspices of the Brookings Institution — in which those knowledgeable in the field and representing different points of view could be brought together. Under effective chairmen the extraneous, emotional issues urged in public by the pressure groups could be soon set aside in the search for the real issues and facts. If these conferences are successful, then the effectiveness of the later presentation to the Congress of the problems in each area will be greatly strengthened. It should be emphasized that much of the groundwork for a tax reform program has already been prepared. In most areas enough research and analysis have been accumulated to permit the development of the program. The problem is that of coming to grips with the basic issues in each area.[g, 12]

Both the emphasis on tax reform and the call for Presidential and Treasury Department leadership clearly meant an active tax program supported at the highest levels.

---

12. The unpublished Brookings paper described by Surrey in Surrey's footnote g is in the Surrey archives at the Harvard Law School Library. Stanley Surrey archives, HOLLIS000601595, 130–6.

The role envisaged in this Report for tax policy was thus completely at variance with the current Treasury posture, under which the top policy people had little interest in tax matters and there was little action in the Congress.

The Report considered matters on which a Presidential statement might be needed in 1961. One subject was that of tax exempt pension plans for the self-employed, being pushed by strong lobbies on behalf of doctors and other self-employed groups. The Report said the entire area of the tax treatment of pension benefits needed examination and urged that an effort be made to defer the self-employed aspect, which was politically sensitive:

> Legislation authorizing pension plans for the self-employed will be introduced early in 1961 (probably Congressman Keogh)[13] and will be backed by strong pressure groups, including the American Thrift Assembly. It is important that Congressional consideration of this legislation should not develop in 1961 to the point where its passage or defeat (or its veto?) becomes a major legislative matter. If consideration of this legislation is to be postponed, at least until 1962, it will probably take a strong Presidential statement to that effect. Moreover, such a statement should come early in the 1961 Congressional session before the legislation gathers force. Thus, it is important that it not be reported by the House Ways and Means Committee. For these reasons, it is recommended that a Presidential statement be so issued at the appropriate time taking the position above discussed.
>
> In brief, that announcement should be along the following lines: Under present tax law inequalities do exist, primarily in the upper brackets, which adversely affect the self-employed person as compared with corporate executives and with shareholder-employees of closely held corporations. However, the Administration is not prepared to resolve these inequalities by extending to the self-employed person the tax preferences presently obtained by corporate executives and shareholder-employees. Those preferences should be reconsidered as a part of the development of the basic tax reform program respecting the elimination of tax preferences and re-examination of tax rates. It will then be possible to consider the best method of achieving pension plan tax equality among the self-employed person, the shareholder-employee, and the corporate executive.
>
> In effect, the hope behind such an announcement would be that the pressure groups pushing H.R. 10 in order to obtain some tax equality in pension plan treatment for the self-employed as respects the treatment now obtained by corporate executives would be diverted into supporting basic tax reform with its possibility of reduced tax rates in the upper brackets as the avenue

13. Congress enacted such legislation in 1962. Self-Employed Individuals Tax Relief Act of 1962, Pub. L. No. 87-792, 76 Stat. 809. The legislation was so strongly associated with its champion, Rep. Eugene James Keogh (D., N.Y.), that the retirement plans it authorizes became commonly known as Keogh plans.

> of tax relief for the self-employed. Certainly, if viewed only as a matter of self-interest, such a result would be of greater benefit to the self-employed person than the authorization of pension plans alone. Viewed overall, it would promote a better tax structure.

The rather lengthy discussion — 12 pages — of issues in the pension area was initially prepared by Mortimer Caplin.

Another urgent issue was the treatment of foreign investment, where the existing tax preferences for that investment and the lobbying in recent years for still more tax benefits were beginning to be viewed with skepticism because of the growing emphasis placed on the large dollar outflow and its effect on the U.S. balance of payments. The Report urged reexamination of the many existing preferences, which were discussed, and essentially evidenced a negative attitude toward tax incentives in this area. Its recommendation was:

> As part of the dollar flow and balance of payment problems, the President may have to take a position on the present treatment under the United States tax law of foreign investment and foreign income. It is recommended that the position taken be along the following lines: The present tax treatment of foreign income requires reexamination to ascertain to what extent existing tax incentives for foreign investment should be withdrawn or modified so as (a) to prevent abuses of those incentives and (b) to confine them to the types of investment activity believed desirable from the standpoint of our general foreign economic policy with respect to the developed and the underdeveloped areas of the world.
>
> This study should also involve a reexamination of the tax treaty program as respects the technical drafting of the treaties and the matters covered in treaties. Approval of pending treaties should be deferred until this study is made.
>
> In a closely related matter, the steps under consideration to implement the Act of Bogota (September 1960) with respect to tax reform in Latin America should be supported.

Finally, there were recommendations for strengthened enforcement activities, all of which called for "imaginative and strong leadership by a determined Commissioner of Internal Revenue, backed by the Treasury Department and the President" — these covered extensive use of the new tool of automatic data processing; attention to the extensive corruption believed to exist in lower levels of the Service in a few of the larger cities; correction of abuses in inventory reporting; and improvement of Service skills to match the skills of the tax bar. There were also recommendations for special studies, covering such topics as tax-exempt foundations, especially the small family-controlled foundations; the feasibility and benefits of an averaging system, the complexity of the tax law; and the cumbersome judicial structure for handling tax matters.

The Task Force Report had the approval of the entire group, though Mr. Ture was really not a supporter of the investment credit. The Report totaled 138 pages, was prepared in a month, and mailed to Sorensen on the target date, December 30. The main burden of writing the Report, as in all such groups, fell on the chairman, and here I found the campaign document and the thinking that went into it very useful. Also, of course, much of my writing in the previous few years had been on tax reform and had covered many of the matters touched on in the Report. But the detailed material on the investment credit, expense accounts, and withholding was really new ground for the entire group. Also some of the other recommendations—for example, strengthening enforcement efforts, the material on pension benefits—were here brought together for the first time. A preliminary summary had been given to Sorensen on December 16, and a conference on the recommendations held at Cambridge on December 17 by the Task Force with Sorensen and David Bell,[14] an economist on the Harvard faculty and now Budget Director designate. During the preparation of the Report I kept in touch with Samuelson and Professor Wilbur Cohen[15] of the University of Michigan, who headed the Task Force on Health and Social Security, so that reasonable coordination could be achieved. One aspect was carefully touched on in the transmittal letter to Sorensen:

> As you are aware, these recommendations of the Report have not been discussed with Chairman Mills of the House Ways and Means Committee or, indeed, any other Member of Congress associated with tax matters. Consequently, you may well want to consider, especially if any publicity is to be given in any way to the Report or recommendations, how it would be appropriate to handle the aspect of Congressional relationships.

1961—Appointment as Assistant Secretary for Tax Policy

In December, while the Task Force Report was being prepared, I was coming under consideration for appointment to a tax policy position in the Treasury. The current custom in the Treasury was to have tax policy handled as only a part of the responsibilities of a person occupying a policy position, usually that of General Counsel. At times the tax policy work was performed by a Special Assistant who did only

14. During the Kennedy administration David Elliott Bell was initially director of the Bureau of the Budget, and later administrator of the Agency for International Development (continuing into the Johnson administration). His varied career included stints on the Harvard faculty and service as an executive vice-president of the Ford Foundation. Eric Pace, *David E. Bell, Budget Director for Kennedy, Is Dead at 81*, New York Times, Sep. 12, 2000, at B10.

15. Working at the Social Security Board from the mid-1930s to the mid-1950s, Wilbur J. Cohen played a major role in the creation and development of Social Security. Later he taught public welfare administration at the University of Michigan. His work in the Department of Health, Education and Welfare (HEW) during the Kennedy and Johnson administrations culminated in a brief stint as Secretary of HEW in 1968. Wolfgang Saxon, *Wilbur Cohen, Leading Architect of Social Legislation, Dies at 73*, New York Times, May 19, 1987, at D30. In 1998 the headquarters building of the Social Security Administration was renamed in Cohen's honor.

that task. I thought these arrangements unsatisfactory because they implied tax policy was not a major Treasury concern. The first arrangement meant that the tax work could be handled by an official along with other important duties, and I knew this could not be done if tax matters were to occupy a major role in Treasury policy. The second arrangement indicated that the tax work was not important enough to warrant being handled by a Presidential appointee. I therefore stated, when asked, that a new position — Assistant Secretary for Tax Policy — be established with jurisdiction over all matters relating to tax policy activities.

I understood through my brother, Walter S. Surrey,[16] a prominent Washington attorney who understood Washington Democratic political circles, that my name was on a number of lists being drawn up by various talent hunters for the President-Elect. After the meeting with Sorensen and Bell, they discussed the tentative Task Force conclusions with Treasury Secretary Designate Douglas Dillon[17] and recommended my appointment to the Treasury. In early January an associate of my brother, Abba Schwartz,[18] spoke directly with Kennedy and received the impression Kennedy was favorable to the appointment. Schwartz conveyed this to me just before DeWind, Caplin and I were to meet in Washington with Dillon to go over the Report. That meeting went well. Dillon had read the Report and asked good questions about several parts. The questions and discussion did indicate, however, that tax policy was a new field for him. He therefore did not have any formulated positions or views, but also seemed free of pre-conceived biases. He seemed disposed to discuss issues in an open, exploratory way without plunging at once into pragmatic, dogmatic or political postures.

The Task Force members met with President Kennedy at the Cambridge home of Professor Arthur M. Schlesinger, Jr.[19] on the afternoon of Monday, January 9, 1961, in a publicly scheduled meeting, to present their Report. All but Mr. Ture were there. We discussed the Report for over an hour. When we presented the investment tax credit, Kennedy asked how much investment would it produce. At that point he left the room to take a call — fortunately, because the "experts" had not asked themselves that question and hence had not thought through the answer. I asked Professor Musgrave for an on-the-spot estimate and he gave the figure of about $3 billion, at a revenue cost of around $2 billion. We gave this to Kennedy, saying it was a rough

16. At the time of his death in 1989, Walter Sterling Surrey was a senior partner in the Washington law firm of Jones, Day, Reavis & Pogue, specializing in international law. He was four years younger than Stanley. *Walter Sterling Surrey, Lawyer*, THE WASHINGTON POST, Feb. 1, 1989, at B7.

17. C. Douglas Dillon served as Secretary of the Treasury from 1961 to 1965. Earlier he had been ambassador to France under President Eisenhower, and later he became president of the Metropolitan Museum of Art. Eric Pace, *C. Douglas Dillon Dies at 93, Was in Kennedy Cabinet*, NEW YORK TIMES, Jan. 12, 2003, at 32.

18. Immigration law expert Abba P. Schwartz served as an assistant secretary in the State Department during the Kennedy and Johnson administrations. Glenn Fowler, *Abba Schwartz, Refugee Expert, Dies at Age 73*, NEW YORK TIMES, Sep. 15, 1989, at B6.

19. Harvard historian Arthur M. Schlesinger, Jr., served as a special assistant to President Kennedy from 1961 to 1963. He wrote two Pulitzer Prize-winning books, THE AGE OF JACKSON (1945), and A THOUSAND DAYS: JOHN F. KENNEDY IN THE WHITE HOUSE (1965). Douglas Martin, *Arthur Schlesinger, Historian of Power, Dies at 89*, NEW YORK TIMES, Mar. 1, 2007, at A1.

estimate. But I certainly realized that we "experts" had slipped in not asking ourselves a crucial question and that Kennedy had the sense to ask it. I doubt I made that mistake again. Yet a decade later the question could still be asked and the economists, who by then had studied the matter, would find themselves really unable to answer it with consensus or a reasonable degree of precision. Professor Musgrave's answer on hindsight was a rational one.

When we discussed "tax reform," Kennedy asked why the issue was important and he seemed to have trouble in pinning down the significance of tax equity and tax fairness.[20] I responded by using an example in the Report, pointing out that persons with the same income pay vastly different income taxes so that we have a whole series of tax rates rather than the single rate structure that most people assume: (add tax exempt)[21] a person with $100,000 of capital gains has a rate of 25%, a married person with $100,000 of oil income has a rate of 32%, a married person with $100,000 of dividend income has a rate of 47%; a married person with a salary or professional income has a rate of 66%. Kennedy liked this illustration of tax unfairness and thought it a useful way to present the picture.

The other Task Force Reports were being made public and Kennedy seemed to assume our Report would be. His press secretary, Pierre Salinger,[22] had told the press that he would "release the Surrey report probably late Monday." I volunteered to Kennedy that the Congressional tax people, especially Chairman Wilbur Mills of the House Ways and Means Committee, would probably not like suddenly to read about these recommendations in the paper and would therefore be prejudiced against them. Kennedy thought quickly about this and agreed, and said the Report would be kept confidential until it could be discussed with Mills and others. I had prepared two summaries, one somewhat detailed running to eight pages and one of two pages, and suggested that the latter be used in any press briefing. Kennedy agreed, and later Salinger briefed the press along the lines of this summary. This excerpt from the Boston Herald of January 10, 1961 indicates the information Salinger released—most of the other papers did not include all this detail:

> During the day Kennedy revealed, through his press secretary, Pierre Salinger: ... That a "taxation task force" which conferred with him at Prof.

---

20. This formulation, "tax equity and tax fairness," was a favorite of Surrey's. There is no indication that for Surrey there was any difference in meaning between "equity" and "fairness." The phrase seems to have been an example of redundancy for emphasis, similar to "cease and desist," "null and void," and, for that matter, "Ways and Means."

21. Presumably Surrey had in mind here something along the lines of, "a person with $100,000 of municipal bond interest income has a rate of zero." Why Surrey left himself a note to add that later, rather than simply adding it at the time, is a mystery.

22. Pierre Emil George Salinger was press secretary for Presidents Kennedy and Johnson from 1961 to 1964. He was briefly a United States senator (D., Cal.), for a few months in 1964. Appointed to fill a vacancy, he lost his bid for a full term. In later years he worked as a television journalist for ABC News. Thomas J. Lueck, *Pierre Salinger, Kennedy Aide, Dies at 79*, NEW YORK TIMES, Oct. 17, 2004, at 42.

> Schlesinger's home had submitted a sweeping report on policy recommendations for 1961.
>
> Recommendations, it was announced, covered measures designed to promote economic growth by stimulating a higher level of private capital formation; legislation to deal promptly with "several more acute abuses and inequities existing under the income tax"; legislation and executive action to beef up enforcement of laws" and to increase the effectiveness of the Internal Revenue Service";
>
> Recommendations for a program of basic tax reform with respect to income, estate and gift taxes, aimed at the elimination or lessening of "existing tax preferences combined with appropriate reductions in tax rates."
>
> The report also covers other tax issues in which a statement of the Administration's views "may be requested or would be appropriate in 1961."
>
> Kennedy himself made no comment on the report. In fact, he passed up many opportunities for comment during the day.[23]

The A.P. release stated a "sweeping shakeup of the federal tax structure" had been recommended in a "secret report from a task force on taxation" and spoke of "selective cuts in both corporate and individual income taxes, but compensating tightening up in some areas which now get special treatment."[24] It also carried some of the detail described in the Boston Herald.

As we prepared to leave, Kennedy mentioned to Professor Caplin that Robert Kennedy[25] had talked to him about Caplin and that the matter was being worked out. Caplin should therefore talk to Robert Kennedy. Caplin, who had taught both Robert and Edward Kennedy at Virginia Law School,[26] had been a candidate for appointment as Commissioner of Internal Revenue and this conversation indicated he would be given that position. As we were leaving, Kennedy then asked me to remain for a few minutes. He said he would like me to join his Administration to work on tax policy and would I do so. I promptly accepted. He asked what position was appropriate and mentioned Under Secretary, but I stated the appropriate position was Assistant Secretary. Kennedy then said an announcement would be made in a few days and the meeting ended. That same day, I informed Dean Erwin Griswold of the Harvard Law School of this situation.

The events of the day really decided the essentials of the 1961–1962 tax program of the Kennedy Administration. I certainly doubt that the President was aware of this and I know that I did not foresee the basic design had thus been formulated. Yet

23. *Kennedy Pledges Rule of Integrity*, BOSTON HERALD, Jan. 10, 1961, at 10 (placement of all quotation marks as in original).

24. *Shakeup in Tax Structure Recommended to Kennedy*, MIAMI HERALD, Jan. 10, 1961.

25. Robert F. Kennedy, the younger brother of President Kennedy, served as Attorney General from 1961 to 1964, and as a member of the Senate (D., N.Y.) from 1965 until his assassination in 1968. Gladwin Hill, Kennedy is Dead, Victim of Assassin, NEW YORK TIMES, June 6,1968 p. 1.

26. Robert graduated from the University of Virginia School of Law in 1951, Edward in 1959. "The Kennedys at Virginia," THE UNIVERSITY OF VIRGINIA MAGAZINE, Winter 2009 available at: https://uvamagazine.org/articles/the_kennedys_at_virginia.

the work that started with the campaign document and ended with the Task Force Report established the tax contours for 1961–1962, and indeed much of 1963–1964. The link was the participation — in part through coincidences — of the same person in the three events, the campaign document, the Task Force Report, and the Treasury appointment to handle tax policy.

On January 11 the Boston Globe in a story by its Washington correspondent stated that I would be appointed the No. 1 tax policy man in the Treasury, either as Assistant Secretary or General Counsel.[27] I had not discussed the matter with the papers and assumed the story came from Salinger's Office. Also on January 11, the Wall Street Journal carried a story giving considerable detail about the Report.[28] It described the "investment credit" and the arguments in the Report why this approach was better than larger, annual depreciation allowances. It also mentioned prompt legislation to repeal the 4% dividend credit and the $50 exclusion dividend, to withhold taxes on dividends and interest, to narrow the definition of what income is eligible to be taxed at the lower capital gain rate, and to tighten the tax treatment of mutual savings banks and savings and loan associations, and in addition reference to loophole closing proposals and a program of basic reform of income, estate and gift taxes. The detail in this article was attributed to task force members, who probably disclosed the information. I assumed that the member involved was Mr. Ture and did not consider the article a helpful one.

The appointment as Treasury Assistant Secretary for Tax Policy was offered by the President on Monday, January 9 and accepted. On Friday the appointment was in a precarious position. Dean McGeorge Bundy[29] called me from Cambridge in the afternoon to say he had been with the President earlier and had been asked to convey this message: The President does not feel that he can get the appointment past the Congress at this moment, since there is strong and clear-cut objection to it. The President said I ought to know this right away and will I stand by.

Shortly thereafter President Kennedy called me: Doug Dillon has received rumbles from the Hill. He had asked Senator Kerr to check and Kerr reported that I was a controversial figure.[30] This — the President said — is to my credit, but he is sorry the

---

27. Robert Healy, *Kennedy Gives Harvard Man No. 1 Tax Post*, Boston Globe, Jan. 11, 1961, at 1. The story, which includes rather detailed biographical information, accurately describes Surrey as "the author of many books and articles on taxation that have given him wide recognition as an expert in his field."

28. *Tax Policy Report for Kennedy Outlines Ways to Spur Economy, Cut Income Taxes*, Wall Street Journal, Jan. 10, 1961, at 3 (Surrey was off by one day on the date of the story). The story identifies Surrey as the leader of the task force, and adds that the report "is considered important because there are indications Mr. Surrey will be given a high Treasury Department post in which he could play a key role in carrying out his own recommendations." The story also asserts that the task force recommendations are "the sort of tax reform House Ways and Means Committee Chairman Mills ... had in mind when he held hearings late in 1959 to solicit views on tax changes from experts."

29. At that time Bundy was dean of the Harvard Faculty of Arts and Sciences.

30. Robert S. Kerr (D., Okla.) served in the Senate from 1949 until his death in 1963. *Senator Robert S. Kerr Is Dead; Wealthy Oklahoma Oil Man, 66*, New York Times, Jan. 2, 1963, at 1. Given Surrey's strong opposition to tax benefits for the oil and gas industry, it is little surprise that a senator from Oklahoma may have opposed his nomination.

problem came up. He would like to have me come to Washington but we don't have to get in a fight immediately. He will wait for two or three days. Try to get the matter straightened out. Find out if Kerr talked to Stam.[31] Talk to Doug Dillon and perhaps it would be worthwhile for me to meet Kerr. Do what I — Surrey — can to find out the situation.

Do what I can! That seemed to me a formidable task. But clearly it had to be performed since I did not want to be in the position of persona non grata in Washington during this Administration. It was clear that if I were blackballed this way this time, that would be a distinct mark opposite my name. So I started on three weeks of telephoning, feeling distinctly unhappy about the whole matter but recognizing that with all the turmoil of a new Administration unless I tried to straighten out the situation no one else would.

On January 16 the Wall Street Journal carried a story headlined "Opposition Rises to Naming Surrey to Treasury Post — He Would Set Tax Policy — His Attacks on Loopholes Trigger Many Protests."[32] The article went on in this vein: "The possibility that an ardent foe of tax loopholes might become the Treasury's tax expert is provoking bitter protests to the Kennedy Administration. Word that … Surrey is being considered for the Treasury post has spurred a vigorous effort by oil companies and other groups to block the appointment. They fear tougher tax treatment if Mr. Surrey gets the job.… Most Kennedy aides had regarded Mr. Surrey's nomination as a sure thing.… For the past week, however, groups that might be hurt by Mr. Surrey's tax

31. Surrey's typescript has "Stan" here, but the intended reference is undoubtedly to Colin Stam, long-time chief of staff of the Joint Committee on Taxation and long-time Surrey nemesis. George Yin has reviewed Surrey's handwritten notes from this period (in the Surrey archives at the Harvard Law Library, Folder 391-2), and reports that the notes make clear that Stam's name came up in the conversations in which Surrey attempted to discover the source of the opposition to his appointment. In one note Surrey asks, "Did Kerr go to Stam?" In another he muses, "[C]an't see turning it down … once started working would quiet down, even with Stam." George K. Yin, "*Who Speaks for Tax Equity and Tax Fairness?" Stanley Surrey and the Tax Legislative Process,* 39 VA. TAX REV. 39, 49–66 (2019) [hereinafter George K. Yin]. As described in the editors' introduction to this volume, much of the "pain and anguish" (as Surrey writes in Chapter 3) Surrey endured in his 1961 confirmation hearing resulted from senatorial umbrage over aspersions Surrey had cast on Congress in his 1957 article, *The Congress and the Tax Lobbyist — How Special Provisions Get Enacted*, 70 HARV. L. REV. 1145 (1957). Given that senators do not routinely peruse the *Harvard Law Review*, it is plausible that Stam brought the article to the attention of some members of the Senate Finance Committee (and perhaps other senators as well). According to Mortimer Caplin, Stam had developed a "strong hatred" of Surrey as a result of the 1957 article. Steve Shashy & Devon Yamauchi, *Talking Shop: An Interview with Mortimer M. Caplin*, 34 VA. TAX REV. 503, 508 (2015). Also according to Caplin, during Surrey's confirmation hearing Stam hovered behind the senators and occasionally whispered to them; Caplin had no doubt that Stam had briefed the committee members on the article. Interview by George K. Yin with Mortimer Caplin, in Charlottesville VA, 3–4 (Oct. 14, 2010). For Yin's thorough consideration of the role Stam may have played in stirring up opposition to Surrey's nomination, *see* George K. Yin, *id* at 71–72, 78.

32. *Opposition Rises To Naming Surrey To Treasury Post*, WALL STREET JOURNAL, Jan. 16, 1961, at 7.

views have been bombarding the Kennedy Administration with protests." The article then briefly covered the series of reforms I had recommended in "speeches, articles and Congressional testimony." The list was reasonably accurate except that it included "tightening mineral percentage depletion allowances" whereas I had instead called for an "objective and comprehensive study" of those allowances. The difference, however, would hardly slow down the oil companies if they were as aroused as the article stated.[h, 33]

I started on over a week of intensive telephone calls. These were some of the principal calls, though not all in this order, and the response:

Dillon: He really had nothing to add, was hoping it would work out and wanted me to stay in touch with him.

Laurence Woodworth[34] (Assistant Chief of Staff (check) of the Joint Committee on International Revenue Taxation and a friend): He believes the objections come from Texas and I should try to check with Representative Frank Ikard[35] from Texas, who is on the Ways and Means Committee. Woodworth did not think the Senate would not confirm, and once I started working the opposition would die down.

My brother: He talked to Representative W. R. Poage[36] of Texas who spoke to Ikard. Ikard said he disagrees with more than half of what Surrey says, but he is one of the most honest and able fellows around. Ikard would support him up and down the line.

Herman Biegel (a Washington attorney and friend, whom I had asked several years ago to handle the legislative end of a tax matter for a Boston client of mine

---

33. For the passage from the debate quoted by Surrey in his note h, *see Transcript of the Third Kennedy-Nixon Television Debate on Issues of Campaign*, NEW YORK TIMES, Oct. 14, 1960, at 20. There are several minor differences between the transcription Surrey quotes and the *Times* transcription; the only difference of any significance is that in place of Surrey's "tax evasion" the *Times* has, more plausibly, "taxation." The editors have revised Surrey's quotation to reflect the *Times* transcription. The debate was a television debate, rather than a radio debate (as Surrey mistakenly describes it).

34. Laurence N. Woodworth was an economist on the staff of the Joint Committee on Taxation from 1944 to 1964. (It is unclear whether he was ever officially Stam's chief assistant. In the resume Woodworth submitted to Congress in connection with his 1977 appointment he indicated he was simply a staff economist during those years, but in his memorial tribute to Woodworth (cited below) Surrey states that Woodworth became Stam's chief assistant in the early 1960s; perhaps Woodworth filled the function without the title.) From 1964 to 1977 he was the chief of staff of the Joint Committee. He died in 1977 at the age of 59, after having served less than a year as the Assistant Secretary of the Treasury for Tax Policy. *Lawrence* [sic] *Woodworth Dies at 59, Administration Tax Policy Expert*, NEW YORK TIMES, Dec. 8, 1977, at 47. Surrey wrote a thoughtful tribute to Woodworth following Woodworth's death. Stanley S. Surrey, *Tribute to Dr. Laurence N. Woodworth: Two Decades of Federal Tax History Viewed from this Perspective*, 32 NAT. TAX J. 227 (1979). Surrey has much more to say about Woodworth in Chapter 10.

35. Frank N. Ikard (D., Tex.) was a member of the House of Representatives from 1951 to 1961. He resigned in 1961 to become an oil industry lobbyist. *Frank N. Ikard; Former Texas Congressman*, LOS ANGELES TIMES, May 3, 1991, at 30.

36. William R. Poage (D., Tex.) was a House member from 1937 to 1978. Richard Pearson, *Former U.S. Rep. William R. (Bob) Poage Dies*, THE WASHINGTON POST, Jan. 4, 1987, at B5.

who had worked with Senator George Smathers[37] on the matter): I said an important person in all this is Senator Smathers who is on the Senate Finance Committee and is a close friend of Kennedy. Could Biegel see what the picture was. (My brother was also asking several Congressman to talk to Smathers).

Henry Fowler[38] (He was by then Under Secretary-designate. I had talked with him on Thursday, January 12, meeting him for the first time. We had a discussion on the scope of the position of Assistant Secretary for Tax Policy, and agreed that direct oversight of the Internal Revenue Service was not within that scope but rested directly with Fowler. However, I would have a direct input on administrative activities that affected tax policy): He said Dillon was for me. I should explore where the objections came from and why. Try to get Kerr in the frame of mind that while some don't like me personally I would be an effective spokesman and acceptable as such.

My brother: He talked to James Webb[39] who was Treasury Under Secretary and Director of the Budget under Truman, knew me in a general way and was close to Senator Kerr. Webb later reported that Kerr said there was no problem as to confirmation or day-to-day operations. Indeed Kerr had not heard anything on it. He was quite reassuring to Webb.

Woodworth: All comments indicate someone from Texas has blocked me.

My brother: Representative Eugene Keogh, from New York and on the Ways and Means Committee, said the opposition Caplin made a strong pitch for the original arrangement — Surrey in Treasury, Caplin as Commissioner.[40] He believes he made an impression on Fowler and Dillon.

Charles Davis (Chicago attorney and a friend):[41] He called to say he talked with Representative Hale Boggs[42] from Louisiana (an oil state) on the Ways and Means

---

37. George A. Smathers was a longtime Democratic politician from Miami, Florida. He served two terms in the House of Representatives and three in the Senate. He was known for his views against communism and for coddling Southern segregationists. *George A. Smathers, 93, Dies; Former Senator From Floria*, New York Times, Jan. 21, 2007.

38. Henry H. Fowler, a lawyer, served as Under Secretary of the Treasury from 1961 to 1964, and as Treasury Secretary from 1965 to 1968. Robert D. Hershey, Jr., *Henry Fowler is Dead at 91; Former Treasury Secretary*, New York Times, Jan. 5, 2000, at A19.

39. James E. Webb was never Under Secretary of the Treasury, but he did briefly serve as executive assistant to Treasury Under Secretary Oliver Max Gardner, prior to Webb's appointment as director of the Bureau of the Budget in 1946. Webb later served as Under Secretary of State (1949–1952), and as director of the National Aeronautics and Space Administration (1961–1968). Bruce Lambert, *James Webb, Who Led Moon Program, Dies at 85*, New York Times, Mar. 29, 1992, at 32. The planned Webb Space Telescope is named in his honor.

40. This sentence does not make complete sense as written, but the editors have left it as-is because it is not clear what Surrey intended.

41. Charles W. Davis was a senior partner in the Chicago law firm of Hopkins & Sutter. In 1949, he was the first chief counsel to the U.S. House Ways and Means Committee, and in 1952 President Harry Truman appointed him general counsel to the IRS. Kenan Heise, *Charles W. Davis, 69, Prominent Tax Lawyer*, Chicago Tribune, Feb. 19, 1987.

42. Thomas Hale Boggs (D., La.) was a member of the House of Representatives from 1947 to 1972, serving as both majority whip (1962 to 1971) and as majority leader (1971 to 1972). He died

Committee and he is not opposed. There was opposition in the Committee, however. Is Senator Kerr doing some trading on this matter on behalf of oil? People are counting on Surrey to demonstrate he doesn't have horns on, and this is to be accomplished with those who have raised doubts. He told Fowler no one can match my experience; why go for amateurs. Was the trouble with Mills?

Lawrence O'Brien:[43] The problem is with the oil companies. We shouldn't delay. Seems to agree there is no fight on the confirmation. I should talk to Ralph Dungan.[44]

Ralph Dungan (an Assistant to Kennedy and a talent hunter): "The flags are up." He is interested in seeing me come down. He has a damn high regard for me but also knows there is strongly expressed discontent in areas where I need support. I should see Kerr and Mills, tell them I am interested in being appointed to the Treasury position, believe I am in the running for it, and I could get their support. Here I blew up and told Dungan that he didn't have the picture straight. The *President* has *asked* me to come down and I had agreed. So the job already was mine and the only problem was to steer it through. Dungan said he didn't realize that, came from the banks and perhaps the Chase Bank, and goes back to the oil companies (there had been some talk Keogh was opposed to the appointment).

He also talked to Abe Fortas[45] who then spoke to Vice-President elect Johnson and reported there was no problem there.

Fowler: He had talked to Lawrence O'Brien, Kennedy's campaign manager and now the chief of liaison with Congress. Both Mills and Kerr said there is a real problem on both tax committees, more in the Senate. Mills said he personally would be pleased with the appointment and the main problems were in the Senate. Kennedy had asked Kerr to look into the matter and it is a pretty substantial problem. Some are for me. How much of the opposition is personal and how much is opposition to tax reform? Are my views too specific? Dillon had told O'Brien no one is better qualified to be an exponent of tax reform and he is all for me. But

(presumably) in 1972, when a small plane in which he was a passenger disappeared in Alaska. *Alaska Jury Declares Boggs Died in Flight*, New York Times, Feb. 8, 1973, at 46.

43. Lawrence F. O'Brien had been the director of the 1960 Kennedy presidential campaign and served as congressional liaison in both the Kennedy and Johnson administrations. He later directed presidential campaigns of other Democratic candidates. From 1975 to 1984 he served, very successfully, as commissioner of the National Basketball Association. Albin Krebs, *Lawrence O'Brien, Democrat, Dies at 73*, New York Times, Sep. 29, 1990, at 29.

44. Ralph A. Dungan was a special assistant to President Kennedy from 1961 to 1964, and ambassador to Chile from 1964 to 1967. Bruce Weber, *Ralph A. Dungan, Aide in Kennedy White House, Dies at 90*, New York Times, Oct. 8, 2013, at A20.

45. Abraham Fortas, who had co-founded the law firm of Arnold & Fortas (later Arnold & Porter) in 1946, was a close associate of Vice President-Elect Johnson. President Johnson appointed Fortas to the United States Supreme Court in 1965. Fortas served only four years on the Court, resigning in 1969 under an ethics cloud. Linda Greenhouse, *Ex-Justice Abe Fortas Dies at 71; Shaped Historic Rulings on Rights*, New York Times, Apr. 7, 1982, at A1. *See also*, Laura Kalman, Abe Fortas: A Biography (1990).

would the appointment endanger tax reform? There is substantial opposition and should they allow it to stand in the way?

Leo Irwin[46] (Chief Counsel to the Ways and Means Committee, and a friend): There is no problem on confirmation; in fact the oil opposition should help there. "We all hope he comes down."

Caplin: He talked to Dillon and Fowler. The question in their minds is will the appointment jeopardize the tax program. They asked Caplin to stay flexible since they may have to turn to him. They are looking for other names and what I had told him changed his viewpoint. He would look into the matter.[i]

Fowler: I wanted to bring him up to date on all the various matters as I saw them. I thought I had good support, and once the appointment was made that would be it and there would be no trouble in the tax committees. He said he would inform Dillon.

My brother: He spoke to Senator Vance Hartke,[47] who is on the Finance Committee and was Chairman of the Democratic Senatorial Campaign Fund. He hasn't heard of opposition but will check. He will support me 100 percent.

Dan Smith (a colleague at Harvard Business School and in charge of tax policy during much of the Eisenhower Administration. We differed strongly on many issues, agreed on others, and had taught a seminar together for a number of years): He called to say he had talked with Mills, who thought it would be a misfortune if Surrey didn't get the job, in view of the others that then might get it.

Biegel: John O'Keefe, Senator Smathers' legislative assistant, spoke to Smathers and Smathers then spoke to the President. Kennedy said I want Surrey but Smathers and Kerr oppose. Smathers said he did not oppose me. "I can live with him and I am in favor of him." Smathers understands Kerr has withdrawn his opposition or has affirmatively approved, assuming he ever did oppose it. Smathers told O'Keefe it is settled and O'Keefe said this can be passed to Surrey.

This was, I believe, on January 24. It was an obviously hectic period and difficult to operate from Cambridge. Yet I felt it better to stay away from Washington since many friends were at work and could do more than I could. My presence in Washington would have made it all seem too personal and would have built up the image of seeking a position rather than clearing the way to a previously offered appointment. Obviously the offer could be withdrawn. In fact, as all these conversations indicated, it was very much up in the air, with uncertainty and rumor adding to confusion and with much else on the minds of the key White House people.

---

46. Leo H. Irwin served as Ways and Means chief counsel from 1949 until 1968, when President Johnson appointed him to the Tax Court. Irwin retired from the Tax Court in 1983. Perhaps his most enduring claim to fame is a poem, "Ode to Conway Twitty," which Irwin included as a footnote to an opinion involving the tax liability of country singer Conway Twitty. Jenkins v. Commissioner, T. C. Memo. 1983-667.

47. Vance Hartke (D., Ind.) was a member of the Senate from 1959 to 1977. Martin Weil, *Sen. Vance Hartke, 84, Dies; Early Foe of War in Vietnam*, THE WASHINGTON POST, Jul. 29, 2003, at B6.

The Inaugural events were taking place. Next followed the intense campaign by the Administration to enlarge the House Rules Committee and this occupied all the White House Congressional efforts. So I had to mark time. I had gathered from Dungan that he would get to my situation after the House Rules Committee battles and obviously he didn't want to antagonize any Congressman during that period. That battle ended successfully on January 31.[48] But the Wall Street Journal was still referring to my situation. On January 27 a round-up article on the first week of the Kennedy era said:

> Watching Cabinet and sub-Cabinet appointments breeze through Senatorial Confirmation formalities, one might easily conclude Mr. Kennedy's desires go almost without challenge. This is in part illusory; some Kennedy appointments are being blocked—by stopping them before he offers them. The liberals blocked Fulbright as Secretary of State; the conservatives are blocking Stanley Surrey as the Treasury's tax policy man. The trick is simply done: An opposing Senator does not threaten to reject confirmation; he just threatens to scuttle any legislative proposals from an unpalatable appointee.[49]

During this period, some media articles were stressing that the Kennedy Administration appears to be "serious about pushing tax reform." Hobart Rowen in a January 24 syndicated article "Tax Reform Gets Push"[50] brought together the Task Force Report, Walter Heller's appointment as Chairman of the Counsel of Economic Advisors—Heller was a Minnesota public finance professor with a background of writing urging tax reform[51]—and Dillon's indicating in his Senate Finance Confirmation hearing that he would push tax reform proposals and indeed had surprised liberal Democrats by opposing the 4 percent dividend credit and the $50 dividend exemption. Dillon's testimony indicated he had fully absorbed the Task Force Report and was cautiously moving to a strong tax reform posture. My views, all in the written record, were stressed and it was said I had written the key article in the 1959 Mills three volume Committee compendium on tax reform—it happened to be the first article and was an overall synthesis. Business Week and Newsweek had articles on tax reform

48. Surrey's typescript has "January 27 (check)" here, but in fact the battle did not end until a narrow House vote (217 to 212 in the administration's favor) on January 31. The vote increased the committee membership from twelve to fifteen, thereby shifting control from a conservative coalition to a group friendly to the administration. John D. Morris, *Rayburn Victory: Speaker Leads Fight to Curb the Power of Conservatives*, New York Times, Feb. 1, 1961, at 1.

49. Henry Gemmill, *First Week: The Kennedy Era Starts with Confusion But Deliberate Caution Also Is Evident*, Wall Street Journal, Jan. 27, 1961, at 6.

50. The editors have not found the newspaper in which the Rowen article was published with the headline quoted by Surrey. For the same article in a different paper, see Hobart Rowen, *Tax Reform May Come with New Administration*, Des Moines Register, Jan. 22, 1961, at 37.

51. Walter W. Heller chaired the Council of Economic Advisers from 1961 to 1964. Before and after his government service he was a member of the economics faculty of the University of Minnesota. Peter T. Kilborn, *Walter Heller, 71, Economic Adviser in 60's, Dead*, New York Times, Jun. 17, 1987, at B11. For more on Heller, *see generally*, Herbert Stein, The Fiscal Revolution in America (1969); J. Ronnie Davis, The New Economics and the Old Economists (1971).

stressing the Task Force Report and my previous writings.[52] I assumed that in some quarters all such articles could only intensify my problems.

Then a new turn developed as several national columnists picked up the episode. Murray Kempton in the New York Post on _____ said it was the first test of the Kennedy Administration[53] (check). On January 27 Jack Steele's column in the Scripps-Howard Newspapers described the entire situation, saying "Lobbying pressure, primarily from the oil and gas industry, apparently has forced the Kennedy Administration to back away from naming one of the nation's top tax experts on tax reform to a key Treasury post."[54] Steele stated my name had been checked with the tax committees, and while there was opposition I would be confirmed. This had been relayed to Kennedy but Congressional sources now reported that my name had apparently been withdrawn. I had met Steele earlier in the year and had given him some material for a series of articles he had written on tax reform. But I had not spoken to him about the current situation.

Marquis Childs in his Washington Post column of February 1 headed "The Urgent Issue of Tax Reform" focused on oil and percentage depletion in counterposing the need for tax reform with the political obstacles in Congress. He ended this way:

> In this connection Capitol Hill is awaiting an appointment in the Treasury that may show which way the wind is blowing. That is for an assistant secretary in charge of tax policy. Reported under consideration is Stanley S. Surrey of the Harvard Law School, a noted specialist on taxation who has performed various missions for the Government.
>
> But the same interests opposing any change in the tax structure regard Surrey with deep suspicion. They are fearful that he would push a vigorous program of tax reform. If this were to be done with the sanction of Secretary of the Treasury Douglas Dillon, who has high marks for respectability in the financial world, it might win acceptance.
>
> "Before my term is ended" the President solemnly said "we shall have to test anew whether a nation organized and governed such as ours can endure."
>
> Here is a firm and significant test.[55]

Drew Pearson on February 2 in a column on oil called attention to the opposition of the oil industry to my appointment.[56] I had not spoken to any of these newspaper

---

52. *Blueprints ... For Washington: High Flying and Hardheaded*, NEWSWEEK, Jan. 23, 1961, at 20.

53. The editors have been unable to locate this article.

54. Jack Steele, *Oil Lobby Blamed for Forcing JFK to Drop Tax Expert*, PITTSBURGH PRESS, Jan. 27, 1961, at 22. According to Steele, "This decision, unless it is reversed by President Kennedy, may doom at the outset his administration's widely advertised tax reform program." Steele also notes that "Professor Surrey is regarded as a courageous advocate of basic tax reform. He has urged a long range program to close so-called tax loopholes, including the 27½ per cent depletion allowance for oil and gas."

55. Marquis Childs, *The Urgent Issue of Tax Reform*, THE WASHINGTON POST, Feb. 1, 1961, at A16.

56. Drew Pearson, *President's Brother Aids Connally*, THE WASHINGTON POST, Feb. 2, 1961, at D3. According to Pearson, "Another critic of oil ... is also facing opposition. Stanley Surrey, Harvard tax expert, was scheduled to be Assistant Secretary of the Treasury. But big oil Sen. Bob Kerr and other friends of oil oppose him. They suspect he is against the oil depletion allowance."

people and did not know how the articles came to be written. But I did regard them as a plus, since they sharpened the controversy in a way that countered the attacks on me.

The controversy had to come to an end, and it did publicly on February 2. Senator Smathers was correct, and again it was the Wall Street Journal that had the information. On February 1 its article was headlined "Kennedy to Ignore Protests, Names Surrey Treasury's Number One Tax Policy-Maker."[57] It went on:

> Mr. Kennedy's intention to name Mr. Surrey to the Treasury tax post was first reported several weeks ago. It provoked a storm of protest from mining companies, building and loan associations and other groups that feared higher taxes would result. A number of influential Senators and Representatives also protested the planned appointment, and for some days Mr. Kennedy debated whether to go ahead. Now he has made up his mind, and the appointment should be announced formally in the next few days.

The appointment was announced in the late afternoon of February 2. It was Ralph Dungan, I believe, who called me, asked in mock seriousness if I wanted to be an Assistant Secretary, and said the announcement would be made in a half-hour. Except for Senator Smathers' report, that was the first time I had heard anything affirmative from the White House.

In retrospect I can really wonder why the decision was favorable. Clearly it was the most controversial of the appointments that were made. Also, the lines were correctly drawn, and the opposition rightly judged the situation. Marquis Childs did have the right analysis. It was hard to visualize myself in the role described in the papers — top Treasury tax man — having all the impact the articles were ascribing to me. Not being in that position but instead teaching classes in Cambridge, "that Surrey" seemed a different person altogether. But seen impersonally and looking at the written record I had created, the controversy had substance. I see as probable key factors in the decision: support from Dillon, support from other White House sources such as Heller and the Council of Economic Advisors,[j, 58] the activities of my brother and others in placing a softening tone on the reported position of some on the Hill, and Senator Smathers' talk with the President.

But there may well have been another crucial factor. Robert Healy, Washington correspondent for the Boston Globe, who earlier had reported on the initial offer, started his February 4 article this way: "Chalk up another win for President Kennedy in appointment of Stanley S. Surrey of the Harvard Law School as the Administration's

57. *Kennedy to Ignore Protests, Name Surrey Treasury's Number One Tax Policy-Maker*, WALL STREET JOURNAL, Feb. 1, 1961, at 8. The story accurately describes Surrey as "a strenuous advocate of tougher tax treatment of many types of income currently getting special tax advantages."

58. The "Library" to which Surrey refers in his note j is probably the John F. Kennedy Presidential Library, which has extensive records of the Council of Economic Advisers. The editors have not attempted to locate whatever material Surrey may have had in mind.

chief tax policy man."[59] It was a serious situation and the easier way out could have been to drop the appointment. While this would have produced some adverse press criticism, that would quickly pass. The President did not take that course and did appoint by then a clearly controversial figure. In that posture, it was a meaningful decision and an indication of where the President stood. From my position I regarded it as a courageous step.

The appointment was trouble to the end. When the official nomination went to the Senate on March 13, after F.B.I. and tax clearances, the Congressional Record stated under Nominations: "Stanley S. Sorrey, of Massachusetts, to be an Assistant Secretary of the Treasury"![60]

Notes

a. Much of this discussion on income tax reform was drawn from my previous writing, such as an article on *The Federal Income Tax Base for Individuals*, 58 COLUM. L. REV. 815 (1958).

b. The collection of campaign speeches contains very few references to tax policy. S. Rept. 994, Part 1, The Speeches of Senator John F. Kennedy, Presidential Campaign of 1960, Senate Committee on Commerce, 87th Cong. 1st Sess. (1961). The statements referred to in the text relate to depletion allowances, tax incentives for investment, and self-employed pension plans.

c. The speech had been delivered on October 12, 1960. It was repeated in text made available for remarks in Philadelphia on October 31, 1960:

> Fifth, we must stimulate plant modernization programs which are vital both to increased production and to building industrial facilities which can compete successfully with the

---

59. Robert Healy, *Kennedy Picked Surrey Month Ago for the Job*, BOSTON GLOBE, Feb. 8, 1961, at 19 (the story's dateline is February 4, just as Surrey has it, but the story did not appear in the *Globe* until February 8). Healy reports, "Surrey is regarded by some Washington attorneys as the best tax expert in the nation." Healy also reports that, in addition to "congressmen from the gas and oil producing states," there were "several Democrats from Northern states with liberal voting records who also were steamed up about the appointment and let their feelings be known to the White House."

60. The final version of the *Congressional Record* accurately reports the nomination of "Stanley S. Surrey [not Sorrey] of Massachusetts, to be Assistant Secretary of the Treasury." 107 CONG. REC. 3798 (Mar. 13, 1961). It may well be that "Sorrey" appeared in the daily (overnight) version of the *Record*, but if so the error was corrected before it could mislead posterity.

It is not clear what else, if anything, Surrey intended to cover in this Chapter. In the draft's table of contents Chapter Six is titled, "A Government Tax Career — Part II, 1961–1969." And in the outline for his memoirs, Surrey summarizes the planned Chapter Six as covering, at least lightly, his entire eight years in Washington in the 1960s: "Assistant Secretary for Tax Policy in Treasury Department under Presidents Kennedy and Johnson — presumably a summary chapter since activities very extensive in both domestic and international areas — legislative and administrative results — describe scene, 1961–1969, use of complete diary." On the other hand, Surrey concludes the story of his nomination with a flourish suitable for the end of a chapter. In addition, if he was planning on writing about the Kennedy-Johnson years, it is a bit puzzling that Surrey, knowing that those years were central to his legacy and knowing that his heart trouble meant he had no guarantee of ample time to finish his memoirs, chose to skip the Kennedy-Johnson years and write instead about his less dramatic later years. If Surrey had continued with Chapter Six, the next topic in chronological order would have been his confirmation hearing. For descriptions of that, see the editors' introduction to this volume, and the more detailed account in George K. Yin, *supra* note 31, at 72–84.

> modern plant of Europe and the Soviet Union. Wherever we are certain that tax revision—including accelerated depreciation—will stimulate investment in new plants and equipment, without damage to our principles of equity, we will proceed with such revision. We will also carefully examine our entire tax structure in order to close loopholes which are unnecessarily depriving the Government of needed tax revenue, and in order to develop tax policies which will stimulate economic growth.

Speeches of Senator John F. Kennedy, note b at 561, 826. I do not know who placed this reference to "accelerated depreciation" in these speeches, but the person had not read the campaign document—or had read it but preferred to use an accepted business phrase rather than the new idea of "investment credit."

d. Up to 1954, the tax law had permitted a business to "write-off," i.e. deduct, the cost of an asset over the period of its useful life, at an annual rate of write-off equal to the cost divided by the useful life; this was called the straight-line method. Hence if a machine cost $100,000 and was expected to last 25 years, the annual deduction for depreciation was $4,000. The 1954 change allowed an annual deduction of 200 percent of the straight line rate but applied to the remaining cost, i.e. in the first year $8,000, in the second year $7,360 (8% of $92,000); this is called the 200 percent declining balance method. This faster method allowed a deduction of 34 percent of cost in the first five years of use of a 25-year asset, as compared with 20 percent for the straight line method.

e. As a member of the American Bar Association Section of Taxation Council, I was a member of a special committee of lawyers studying withholding to determine the position of the Section. This Committee was active at the same time as I was working on the Task Force Report. The Committee met in December 1960 with Treasury and Internal Revenue Service representatives. I gained two impressions—the Treasury really had done little hard thinking and was instead defending a policy position previously taken; the technical Service personnel believed withholding would work and would have liked to see it pushed, but were reluctant to say this expressly because of Treasury opposition to the basic idea. The committee later recommended against a withholding system.

f. As to two areas that later took on importance—oil and percentage depletion, home ownership and the deduction for mortgage interest—the following was all that was said:

> "Percentage depletion—A re-examination of the present rates and their relationship to cost depletion."
>
> "Personal expense deductions—The issues here relate primarily to the deduction for personal interest and for state and local taxes, and the corresponding part of the standard deduction; attention should also be paid to abuses of the charitable deduction."

g. During this period I was also preparing a lengthy paper for the Brookings Institution, which had been given a large grant by the Ford Foundation for a major research project in Studies in Government Finance. My paper, prepared at the request in ____ of Brookings and turned in on January 14, 1961, was on the "Agenda for Consideration of Tax Research Topics Possessing a Significant Legal Orientation." It turned out to be a lengthy, detailed paper, 59 pages in length. Some of the topics paralleled those in the Task Force Report; others involved research themes seeking exploration needed generally to guide legislative action—for example, a topic on the effects of tax rules on the conduct of activities in our society, here referring to such matters as capital gain rules, estate planning tax techniques, employee fringe benefit tax rules, the tax treatment of charitable contributions and the effect on the creation of family foundations, where the inquiry was to ascertain whether, to what extent, and in what direction tax rules had distorted family and business activities away from their otherwise normal patterns, together with a study on the techniques and tools required to predict the likely social, economic and political consequences of proposed tax rules. Or a topic on the considerations that should be weighed, once it is decided that a specific objective be sought by Government, whether that objective should be reached by a tax technique or by a direct budget expenditure technique.

The paper in its conclusion suggested various ways to make the projected Brookings research useful, and here suggested "confrontation conferences," of the kind mentioned in the Task Force Report, in areas where sufficient data already existed so as to clarify the points of agreement and disagreement and thereby focus attention on the judgments necessary to policy decision. Where sufficient data did not exist, "planning conferences" should be held to obtain informed consensus on the lines which immediate research should take to set the stage for policy judgments.

I was a member of the Advisory Committee established under this project.

h. Candidate Kennedy had carefully steered his way around the subject of percentage depletion calling essentially for a study; see The Speeches of Senator John F. Kennedy, Presidential Campaign of 1960, note b, 1060, 1122. In the third radio debate with Candidate Nixon, Kennedy said:

> "There are about 104 commodities that have some kind of depletion allowance, different kinds of minerals including oil. I believe all of those should be gone over in detail to make sure that no one is getting a tax break, to make sure that no one is getting away from paying the taxes he ought to pay. That includes oil, it includes all kinds of minerals. It includes everything within the range of taxation. We want to be sure it is fair and equitable. It includes oil abroad. Perhaps that oil abroad should be treated differently than the oil here at home ... I can assure you that if I am elected President, the whole spectrum of taxes will be gone through carefully and if there is [sic] any inequities in oil or other commodity, then I would vote to close that loophole."

i. In the Kennedy Library President's Office files on Staff Paper (Dungan) there is an undated memorandum to the President from Dungan: "Just a reminder you wanted to talk to Wilbur Mills about Stan Surrey for the tax policy job in Treasury."

j. [Add CEA material from Library].

SEVEN

A Law School Professor

Part II, 1969 to Date

With the end of the Johnson period and the change from a Democratic to a Republican Administration, as a Presidential Appointee as Assistant Secretary of the Treasury (Tax Policy) I had necessarily to resign. Indeed, the incoming Attorney General, John N. Mitchell, as quoted in the Bond Buyer, had said I would be the first official to be fired.[1] Perhaps his statement stemmed from my 1968 Treasury work diminishing the importance of industrial revenue bonds,[2] a field in which Mitchell was among the innovators and chief practitioners.[3] But obviously I would not wait to be fired![4]

What next? In a sense I was at the same crossroads as when earlier in 1947 I had also resigned a Treasury position. There were obvious openings in private practice at respectable remuneration. But this time I had experienced a career as a professor whereas in 1947 a teaching career was almost an uncharted area. I had no hesitation in deciding to return to Harvard Law School. The school is kind to its professors

1. After having directed Richard Nixon's 1968 presidential campaign, John N. Mitchell served as attorney general from 1968 to 1972, when he stepped down to direct Nixon's 1972 reelection campaign. In 1975 Mitchell was convicted of several Watergate-related crimes, for which he served nineteen months in prison. Prior to his involvement in presidential politics, Mitchell had been among the nation's leading municipal bond lawyers, for part of that time as a partner with Nixon, in Nixon, Mudge, Rose, Guthrie, Alexander & Mitchell. *John N. Mitchell Dead at 75, Major Figure in Watergate*, New York Times, Nov. 10, 1988, at A1.

2. An industrial revenue bond (IRB) involved an arrangement under which a state or local government acted as a conduit for borrowing by private industry, thereby extending to the corporate borrower the governmental ability to pay tax-exempt interest on its bonds. With Surrey as the driving force, in March of 1968 Treasury issued proposed regulations that, if finalized, would have ended the tax-exempt status of IRB interest. *Tax Rules for Industrial-Revenue Bonds Formally Proposed by IRS; Hearings Set*, Wall Street Journal, Mar. 25, 1968, at 19. This spurred Congress into action; in June Congress passed legislation treating interest on "industrial development bonds" as taxable, with an exception for bond issues of $1 million or less. Revenue and Expenditure Control Act of 1968, Pub. L. No. 90-364, § 107, 82 Stat. 251, 266 (codified at former IRC § 103(c)).

3. A 1969 *Los Angeles Times* story described Mitchell as having been a leading innovator as a municipal bond attorney. Murray Seeger, *Mitchell Vetoes Tax on Municipal and State Bond Income*, Los Angeles Times, Apr. 26, 1969, at A1 ("Mitchell, while in private practice, was credited with suggesting the formation of public corporations which could borrow money through tax-free bonds without going through the normal government process of getting voter approval.").

4. Surrey was the first high-level Treasury official from the Johnson administration to resign following Nixon's election, on January 16, 1969. Robert B. Semple Jr., *Most Nixon Aides in Top Echelons Still Unnamed*, New York Times, Jan. 18, 1969, at 14.

who resign to work in government and then return. There is no practice, as in the rest of the University, of filling the position with another professor. Since the number of professorships in each department of the university is almost a fixed number and permission to be on leave of absence is restricted to two years, a professor who resigns takes his or her chances. The Law School, however, has no stated number of professorships and can be quite flexible in professional appointments. The School had in various ways indicated I would be welcome, and indeed had not filled my chair as Jeremiah Smith Professor. So I returned in April in 1969 to resume my teaching of tax law.

Teaching and Writing

The tax aspects of the School had changed. Professor Ernest Brown,[5] discouraged by the Vietnam era of students, had left for a position in the Department of Justice. Dean Griswold was the Solicitor General of the United States and Derek Bok had succeeded him as the Dean.[6] Professor William Andrews had come on the faculty to teach taxation, and visiting professors had participated.[7] Elisabeth Owens of the International Tax Program, and the first woman professor at the school,[8] was now handling the International Tax Course. Oliver Oldman,[9] also now a professor, was directing the International Tax Program. Also, the proliferation of tax law—for which I had a responsibility!—demanded different courses. The general tax course had been split in two parts, a basic course on the taxation in general of individuals and corporations, and an advanced course on taxation of corporations and shareholders. Estate and gift taxation was removed from the earlier basic course to emerge as a separate course in Estate Planning, handled by property law teachers, and Estate and Gift Taxation, handled by the tax side.

I soon found out that I needed a large amount of retooling to teach tax courses. Life as an Assistant Secretary does not require the reading of all decided cases, law review articles, all Treasury rulings and so on. New modes of tax practice had also

5. For more on Ernest Brown *see* Chapter 3, note 58.

6. Derek Bok was dean of Harvard Law School from 1968 to 1971, and president of Harvard University from 1971 to 1991 (as well as acting president from 2006 to 2007). He has written six books on higher education, including DEREK BOK & WILLIAM G. BOWEN, THE SHAPE OF THE RIVER (1998) (on affirmative action).

7. William D. Andrews was on the Harvard Law faculty from 1961 until his retirement in 2007. He was among the leading tax theoreticians of his generation; his work was typically more theoretically sophisticated but less practically oriented than Surrey's. Perhaps his most influential article was his classic argument for replacing the income tax with a progressive consumption tax. William D. Andrews, *A Consumption-Type or Cash Flow Personal Income Tax*, 87 HARV. L. REV. 1113 (1974). He died in 2017. *Leading Tax Scholar Bill Andrews '55: 1931–2017*, HARVARD LAW TODAY, May 31, 2017.

8. For more on Elisabeth Ann Owens *see* Chapter 5, note 21.

9. International tax law scholar Oliver Oldman taught at Harvard Law School from 1955 to 1993, directing Harvard's International Tax Program from 1964 to 1989. *Oliver Oldman, Expert in International Tax, 1920–2008*, HARVARD LAW BULLETIN, Dec. 9, 2008.

developed. The casebooks which I had earlier used — the Surrey-Warren income tax book and the Warren-Surrey estate and gift tax book — were clearly outdated. The first step in meeting these changes, apart from a large amount of reading of back materials, was to revise the casebooks. I had decided that the income tax book had to be split into two books to match the separate course developments. I was fortunate to obtain for this revision as co-editors, Professors Paul McDaniel and Hugh Ault of Boston College Law School. McDaniel after considerable experience in tax practice in Oklahoma had served in the Treasury for a brief period overlapping with my stint. Indeed, Paul's coming to the Treasury was the outcome of a talk I had with an Oklahoma tax lawyer, ____, whom I knew, who kept pressing me on the observation there was no one on my legal staff who understood oil and gas law. I turned the tables by saying that he had the responsibility of recruiting for me an able lawyer knowledgeable in that field. He responded nobly by sending McDaniel from his firm to me. Later, after I left, Paul would have been Associate Tax Legislative Counsel (?) but a Republican senator from Oklahoma refused on political grounds to approve the appointment — luckily, I think, for McDaniel in the end. He became the tax assistant for a short period to Senator Albert Gore, who as a maverick member of the Senate Finance Committee had taken decidedly progovernment tax positions. Paul then went into teaching at Boston College.[10] Ault, somewhat younger, had practiced law with Bingham, Dana & Gould in Boston before coming to Boston College.[11] These two handled the initial task of updating the material while I reviewed the organization and content.[a] Federal income taxation, Vol. 1 appeared in 1972, and Vol. 2 in 1973.[b, 12] The estate and gift tax book was done with McDaniel and Harry L. Gutman, a Boston practitioner, also teaching part-time at Boston College, and later a professor at the University of Virginia Law School.[13] It appeared in 1977 as Federal Wealth Transfer Taxation.[c] As before, the books emphasized tax policy issues along with the nuts and bolts and drew on a wide variety of materials: court decisions, Congressional documents, Treasury reports, articles, etc. The materials in these books are more detailed than in other

---

10. Paul R. McDaniel divided his lengthy career among the law schools of Boston College, New York University, and the University of Florida. *Eminent Tax Scholar and Professor Paul R. McDaniel Dies at Age 74*, NYU Law News, Jul. 20, 2010. His most notable collaboration with Surrey was not the casebook, but Stanley S. Surrey & Paul R. McDaniel, Tax Expenditures (published in 1985, the year after Surrey's death).

11. Hugh J. Ault took emeritus status at Boston College Law School in 2012, after a long and distinguished career as an international tax law scholar. He remains active as a scholar. Hugh J. Ault, Brian Arnold & Graeme Cooper, Comparative International Taxation: Structural Analysis (4th ed., 2019).

12. As far as the editors have been able to determine, no book labeled as the second edition of Volume 1 was ever published. Most likely Surrey inserted the blank in his note anticipating that a second edition would be published before the publication of his memoirs. In lieu of a second edition was the posthumous (for Surrey) publication of Stanley S. Surrey, Paul R. McDaniel, Hugh J. Ault & Stanley A. Koppelman, Federal Income Taxation: Cases and Materials (1986).

13. Harry L. (Hank) Gutman was chief of staff of the Joint Committee on Taxation from 1991 to 1993. Before that, he had taught at the University of Virginia Law School (1984–1989), and at the University of Pennsylvania Law School (1989–1991). He is currently of counsel with the Washington law firm of Ivins Phillips Barker.

taxation case books, and along with the policy discussions, do present a challenge both to teachers and students. The inclusion of both policy issues and detailed case law and Treasury materials is a tough assignment and casebook preparation is a demanding task. The ever growing, ever changing tax world makes the task much harder than in many other fields of law.

The teaching of taxation courses was more demanding than in my first career as a professor. The subject matter had grown to be so complex and vast that selectivity was important. The reading load on the students likewise increased. Class preparation in itself had lowered, partly as the result of changes in student approach to law school growing out of the Vietnam unrest and partly because of the tug of non-course activity—journals, clinical activities, work in outside jobs. I found it was desirable to organize a class in groups of three or four, prepare questions in advance for each assignment, and make two or three groups responsible in turn for each assignment. This did result in informed class discussion of the questions. While many teachers in this period were moving gradually towards more and more lecturing in class I stuck to question-and-answer dialogue. Taxation is also a difficult subject because students are not familiar with close reading of the language of statutes and regulations, watching every word and catching its changing significance under different situations. They must constantly be forced to focus on the language in the light of the questions, and not be permitted to think great thoughts about policy issues or the future of America until they understand the present rules and how they came to be in the law. Also it is hard to combine nuts and bolts and policy issues, since student preference divides between which should be emphasized. As a result of a system of course evaluation by students which was inaugurated in the 1970s a professor was made fully aware of not being able to satisfy every student. Some students find taxation boring, while others to their surprise find it interesting, especially those who see that important policy issues underlie the dry, technical, complex statutory language. For some the professor is the best in the school; for others he or she shows the evil of the tenure system. I had a hard time keeping the reading to a rational level, largely because of an acquaintance with so many facets of taxation. Indeed, invariably I was told by students that my courses required far more work than the credit allowance normally called for.

Another problem in teaching taxation is the unfamiliarity of most students with the business world. During their college years and for about half a year in between college and Law School in the world outside, their experiences tend to such fields as political campaigns, Congressional interns, social welfare programs, travel, etc., but rarely to activities that would give him insight into what is a corporation or partnership, how business is generally conducted, pension arrangements and the like. They are thus long on political and social knowledge but very short on business, and also economics despite some general college courses on that subject. As a result many of the facts and operational decisions described in the materials, which because of the broad coverage of taxation develop in the business scene are strange to them. They must learn—and be taught—both tax law and the milieu in which that law is applied.

At the Law School I of course concentrated on federal taxation. With the other tax professors I taught the basic course and the advanced corporate course, along with estate and gift taxation and international taxation. I again gave my seminar in current tax policy, which I taught jointly with Professor Richard Musgrave, an eminent public finance specialist who held a joint appointment in the Law School and Department of Economics. After he retired, I continued with other economists, always finding one who, while knowing the economic jargon, equations and models, could depart from them to explain public finance issues to law school students with, almost entirely, little background in economics. For a while I taught Legislation and also a seminar, which grew to a class, in Tax Aspects of Urban Problems (?).

The teaching of federal taxation, especially if one desires to diversify, is a difficult task. It is necessary to be current in tax theory, tax policy, and the rules of an ever-changing tax system as articulated in statutory law, administrative action, and judicial decisions;[d, 14] in what is being said and written about in the current literature; in what is practiced in law offices and accounting firms since they are at the cutting edge. To this is added the task of preparing materials, writing articles and books, giving lectures, attending lectures and conferences, and so on. Keeping abreast of current policy issues requires consulting activities, formal and informal, with the various governmental tax centers and their key figures in Congress and the Executive; and testifying at public hearings, and knowing about and sometimes participating in the public activities of a variety of organizations in the tax field; and in following policy movements in other countries. This variety of tasks—and I undoubtedly have failed to list some more—must be met over the range of the entire federal tax system—individual taxation, corporate taxation, estate and gift taxation, international taxation, and often the special excise taxes. All in all it is a hard life—unless this is what fascinates you and meets the demands of your curiosity.

Using my Treasury background, I continued to write on tax subjects. In 1972, the Harvard University Press published "Pathways to Tax Reform,"[15] an extension of several previous law review articles and the first book written on the subject of "tax expenditures," a subject whose unfolding is considered in Chapter Eleven.[16] In that year, two colleagues, Oliver Oldman of Harvard Law School and William F. Hellmuth, then of McMaster University and now of Virginia Commonwealth College (formerly with me in the Treasury as Deputy Assistant Secretary in 1968),[17] published a selective collection of speeches I gave as Treasury Assistant Secretary.[e] A variety of articles

14. There are two volumes of regular decisions of the Tax Court published each year. This does not include, however, Tax Court memorandum decisions, which are not officially published, but which have precedential value, and which are collected into volumes by commercial publishers.

15. Stanley S. Surrey, Pathways to Tax Reform (1973).

16. Although Surrey planned a Chapter Eleven, "Tax Expenditure Analysis—A New Fiscal Concept, 1968 to date," there is no known draft of that chapter.

17. Hellmuth joined the faculty of Virginia Commonwealth University in 1995 and remained there for the rest of his career. Surrey and Hellmuth coauthored an important essay in the early debates over the concept of tax expenditures. Stanley S. Surrey & William F. Hellmuth, *The Tax Expenditure Budget—Response to Professor Bittker*, Nat. Tax J. 528 (1969).

followed — on tax simplification,[18] on descriptions of the background and legislative paths of several major tax acts,[19] on international topics,[20] [Check]. A number of these articles were published abroad after translation [Check].

An interesting episode was an appearance on William F. Buckley's talk show "The Firing Line."[21] The subject of course was taxation. Buckley had material prepared for him on various current topics and covered these with his questions. I could see, knowing the field, that he certainly was as quick a learner as his reputation indicated. But, again Treasury experience at Congressional hearings was useful. I was able to give my answers to his questions and then go on to turn the conversation to what I had desire to get on the record. I found it was necessary to concentrate hard on Buckley's questions, since they were often phrased in a complex manner and with unusual words. We did cover a lot of ground and I believe I held my own and was not overpowered as are many of his participants. At least, after it was over Buckley said I handled the program very well.

The Brookings Institution

In Chapter Six, I described my close association during Treasury years with The Brookings Institution through Joseph Pechman, Director of Economic Studies.[22] This association continued when I returned to Harvard. Pechman had secured financing

---

18. Stanley S. Surrey, *Complexity and the Internal Revenue Code: The Problem of the Management of Tax Detail,* 34 LAW & CONTEMP. PROBS. 673 (1969).

19. Stanley S. Surrey, *The Tax Reform Act of 1969 — Tax Deferral and Tax Shelters,* 12 B.C. INDUS. & COM. L. REV. 307 (1971); Stanley S. Surrey, *Reflections on the Tax Reform Act of 1976*, 25 CLEV. ST. L. REV. 303 (1976) [hereinafter *Reflections on the Tax Reform Act of 1976*].

20. Stanley S. Surrey, *Changes in U.S. Taxation of Business Abroad: The Possible Alternatives,* 32 J. TAX'N. 312 (1970); Stanley S. Surrey & David R. Tillinghast, *General Report on Allocation of Incomes and Expenses Between Related Entities,* 56b C. DE D. FISC. INT'L 1 (1971).

21. Political pundit William F. Buckley, Jr., was arguably the most influential American conservative public intellectual of the second half of the twentieth century. Among many other things, he founded *National Review* magazine, and hosted the public affairs talk show *Firing Line* for an amazing 1,504 episodes over thirty-three years. His 1968 television debates with Gore Vidal, in which Buckley famously and disastrously lost his temper, are the subject of a 2015 feature-length documentary, *Best of Enemies.* For a biography, *see* CARL T. BOGUS, WILLIAM F. BUCKLEY JR. AND THE RISE OF AMERICAN CONSERVATISM (2011). The entire one-hour episode with Surrey is available for streaming online at Firing Line broadcast records, *Tax Reform*, HOOVER INSTITUTION ARCHIVES (Jan. 21, 1974), https://digitalcollections.hoover.org/objects/6301, and is required viewing for anyone interested in Surrey. Buckley begins by introducing Surrey as "that slightly mysterious figure who, by his own admission, was the major architect of the Tax Reform Act of 1969, considered a step in the right direction by some critics of tax policy, considered by others one of the most maladroit pieces of tax legislation in American history." Although the discussion is civil throughout, and Surrey and Buckley even find a few points of agreement, Buckley goes straight at Surrey's policy vulnerabilities. The episode is described and discussed in more detail in the editors' introductory essay.

22. If Surrey wrote the portion of Chapter Six he describes here, it has been lost. The Brookings Institution is among the oldest and most influential of American think tanks. Founded in 1916, its stated mission is "to conduct in-depth research that leads to new ideas for solving problems facing society at the local, national and global level." The Brookings Institution, *About Us*, https://www.brookings.edu/about-us/. On the think-tank political spectrum, Brookings is generally regarded as

for annual conferences on fiscal topics he selected. He and I would first consult on a desirable topic for each of these conferences. After the topic was selected we would then consider the subtopics to be covered and their time allocations. These conferences generally occupied two full days. Next, we would discuss the participants, those to be asked to prepare papers and those to be invited. My input here was mainly the suggestion of appropriate legal and accounting participants, though Pechman himself knew some of the possibilities and I in turn knew some of the appropriate economists. When the papers were prepared I read some of the main papers and gave my comments to Pechman followed by a discussion of the program order under each subtopic in the light of the papers.

I attended all of the conferences as a participant, one of the minority of lawyers since the economists usually had the main roles. Pechman would then ask me to be the chairman for the concluding session, whose purpose was to summarize the earlier discussions and ascertain the lines of consensus and disagreement. In this role both my Treasury and teaching experience were helpful. The job of a chairman requires a willingness to put direct questions to participants, to drive through the ambiguities or irrelevances often present in answers, to tactfully press confrontation between differences of opinion so that the precise differences are made clear, and to keep the discussion going. This job, as any chairman knows, requires a knowledge of the subject in hand, the more knowledge the better, and a willingness to be confrontational in a polite but firm way. Passivity as a chairman generally produces an inconclusive conference, with too many unresolved matters and differences hanging in the air. Fortunately, given the Treasury experience, I was able to prod the economists to explain their views in language that non-economists—and the Chairman!—could understand and then cross-examine. There was also the reverse matter of making the lawyers and accountants understandable to the economists! One had to force all these disciplines to strip away their technical jargon and references—lawyers referring to Code section numbers are of no help to economists and economists expressing themselves in the shorthand *they* use when talking within the fraternity are no help to outsiders.

The topics Pechman and I chose were in the forefront of either currently active issues or in areas where we saw ferment and thought a conference would help in the further development of the area. These conferences were regarded as highly successful. Out of each conference Brookings published a book containing the prepared papers and then a summary, by a Brookings staff member, of the discussion, consensuses and disagreements. Each of these books represented a major contribution to thinking on the chosen subjects.[23]

---

center-left. Joseph A. Pechman, a leading public finance economist, was Brookings' director of economic studies for more than two decades. His book, FEDERAL TAX POLICY (5th ed., 1987) was a standard reference work in the field. *Joseph A. Pechman is Dead at 71; Aided 1986 Income Tax Changes*, NEW YORK TIMES, Aug. 21, 1989, at B8.

23. *See, e.g.*, INFLATION AND THE INCOME TAX (Henry J. Aaron, ed., 1976); COMPREHENSIVE INCOME TAXATION (Joseph A. Pechman, ed., 1977); CHARLES E. MCLURE, MUST CORPORATE INCOME BE TAXED TWICE? (1979); WHAT SHOULD BE TAXED: INCOME OR EXPENDITURE? (Joseph A. Pechman, ed., 1980).

National Tax Association

The National Tax Association is the one tax organization in the United States that combines federal, state and local fiscal personnel and also administrators, economists, lawyers, and accountants, both practicing and academic.[24] Its activities primarily are an annual conference and publication of a quarterly, the National Tax Journal containing a variety of articles. In 1971 the NTA inaugurated the practice of also holding an annual two-day Washington symposium on current tax subjects, generally from a tax policy aspect. Laurence Woodworth, the chief of the Joint Committee Staff and a close friend, was active in the NTA and persuaded me to participate on the program committees for these symposia, sometimes as the Chairman and sometimes as a member. A program committee has the usual difficult assignments—pick the main topic or topics, the speakers including the Congressional or top administrative persons to give the luncheon talks, and the chairmen for the various sessions. For the NTA symposia the task is complicated by the need to satisfy two almost distinct audiences, those interested in federal taxation and those interested in state and local taxation. The proceedings of the symposia are published in the September issue of the National Tax Journal.

The following is a partial list of some of symposia topics:

[Insert later][25]

On the whole these meetings were regarded as well conducted and highly useful, since they were among the very few meetings focused on tax policy. One outstanding symposium was the May 1978 meeting held as a memorial to Laurence Woodworth, who had been appointed Treasury Assistant Secretary for Tax Policy in 1977 and who suddenly died of a stroke in December of that year. The topics centered on tax policy since this was the major concern of Woodworth's career as the Chief of the Joint Committee Staff for many years. He and I had been close friends and allies throughout my Treasury years and the following period on both policy issues and technical decisions. I was the Chairman of the Program Committee and chose to

---

24. Founded in 1907, the National Tax Association accurately describes itself as "the leading association of scholars and professionals dedicated to advancing the theory and practice of public finance, including public taxing, spending, and borrowing." National Tax Association, *About*, https://www.ntanet.org/about/. For a history of the NTA's gradual transformation from an organization with an eclectic membership divided fairly evenly among lawyers, business representatives, academic economists, and government officials, to an organization dominated by academic economists today, *see* Ajay K. Mehrotra & Joseph J. Thorndike, *From Programmatic Reform to Social Science Research: The National Tax Association and the Promise and Peril of Disciplinary Encounters*, 45 LAW & SOC'Y REV. 593 (2001).

25. Surrey's planned insert could have included the following: FISCAL PROBLEMS OF FEDERALISM (1971), FISCAL DECISION MAKING (1972), FEDERAL TAX REFORM (1973), NEW DEVELOPMENTS IN TAX ADMINISTRATION AND PENSION PLANS (1974), THE TAXATION OF INCOME FROM CORPORATE SHAREHOLDING (1975), URBAN FISCAL PROBLEMS (1976), TAX AND BUDGET SIMPLIFICATION (1977), ENERGY TAXATION (1978), FEDERAL TAX POLICY AND THE TAX LEGISLATIVE PROCESS (1979, the Laurence N. Woodworth Memorial Symposium), AND PUBLIC FINANCE IN THE 1980S (1980).

assign to myself the writing of the memorial tribute. As far as I know it remains the only description of Woodworth's career and his many contributions to the federal tax system.[26] One part of this symposium was interesting in a different way. I persuaded Wilbur Mills, who had gone into retirement, making no public appearances, after resigning as Ways and Means Committee Chairman and leaving Congress. I thought the occasion was just the right one for Mills to come out of his retirement since he had known Woodworth for many years and had respected his assistance. He willingly agreed and in his customary effective style, shaped in years in Congress, paid tribute to Woodworth.[27]

As a result of my program activity, I became acquainted with Harry Olsher,[28] who as president of a small foundation in Washington, the Fund for Public Policy Research, was at that time financing The National Tax Journal and the symposia as well as some of the Brookings conferences. This acquaintanceship resulted in my obtaining from Olsher the almost total financing of the newly-instituted American Law Institute Income Tax Project, described in Chapter 8. As another development, I was asked to be the Vice-President of the NTA, a position held for one year and invariably followed by appointment as President for a year. The presidency rotates among academics, administrators, generally from the state field, and tax executives with private companies. The chief task of the President is to deliver the annual opening address.[29] I decided to make this a full-fledged discussion of current tax policy issues. The title, "Our Troubled Tax Policy: False Routes and Proper Paths to Change," accurately indicates the substance of the talk. As to the false routes, I was sharply critical of some current policies and policy thinking — supply side economics, the urgings of some for a shift from income to consumption taxes, the push for integration of the corporate and individual income taxes, and the growth of tax expenditures. I also sharply criticized econometric economists whose testimony before Congressional Committees was based on their computer models and printouts, a method that often awed the Congressman who rarely inquired as to the assumptions on which the models were based or why the models always seemed to support the viewpoints which the economists, following their individual biases, presented to the committees. As to the proper paths I stressed [an increased emphasis on tax expenditure analysis, and a

26. Stanley S. Surrey, *Tribute to Dr. Laurence N. Woodworth: Two Decades of Federal Tax History Viewed from this Perspective*, 32 NAT. TAX J. 227 (1979) [hereinafter Stanley S. Surrey, *Tribute to Dr. Laurence N. Woodworth*].

27. Wilbur D. Mills, *Tribute to Dr. Laurence N. Woodworth*, 32 NAT. TAX J. 323 (1979) [hereinafter *Tribute to Dr. Laurence N. Woodworth*].

28. Prior to his work with the Fund for Public Policy Research, Harry Olsher served on the staff of the House Committee on Banking and Currency, chaired by Wright Patman (D., Tex.). The *New York Times* described Olsher, in that capacity, as "a cantankerous, dapper fellow who somehow manages to surround each study with all the fog and suspicion of a Charlie Chan film." Robert Sherrill, *'The Last of the Great Populists' Takes on the Foundations, the Banks, the Federal Reserve, the Treasury*, NEW YORK TIMES, Mar. 16, 1969, at SM24. Olsher was the president of the Fund for Public Policy Research for the entirety of its existence, from 1969 to 1985. *Harry A. Olsher,* THE WASHINGTON POST, Dec. 27, 1996, at D4.

29. Surrey was NTA president in 1979–1980.

concerted attack on tax shelters.][30] During my term as president, I decided to obtain a survey of current problems faced by the NTA and suggested methods to solve them. I was concerned, for example, about the aging of its membership; the often lack of systematic choice of topics for the symposia and annual conferences, which at times turned without coordination year to year on those who happened to be in charge each year, the chairman of the symposia program committee being selected by the Vice President and the annual conferences being chaired by the person appointed by the President. To meet my concern, after consultation with old hands and new hands, I appointed a study committee. While its Report largely met most of my expectations, it was not followed by much activity on the part of succeeding chairmen, an indication of the difficulties in changing the status quo prevailing in an organization with a long history.

The year as president essentially ended my connection with NTA activities, as a matter of choice. Time did not permit their continuation.

Political Activities

In 1972 Senator George McGovern was nominated as the Democratic candidate for the Presidency. I did not know the Senator and had not really participated in his campaign for the nomination. I had a severe heart attack in March 1972 and simply was sidelined from all activity for the spring and early summer months. But I could read the newspapers and I became convinced that in the field in which I did have expertise McGovern was getting unorganized and often amateurish advice. For example, some of his advisers had pushed him into urging a negative income tax—payments of amounts to, rather than positive taxes paid by, low income recipients. But McGovern did not fully understand the proposal and was not carefully, as far as I could tell, briefed on its details and the debating points that it would produce. As a result Senator Humphrey, with a few deft observations, simply made the recommendation as described by McGovern appear rather silly.[31]

30. Stanley S. Surrey, *Our Troubled Tax Policy: False Routes and Proper Paths to Change*, 73 PROCEEDINGS OF THE ANNUAL CONFERENCE OF THE NATIONAL TAX ASSOCIATION 1 (1980); *reprinted* in 12 TAX NOTES 179 (1981). For a more detailed description of Surrey's address, *see* the editor's introduction to this volume. It is striking that in this draft of his memoirs Surrey included (apparently from memory) an accurate and rather detailed description of his denunciation of "false routes," while leaving a blank (presumably to be filled in later, after having reviewed the address) where the "proper paths" belonged. (The material in brackets in the text is supplied by the editors in place of Surrey's blank.) This might not be surprising, however, to one who has read the address; in the address Surrey's fervor is directed much more at denouncing the false routes than in praising the proper paths.

31. Jack Rosenthal, *Growth of an Issue: McGovern Dilemma*, NEW YORK TIMES, Jul. 8, 1972, at 10 (reviewing campaign developments relating to McGovern's proposal for a $1,000-per-person annual demogrant, including McGovern's having told an interviewer than he could not state the cost of the program, and Hubert Humphrey (McGovern's leading rival for the Democratic nomination) pointing out during a primary debate that it was not that difficult to multiply $1,000 by a national population of 210 million).

As a good Democrat and tax professional this was disheartening. I went to my colleague, Professor Abe Chayes,[32] active in Democratic politics and the McGovern campaign, and suggested that a tax advisory committee should be appointed. He passed the suggestion along and I was soon informed that this Committee would be established, with Adrian DeWind, a friend and my successor in my first Treasury career, and a highly successful, liberal, New York tax attorney. We put together a committee and held our first meeting in New York in late July. It was essentially a new group composed jointly of academics, including economists, practicing tax lawyers DeWind and I knew, plus several handed to us by the McGovern staff.[33] At our first meeting we agreed on a tentative agenda with assignments parceled among the members.

Our work essentially was a rescue operation—how to make McGovern's negative tax approach look reasonable from both policy and technical standpoints and to suggest additional proposals that would not be dismissed by those in the electorate who worried about tax matters as being too extreme or impractical but at the same maintain an image of tax liberalism and concern for low and middle income taxpayers. After a few meetings we settled on a program along these lines: Tax reforms raising $22 billion in additional revenue by 1975, including: ending preferential rates for capital gains; elimination of the tax-free step-up in basis at death; reform of depletion allowances; replacing the tax exemption for municipal bond interest with a nontax direct subsidy to state and local borrowers; allowing deductions for investment interest expense to offset only investment income; replacing accelerated depreciation with slower, more economically accurate depreciation allowances; revising the investment tax credit to reward only *increased* investment; and lowering the top marginal tax rate to 48 percent on both earned and unearned income.[34]

Then a number of us, including DeWind and I, presented the program to McGovern and his political advisors in a meeting at his Maryland home. The pros and cons of several issues which could go either way were examined and placed on hold. But the program as a whole pleased McGovern, and it was made public in an August 29 McGovern speech to the New York Society of Security Analysts.[35] I doubt that

---

32. Abram Chayes was a leading state department official in the Kennedy administration and a professor of international law at Harvard for over 40 years. He was also a top advisor for Senator George McGovern and worked on Jimmy Carter's 1976 presidential campaign. David E. Rosenbaum, *Abram Chayes, John Kennedy Aid, Dies at 77*, New York Times, Apr. 18, 2000.

33. In addition to Surrey and DeWind, the members included Joseph Pechman, Mortimer Caplin, and economist Ed Kuh of MIT (McGovern's chief economic adviser). Hobart Rowen, *McGovern Group to Meet on Tax Reform Proposals*, The Washington Post, Jul. 26, 1972, at D10.

34. The list of proposals in the text is supplied by the editors to replace Surrey's direction to himself to "insert later." The list is based on McGovern's tax policy speech of August 29, and on the assumption (supported by Surrey's account here) that McGovern's speech does not differ from what the committee had recommended. For McGovern's speech (to the New York Society of Security Analysts), *see Excerpts from Senator McGovern's Address Explaining His Economic Program*, New York Times, Aug. 30, 1972, at 22.

35. *Id.* Not only were McGovern's proposals consistent with Surrey's tax policy views; McGovern seemed also to borrow much of his rhetoric from Surrey: "Let us not impose taxes in bold print and then give them back in fine print to a favored few. Let us treat all taxpayers alike, no matter how they

the program had any influence in the campaign one way or the other. It is best in a campaign, as I learned in the Kennedy campaign, to stay away from tax issues, since they have a capacity whatever their merits largely to annoy rather than please people. In the McGovern campaign, an organized, moderate program was necessary in an effort to dispel the highly negative results of the tax views he had expressed in the pre-nomination period. I recall one fascinating sidelight of the visit to McGovern's home. The first news of the Watergate break-in arrived at his house around noon that day. On hearing it, McGovern's immediate comment was "I bet John Mitchell is behind this." Politicians really know each other!

My next political interlude came with the Carter nomination campaign and then the election campaign. This is a long story in itself which started my third Government career, this time as both a Treasury and White House consultant, along with being a Kennedy advisor. How this developed and was managed is described in Chapter 10.

Legislative Activities

During the Nixon and Ford Administration I had little direct contact with the Treasury Department. Though my successors—Edwin S. Cohen as Assistant Secretary and John Nolan as his Deputy—were friends,[36] they saw me, correctly, as a Democrat and too liberal for them, particularly Cohen, and certainly for the Republican Administration. But an outsider has a role to play and I found a number of openings.

Early in 1971, the Treasury suddenly abandoned the administrative rules I had established for the depreciation of assets used in a business. Those rules, more fully described in Chapter 6,[37] were based on allowable depreciable class lives determined as best we could on the available evidence on the actual use of assets in the various classes.[38] As a safeguard, a reserve ratio test was also adopted which, in its technical operation, would indicate whether any particular company using these class lives

---

make their living. Let there be no more mythical tax paupers who in fact receive hundreds of thousands of dollars in real income but pay little or nothing in taxes."

As to the demogrant proposal, which had caused him so much grief, McGovern said only, "I have asked some of the nation's leading economists to continue to work on the issue," and that "the ultimate resolution of that question must be the subject of careful study by both the Congress and the executive branch."

36. Edwin S. Cohen served in the Nixon administration, first as the assistant secretary of the Treasury for tax policy, and later as undersecretary. He divided the rest of his lengthy career between private practice and teaching at the University of Virginia Law School. Wolfgang Saxon, *Edwin S. Cohen, 91; Helped Formulate Nixon Tax Programs*, NEW YORK TIMES, Jan. 8, 2006. He authored a lengthy and entertaining autobiography, A LAWYER'S LIFE: DEEP IN THE HEART OF TAXES (1994).

After serving as Treasury deputy assistant secretary for tax policy from 1969 to 1972, John S. Nolan rejoined the Washington law firm of Miller & Chevalier, where he practiced until his retirement in 1998. *Lawyer John Stephen Nolan, 73, Dies, Former Treasury Official was 43-Year Member of D.C. Firm*, THE WASHINGTON POST, Jan. 21, 1999, at B7.

37. If Surrey wrote a draft of a portion of Chapter Six dealing with this topic, it has been lost.

38. REV. PROC. 62-21, 1962-2 C.B. 418.

for taxpayers was in its own situation experiencing asset lives whether longer or shorter than the class lives themselves.[39] If so, an adjustment whether unfavorable (required to go to the longer lives for tax purpose) or favorable (allowed the shorter lives) to the company was required. On the basis of careful Treasury analysis and the general opinion of the accounting profession this reserve ratio test was technically an accurate indicator of the asset lives in actual use. The combination of class lives and the reserve ratio test was designed to place tax depreciation on a course that follow economic depreciation, and thereby avoid distortion and litigation. As a taxpayer safety valve, a "facts and circumstances" situation could produce a special determination based on that approach where the facts and circumstances adequately supported the differentiation.

But these rules were abandoned by the Treasury in 1971. The cause for the abandonment was not the invalidity of the rules but the fact that in their actual operations companies could not meet the reserve ratio test. This situation meant that an adjustment would have to be made to lives longer than the permitted class lives, and a resulting increase in taxes because of lower deductions for depreciation. But the situation really meant that industry simply did not behave as it had strongly asserted would be the case when the rules were earlier established. Industry then said that assets were being replaced far more rapidly than the previous permitted allowances. These assertions had pushed the class lives toward the shorter end of a possible range in the various classes. The failure of industry to live up to its assertions — not an untypical situation in these matters — created a dilemma for the Nixon Treasury. Under the rules it either had to handle a large volume of "facts and circumstances" pleas as companies sought escape from their own practices, which would involve a large administrative load, or else follow the results of the reserve ratio test and assert a large number of tax deficiencies. While some in the Treasury might have taken the latter course, or at least extended the time for compliance with the reserve ratio test, the political considerations appear to have dictated a third solution. This was to drop the reserve ratio test and, departing from a standard of economic depreciable lives, allow companies to use tax depreciable lives 20 percent shorter than the guideline class lives (or in some cases 20 percent longer). This pleased industry since it took the companies off the hook, and at the same time introduced the concept of using tax depreciation as an incentive, through increased cash flow from lower taxes, to more rapid acquisition of assets — at least that is always the theory if not the result.

This action — styled "asset depreciation range" — ADR — was to be taken by administrative action through a Treasury Regulation.[40] A number of academics and practicing lawyers, however, who disagreed with the basic policy behind the move,

---

39. *Id.* at 435, supplemented by REV. PROC. 65-13, 1965-1 C.B. 759. For a more detailed description of income tax depreciation rules in the 1960s, *see* Henry J. Lischer, Jr., *Depreciation Policy: Whither Thou Goest*, 32 SW. L. J. 545, 556–63 (1978).

40. Treasury announced its proposed asset depreciation range (ADR) regulations in March of 1971. 36 Fed. Reg. 4885 (Mar. 13, 1971). It adopted the final regulations three months later. Treas. Dec. 7128 (Jun. 22, 1971), 1971-2 C.B. 132. For Treasury's rationale for the ADR approach, *see* Announcement 71-76, 1971-2 C.B. 503, 512-17.

also thought such Treasury action was not authorized by the statute. They read the statute as requiring the use of economic lives. Feeling strongly on both matters, I and several others decided to oppose the Regulation. We would do this in two ways; opposition at the Treasury hearing on the proposed Regulation, a move which we recognized would not stop the issuance of the Regulation, and a court proceeding to enjoin the Treasury from putting the Regulation in effect. This second step was novel and there was little or no precedent on the success of such a legal proceeding. A preliminary but basic question was whether there was legal standing before the court for our plaintiffs to bring the action at all, they not being taxpayers whose own tax liability was involved, the usual tax litigation situation, but rather third parties protesting the generosity of the Treasury toward a certain group of taxpayers.[f, 41] We picked as plaintiffs a number of persons, each of whom could claim a different basis for standing: A Congressman, a company which met the ratio reserve test, [Check].

With the assistance of a law school student, I prepared the basic tax brief for the case. A District of Columbia public interest organization would handle the standing issue and Bernard Wolfman, a well-known tax attorney in Philadelphia, who had appeared at the Treasury hearing, would handle the tax aspects of the court proceedings.[42] Our brief was convincing to us. It must have also worried the Treasury Department. As a part of a proposed 1971 Revenue Act, the Treasury recommended statutory enactment of the ADR system. This step, if successful, would end our legal action, since Congress clearly had the authority to change depreciation for tax purposes from the standard of economic depreciation to an incentive ADR approach.

Liberals in Congress opposed the Treasury ADR proposal and our brief was placed in the Hearings record[43] [Check]. While a few marginal items were stripped away, the House accepted the Treasury proposal. In the Senate the proposal was approved

41. The general rule is now well settled that third parties lack standing to challenge the government's unduly favorable tax treatment of others. Simon v. Eastern Kentucky Welfare Rights Organization, 426 U.S. 26 (1976); Allen v. Wright, 468 U.S. 737 (1984).

42. In the early 1970s Bernard Wolfman was dean of the University of Pennsylvania Law School (and not, as Surrey implies, in private practice). Wolfman had been dean since 1970 and had been on the Penn Law faculty since 1963. Wolfman moved to Harvard Law School in 1976 and remained there until he retired in 2007. He wrote on a wide range of tax topics, including corporate tax and ethics in tax practice. Douglas Martin, *Bernard Wolfman, 87; Sought Tax Overhaul*, New York Times, Aug. 31, 2011, at B18.

The "District of Columbia public interest organization" handling the standing issue was Common Cause, working in conjunction with consumer advocate Ralph Nader. *Suit to Bar Easing of Depreciation Guides Filed by Nader, Common Cause, and Others*, Wall Street Journal, Jul. 8, 1971, at 6. The story describes Wolfman as "chief counsel" for the challengers; it does not mention Surrey.

43. The Ways and Means Committee, the Finance Committee, and the Joint Economic Committee all held hearings in 1971 at which the ADR system was both attacked and defended. However, the editors have not found the brief described by Surrey in the records of any of those hearings. (Surrey's "check" indicates he had doubts on this point.)

by a one-vote margin.[44] But this was the high point of opposition to using the depreciation deduction as an incentive. Indeed, as seen later, once industry got used to ADR benefits, it wanted more and received more—much more—from the Reagan Administration in 1981.[g, 45] Throughout the Hearings and debates, Laurence Woodworth, Chief of Staff for the Joint Committee, officially a neutral advisor but with a liberal tax reform bent which he expressed, softly, when he could, went to considerable length to describe its problems. He really did not want the proposal to be adopted. But his negative statements were no match for the Treasury presentation. Woodworth, as was his custom, relied in such situations on a general, but not a detailed, analysis of a proposal and on an ability on the spot to state arguments which he thought would appeal to the Committee members. But the Treasury came fully armed with data and tables, some relevant and some not, some accurate and some questionable. They scattered their material over a wide area but principally relied on data showing American industry was not receiving as generous depreciation deductions as were provided in other countries, which result they claimed meant automatically a loss of American competitiveness in world markets. These international comparisons are always suspect, for while presented with the assumption that the situation is caused by the one factor the proponents seek to change favorably to them, so many other differing factors are present to make a single aspect almost meaningless by itself. But the comparisons are debating points and very often succeed in Congress.

Another 1971 Treasury proposal involved favorable tax treatment to U.S. corporations exporting goods abroad. The Commerce Department had been peddling the idea for a number of years. In 1968 the then Treasury strongly rejected the proposal and it lay dormant in most of the government departments concerned. But not in the Commerce Department. In 1970 and again in 1971 Commerce urged its proposal on the Nixon Administration. Seeking tax measures favorable to business, the Commerce proposal became Administration policy and the Treasury recommended it for the 1971 Act. The proposal would enable exporters to determine the cost of goods exported—in order to separate an overall export profit into its two segments, manufacturing profit and sales profit—on a formula basis that produced a cost lower than that resulting from application of the existing standard of an arm's length approach. The latter approach relied on prices at which manufacturers sold to exporters in an independent market. Under the proposal the goods, with their low cost, were treated as sold to a so-called DISC subsidiary of the manufacturing company. DISC stood for Domestic International Sales Corporation. The subsidiary was a paper corporation, which in turn was treated as the exporter. Its sales profit, computed on its sales price less its arbitrary low cost, which meant a large fictitious sales profit, was

44. For the resulting legislation, *see* Revenue Act of 1971, Pub. L. 92-178, § 109, 85 Stat. 497, 508 (formerly codified at IRC § 167(m)).

45. The rules of the "accelerated cost recovery system" (ACRS) enacted in 1981 were unprecedentedly generous; for example, the "recovery period" for a building was a mere fifteen years, regardless of the building's actual useful life. Economic Recovery Tax Act of 1981, Pub. L. No. 97-34, § 201, 95 Stat. 172, 203 (codified at IRC § 168).

then to be currently exempt from income tax as long as it was invested in export assets. This condition was an illusory hurdle since investment in the export receivables qualified. The deferral of tax would end only when investment in exports assets declined. But this was to be expected, if at all, only in a distant future, so distant that deferral turned basically into exemption, which always is the end result of a deferral. [Give figure][46] The stated purpose of this elaborate exercise was to provide incentive, through the tax system, to the export of American goods.

Those outside the Administration considered the entire "Rube Goldberg"[47] arrangement to be pretty silly. Even business thought that is how it would appear to Congress and it would not be seriously considered in legislation. But the Treasury was adamant in its defense and again presented its numbers, this time less relevant and less accurate than in the ADR controversy. I was among those who opposed the measure, considering it a waste of government revenue because it would have hardly any effect on our exports. It simply financed normal exports and made funds from the "deferral" of tax available for non-export purposes. Jointly with ____, then an Assistant Professor in the Harvard Economics Department, we wrote a piece for the Washington Post business section strongly attacking the proposal.[48] I had inserted into the Hearings a longer, more detailed argument, which I must state really demolished the idea.[49] But logic, even supported by debating points countering the debating points of the other side, does not always prevail in these matters. Woodworth also opposed DISC and tried to stop it before the House Ways and Means Committee. But by then business, seeing that the Treasury was really serious about the proposal and would work hard for it in Congress, began to view it from this different perspective. After all, Congress would have some difficulty, if industry pushed for the proposal and presented its arguments — typical of those used in support of an incentive business desires — to turn down a strong Treasury desire to give the funds to business. But the Committee members really disliked the proposal and wished Treasury would forget it. Treasury would not. The Committee therefore compromised and allowed a tax

46. It is not clear what sort of figure Surrey intended to give here. In general, the benefit to a taxpayer of deferring \$1 of tax to a future year equals the amount by which \$1 exceeds the present value of the future tax liability. The present value of the future tax liability decreases — and thus the benefit of deferral increases — with the length of the deferral period and with the discount rate (which is a function of prevailing interest rates). With a deferral period of ten years and a discount rate of 8 percent, for example, the present value of the future tax liability is about \$0.21, with the result that the benefit to the taxpayer of the deferral is about 79 percent of the benefit of permanent exemption. For more on the DISC proposal, see generally, Donald Lubick and Gerard Bannon, *Stanley S. Surrey and the Quality of Tax Policy Argument*, 38 NAT. T. J. 251, 255 (1985).

47. Rube Goldberg (1883–1970) was famous for his cartoons depicting ludicrously complicated machines to perform tasks that could be accomplished much more simply.

48. Surrey published two anti-DISC essays in the *Post*; neither is coauthored. Stanley S. Surrey, *DISC: A Billion-Dollar Tax Loophole Hidden in New Economic Policy*, THE WASHINGTON POST, Sep. 19, 1971, at E1; Stanley S. Surrey, *DISC: Tax Windfall on Top of Trade Windfall*, THE WASHINGTON POST, Oct. 24, 1971, at L1.

49. *Hearings Before the Comm. on Finance*, U.S. Sen., 92nd Cong., 1st Sess., on H.R. 10947, at 725–38 (1971) (written statement of Stanley S. Surrey).

deferral for half of the export profit. In this form DISC passed an also skeptical Senate, with now really aroused business interest and the Treasury overcoming considerable opposition.

So DISC went into law.[50] From then on it was all downhill. The opponents of DISC had succeeded in requiring an annual report from Treasury on its effectiveness in the export world. These annual reports, prepared by objective Treasury economists, and despite a contrary cover paper by Treasury political officials during Republican Administrations, show DISC had an almost negligible effect on exports and was only a tax boon to the large corporations that are our major exporters.[51] Thus, ______________________________.[52]

An attack on DISC in 1976 led to placing the provision on an increase in exports basis, so that only those profits in excess of a prior moving average were eligible.[53] Abroad DISC was attacked by other countries as in violation of the General Agreement on Tariffs and Trade (GATT), and a GATT panel so found, declaring it an export subsidy contrary to GATT rules.[54] The panel could hardly have found the contrary, since business and the Treasury had said before that this is exactly what it was. The Carter Administration tried to eliminate DISC in its 1978 tax reform proposals, but all those proposals ended en masse in defeat. The Dole Act of 1982 did cut back on DISC, [reducing the tax benefit from the DISC provisions by 15 percent.][55] I must conclude that the attack on DISC, in which I was in the forefront, had some success.[56]

In 1973 Chairman Wilbur Mills of the House Ways and Means Committee decided to hold hearings on tax issues. Mills was seeking some tax reforms, with a number of the Committee members, especially younger members, pushing for this position. The younger Representatives not on the Committee were also pushing along the same line in the Democratic caucus. I was asked to be on the opening panel, which had been assigned the overall subject of "Objectives and Approaches to Tax Reform and Simplification." The other members of the panel were Dan Throop Smith, Joseph Pechman, Norman Ture, and Boris Bittker.[57]

---

50. Revenue Act of 1971, Pub. L. No. 92-178, Title V, 85 Stat. 497, 535.

51. *See, e.g., Comm. on Ways and Means*, Third Annual Report of the Department of the Treasury on the Operation and Effect of the Domestic International Sales Corporation Legislation (for Fiscal Year 1974) (1976).

52. Not knowing what Surrey intended here, the editors have let stand Surrey's blank.

53. Tax Reform Act of 1976, Pub. L. No. 94-455, § 1101, 90 Stat. 1520, 1655.

54. *DISCs' Validity is Challenged by GATT Panel: Group Decides Tax Benefits of Firms are Subsidies, Violating Trade Rules*, WALL STREET JOURNAL, Nov. 5, 1976, at 18.

55. Tax Equity and Fiscal Responsibility Act of 1982, Pub. L. No. 97-248, § 204(a), 96 Stat. 324, 423.

56. Surrey does not mention the Deficit Reduction Act of 1984, which became law in the month before his death. The Act generally replaced the DISC regime with a new regime for "foreign sales corporations" (FSCs), although it gave small businesses the option of an interest-charged DISC regime (IC-DISC) requiring a DISC to pay interest on deferred income. Deficit Reduction Act of 1984, Pub. L. No. 98-369, § 801, 802, 98 Stat. 494, 985, 997.

57. Boris I. Bittker served on the faculty of Yale Law School from 1946 to 1983. He was Surrey's only real rival as the leading mid-century tax scholar among professors in U.S. law schools. Although

Many years earlier, in a Mills Hearing in 1959 on Tax Issues, I had been the first speaker.[58] Largely out of sentiment I desired to be in the same position on this panel. Just before the Hearing opened, I mentioned this to John Martin, then Chief Counsel of the Committee whom I had known in my Treasury capacity.[59] John had already arranged the speakers in a different order, though as yet he had not informed them of that order. He kindly consented to my request, and then told Mills of the revised order. In my opening remarks I made mention of my prior appearance, saying: "I would like to mention what could be considered a sentimental note. I did happen to be on the first panel in 1959. As a matter of fact, I also started off as the first witness on that panel. We have come a long way since then under the leadership of this committee."[60] I chose as my presentation the subject of "the basic objectives of tax reform," of which the "prime objective ... is to achieve greater fairness in the Federal tax system and to restore the confidence of the public in that system," and the second objective is "restor[ing] efficiency and economy in the expenditure of government funds."[61] With a panel composed of persons coming with different biases, there ensued after the oral presentations the usual discussion of the conflicting views on the various topics. In such a position one has to be alert to match the debating points being made, and to do so in a way that Committee members attending the Hearing may follow and perhaps remember. A Committee member really listening could in this process gain some understanding on what tax professionals thought "the shouting was all about."

In this period of the 1970s I became a steady advisor on tax matters to Senator Edward Kennedy.[62] I had not really known the Senator in my Treasury period but I had talked with Carey Parker, his legislative assistant who covered tax matters among his duties.[63] Parker is an extremely able person, with intellectual and political per-

---

Bittker wrote scores of influential articles, his magnum opus is the multi-volume treatise, FEDERAL TAXATION OF INCOME, ESTATES AND GIFTS (1st ed., 1981). The Bittker-Surrey debate on the tax expenditure concept is described by the editors in their introduction to this volume. It is a bit puzzling that Surrey scarcely mentions Bittker in these memoirs; presumably Bittker would have been more prominent in Surrey's planned chapter on tax expenditures. Memorial tributes to Bittker are at 115 YALE L. J. 737–54 (2006). Josh Duboff, *Law Scholar Bittker Dies at Age 88*, YALE DAILY NEWS, Sep. 15, 2005.

58. *Income Tax Revisions, Panel Discussion Before the Comm. on Ways and Means, House of Representatives*, 86th Cong., 1st Sess., 6 (1959). Surrey discusses his 1959 testimony in Chapter Three.

59. John M. Martin, Jr., was on the staff of Ways and Means from 1956 to 1981, retiring as chief counsel in 1981. *John M. Martin Jr.*, THE WASHINGTON POST, May 17, 2012, at B7.

60. *General Tax Reform, Panel Discussions Before the Comm. on Ways and Means*, House of Representatives, 93rd Cong., 1st Sess., on the Subject of General Tax Reform, Part 1, 9–10 (1973).

61. *Id.* at 10, 12. In furtherance of the second objective, Surrey urged the Committee to "make the proponents of these [tax] expenditures justify as Government priorities the amounts that are being spent through the [tax] system, the manner in which they are being spent, and the way the recipients are obtaining these funds." *Id.* at 12.

62. Edward Moore (Ted) Kennedy (D., Mass.), younger brother of John and Robert Kennedy, served in the Senate from 1962 until his death in 2009. *See generally* ADAM CLYMER, EDWARD M. KENNEDY: A BIOGRAPHY (updated ed., 2009) [hereinafter ADAM CLYMER].

63. For more on Carey Parker and his role as an advisor to Ted Kennedy, *see*, Carey Parker Interview (Sept. 22, 2008), Edward M. Kennedy Oral History Project, Miller Center Presidential History Project, University of Virginia.

ception, and clearly the dominant person for Kennedy on legislative matters. Parker began to call me for my opinion on various tax issues. Somewhat later, Professor Paul McDaniel, my colleague on the casebooks and in other matters, began to assist Parker, whom he had met when McDaniel was an assistant to Senator Gore.[64] Soon we were pretty much among the few persons Parker really relied upon for informed views on tax legislation, informed both as to substance and Senator Kennedy's posture in the Senate. The Senator suddenly became very interested in tax issues in the Senate. Before he had other matters on his mind and while usually casting a liberal, reform vote on tax legislation, did not seriously participate in the floor debate. Not being a member of the Senate Finance Committee and not having a real background on tax issues, he left the subject to his friends on the Committee, following their lead. But in 1976 he suddenly turned into a leader on tax legislation.[65] McDaniel and I were increasingly being called on for policy guidance, with McDaniel taking the principal role but also checking to get my views so that we would present Parker and Kennedy with a united view. They had neither the time nor patience to listen to a McDaniel-Surrey long conversation on sorting out issues, clarifying each of our positions and agreeing on the advice we thought was sound.

Kennedy began in Senate floor debate to oppose Senator Russell Long, Chairman of the Finance Committee.[66] Long was then a powerful figure in Congress, with an excellent, fast thinking mind and a formidable debater. Most senators simply decided that, given his qualities and his rather deep—for a Senator—knowledge on tax issues, and aided as he was by the staff of the Joint Committee which in the Senate was really his staff, there was simply no point in tangling with him. But, on matters on which Senator Kennedy had been well briefed, Kennedy decided to try an opposition role. Picking the issues on which to tangle, Kennedy found, somewhat I believe to his amazement and certainly to his delight, that he could hold his own with Long. It really pleased Kennedy to defeat Long on an issue, not because of any personal antagonism but from the confidence he gained in besting Long on the latter's territory.

Kennedy soon became the leading tax reformer in the Senate, and was looked to by other like-minded Senators for substantive positions and legislative tactics. The major 1976 Revenue Act in the Congress was the high point of tax reform in the

---

64. Albert A. Gore (D., Tenn.) served in the Senate from 1953 to 1971. He was the father of Vice-President Gore. Irvin Molotsky, *Albert Gore Sr., Father of the Vice President, Dies at 90*, New York Times, Dec. 6, 1998, at 67.

65. "Kennedy took on yet another intellectual challenge in 1976, tax reform." Adam Clymer, *supra* note 62, at 238. Clymer mentions both McDaniel and Surrey in this connection.

66. Russell B. Long (D. La.), son of the legendary Huey P. Long, was a senator from 1948 to 1987, and chairman of the Finance Committee from 1966 to 1981. As Surrey notes, Long was a formidable Finance Committee chairman because of his deep knowledge of tax law and policy, his debating ability, and his extensive experience with the Senate legislative process. He is credited with one of the more memorable tax policy quips: "Don't tax you, don't tax me, tax that man behind the tree." John H. Cushman Jr., *Russell B. Long, 84, Senator Who Influenced Tax Laws*, New York Times, May 11, 2003, at 40. For a recent scholarly biography, *see* Michael S. Martin, Russell Long: A Life in Politics (2014).

Senate. Kennedy prepared very thoroughly for this legislation, reading carefully the material that we and others had written for him. Once, he and Paul spent a long afternoon in my Cambridge home going over some material, remarking now and then, "well there goes my small business support," and so on, as he clearly saw the political aspects in Massachusetts of certain tax positions.[h] It was almost a revelation to McDaniel and me to see the concentration with which the Senator pored over the materials in this period before the debate, devoting long hours to a subject that is difficult, and to those not interested in its technicalities a dry, often boring task. Kennedy persevered and quickly absorbed the material, so he was soon in a position to handle it with confidence.

Kennedy asked McDaniel and me to prepare a primer on the tax issues that would come before the Senate, a primer written in language a Senator and his assistants could understand. The primer was to describe the issues and strongly support the reform positions. We undertook the task with the assistance of Joseph Pechman, in his private capacity and not as a Brookings Institution executive. (One can readily observe that the same names — such as Pechman — constantly reappear in this narrative, and see thereby that the tax reformers were a small closely-knit group.) The task had to be accomplished in a few weeks to be ready for the Senate floor debate. We met the deadline by deciding on the pertinent topics and then assigning them to lawyers and economists, whom we personally knew as both really informed in the particular topics and in sympathy with the positions it had been decided the Senator would take. We then edited the pieces, each a few pages in length and overall 173 printed pages,[67] to be sure they would be informative, accurate, and above all understandable by the Senators. Paul and I considered we had had sufficient contact with Congress to regard ourselves as expert authorities on what a Senator would understand! The final product, entitled "Compendium of Papers on Federal Tax Reform," was in mimeograph form distributed by Kennedy and became the "bible" for his group in the floor debate on the 1976 Act.[68] Paul was, for these debates, appointed by Kennedy as an assistant so that Paul could have the privilege, accorded by Senate practice to the Senatorial assistants, of being present on the senate floor. With Paul sitting alongside him and being immediately available for advice and information, Kennedy coordinated the efforts of those Senators desirous of tax reform, with the lead on various issues assigned to sympathetic Senators in a strategic position (often meaning no serious problems in their State with the position being pushed) to take that role. The Kennedy group succeeded on a number of matters either in striking or modifying portions of the Committee bill or in adding proposals they favored. [Check — can I specify some of these matters?][69]

67. The page count is not for the mimeographed material, but for the material as it was later published. STANLEY S. SURREY, PAUL R. MCDANIEL & JOSEPH A. PECHMAN, FEDERAL TAX REFORM FOR 1976: A COMPENDIUM (1976).

68. Kennedy had the compendium printed in full in the *Congressional Record.* 122 CONG. REC. 22283–22319 (1976).

69. In an article reviewing the politics and substance of the 1976 Act, Surrey noted several modest successes of the Kennedy-led Senate tax reform group: applying at-risk rules to limited partnerships

Kennedy remained a strong believer in tax reform. But the Carter Administration, though also on the reform side, was too cautious for the Senator and he decided to turn to other legislative issues, such as health care. His relations with Carter on tax and other matters became strained. In this period I was a White House consultant on tax matters, but still kept my relationship with the Senator and Carey Parker, as well as with McDaniel who continued as the Senator's principal tax advisor. These intersecting relationships obviously made for careful, but open, conduct which will be described in Chapter 10.

Throughout the 1970s when Woodworth was Chief of the Joint Committee Staff we kept in close touch with each other. I was fully free to speak to him at any time on current legislation, suggesting positions and tactics. He in turn felt free to call on me for assistance, knowing that the assistance would provide the positives and negatives on an issue and above all, would not be such as to jeopardize Woodworth's position before the Congress. In this period Woodworth was the dominant tax figure on the Hill. The Republican Treasury had little credibility before the Democratic Tax Committees, so that Woodworth had the field to himself. Treading carefully, for an outward objectivity was necessary to protect him from the Republicans and Democrats on the Committees who had conservative bents—and there were a number of these—Woodworth steered the Committees to reform positions. These positions had the backing of Mills, the young Representatives in the House and the Kennedy group in the Senate, the latter often on many subjects about equal to the opposition. The reforms in this period, especially in 1975 and 1976 when Woodworth was playing his role to the fullest, are in very large measure his doing. I was throughout a constant, willing ally.[i, 70]

I had a somewhat similar role, albeit in an entirely different setting, in advising the public interest tax groups that were starting their work in Washington. One group was led by Tom Field, an enterprising tax attorney whom I had met when he was in my Treasury office.[71] Tom was a liberal tax reformer in that he was conscious of the special preferences in the tax system and devoted all his energies to an attempt to attack them. He established a tax periodical, Tax Notes, which rapidly became must reading for those who desired to keep current on tax legislation and policy and to

---

(except real estate), defeating a proposal for a sliding scale of capital gains rates, and defeating a proposal to reduce the maximum tax rate on up to $100,000 of investment income. *Reflections on the Tax Reform Act of 1976*, *supra* note 19, at 305–06.

70. Surrey discusses Woodworth's work with the Joint Committee in the 1970s in some detail in his tribute to Woodworth. Stanley S. Surrey, *Tribute to Dr. Laurence N. Woodworth*, *supra* note 27.

71. Former Treasury lawyer Thomas F. Field founded Tax Analysts in 1970, for the purpose of defending the public interest in the tax arena by research, lobbying, litigation and publishing. In 1972 Tax Analysts began publishing *Tax Notes* as a weekly journal of tax news and analysis. It soon became—and remains today—the tax policy journal of record. In addition to the weekly publication of *Tax Notes*, Tax Analysts now publishes a daily edition, as well as specialized journals covering state tax and international tax. Field stepped down from his leadership position in 2001. Tax Analysts, *About Tax Analysts: History of Tax Analysts*, http://www.taxmuseum.org/www/website.nsf/Web/HistoryOfTaxAnalysts?OpenDocument. *See* also, Joseph J. Thorndike, *The Battle for Transparency in Tax*, FORTUNE, Aug. 5, 2020.

be informed of the maneuvering in Congress and Treasury. Tom also formed Taxation With Representation, engaged in public interest lobbying on tax issues in Congress.[72] While in a sense originally a one-man office, Tom could draw on the close group of reform-minded experts to advise him on the substance and tactics of his work. I was a member of this group and gave Tom all the encouragement and assistance I could. The other principal group was formed by Ralph Nader, called Citizens for Tax Justice.[73] It was first run by Tom Stanton, a Harvard Law School graduate, who, to his later chagrin, had never taken a tax course while at law school, looking down at the subject.[74] But Tom did know I taught Taxation and turned in this direction for assistance. Soon thereafter, the leadership of the small group was filled by Dean C. Tipps, also a recent law school graduate[75] (correct? which?). Tipps was a superb tax lobbyist, who easily could have earned a six-figure salary working for a major corporation or trade group. Congressmen liked him, even the conservative members, appreciated his directness, honesty, and complete understanding of legislative tactics and nuances. He soon became an important figure among the Ways and Means Committee tax reformers, helping to organize them on various issues and suggest tactics and debating points. Stanton had passed me along to Tipps, and we at once liked each other. We had the same views on most issues and I was able to fill Tipps in on their substantive background, which he lacked. In turn he would inform me how legislative matters were progressing and predict their outcome, always with a high rate of accuracy. He was an important ingredient in the tax reform movement during the Republican Administrations. When the Republicans[76] arrived Tipps switched to environmental mat-

72. In Regan v. Taxation with Representation of Washington, 461 U.S. 540 (1983), Field's organization argued that the denial of tax-exempt status under IRC § 501(c)(3) to organizations engaged in lobbying was unconstitutional. The Supreme Court upheld the constitutionality of the challenged rule, but noted that it was permissible for a § 501(c)(3) organization (eligible to receive tax deductible donations, but not permitted to engage in substantial lobbying) to be affiliated with a § 501(c)(4) organization (permitted to engage in substantial lobbying, but not eligible to receive deductible donations).

73. Ralph Nader and associates founded Citizens for Tax Justice (CTJ) in 1979; according to its website, CTJ works "[a]gainst the armies of special interest lobbyists for corporations and the wealthy," in order "to ensure working people have a voice in the development of our nation's tax policies." Citizens for Tax Justice, *About*, https://www.ctj.org/about/. On Nader's lengthy and high-profile career as attorney, activist, consumer advocate, and third-party presidential candidate, *see* JUSTIN MARTIN, NADER: CRUSADER, SPOILER, ICON (2002).

74. Thomas H. Stanton writes and teaches at Johns Hopkins University in the areas of risk management, federal credit and benefits programs, government corporations, and government regulation. He has written several books, including WHY SOME FIRMS THRIVE WHILE OTHERS FAIL: GOVERNANCE AND MANAGEMENT LESSONS FROM THE CRISIS (2012).

75. Dean C. Tipps became the founding director of CTJ in 1979, and served in that capacity until the mid-1980s. He later spent twenty-two years as the executive director of the California State Council of the Service Employees International Union (the largest union in California), retiring in 2008. For a tribute to Tipps upon his retirement, *see* 154 CONG. REC. 8084 (2008). Tipps was not, in fact, a law school graduate as Surrey supposed; his highest educational attainment was a master's degree in sociology from UC Berkeley.

76. Surrey has "Democrats" here, rather than "Republicans," but in context it is clear he is referring to the arrival of the Reagan administration in 1981.

ters and was succeeded by Robert McIntyre, a quieter person, perhaps not as skilled in lobbying, but a tireless worker for tax reform.[77] His activities were overshadowed, of course, by the Treasury while it was in Democratic hands. But they became more important, though perhaps not with the same effectiveness as before, in the Reagan Administration. His office developed the ____, a useful monthly on federal and state tax facets.[78] I also liked McIntyre and continued to be of assistance to his group.[j]

Tax Organizations

On my return to Law School I soon began to play a role in a number of organizations active in the tax world. On the domestic side I initiated the second American Law Institute Income Tax Project, obtaining the financing for the Project, planning its program, scope and personnel, and then becoming the Project Supervisor. This was a role to continue for the entire life of the Project, over a decade.[k] I have previously mentioned my participation in the activities of The National Tax Association.

The international area was also a field of interest and considerable activity on my part. I mention here only the highlights, reserving a full description to Chapter 9. Thus, for one year, 1968, while in the Treasury I was the United States Member of a new United Nations unit, the Ad Hoc Group of Experts on Tax Treaties Between Developed and Developing Countries, and thereafter the Special Advisor to the Rapporteur of this Group.[79] I soon became the person that largely shaped the Group's program, focused its deliberations, arbitrated the conflicting positions of the members, and wrote the principal conclusions for its Reports. The group's work over more than a decade produced the U.N. Model Tax Treaty, most of which I had drafted.[80] Another international organization in which I participated throughout was the International Fiscal Association, the largest international tax organizations, with over 5,000 members [Check],[81] composed of all types interested in the international tax world: tax executives, tax lawyers, tax accountants, Government tax officials, and fiscal economists. In 1969, when a reorganization of the governing structure of IFA

77. Robert S. McIntyre was associated with CTJ for nearly four decades, beginning in 1980 as director of federal tax policy, becoming executive director upon the departure of Tipps, and retiring in 2017. Unlike Tipps, McIntyre was a lawyer, with a JD from the University of Pennsylvania and an LLM from Georgetown. *See generally* Jasper L. Cummings, Jr., *Robert S. McIntyre: Interview*, 33 A.B.A. Section of Taxation News Quarterly 5 (Summer 2014) (a wide-ranging interview near the end of McIntyre's CTJ career).

78. CTJ currently produces a weekly email newsletter, the *Tax Justice Digest*. The editors have been unable to determine whether the monthly publication Surrey describes was of the same name.

79. For the group's first report, *see* United Nations, *Tax Treaties between Developed and Developing Countries* (1969). Surrey is listed as the sole member of the group from the United States. *Id.* at 5.

80. United Nations, *Model Double Taxation Convention between Developing and Developed Countries* (1980).

81. Today the International Fiscal Association describes itself as "the leading non-governmental, international organization dealing with tax matters," with more than 12,500 members worldwide. USA Branch of the International Fiscal Association, *Welcome to IFA USA!*, https://www.ifausa.org/.

occurred, I was appointed the United States member of its Permanent Scientific Committee. This group — with its wonderful title — was responsible for the entire planning of the substantive part of the program for its annual meetings, styled "Congresses." These meetings, with their attendant documentary material, discussion sessions, and seminars, were the principal substantive activity of the IFA. Thus the PSC was at the center of the IFA work and on it depended the quality and content of its contributions to knowledge. The PSC decisions were thus crucial to the organization's continued vitality. Representing the largest branch in IFA, the U.S. Branch [Check],[82] and because of my continued membership soon having a position among the seniors of the PSC, I was able fully to participate in the Committee's decisions.

Another international activity was of a different character. In 1980, on behalf of the Western Asia (to us the Middle East) Office, located in Beirut, Lebanon, of the United Nations Development Program, I made a month's tax survey of three member countries, North Yemen, Saudi Arabia and Syria. This was a fascinating trip, to an area I had never visited, and while I worked hard, the month passed quickly. I then, by an indirect route, went to Israel on a Lady Davis Fellowship for several months to teach a seminar in the Law School of Hebrew University.[83] Here I wrote my U.N. report on the Arab tax systems — admittedly quite a Middle East combination.[84]

Law School Activities

An academic has much more to do than pursuing teaching and studies in substantive fields. Harvard Law School operates to a large extent through Committee deliberations which end in a faculty consideration of the matters. While a Dean does exert some centralized leadership, the faculty, through the Committees and its meetings as an entire body, really makes the basic decisions on the direction and policies of the School. In my first tour of duty in the 1950s I did not serve on any Committees. The then Dean, Erwin N. Griswold, evidently considered my work as Director of the International Program in Taxation a sufficient contribution to the School's activities. Matters did change, however, when I entered upon my second tour of duty.

My return to Harvard coincided with the peak of the Vietnam student unrest in academic institutions. In the Spring of 1969 some Harvard students as part of the activities prompted by that unrest occupied the Administrative Offices of the Uni-

82. Today the USA branch of the IFA claims only to be "one of the largest IFA branches, with nearly 1,000 members." *Id.*

83. The Lady Davis Fellowship was established in 1973 by the Lady Davis Fellowship Trust to fund visiting scholars, post-doctoral researchers and doctoral students from abroad to teach, study and participate in research in Israel at the Hebrew University in Jerusalem and at the Technion Institute of Technology in Haifa.

84. Surrey has much more to say about these Reports in Chapter 9, where he covers all of the international activities described here in greater detail.

versity for several days.[85] One of the occupiers and leaders was a Law School student and the faculty considered suspending him. A large part of the student body was solidly against suspension. They made faculty meetings impossible in the usual Law School room, through blocking the halls and clamoring to attend the meetings. The faculty moved to another University Building, Holyoke House, in a room reached only by elevators and there voted suspension. The student protests at this action forced the faculty to hold a mass meeting of the student body to discuss the suspension. I had been working with some other faculty members and several students in a loose group to meet with the Dean on the situation. A previous meeting, held prior to my return, had been a rather disorganized affair with the Chairman having difficulty in controlling its conduct. It was decided that I should conduct the second meeting. Perhaps student unfamiliarity with me as compared to other faculty members, because I had not yet started to teach, led to the selection. In any event I agreed to the assignment, provided a student would act as Co-Chairman. This was arranged and the meeting held. I explained the ground rules, such as alternating speakers and time allotments. The first speaker for the faculty was Professor James Vorenberg, years later its Dean.[86] He spoke slowly and with a large amount of detail. Soon he had reached his time limit but was continuing to talk without any indication he would soon end his speech. I informed my student Co-Chairman I was going to stop Vorenberg, and he thought that would be too strict. But I had decided my credibility as Chairman rested on stopping him, so I broke into his talk saying he had one minute in which to finish. Vorenberg was quite startled by this, but did finish. The students appreciated this firmness with a faculty member and the meeting proceeded in an orderly fashion, with the student and I taking turns as Chairman. After several hours, some of the students opposed to the suspension began strongly to push a motion to adjourn, pointing out that the Dean had previously left the meeting. I thought this a serious error on his part but ruled the motion out of order, saying there were some persons desiring to speak who had been patiently waiting. Despite a variance with parliamentary procedure my ruling was accepted and the meeting later ended.

Thus, I had been dragged into problems of the School relating to its students.[87] A basic issue was the desire of a significant number of students for more student

---

85. Actually, the student occupation of Harvard's University Hall lasted only seventeen hours. At the request of Harvard's administration, more than 400 state and local police swarmed Harvard Yard, many of them charging into University Hall and dragging out students by the hair. Robert Reinhold, *400 Police Quell Harvard Uprising*, New York Times Apr. 11, 1969, at 1.

86. James Vorenberg, a leading criminal law scholar, served on the Harvard Law faculty from 1962 to 1989, the last eight of those years as dean. William Glaberson, *James Vorenberg, Watergate Prosecutor's Right-Hand Man, Dies at 72*, New York Times, Apr. 13, 2000, at C21.

87. In his memorial tribute to Surrey, Bernard Wolfman wrote, "His open-mindedness and his innate understanding of the needs and drives of young people led his dean to appoint him the faculty's liaison with students during periods of unrest and distrust. Despite the age gap and the availability of younger professors, it was Stanley Surrey whom both the students and faculty trusted to mediate. His integrity and his pragmatism achieved solutions that benefited the law school as a whole and made the educational process more effective for all...." Bernard Wolfman, *Statesman, Scholar, Mentor*, 98 Harv. L. Rev. 343, 344–45 (1984).

participation in the conduct of the School and its decision-making process. This desire was of course a move that students at many other educational institution were vigorously pushing. The Dean's response was to appoint a Committee of three faculty members—Abe Chayes, Charles Haar[88] and myself—to consider the matter in depth with a student group. I surmised, correctly I believe, that the Dean [Derek Bok—eds.] had chosen us because we all had experience in the Federal government and therefore he assumed, again correctly, that we knew when to compromise, when to yield and when to stand firm.[1] Haar had little interest in the task, so Chayes and I met with the students over a long period of time. We readily agreed with their basic demand of more participation in formulating School policies, so that the issues were those of shaping rational methods of participation. The meetings were friendly and cooperative, with the students recognizing our sympathy with their basic goal. Out of this Committee's work there developed significant changes in the process of student participation. We recommended, for example, that students fully participate along with faculty members on all committees except Appointments and Admissions; that a Student Council be formed with elected members from each of the three classes; that this Council be free to discuss issues and present recommendations to the faculty; that the Council select the student members of the committees; that the student members of committees be allowed to attend faculty meetings, in non-voting capacity but free to speak, when recommendations of their committees were on the floor; and that through a lottery a specified number of other students who desired to do so could attend faculty meetings as non-voting members but able to speak. The faculty accepted all these recommendations and the School process thus changed significantly.

My next major assignment was to chair the newly appointed University Advisory Committee on Shareholder Resolutions (ACSR). Various public interest groups, churches and others, had begun the practice of formulating resolutions that they recommended be placed before corporate shareholders in connection with the annual corporate meeting. These resolutions ranged over a wide area of the concerns of the groups—the manufacture of munitions for Vietnam; the appointment of women and blacks to corporate boards; the participation of corporations in state political campaigns; activities in South Africa; compliance with environmental safeguards; and on and on. The sponsors of the resolutions would then seek proxies from the institutional investors, such as Harvard, that held blocks of stock in the corporations involved. The Fellows of Harvard University—its governing body—had handled this chore but, since there had been few resolutions in the past to consider, standards for decisions on proxies had not been established. The students were demanding a wider School participation in the decisions on these proxies. President Bok in response, formed the Committee, composed of five alumni representatives, selected by the Alumni Association, five faculty members drawn from the various faculties, and five

88. Charles M. Haar, a leading scholar of land-use and environmental law, served on the Harvard Law faculty from 1952 to 1991. David W. Dunlap, *Charles M. Haar Dies at 91; Used Courts to Clean Boston Harbor*, New York Times, Jan. 17, 2012, at A19.

student members selected by students.[89] The Dean said he was suggesting my name for the Law School.[90] I replied the field was completely strange to me for I was a tax lawyer and not a corporate lawyer, and the School had a number of the latter. Nevertheless he requested me to participate and I agreed. Next, Bok, previously on the Law School faculty, called to say that since I was the only lawyer it was natural that I should be the Chairman. While the complete logic of this position escaped me I was hardly in a position to deny that there was some merit in his viewpoint, and so I became Chairman.

Our meetings started in just about the same state of ignorance on everybody's part, for this type of proxy movement was new. Moreover, each of the members was an unknown to the others, both within the five-member groups and among the groups. The order of decisions on the proxies was determined by the various dates on which the corporations involved would hold their annual shareholding meetings. There was really little solid information at hand on these resolutions, although one public interest group [Check] had started a service that collected the resolutions and gave some pro and con background on each.[91] The proponents of the resolutions and the corporations in some cases supplied brief descriptions of their positions.

At the outset I decided the only way to proceed was to achieve two objectives: one, a full discussion in which all members joined and two, the avoidance of block voting, i.e., alumni, faculty and students each sticking together as a block. At first there were suspicions all around, with alumni expecting students to be wildly liberal or radical, students expecting alumni to be horribly conservative, and the faculty to be unworldly. But very quickly these preconceptions disappeared. The discussions brought out opinions formed by the members as individuals, and not by groups. I encouraged the students, sometimes awed by alumni successful in life, to speak out, quietly advising them they would be listened to by alumni and faculty if they advanced their positions in a sensible, calm way that carefully responded to the views of others. Here, as elsewhere, I have always found that students can make valuable contributions to University problems, with the exception of those few students blindly led by passionate commitment to a group goal. We also held a general student meeting at which the views of non-member students could be obtained.

Our practice was to vote on each resolution, with dissents and abstentions permitted but no names mentioned. Each decision was accompanied by a brief written explanation of the reasoning on which the decision was based. The decision was then forwarded to the corresponding committee of the Fellows for their action,

89. The names and brief profiles of the original ACSR members can be found at *ACSR Members in Profile*, HARVARD CRIMSON, Mar. 16, 1973 (identifying Surrey as chairman).

90. The law school dean, unnamed by Surrey, was Albert M. Sacks, who was a member of the Harvard Law faculty from 1947 until his death in 1991, and dean from 1971 to 1981. His specialties were legal process and constitutional law. Alfonso A. Narvaez, *Albert M. Sacks, 70, Harvard Law Dean and Noted Teacher*, NEW YORK TIMES, Mar. 23, 1991, at 28.

91. This is probably the Corporate Information Center, an affiliate of the National Council of Churches directed by Frank P. White. *See* Marilyn Bender, *Investment Missionary: 'Minister with Portfolio' Helps Churches Question Corporations' Behavior*, NEW YORK TIMES, Apr. 15, 1973, at F7.

which would be the formal position of Harvard on the proxy solicitations. Our committee work was appreciated by the Fellows, for they recognized the care with which decisions were made and that we had avoided the danger of block voting. In only a very few instances did the Fellows' decision differ from ours,[92] and these situations were discussed by the two committees, with the discussions sometimes indicating that more study and information was needed on both sides, with this task falling on the ACSR. The final action on a proxy was announced in the Harvard Gazette, with the ACSR views.

I remained as Chairman for two years, with the composition of the Committee otherwise changing. We grew more sophisticated in our understanding of the issues involved and, since a number of resolutions followed the same pattern, took positions that were then applied to similar resolutions in a group. I recall our most difficult assignment was a resolution pushed by farmers whose fields were adjacent to a power plant that emitted gases allegedly harmful to crops. The Washington environmental authorities had tentatively decided that certain smokestack construction was necessary to prevent the emission of the gases. The company resisted, claiming the changes were neither needed nor desirable and the cost would be too great. One of the organizers of the farmers, an astute person and able speaker, came to Harvard to address the undergraduate students and soon obtained over a thousand signatures on petitions to Harvard to support the proxy solutions.[93] Obviously there were a number of technical issues on which nearly all members had no understanding. One of our members, luckily, was a chemist and he was commissioned to make a quick study [Check—who was this or did we get a faculty specialist].[94] On the basis of the information so gathered we decided in favor of the proxy and the Fellows agreed.[95]

While our decisions were not momentous events in the corporate world, there were factors present that gave the decisions a considerable importance. A majority of shareholder votes decided the issue at the shareholder meeting, but if a resolution obtained a 3 percent shareholder vote it automatically was on the agenda for the next annual meeting. Many corporate executives were sensitive to public opinion

---

92. In 1973 the Fellows abstained from voting Harvard's Mobil Oil stock, instead of following an ACSR recommendation of a vote in favor of a shareholder resolution to require Mobil affiliates in South Africa to adopt programs to establish equal employment opportunities. Also, in 1973, the Fellows declined to follow ACSR recommendations relating to Continental Oil and IBM. Seth M. Kupferberg, *ACSR Ignored by Corporation on Mobil Vote*, Harvard Crimson, May 4, 1973.

93. Nicholas Lemann, *Bok Receives ACORN Petition on Arkansas Power Facility*, Harvard Crimson, Nov. 20, 1973.

94. There were no chemists among the original five faculty members of ACSR.

95. The dispute was between Arkansas Power & Light, a subsidiary of Middle South Utilities, and Arkansas Community Organization for Reform Now (ACORN). Contrary to Surrey's account, it was not a proxy dispute. Rather, ACORN wanted Harvard to use its stock interest in Middle South to pressure Arkansas Power & Light into more environmentally responsible behavior. Richard J. Meislin, *Farmers Square Off with a Utility*, Harvard Crimson, Nov. 10, 1973. As Surrey writes, ACSR recommended that Harvard do as urged by ACORN. The Fellows accepted the recommendation, sending a letter to Middle South calling for more pollution controls. *Finally, A Word on AP & L*, Harvard Crimson, Apr. 27, 1974; Nicholas Lemann, *A Game of Pressure*, Harvard Crimson, May 22, 1974.

and very often to the opinion of the academic institutions that had invested in their shares. Consequently, even though the proxies never obtained a majority, corporate executives were forced to focus on issues, which they would otherwise have neglected or had handled at a lower level, when institutions such as Harvard, Yale, a church group, sometimes an insurance company (TIAA, for example), perhaps an investment house, voted for a particular resolution. ACSR positions were not taken lightly on our side, for Harvard could not risk or want simply a knee-jerk reaction to every criticism of corporate activities. Our discussions were thorough and relatively free of an anti-business bias. The successful operation of the ACSR in the first two years of its life firmly embedded the committee in the Harvard decision process on these proxies, and the committee has continued to function along the lines our group developed at the start.

A variety of other assignments were placed on me by the Dean,[96] and though I often could point to lack of experience, he stuck to his request. A faculty member rarely refuses a request by a Dean to handle an assignment, unless he truly believes the choice is a poor one for strategic or other reasons, and this seldom happens. Deans do know their faculties and which professors can fill particular slots. One assignment was of my own choosing. When the Kennedy School of Government was formed there was joined to it an Institute of Politics. As the name implies the Institute was designed to acquaint students with the role of politics, in the large sense of the word, in both our governmental affairs and everyday pursuits. The Law School was entitled to a representative in the Institute activities. I had never paid much attention to the Institute but gradually saw the importance and interesting work that it promised. When the representative initially chosen decided to leave his faculty position, I asked the Dean to appoint me as the representative. He readily agreed, happy to be relieved of the problem of selecting and getting the agreement of a faculty member to serve.

The main function in which these representatives participated was the selection of Institute Fellows. The Institute offered five or six Fellowships each term to persons participating in political life. Participation was very broadly defined, for it covered elected officials at all levels, officials of that character who had left office or lost elections, lobbyists for business or labor, public interest activists, newspaper and TV reporters who handled Government affairs, appointed officials in the executive branch, Congressional staffers, and so on. Various balances were sought each time around, Democrats and Republicans of various shades, women, minorities, federal and state persons, a person from abroad. The Fellows were required to give a non-credit seminar, mainly for undergraduates, of their own choosing and to pursue some research in their fields. But mainly they were free to roam at Harvard, and what they gained from five months of such roaming in a university depended on their initiative and personality.

96. Again, the unnamed law school dean is Albert M. Sacks.

The Institute had established an Advisory Panel on Fellowships to meet several times a year to consider the persons who had been suggested for a position as Fellow. Its membership came from various parts of the University and representatives of students. The latter had a special interest in the seminars and in the ability of Fellows to serve as role models for a varied student body with interests, firm or vague, in "politics." The suggestions came from an ever widening network of friends of the Institute, former Fellows, the Panel itself. The Panel's function was advisory, with final decision resting in the Director of the Institute. I sat for several years on the Panel. Then when Jonathan Moore,[97] a liberal Republican, with a fast-moving creative mind and a wide range of knowledge of the political world who had served in several government positions, became Director, he asked me to chair the Panel. The Chairman's role was to obtain free discussion of the names on a list supplied by the Director and his assistant who worked with the Fellows. An aspect I considered important was to give the student members of the Panel the realization that their views would be taken seriously and were just as important, even more so in some cases, than the other representatives. Each prospective candidate thought appropriate for the Institute to consider was interviewed by several faculty persons and Institute leaders, and also by the students. I and others considered important the opinions of the students as to how other students would react to the interviewee and whether he or she was likely to lead a seminar attractive to students. This had not always been the situation, and in the early years of the Panel the students saw themselves as a distinct notch lower than the other members. On becoming Chairman I met with the student representatives and after hearing and discussing their activities, strongly told them they should participate fully, present their views whenever they chose and their comments would be respected. The students welcomed this and soon found that the other Panel members respected carefully considered and ably articulated student views. While initially I participated in some Institute decisions on other activities, I found that my time did not permit this participation. But the Director asked me to continue as the Chairman and I kept this connection with the Institute. Also, when the Institute established a week-long seminar for newly elected Congressmen, I handled the session on taxation issues.

At the Law School, I became the Chairman of a faculty committee to oversee the allocation of a large Ford Foundation grant to support faculty research on projects chosen by those who desired to participate. The grant enabled the School to finance a period of research free from teaching duties and also a summer stipend. A faculty member, Laurence Tribe,[98] was the active Director of the enterprise and the Committee

97. Jonathan Moore directed the Kennedy School's Institute of Politics from 1974 to 1986. Later he was instrumental in the creation of the Kennedy School's Shorenstein Center on Media, Politics and Public Policy. Sam Roberts, *Jonathan Moore, Academic and Public Servant for 6 Presidents, Dies at 84*, New York Times, Mar. 14, 2017, at B14.

98. Laurence H. Tribe, Carl M. Loeb University Professor, joined the Harvard Law School faculty in 1968. He has long been, and remains today, among the nation's leading authorities on constitutional law. His treatise, American Constitutional Law (3rd ed., 2000), has been enormously influential.

had a minimum amount of activity, largely advising Tribe here and there on situations in which he was in doubt. This work led to a much broader assignment. As the Ford grant ran out the Dean desired that the School in some fashion make additional research funds available for the faculty. At this time, besides a half-year sabbatical every seven years, a faculty member could obtain a half year for research, being paid his regular salary. The Dean formed an informal committee composed of Frank Sander,[99] Charles Nesson,[100] and myself to develop a project for him. In the air was the suggestion of a summer research program. We explored this idea in detail and gradually formed a suggested program. The program would provide a fixed stipend, the same amount to each participant regardless of individual faculty salary levels, for a month's research that promised to lead to publication of the research results — a book, an article, and in special instances materials for a new or revised law school course. Those participating had to agree to spend a full month at the Law School in a continuous period, so that research momentum would not be affected by vacations or outside activities. A committee would consider applications for these stipends, there being no limit on the number of participants, to determine that the intended research and time frame met the terms of the program. Each participant at the end of the summer was to provide the Committee with an informal report on what was accomplished and the likely nature and time for publication.

After we had formulated a tentative detailed description of the program and its requirements the Dean circulated the faculty for comments. The comments were highly favorable and only a few suggestions for changes were made. The Dean then, with the approval of President Bok, instituted the program in the summer of 1979.[101] The program was an immediate success, with perhaps half the faculty participating [Check]. The requirements were fully met in each case and Committee monitoring was thus made easy. Of course, the program was open to some abuse. A faculty member who hitherto had performed research activities while the School was in session could postpone a month of that research until the summer and thus receive a stipend under the program. But, I believe wisely, we simply ignored the possibility of such maneuvering and found that the faculty did not engage in this game-playing. The program did accomplish its aim, to increase faculty research and publication, and to allow those faculty members, especially the younger members, desirous of increasing their funds not to have to resort to consulting positions or teaching in a summer session at another law school. The program was continued, and the original committee handled the oversight on behalf of the Dean for a number of years.[m]

---

99. Frank E. A. Sander, a pioneer in alternative dispute resolution, served on the Harvard Law faculty from 1959 until his retirement in 2006. *In Memoriam: Frank E. A. Sanders '52, A Pioneer in the Field of Alternative Dispute Resolution (1927–2018)*, HARVARD LAW TODAY, Feb. 27, 2018.

100. Charles R. Nesson, the Weld Professor at Harvard Law School, joined the Harvard Law faculty in 1966. He has had a long, varied, and high-profile career. His extensive scholarly interests include evidence law and the law of the internet.

101. Tammy Jacobs, *Dean Says Tuition Hike will be $375*, HARVARD LAW RECORD, Mar. 23, 1979, at 1, 4 (indicating the tuition increase was needed to finance, among other things, "a new summer program to aid faculty research").

One of the last assignments the Dean gave me was to chair a committee to oversee the functioning of a newly formed Legal Services Institute. A faculty committee given the task of recommending methods of providing clinical legal education to students had suggested the Institute. Essentially it was the concept of Professor Gary Bellow,[102] the principal teacher in the clinical area and an ardent proponent of such training. The Committee developed a plan for an Institute to be conducted jointly by Harvard Law School and Northeastern Law School, to be funded for several years principally by a grant from the Federal government's Legal Services Institute with supplemental funds contributed by the Law School. Several faculty members who volunteered for the work were to handle the courses given by the Institute, which courses would receive full school credit for the participating students. The students were drawn from volunteers in the third-year class to spend a full year at the Institute, taking its clinical courses and participating in its legal aid activities. A considerable number of the faculty were very dubious about the desirability and feasibility of such an Institute. The faculty therefore decided to proceed with the plan on an experimental basis for several years, with a faculty committee to oversee its operations, and then recommend appropriate further action.

It was this oversight committee, small in number and with participants from both Harvard and Northeastern, that the Dean asked me to chair. I again pleaded, a true plea, that I had absolutely no experience in the clinical field. But the Dean persuaded me that both of the sectors of the faculty divided on the plan would accept me as an impartial Chairman, and I again agreed. Professor Bellow and his staff established the Institute in a building in Jamaica Plain, a part of Boston in which resided a relatively low income group with large number of Hispanics and blacks [Check].[103] The Institute offered the residents in the area a full-fledged legal assistance office to help them with their problems. The students were trained by the staff to participate in this caseload.

The Institute had expected a fairly sizable enrollment and was disappointed when only eight or so Harvard students applied, with about an equal number from Northeastern and a few from other law schools. The requirement of a whole year's clinical study made students who earlier had expressed an interest in clinical work and then a public interest practice after graduation (the latter was not required for participation, it being sufficient to express a present interest in such post-law school activity) think more carefully about their plans. These second thoughts kept the number of students still willing to go ahead to a handful. The Institute proceeded with its work, since it had a full legal assistance docket and courses already arranged.

---

102. Gary Bellow was a pioneer in both clinical legal education and the provision of legal services to the poor. He founded a clinical program at Harvard Law School when he joined the faculty in 1972, and he remained at Harvard until his death in 2000. William H. Honan, *Gary Bellow, 64, Advocate of Legal Services for the Poor*, New York Times, Apr. 15, 2000, at A13.

103. A brief history of the Legal Services Institute describes Jamaica Plain of the late 1970s and early 1980s as a "diverse urban neighborhood." Shira Shaiman, The Hale and Dorr Legal Services Center of Harvard Law School, 1993–2003 (2003), at 11 [hereinafter Shira Shaiman].

Our committee, which had both Harvard and Northeastern members, spent the first year and a half in advising the Institute and the two law schools on a variety of operating details, such as the arrangement and content of the courses, the allocation of school credit among the courses, tuition costs for students from other schools, the relationships between the two law schools (fully cooperative with no rough spots) and the like. In the spring of the second year we started to develop a plan of evaluation of the Institute, which we could send to the Faculty. But suddenly the Legal Services Institute, now with a limited budget under the Reagan Administration, informed the School that no further grants would be made. Since the Institute was an expensive operation which Harvard alone could not finance and since the School had not formulated a decision on a long range future for the Institute, it was decided not to continue its work into a third year.[104] But the Dean did desire an evaluation of its operations for the two years of its existence. Our committee had neither the time nor rounded experience required for a careful evaluation. I therefore arranged for three persons with the appropriate experience to conduct an on-the-spot evaluation covering three distinct aspects: the students' reaction to their training and activities; the quality and logistics of the legal assistance provided to clients; and the quality and utility of the courses conducted at the Institute. The three experts made their reports and the committee submitted to the faculty an overall statement plus the reports. Those reports were partly negative on the students' reactions, especially their views on day-to-day administration; quite praiseworthy on the legal assistance; and not very illuminating on the courses. Our committee gave no hard and fast recommendations, but said the evaluations spoke for themselves. We said that the faculty had to rethink the clinical offering, especially against the high costs involved, and consider alternatives. But on the whole the report had the distinct tone that the two aspects of the Institute — clinical training and legal assistance — were appropriate for the School to continue within a framework that was manageable and affordable. The School has continued to experiment in this area, especially by shortening the commitment of student time which made it possible to attract more students, a closer coordination with regular Law School courses in the clinical area, and with the legal assistance provided in association with Greater Boston Legal Services.

In Retrospect

As I write this chapter I am somewhat taken aback by the variety and number of activities I pursued, in addition to a full teaching load of two courses a term. It is difficult to remember how time was made available for those pursuits. Of course the activities outside the School — the American Law Institute, the International Fiscal

104. Rob Woolmington, *LSI Fate All But Sealed*, HARVARD LAW RECORD, Jan. 22, 1982, at 1. The story describes the Institute's creation, operation, and demise. For another account of the same events, *see* SHIRA SHAIMAN, *supra* note 103, at 10–13. As Surrey notes, law students worked at the Institute for only two academic years, 1980–81, and 1981–82.

Association, the United Nations work, for example — did widen my knowledge and had a considerable input into my regular courses. Also in addition to the activities described or noted in this chapter, there were other activities that are described elsewhere, such as additional international activities, a government consulting arrangement throughout the years of the Carter Administration,[105] and the continuous work on developing the tax expenditure concept. All in all, I now more fully perceive in retrospect how varied and active was my second teaching phase and how a Harvard base of operations led to one project after another. It was a very fruitful dozen years. And throughout I was able to keep a schedule of thirty day cruises each summer in my Ericson 35 sloop purchased in 1973 after my heart attack (my first cruising sailboat was a Galaxy 32, purchased in 1958, one of the first fiberglass boats built on the East Coast), cruises which took my friends and me throughout the Maine Coast and the Canadian Maritime Provinces.[n, 106] Tax talk was not allowed on these cruises and legal talk held at a minimum, though some of my friends were lawyers and judges, but others were architects, businessmen, and a retired old salt.[107]

After writing this chapter and reflecting on its contents, I was surprised to see how crowded with activity this decade as a professor once more had been. I have really mentioned only the highlights and naturally many an activity is left unmentioned. In a sense, in diversity and intensity of work, it resembled the Treasury period, though there of course diversity and intensity had taken different forms. But the decade does underscore the large degree of variety that a career in taxation does offer and how different that career can be from the cut and dried view many have of the tax field.

Notes

a. In March 1972 when I suffered a severe heart attack (massive coronary infarct), these two professors took over my courses until the end of the term.

b. Surrey, Warren, McDaniel and Ault, Federal Income Taxation, Cases and Materials (1972, 1973). Volume 2 was revised in a Second Edition in 1980 and Volume 1 in ___. Dean Warren's

105. Surrey describes his work with the Carter administration in Chapter Ten.

106. The three articles Surrey mentions in his endnote n are: Peter Murray & Stanley Surrey, *Newfoundland Soundings … Remote, Raw, Grand*, Sailing, Mar. 1981, at 51–55; Peter Murray & Stanley Surrey, *Whales, Williwaws and Iceberg: A Newfoundland Cruise*, Sailing, Mar. 1982, at 31–35; and Peter L. Murray & Stanley S. Surrey, *Chasing the Sun in the Gulf of St. Lawrence*, Sailing, May 1983, at 72–73. A fourth article, describing a cruise during which Murray and Surrey were trapped for nine days in ice in Saglek Bay, Labrador, was published a few months after his death. Peter L. Murray and Stanley S. Surrey, *Locked in Labrador*, Sailing, Dec. 1984, at 34–37. Peter L. Murray is of counsel with the Portland, Maine, firm of Murray Plumb & Murray, which he cofounded. He is a frequent visiting professor at Harvard Law School. His areas of expertise include evidence, comparative law, and trial advocacy.

107. Speaking of salt, the reader may want to take Surrey's claim of no tax talk on cruises with a grain or two. Later in his memoirs Surrey reveals that he wrote an article on corporate tax integration while on a cruise (Chapter Eight, Surrey's note o), and that on another sailing trip he had long telephone conversations relating to tax policy positions of the Carter presidential campaign (Chapter Ten). But Surrey made the calls from pay phones on docks, rather than from his boat, so perhaps he escapes on a technicality.

name was carried over from the earlier books, but he did not participate in the new volumes. Supplements to the volumes were published from time to time.

c. SURREY, WARREN, MCDANIEL AND GUTMAN, FEDERAL WEALTH TRANSFER TAXATION, CASES AND MATERIALS. The book was revised in a Second Edition in 1982.

d. As an illustration of current material, *each year* there are statutory changes with the new laws, committee hearings and reports, Congressional debates; two volumes of tax decisions of the upper courts; three [check] volumes of Tax Court decisions; two volumes of administration actions, Treasury speeches and other Congressional documents. All of this is the accumulation of information that pours in once a week mainly through the current output of the commercial tax services under the various taxes. Interspersed with this current deluge are the articles in law reviews, accounting journals, etc., that must be read and others scanned, books to be examined. I undoubtedly have omitted some other facets, but the above description should be sufficient to indicate the reading that must be done each week, each year.

e. TAX POLICY AND TAX REFORM: 1961–1969, SELECTED SPEECHES AND TESTIMONY OF STANLEY S. SURREY, Edited by William F. Hellmuth and Oliver Oldman (Commerce Clearing House, Inc., 1973). Even on a selective basis I had managed to fill 741 pages!

f. A slender precedent at the time for our standing might be found in a Federal District of Columbia Court decision allowing black parents to enjoin the IRS from granting tax exempt status to Mississippi schools practicing racial discrimination, Green v. Connally, 330 F.Supp. 1150 (D. D.C., 1971), *aff'd without opinion* sub. nom. Coit v. Green, 409 U.S. 997 (1971)). But the legal rules for this type of third party action were in an initial stage and confusing. The issue has not yet been clearly resolved [Check].

g. Robert S. McIntyre, Inequity and Decline: How the Reagan Tax Policies are Affecting the American Taxpayer and the Economy (1983).

h. A word on the perils of having a Senator in for a visit at home. It was not long before Kennedy lit a cigar. But cigars are high on my wife's negative list. After greeting the Senator, my wife had retired upstairs. I saw I was in a no-win position. Paul simply observed the scene. I decided that this time the Nation's interests came first and if the Senator concentrated best when he was smoking, so be it. There was not full agreement on my wife's part, putting it mildly, as I learned after Kennedy left.

i. Cite National Tax Journal.

j. *See* ROBERT S. MCINTYRE, INEQUITY AND DECLINE: HOW THE REAGAN TAX POLICIES ARE AFFECTING THE AMERICAN TAXPAYER AND THE ECONOMY (1983).

k. The Project is described in detail in Chapter 8.

l. Chayes had been the Solicitor in the State Department (similar to a General Counsel) and Haar an Assistant Secretary in HUD.

m. Harvard also in the summer conducted a two week Summer Session for practicing lawyers. The teaching was done entirely by the Harvard Law School faculty who through lecture and selectivity reduced their regular courses to the time frame of the Session, one or two weeks of one and a half hours for each class. It was decided that a faculty member who met the requirements of both programs, the Summer Session and the Summer Research Project, could participate in both activities. This made for a full summer, but one with an appropriate remuneration.

n. For those more interested in sailing than taxation or law school life, let me refer to three articles, written together with Peter Murray, in Sailing magazine on these cruises; [Give titles and dates].

EIGHT

American Law Institute

Part II, 1973 to Date

The Beginning

On my return to Harvard Law School in 1969 I again became engaged in teaching courses in Taxation. I found the course that required the most preparation was that on the taxation of corporations and shareholders, called Advanced Taxation: Corporate Transactions. In my Treasury policy position I only infrequently dealt with that area of the Code, since in that period relatively few legislative issues involved this aspect.[a] It is an area, however, which is central to tax practice, and tax planning for businesses is the focus of most law firms. That practice is built, of course, on the Code and case law, but to a greater extent than elsewhere it involves Treasury Regulations, Rulings, and the most current material of all, private letter rulings.[b, 1] The work goes beyond a knowledge of this material — for it extends to the tax plans and maneuvers that build upon it and reside in the minds and files of tax lawyers. It is these plans and maneuvers that become the cases and Regulations or statutory revisions often years later, and by then this cutting edge of tax practice has developed new plans and maneuvers.

A tax professor, unless his school permits him to engage in a constant active consulting practice — and Harvard does not — can only obtain snatches of the planning work of the law firms, and even knowing this much involves some regular contact with a law firm and tax lawyers. In my situation, I learned what I could from weekly lunches with the tax department, among the best, of a Boston law firm, Bingham, Dana and Gould, and the luncheon meetings every third week of the Boston Tax Forum, a group of senior tax practitioners in Boston, in which Harvard tax professors were automatically made members. The main teaching work of a professor in the corporate tax course attempts to help the students find their way through the Code sections relating to corporate formation, distributions to shareholders, liquidation, and reorganization — probably the most intricate part of the Code.[c] I found that my efforts to relearn this material — I had taught it on my first law school tour — were

1. For the court's decisions referred to in Surrey's note b, *see* Tax Analysts & Advocates v. Internal Revenue Service, 505 F.2d 350 (D.C. Cir. 1974); Fruehauf Corp. v. Internal Revenue Service, 522 F.2d 284 (6th Cir. 1975), *vacated*, 429 U.S. 1085 (1977). Following the judicial decisions, in 1976 Congress amended the Code to provide that private letter rulings (with redactions) are open to public inspection. Tax Reform Act of 1976, Pub. L. No. 94-455, § 1201, 90 Stat. 1520, 1660 (codified at IRC § 6110).

frustrated by this intricacy. It was difficult to find a logical orientation since consistency and orderly development did not characterize the Code provisions or cases. The borderlines were twisted, not fixed, often murky or unmarked. The Treasury Rulings, of which there are many, constantly either contained elaborate development of an unforeseen interpretation or simply announced an interpretation without discussion or reasoning. The students thus saw much of the course as a game of continually pulling rabbits out of a hat.

I discussed my problems with Professor William Andrews, who had come to Harvard in 1961 from the Boston firm of Ropes and Gray, and whose specialty was corporate taxation.[2] Andrews had an excellent mind that penetrated deeply into the framework of the field and could, to the best one was able, hold all the inconsistent patterns together in his thinking. Thinking of the work I did in the earlier American Law Institute Tax Project,[d] I asked him if a thorough study of the field could improve the situation. He thought it could, but perhaps only if new approaches were permissible within the study.

At this time, Leonard Silverstein,[3] a Washington tax attorney,[e] talked to me about *his* problems with the Code provisions on the taxation of partnerships and partners. Apparently some cases that he had in his office illustrated for him that these Code sections left unanswered the rules in many of the day-to-day situations, especially real estate transactions. Tax shelters — real estate, oil, farming, motion pictures, almost anything — were all the vogue and these shelters used the partnership form as the vehicle for their operation.[f] Silverstein asked me if I thought the American Law Institute (ALI) would undertake a study of the partnership area, and said that Tax Management, Inc., which he headed as a division of the Bureau of National Affairs, a Washington organization — this division publishes tax material and had been founded by Silverstein years ago — would contribute some funds for a study.

Out of this background I developed the idea of a major ALI income tax project that would cover both corporations and partnerships, and perhaps more. I discussed such a project with Professor Herbert Wechsler of Columbia Law School, the Director of the ALI.[4] He liked the idea, remembering that the initial ALI Tax Project in the late 1940's and throughout the 1950's had held the interest of the membership and also brought in many new members. The project was fine, acceptable — but the ALI

2. William Andrews is identified in Chapter Seven, note 7, as one of Surrey's longtime Harvard Law School colleagues.

3. Leonard Silverstein co-founded the Washington law firm of Silverstein and Mullens in 1960. Remarkably, he continued to work at that firm — and, following a merger in 2000, at Buchanan Ingersoll & Rooney — until his death in 2018. In 1959 Silverstein created the BNA Tax Management Portfolios, which continue today as the Bloomberg Tax Management Portfolios. Adam Berstein, *Leonard Silverstein, D.C. Arts Patron and Top Tax Lawyer*, THE WASHINGTON POST, Feb. 16, 2018, at B5.

4. Herbert Wechsler, a leading scholar of constitutional law, criminal law, and the federal courts, was on the faculty of Columbia Law School from 1933 to 1978, and director of the ALI from 1963 to 1984. Among his many accomplishments, he successfully argued before the Supreme Court the landmark First Amendment case of New York Times v. Sullivan, 376 U.S. 254 (1964). Tamar Lewin, *Herbert Wechsler, Legal Giant, Is Dead at 90*, NEW YORK TIMES, Apr. 28, 2000, at C21.

had no funds to finance it. If I wanted the project to be undertaken, I would have to find the funds! This answer put me in an unusual position, that of both developing the substantive project and getting it financed. The first part of the task represented familiar ground, but the second was not my forte.[g, 5] Silverstein's contemplated grant would not be enough. Moreover, I thought the project would attract more interest if it first studied the corporate area, and this held no interest for Silverstein who strongly wanted his study of partnerships.

At this point I turned to Harry Olsher,[6] President and sole guiding hand of the Fund for Public Policy Research, a small Washington foundation with about $300,000 annual income. Olsher's chief—probably sole—interest was in fiscal policy. He had for a time financed activities of the National Tax Association and was currently financing the Brookings Institution annual tax conferences, along with an annual index to fiscal studies and some other such publications. I had come to know Olsher through my work on NTA seminars.[h] I gathered from Olsher that he had just about lost interest in financing Brookings, which had been his largest use of funds. I mentioned the proposed ALI project to him and he expressed interest, in large part founded on a confidence he had developed in my tax activities. With that indication of interest, I then suggested he talk it over with two of his close advisors, Laurence Woodworth, Chief of the Staff of the Joint Tax Committee, and John Nolan, Olsher's attorney. He did, and both favored the project. Olsher then agreed to finance the project, covering corporations and partnerships. Silverstein, somewhat annoyed at the choice of corporations as the first study, nevertheless agreed to have Tax Management, Inc., contribute $40,000 on my assurance that partnerships would come next.

With the financing in hand, I next prepared the structure of the study. The earlier ALI income tax project involved a Chief Reporter and an Associate Reporter who worked under the direction of a small Tax Policy Committee, composed of prominent persons in the field, that made the final decisions. The Reporters covered the entire Code, with one or two consultants for the more important parts. I decided on a new format for our study. We would have a Reporter for each part of the study, with an Associate Reporter if this were desired. A consultants' group of about fifteen members, or so, composed of outstanding tax practitioners and academics working in the corporate area, would be the principal advisors to the Reporter. These consultants represented both geographical and professional diversity, the latter ranging from lawyers in very large firms with major corporations as clients to some in somewhat smaller firms with lesser size clients. The overriding factor in choosing these consultants was their reputation for objectivity when participating in a study of the type the ALI pro-

5. Surrey appears to be uncharacteristically modest in recounting his first foray into fundraising. In 1952, the Ford Foundation provided the initial funding for the International Tax Program directed by Surrey, and by 1960 the Ford Foundation was a significant supporter of the World Tax Series, which produced several monographs on taxation in different foreign jurisdictions. Bruce A. Kimball and Daniel R. Coquillette, The Intellectual Sword: Harvard Law School, the Second Century 511 (2020).

6. For more on Harry Olsher, *see* Chapter Seven, note 28.

duces. These are lawyers who understand that whatever they may plead in briefs before the IRS or the courts and whatever weaknesses or unknowns in the Code they may utilize in their tax planning, the clients' hats must be left behind when the lawyers are in the role of ALI consultants. This does not mean a view that the Treasury is always right or that the result most favorable to the "Government side" must be sought. Rather it means a clear willingness to balance as well as one can the interest of taxpayers and Government, and the work of the representatives of both, in devising an appropriate structure for the Code. Add to this ingredient an ability to think clearly in tax policy terms and to envisage structures that could depart significantly, if appropriate, from the law they knew, and you have the qualities sought in choosing consultants.

I also established the practice of having a prominent member of the Section of Taxation of the American Bar Association appointed as the liaison between that Section and the ALI study. In this I informally sought a person who had the knowledge and qualities of the consultants. This liaison member was a full voting member of the group and his function was not to represent the Section or press the views it might have on the subject, but rather to have an intimate knowledge of the decisions in the study so that he could report to the Section on the study. Preliminary drafts would be prepared by the Reporter and discussed several times in two- or three-day meetings a year with the consultants. The Reporter would be guided by the consensus of the consultants, though he could express his preference for his own approach if it differed from that consensus. Then the Reporter would prepare a revised draft to be discussed in a November meeting of the Tax Advisory Committee. This Committee, to meet once a year, would be composed of around 75 lawyers, chosen on a variety of criteria — standing in the profession, government or academic background, major area of practice, geography, types of clients, and so on. The goal was to obtain a widely representative group capable of intelligently judging the work of the Reporter and the Consultants. As far as possible, given the desire for a wide representation, here also an ability to be objective was an important factor. The net result of this selection process would produce a Committee that was somewhat more receptive to structural change than the average tax lawyer, who is very much inclined to think in terms of existing law rather than statutory change and generally uses whatever are the tools an existing statutory system may offer, thus taking in stride as a guide the rules legislated by the Congress from time to time. The selection process for the Committee meant that if it could not be persuaded to approve a suggested change, it was highly unlikely that the tax bar as a whole, and the professional tax organizations, would support the change. But the opposite did not follow, for acceptance by the Committee was no guarantee of agreement by the general tax bar. However, the Committee's acceptance was almost certain to be a sine qua non to ALI adoption of the change.

After consideration by the Tax Advisory Committee, a draft would then follow traditional ALI procedures. First it would be presented as a Discussion Draft to the December meeting of the Council of the Institute, a group of about fifty lawyers chaired by the President of the Institute. The members, drawn from the ranks of outstanding judges, practicing lawyers, and academics, were mostly on the elderly side. On the whole they were generalists and not specialists in particular areas. Of those in attendance at a meeting, only about three or four were really familiar with tax law. This situation created two problems for a Reporter presenting a draft. A position strongly taken by one of the Council tax specialists, even if a spur of the moment thought and not carefully considered, could easily sway the Council generalists—after all, it was a tax lawyer talking. At the other end, a position also strongly voiced by a generalist who of necessity did not know how the position fitted with the rest of the tax structure, could if persuasively argued albeit in generalist terms also sway the Council. A Reporter had to speak quickly and with confidence, with arguments appealing to both specialist and generalist, to prevent a Council approval of these suggested changes in the draft which the Reporter considered not to be desirable. A draft then moved to the next stage—consideration by the membership of the Institute in attendance at the annual May meeting—either approved by the Council, with any changes the members agreed upon, as a Tentative Draft or be sent to the annual meeting, again with the changes, as a Discussion Draft. The Council nearly always moved a draft along either route rather than rejecting it.

The Reporter would then present the draft to the membership in May. After the presentation, there was floor discussion either pro or con or with a different approach entirely. While the Institute membership as a whole is also that of generalists, there is a significant group of tax specialists, so here again comments came from both directions. Suggested amendments were put to a vote of those present, and if adopted became a part of the draft. If the Reporter and Director then decided to put the draft, as amended, to the membership for approval or disapproval, a vote decided the question. A Reporter, with the approval, usually granted by the Director although he generally desired to keep projects moving, could simply present a draft for discussion without a vote, stating that the floor comments would be considered in a revision of the draft to be presented at a later meeting. A tax draft was usually allocated a half-day slot on the program. If a draft was approved, it would be published as the Institute's position on the subject. If a draft did not obtain approval or if a Reporter decided it was the part of wisdom not to force a vote, the draft would be published as the Reporter's Notes.

Obviously, all these steps along the road—Reporter's Study, Consultants' meetings, Tax Advisory Committee meeting, Council meeting, annual membership meeting—meant a time-consuming process. After a Reporter first presented his thinking to the Consultants it would usually take a year for the material to reach the May meeting. But the time spent all added to careful consideration by groups with varying backgrounds and this contributed to the respect accorded to Institute publications. Following his practice, the Director would attend all these various meetings.

This then was the process I planned for the corporate taxation study and any other study to follow in the tax project. I would take the role of Supervisor of the entire project, a new Institute position. In that role I would first present a project to the Council for its approval. On its approval, I would then select the Reporters, consultants, and Tax Advisory Committee membership, all of whom had to be approved by the Council, after first being checked by the Director — the approval invariably being granted. Naturally I sought the advice of experienced friends for these choices, and checked with the chosen Reporter the other personnel. This done, I had to work out with the Reporter and consultants the schedule of topics within a particular study. Also I would read all the drafts, discuss them with the Reporter, attend all meetings taking an active role to the degree I thought advisable in sharpening discussion and pressing differing views to consensus or decision by vote and in general keeping a study moving along its scheduled track. While I would at times present my own opinions, I always left the final decision to the Reporter when we differed.

Subchapter C Study

This procedure was first presented to the Director and then the Council, and met with its approval at a December 1973 meeting. It was announced to the Institute at its May 1974 meeting.[i] I chose Andrews as the Reporter for the corporate study and selected an admirable group of consultants.[j] In the summer of 1974 the consultants met to hear the Reporter's plan for the project. He presented as the first half of the project a suggested thorough analysis of the rules regarding corporate acquisitions and mergers, and discussed several innovative approaches. The consultants sharpened these thoughts and the project was launched. It was titled "Subchapter C Project," after the part of the Code that dealt with this subject. An agreed set of basic assumptions under which the study would proceed was made. These assumptions reflected major policy issues, some partly economic in nature and some political, on which it was thought advisable for the Institute not to speak, since the issues were both fairly well imbedded in current tax policy and were matters as to which Congress and others were not likely, and properly so, to regard the Institute as having a specialized expertise. But, given these assumptions, the entire Code's technical structure was open for consideration under the project. The basic assumptions were: gains and losses are required to be realized before taken into account; separate computation of corporate and shareholder taxable income will generally continue; there would be no "integration" of the corporate and individual income taxes, and that distributed corporate earnings would bear the burden of both corporate and individual income taxes; capital gains and losses will be treated differently from ordinary income and losses.

Over the next two years Andrews prepared six preliminary drafts, considered at two meetings a year of the consultants and, starting in 1976, by the Tax Advisory Committee. The 1976 Annual Institute Report contained this reference:

> The preliminary drafts deal in an integrated way with acquisitions which are accorded differential treatment under present law depending on whether they are incident to a reorganization, as defined. A major target is to make

> explicit the extent to which tax consequences in this area are effectively elective and to disassociate permissible elections from essentially irrelevant choices of corporate procedure. It is anticipated that this phase of the study will soon be ready for submission to a larger tax advisory group that is about to be established and that recommendations will be presented to the Council and the Institute during the coming year. Meanwhile, the other major phase of the work on corporations and shareholders, dealing with distributions by continuing corporations, will begin this summer.[k]

The consultants were amazingly conscientious in their attendance and participation in framing conclusions. They did their homework of reading and reflecting on the Reporter's Drafts, and then engaged at the meetings in intense, analytical discussion of all the possible changes in an area. A comment by one consultant prompted a thought by another, and so it went. At all times the Reporter would either be defending the positions taken in his draft or agreeing that a suggestion arising from the discussion was the better approach. The views of the consultants were sometimes unanimous, sometimes sharply apart. If the latter, a vote would be taken. If the vote was strong for a particular position, the Reporter would adopt it. If the vote were closely divided, more thinking on the Reporter's part was required. Each consultant had his own style and forte. Some were constantly suggesting variations from the Reporter's approach; others specialized in destroying many a suggestion by pointing out how he would plan to avoid taxes under its weaknesses; others were quiet but spoke when a suggestion perhaps acceptable in a big city law practice would not be practicable in a smaller practice. The predominant character of the meetings was a great enthusiasm for the work and an always friendly, harmonious discussion despite often complete cleavages in approach. Two days of this rigorous analysis was about all a meeting could take, for the unrelieved discussion at a high pitch was a drain on energies and thoughts. But the consultants welcomed the change from their usual law practice routine, for the meetings gave them a chance to use their expertise in an entirely different, fascinating way, that of building a new structure through analyses of issues that were often new and strange, all this being performed in a discussion with some of the sharpest minds in the field.

The meetings of the Tax Advisory Committee were also interesting though in a different way. At this point, a new structure was not being built but rather a structure already fashioned by the Reporter and consultants was being exposed to criticism from a wider, more varied audience. But even here the discussion was at a level that required fast thinking on the part of the participants — should they agree or disagree with a criticism or suggest a different approach, perhaps a compromise that satisfied the varying objections. Often differences of opinion were put to a vote, usually when a Reporter felt he would get a favorable response to a point in his draft, either in its original form or amended on the spot in accepting a floor suggestion, or when he could live with either of two positions. When a Reporter sensed that the meeting would not approve his position, he settled for discussion and agreement to rethink the matter, rather than obtain a negative vote. At the next meeting, after some rethinking by the Reporter and with improved presentation and argumentation, the vote would often be in support of the Draft.

In 1977, Tentative Draft No.1 was presented to the Institute.[7] It had the strong approval of the consultants, Tax Advisory Committee and Council. The 1977 Annual report of the Director states:

> Federal Income Tax. This is the first submission to the Institute deriving from the project to reexamine Subchapters C and K of Chapter 1 of the Internal Revenue Code, dealing respectively with corporate distributions and adjustments and with partners and partnerships. It is concerned only with Subchapter C and focuses primarily on corporate acquisitions, which are now subject to extremely different treatment if they meet the technical definition of a "reorganization" than if they do not. A very different approach to the problem is proposed.
>
> The issues are too complex to be summarized in this report but I can say, as one who has attended all the meetings of the reporter with the gifted bodies of consultants and advisers, that the material presented in the draft will be of interest not alone to the tax specialist. The problems posed and the solutions canvassed should intrigue the Institute in general, if only as an illustration of the variousness of the economic possibilities that must be kept in mind in framing a tax policy that is both viable and fair.
>
> The time we can devote to the consideration of this subject is too brief to permit judgment at this meeting as to many issues of detail. The question to be emphasized on this first reading is, accordingly, whether the approach that has been taken is constructive. The Council went no further than to reach agreement that it is, given the basic premise of the present law that separate taxes should be imposed on a corporation and its stockholders, with different events determining when taxable income has been realized. Much that is here discussed and proposed would still be relevant, however, even if that premise should be modified by integration of the taxes in some form.[1]

The Draft was approved by the Institute almost unanimously.

It is necessary here only to summarize the approach of this Draft, an approach that departed greatly from the existing structure: the treatment of acquisitions of a corporate asset or stock (called reorganizations under present law) would be elective; in the absence of an election stock acquisitions and statutory mergers would be carryover-basis acquisitions and asset purchases would be cost-basis acquisitions; this system would prevail whether the acquiring corporation used stock or cash to make the acquisition; the purchase of the subsidiary's stock would be treated like a purchase or sale of the subsidiary's assets; exchanges of stock at the shareholder level would be tax-free without any limitation except those involved in defining an

7. American Law Institute, Federal Income Tax Project, Tax Advisory Group Draft No. 1 (Sep. 28, 1976).

acquisition, so that investor non-recognition would not depend on an acquisition qualifying as a reorganization.

A full discussion is contained in a book written by Andrews, as the concluding part of a Reporter's assignment.[m] This book is a major contribution to the literature on corporate taxation. It led the Treasury and technical staffs to utilize some of its material in the 1982 Act revisions of a part of the relevant Code.[8] Other material is being considered as technical discussions on corporate acquisitions proceed in governmental circles.[n, 9]

The second part of the Subchapter C study involved corporate distributions—dividends to shareholders, distributions in redemption of stock, distributions in partial or complete liquidations, and payments of interest and principal to lenders to the corporation. At the outset of the work on this part a major change in policy was developing in government circles. It was earlier stated that one basic assumption of the study was the continuance of the classical treatment of the corporate and individual income taxes, which meant a separation of the two taxes without a reflection, when the individual's tax on a dividend was computed, of a corporate tax having already been paid on the earnings behind the dividend. The opposite treatment was styled "integration" under which, as exemplified in several European countries, a shareholder received a credit against shareholder income tax on a dividend for a part of the corporate tax on the earnings behind the dividend. Integrations could also involve a deduction of part of the dividend at the level of the corporate tax or, much the same, a lower corporate tax rate applied to distributed profits. But while the classical treatment had long characterized the U.S. tax system, in 1977 the Treasury announced consideration was being given to a change to an integration approach.[10] Laurence Woodworth, then Assistant Treasury Secretary for Tax Policy, had come to the Treasury with a plan of "full integration"—taxing shareholders on annual corporate profits whether or not distributed, with full credit for the corporate tax. He would couple this system with an elimination of the capital gain preference on the sale of assets, including assets other than corporate stock. When Woodworth first mentioned these thoughts to me, before he went to the Treasury, I warned that there would be no one in the corporate world providing support for full integration. There would only be some academics, mostly economists, who had for years thought along this line, albeit in a manner usually detached from the attitudes and practicalities of the real world. I also said that "partial integration" was both difficult and inadvisable, and further that his capital gains trade-off was not the fulcrum to move the system to integration.[o]

---

8. Presumably Surrey had in mind here the enactment in 1982 of IRC § 338, providing for elective tax treatment of certain acquisitions of corporate stock. Tax Equity and Fiscal Responsibility Act of 1982, Pub. L. No. 97-248, § 224(a), 96 Stat. 324, 485.

9. *Staff of the Senate Comm. on Finance, The Reform and Simplification of the Income Taxation of Corporations*, 98th Cong. 1st Sess., S. Prt. 98-95 (1983). The Report explains that the ALI's proposals "form the starting point for the staff proposals on acquisitions and liquidations." *Id.* at 2.

10. Department of the Treasury, Blueprints for Basic Tax Reform 68–75 (1977).

But on going to the Treasury Woodworth announced his thoughts. My reaction proved immediately to have been correct, for the business world would not buy "full integration." No matter what the economists thought, corporate executives and directors were not going to support a proposal that taxed shareholders on profits not distributed to them — some shareholders would not have the funds to pay the tax — nor were they keen on making the distributions that could provide the funds, but instead wanted the profits to remain at the corporation's disposal. Woodworth retreated almost at once to "partial integration" and many economists followed him, saying half the loaf would do. But these economists were willing to close their eyes to the large tax windfalls partial integration would mean to well-to-do shareholders, and the major part by far of corporate stock is owned by those shareholders. The business community was uncertain and divided on partial integration: it did mean benefits to shareholders, but those benefits would come only if dividends were distributed. Many in the business world thought this would bring shareholder pressure for larger dividends, and this pressure was distinctly not desired by corporate managers. Finally, partial integration was turning out to be far more complicated and with more cross-currents than the Treasury initially had seen. For one, a shareholder credit for a corporate tax paid could only be allowed if a corporate tax had actually been paid. But many a corporation with book profits to support dividend distributions had, because of the many tax preferences available to corporations, actually paid no or little tax so the credit would not be available to their shareholders — this could make for difficult management explanations why these shareholders, who saw themselves worse off than the shareholders in other corporations who did receive credits, were really not in that position, since for them more after-tax profits were realized by their corporations. As another obstacle there was the obvious question of how to treat tax-exempt institutions — would they still get a refundable credit though the dividends they received were not taxed.[p]

For the Reporter[11] and the ALI this sudden possible change in a basic assumption meant rethinking about the second phase of the project. Should the project shift to a study of how best to implement integration. A few consultants and many in the Tax Advisory Group strongly favored this shift. I opposed it, since there was no guarantee the country would turn to integration and, moreover, other groups were busy devising or exploring implementation plans. The Director and Council awaited our decision. We — Reporter, consultants and I — decided not to make this shift but instead the Reporter could in his study take account of the fact that dividends, not being deductible by the corporation, were taxed more heavily than interest payments, which were deductible. This fitted with the Reporter's own thoughts from the outset, since he disliked the favorable treatment of corporate debt compared to that accorded to corporate equity. The Reporter's approach here was to allow a corporation paying dividends on new shareholder investment — so that

11. Here, and in the remainder of Surrey's discussion, "the Reporter" is William Andrews. It is unclear why Surrey persists in calling Andrews "the Reporter" rather than referring to him by name.

prior investment made under different premises would not receive a windfall—a deduction comparable to a rate approximating the going rate on corporate debt. This approach would be a tax plus for corporations and shareholders. But the Reporter wanted also to eliminate the tax advantages of corporations buying back some of their stock in the open market rather than using the funds to distribute a dividend. Since the buy-backs were at capital gain rates on any profit in the stock sold to the corporation but the dividends were taxed at ordinary rates, this approach was a tax minus for corporations and shareholders. The consultants were divided on these suggestions, more favoring the first aspect than the second, and closely divided on whether the package as a whole should be accepted or rejected and whether the first part could be accepted without the second. When the matter came to the Tax Advisory Committee there was even stronger support for a dividend deduction parallel to the interest deduction but stronger opposition to the corporate buy-back proposal. If left to a vote on the package it would likely be rejected, to be followed by a vote favoring adoption of only the deduction proposal.

The Reporter desired the package. On its presentation to the Council the reaction seemed much the same as in the Tax Advisory Committee. But the Council simply passed the draft containing both proposals on to the Institute for discussion. As stated in the Director's Annual Report for the 1979 meeting this course was followed:

> Tentative Draft No. 2 (Subchapter C). Professor Andrews and his Consultants and Advisors have been engaged since 1975 in the intensive study of the treatment for federal income tax purposes of corporate acquisitions and distributions under Subchapter C of the Internal Revenue Code. The first submission based upon this work, addressed to problems incident to acquisitions, was before the Institute two years ago (Tentative Draft No.1) when the "theory and approach of the proposals" received tentative approval, reserving judgment as to matters of detail. A.L.I. PROCEEDINGS, 54th Annual Meeting, p. 393.
>
> This second submission is addressed to problems incident to distribution, especially the stark distinction in the treatment at the corporate level of payments constituting dividends and interest. The present position and the proposals for change are clearly summarized in the Reporter's Introductory Memorandum (pp. xvii–xxv) and Introduction (pp. 1–34). I cannot usefully elaborate upon those statements. It is, however, well to emphasize that these proposals are unique in the suggested method of alleviating the special burden now imposed on equity financing, while avoiding any windfall with respect to equity in place. Whether one agrees or not, I do not hesitate to state my own conviction that this draft is a brilliant exposition of the problems and constructive contribution to their possible solution.
>
> In submitting the draft to the Institute, the Council went no further than to express the judgment that the study is important, and that the proposals are significant and merit widespread discussion. It may be wise for the Institute similarly to forego any effort at this stage to reach more definitive

> conclusions, focusing instead on the full exposition and discussion of the bases and the implications of the draft.[9]

The presentation at the 1979 meeting thus involved only discussion but no effort to obtain a vote. In the ensuing year the Subchapter C study had been completed by the Reporter and Consultants with recommendations, highly innovative, on the treatment of loss carryovers. In the meantime I reached the firm conclusion that the attitude of the Tax Advisory Committee would predominate at the Institute meeting, and was strengthened in this view by corridor talk with many experienced Institute members. I therefore suggested to the Reporter and the Director that the matter not be pressed to a vote, believing it better to have both proposals on the books as neither approved nor disapproved, rather than with the dividend part approved and the buy-back part rejected. They agreed and this was the final outcome. The Director's Annual Report for the 1980 meeting reflects this view, also taken by the Council:

> Subchapter C. When Tentative Draft No. 1 was before the Institute in 1977 and the "theory and approach of the proposals" were approved (A.L.I. Proceedings, 1977, p. 393), it was understood that the recommendations with respect to the treatment of corporate acquisitions would not be complete until attention was accorded to the problem of loss carryovers. That omission is corrected by Tentative Draft No. 5, which deals exhaustively with the carryover of net operating losses and with related and collateral matters.
>
> The prime thrust of the main proposal is, as the Reporter puts it (T.D. No. 5, p.2), to "require an allocation of post-acquisition earnings, in effect, among the parties to an acquisition or combination transaction," allowing a prior loss carryover "only against subsequent earnings allocable to continued investment of the capital of the loss corporation." Thus "the mode of limitation" of the permissible deduction is refocused "away from the loss carryover itself toward the earnings against which it may be deducted."
>
> Simplicity of concept does not, of course, avoid complexity in the details of application. It is, however, fair to say that on both points the present submission has been viewed with enthusiasm by the Consultants, the Tax Advisory Group and the Council. Even those who favored the elimination of all limitations on the carryover tend to support the recommendations as a viable proposal that would effect a real improvement in the law.
>
> When these formulations have been perfected at the meeting, it is hoped that the Institute will finally approve the acquisition proposals derived from Tentative Draft No. 1, as resubmitted (pp. 157–72) in and supplemented by Tentative Draft No. 5. The council has approved this course.
>
> It is not proposed to ask for Institute approval of the treatment of corporate distribution and Tentative Draft No. 2 of 1979 but rather to publish the work as a Reporter's Study, possibly as an appendix to the book on acquisitions. That will preserve much useful and imaginative analysis, while recognizing

that the legislative recommendations are not thus far supported by a sufficient consensus for their promulgation.[r 12]

So ended the Subchapter C corporate study. It produced innovative thinking in the area and is bound to have an influence on future developments. All involved regarded the project to have been successful and fully worth the time and hard thinking of all the participants.

Subchapter K Study

When the Subchapter C study was well underway I turned to organizing the Subchapter K study. Subchapter K contains the Code sections relating to the taxation of partners and partnerships, and had been adopted in the Code nearly thirty years ago as a result of the recommendations of the earlier ALI project. These sections had scarcely been changed in the intervening years, and the basic focus of the new study was to be whether and where changes should be made. As stated earlier, the rise of the tax shelter use of partnerships had brought pressures to bear on these Code sections and various problems of their interpretation and application were surfacing in tax planning and court decisions. The first step in this second project was the choice of a Reporter. Since the Institute nearly always used professors as the Reporters for its projects, I carefully examined the list of tax professors who taught a course on Partnerships or who were said to be experts in the area. This search was not productive. Since much of the problems to be discussed lay in the realm of tax planning and law firm practice, the Reporter necessarily had to have a sure grasp of that practice, and hardly a professor met this requirement. Also, together with a knowledge of the world of practice, the Reporter needed a maturity and standing sufficient to command the immediate respect of the consultants and the Tax Advisory Committee.

I had been impressed by one of the consultants in the Subchapter C study who also practiced in the partnership area. This was Richard Cohen, a partner in the New York law firm of Lord, Day and Lord.[13] I checked with the Director on whether a practicing lawyer would be acceptable to him and the Council, and after an affirmative answer, I broached the subject with Cohen. He was intrigued by the proposal, having already experienced the intellectual pleasure that ALI work provides. The problem was whether the firm—and his family—would allow him the necessary time to spend on the study. After some reflection he agreed and the Institute announced his appointment in 1976 in the Report of the Director:

---

12. The hearing cited in Surrey's note r led to a set of ALI-inspired recommendations by the staff of the Senate Finance Committee. *The Subchapter C Revision Act of 1985, a Final Report Prepared by the Staff* (S. Prt. 99-47, 99th Cong., 1st Sess. (1985)). That in turn led to 1986 legislation adopting the ALI approach. Tax Reform Act of 1986, Pub. L. No. 99-514, §621, 100 Stat. 2085, 2254 (codified at IRC §§382, 383).

13. Richard G. Cohen was the reporter for the ALI's partnership tax project from 1976 to 1984. In 1985 Cohen left Lord, Day & Lord to become a partner with the New York law firm of Winthrop, Stimson, Putnam & Roberts. He died in 2012.

> The project also contemplates a study of the problems posed by Subchapter K of the Code, concerned with partnerships. I am happy to report that Richard G. Cohen of New York, who has been serving as a consultant in the work on corporations, has accepted appointment as Reporter for Subchapter K. A separate committee of consultants on this subject will be designated shortly by the Council.[s]

We now had two projects underway, with current financing coming only from the Fund for Public Research.[t] I selected a group of Consultants for this Subchapter K project. Many of the Subchapter C consultants carried over, since their practice related to both corporations and partnerships, and in addition a good working relationship had been already established. A few new names were added to complete the group, including a consultant from Texas familiar with oil and gas partnerships, Richard Freling,[14] and Arthur Willis,[15] the father figure in partnership taxation through his long experience in the field and his authoritative books on partnership taxation.[u] Also, some additional persons with a strong background in the taxation of partnerships were added to the Tax Advisory Committee.

Since the Reporter and many of the consultants already had ALI experience through the Subchapter C work and knew how a Reporter and the consultants were expected to function in these studies, and since the new members were fast learners and caught the spirit and mode of operation, the work rapidly got underway. At the initial meeting of the Consultants a young partner, William A. Rosoff,[16] in the Philadelphia firm of Wolf, Block, Schorr and Solis-Cohen, impressed all of us very favorably. Rosoff had been suggested to me by Jerry Kurtz,[17] the senior tax partner in the firm and whom I had asked if he wanted to be a consultant, especially because of his intellectual qualities, balance and real estate tax experience, a field in which the partnership form is the operating norm. He said Rosoff in the firm would do far better as a consultant because his knowledge of real estate partnerships exceeded Kurtz's by far. Kurtz's

---

14. Richard Alan Freling is of counsel with the Dallas office of the Jones Day law firm. In his decades of active tax practice in Texas, Freling began with Jenkins & Gilchrist, later moved to Johnson Gibbs, and still later to Jones Day. For an oral history of his career (as of 2010), *see* Tax Section State Bar of Texas, *Texas Tax Legends: Richard A. Freling 10/14/2010*, http://www.texastaxsection.org/DrawLegalLegendVideos.aspx?VideoID=9.

15. Arthur B. Willis practiced tax law in Los Angeles for almost four decades, much of that time as a name partner in Willis, Butler & Schiefly. He also regularly taught partnership tax at the University of Southern California Law School. His highly regarded treatise on partnership taxation remains updated and in print, four decades after his death. ARTHUR WILLIS, PHILILP POSTLEWAITE, & JENNIFER ALEXANDER, PARTNERSHIP TAXATION (8th ed., 2017). *Lawyer Helped Both Business, U.S. on Taxes*, LOS ANGELES TIMES, Mar. 9, 1981, at 28.

16. William A. Rosoff was a partner with Wolf, Block, Schorr & Solis-Cohen from 1975 to 1996. He later served for more than a decade as president of Advanta Corporation. Since 2011 he has been of counsel with the Dechert law firm.

17. Jerome Kurtz became IRS Commissioner during the Carter administration, and in that role led the IRS's charge against tax shelters. Surrey was one of Kurtz's teachers at Harvard Law School, and he recruited Kurtz to Treasury in 1966. Emily Steel, *Jerome Kurtz, Leader of I.R.S. During Carter Era, Dies at 83*, NEW YORK TIMES, Mar. 5, 2015, A25.

recommendation was all I needed and I named Rosoff as a consultant, the youngest in the group and not really known outside Philadelphia. Kurtz's judgment was right on the mark. I soon saw that Cohen, combining active practice and the Reporter's position, really lacked the adequate time necessary for the study. Cohen readily welcomed assistance and I suggested Rosoff as an Associate Reporter. Cohen at once agreed, thankful he would have someone able to share the work. The two Reporters worked well together. Cohen was a thoughtful person, at first reluctant to press his views strongly or to obtain confrontation with the consultants. But he had a good grasp of the subject and the instinct for the proper decision. He also had no pride of authorship and willingly accepted suggestions from me and the others. Rosoff was a somewhat more rapid thinker, sometimes jumping too fast to a conclusion, but completely open-minded and receptive to suggestions. Rosoff really worked on an equal basis with Cohen and the two divided the material between them.

As the study progressed it became clear it was of a totally different nature compared with the Subchapter C work. Subchapter C, as we said earlier, was a complex maze of arbitrary, often inconsistent rules, lacking any orderly pattern, so that a basic restructuring using new premises and techniques was required if there was to be real improvement. In contrast, as the Reporters made their survey of Subchapter K, they found a relatively orderly pattern, with rules that followed along on a logical, consistent path. To be sure over the years gaps had been revealed, some provisions required clarification and strengthening, and the rules needed testing and amplification to meet the new burdens cast upon the partnership form. The Reporters decided that the basic structure of the partnership sections was sound. This structure, unlike the separateness of corporations and shareholders that characterized Subchapter C, treated the partnership as only a reporting unit rather than a taxpayer on its profits. Instead, the partnership profits are allocated to the individual partners and taxed to them as the only taxpayers in the unit. While the structure thus involved only one set of taxpayers, the fact that the determination of their taxable income from the partnership was made at the partnership level presented its own technical problems. Some of these related to whether appreciated property contributed by a partner kept its original basis where the contribution was matched by money from the other partner, whether the determination at the partnership level of the components of its overall income, with many components subject to different treatment under general Code rules, carried over to the partners with the same differing treatment.[18] Questions of interpretation arose on the proper treatment for the admission of new partners and the retirement of present partners. Perhaps the rules under the greatest pressures were those governing the allocation of the partnership income among the partners, since in many a tax shelter and even a non-tax shelter partnership,[19] strenuous efforts were often made by the partnership and partners to allocate components of gross income and deductions in such a way that those allocated components best meshed—

---

18. Although "same differing treatment" is puzzling at first reading, it makes sense in context; thus, the editors have left it as-is.

19. Surrey has "partnership-partners" here; the editors have changed it to simply "partnership."

from the viewpoint of obtaining the least tax liability at the partner level—with the components the partners had from other income sources.

On the whole the Subchapter K work proceeded with fewer serious differences of opinion. The drafts moved along from problem to problem, covering discrete provisions in orderly fashion. The first presentation to the Council in 1978 provoked minor suggestions, and these drafts went to the Institute in May 1979.

> Tentative Draft No. 3 (Subchapter K). Of all the innovations and reforms in the 1954 revision of the Internal Revenue Code, none was more explicitly derived from the prior studies of the American Law Institute than Subchapter K, the first systematic statutory treatment of partners and partnerships for federal income tax purposes. Subsequent reexamination of the statute by the Institute and others led to recommend changes which, upon the whole, were not enacted, though amendments were made in 1976 and again in 1978. Given this background, the proposal that the Institute return to the consideration of tax problems necessarily envisaged a new study of Subchapter K. Three years of work by the Reporters and their Consultants, helpfully reviewed by the Tax Advisory Committee and the Council, produced the submissions now presented in this draft.
>
> The analyses in the proposals are pervasively influenced by the judgment that the income of a partnership should so far as feasible be taxed to the partners as though each of them were directly conducting his proportionate share of the partnership business. It is recognized, however, that countervailing factors may call for deviation or departure from this "pass-through" model and much of the draft is devoted to appraising the adequacy of the reasons for particular departures, both those presently in force and those proposed. The significant recommendation of a "full fragmentation" approach to the characterization of gain or loss on disposition of a partnership interest, as opposed to the collapsible assets approach of present law, is an important case in point....
>
> A major target of the work on Subchapter K has been to simplify the statute and, in the case of Part E, the regulations, which even to the tutored eye appear excessively opaque. It is believed that progress has been made but here, as elsewhere, it is limited by the complexity of the problems that must be faced....[v]

We were now having a full day at the Annual Meeting allocated for the Tax Project, with two studies working in tandem. Two studies at a time were the maximum, for the Institute meeting schedule, covering other work of the Institute, could only allocate a day to tax matters. And, just as important, two studies were all that Reporters, Consultants and Tax Advisory Committee could handle.

The rest of the Subchapter K project went along with the same ready acceptance by the Institute. The various Annual Reports of the Director summarize the progress. The 1980 Annual Report states:

> Subchapter K. The first submission dealing with the income taxation of partnerships and partners was considered by the Institute last year (Tentative

Draft No. 3). The general approach, adopting insofar as feasible a "pass-through" model for taxing partnership income, and specific recommendations with respect to some eight problem areas were approved.

Tentative Draft No. 4 extends the study to six more sets of problems: The closing of the partnership taxable year for a deceased partner; like-kind exchanges of partnership interests; basis adjustments upon the purchase or transfer of a partnership interest; loss or gain on non-partnership transactions between a partner and the partnership; the timing of corresponding items of income and deductions arising out of transactions between a partnership and a partner or a related person. The solutions offered have on the whole commanded the assent of the Consultants, the Tax Advisory Group and the Council. The recommendations deal, however, with matters that have great practical significance for all of us. They merit close attention.[w]

The 1981 Report states:

Federal Income Tax Project: Subchapter K, Tentative Draft No. 7....

The idea of treating the partnership as an entity for purposes of audit, with significance attached to the result in dealing with the tax returns of members, has been advanced before but its detailed development in this formulation differs to some extent from previous proposals. The Consultants, the Tax Advisory Group and the Council heartily endorsed the plan. The same may be said of the recommendation to avoid so far as possible the stringency of the "resemblance" test for determining the unincorporated entities that may qualify for passthrough taxation as partnerships.

The draft also suggests restrictions on the use of limited partnerships as vehicles for the pass-through of losses and other tax benefits. These proposals have the support of the Consultants and the Council. The Tax Advisory Group articulated problems of significance but still regarded the suggestion as a useful contribution, warranting further effort to perfect its terms.[x]

The work was concluded in 1982 with final approval by the Institute. The 1982 Annual Report states:

Federal Income Tax Project: Subchapter K, Tentative Draft No. 8....

The present proposals have the general support of the Consultants, the Tax Advisory Group and the Council. Their evaluation and disposal by the Institute will permit us to republish the entire work as an Official Draft. It will be a fitting sequel to the volume on corporate acquisitions and distributions under Subchapter C that has just been published.

As was the case in prior drafts relating to Subchapter K, the problems dealt with are for the most part independent of each other. There run through all, however, the unifying questions whether and how far the "pass-through" model favored at the start (see Tentative Draft No. 3, p. 10) can be employed or faces difficulties justifying deviation. Parts T through Y are particularly

> interesting in this connection, dealing with the problem as it arises under illustrative Code provisions drafted without partnerships in mind. Part Z then presents a challenging attempt to formulate in general terms the considerations to be weighed in resolving such an issue, offering a statutory guide for interpretive regulations[y]....

The study thus took six years to be completed. A book describing all the material and recommendations was published by the Institute in 1984.[z] It is still too early to see what others will do with the material. The ABA Section of Taxation had commenced an examination of the recommendations, but this was slowed by the death in 1982 of John Sexton, a Consultant and also a highly regarded member of the Section with a recognized expertise on the taxation of partnerships.[20]

The ALI study, along with other groups, had carefully considered a plan to completely revise the method of auditing partnerships and partners, including court procedures. The Reporters and Consultants here worked closely with the other groups. The result was the 1982 legislation embodying in general the government and practitioner consensus on the new procedure.[21]

It is inevitable that statutory or regulatory changes in the partnership area will be made in the future, and the ALI study will always be at hand to draw upon. This is what the ALI as an organization expects to happen with its studies. It is not a lobbying organization and does not therefore as an organization pressure Congress or the Treasury to consider its recommendations. Rather, those recommendations are on the table, with other organizations, lawyers, and government staffs free to consider and utilize when the government or taxpayers turn to legislation in the particular field—an event whose timing is pretty much unpredictable and likely to emerge all of a sudden. Often, in this situation, the ALI studies are the only coordinated material with which to begin the legislative staff work.[22]

Subchapter J Study

Subchapter J of the Code, governing the tax treatment of trusts and estates, is the third of the Code subchapters that are the grist for most law practice. There is probably more specialization in the trust and estate area than in corporations and partnerships,

---

20. John J. Sexton practiced tax law with the Washington firm of Arent, Fox, Kintner, Plotkin & Kahn. *John Sexton, 52*, THE WASHINGTON POST, Dec. 30, 1982, at B8.

21. Tax Equity and Fiscal Responsibility Act of 1982, Pub. L. No. 97-248, §402, 96 Stat. 324, 648 (originally codified at IRC §6221 to 6231).

22. One notable instance of Congress following an approach suggested by the ALI is outside of Subchapter K. In the anti-tax-shelter passive loss rules enacted in 1986, Congress provided that losses of limited partners were automatically subject to the passive loss restrictions. Tax Reform Act of 1986, Pub. L. No. 99-514, §501, 100 Stat. 2085, 2233, 2237 (codified at IRC §469(h)(2)).

but large firms have their trust departments and for smaller firms it is a significant part of their work for their individual clients, especially their more well-to-do clients. Here also, the Code reflected almost in its entirety the recommendations of the earlier ALI study. There had been some subsequent legislative changes but the sections largely were those that had been drafted by the ALI. I therefore considered it only fitting that our new ALI study covered this Subchapter.

As usual, the first step was the choice of a Reporter. Professor Emeritus A. James Casner of Harvard Law School was the father-figure in this field,[23] through his nationwide lectures and publications on trusts and estate planning.[aa] Also, Casner had been the ALI Reporter in a project, commenced in 1961 and concluded in 1968, on the Estate and Gift taxes, the Code sections of which governed the estate and gift tax treatment of trust arrangements.[24] The Director and I considered it appropriate to ask Casner if he wished to be the Reporter for the Subchapter J project. A little to my surprise he accepted at once, though he already had what others would call a full schedule in his work as the ALI Reporter on the Restatement of "Property: Donative Transfers," and his lecturing and writing. To make room for the ALI tax work Casner put off a plan to teach at one of the other Boston law schools.

The choice of consultants proved more difficult than in the other projects. The people to draw upon were fewer in number, and generally less well known in the tax profession at large than the Subchapter C and K consultants. Also, it was harder to gauge the rate at which they would fit into the ALI standard of objective consideration of the issues. Trusts for some lawyers are utmost sacred instruments that permit wide flexibility in planning the use and disposition of family property. They were also instruments that, through an astute combination of this flexibility and threading both carefully and ingeniously through the tax provisions, could markedly reduce the income tax liabilities of a family group. Moreover, the wealthier the family, the greater the flexibility and ingenuity that was applied and consequently the greater the effectiveness in producing tax benefits.

Casner knew all the various maneuvers used in trust tax planning for he had used them over the years in a significant consulting practice. He was, all in all, an obvious choice for Reporter. But before I made my recommendation I talked with Casner to allay fears and doubts some had that his practice and extensive knowledge would keep his recommendations too close to the status quo. I knew that other academics

---

23. A. James Casner joined the Harvard Law School faculty in 1938 and served as a full-time member until 1977. He was widely recognized as *the* authority on all aspects of estate planning, including gift and estate taxation and income taxation of trusts. *A. James Casner, 83, Harvard Law Professor*, NEW YORK TIMES, Sep. 4, 1990, at D11.

24. FEDERAL ESTATE AND GIFT TAXATION: RECOMMENDATIONS OF THE AMERICAN LAW INSTITUTE AND REPORTERS' STUDIES (1969). Although the publication date was 1969, the ALI had adopted the recommendations in 1968. For a broad history of U.S. trust law, see generally, Lawrence M. Friedman, Dead Hands: A Social History of Wills, Trusts, and Inheritance Law (2009).

who taught trust law, and also some practitioners, wanted a thorough new look at the field. My conversation with Casner enabled me to put these worries at rest, for he expressed a desire to consider some far-reaching changes. This was a side of Casner that few appreciated, a willingness to step away from his practice and hard-earned investment in the present law to look at the essential tax fairness that should mark the trust provisions. Those provisions—and Casner in using them—had helped many a wealthy family. But basically he thought those provisions were both abused and often wrong, and major corrections were needed. Many have overlooked this tax reformer streak in the Casner personality. And yet at times in the past he had talked in tax reform terms. One example was his strong, right to the point, testimony before the House Ways and Means Committee in its 1976 Hearings on Federal Estate and Gift Taxes[bb] in which he said that the estate tax was only an elective tax. Clients could pay it or not, for lawyers could clearly outline both the paths to payment and the paths to escape. He forcefully said far-reaching remedial measures were necessary if the escape paths were to be blocked, including an end to the mechanics that permitted the tax to be skipped through several generations—children, grandchildren, even great-grandchildren—as each generation enjoyed the family wealth. The essential building block for this "generation skipping" escape was the trust device. Casner as the ALI Reporter for its 1960's estate and gift tax project had done his best to obtain recommendations designed to end such abuses. But a conservative group of consultants and conservative members of the Institute often blocked his proposals.

The Director and Council readily approved my recommendation and the Subchapter J study was announced in 1980:

> Subchapter J. As I reported last year, the Fund for Public Policy Research, which has provided the main support for our work on the federal income tax, enlarged its subvention to permit the study to include the income tax treatment of estates and trusts. The Council designated Professor A. James Casner as Reporter for this portion of the work ...[cc]

Consultants were also appointed, with Casner and I jointly putting the group together. This proved a harder task than for the two prior studies, since the field was more limited and assured objectivity more difficult to find. We ended with the majority of the consultants new to ALI methods.[dd] This newness showed immediately when Casner presented some tentative recommendations at the first meeting. Some Consultants simply couldn't conceive any change was needed. The then-present trust tax rules were working well for them and their clients and why disturb a satisfactory situation?[25] A strong strain in this view was that trusts offered useful, flexible tools to govern the handling and disposition of a family's property. This highly useful non-tax use—not disputed by anyone—was the prime consideration in their minds. Since these non-tax uses were essential to an intelligent disposition of a family's wealth, ipso

25. The editors have changed Surrey's "present" to "then-present" for clarity.

facto the accompanying tax rules could not be called abuses. Even if the end result meant lowered family taxes, this was but a side effect of the desirable, necessary non-tax purposes served by trusts.

This attitude—that an admitted bona fide non-tax reason automatically makes it inappropriate to change an accompanying favorable tax provision—is widespread among many lawyers and their clients. A good business or family reason for a transaction automatically validates the applicable tax rule, and any consequent tax benefit is an appropriate corollary of the non-tax use. It is difficult to persuade those with this view that the non-tax reasons for trusts cannot justify the unfairness that may result under the tax rules, and that the lawyers could keep their non-tax uses of trusts but the family would on the other hand have to pay its fair share of tax.[ee]

Under the tax rules at that time, if property were put in trust form by a grantor during his life, this automatically added a new taxpaying unit to the family group, with its schedule of tax rates that were often lower than the grantor's. A typical trust was for just over ten years for the benefit of a child, with the property to return to the grantor at the end of the ten-year period. Ten years was the magical statutory number, for the income of trusts with a lesser duration would still be taxed to the grantor.[26] In the ten-year period the trust, for example, could furnish the income for a college education at a tax rate considerably lower than the grantor's rate. Largely only families in the well-to-do class could place property in trust for such a time period. Another use of the trust device was to ensure an aging parent or a sickly relative of an income for life, with the trust property to return to the grantor at the death of such a trust beneficiary. This also provided support for the beneficiary at a family tax rate lower than that which would be obtained if the grantor paid the support directly from after-tax income.[27] Still another use of a trust was for a father (generally fathers had the wealth, though in some cases it was mothers), to place property in the trust, with no possibility of return to the grantor, but with discretion in the trustee to accumulate the income or pay all or part of it to those children of the grantor who on a given year needed additional funds, because of illness or entering a new business or having a child of their own.[28] The Code required in some detail that the trustee be such as to give an aura of independence from the grantor, so that it might appear that the decisions were those of the trustee and not the father. But a bank or a lawyer or a brother or a best friend could be the trustee, and it was a commonly accepted view that the father's wishes would be honored by these trustees with "independence" existing only on paper. In nearly all cases if the father year in, year out provided for children directly out of his after-tax income, the total tax liability of the family would be greater. The trust device simply shifted a part of the taxable income to the trust, and a split income nearly always reduces overall liability. The trustee was in effect a

26. Former IRC § 673(a).
27. Former IRC § 673(c).
28. IRC § 674(c).

member of the family, but the type of member that placed some of the family income in a lower tax bracket than that of the father. These uses of a trust could only be made by a family member with propertied wealth—earned income would not produce the tax result since under the rules that type of income must first be taxed to the earner before it is distributed to others. Moreover, usually a rather large amount of propertied wealth was required, for fathers were often reluctant to place some of their assets in the trust unless a significant amount of assets still remained as the father's own property—suppose the father or mother became ill, or the father's business faltered, and the children were ungrateful.

Casner proposed to make the income in all these situations still taxable to the grantor unless the trust income was irrevocably to be distributed to a beneficiary, with no possibility of the trust assets to return to the grantor. This proposal at once produced a disagreement with many of the consultants and later with the Tax Advisory Committee. The opposing argument always was that these trusts were made for a good social purpose—to educate children, to take care of a parent, and so on—and therefore the tax rules should not place a burden on their use. Casner relied mainly on the argument that only the well-to-do with property wealth could escape taxes through these trusts and this was inequitable. It was only later that, at my urging, he pointed out the illogic of the opposition—a good social purpose does not automatically support lowered taxes. Working for a living for a family is a good social purpose, but salaries and wages are taxable.

The second main Casner proposal dealt with the taxation of trusts, created by the grantor, after the grantor was dead, so that taxation to the grantor could not be the solution. Here he proposed that the trust income be taxed entirely at the top rate of tax. He knew that many such trusts—ones whose creation he had advised—were vehicles to keep the family tax liability as low as possible through a combination of discretionary distributions made by the trustee annually to those family members who happened to be in low tax brackets and with the accumulation of some of the income in the trust itself, usually whose tax bracket was considerably below the top bracket.[ff] Casner focused on the manipulation and consequent escape from tax that this device produced, and therefore recommended that the top tax rate would apply to the trust income unless irrevocably designated for a beneficiary, and only then would a distribution to the beneficiary be taxable instead of to the trust. The proposal was essentially similar to the grantor proposal, but with the top tax rate substituted for the grantor's rate since the grantor was dead.

But here also where Casner saw tax escape many lawyers saw only the use of trusts as sensible family planning in the light of an unpredictable future—why should income be given irrevocably for child A who might become a wealthy entrepreneur and didn't need the income while child B, who either became ill, was a struggling artist, etc., desperately needed funds. A trustee such as a bank could, with its discretion in the distribution each year of the trust income, sensibly handle these changing family situations. Here also there was this sharp divergence of viewpoint earlier described under grantor trusts.

Casner therefore did not press either proposal to a vote by the consultants, the Tax Advisory Group or the Council. He continued this position at the 1981 Institute meeting:

> Federal Income Tax Project: Subchapter J, Draft No. 6, A Discussion Draft. This draft reflects the extension of the Institute's examination of federal income tax problems to Subchapter J of the Code, concerned with the income of estates and trusts.
>
> The central problem addressed by the Reporter is the extent to which a donor should be able to reduce the tax burden on income-producing property by establishing a trust as the taxpayer, rather than the settlor or the beneficiary. Present law limits the possibility of achieving this result but the Reporter leaves no doubt of his view that the current restrictions are both too complex and too relaxed.
>
> The alternative propounded in the draft is "that a trust should not be a separate taxpayer with a separate rate schedule, at least during the creator's lifetime." The implications of that position are developed in detail, with helpful illustrations and sustained consideration of the extent of its divergence from existing law. Excluding the trust as a tax entity requires, of course, turning to the creator or to an identifiable beneficiary. The "General Rule" presented in the draft delineates the situations where it is submitted that the target ought to be the settlor, postponing at this stage the questions when or whether it should be the beneficiary.
>
> The Consultants, the Tax Advisory Committee and the Council discussed the questions raised by this material, without as yet taking positions on the answers they should have. The draft we have before us is, accordingly, denominated a "Discussion Draft." It is hoped, however, that the Institute's deliberations will point the way to the solutions that should ultimately be put forward and endorsed.[gg]

At this meeting it became clear that Casner could not persuade the members to his view. There were the arguments mentioned above of "a good social purpose," presented by some who pushed it as a debating point. Lawyers representing large institutions, such as trust companies, advanced arguments against the proposals, though knowing full well that, for the trusts of the wealthy, the Casner view was realistic.

But here a new strand developed. Casner had argued that trusts were created to manipulate tax results for the family, and perhaps the trusts he had seen and structured as a consultant in his practice had this essential characteristic. But many an Institute member, perhaps from a smaller town or with a smaller practice, genuinely believed that tax manipulation did not play a role, even a minor role, in the reasons for which they created trusts. Casner seemed not to recognize this viewpoint, or at least not to bridge the gap between these members and his view of the area. Moreover, Casner was not always a persuasive advocate. He sometimes parried a member's argument or viewpoint with a joke, such as if he had known the member as a student, "That isn't what I taught in class" or "You must not have paid attention in class." His answers gave the distinct impression his views were immovably grounded by his perception of trusts as used by the wealthy and as unwilling to discuss the other viewpoint on the merits. Moreover, Casner's draft largely consisted of his proposals and examples of their application, with hardly any articulation of reasons for the proposals or any discussion of other viewpoints. Hence an Institute member not very familiar with trust taxation received no help from reading the draft material. The President, Director and I a number of times mentioned this to Casner, but he could not change a style to which he had become accustomed.

There was, however, another aspect of the situation that worked in Casner's favor. He was urging reforms in trust taxation that were needed if this part of the tax law was to become more equitable with far fewer escapes from tax. Later, in a position of compromise, he would have to pull back to some extent. But only a Casner could have pushed his suggested reforms. A younger professor or lawyer (assuming the latter would even hold those views) simply would have in effect politely been laughed down or ignored and such proposals would have died at once. Only the fact that Casner was Casner and people were aware of his vast experience, and knew that he could devise a trust plan—and had—that was equal to or better than their ingenuity produced, made it possible for the proposals to be seriously considered. After all this was *Casner*, the father-figure, making the proposals and many members paused to reflect that there must be some soundness in his proposals. And so the proposals stayed alive.

Casner essentially stuck to his proposals at the next year's consultants' meeting. Some of the consultants, becoming attuned to the Institute's objective approach and willing for the first time to move away from the work they performed day-in and day-out for clients were now more receptive to Casner's treatment of grantor trusts. But there was still only a divided view on post-grantor death trusts. At the previous Council meeting, one Council member stressed the value of having a small family trust managed by a family member, since he thought this was a useful device for the family, and should not be forced to have its income taxed at the top rate of tax but at its own rate. Casner then worked this thought into the treatment of post-grantor death trusts, but it brought its problems of what was "small" and even here who should be permitted to qualify as the trustee—a relative of the grantor, a friend, a bank, and so on. The consultants did desire to move in this direction and Casner accepted the view. This departure from using the top tax rate in all cases necessitated a requirement that the income of all trusts created by the grantor be aggregated, since otherwise the use of multiple trusts for the family beneficiaries would entirely defeat his plan.

The Tax Advisory Group in 1981 was still cool to Casner's proposals. But at this point almost by chance a new turn was taken in the proposals. Joseph Kartiganer, a trust lawyer from White and Case in New York, had become a consultant as liaison for the College of Probate Counsel.[29] He wrote a letter to Casner shortly before the

29. Later in his career Joseph Kartiganer practiced tax law with the New York firm of Simpson Thacher & Bartlett and was a frequent lecturer at Columbia Law School. He is currently retired.

November Tax Advisory Committee meeting suggesting a new approach but based on the same policy objectives contained in the Casner proposals. I called Kartiganer who said he had tried out his approach on his Probate College colleagues and it was acceptable to them. As to grantor trusts, he shifted the focus from taxing the grantor on a trusts' income to taxing the trust itself but at the grantor's rate. This shift in approach did not produce significant differences in tax result. But it apparently was cast in a form more acceptable to the lawyers since it did not tax the grantor on the trust's income but left the trust as a taxable entity with only its tax rate affected by the grantor's position. It also made some of the operative techniques simpler; for example, under Casner's approach in the situation where the grantor did not have sufficient income of his own to cover the tax on both his income and the trust's income a mechanism was required to allow the grantor to obtain funds from the trust. Kartiganer also had a proposal for post-death grantor's trusts which focused on the trust as a new taxpayer and did not involve the use of the top tax rate. On the second day of the Tax Advisory Committee meeting I asked Casner to have lunch with Kartiganer and listen to his suggestions. Casner did and considered them to be an improvement. So in the afternoon he shifted from his approach to the Kartiganer approach. Naturally there was confusion and insufficient discussion, but the committee seemed willing to accept this new approach though a vote was not taken.

At the council meeting in December Casner orally described his new approach, still in a formative stage. The Council could do little but give it tentative approval and permit him to present it to the annual meeting:[30]

> Federal Income Tax Project: Subchapter J, Tentative Draft No. 9....
>
> Draft No. 6 of last year dealt only with the questions whether and when the settlor may reduce the tax burden of income-producing property by establishing a trust as the taxpayer, with a separate rate schedule, rather than having the income taxed to himself or to a beneficiary. This submission proposes answers to those questions and deals in addition with the questions when the tax burden should fall on a beneficiary of the trust or on the trust as a separate entity, and if the latter, at what rate.
>
> The central focus of the draft is the general policy of eliminating the trust as a separate income tax entity with its own graduated rate scale to a much greater extent than that result has been achieved by the *Clifford* case, on the one hand, and the throwback rule upon the other, with their respective statutory formulations and inordinately complicated qualifications and exceptions....
>
> An earlier draft addressed to the problems here considered was reviewed by the consultants and by the Tax Advisory Group and, in the light of those

30. The way Surrey introduces the block quote suggests he is quoting Casner. In fact, as with all of Surrey's quotations from ALI annual reports, the person quoted is ALI Director Herbert Wechsler.

> discussions, revised significantly in the preparation of the Council Draft. Since neither the consultants nor the Tax Advisory Group took formal votes on any issue, we do not know how far these proposals would be approved by either body. My impression as an observer is that their opinion would be divided, with support of substance in both groups.[hh]

Casner did so, but again the presentation was unsatisfactory because there had been insufficient time fully to analyze the new approach. At the end of Casner's description of the grantor trust proposal, motions were made to abandon the study and there was a good chance those motions would prevail. A hasty conference between President Perkins,[31] Hugh Calkins,[32] a Council member who had been an active participant in the discussions, and me produced my suggestion that Calkins simply move to continue the study, taking account of the discussion at the meeting. Calkins did so and once more Casner obtained a reprieve.[ii] He spent little time on the second main proposal and it likewise was not put to a vote.

Casner presented the consultants later in 1982 with the proposal modified along Kartiganer's approach. There was general approval of the draft, with changes suggested in the rules for discretionary trusts. It was the consultants' view, though divided, that a grantor or trust should not be taxed under the methods in the proposal if the trustee, though required to distribute each year's income, could exercise discretion as to whom it would be distributed. After this meeting I suggested to Casner that Kartiganer and Richard Covey,[33] a highly experienced trust lawyer, counsel to the American Bankers Association, and a consultant with a mind of his own, come to Cambridge to discuss a number of policy and technical issues. The conference was productive, because it produced agreement on some issues and clear-cut, articulated division on other issues. Casner then went before a February 1983 meeting of the Council. Here he ran into pressure to modify still further the rules as to discretionary trusts, to permit discretion in the trustee both to distribute or accumulate without being taxed along Casner's lines. Here the "good trust view" surfaced again, though by a close vote, with the argument that such discretionary trusts made sensible family planning, with the proponents of this view unwilling to accept the argument that this allowed the grantor to have his cake (a lower family tax liability) and also to eat it (by in effect controlling the annual use of the income through his "suggestions" to the trustee). Where accumulation did occur a post-grantor death trust was to be taxed at 60 percent

---

31. Roswell B. Perkins was president of the ALI from 1980 to 1993. He practiced law with the New York firm of Debevoise & Plimpton for more than fifty years, from 1949 to 2001. *In Memoriam: Roswell B. Perkins*, ALI NEWS, Mar. 11, 2019, https://www.ali.org/news/articles/memoriam-roswell-b-perkins/.

32. Hugh Calkins had a long career practicing tax law with the Cleveland firm of Jones Day. Dennis B. Drapkin & Raymond J. Wiacek, *In Memoriam: Hugh Calkins*, 68 TAX LAWYER 1 (2014).

33. Richard B. Covey is senior counsel with the New York law firm of Carter Ledyard & Milburn, with more than four decades of estate planning experience. He has received national media attention for pioneering the so-called Walton grantor retained annuity trust, which Covey estimated in 2013 had cost the federal government more than $100 billion in lost tax revenue. Zachary R. Mider, *An Accidental Tax Break for America's Wealthiest People*, THE WASHINGTON POST, Dec. 29, 2013, at G3.

of the top rate on the first $40,000 of its income, and the balance at the top rate. The Council then approved the draft and it went to the 1983 Annual meeting:

> Federal Income Tax Project (T.D. II): Subchapter J, Taxation of Trust Income. . . .
>
> This draft presents what are now thought to be mature conclusions on most of the important issues thus far raised. General Rule No. I has been modified to narrow the circumstances in which the income of a trust will be taxed to the creator in his lifetime, substituting in part for that mechanism a tax on the trust as an entity measured, however, not by an independent progressive scale but rather by the marginal rate of the creator. At the same time the definition of a "required distribution" that shifts the burden of the tax from the creator of the trust to the beneficiary has to some extent been widened, preserving *pro tanto* the tax consequences accorded to the fact of distribution under present law.
>
> General Rule No. II, applicable after the death of the creator, also has been modified to relax the definition of "required distribution." Moreover, in situations where the tax falls on the trust as an entity (without the deduction for distribution), the rate of tax has been ameliorated by the introduction of a two-step progression (60 percent of the top rate for an unmarried individual on the first $40,000 of taxable income and the top rate on any excess).
>
> These adjustments of the prior formulations are designed to assure that the income tax does not penalize use of the trust for conventional family planning unrelated to tax saving and to facilitate the mechanisms of administration and collection. Coupled with numerous improvements of detail, the revision greatly strengthened the support of the Consultants and Advisers for the substance of this draft. That such support is now substantial is quite plain. Whether the Institute subscribes to that appraisal is a question of importance for the future of Subchapter J.
>
> There are issues, I should add, on which division of opinion is reflected in alternative positions. It is important that the meeting focus on the choices to be made, though the alternatives can be preserved if no consensus is achieved.[jj]

At this meeting Casner made a strong and better articulated defense of his proposals. The votes on the alternatives mentioned in the above quotation — allowing full discretionary trusts whereas Casner desired restrictions — went for the first viewpoint. Floor discussion on the basic proposals then followed, with strong pro and con speeches. A motion to reject the study was made. The Director intervened to say it was not only Jim Casner speaking but that the consultants, Advisory Committee and Council had approved the draft. We expected the vote to be close but to our surprise Casner was sustained by a two-to-one majority. This presumably occurred because the bulk of those in attendance, not specially versed in trust taxation, decided to vote "with the establishment." Also, the greater liberality allowed discretionary trusts satisfied many of the prior objectors; for example, Malcolm Moore,[34] prominent in the ABA Section of Property, Probate and Trust Law—a Section whose Council at an earlier annual meeting had presented its formal conclusion that the study be dropped—spoke in favor of the proposals.

What would Casner's proposals accomplish? They would end the tax advantages of short-term grantor trusts—the ten year trust for my son or the trust to my mother for life. They permitted discretionary trusts, with anyone allowed to be the trustee, even[35] the grantor[kk] but with accumulated income to be taxed at the grantor's rate. As to post-grantor-death trusts, the proposals by taxing accumulated trust income at the special two-step rate made the complex and apparently not observed "throw-back rule" unnecessary. The proposals also solved the multiple trust problem by requiring aggregation of all trusts created by the grantor. The overall result was a balancing of Casner's views and the views of those who believed "good family trusts" should not have the consequence of higher taxes than at present. Whether the proposals will commend themselves to Government staffs or tax groups working on tax legislation is, like all these tax studies, a question for the future. [Later add estates and book.][36]

International Aspects of U.S. Income Taxation

In 1981 Mervin M. Wilf of Philadelphia suggested to me that the Institute undertake a study of the Code rules governing the international aspects of U.S. income taxation.[37] Paul Wolkin, Associate Director, who had discussed the subject several times with

34. Malcolm A. Moore had a long, distinguished career as a tax, trusts, and estate planning attorney. He retired in 2016 as a partner at Davis Wright Temaine LLP in Seattle, WA. In 1982, he was chair of the American Bar Association's Real Property, Probate, and Trust Law Section. *Malcolm A. Moore Presented with Albert Nelson Marquis Lifetime Achievement Award*, MARQUIS WHO'S WHO, Mar. 29, 2019.

35. Surrey has "given" here, but presumably he intended "even."

36. The ALI published the proposals the year after Surrey's death. AMERICAN LAW INSTITUTE, FEDERAL INCOME TAX PROJECT, SUBCHAPTER J: PROPOSALS ON THE TAXATION OF TRUST AND ESTATE INCOME AND INCOME IN RESPECT OF DECEDENTS (1985). In the Foreword to the published proposals, new ALI Director Geoffrey C. Hazard, Jr., commented, "The project has already made a major contribution to development of income tax law and policy, as indicated both in the Treasury tax proposals promulgated in the fall of 1984 and the President's proposals promulgated in the spring of 1985." *Id.* at xiii. The Tax Reform Act of 1986 tightened the grantor trust rules for reversionary interests along the lines recommended by the ALI. Tax Reform Act of 1986, Pub. L. No. 99-514, § 1402, 100 Stat. 2085, 2711 (codified at IRC § 673). The Act also greatly reduced the potential tax advantage of shifting income tax liability from an individual to a trust, by providing that all but the first $5,000 of taxable income of a trust was taxed at the 28% top marginal rate applicable to individuals. *Id.* § 101, 100 Stat. at 2096 (codified at former IRC § 1(e)).

37. Mervin M. Wilf practiced tax law with his own Philadelphia firm, Mervin M. Wilf, Ltd, and with the Boston firm of Hale & Dorr.

Wilf, agreed.[38] I was at once sympathetic, for I taught International Taxation, and over many years had a real interest in the field. Moreover, this aspect of U.S. income taxation, in the entire history of the income tax, had never been systematically studied in the manner of an ALI study.[ll] The earlier 1954 ALI study touched on the area, but only as a small part of the then Code, since international taxation at that time was a very minor subject. The Director agreed and the usual course of events ensued for this study. First the Reporter. On this matter I had no doubts at all, for I considered David R. Tillinghast, an international tax lawyer with Hughes, Hubbard and Reed in New York, clearly the outstanding choice.[39] Tillinghast had been in the Treasury when I was there and later we had worked together on a number of International Fiscal Association projects. We work well together and after discussion can reach agreement on almost any matter on which we started from divergent approaches. Tillinghast was highly intelligent, articulate, with great experience in his field, had taught part time at New York University Law School, respected by all, and possessed of a secure balance in the taxpayer-government axis. To my immense relief Tillinghast agreed to be the Reporter — was enthusiastic about it. I then observed that being still engaged in an active practice he would need help and for this purpose suggested Professor Hugh J. Ault of Boston College Law School.[40] Ault was also a close friend, we collaborated on casebooks, his teaching specialty was international taxation, his command of foreign languages had enabled him to practice at intervals in France and West Germany and to teach in West Germany. I thought Ault was the best international tax law professor in the field. Again to my relief Tillinghast at once accepted the suggestion and Ault readily agreed. Next the consultants. This was in one sense not a difficult task, for this field of international tax law had attracted a number of specialists, not large in terms of other aspects of tax practice, but very able and possessed with the necessary objectivity; many had at one time or another worked in the Treasury. The problem was to keep the number of consultants to a reasonable figure. Tillinghast, Ault and I worked hard on this and ended with a first-class group. The Council approved these choices and the study was announced in 1981.[mm]

We first agreed on the basic assumptions — the very basic policy positions in the present system which we would not attempt to change: no general end to "deferral" of a U.S. parent's tax on earnings of its foreign subsidiary, but the general concept of taxing currently the "tax haven" earnings of foreign corporations will be continued; the U.S. will continue to grant a credit for foreign income taxes; there will be no integration of corporate and shareholder taxation in the U.S.; partnerships will remain

38. Paul A. Wolkin had a long career at the ALI, much of it focused on the delivery of continuing legal education. *Paul A. Wolkin, 78, A Legal Educator*, NEW YORK TIMES, Nov. 11, 1995, at 13.

39. After his time at Treasury in the 1960s, David R. Tillinghast had a long career in international tax law, retiring from Baker & McKenzie in 2012. He taught part-time for many years at New York University Law School, where an international tax lecture series is named in his honor. *In Memoriam: David R. Tillinghast*, NYU LAW NEWS, Aug. 23, 2018.

40. For more on Hugh Ault, *see* Chapter Seven, note 11.

non-taxable entities; specific policy-oriented provisions, such as exemptions of earned income from foreign sources, DISC deferral of tax.

Next came an overview of the study. It was decided to commence first with the consideration of the United States tax rules applicable to foreigners receiving income from U.S. activities or investment. The Reporters prepared drafts giving their suggestions for the "source rules"—to determine when was there income from U.S. sources which the U.S., as the country of source, could appropriately tax. These source rules were discussed at the first meeting of the consultants. Our choice for this group proved correct, for the group at once engaged in an informed, objective, high level analysis of the rules presented by the Reporters. With some changes made after the consultants' meeting, the Reporters presented the source rules material to the Tax Advisory Committee and there it had full acceptance. The Council, very favorably impressed by the Reporters' presentation and answers, approved and this part of the draft went to the 1983 Institute meeting:

> Federal Income Tax Project (T. D. 10): International Aspects of United States Income Taxation....
>
> The decision to include this subject in the Project was taken in the view that a systematic study of this area of tax law, with emphasis upon the appraisal and critique of its animating policies, would be helpful to practitioners, to government officials and to Congress. That this expectation was well founded has been confirmed, I think, by the reception thus far given to the work of the Reporters. The Institute's evaluation of the sample of that work presented here will, of course, provide the acid test.
>
> The contemplated study is readily divided into two main parts: first, the taxation by the United States of American citizens, residents and corporations deriving income from activities abroad; and second, our taxation of foreign individuals and enterprise deriving income from activities or investments here. Both aspects of the subject will be dealt with and their close relationship is clear.
>
> ...
>
> This draft powerfully illustrates a point that I have made before in connection with the Federal Income Project, that very frequently one need not be a specialist in taxation to participate constructively in the consideration of the problems involved. Surely the issues that must be confronted here lie in the broad domain of conflicts or foreign relations law or even commercial law (the passage of title rule), not in the realm of technicality. The Institute will view them, I am sure, in that perspective.[nn]

The Institute agreed with little discussion. In the meantime the Reporters had been considering with the consultants the techniques appropriate to tax income from sources in the United States, as previously decided. Here one of the main changes suggested by the Reporters was to impose a tax, in addition to the regular corporate tax, on the profits of a branch in the United States owned by a foreign corporation.

This device was to be in place of the present, rather cumbersome, rule that considers a dividend paid by the foreign corporation out of its U.S. branch profits as a dividend from U.S. sources and therefore the foreign corporation must act as a withholding agent for the United States, collecting a withheld tax on its dividends, with the funds so withheld to be transmitted to the United States.

[Add future work.][41]

Federal Estate Tax Treatment of Generation-Skipping Transfers

After the International Tax study was launched I met with some of the consultants on the various studies to obtain suggestions for any future ALI studies if funds can be found. The meeting was not very productive, except for the principal suggestion that a study be made of the role of "interest" in tax law. There was, however, one study which did intrigue the group, and this was a study of the generation-skipping provisions added in the 1976 Act. This subject requires a word as to its historical background.

"Generation-Skipping" is the term applied to a trust created, say by a father in his will, the income, and if necessary some of the principal, in the trustee's discretion to be distributed among his children and their wives, and perhaps nephews and nieces—the first generation with interests in the trust but no direct ownership of the trust assets since these assets technically belonged to the trustee. After the death of these beneficiaries the trust could either be terminated, and the assets turned over to grandchildren, or if the father had so desired on the creation of the trust, ownership of the assets would remain in the trustee with similar discretion as to the grandchildren—the second generation—and then in some cases, to great-grandchildren—the third generation. An estate tax would be paid on the value of the trust's assets on the father's death, but thereafter, since ownership of the assets did not leave the trust, the estate tax on the first generation, on the second generation, and if the trust still continued on the third generation, was not imposed—i.e., generations were "skipped". A wealthy family in this fashion could escape payment of an estate tax for perhaps one hundred

41. The results of the ALI project were published in 1987, three years after Surrey's death. FEDERAL INCOME TAX PROJECT, INTERNATIONAL ASPECTS OF UNITED STATES INCOME TAXATION, PROPOSALS OF THE AMERICAN LAW INSTITUTE (1987). Although the study was not formally published until after the enactment of the Tax Reform Act of 1986, it had been substantially completed and approved by the ALI in time for Congress to consider it during the 1986 legislative process. Reporters Tillinghast and Ault were "gratified that this study contributed directly to the development of several of the provisions that were included in that legislation." *Id.* at xiii. For example, the study's proposal for a "branch remittance tax" (described by Surrey in the text) was adopted (with various technical modifications) in the 1986 Act. *Id.* at 140–57 (describing the proposed branch remittance tax); Tax Reform Act of 1986, Pub. L. No. 99-514, § 1241, 100 Stat. 2085, 2576 (enacting the branch profits tax, codified at IRC § 884).

years. Obviously, with the estate tax being skipped in this fashion, a family's wealth was bound to increase since no portion went to the government in estate tax.[oo]

These generation-skipping trusts were not fanciful arrangements just on paper for lawyers and clients to dream about; a significant portion of the family wealth in the country followed this route. Tax reformers for years had urged that the rules permitting such generation-skipping be abandoned and in their place there be substituted the policy of applying the estate tax once each generation. Articles were written, studies made, conferences held, and even Congressional hearings, but Congress did not act.[pp] The pressure for reform did not go unchallenged, for trust companies, banks and lawyers strongly defended the rules.

In 1976, however, the Congress made one of those sudden quantum jumps that characterize tax legislation. In that year the President and many groups were pushing hard for an increase in the estate tax exemption from $60,000 to $150,000. The parade was initially led by the farm organizations, but soon the small business organizations joined. Their plea was the lack of funds to pay the estate tax, and to prevent the sale of farms and business by their family owners, the estate tax had to be made more lenient. Despite the lack of proof for this proposition, the parade was favorably viewed by the Congress and an increased exemption appeared certain. Of course, there stayed in the background lawyers for clients whose estates consisted of diversified securities — by far the largest number of decedents — who wisely did not appear openly in the ranks of the parade but favored its goal. When it became clear the exemption would be raised to $175,625 (in the form of a $47,000 credit against the tax) — so that less than 2 percent of decedents would be subject to tax as compared with 7 percent under the $60,000 exemption, the tax reformers led quietly by the Joint Committee Staff proposed legislation to cure the generation-skipping trusts. The Republican Treasury strongly opposed the suggestion, though it favored the exemption increase. But a deal was cut in the Senate; the exemption was increased and anti-generation-skipping legislation adopted. The Ways and Means conferees accepted the bargain. On the House floor, however, the groups opposing the generation-skipping legislation mustered their forces. The farmers — and their Congressmen — were in a dilemma, for the choice lay between either both pieces of legislation or neither. The deal held firm by a close vote and anti-generation-skipping legislation entered the Code.[qq, 42]

Then came the counter-attack. With their higher exemption secure the farmers went back to their farms and the small businessmen to their businesses. This left the banks and trust companies and estate planning lawyers to mount a strong attack on the new generation-skipping rules.[rr, 43] They had some ammunition, for the 1976 rules had been hastily drafted and presented a large degree of complexity. It was not a complexity that could not be understood with patient reading but a complexity that

---

42. Tax Reform Act of 1976, Pub. L. No. 94-455, § 2006, 90 Stat. 1520, 1879 (codified at former IRC § 2601 to 2622).

43. Surrey recounts the short unhappy life of carryover basis at death (the subject of Surrey's note rr) in Chapter Ten.

was seized upon as impractical and unworkable. Moreover, critics would argue that the whole exercise was for naught since the statute had gaps that astute tax planners for the wealthy could utilize while the less astute, less experienced, more numerous small firms, with less wealthy clients, could not perceive or utilize. Wealth here meant at least several millions of dollars and rose to half a billion; indeed, a family with the latter wealth had under the prior laws paid only minor amounts in tax[ss] as generations were skipped, and would be able largely through weaknesses in the new legislation to duplicate this performance. The attack was made in strength and 1983 seemed the crucial year, since then the new rules came fully in effect.

Back now to our ALI informal meeting on new projects. Some members of the ABA Section of Taxation, who favored generation-skipping restraints, said that perhaps the ALI through a technical study could devise rules that were both workable and effective, and these rules might appeal to the Congress as a compromise position. In thinking about this, and reading the ABA testimony at Senate Hearings held on proposed repeal, I noticed that the attack was both strong in tone and replete with cliches and "horribles," but without any indication at all that a real problem of tax equity existed because of these generation-skipping trusts. Yet every lawyer versed in the field understood that such a problem did exist. I mentioned the possibility of a study to the Director and Council but they were uncertain the ABA would not at once attack such a project even before it was launched. I therefore asked two top ABA Tax Section officials to approach the ABA, which meant its Real Property, Probate and Trust Law Section, to determine if this opposition did exist. Since the latter group did not deny a problem existed or at least did not deny that consideration could be given to ascertain if a problem did exist, they stated they would not oppose the project if it covered both aspects: did a real problem exist and if so what was a rational cure. The ALI Council agreed and this study was launched.

I desired a quick study with the hope that our work could emerge before Congress repealed the generation-skipping rules or altered them. I selected Professor Harry L. Gutman of Virginia Law School as the Reporter.[44] Gutman had been in Boston law firm estate practice, collaborated on estate and gift tax materials with me, worked for several years in the Treasury on estate tax issues, and was now teaching estate taxation at Virginia Law School. He was intelligent, fast thinking, open to suggestions and—highly important—ready to meet my proposed quick timetable. As Associate Reporter I selected Joseph Kartiganer who had proved so helpful in the trust project—an experienced lawyer, with an imaginative, creative mind that could look far beyond current rules, and also open to suggestion. I decided in the interests of time

44. Harry L. ("Hank") Gutman began practicing tax law in Boston and was in the U.S Treasury Department from 1977–80. Afterwards, he taught tax law at the University of Virginia and the University of Pennsylvania. In 1991, he became Chief of Staff of the Congressional Joint Committee on Taxation. From 1999–2015, he was part of KPMG's Washington National Tax Practice. Most recently, he was Of Counsel at the law firm of Ivins, Phillips & Baker. *Former Tax Committee Chief of Staff Joins Ivins*, Aug. 4, 2016, *available at*: https://www.prnewswire.com/news-releases/former-tax-committee-chief-of-staff-joins-ivins-300309352.html.

to keep the number of consultants small, seven in number plus three liaison members for I desired to have a fully representative group.[tt] The study was announced at the 1983 Annual Meeting:

> A New Tax Project: The Federal Estate Tax Treatment of Generation-Skipping Transfers. On the recommendation of Stanley S. Surrey, the Supervisor of the Federal Income Tax Project, supported by a distinguished group of advisers, the Council approved a study of the problems presented by the generation-skipping provisions of present law, with a view to devising an appropriate statutory solution, if that is possible. Harry L. Gutman of the Law School of the University of Virginia has been designated Reporter and Joseph Kartiganer, New York, NY, Associate Reporter …
>
> The project will be supported by a grant from the Fund for Public Policy Research. The completion of the study is expected in two years.[uu]

We now had for the first time three ALI studies in progress, the completion of the Subchapter J study, the continuation of the International Tax Study, and the Generation-Skipping Study.

Gutman prepared a long summary of the prior studies. He included a Treasury announcement made in 1983 providing its proposal for revision of the rules. Gutman and Kartiganer then presented the issues and possible solutions to a consultants' meeting in June, 1983. The majority of consultants either agreed that a real problem existed or that they would hold such a decision in abeyance until the range of possible solutions was discussed at the next meeting.

[Give future developments.][45]

Notes

a. The Treasury in this period did promulgate a complete revision of the consolidated return regulations, and several minor changes in the reorganization sections were enacted. Also the personal holding company rules were tightened.

b. These rulings were later, by court decision, required to be made public.

c. Very specialized sections may perhaps involve more intricate detail, such as the taxation of insurance companies, but most practitioners do not become involved in such a specialty.

---

45. At the time of the ALI's 1984 Annual Meeting, it appeared that Congress was on the brink of repealing the generation-skipping tax (GST). For that reason, the members were presented with only a discussion draft; no votes were taken. FEDERAL ESTATE AND GIFT TAX PROJECT, STUDY ON GENERATION-SKIPPING TRANSFERS UNDER THE FEDERAL ESTATE TAX (Discussion Draft No. 1, Mar. 28, 1984); Roswell B. Perkins, *President's Letter*, 6 ALI REPORTER 1, 8 (Jul. 1984). As it happened, Congress did not repeal the GST in 1984, but the ALI nevertheless did not revisit the project in later years. In 1986 Congress repealed the 1976 version of the tax (with the repeal retroactively effective to 1976) and replaced it with a fundamentally redesigned tax on generation-skipping transfers. Tax Reform Act of 1986, Pub. L. No. 99-514, § 1431, 100 Stat. 2085, 2717 (codified at IRC § 2601 to 2663). The 1986 legislation is in agreement with the ALI study in some respects; for example, the legislation imposes a tax on "direct skips" as recommended in the 1984 discussion draft.

d. *See* Chapter 4.

e. *See* Chapter 7.

f. For an early description of tax shelters and their operative techniques, *see* SURREY, PATHWAYS TO TAX REFORM (1973), Chapter IV.

g. Nor had I been lucky in a previous fund raising effort. I had developed the idea of a Harvard Center for Fiscal Studies, in which the Law School would play the chief role, in association with the Economics Department and the Business School. The project was discussed informally with several foundations without any encouragement until we approached the Ford Foundation; there it was met with interest. A full description of the project, signed by the heads of the three University segments and calling for $3 million, was then submitted to the Ford Foundation. The project was viewed favorably and had cleared all the hurdles, including the Vice Presidential level of the Foundation. We were informally assured the board would approve it. But at the meeting at which it was to be approved, the board drastically revised its grant goals and our project fell outside the new directions. We thus lost our $3 million, and this ended my venture into fund raising.

h. *See* Chapter 7 for the relationship with Olsher.

i. *See* the Annual Report, 51st Annual Meeting (May 21–24,1974) 12–14.

j. The initial consultants were M. Bernard Aidinoff, New York; Boris I. Bittker, Connecticut; Walter J. Blum, Illinois; Richard G. Cohen, New York; Martin D. Ginsburg, New York; Don V. Harris, Jr., District of Columbia (ABA Liaison); Vester T. Hughes, Jr., Texas; Howard G. Krane, Illinois; Harry K. Mansfield, Massachusetts; Leonard L. Silverstein, District of Columbia; Laurens Williams, District of Columbia; James H. Wilson, Jr., Georgia; and Bernard Wolfman, Pennsylvania. Later Bittker dropped out, and James B. Lewis of New York and Professor Marvin A. Chirelstein of Yale Law School joined the group. Chirelstein left after a year. The ABA Section of Taxation Liaison was Don. V. Harris, Jr. (to 1975) and K. Martin Worthy (from 1975), both of the District of Columbia.

k. Annual Report, 53rd Annual Meeting (May 18–21, 1976) 11–12.

l. Annual Report, 54th Annual Meeting (May 17–20, 1977) 9. The last sentence relating to integration of the corporate and individual income taxes, and also the mention of Subchapter K, will be discussed later.

m. American Law Institute, Federal Income Tax Project, Subchapter C, Proposals of the American Law Institute on Corporate Acquisitions and Dispositions, and Reporter's Study on Corporate Distributions (1982).

n. Refer to Senate announcement referring to ALI.

o. These matters had been discussed at a July 1975 seminar of the National Tax Association, which Woodworth chaired, and at which I made a brief oral observation supporting the viewpoints mentioned in the text. Later I wrote an article on this for the National Tax Journal (*Reflections on Integration of Corporation and Individual Income Taxes*, 28 NAT. TAX J. 335 (1975)) — an article written by the way while on a cruise and waiting for a crew change in the little harbor of Cutler, Maine. I must add my boat did not have a tax library!

p. All of the many problems involved in integration were aired at an Oct. 1977 Brookings conference, and a book written in the light of that conference, Charles E. McLure, Jr., Must Corporate Income Be Taxed Twice? (The Brookings Institution, 1979). Earlier the Harvard Business Review had asked McLure to write an article favorable to integration — his then position, greatly modified in his later more skeptical book — and me to write on the opposite side. I suggested to McClure that instead of pro and con articles, which usually are like unseen ships crossing in the night, we write a joint article presenting the issues we considered had to be discussed and faced. This appeared as Surrey and McLure, *Integration of Income Taxes: Issues for Debate*, 55(5) HARV. BUS. REV. 169 (1977).

q. Annual Report, 56th Annual Meeting (May 15–18, 1979), 12–13.

r. Annual Report, 57th Annual Meeting (June 10–13, 1980) 9–10. The work on corporate distributions is described in Andrews' book, Reporter's Study, *supra* note m. The proposals on loss carryover are included in the Andrews book, *supra* note m, as proposals of the Institute. These proposals have formed the framework of the initial study in 1983 by the Congressional tax staffs, discussed at *Carryover of Net Operating Losses and Other Tax Attributes of Corporations:* Hearing Before the Subcomm. on Select Revenue Measures of the Comm. on Ways and Means, 98th Cong., 1st Sess. (September 22, 1983).

s. Annual Report, 53rd Annual Meeting (May 18–21, 1976) 12.

t. The 1978 Annual Report, 55th Annual Meeting (May 16–19), 1978) 12, stated:

> Those who have followed the Tax Project will be well aware that progress has been slower than we thought that it could be, but we are not alone in finding that constructive tax revision is a task of greater difficulty than it was congenial to suppose. It is, therefore, a matter of immense importance that the Fund for Public Policy Research has recently advised that it will extend its support of the Tax Project through calendar year 1982. To the Fund and to its able and devoted President Harry A. Olsher, who has attended all our meetings on the Project, I express the Institute's appreciation.

u. Willis, Partnership Taxation (2d ed. 1976). The full list of consultants chosen included M. Bernard Aidinoff, William D. Andrews, Hugh J. Ault, Walter J. Blum, Richard Freling, James O. Hewitt, Martin D. Ginsburg, Sherwin Kamin, Howard G. Krane, Donald Lubick, John S. Pennell, William A. Rosoff, John Sexton, Arthur Willis, and Bernard Wolfman. Joseph P. Driscoll, also from Texas, was the ABA liaison. Lubick did not participate since he had become a government official.

v. Annual Report, 56th Annual Meeting (May 15–18, 1979), 13–14.

w. Annual Report, 57th Annual Meeting (June 10–13, 1980) 10.

x. Annual Report, 58th Annual Meeting (May 19–22, 1981) 8–9.

y. Annual Report, 59th Annual Meeting (May 18–21, 1982) 10–11.

z. Federal Income Tax Project, Subchapter K: Proposals of the American Law Institute (1984).

aa. *E.g.*, A. James Casner, Estate Planning (6 volumes, 1980, and annual supplements).

bb. Federal Estate and Gift Taxes: Public Hearings and Panel Discussions Before the Comm. on Ways and Means, House of Representatives, 94th Cong., 2nd Sess., 1333–1336 (1976).

cc. Annual Report, 57th Annual Meeting (June 10–12, 1980) 10.

dd. The Consultants were William D. Andrews, Harvard University Law School, Cambridge Massachusetts; J.H. Butala, Jr., Cleveland, Ohio; Henry Christensen, III, New York, New York; Stephen T. Dena, Orlando Florida; Dic L. Dorney, Detroit, Michigan; Mary Louise Fellows, University of Illinois College of Law, Champaign, Illinois; Douglas A. Kahn, University of Michigan Law School, Ann Arbor, Michigan; Sherwin Kamin, New York, New York; James B. Lewis, New York, New York; Harry K. Mansfield, Boston, Massachusetts; Malcolm A. Moore, Seattle, Washington; Leo L. Schmolka, New York, New York; and James M. Trapp, Chicago, Illinois. Arthur L. Klein was the ABA Liaison. As the study progressed and it became clear that Casner's views were producing sharp divisions in the group, an additional Consultant was added as liaison with an organization also interested in trust taxation—Joseph Kartiganer, a trust specialist with the firm of White and Case in New York as liaison for the College of Probate Counsel. Malcolm Moore, already a member of the group, was prominent in the American Bar Association Section of Property, Probate and Trust Law. Both organizations had been strongly critical of the Casner approaches and were conservatively oriented to the status quo.

ee. This trust discussion was reminiscent of the argument in the 1960's that a separate corporate surtax exemption should be available for each subsidiary in a corporate chain because this multifold use of subsidiaries was chosen for valid non-tax business reasons, including compliance with state laws. The view that the whole chain was in reality one large enterprise entitled to only one exemption just didn't enter a Congressman's mind—or perhaps was adroitly kept from so entering—and the many exemptions persisted despite Treasury attack. Woodworth and I in the 1968 Treasury tax recommendations decided to handle the recommendation differently. We suggested that the Code specifically state that in the first year thereafter a corporate chain was entitled to 500 separate surtax exemptions with the number dropping to 250, then to 100, and so on until it came to one. This proposed statutory formulation sharply disclosed the ridiculousness of the situation, and the single surtax exemption rule was adopted in 1969.

ff. There was a Code rule that if trust income accumulated over a number of years was eventually paid to a beneficiary, the beneficiary had to spread the income back over prior years—the "throwback rule"—and often this raised the total tax liability of the beneficiary. But Casner considered the rule unworkable and not applied in practice.

gg. Annual Report, 58th Annual Meeting (May 19–22, 1981) 9–10.

hh. Annual Report, 59th Annual Meeting (May 18–21, 1982) 11–12.

ii. At this point I suddenly suffered what later was diagnosed as a ventricular arrhythmia (rapid, irregular heartbeat) and for a moment fell asleep. I awakened, stayed about fifteen minutes to hear the end of the first proposal, and then left the platform. The result was an ambulance trip to the intensive care unit of a Philadelphia hospital and an overnight check, which produced no disturbances. On my return to Cambridge, my Boston cardiologists believed it had been an arrhythmia and sent me to a hospital. They were correct in their diagnosis since a similar episode happened again while in the Boston hospital. We then started on a long course of testing a variety of experimental drugs. After about ten weeks in the hospital over a period of three stays, the doctors were satisfied they had the right combination. I was discharged with a diet of about ten different pills, fifteen in all each day!

jj. Annual Report, 60th Annual Meeting (May 17–20, 1983) 9–11.

kk. Present law has elaborate rules as to who is regarded as an "independent trustee." Nearly all in the trust field, even the two bank officials in the consultants' group, agreed that this independence existed in form but not in fact. Casner preferred to retreat only so far as to allow a discretion in the manner of distribution, but with a requirement that the entire trust income be subject to required distribution. The Council and Institute preferred that the discretion not be so limited.

ll. In 1963–64 the Treasury, in conjunction with a group of investment company and other corporate officials, had studied some aspects of the taxation of foreigners with income from U.S. sources, and the results of this study were legislated in the Foreign Investors Tax Act of 1966, Pub. L. No. 89-809, 80 Stat. 1539. But the study was only a partial one, with some aspects being economic policy decisions and not technical tax matters.

mm. The Consultants were Melvin S. Adess, Chicago Illinois; M. Bernard Aidinoff, New York, New York; Gerald T. Ball, London, England; George W. Beatty, Washington, DC; Richard G. Cohen, New York, New York; Harvey P. Dale, New York University School of Law, New York, New York; Richard M. Eigner, San Francisco, California; Joseph H. Guttentag, Washington, DC: John B. Jones, Jr., Washington, DC; Jerome B. Libin, Washington, DC; John S. Nolan, Washington, DC; Robert H. Preiskel, New York, New York; Richard C. Pugh, New York, New York; Sidney I. Roberts, New York, New York; H. David Rosenbloom, Washington, DC; and Mervin M. Wilf, Philadelphia, Pennsylvania. Carl L. Estes, Houston, Texas was the liaison for the ABA Tax Section and Robert J. Patrick, Washington DC was the liaison for the U.S. Branch of the International Fiscal Association. Tillinghast and I, wanting these two as part of the group, had arranged their designation. Several lawyers and professors with experience in the international tax field were added to the Tax Advisory Committee.

nn. Annual Report, 60th Annual Meeting (May 17–20, 1983) 8–9.

oo. Other, considerably less used devices to skip a generation, were a legal life interest to a child, remainder to grandchild (a one generation skip); an outright gift, not in trust, from grandfather to grandchild (also a one generation skip).

pp. *See* references, page 938, in STANLEY S. SURREY, WILLIAM C. WARREN, PAUL R. MCDANIEL AND

HARRY L. GUTMAN, FEDERAL WEALTH TRANSFER TAXATION (2d. ed. 1982); Hearings, note bb above.

qq. Surrey, *Reflections on the Tax Reform Act of 1976*, 25 CLEV. ST. L. REV. 3030 (1976).

rr. As a part of this same 1976 legislation, the Code was also amended to provide for a carryover of a decedent's basis on the assets that passed to his heirs, in place of the rule that gave the heirs a basis equal to value at the decedent's death — a rule that permitted any appreciation of the asset while owned by the decedent to escape income tax. This reform fell in 1980 under a strong attack led by the American Bar Association and lawyers.

ss. George Cooper, *A Voluntary Tax? New Perspectives on Sophisticated Estate Tax Avoidance*, 77 COLUM. L. REV. 161, 222 (1977).

tt. The consultants were: William D. Andrews, Harvard Law School, Cambridge, Massachusetts; A. James Casner, Harvard Law School, Cambridge, Massachusetts; Richard B. Covey, New York, New York; James B. Lewis, New York, New York; Daniel I. Halperin, Georgetown University Law Center, Washington, DC; Vester T. Hughes, Jr., Dallas, Texas; and Mildred E. Kalik, New York, New York. The liaison from the ABA Tax Section was Doris D. Blazek, Washington, D.C.; from the ABA Real Property, Probate and Trust Law Section, Jackson M. Bruce, Jr., Milwaukee, Wisconsin; and from the American College of Probate Counsel, John A. Wallace, Atlanta, Georgia.

uu. Annual Report, 60th Annual Meeting (May 17–20, 1983) 13.

NINE

International Activities

Part II, 1969 to Date

The return to Harvard did not mean an abandonment of participation in the world of international taxation. While I was no longer involved in formulating the United States official tax policy in this area, the transition to a non-governmental status did allow for work in fields that were not open while I was an official. These fields — and my relationship to them — form the substance of this Chapter.

International Fiscal Association

The International Fiscal Association — IFA — is a unique international private body.[1] It is the largest organization that concerns itself with the rules and issues that impinge on international tax activities, broadly construed. It is formally a grouping of national branches in many countries — 25 persons can constitute themselves an IFA national branch and membership in a branch automatically means membership in Central IFA; persons in countries without a branch can also become members. The membership of IFA covers the range of those interested in international tax matters. The largest group are tax executives of business firms, followed by lawyers, accountants, government officials and academics, in about that order. There are around 6,300 members, and about 40 national branches. Central IFA is the parent body that controls the activities of IFA as an international organization, while the national branches are free to pursue their own activities in their respective countries, such as conferences, meetings, joint sessions with branches in other countries and so on.

IFA has two sides to it, which come together at its annual Congresses. One is social, with IFA members gathering once a year for a week in an international setting under a carefully organized program that except for the location does not vary in its format. Thus, there are receptions with the mayor of the city in which the Congress was held and by IFA itself, an evening spent on a cultural activity depending on what the city offers — a concert, a ballet, an opera. One full day is set aside for sightseeing — a tour through the countryside, or a visit to some monuments, castles, smaller cities, scenic areas, that can be covered conveniently in a day. Persons attending are

1. Today the International Fiscal Association describes itself as "the leading non-governmental, international organization dealing with tax matters," with more than 12,500 members worldwide. USA Branch of the International Fiscal Association, *Welcome to IFA USA!*, https://www.ifausa.org/.

given a choice among several different activities, and travel by buses is organized by various languages—English speaking buses, French speaking, German, and Spanish—with guides to match the language designated for the bus. The meetings end with a formal dinner and dance, with a large majority treating it as a black tie affair. Since about half of the members bring their wives or other persons—they are all referred to as "accompanying persons"—the affairs are really social. There are museum trips, dress shows, local city tours, special events organized for the accompanying persons during the periods when the members are engaged in the substantive meetings. Since most members and the accompanying persons gather each year, there is a "we meet once more" atmosphere that prevails. Each Congress is located in a different city and country—Copenhagen, Paris, London, Vienna, Rotterdam, Brussels, Sydney, New York, Madrid, West Berlin, Montreal, Venice; this variety adds to the conviviality and social aspect of the Congresses. The expenses of a Congress are borne by the fees charged for the Congress and by the branch of the country in which it is held, with corporations, banks, law firms, accounting firms, and so on solicited by the local committee charged with arrangements.

But IFA also has its serious side. Essentially its professional activities are based on comparative tax law studies in fields chosen in advance. For each Congress two topics are selected well in advance and the national branches are asked to select a Reporter or Reporters to prepare a country description report on the subject as treated in the particular country. A General Reporter, with a familiarity on the subject, is chosen by Central IFA to prepare a Directive indicating the aspects of the topic to be covered by the National Reports and the structural organization of these Reports. The General Reporter receives the National Reports and, using them as a base, prepares a summary of the treatment of the topic, and also makes suggestions for future changes or studies. The General Report, in English, French, German and Spanish, and the National Reports, written in the language preferred by the Reporters, but accompanied by a short summary worded in each of the other languages, are brought together in a volume (Cahier) published by Central IFA. Each Congress involves two main topics, so that annually two volumes are sent to all members. These volumes are by far the most informative comparative law treatment of the subject covered and are a unique and valuable contribution to the field.[2]

Illustrative of the topics covered are:

International Problems in the Field of General Taxes on Sales of Goods and Services (1983)

Tax Avoidance/Tax Evasion (1983)

The Tax Treatment of Interest in International Economic Transactions (1982)

Unilateral Measures to Prevent Double Taxation (1981)

---

2. For a complete list of the volumes produced by the IFA (two per year, for most years), *see* IFA, *Cahiers titles since 1939: A complete list of the volumes published since 1939*, https://www.ifa.nl/cahiers/cahiers-titles-since-1939.

Rules for Determining Income and Expenses as Domestic or Foreign (1980)

Inflation and Taxation (1978)

Each Congress opens with a program of talks interspersed with music. The principal speaker is usually the Finance Minister of the country, or a suitable alternate. Other officials concerned with fiscal policy speak, and also the President of IFA. Next comes a day devoted to an oral discussion of a topic, with any member free to present views on the Reports or the topic. The topic discussion is opened by a panel of four or five members. Then a Resolutions Committee of six or so members, chosen for geographical diversity and knowledge of the topic, prepares a Resolution on each topic. These Resolutions, based on the Reports and the oral discussions, are designed to reflect the views of those present on the topic — trends to be pursued, policies to be encouraged or discouraged, changes that should be made. They are thus substantive in nature and designed to place IFA on record on the topics overall. Occasionally the Resolutions take the form of a precis of the discussion when it is thought, perhaps because of a wide diversity of substantive views, desirable only to summarize the discussion. The Resolutions are then presented to the Congress for discussion and invariably adoption, though sometimes with amendments. The discussions of the topics and later the Resolutions are handled by simultaneous translation, with English, French, German, and Spanish as the languages used.[a, 3]

In addition to the discussion of the two topics there are seminars, one or two in number, conducted by panels. These seminars cover areas that do not lend themselves to descriptive reports by each branch and often touch on fiscal policy issues rather than the substantive aspects of a particular field, as in the two main topics.[b] Some examples of Seminars are:

Imputation Systems — Objectives and Consequences (1982)

Taxation of the Income from the International Seabed (1981)

Recourse to Tax Havens — Use and Abuse (1980)

U.N. Draft Model Taxation Convention (1979)

The Revised OECD Model Double Taxation Convention on Income and Capital (1977)

The main affairs of IFA are conducted by two standing committees. One is the Executive Committee, composed of members and alternates selected from the General Council, in turn composed of members of each national branch of IFA. This Committee chooses the location of each Congress, sees that the country selected has an adequate committee properly to plan the week's activities, approves the overall arrangements for each Congress, reviews the Resolutions before their presentation to a Congress but nearly always makes no changes, and acts on any policy matter affecting IFA, e.g., dues, new branches.

3. The IFA now calls the publications mentioned in Surrey's note a Congress Reports.

The second standing committee is the Permanent Scientific Committee (PSC)—a wonderfully portentous title. This committee is composed of around 12 to 13 members, nominated mainly by the larger and important national branches. Thus the United States, West Germany, France, Switzerland, Italy, the United Kingdom, Belgium, are invariably represented. The other memberships rotate in an informal fashion, decided by the Executive Committee. Thus, Spain, the Scandinavian countries, Australia, Israel have held membership on the PSC. The PSC is the substantive arm of IFA. It chooses the topics for the annual Congresses and the General Reporters. It also chooses subjects for the half-day Seminars held at each Congress along with the discussion on the two main topics. The format of the various substantive discussions is developed by the PSC, such as having a panel presentation for each main topic. The personnel for these activities—the Chairman, the Discussion Leader, and the membership of the panels and Resolutions Committee for each subject—are selected by the PSC. Selection is based on the combined criteria of ability, knowledge, language diversity, and geographical diversity. While the selections have to be ratified by the Executive Committee, this is pro forma. But the Executive Committee does choose the Chairman of the PSC and the countries to be members. The Secretary of IFA, a person from the Netherlands, and the head of the Bureau of International Documentation located in Amsterdam, are ex officio members of the PSC.

The PSC thus occupies a central role in IFA, having the responsibility to provide interesting and important subjects, and competent personnel for the various sessions. It was on this committee that in 1969 I became the United States Representative. This role came in a rather curious way.

As IFA—started in 1939—grew in membership and importance, its activities came to be directed in the main by the tax executives of major firms. This was especially so in the case of the U.S. Branch. The dominant figure in IFA—and also the U.S. Branch—was its President, Mitchell B. Carroll, a New York international tax attorney who often represented business interests as a lobbyist before the Congress.[4] (Who was PSC member before me?)[5] In the 1960's as a Treasury official I really first became seriously aware of IFA, though I had been a member before this. I saw that its Resolutions were nearly always pro-business and anti-government.

4. Mitchell Benedict Carroll, international tax lawyer, was elected president of the IFA in 1950 and was named IFA's honorary president for life in 1971. For a discussion of Carroll's efforts in the 1930s and 1940s to bring about tax treaties between the United States and other Western Hemisphere nations (describing Carroll as "a charismatic figure [who] had the trust of many Latin American experts in the field of taxation"), *see* Jose Antonio Sanchez Roman, *The Challenge from the Periphery: Latin America's New Deals and the Shaping of Liberal Internationalism in FDR's Era*, 61(2) Rev. Bras. Polit. Int. 1, 16–19 (2018).

5. The answer to Surrey's parenthetical question is more complicated than he probably supposed. The 1969 IFA Yearbook lists both Surrey and Leif Muten as PSC members from the United States. However, Muten was a Swedish national, affiliated with the United States only in the sense that he was then working for the International Monetary Fund in Washington. It appears that Surrey was the first PSC member with American citizenship. Email from H. A. Kogels to Lawrence Zelenak, September 21, 2020.

For this reason I did not have my office make it a practice to participate in the annual Congresses. Only once did I send a representative, and that was in 1964 to a Congress considering the subject covered by our Subpart F, controlled subsidiaries especially in tax havens, and here the Resolution was adverse to the U.S. view. I also saw that the Resolutions had little real world effect on Congressional decisions, largely being material to be used by business as debating points. So in my set of priorities IFA held a low ranking.

In 1969, shortly after my return to Harvard, several top U.S. tax executives asked me to become the U.S. representative on the PSC. I was really startled by the request, and stated they knew that my views on international tax matters often differed from theirs. But they had thought about this, and had not been deterred. They said IFA was going through a period of reorganization to make it a more vital and representative body, and the "old guard" was turning over affairs of IFA — and the U.S. Branch — to a broader and more balanced group. While they knew my views, they also said they considered me fair and open-minded, and with a stature and knowledge that could make the U.S. point of view on PSC affairs a significant matter.

So it was in this capacity I attended my first IFA Congress, in Rotterdam in 1969, and met with the PSC as the U.S. representative. A reorganization was indeed taking place. Mitchell Carroll was to be President for only a few years, and the Presidency was to change on a two-year basis. The new PSC Chairman was Raoul Lenz, a Swiss tax attorney, for a while in the Swiss diplomatic service.[6] In 1969 he was not widely known. But it took only the first meeting under his guidance for me, and others, to see that his choice was most fortunate. He was in command at all times, but in a fashion that allowed members freely to express their opinions. He would forcefully state his views, but did not make them decisive. Instead he sought a rational consensus on each point. His international tax experience was adequate to the task, and expanded as the years went on. He was conversant in four languages — English, French, German and Italian — and while the meetings were conducted in English, out of sympathy with my and one or two other members' lack of languages besides English, he could thus interpret for a member who felt his point could be better stated in his own language.

The PSC itself in addition to the new Chairman was changed into a less conservative body, for example with Pierre Kerlan,[7] a government official, as the French member, besides myself as the U.S. member.

As the years went by the PSC made significant changes in the substantive work of the Congresses. More care was taken on the selection of the topics, panels were

6. Swiss international tax lawyer Raoul Lenz co-founded the law firm of Lenz, Schluep, Briner & de Coulon in Geneva in 1951. The firm merged in 1991; the merged firm, Lenz & Staehelin, is the largest independent law firm in Switzerland.

7. Pierre Kerlan served in the French Ministry of Finance in high-level international tax positions in the 1960s and 1970s. He co-authored a volume as part of the World Tax Series of Harvard Law School's International Program in Taxation. MARTIN NOOR & PIERRE KERLAN, TAXATION IN FRANCE (1966).

introduced into the discussions to give them better focus, the discussions were organized in substantive time periods, replacing the previous everything at once pattern, seminars were instituted, the composition and activity of the Resolutions Committee became more balanced, the General Reports became more organized and more guidance was given to the National Reporters so that the annual volumes met higher standards.

The PSC each year holds two meetings, generally at the site of the forthcoming Congress, with one in the February before a Congress and one just before the opening of a Congress. Since most PSC members came from European countries, the meetings were always in Europe. I was the member who had the largest journey to make for the occasion, so the February meetings were held on the weekend before Washington's birthday to accommodate my law school duties.

From the start I took a positive stance in the PSC discussions, making my views known and trying graciously to sustain discussion with those of a contrary viewpoint. I became friendly with Raoul and we respected each other's views, be they in agreement or disagreement. Also, within the PSC I generally gave my support to Raoul. He merited this, for his views were clearly expressed and open minded, and his chairmanship was always constructive. As the years went by I became a senior member of the PSC. Besides Raoul and the two ex-officio members I was the only one who went back to 1969.

I made it a careful practice to check whenever possible with the officers of the U.S. Branch. Fortunately the leadership of the Branch had fallen to broad-minded persons able to recognize the claims of both taxpayers and tax authorities. Thus, I would ask for suggestions whenever a U.S. slot was allocated on a panel or the Resolutions Committee, or as a General Reporter, and also suggestions for topics. At various meetings of the U.S. Branch I sought ideas for making the Congress discussions more interesting. In part this pointed to always having Discussion Leaders who were both knowledgeable and strong. In the PSC I pushed for more than geographical diversity in the Discussion Leader, seeking experience as well, and also to lessen the practice of falling back on PSC members as Chairmen.

I did act as the General Reporter for the 1971 Washington Congress on the subject of "Criteria for the Allocation of Items of Income and Expense Between Related Corporations in Different Countries, Whether or Not Parties to Tax Conventions," essentially the area covered by our Regulations under section 482.[8] I took the precaution of having David Tillinghast, a leading New York international tax practitioner who had worked with me in the Treasury as the first International Tax Counsel, to be Co-Chairman. In this way our Report would be well-balanced and not open to criticism because of my section 482 views. Dave and I also sat as members of the panel in London on "Allocation of Expenses in International Arms Length Transactions of Related Corporations." At the Mexico City 1974 Congress, I co-chaired with a Mexican attorney a seminar on _________.

---

8. *Criteria for the Allocation of Items of Income and Expense Between Related Corporations in Different States, Whether or not Parties to Tax Conventions,* 56b C. DE D. FISC.INT'L (1971).

I also acted as General Reporter in the Jerusalem Congress on "Tax Incentives As an Instrument For Achievement of Governmental Goals," choosing Emil Sunley as a fellow Co-Chairman because I desired an economist to play a role.[9] This Congress gave me the opportunity, through the work of the National Reporters and our General Report, to acquaint a wider audience[10] with the subject of tax expenditures.[c] Incidentally, I also delivered the opening speech of the Varna, Bulgaria, 1977 Congress of the International Institute of Public Finance, a much smaller organization, with no social side and composed nearly entirely of fiscal economists (the lack of a social side should not be laid to economists as members!). It does have members from the Communist-controlled countries and alternates its meetings between East and West. The Varna Congress, on "Subsidies, Tax Reliefs and Prices," similarly afforded me the chance to expound on tax expenditures before a different group and to include topics relating to tax expenditures in the agenda for the meeting.

At the Sydney 1978 Congress I was awarded a Silver Medal by the Bureau of Fiscal Documentation, an organization related to IFA. This came as a complete but welcome surprise. Given my general views on tax policy it was encouraging that those who worked in IFA and often held differing views accepted me as constructive person in the international tax field.[d]

The PSC membership, and the IFA activities, widened my acquaintance both on international tax matters and with persons in the various countries who were informed and capable. This knowledge in turn was utilized in my International Taxation course and in views I expressed to the Treasury or Members of Congress. For these reasons, I always aimed at having IFA topics that would widen knowledge on controversial subjects, such as the allocation of income and expenses, tax havens, the foreign tax credit, and so on. Invariably the material developed on a topic confirmed my view that an appropriate U.S. tax policy, as I saw it, was generally not out of line from the viewpoints and activities in other countries. I believe that the information thus developed provided useful support to those interested in reform changes in U.S. policy or in maintaining reform positions then in effect.

United Nations Ad Hoc Group of Experts on Tax Treaties between Developed and Developing Countries and the U.N. Model Treaty

In 1967 while I was still in the Treasury Karl Lachmann, the Chief of the International Tax Section of the Fiscal and Financial Branch in the Department of International Economic and Social Affairs of the United Nations came to see me on a

9. *Tax Incentives as an Instrument for Achievement of Government Goals,* 61a C. DE D. FISC. INT'L (1976).

10. Surrey has "provide a wider acquaintance" here, rather than "acquaint a wider audience"; the editors' change clarifies what appears to be Surrey's intended meaning.

U.N. activity which he desired to organize.[11] I knew Karl from the Harvard International Tax Program work and respected his ability and desire to have the U.N. participate constructively in the international tax field. Karl said he was attempting to have the U.N. form a group of tax experts from both developed and developing countries to work on a Model U.N. Tax Treaty that could be used in negotiations between such countries. The background for the effort was this: In 1963 the OECD (Organization for Economic Cooperation and Development) Fiscal Committee had after considerable years of effort developed a model double taxation treaty.[e] The OECD is composed mainly of the European countries, plus the United States, Canada and Japan. Almost all of its members would rank as developed countries. In the Treasury I had agreed that the United States would be a party to the development of that treaty. On its publication it immediately became the basis for negotiations between developed countries since they had participated in its formation.

In the late 1960's developed countries sought to negotiate double taxation treaties with developing countries and presented the OECD Model as a starting point for the negotiations. But soon the more astute negotiators from the developing countries saw the problem for them in using the OECD treaty. That treaty, in its solution to the elimination or reduction of double taxation, was based on relinquishment of jurisdiction to tax by the country of the source of the income. This was supplemented, where taxation at source remained, by provision for a foreign tax credit or exemption of foreign income in the country of residence. As between developed countries, this solution worked reasonably well for they were both countries of the source of income through investment or trade from the other countries and also countries from whence investment or trade originated. Hence no country appreciably lost tax revenues under the OECD Model—the revenue lost through relinquishment[12] of source jurisdiction was made up either through the revenue gained by consequently lower foreign tax credits, or in exemption countries through an increase in profits of their enterprises.

But developing countries were almost entirely countries of the source of income, and did not have enterprises engaged to a significant extent in investment or trade in other countries. The OECD Model, with its emphasis on reduction in source taxation, thus would mean for these developing countries a revenue loss without a compensating revenue gain. Many developing countries were therefore dissatisfied with the OECD Model. But, often being new to international tax negotiations, they lacked the experience and insight necessary to reshape the OECD Model in a direction to benefit them.

Lachmann perceived this problem and thought the U.N., through convening a group of experts from developed and developing countries, could frame a model

11. Karl Edward Lachmann, a native of Berlin, came to the United States in 1937 and worked for the federal government in various capacities (including assisting with the Nuremberg prosecutions) from 1938 to 1947. He then joined the recently founded Office of Economic Affairs of the United Nations. Lachmann died in 1968, just a year after the conversation Surrey relates. *Karl Edward Lachmann, Fiscal Aide at U. N., 53*, New York Times, Aug. 31, 1968, at 23.

12. Surrey has "reimbursement" here, but clearly he intended "relinquishment" (note the mention earlier in the same paragraph of "relinquishment of jurisdiction").

treaty suitable to double taxation negotiations between such countries. It was a bold enterprise that could well collapse at the start if each side became political or intransigent. I told Karl I was hesitant to commit the U.S. to membership in this group, fearing a political attack on our tax policies and on our[13] large foreign investments. But Karl persuaded me that the enterprise could succeed, and indeed the chances would be increased if the United States took a strong but constructive position in the discussions of the Group. I therefore gave the consent of the Treasury to this effort, with the State Department following our leadership.

The U.N. in 1967 then formally organized the Ad Hoc Group of Experts on Treaties Between Developed and Developing Countries. The Group initially consisted of eight developed countries and ten developing countries.[f] Each country presented the U.N. with the name of its representative and the U.N. appointed the person as a Group Member. Though thus nominated by their Governments, the members acted in their personal capacity as experts and not as official representatives, though the distinction was meaningful only as an effort to keep the Group from becoming a political body. The developed countries named as members their ranking official in the international taxation field, the career person whose responsibility it was directly to negotiate double taxation treaties. The developing countries usually named their Tax Commissioners, as generally they were the officials responsible for negotiations. Karol Krcmery and his office acted as the Secretariat for the Group.[g, 14]

The first meeting of the Group was in Geneva in December 1968. I decided to attend as the U.S. member along with Nathan Gordon, an economist who usually represented the United States in treaty negotiations.[15] A member from a developing country, Sudan — not a tax expert — was chosen as the Chairman.[16] Also, as observers, were officials from the OECD Fiscal Division, International Monetary Fund, International Fiscal Association, International Chamber of Commerce, and a few countries. Observers could participate in the discussions but not directly in decisions of the Group. The Group decided to use the OECD Model as the procedural basis for the discussions, but with the understanding that its substantive conclusions were in no way binding on the Group. The first meeting consisted of general discussions on the main articles of the OECD treaty, with various countries stating their general positions. Interestingly, only one developing country — Argentina — took the position that source jurisdiction should be exclusive. Argentina itself did not tax its residents on foreign income. The other developing countries recognized that the developed coun-

---

13. The editors have inserted the second "on our" in the sentence to clarify that Surrey did not fear large foreign investments; rather, he feared a political attack on large foreign investments of U.S. corporations.

14. Karol Krcmery, a Czechoslovakian lawyer, had worked for the United Nations since the late 1940s.

15. Nathan N. Gordon served in the Treasury Department for 35 years, retiring in 1975 as deputy assistant secretary for tax policy. *Nathan N. Gordon Dead; Ex-Treasury Official, 61*, NEW YORK TIMES, Sep. 15, 1976, at 48. Surrey discusses Gordon and his untimely death, *supra*, Surrey's note c.

16. Hamzah Merghani of Sudan was the chairman.

tries, who generally taxed their residents on a worldwide basis, had a legitimate claim on some revenue from international transactions. This could scarcely be otherwise, for some developing countries, such as India and the Philippines, themselves exercised worldwide jurisdiction. But, as expected, all developing countries took the position that the extent of source jurisdiction under treaties had to be expanded over that set forth in the OECD Model. In varying degrees the developed countries recognized the need for this greater source jurisdiction and that more flexibility was required. In the few negotiations that the United States undertook with developing countries I had already taken the policy position that those countries should not be called upon to make the revenue sacrifices required by the OECD Model, but that our aim should be to lessen source jurisdiction to the extent that it would produce an excess foreign tax credit for our investors. After all, the U.S., attempting through our foreign aid programs to assist developing countries, could hardly turn around and ask those countries to relinquish significant tax revenues they would use for their development. Hence, in the U.N. Group the United States was the country, or at least one of the countries, most open to recognizing the merits of the general positions taken by developing countries.

The first meeting was highly successful in producing a non-political discussion based on tax expertise and not the Developed World-Third World atmosphere that marked many U.N. meetings. The sufficient diversity of viewpoints that exists within both developed countries and the developing countries went far to eliminate a political content from the discussions. Also, each member, with only a few exceptions, being a tax expert familiar with the field, the members immediately talked with each other as tax experts and not politicians. In addition, the members were of high quality and persons with both ability and the necessary flexibility to make progress possible.[h] The success of the first meeting made it clear that continuation of the Group would be productive, as Lachmann had earlier hoped. A second meeting was set for 1970, with an agenda and background papers to be prepared by the Secretariat with additional material from member countries to the extent they desired.

By this time I had left the Treasury and could no longer be the U.S. member, so Gordon took my place. Krcmery then asked me to associate myself as an Advisor to the Secretariat so that I could work on the preparation for the meeting and also attend the meeting. I agreed, on the condition I have an official title and sit on the platform with the presiding officials. We decided on the title of Special Advisor to the Rapporteur. In this capacity I then attended the second meeting. It soon became clear that a vacuum existed in the members of the Group chosen as its official leadership. With all the good will in the world, they either did not possess the tax expertise and background necessary to keep the discussions focused and to develop consensus positions.[17,i] Krcmery himself did not have the standing or experience needed to handle a strong Group. He was not a tax technician, and his strength lay in finding ways to

17. The "either" in this sentence is missing its "or." Not knowing what "or" clause Surrey might have intended, the editors have left the sentence unchanged.

placate any member who found fault with the arrangement, to oversee the distribution of materials, to keep the summaries moving along, to keep the documentation in order, and the like.[18]

As a result the working methods soon developed with my sitting next to the Chairman and either advising him or participating directly in the discussions. I saw my role, not as an advocate for any position but, through discussion and questions, as one of narrowing and sharpening differences and searching for consensus positions that the Group would support. The Group did not vote on any matter and the meeting summaries (which were prepared by Krcmery's staff and special outside assistants utilized for the meetings) did not name any member or country, but only said a member or members from a developed country stated or suggested such and such, etc. This procedure went far to prevent the development of a political atmosphere. At the same time it increased the task of finding a consensus position which a majority would support, with dissents allowed, though again not by my name. Hence I undertook after the discussion of a topic to write a brief memorandum stating the consensus I considered that had developed and then to present this to the Group for discussion and possible changes. Fortunately, without any formality, both the developed countries and the developing countries accepted my acting in this role. The developing countries were aware of my general sympathy for their position and willingness to clarify their arguments and positions, which were not always clear because of their lack of experience. The developed countries saw me as an expert who was experienced and fair, as familiar as they were with the issues and positions. When the final report of the meeting was prepared, I wrote the portions dealing with the conclusions of the Group and also drafted suggested treaty language embodying these conclusions.

Finding a consensus in a Group of this nature is a delicate task. In many instances in the discussions the members appeared strongly to assert opposing views. Yet a consensus, once stated often produces a consensus simply because it is stated—provided the consensus reflects a proper balancing of competing views. The statement of a consensus has the effect of allowing members to see some of their positions reflected and to appreciate that useful compromises could be made. Such a consensus, and the guiding of discussions that preceded it, had to be handled so as not to make a member lose face or be driven to an extreme position from which he could not escape. Obviously, the person having the task of finding the consensus must be well experienced in the field, so as to appreciate the factors involved in disagreements and pick up nuances and openings that could lead to the consensus. He must be regarded as experienced, unbiased and frank, and perceived clearly as a person to be trusted to be fair in his judgments. All in all, the task is both demanding and fascinating.

In this sort of happenstance manner, although I came from the United States, I was accepted by all members as the catalytic agent to keep the meetings on useful tracks.

---

18. One is reminded of Antony's description of Lepidus in William Shakespeare, Julius Caesar act 4, sc. 1 as "a slight unmeritable man, meet to be sent on errands."

This second meeting also went well and a third meeting was scheduled for 1971. For this meeting I aided Krcmery in obtaining persons to write papers for the Secretariat to be utilized at the meeting. I also advised him in general on the agenda and appropriate documentation. We worked well together and Krcmery welcomed my assistance. The Group proceeded at a careful pace, sometimes reaching a specific conclusion and on other issues deciding that the particular matter had to be left to the negotiations themselves, with the contours of the issue being spelled out by the Group.

Krcmery was fully content to let me continue to have the burden — and opportunity — to handle the substantive side. This same arrangement continued after the Chairman, Mr. Merghani, died and was succeeded, in the Sixth Meeting by A.N.E. Amissah from Ghana, a former judge and law school dean but not a tax expert.[19] Both Merghani and Amissah were strong characters who could run a meeting well and in general perceive the issues being developed. Both also appreciated my participation and cooperating with them by advising when I thought a topic had been exhausted or time should be allowed to let the members reflect and talk informally on an issue.

In 1974, a preliminary paper was prepared by the Secretariat with the assistance of some members and myself, entitled "Guidelines for Tax Treaties Between Developed and Developing Countries."[j] This paper, summarizing the work to date, was designed to demonstrate that progress was being made and the basis of a model U.N. treaty was forming. During the years, the membership of the Group was changing as persons retired from their governmental positions or some countries were added. At the outset the developed countries that participated most often were France, Germany, the United States, Switzerland, and often the Netherlands and Japan. They were all represented by strong personalities with long experience in negotiation and who had known each other over many years. On the whole the first three were perhaps the most sympathetic to positions taken by the developing countries, with Germany sometimes motivated by a strong desire to win the good will of developing countries as a step in its national policy of increasing its investment in those countries. In the developing country group, India, Sri Lanka, Israel and the Philippines took the leading role. The only Latin American countries represented were Argentina, which through insistence on exclusive source jurisdiction had rather isolated itself from making a contribution, and Chile whose initial representative rarely spoke.[k, 20] The African countries also rarely spoke. Over the years there were some changes in leadership through changes in the Group. Some members retired from their government posi-

---

19. Austin Neeabeohe Evans Amissah was a Ghanian appellate judge (1966 to 1976), dean of the University of Ghana Law Faculty (1969 to 1974), and briefly attorney general of Ghana (1979). Later he served as a judge of the Court of Appeal of Botswana (1981 to 2001, including as president of the Court from 1988 to 2001). Patrick Smith, *Obituary: Justice Austin Amissah*, THE INDEPENDENT, Feb. 8, 2001, at 6.

20. Milka Casanegra de Jantscher (mentioned in Surrey's note k) joined the staff of the International Monetary Fund in 1972. Before that she was assistant commissioner for planning and research in the Chilean Internal Revenue Service.

tions and were replaced; some developing countries were added to the Group. The Latin American voice was strengthened by the addition of Brazil, whose representative, F.O.N. Dornelles, was a forceful, intelligent advocate of his positions and one who came bluntly right to the point without any effort to appease others.[21] Later the Latin American voice was also increased through a change in the Argentine representative. The new member, unlike his predecessor, had been a treaty negotiator and held strong views expressed but at great length. As the representation of the Asian countries, with the exception of Pakistan, diminished in forcefulness and skill, the Latin American changes pushed the Model closer in a number of instances to the desires of developing countries.

In 1977 a significant change occurred in the U.N. Secretariat. Pierre Benoit, an agricultural economist from Haiti, was appointed the Head of the Fiscal and Financial Branch of the Department of Economic and Social Affairs.[22] Benoit, an intelligent but extremely sensitive person who trusted no one, had no experience in the tax area. This lack of experience contributed to his distrust and stubbornness, for he always realized he could not match the experience of the Group. While he worked hard and read the material, his lack of a tax background prevented him from understanding the pertinent issues and the interconnections among the various doctrines and disputed areas. When Benoit took over the U.N. Secretariat in 1977, Krcmery was relegated to a back seat. The 1977 meeting of the Group went on as before, and my role was unchanged. At this point I decided that more progress could be made if the Group's decisions were set forth in treaty language with commentary, following the OECD style. I informed Krcmery of this and he approved but warned that Benoit may later turn against the idea. The material was prepared by Harvard graduate students and editors of the Harvard International Law Journal, and it was an excellently done piece. It appeared in 1978.[1] Unfortunately it carried a title of 1978/U.N. Draft, for the suggested U.N. draft convention, though there was a clear explanation it was a Harvard draft based on the U.N. work to date. But Benoit was furious, stating it was a misrepresentation.[23] Krcmery did not indicate he had been informed of the work and I did not point this out.

---

21. Francisco O. N. Dornelles is a Brazilian lawyer, economist, and politician. He was briefly Brazil's Finance Minister (1985) and served as vice governor of Rio de Janiero from 2015 to 2019.

22. J. Pierre V. Benoit was the assistant director of the Centre for Development Planning, Projections and Policies, United Nations Secretariat, in charge of the Financial Resources Development Branch. United Nations, *Tax Treaties Between Developed and Developing Countries, 7th Report*, 3 (ST/ESA/79, 1978). In the entirety of Surrey's memoirs, Surrey's expressed dislike of Benoit is rivaled only by his comments on Colin Stam.

23. The article Surrey cites in Surrey's note 1 consists entirely of description and analysis (without the inclusion of proposed treaty language), and clearly indicates Surrey's authorship. Thus, Surrey's article could not have been the cause of Benoit's unhappiness. Rather, Benoit must have been upset over something Surrey does not cite—a complete draft of a model treaty, with proposed official commentaries, prepared by Harvard Law students. *Proposed Draft Double Taxation Convention for Use Between Developed and Developing Countries with Explanatory Commentary*, 19 Harv. Int'l L. J. 67 (1978). The "Proposed Draft" immediately follows Surrey's article in the same journal issue. Although the introduction of the "Proposed Draft" states that the draft and commentaries "were prepared for

From the start of his appointment Benoit had appeared to resent my assistance to the Group, apparently because he saw it reflecting adversely on the competence of the Secretariat and his own competence—he was correct on both points. After the Harvard material was published, Benoit became in effect a personal enemy. While it annoyed him immensely, I continued in my advisory capacity, with the different title of Special Advisor, or Special Advisor to the Bureau. The Group clearly understood that Benoit lacked sufficient capacity to assist them, and my participation was important. In 1979, at a meeting of a Drafting Committee (where I acted as Special Advisor to the Committee) of the Group in New York, Benoit presented both a draft treaty with commentary—nearly entirely similar to the Harvard work—and historical material on the development of double taxation treaties. He also inserted, as conclusions of the Group, some observations. The Group, led by Dornelles, firmly rejected this latter material as not being conclusions of the Group. The Group also made necessary changes in the descriptive material. The final document emerged as the "Manual for the Negotiation of Bilateral Tax Treaties Between Developed and Developing Countries."[m] The articles of a proposed treaty were described as "Guidelines". Designed to provide background for developing countries, the purpose and concept of the Manual were fully sound, though it was premature to issue such a document. But Benoit did not have the experience or background equal to the task and a weaker, less useful document resulted.

I continued in my role through the final meeting in 1979 in Geneva, which produced a complete Model.[n] The Model was prepared by using the drafts of the various articles agreed to in the prior meetings, plus OECD language when the OECD wording was satisfactory to developing countries.[o] Since I had written the proposed treaty language for the Reports on the prior meetings, I was in effect the author of the U.N. Model and recognized as such by the Group. A Commentary, based on my material in the prior Reports, was included, and where relevant the OECD Commentary was inserted, in a manner that distinguished it from the new U.N. material.

A convenient way here to summarize the U.N. Model and its relation to the OECD Model is to quote from a monograph I wrote on the Model, as mentioned later:

> The basic departure from the OECD Model is, thus, the emphasis placed by the U.N. Group on taxation at the source. That emphasis ... compelled the Group to explore what is involved in the exercise of source taxation more than did the OECD Model. This exploration did not focus solely on the exercise of source jurisdiction by developing countries. Every developed country, though it may stress residence jurisdiction, also exercises source jurisdiction. Thus, the developed countries in the Group also had, with respect to their own taxes, an interest in the exploration of the factors involved in source

eventual submission to the United Nations Secretariat by ... students at Harvard Law School" (*id.* at 70), and that the draft is "not an official United Nations document" (*id.* at 68), it also states (*id.*) that "the purpose of the following draft treaty [is] ... to reflect the work of the Group of Experts" and that "it is the only draft covering the entire scope of the U.N. group's work." A disinterested reader might conclude that there was more substance to Benoit's grievance than Surrey acknowledges.

jurisdiction. Given this basic emphasis on source jurisdiction, the U.N. Model focusses on the delineation of the exercise of such jurisdiction with respect to the various classes and items of income. This focus is a major aspect of the U.N. Model.[24]

I, and other members of the Group, had been urging the U.N. officials above Benoit to provide wide dissemination of the model treaty among developing countries. They agreed with the objective, but felt constrained by the stringency of funds that prevailed in the U.N. As one method of dissemination I wrote a monograph describing the treaty, its departure from the OECD model and the reasoning behind the departures. This monograph, *United Nations Model Convention For Tax Treaties Between Developed and Developing Countries, A Description and Analysis*, about 85 pages plus the Model as an appendix, was published in 1980 jointly by Harvard International Tax Program and the Bureau of International Documentation in Amsterdam.[25] I also persuaded IFA to hold a seminar on the U.N. Model at its Copenhagen 1979 Congress; a seminar on the OECD Model covering the 1977 changes in that Model had been held at the Vienna 1977 Congress. The Copenhagen Seminar, of which I was the Chairman, took a favorable approach to the U.N. Model, and one speaker, L.J. Griffeon of the Netherlands, gave illustrations of the extent and manner in which the Model was beginning to influence negotiations. Its influence was in part a matter of the knowledge and understanding that a particular developing country had of the U.N. Model. It does appear that the Model is having an influence, such as in the permanent establishment area, where more activities in the source country are defined in a treaty as permanent establishments and therefore under the structure of the treaty remain taxable by the source country.[26] The OECD treaty in these situations would restrict source taxation.

Incidentally, one point which I expected to arise in the U.N. meetings, and which did arise, was the issue of tax sparing.[27] Either as a matter of believed logic or a matter of knee-jerk dogma, the developing countries pushed for inclusion of tax sparing in the U.N. Model. The developed countries, other than the U.S., had tax sparing clauses in their treaties with developing countries. Some of the members from the developed countries with such treaties did not have much regard for those provisions, but the provisions were there and the members could not object. The German member, often

---

24. Stanley S. Surrey, United Nations Model Convention for Tax Treaties Between Developed and Developing Countries: A Description and Analysis 10 (1980) (footnotes omitted). The editors have omitted most of Surrey's lengthy block quotation from this work.

25. *Id.*

26. For a large-scale recent study of the influence of the U.N. Model Treaty on actual treaties, *see* Wim Wijnen & Jan de Goede, *The U.N. Model in Practice, 1997–2013*, 68 Bull. Int'l Tax'n 118 (2014). Eric Zolt has summarized the mixed results of the study; on the one hand, the U.N. Model Treaty "has clearly influenced treaty practice," but on the other hand, "for many U.N. provisions, the adoption rates are remarkably low." Eric M. Zolt, *Tax Treaties and Developing Countries*, 72 Tax L. Rev. 111, 125 (2018).

27. Surrey describes an earlier tax sparing controversy, and his opposition to tax sparing, in Chapter 5.

following the German policy of "being kind" to developing countries, did push hard for acceptance of tax sparing. But the U.S. member obviously strongly objected. Many of the developing countries did agree with the arguments and points made by the U.S. member and would have been willing to drop the controversy. But since some developing countries pushed hard for it, Brazil and Argentina among them, the issue would not disappear. Accordingly, there is rather strong language in the Sixth Report and the Commentary on Article 23 favoring tax sparing but indicating one developed country disagrees.[28] The U.N. Model Treaty itself in its Article 23, Methods for the Elimination of Double Taxation, does not refer to tax sparing.

With the U.N. Model Treaty finished, the question arose whether the Group should continue in existence. The members of the Group desired to do so and Benoit shared this view. The Economic and Social Council then continued the Group changing its name somewhat to "Ad Hoc Group of Experts on International Cooperation in Tax Matters" adding some additional countries and dropping others,[p] and stating an agenda.[q] An important item on the agenda was that of tax avoidance and evasion in international tax matters, and this subject was scheduled for a December 1981 meeting in Geneva. On my return I sent Benoit memoranda on how some documentation could be prepared, such as a questionnaire which would make the members focus in advance on the issues and, since most were removed from daily contact with these issues, could prompt them to have the responsible administrators provide material. I also suggested that each member evaluate which were the most pressing problems his country faced and what solutions he thought would be useful. Much of these suggestions derived from a recent conference on the same subject which the Harvard International Tax Program and the German Foundation for International Development, with the cooperation of the relevant German and U.S. tax authorities, held for a group of developing countries in May, 1980.[r] The U.N. had been asked to join but Benoit could never get beyond the formal manner in which the sponsors of the Conference were stated. The Conference was successful in developing material and viewpoints on the subject.

Benoit disregarded my suggestions and would not even circulate the summary made of the Berlin meeting. With no documentation being prepared by the Secretariat, Benoit did have the good sense to select a knowledgeable Chairman and found him in the U.K. member, M.H. Collins.[29] He had been in charge of international matters for the United Kingdom Inland Revenue, was a hard, intelligent worker, and had prepared material on some aspects of international tax avoidance for the OECD Fiscal

---

28. "Many members from both developed and developing countries agreed with the view that tax-sparing credits should be included in treaties between developed and developing countries, where the developed country uses the credit method. However, a member from a developed country expressed the view that for a variety of reasons tax-sparing credits were not an appropriate tool for economic development." United Nations, *United Nations Model Double Tax Convention Between Developed and Developing Countries*, 185 (ST/ESA/102, 1980).

29. Maurice Hugh Collins had a long career with Inland Revenue, largely devoted to the negotiation of tax treaties. He chaired the U.N.'s Ad Hoc Group of Experts on International Co-operation in Tax Matters from 1981 to 1990. Tony Collins, *Maurice Collins Obituary*, THE GUARDIAN, Mar. 20, 2019.

Affairs Committee. He prepared overall descriptive material, largely based on the OECD papers, and this was the only documentation presented. Benoit did not want to invite me to assist and in the end reluctantly said I could be present as an Observer. Countries not members of the Group could attend as observers and also certain international organizations, such as IFA, and these observers were allowed to participate in the discussion but not directly in the formulation of final views. To strengthen my status I also arranged to be a representative of IFA if that step became necessary.

At the conclusion of the first day I told the Chairman I would be available to help him and he thankfully and immediately accepted my offer. I thus participated in really the same manner as in prior meetings, writing some material for the Chairman, asking questions and making observations in the discussions, and attending as a member all meetings of the Drafting Committee, a sort of Executive Committee composed of the officers elected for the meeting.

Because of the lack of adequate background preparation and documentation, the meeting achieved very little and the Report is largely a description of prior material from OECD and elsewhere.[s] The Group scheduled another meeting for December 1983. It also, on its own momentum, wrote an overall statement of the functions of the Group, such as keeping an eye on developments under the U.N. Model Treaty. Further, the OECD Members of the Group, recognizing the inadequacy of Benoit's leadership, proposed that an interim Steering Committee be given the task of preparing for the next meeting. The developing countries fully endorsed this suggestion. However, Benoit dropped this idea in the Resolution he drew up for the Economic and Social Council.

At this stage it is difficult to assess the future prospects for activities of the Group. Its membership is clearly composed of competent officials, used to working with each other and across any political lines. It thus has the potential for making important contributions in the field of international taxation. It could certainly do this with an efficient, knowledgeable Secretariat. The answer is not yet clear.[t, 30]

Some Other Countries

JAPAN

In 1972 Professor Carl Shoup (then Emeritus) and I were invited, with our wives, to come to Japan by the Ministry of Finance. The trip largely consisted of lectures at Tokyo University, speeches before tax and business groups in Tokyo and Osaka,

---

30. At the third meeting of the Group, in December of 1985—the first meeting since Surrey's death more than a year before—Benoit was still serving as secretary of the Group. At the opening of the meeting, Benoit "paid tribute to the memory of Professor Stanley Surrey of Harvard University, who had been for many years an adviser to the United Nations Secretariat and in that capacity had made a most valuable contribution to the work of the Group and to that of its predecessor...." Report of the Ad Hoc Group of Experts on International Co-operation in Tax Matters on the Work of its Third Meeting, 3 (ST/ESA/203, 1987).

and discussions on tax problems with Ministry of Finance officials. While our wives were on the trip, they often in effect travelled second class. Thus, one highlight of the trip was an award, Order of the Sacred Treasure, Second Class (the Order given to foreigners) which I received from Prime Minister Tanaka in his office — on October 3, my birthday, as I informed him.[31] Our wives were not invited. Then, at another reception while our wives and Japanese women were talking, the Japanese officials decided to leave, and took us along. It was only when one Japanese woman told my wife "Your husband is leaving" did she get the word.[32]

A trip under the auspices of a Ministry of Finance is a top level experience, since that Ministry is important in the Government structure, and has young, capable persons to act as guides. Also, it can draw on its Regional and local offices to shepherd us when we arrived in their cities. Professor Hiroshi Kaneko of Tokyo University, a friend, also accompanied us.[33]

My wife and I returned to Japan in 1978 at the invitation of the Japanese Foundation. We travelled during my sabbatical and made it an around the world trip. In London I lectured at seminars in the London School of Economics [Check]; in Iran we were tourists; in India I lectured at a course given in New Delhi by the U.N. Centre on Transnational Corporations; in Indonesia I consulted at length with government officials and lectured on international tax matters — they reciprocated by giving us a tour through Indonesia and Bali; we came as tourists to Hong Kong; and then in Japan, our longest stay, I again lectured somewhat on the order of the 1972 trip. I was interviewed by Japanese historians on my recollections of the Shoup Mission. Professor Kaneko accompanied us on a trip to southern Japan, and we were handed from Tax Office to Tax Office, which took care of all the arrangements.

THE MIDEAST — THE ARABIC COUNTRIES (OR WESTERN ASIA)

In December, 1979, while at the U.N. Treaty Group meeting I received a New York call from Mr. Richard Pau U, Chief Regional Commission's Liaison Unit from the U.N., asking if I would undertake a tax mission for the Western Asia (ECWA) office of the U.N. Development Organization (?).[34] I tentatively agreed, and later in New York at a meeting with Mr. Pau U and Mr. Basim A. Hannush, the head of

---

31. Kokuei Tanaka was prime minister of Japan from 1972 to 1974. His political career was clouded by scandal. In 1983 he was convicted of accepting $4.5 million in bribes from Lockheed Corporation. James Sterngold, *Kakuei Tanaka, 75, Ex-Premier and Political Force in Japan, Dies*, New York Times, Dec. 17, 1993, at B14.

32. Surrey does not explain why he could not have conveyed "the word" to Mrs. Surrey himself.

33. Hiroshi Kaneko was a member of the law faculty of Tokyo University from 1953 to 1991. He is currently an adviser to the Tokyo law firm of Nagashima, Ohno & Tsunematsu.

34. The Commission was established by the Economic and Social Council of the United Nations in 1973, as the Economic Commission for Western Asia (ECWA). It was renamed the Economic and Social Commission for Western Asia (ESCWA) in 1985.

ECWA, the Mission was firmed up.[35] I was to visit three countries falling under the jurisdiction of that office, spending a week on each. Earlier I had received, without applying, a Lady David Fellowship to teach a semester at the Law School of Hebrew University in Jerusalem. I decided to undertake both assignments, and therefore arranged a leave of absence from Harvard for the Spring 1980 term.

After a PSC meeting of IFA in Paris, I flew to Beirut in late February 1980, the location of the ECWA. Beirut then was relatively quiet on the surface, but one kept off the streets at night, carefully observed the checkpoints and took the roads that were treated as safe. The U.N. officials spent several days describing my Mission. Essentially they desired to obtain an assessment of the extent to which the tax systems of three countries — North Yemen, Saudi Arabia, and Syria — could sustain economic development projects in those countries. I found the ECWA economists, and others, somewhat naive as to what such a mission could accomplish in a week and also relatively uninformed (or informed in an almost abstract, academic way) about these tax systems. Only the head of the office, Dr. Hannush, was realistic. He said I was to give them a view from the "top of the pyramid." And that was all I was expected to accomplish.

As a guide, interpreter, associate, companion, I was joined by Dr. Adnan Mardini, a Syrian. He was Regional Advisor in Development Finance in ECWA. Dr. Mardini had a graduate degree from American University in Washington, had spent some years in the United States, and before joining the U.N. was a Deputy Finance Minister in Syria.[36] While not a tax specialist, he had a good grounding in economics and fiscal matters. Above all, he was a delightful and intelligent companion, who worked most cooperatively. His knowledge of the countries and their officials was very helpful in getting me started in a country. I was careful not to discuss my Lady Davis Fellowship.

YEMEN ARAB REPUBLIC (NORTH YEMEN)

The Mission took place in March, 1980. We first drove to Damascus, where Dr. Mardini lives with his American wife, and which he visited every weekend. From there we flew to Sanaa, the capital of the Yemen Arab Republic (North Yemen). I must admit that when I first heard of the Mission I had to look for North Yemen in an atlas.[37] It is not much of a country. The authority of the Central Government does not fully extend to the borders, and local tribes often go their own way. The country is really an underdeveloped country.

Sanaa is not an impressive place. Indeed, on the contrary its general atmosphere is that of a relatively poor city — few streets in good shape, non-descript buildings,

35. Basim A. Hannush, a Harvard-educated economist, was with the ECWA (and its successor ESCWA) from 1963 to 1991.

36. Mardini's 1965 American University doctoral dissertation had been on "Monetary Policy in Syria (1945-1956)."

37. Anyone looking for the country of North Yemen in an atlas today would be disappointed; the two Yemens merged in 1990.

many people poorly dressed. It also had the air of a city whose customs were not twentieth century—men nearly always wearing daggers of various degrees of utility and value in their belts, black robed and fully veiled women, the custom of nearly everyone chewing the narcotic khat on Friday. Our hotel in the city was a minus two star place, relatively clean but old and somehow having an air of being more broken-down than it was. We ate our meals there, which were modest and not sickness producing, compared with our one dinner at the Holiday Inn [Check] outside the city which ended with a real stomach upset later at night.[38]

Essentially our pattern of working was to start with the Ministry of Finance, through a telephone call by Dr. Mardini, to obtain overviews of the tax system, their thoughts of its adequacy and possible changes, their views of tax administration, the development plans for the country and the relationship of the tax system to those plans. A similar discussion with the Minister of Development centering on the last point followed. In these interviews Dr. Mardini and I used a "team approach." He would supply the opening pleasantries, to be followed by very general conversation. At the proper point, Dr. Mardini, using a variety of techniques, would advise me when I could begin serious questioning. I did nearly all of the questioning, probing as deeply but delicately as I could. Whenever the questioning became perhaps embarrassing for the official or too severe, Dr. Mardini would signal me to change to another subject. Of course, where English was not spoken, he interpreted for me. Through these devices nearly all of our interviews were productive and pleasant.

We obtained from several sources a detailed description of the tax system and the revenues raised through each tax measure, a task which required considerable probing because the details are not readily available in one document. We noted the areas of weakness in the structure and the "escapes" of the well-to-do in the society.

The next main step was to obtain a picture of the state of tax administration—the methods of collection, the degree of compliance, the priorities of the tax administrators, the education level and training of the employees, the overall attitude of the administrators, the possibilities for improved administration and the revenue consequences. This task involved a number of meetings with the Director-General and his staff. We found the Director-General, Yahya Al-Haddy, a very able, imaginative, ingenious, hard-working and responsible person. He knew the weaknesses of the present administration, despite only a year in his position (he previously had been the Director-General of Customs), and earnestly desired improvements. We, of course, bombarded him and his staff with questions, which he answered in a straight-forward manner, not sliding or polishing over defects or problems in administration. His interest in our questions and suggestions was so keen that later, on his own motion, he interviewed us with a list of questions he had prepared. We also interviewed other persons, such as the accounting professors in the college and the International Bank Staff members of a lengthy mission to Yemen (of which ECWA was apparently completely unaware).

38. The only Holiday Inn in Yemen today is in Mukalla, an eleven-hour drive from Sana'a. The editors have not determined whether there was a Holiday Inn in or near Sana'a in 1980.

It may help to illustrate our impressions by quoting from a summary in my Report:

> Overall, there should be cautious — but hopeful — optimism as to improvement in the tax structure and tax administration — *if* the government remains stable, *if* the direction of tax administration remains in capable hands, *if* there is continued and even increased expert assistance from outside, and *if* the requisite patience for steady and not over-hasty steps is maintained, along with increased public education on the reasons for improved tax administration and compliance. These of course are major conditions, but they are by no means insurmountable. Rather, they appear to be within the scope of a cautiously optimistic yet reasonable outlook.[39]

SAUDI ARABIA

After a week in Sanaa we flew to Riyadh, the capital of the country. Without Dr. Mardini I probably still would be at the Sanaa airport, so crowded and unorganized is that airport. Riyadh was quite a contrast — numerous major hotels, impressive government office and business buildings, a modern hospital, all mixed with areas in different stages of construction. The city did not have the sense of charm or uniqueness one got in Sanaa through seemingly stepping back through decades, but instead we were plunged into a city hustling to complete its change to the modern world and without time to spend on public amenities and scenic areas.

Our work in Saudi Arabia took a completely different approach. The fiscal officials in Saudi Arabia pay hardly any attention to requests by ECWA — a matter which ECWA did not mention to me. As a result it was impossible to interview officials in the Ministry of Finance — a telephone call by Dr. Mardini produced a request for a written request and our purpose; this was sent, in English, but returned with the demand that it be written in Arabic, though the officials spoke English; the request in Arabic produced the reply that the Minister of Finance was in Jidda and his permission was needed; a telegram had been sent to him but he had not replied. These exchanges occupied our week in Riyadh, and the type of interviews that took place in Sanaa could not be duplicated.

We then turned to other sources. A team from the London-based Stanford Research Institute-International was working on development plans and had information on the tax system. Saudi Arabia does not have an income tax on resident companies or on individuals. It does impose a tax on foreign corporations engaged in business in Saudi Arabia, with a special tax on oil companies — the amounts in 1977–1978 were 671 million S.R. for the first and 98,665 million S.R. from the latter (exchange rate at the time of the Mission was 3.15 S.R. to $1.00). Oil royalties also produced 31,817 million S.R. With these amounts of revenue, the Stanford people were not thinking about a domestic tax structure, nor did they appear to spend sleepless nights on what

39. The editors have omitted most of Surrey's lengthy quotation.

might happen if oil revenues declined. The emphasis on "taxes" is only on "negative taxes," i.e., subsidies to support lower gasoline prices, flour prices, housing, etc.

Most of the work under the income tax on foreign corporations is, for the private sector, performed by chartered accountants. We obtained our knowledge of the state of tax administration through an interview with a prominent accounting firm. The accountant we met thought the tax administration was effective and aware of modern problems, such as transfer pricing. There are a handful of lawyers involved in the legal disputes that occurred in tax practice, and an interview with one produced the view that the staff of the Tax Department was competent to handle these disputes. This lawyer was the only person interviewed who thought the country should introduce a low rate domestic income tax so that the public would become accustomed to paying taxes. An interview with a university group informed us that a fairly large number of graduates in the economics field take the customary public finance courses. University students are given a free education but in return on graduation work for the government for a period of time.

My summary for Saudi Arabia was as follows:

> Overall Conclusions and Recommendations
>
> From the above material it is clear that overall conclusions and recommendations must indeed be brief. The development plan is financed almost entirely by oil revenues and apparently this process will continue into an indefinite future. The administration of the income tax on foreigners (and presumably also that on oil companies) appears to be proceeding without serious difficulties, though the information obtained on this aspect, as explained above, was somewhat scanty. There is no present serious consideration being given to the imposition of a customary income tax (the present minor Zakat apart) on Saudi nationals. Whether or not consideration should be given to that subject is a matter on which the Mission cannot be expected to give any conclusion.[40]

SYRIA

From Saudi Arabia we flew to Damascus in Syria. Damascus is a pleasant city, presenting both the old and the new. But in some intangible way one senses that an authoritarian hand is always present. The hand is not always in control, and Dr. Mardini would not drive in certain areas for worry about bombs.

We found the tax authorities very accommodating, granting all the interviews we required. Syria is moving to modernize its tax administration, and a team of French experts is engaged in computerizing many aspects, such as lists of taxpayers' returns, delinquencies, etc. A large section of business is government owned, so that the income tax is mainly aimed at smaller businesses and the professions. The tax therefore

40. The editors have omitted most of Surrey's lengthy quotation.

does not play a large role in financing development plans, which rely on the surpluses of the public enterprises and foreign assistance. Our interviewing was similar to that in Sanaa, but with more officials involved and a higher order of activity and sophistication. The collection of adequate data is emphasized and there is a Directorate of Research and Studies charged with obtaining data and studying changes in the tax system, through economic and legal research and some comparative work on fiscal legislation in other countries. We learned later that a recent International Monetary Fund Report had been prepared on Syria, of which ECWA was either ignorant or didn't think, erroneously, would be helpful in our work. Nor did any of the Syrian officials mention the document.

My overall conclusions were:

> The overall conclusions regarding the contribution of the tax system to development planning is that, given the large public enterprise sector, the contribution made through taxation of the private sector must naturally be minor, even considering improvement in tax administration or new taxes. The fact that the income tax applies to the public enterprises and as such for 60 to 70 percent of the commercial profits tax is just really, as far as revenue is concerned, an accounting or classification matter. The major contribution to development, apart from foreign assistance, are the surpluses available from the public enterprises.

Dr. Mardini drove me from Damascus to Beirut, then a pleasant scenic drive with only a few checkpoints and no difficulties at the border. I spent several days in Beirut discussing the Mission and Report with the ECWA officials. Then my hasty tour of the four Arabic countries ended.

After my Report was prepared and typed — 70 pages — I sent it to Mr. Hannush of ECWA through Mr. Pau U. The Report was read in ECWA and written comments made by Dr. Mardini and Dr. Kazemi, Senior Economic Affairs Officer.[41] Those of Dr. Mardini were minor and those of Dr. Kazemi completely unrealistic. He desired an evaluation of the "buoyancy and elasticity" of the tax system. He also stated:

> The raising of revenue, important as may be, should not be construed as the only overriding function of the tax system. The impact of the tax system on growth (i.e., the allocation function) and prices (stabilization function) and its burden on capital and labor (distribution function) also need to be examined, however briefly. The general guidelines which will emerge from such an examination should provide the basis for a more elaborate and purposeful evaluation of these aspects of the tax system in line with development objectives and priorities and within the overall framework of the fiscal policy operating under the economic and social system prevailing in the country(ies) concerned.

---

41. Shamsuzziker Kazemi was with the ECWA from 1977 to 1982. He later served as Afghanistan's ambassador to the United Nations in Geneva. His 1970 doctoral dissertation (University of Glasgow) was on "Some Aspects of the Afghan Tax System with Particular Reference to the Income Tax Law."

It was not clear whether he thought my Report should have supplied the answers to these issues, or whether ECWA should proceed with research on these issues as the next step of work in the tax field. If the former, it portrays a naive ignorance of what a week's visits in each country can accomplish and the lack of data on which to attempt any thoughtful answers on the matters he mentioned. If the latter, then all one can do is wish him luck and hope he has a long tenure in ECWA or can afford missions for longer than one week.[u]

ISRAEL

After concluding the U.N. Mission I flew to Greece where my wife joined me. In Athens, at our Embassy and the Israeli Embassy, I obtained a second U.S. passport with an Israeli visa. Since I was to earn money in the country, a tourist visa which can be kept separate from a U.S. passport, not stamped in Israel, and which eliminates problems with Arabian travel, would not do and the separate passport was necessary. We then visited Crete and Rhodes, returned to Athens and flew to Israel, arriving around the first of April.

My wife and I had been to Israel several times when I was a Treasury official, so we already had taken trips in the area. The Hebrew University officials found us an apartment in a building the University owned in a housing development near the University on Mount Scopus in East Jerusalem. The Law School is in that part of the University. Our apartment was not the most comfortable abode, sparsely furnished, and cold since it had been unoccupied during the winter and the heat in the building was now turned off. The person from the University office that oversees University Buildings was a hard bargainer, and my wife had long arguments with him about obtaining more linen, some floor heaters, more cooking dishes, light bulbs, etc. We ended by often buying additional items. The apartment was convenient, however, with a bus route to the University close by and also a shopping center. The area—and the University—offered many scenic views of the mountains and the desert on one side and West Jerusalem on the two other sides.

At the Law School I was given a small but useful office. I soon learned that the facilities were sparse—secretarial and xeroxing help on the minimal side, but cheerfully it worked out. My obligation on the Fellowship[v, 42] was to give a seminar once a week on tax policy over a three month period. This had been arranged by Professor Aaron Yoran, the taxation member of the Faculty.[43] I soon discovered that knowledge of the English language was a significant problem. Professor Yoran had asked me to give a lecture to his International Taxation class on a day he had to be away. It was a reasonably large class, say 75 students. After a brief intermission, I found that con-

42. Henriette Marie Meyer (1872–1963) was a Canadian philanthropist. After her husband, Sir Mortimer Davis, was knighted in 1917, she was generally known as Lady Davis.

43. In addition to being a senior lecturer with the Hebrew University law faculty, Aaron Yoran directed the Harry and Michael Sacher Institute for Legislative Research and Comparative Law (also at Hebrew University).

siderably less than half the class reappeared. I had thought the lecture was going well and interesting, so at the end I inquired about the absences. I was told that many of the students could not follow a lecture in English—and that was that. The seminar, partly for the same reason, had only a few students. But some other professors and government officials attended, so that the group permitted interesting exchanges. Obviously, much of the work was on a comparative law basis. I had discussed with Yoran topics that would be of interest in both the United States and Israel, prepared some xeroxed material on them, and then conducted the seminar along Socratic dialogue lines. I think it went well. I gave a brief examination to the students taking the course and read the papers on the plane—obviously all passed.

The seminar was my only official duty. While I was free to attend Faculty meetings and other Law School activities, since they were conducted in Hebrew it was my turn to stay away. I spent my time just finishing my U.N. Report, having it typed by a student, and then sent to Beirut via my Harvard office. The rest of my time was spent on initial writing of some chapters for a book on Tax Expenditures.[44]

The Law School Faculty was a combination of elderly professors, some of whom did not speak English or even were aware of my presence, and younger professors who spoke English, had taught in American law schools and were very familiar with our methods. The younger professors were all bright, had a wider legal knowledge than most U.S. professors, since they were—had to be—familiar with Israeli law, the law under the U.K. mandate, old Hebrew law, and a good deal of Continental European law, plus U.S. law. They were both friendly and busy. They often had a morning coffee break in a faculty lounge and I met with them. Law School salaries are low—including those paid under the Lady Davis Fellowships—and many faculty members had consulting positions or part-time teaching arrangements elsewhere.

Weekends were occupied with tours through the Old City and surrounding areas, trips in a rented car through northern Israel and then Tel Aviv—being carefully warned to stay away from certain cities where trouble was likely to be brewing. (Two weeks after we left a bomb was exploded at the bus stop I had used.)[45]

In Israel there were dinners and visits with persons we had met on our previous trips. In all, out time was fully occupied, and I was able to complete a number of draft chapters for a Tax Expenditure book.

My Middle East (Western Asia) expedition was thus an interesting episode. The differences among all the countries visited, together with this first trip to Arabic countries, provided interesting contrasts. Obviously, all the contrasts are not absorbed in a week, but the variety is stimulating. So also are the basic conflicts—probably Dr. Mardini and certainly others would wonder about a Lady Davis Fellow. Equally,

44. Presumably the reference is to what became STANLEY S. SURREY & PAUL R. MCDANIEL, TAX EXPENDITURES (1985), which was published the year after Surrey's death.

45. Surrey's description of a week he spent away from Israel during his Fellowship is omitted. He spent the week in Berlin at a conference exploring the possibility of establishing training programs in various developing countries, modeled on the Harvard International Tax Program.

many persons in Jerusalem found it hard to understand my travelling with a Syrian for a month. The information I obtained on tax structure and policy in these countries did not differ from what I knew of the rest of the world. The range of technique from the experts in Israel down through Syria and then to Yemen would be matched by a trip from Japan through some Latin American countries and on to many African countries.

Looking back, I can see how much I learned from these international activities. To some degree the learning was reciprocated, through the formulation of the U.N. Model Treaty and the growing standards of IFA, to which I contributed. These international activities made for a pleasant mix with the domestic pursuits that also occupied the same years.

PEOPLE'S REPUBLIC OF CHINA

In August 1980, the Harvard International Program in Taxation conducted a one-month seminar in China on tax law and policy. The seminar was arranged by Professor Jerome Cohen, then Director of the Harvard East Asian Program.[46] The purpose was to give an intensive introductory course in taxation to a group of Chinese officials that would presumably work in the tax area once the Chinese system of taxation would be modernized. Since China then had no real income tax the seminar focused on that subject. Professors Oliver Oldman of Harvard, Robert Hellawell of Columbia,[47] Richard Pomp of Connecticut,[48] Harvey Dale of New York University[49] and myself were the principal lecturers in the program. The officials who attended were top level persons in the Ministry of Finance and tax officials from all parts of China. The sessions, for each morning of the month, were held at a college in the city of Dalian, near the place formerly called Port Arthur. We had sent basic materials to the Chinese in charge some months ago, and these had been translated. The students, so to speak, spent a month going over the materials.[50] I was scheduled for the last week.

My wife and I flew to Peking and then Dalian, at both places being in the hands of young personnel from the Ministry of Finance. It was fascinating to be among the

---

46. Jerome A. Cohen is arguably the leading American scholar of Chinese law and government. He directed the East Asian Legal Studies Program at Harvard Law School from 1964 to 1979. He spent the following decade in legal practice with the firm of Paul, Weiss, Rifkind, Wharton & Garrison. In 1990 he joined the faculty of New York University Law School, where he remains today as a professor and as the director of NYU's U.S.-Asia Law Institute.

47. Robert Hellawell was on the faculty of Columbia Law School from 1964 until his retirement in 1989. Prior to joining the Columbia faculty, he had held high-level positions in the Peace Corps during the Kennedy and Johnson administrations. He died in 2001

48. Richard D. Pomp is the Alva P. Loiselle Professor at the University of Connecticut Law School. He is a leading expert on state and local taxation.

49. Harvey P. Dale is a scholar of international tax law and a pioneer in the study of philanthropy and the law. He is on the faculty of New York University Law School, where he is University Professor of Philanthropy and the Law and director of the National Center on Philanthropy and the Law.

50. The editors are puzzled as to the function of "so to speak" in this sentence, but have left the sentence as Surrey wrote it.

earlier visitors to China once the country was opened to foreigners. I believe our seminar was among the first, if not the first, to be conducted by American professors. We stayed in a comfortable resort hotel on ____________________________,[51] and ate our meals there, Chinese style. There was time for us in the afternoons to visit the surrounding areas—the large port, shops in the city, small manufacturing firms, an agricultural commune, a seaside resort. Naturally, the curiosity on both sides was quite large. We were followed by groups of Chinese at all the places. Professor Cohen speaks Chinese and were we thus able to ask the questions that interested our group and understand the replies.

My role in the seminar was to cover parts of the United States tax system that related to international transactions. I thus spoke, as I recall, on our section 367 involving transfers of assets from U.S. parents to their foreign subsidiaries and liquidations of such subsidiaries; Subpart F involving American-owned corporations located in tax havens; the general treatment of receipts from abroad and from sales of stock in U.S.-owned foreign companies; and other similar matters. It was hard going to present these subjects to persons who had never dealt with an income tax. The lecturing was aided by the method of interpretation, with the Chinese interpreters—top level tax officials and a professor of economics—interpreting on a sequential system. I would speak a few sentences—as simply as I could—and then have time to prepare the next group of sentences while the interpretation of the first set of sentences was being made. As is usually the case with such interpretation, the interpreter would often take twice as much time as when I spoke. Apparently the interpreter was doing his best to amplify and clarify my remarks for the class. Professor Cohen attended the sessions and occasionally would correct the interpretation, though the subject matter was as new to him as to the Chinese except that he could follow my remarks and check the interpretation. We found the interpretation was excellent, made more so by the complexity of the material.

A part of my assignment was to cover the subject of bilateral income tax treaties. These treaties, initially largely between developed countries, were designed to eliminate double taxation of income arising in one country and received by residents of the other country. The treaties were beginning to extend to a developed-developing country pattern and, as described earlier, the U.N. was working toward a model treaty for that pattern. I knew the class would be interested in what in the future—after China had established a basic income tax system—could be a United States-China treaty. So I simulated a negotiation between India and the United States, with India as a developing country making various demands, either in line with the U.N. Model or beyond, such as asking for a tax sparing credit which the United States would not concede. The class, which I am sure could transform this presentation into a United States-China treaty, was interested in the situation. We really found them interested in all of our lectures, for the talks opened new insights to them which they would comprehend in a professional way.

51. Probably Golden Pebble Beach.

When our week is Dalian was over we returned to Peking, after an extra night stay because the Peking-Dalian DC3 had to await shipment of a part to enable it to be airborne again. The stay in Peking was for the most part devoted to touring that area. Ministry of Finance young employees were again our guides, and using a car made available to us, conducted us to as many of the sights to visit as could be done in the time available. It has been, as I said in regard to trips to Japan, very helpful in a foreign country to be in the hands of the Ministry of Finance, for those hands open all doors. China was even a special case — as my guide told my wife: "It is a great responsibility I have in taking care of Professor Surrey since he is a very old man." Knowing the Chinese veneration for the wisdom of the elderly, I took this as a high compliment.

During the week in Peking I met several times with the Commissioner of Taxation and his staff to discuss tax issues and to answer questions on the U.S. tax system. These are able officials, forced to shift their thinking from an almost obsolete tax system to a modern approach. In the years that followed they received advice, often conflicting, from all sorts of American "experts", lawyers, accountants, tax executives, academics. Slowly they were evolving their own variations of the modern income tax.[w] The process continues, as do initial negotiations on a United States tax treaty.[52]

Our trip to China was far too short. But at the end of our stay in Peking we were off to Copenhagen for the 1980 IFA Congress.

Notes

a. IFA publishes annually a Yearbook summarizing the events of each Congress; *e.g.*, the opening speeches, a report on the discussions of each topic, the Resolutions adopted, a report on the Seminar, and also lists of national branches, officials and members.

b. The papers delivered by the members of a Seminar panel are published by IFA in a separate annual monograph.

c. A sad event occurred at the Jerusalem Congress when the recent Chairman of the U.S. Branch, Nathan Gordon, died from a heart attack. Gordon, an economist, was the career Treasury person specialized in international tax matters and had obtained prominent recognition in the field. The Georgetown journal, *Law and Policy in International Business*, dedicated a 1978 issue (called "Issues in International Taxation") to him, and for it Pierre Kerlan, Gordon's French counterpart, and I wrote "in memoriam" pieces. Stanley S. Surrey, *Foreword*, 10 L. & POL'Y IN INT'L BUS. v (1978); Pierre Kerlan, *A Tribute to Nathan Gordon, an Eminent International Tax Expert*, 10 L. & POL'Y IN INT'L BUS. xi (1978). I also wrote an article, Stanley S. Surrey, *Reflections on the Allocation of Income and Expenses Among National Tax Jurisdictions*, 10 L. & POL'Y IN INT'L BUS. 409 (1978), which attempted to state governing principles and to define the relationships between our section 482 and section 861 Regulations.

---

52. The tax treaty between China and the United States was signed in 1984 and became effective in 1987. Income Tax Convention, United States — The People's Republic of China, Jan. 1, 1987, S. TREATY DOC. NO. 97-24.

d. The Managing Director of the Bureau, Prof. J. Van Hoorn, Jr., made the following kind remarks on the presentation of the Medal (Bulletin for International Fiscal Documentation, December 1978, p. 542):

> During its last meeting, in May this year, the Bureau's Board of Trustees decided to celebrate the Bureau's fortieth anniversary by creating an Award. This Award is very simple and is granted, not in recognition of work done on behalf of the Bureau itself but, more generally, to those who have devoted themselves in an outstanding way to the furthering of knowledge, thinking and research in the field of international taxation. It was further decided to grant the Award — a silver medal — for the first time during this Congress which happens to occur in the very week that forty years ago the Bureau started its work.
>
> There is a man in this audience today who, over many years and not always in agreement with the ideas, wishes and experiences of others, has devoted himself wholeheartedly to matters of international taxation as a scholar, as an administrator, as a scholar again, as a consultant to international organizations. This man, whose ideas are controversial to some and agreeable to others, was and is involved in the creation and development of an instrument to educate and train people from many developed and above all less developed countries, an instrument of which few if any people will deny the significance and efficacy. I am happy that this man is also one of the most active members of I.F.A. He is a modest man, and he is not even aware of what I am about to say.
>
> I am very pleased that the Bureau's Board of Trustees have authorized me to honour and acclaim
>
> Professor Stanley S. Surrey
>
> by making him the first recipient of the Silver Medal of the International Bureau of Fiscal Documentation, because of the outstanding quality of his many and varied achievements in the international tax area in which both I.F.A. and the Bureau have been operating for forty years and which are so numerous that it would take too long to specify them. May I just mention his involvement in the International Tax Program of Harvard Law School and in the work of the U.N. Group of Experts on Tax Treaties between Developed and Developing Countries.
>
> Many have benefited from the Program and several of those are among us now. The work of Prof. Surrey as rapporteur to the U.N. Group is perhaps even of wider significance in the development of international tax law, as not only those among us who participated in the U.N. Group are aware.

e. OECD, *Draft Double Taxation Convention on Income and Capital* (1963).

f. The developed countries were: France, Federal Republic of Germany, Japan, Netherlands, Sweden, Switzerland, United Kingdom, United States. At the second meeting, Norway was added. The developing countries were: Argentina, Chile, Ghana, India, Israel, Pakistan, Philippines, Sudan, Tunisia, Turkey. At the third meeting Ceylon (Sri Lanka) was added. At the fifth meeting Brazil was added.

g. Lachmann had died before the meeting and had been succeeded in the U.N. by his Assistant, Krcmery, who was not a tax expert.

h. A report on the meeting, covering the discussion and some of the documentation, was published by the U.N. as "Tax Treaties between Developed and Developing Countries" (1969, E/4614, ST/ECA/110).

Reports were published for all succeeding meetings:

Second Report (1970, E/4936, ST/ECA/137)

Third Report (1972, ST/ECA/166)

Fourth Report (1973, ST/ECA/188)

Fifth Report (1975, ST/ESA/18)

Sixth Report (1976, ST/ESA/42)

Seventh Report (1978, ST/ESA/79)

Eighth Report (1979, ST/ESA/101)

i. Mr. A. Scheel of Norway had become the Rapporteur.

j. ST/ESA/14.

k. At the Second Meeting, Chile had been represented by Milka Casanegra, a knowledgeable person who took an aggressive stand on preserving source jurisdiction.

l. Stanley S. Surrey, *United Nations Group of Experts and the Guidelines for Tax Treaties Between Developed and Developing Countries*, 19 HARV. INT'L L. J. 2 (1978).

m. (1979), ST/ESA/94. In addition to the Guidelines, the Manual contained an historical overview of tax treaties; material on international tax evasion and avoidance taken from a memorandum which George Beatty of the United States and I had earlier prepared for the Group; observations on the Guidelines taken from earlier Reports; suggestions relating to the application of the Guidelines on mutual agreement procedure, allocation of receipts and expenses, and exchanges of information, verbatim from earlier material I had prepared for the Reports, as were the observations on the Guidelines; and a note on procedural aspects of tax treaty negotiations written by the U.S. Member.

n. United Nations Model Double Taxation Convention Between Developed and Developing Countries (1980, ST/ESA/102).

o. The OECD had revised its model in 1977, Model Double Taxation Convention on Income and Capital, Report of the OECD Committee on Fiscal Affairs (OECD, 1977), and this revision was reflected in the U.N. Model.

p. The countries in the Group were now: Argentina, Austria, Brazil, Chile, Egypt, Finland, France, Federal Republic of Germany, India, Indonesia, Israel, Jamaica, Japan, Mexico, Morocco, Netherlands, Nigeria, Pakistan, Spain, Switzerland, Syrian Arab Republic, United Kingdom, United Republic of Cameroon, United States.

q. United Nations, Economic and Social Council Res., 1980/13, Supplement No. 1, 12 (April 28, 1980).

r. German Foundation for International Development/Harvard Law School International Tax Program, Summary of the Proceedings of the International Conference on International Tax Avoidance and Evasion (19–23 May 1980, Berlin (West)).

s. International Co-Operation in Tax Matters, Report of the Ad Hoc Group of Experts on International Co-Operation in Tax Matters on the Work of its First Meeting (1983, ST/ESA/128).

t. Not being invited to the 1983 meeting and somewhat weary of the conflict with Benoit, I did not make an effort to attend. The meeting dates also conflicted with a meeting of the ALI Council which I had to attend. In 1981, with the same conflict, I did make an intermediate hasty trip from Switzerland to the United States and back. But with no encouragement from Benoit, to do this again would be too much discomfort.

u. Apparently ECWA intended to amplify my Report with material prepared presumably by Dr. Kazemi and then to publish it. However, as far as I know, this was not done. Also ECWA said it was contrary to U.N. policy for me to publish the Report and I did not do so. I have a suspicion that the certain coolness that developed in ECWA after they received my Report was occasioned by my secretary, when she sent the Report and without realizing the consequences of her error, wrote that I could be reached at the Law School of Hebrew University in Jerusalem.

v. The Lady Davis Fellowships were endowed by Lady Davis, a Canadian. An office in Jerusalem selects Fellows through allocation to various parts of the University and in turn receives nominations.

w. The Chinese tax system as it existed in 1979 is described in Richard D. Pomp & Stanley S. Surrey, *The Tax Structure of the People's Republic of China*, 20 VA. J. INT'L L. 1 (1980). The evolving modern tax system, as of 1981, is described in Richard D. Pomp, Stanley S. Surrey & Timothy A. Gellatt, *The Evolving Tax System of the People's Republic of China*, 16 TEX. INT'L L.J. 11 (1981).

TEN

A Government Tax Career

Part III, 1969–1980

After my resignation from the Treasury Department in 1969, I concentrated on re-entry into the Academic world. But I found it difficult to keep Washington tax and political affairs out of my mind and time. As described in Chapter Seven, I was vocal in opposition to proposals of the Nixon Administration, such as the new depreciation rules and DISC. As also described there I participated as a tax advisor to Senator McGovern in his 1972 campaign. Then, as Senator Kennedy became interested in tax reform, I was one of his advisors, especially in the period 1974–1976 when he was an active participant in legislative matters in the tax area.

A wholly new venture commenced in 1975 that was to lead me to a third Government career. In 1976 Governor Jimmy Carter was engaged in an active—very active—campaign for the Presidency. Around the end of February, 1976, I received a phone call from Carter headquarters: Carter had said in a speech that if elected he would consider wholesale elimination of income tax deductions, including the deduction for home mortgage interest and property taxes.[1] This elimination of deductions would permit an overall reduction in tax rates. The caller said the speech was causing a strong press opposition.[a] Carter that very evening was to debate the campaign issues with the other candidates and this subject was bound to come up. What should Carter say? Obviously, the question may be translated into "What does he do to dig himself out of this hole?" As a quick response, I said he could stress that the interest deduction for homeowners was "upside down," in that the deduction was allowable against the highest income tax bracket of the taxpayer. Thus, the wealthier the homeowner, the larger the amount of mortgage interest that the Government was paying through the deduction (70 percent for a person in the top bracket), and on the other side a homeowner exempt from tax because of a large family received no government assistance. Carter could say *this method* of assisting homeowners—and he is all for such assistance—is unfair and should be reexamined to find a better solution. As predicted, the other candidates jumped all over that part of Carter's speech. Unfortunately, either the answer was not un-

1. Carter had been saying for weeks that he favored repeal of many income tax deductions, without specifying which deductions. But at a forum on February 23, he answered a specific question about the deductions for home mortgage interest and property tax, saying both should be repealed. Adam Clymer, *From the Mouth of Jimmy Carter*, The Baltimore Sun, Feb. 29, 1976, at K3.

derstood by my caller or in turn by Carter and he fell back on lame talk about the tax system needing reexamination in general, without realizing he could have put others on the defensive.

This call started a link with Carter's campaign and I continued to receive other calls seeking background information. Then in the summer of 1976, the tax work for the campaign was formalized. Joseph Pechman, a close friend at the Brookings Institution, and I were asked to chair a Tax Task Force to provide background material for the campaign. We formed this group, composed obviously of our friends, lawyers and economists, who possessed a close acquaintance with the subjects Pechman and I decided to cover. These subjects were parceled around the members of the Task Force and others, who were asked to prepare brief memoranda on the subjects. Pechman and I went over these memoranda, to check content and understandability at the level of campaign headquarters which did not have a tax specialist. That summer I was sailing in Cape Breton and Nova Scotia. To receive material from Pechman I enlisted my crew as couriers, and as a new member came on board for his leg of the sail he had with him a packet of papers from Pechman. I read these, made my changes, and then whenever we came to a port where I could make a phone call I discussed the changes with Pechman. I remember with embarrassment using for an hour the only pay phone on a dock in East Boothbay Harbor with a number of tourists obviously fretting and wrathful. This procedure had all the earmarks of a haphazard approach, but it did work smoothly. Over twenty-four memoranda were prepared. They were brief, gave background, pros and cons, and conclusions on the policy approach that should be taken if the subject arose in the campaign—and for thought later on if Carter won.[b] Carter wisely did not talk much more on specifics of the tax system, but stuck to generalities and the theme that the tax system was a "disgrace" and required complete revision. On nomination, in his acceptance speech he said:

> It's time for a complete overhaul of our income tax system. I still tell you it's a disgrace to the human race. All my life I have heard promises of tax reform, but it never quite happens. With your help, we are finally going to make it happen and you can depend on it.[2]

We found later that the generality of this statement was matched by the generality of Carter's knowledge of the tax system, and he had to be told what "disgrace" and "revision" specifically meant.

As another part of the campaign, I went to Washington for an afternoon session of "experts" assembled to help brief Senator Mondale for his Vice Presidential debate with Senator Dole. Mondale was rather surprised and gratified that I would make the trip just for this one reason. It never occurred to me not to consider the meeting and my participation on the tax side as something I could decide to skip. Each of us asked Mondale some questions in our field of expertise—I asked, for example, "Did

---

2. *Transcript of Carter Address Accepting Democratic Nomination for Presidency*, New York Times, Jul. 16, 1976, at 10. The *Times* transcript has "feel" where Surrey has "still tell," and "happened" where Surrey has "happens."

he favor a sales tax?" — and then gave our comments on his replies — "No" was the answer to my question.

In the fall of 1976, one of my colleagues, Professor Charles Fried, a good friend with a next-door office, but distinctly conservative on fiscal matters, wrote a New York Times Op-Ed piece criticizing Carter's tax talk.[3] I wrote a reply, at the suggestion of Carter headquarters, which I sent to the Times but which through a mix-up was not used. However, it does provide the defense I saw for a "Carter Program":

GOVERNOR CARTER'S TAX PROGRAM

By Stanley S. Surrey

Taxation is a complicated matter and even a colleague of mine at Harvard Law School, Charles Fried, showed his confusion when he criticized Governor Carter on this page last week.

Professor Fried created a tax program which he then proceeded to criticize — but it is not Jimmy Carter's program. Specifically, Fried's article either stated or implied that Governor Carter's tax reform would involve: heavier taxes on middle income taxpayers in order to provide tax reductions for those making lower incomes; and the elimination of deductions for homeowner's mortgage interest and property tax payments and for charitable contributions.

Governor Carter has made it clear that his tax reform would involve lower not higher taxes for the broad range of low and middle income taxpayers in this country. The Carter program does not envision taking money from those above some arbitrary income level in order to give it to those below. Governor Carter has specifically stated that he will not eliminate the deductions for homeowners and for charitable contributions.

What Governor Carter *has* advocated is a tax system in which all taxpayers, including corporations, pay their fair share and which is simple enough so that the average taxpayer can fill out his own return. Presently we have a tax system in which numerous individuals and corporations with substantial income pay little or no income tax. Governor Carter is stating that if we are to continue to have broad public support for our tax system we must reform it to eliminate those abuses. The fact is that through such tax reform the goals of Governor Carter can be accomplished without requiring — contrary to Professor Fried's article — either that middle income people will have to pay higher taxes or that punitive tax rates must be imposed at the top.

No one can reasonably expect a complete tax reform plan to be developed during a political campaign. But Governor Carter has indicated the direction

3. Charles Fried, *Carter's Tax Program*, New York Times, Aug. 18, 1976, at 28. Charles Fried, the Beneficial Professor of Law, has taught at Harvard Law School since 1961, with breaks to serve as United States solicitor general (1985–1989) and as associate justice of the Supreme Judicial Court of Massachusetts (1995–1999). His wide-ranging scholarly interests include contracts, torts, constitutional law, and law-and-philosophy.

in which he would move as President by specifically proposing the elimination of certain special provisions, such as the deferral provisions which encourage our corporations to invest abroad rather than at home; the DISC provisions which provide a tax reduction for corporations to do what they would do anyhow, i.e., export their products to profitable foreign markets; tax shelters which wealthy individuals and corporations use to invest in ventures primarily for tax write-offs rather than the expectation of economic gain; and expense provisions which permit tax deductions for lavish entertainment and travel.

The essential point to be understood is that official estimates show that there are $100 billion worth of special tax benefit provisions in the tax laws. As indicated above, Governor Carter has supported the retention of certain of these. But there are many others which serve only special interests or no longer fulfill the purpose for which they were originally intended or meet needs which could be handled more efficiently through other means. The closing of these special provisions will indeed provide enough tax revenue to permit significant tax relief for low and middle income taxpayers.

The Ford Administration, on the other hand, eschews any interest in genuine tax reform. Thus, in this year's struggle for tax reform, the Administration defeated the effort to repeal the deferral of tax on foreign profits and the DISC provisions.

Instead of tax reform President Ford proposes tax reductions for corporations. He also proposes tax reductions for individuals, but unlike the reductions for corporations which are real, the reductions for individuals are illusory. Tax cuts which he says are designed for individuals are entirely offset by the repeal of existing tax benefits (specifically, the per capita tax credit and the earned income credit for poor working families) and by an increase in social security and payroll taxes. In fact, under Mr. Ford's proposals, working families earning up to $8,000 a year will actually lose money and be worse off than they are under present tax laws. This is tax reform in reverse.

The basic issue really is whether the public wants a just tax system. A Ford Administration cannot be expected to deliver on the promise of more equitable tax laws because it has never made that promise. Jimmy Carter has made tax justice in the form of a simpler, fairer tax system a major focus of his campaign and has pledged that a Carter Administration will deliver on that promise.

In September, W. Bowman Cutter, a Carter supporter, and former Rhodes Scholar, was asked to hold meetings to develop a detailed program in the tax field.[4] Cutter in

4. Economist W. Bowman Cutter served as executive director for the budget in the Office of Management and Budget from 1976 to 1981, and with the National Economic Council from 1993 to 1996. He has also been a partner in the accounting firm of Coopers & Lybrand (1981–1983) and managing director of the Warburg Pincus private equity firm (1996–2009). Surrey's typescript has a blank in place of "Rhodes Scholar" (the editors' best guess as to what Surrey had in mind).

turn asked Roger Altman (later to become Assistant Secretary of the Treasury for Domestic Finances) from a New York investment firm to help him.[5] They asked certain people to attend these meetings, such as Pechman and me, and others invited themselves. Neither Cutter nor Altman knew much about the tax field and the meetings roamed over many subjects without producing a specific program. The meetings were hardly helpful in charting a future course, though they did provide Cutter, who became Executive Director of the Office of Budget and Management with a background of the tax issues. In preparation, Pechman and I held a meeting on September 1, 1976, with a small group to produce specifics. Thereafter, various meetings were conducted by Cutter, with a shifting membership in attendance. Later Bowman, Pechman and I discussed possibilities for the position of Assistant Secretary for Tax Policy. I expressed the view that this person preferably should be a lawyer and not an economist since much of the day-to-day work and appearances before Congress involved matters closer to a lawyer's talents than to an economist. I would make an exception for Larry Woodworth, the Chief of Staff for the Joint Committee on Taxation, because of his familiarity with tax legislation and the Congress over many years.

I was in St. Croix in December 1976 when Larry Woodworth called me to say he was to be Assistant Secretary in the Carter Administration. He previously in the summer had told me he was about ready to leave government for an academic position. But Carter's election as a "tax reformer," perhaps the urging of the two tax chairman, Senator Long and Representative Ullman,[6] that he take charge, but more important the desire by Larry to be a crucial part of the tax action in a post with access to the President persuaded him to desire the position. Once that desire became clear in Larry's mind, the rest followed. Calls by Long and Ullman to the Carter circle, perhaps to Carter himself, settled the matter, for the request of the two most powerful Congressional persons in tax matters could scarcely be denied. I do not recall much earlier speculation on who should obtain the position, though I suspected Pechman desired it and had made his wishes mildly known. But no one could match Larry's credentials, his own record and his supporters.[c]

Larry was a savvy person with no ego problems. He knew his new position would be difficult — it always is — and he both wanted the best assistance he could get and he knew who could give it. He told me in his phone call that he had asked Jerome Kurtz, a lawyer in Philadelphia, who had been the Tax Legislative Counsel in the last

5. Investment banker Roger Charles Altman served as assistant secretary of the Treasury for domestic finances from 1977 to 1981, and as deputy secretary of the Treasury from 1993 to 1994. After his second stint at Treasury he co-founded Evercore, an investment banking advisory firm, of which he is currently senior chairman.

6. Albert Conrad Ullman (D., Ore.) was a member of the House of Representatives from 1957 to 1981, and chairman of the Ways and Means Committee from 1974 to 1981. His electoral defeat in 1980 — unusual for a powerful committee chair — was attributed by some to his support for a federal value-added tax. John T. McQuiston, *Al Ullman, Former Congressman, Dies at 72*, New York Times, Oct. 13, 1986, at A20.

years of the period when I was in the Treasury, to be Commissioner of the Internal Revenue.[7] For his top economist, a Deputy Assistant Secretary position, he had the acceptance of Emil Sunley, at Brookings but with experience in the Office of Tax Analysis in the Treasury when I was there.[8] For his top legal assistant, also a Deputy Assistant Secretary, he sought Donald Lubick, a Buffalo lawyer who had been the Tax Legislative Counsel the first years of my Treasury period.[9] And for Tax Legislative Counsel he wanted Daniel Halperin, a New York lawyer but earlier on the staff of that office whom I had asked to come to the Treasury.[10] These choices were wise and for me flattering since Larry wanted to put back in top Treasury positions persons I had earlier brought into the Treasury. Larry asked me to call Kurtz and Lubick to persuade them to accept their offers. Kurtz responded with enthusiasm, he really liked the idea of being Commissioner and I knew he obviously had the talents to be an excellent official. Lubick on the other hand was very negative about the offer. He thought, having been at the same level with Kurtz, he also deserved a Presidential appointment, which would not be involved in a Deputy Assistant Secretary position. Probably he also thought he was a logical choice to be the Assistant Secretary. But I talked at length to persuade him to leave aside these personal feelings and accept Larry's offer. I pointed out that the tax field had a high Presidential priority and also that Larry was not a person who liked to develop specifics and weave them into an overall program. Lubick as Deputy Assistant Secretary would have this task, so that he would be in a key post. Lubick finally agreed and came to Washington. When in Congress Larry often did not go over much material produced by his staff and made public. Also, his staff, knowing Larry's lack of or dislike for administration of an office, simply went ahead and held the conferences and did the studies thought advisable. In saying this to Don I was not intending to denigrate Larry's abilities, but

7. Jerome Kurtz served as Commissioner of Internal Revenue from 1977 to 1980. In later years he was first a partner in the Washington office of the law firm of Paul, Weiss, Rifkind, Wharton & Garrison, and then on the faculty of the New York University School of Law. His *New York Times* obituary notes that Surrey recruited Kurtz to Treasury in 1966 to work as tax legislative counsel, and that Surrey "had a major influence on [Kurtz's] philosophy toward tax policy." Emily Steel, *Jerome Kurtz, Leader of I.R.S. During Carter Era, Dies at 83*, NEW YORK TIMES, Mar. 3, 2015, at A25.

8. Emil M. Sunley served as deputy assistant secretary of the Treasury from 1977 to 1981, after which he became a principal with the accounting firm of Deloitte & Touche (and predecessor) (1981–1992), and later assistant director of the fiscal affairs department of the International Monetary Fund (1992 until retirement in 2006).

9. Donald C. Lubick served as tax legislative counsel in the Kennedy and Johnson administrations; as deputy assistant secretary for tax policy, and later as assistant secretary for tax policy, in the Carter administration; and as assistant secretary for tax policy in the Clinton administration. When not in government, he was (until his retirement) a partner in the Buffalo-based law firm of Hodgson, Russ, Andrews, Woods & Goodyear. The Donald C. Lubick Symposium Series of the Tax Policy Center is named in his honor.

10. Daniel I. Halperin is the Stanley S. Surrey Professor of Law, Emeritus, at Harvard Law School. Before coming to Harvard, he taught at the law schools of the University of Pennsylvania (1970–1977) and Georgetown University (1981–1996). He served at Treasury during the Carter administration, first as tax legislative counsel and later as deputy assistant secretary for tax policy. He has written extensively on the income tax treatment of retirement savings, tax-exempt organizations, and income tax timing issues.

rather to show Don the wide scope he would have to develop his own ideas and coordinate the Treasury staff. As fate worked out in a year he was Assistant Secretary after Woodworth died.

Clearly Larry had chosen his staff well. He had worked with each of them while he was in Congress and knew their talents and cooperative approach. The tax bar recognized that a competent, talented group was to be in the Treasury in the new Administration. The appointments were obviously pleasing to me, for my friends were now in the positions of control and my link to the Treasury was secure. Soon after taking office Larry and Lubick asked me to become a regular Treasury consultant, on a formal, public basis. So once again I was back in the Treasury on an official basis, changing from Assistant Secretary to an official advisor to the Assistant Secretary and his staff—and to friends of many years. We could talk frankly and easily with each other, and my efforts were directed to making Larry and his office a successful operation. The enthusiasm and morale of his staff were high, for they knew their principal task was to prepare in 1977 a tax reform program for a President that had promised tax reform. The new Treasury Secretary, W. Michael Blumenthal, was an intelligent person, presumably free from any fixed preconceptions regarding tax policy.[11] The President wanted a strong tax reform program and Larry had that program in his head. With spirits high, the group did not perceive that a cloud was forming that would affect their work.

President Carter had decided that his first major legislative program would be in the energy field. He developed this program by working almost in secret with his energy advisors. They made the decision to use the tax system as the vehicle to carry the program—tax credits for certain activities, a denial of deductions for other activities, and excise taxes on other activities [Check].[12] The energy advisors may well have been experts in the energy field but they certainly lacked a tax background. For example, their recommendation to use the tax system as the mechanism to achieve a non-tax program, adding more tax expenditures, was directly contrary to what was the necessary approach of a tax reform program, that of reducing tax expenditures and instead to use direct programs to accomplish desired goals and not the tax system. The energy program was shaped almost exclusively by the President and his energy advisors, and the Treasury was scarcely consulted. Larry learned of the proposed program shortly before its submission to Congress and could do little to improve it. Apparently, Larry did not resist the basic decision to use the tax system. He had not objected before when the House Ways and Means Committee itself in 1975 tried to

11. W. Michael Blumenthal served as secretary of the Treasury from 1977 to 1979. He had served in the State Department during the Kennedy and Johnson administrations. Immediately before his appointment as Treasury secretary, he was the chairman and CEO of Bendix International. Following his time at Treasury he served for a time as chairman and CEO of Unisys, after which he became a limited partner in the investment bank Lazard Freres & Co.

12. Exec. Office of the President, The National Energy Plan (1977). Although the plan relied heavily on both credits and excise taxes, it did not (contrary to Surrey's recollection) feature deduction denials.

use the tax route to solve energy issues, especially through tax regulatory measures such as a higher gasoline tax and a "gas guzzler" tax but also including tax incentives. While Larry may have thought that tax incentives complicated the tax system and were generally ineffective, he did not resist their use by the Committees. So Larry may not have been inclined to resist when the President in 1978 chose the tax route, both for regulatory and incentive measures. Perhaps Larry thought the die was cast so that advice to stay away from the tax system would be unacceptable and weaken Larry's effectiveness in the Administration. Larry may have thought he could, as the program went along, fix up its weaknesses just as he always had done before in the Congress when tax matters were involved.[d]

When the energy bill was in the committee stage in the House, the Administration pushed hard for the bill. This pressure left the Ways and Means Committee members in a tired state. Also, they had developed a negative attitude toward the Administration, an attitude engendered by what they regarded as a poor performance by Department of Energy personnel — inaccurate data for example — and ineptness of the Administration in its dealings with the members. In the Congress itself, the energy proposals had a divisive effect, setting liberals against conservatives on some issues and producing other divisions on other issues. The feelings induced by the energy bill tended to exacerbate the problems that various committee members were experiencing through other Administration decisions or reactions on matters in which they were involved. All in all, certainly the Treasury, as well as other observers, saw the atmosphere in the Ways and Means Committee "poisoned" by the events surrounding the energy bill. If tax reform had come first before the Committee, life in their view would have been different. But tax reform was not ready to come first and in any event the President perceived energy as his first major measure.

The damage done to a tax program by the energy proposals was not fully recognized in the Treasury, and work on the tax program proceeded at a hard pace. In April 1977, Larry called a major meeting of his entire staff, some non-Treasury persons, and representatives from the Congressional Staff of the Joint Committee. The purpose of the meeting was to obtain reactions from those not on the Treasury staff. Larry made it at once clear that he did have a grand design for a major change. He would propose, as one part of a package, "full integration" of the corporation tax with the individual income tax, by including directly in shareholder income the proper share of corporate income and ending direct tax payments by corporations. Accompanying this, in the name of simplicity, Larry desired to eliminate the special treatment of capital gains and then, as a counter-weight, reduce the top rate of tax to 50 percent.

Larry had talked with me about such a plan in the summer of 1976 when he was working on a capital formation study. I listened and then said that after announcing the plan — which presumably would have been while he was still the Chief of Staff — he could look behind him and find no one following him. Full integration was a dream goal of most economists but one yet to be adopted by any country. But Larry was entranced by this goal of the economists and more strongly by the concept of his entire package, which would of course become a major change in tax policy.

When Larry proposed at this meeting his idea of "full integration" both Pechman and I reacted negatively to the stress Larry was placing on this elimination of double taxation, which is the goal of any full integration plan. A discussion followed of "full integration," and also of "partial integration," which is really dividend relief since the tax status of dividends would be changed either by allowing a dividend deduction at the corporate level or allowing a shareholder a credit for all or a part of the corporate tax paid on the earnings behind the dividend but "grossing up the dividend" by the allowable credit. The business community was beginning to stress "capital formation" as the goal of tax reform, a goal that was only a third priority to the Treasury after the goals of equity and simplification. As a result of this approach of business, there was a discussion of integration in relation to capital formation, with views divided on whether or not greater capital formation would be induced.

After "integration" was examined, the group turned to a tour of what were the usual proposals made by tax reformers. If partial integration were sought, which meant lower taxes for upper-bracket shareholders — by far the largest group of shareholders — then the tax on capital gains should be increased by taxing such gains in full and also at death taxing as income any appreciation in the value of the decedent's assets. Both Pechman and I urged a strong, broadly ranging, overall program, which would give the Treasury room to maneuver once Congress started to work over the program. Larry seemed to be aiming for a somewhat less broad program closer to what he considered Congressional reaction would be.

As Treasury work on the program progressed, Larry became aware of a change that had occurred in the relationship between Treasury formulation of tax policy — or other policies — and White House review. Larry in taking his job probably had in mind the period when I was in the Treasury and he was working closely with me. Then, as he perceived, the Treasury led the way in the formulation of tax proposals and the White House usually concurred without much discussion. But in the succeeding years the White House had been moving to a larger role and in the Carter Administration this move was pronounced. Stuart Eizenstat, the able head of the White House policy staff, desired that Treasury at all times keep the White House consulted on the program it was developing.[13] This oversight function presumably stemmed from Carter's desire to immerse himself in the details of programs as they took shape. At one point he asked the Treasury for a list of all tax expenditures and what action the Treasury was taking on each one. Eizenstat had as his tax man Robert Ginsburg, a young lawyer, who did not have a tax background.[14] To strengthen the

13. Stuart E. Eizenstat was President Carter's chief domestic policy adviser from 1977 to 1981. His later positions have included deputy secretary of the Treasury (1999–2001) and U.S. ambassador to the European Union (1993–1996). He currently heads the international practice of the Washington law firm of Covington & Burling.

14. Robert Ginsburg served as associate director for tax policy (among other things) under Eizenstat in the Carter administration. A graduate of Harvard Law School, he came to Washington from the Wall Street law firm of Cravath, Swaine & Moore. Ginsburg's tax policy conflicts — based on "philosophical as well as personal differences" — with Treasury Secretary Blumenthal were so sharp as to be covered by the *New York Times*. Clyde H. Farnsworth, *Eizenstat is Helping to Fill a Vacuum*, NEW

White House capability to review Treasury proposals, in the spring of 1977 Eizenstat asked me to be a White House consultant on tax policy. He knew of my Treasury association, but considered it a plus since I would have complete knowledge of what was desired by each group and could explain one group to the other as I perceived a particular issue.

As a White House Consultant my main task was the education of Ginsburg. Ginsburg was a quick study and apparently had Eizenstat's confidence. He would go over the Treasury's proposals with me, have me explain both the proposals and their relation to the issues, talk over the suggestions he had in mind, encouraging some and discouraging others. Ginsburg's general motivation was for a very strong reform-pitched program, stronger than Woodworth or at times Lubick desired. This attitude stemmed from Eizenstat's views and they in turn reflected what Carter appeared to desire. I thus became almost an arbitrator, explaining the Treasury and its arguments to Ginsburg and then explaining Ginsburg to the Treasury. Thus our arrangement[15] was somewhat anomalous, but I had the confidence of the Treasury Staff and quickly also was fully trusted by Ginsburg.

Another force soon added an additional facet to my dual role. Senator Kennedy, a leader of the tax reform group in the Senate consideration of the 1976 Act, desired to push the Carter Administration on tax reform along lines he considered desirable. This was but one of the signs that Kennedy wanted to keep Carter hewed to liberal proposals and to work with him only as long as Carter had that approach. I had been an active advisor to the Senator in 1976, along with a colleague, Paul McDaniel of Boston College Law School. Paul was now advising Kennedy on this new 1977 program and, as we had worked together in the past, wanted to talk the program over with me. I informed Eizenstat of this request and he said I could also continue as an advisor to Kennedy's staff and McDaniel. Three hats—but all labelled "tax reform"! Kennedy announced his program in July 1977.[16] It was a strong program, based largely on McDaniel's approaches and not proposing any integration of the corporate and individual income taxes. It stressed tax relief to lower brackets, a tightening of preferences in the upper brackets, mainly as to capital gains and personal deductions (e.g., home mortgage interest, charitable contributions, state taxes), and an attack on tax shelters.

In the meantime Larry soon realized "full integration" would have only the support of academics. But with some integration as his goal he retreated to "partial integration." This was a really backward step in the eyes of many tax reformers, since it conferred distinct benefits to the upper brackets in view of their large shareholdings. Larry soon discovered two other problems with his partial integration proposal, which he coupled

---

York Times, Dec. 3, 1978, at F2. Events recounted by Surrey later in this Chapter suggest some reasons for the Ginsburg-Blumenthal animosity.

15. Surrey has "argument" here, but presumably "arrangement" was intended.

16. *Edward Cowan, Kennedy Presents His Proposals for Tax 'Reform',* New York Times, Jul. 2, 1977, at 7 (summarizing Kennedy's 41-page list of proposals, and noting that McDaniel was Kennedy's principal tax policy adviser).

with taxing capital gains as ordinary income. The package would not hold together. The business community was divided on integration, not at all sure it wanted even partial integration, unsure what such integration really involved, and what its effect would be.[e, 17] Moreover, there were many technical problems to be solved, more than had been anticipated.[f] The securities industry—investment houses and brokers—and the real estate industry were clear that they did not want an increase in the capital gains tax, even with the inducement of the fifty percent top rate. Another Congress could raise that rate but the concept that capital gains were just like other forms of income could well persist. Arguments based on "simplification" were certainly not the lever to move them from their position.

Larry also found that in devising a tax program he now had more actors to satisfy than when he was in Congress. In the Executive Branch there were other parts of the Treasury (e.g., on international matters), the Secretary himself, other Executive Departments, the Council of Economic Advisors, the White House Staff and, of course, the President. Larry's immediate task was to shape the program that could obtain consensus approval of all these actors. But Larry also kept looking ahead to shape the program so that it would be acceptable to his former masters, Chairmen Ullman and Long, and their Committees. Larry soon began to see the problems in satisfying both worlds. The pursuit of Congressional advance acceptance meant compromise in advance, perhaps a path congenial to Larry's style. But a President and a White House Staff intent on major tax reforms, because of the President's campaign commitment and his personal inclination, wanted bolder proposals and fewer compromises. The Secretary was somewhat in between, at first accepting major reforms—even Larry's key ideas earlier mentioned—but then moving away from a strong position as the business community raised its objections and the Secretary succeeded Budget Director Lance as the Administration's contact with that community.[18] Indeed, the role Larry appeared to undertake was not really doable in the larger scheme of things. Essentially the Assistant Secretary for Tax Policy must be an advocate for the President's views and programs. If too much is compromised at the start in anticipation of expected Congressional response, the President does not obtain the quality of advice or the maneuvering positions to which he is entitled and which he needs to have.

The Treasury in the summer of 1977, after considerable back and forth discussion with Ginsburg, formulated its initial version of a tax reform position. This development occurred in stages. First came a July 15, 1977, long memorandum to be used

17. For press coverage of the Business Roundtable proposals mentioned in Surrey's note e, *see* Deborah Rankin, *Business Executives Ask Tax Shift*, New York Times, Jul. 13, 1977, at D15 (stating that the Roundtable "was undecided about what method [of corporate integration] should be followed").

18. Georgia banker Thomas Bertram Lance served only eight months as director of the Office of Management and Budget, before resigning in response to allegations of financial misconduct. In 1980 a jury acquitted Lance of nine counts of bank fraud; the jury deadlocked on two other charges, and the Justice Department then dropped those charges. Robert D. Hershey Jr., *Bert Lance, Carter Adviser, Dies at 82; Accusations Cut Washington Stay Short*, New York Times, Aug. 16, 2013, at A21.

as a discussion paper with the White House and Council of Economic Advisors. It was a broad program, with reduced partial integration as one choice among others for business tax reduction, but also continuing the treatment of capital gains as ordinary income. After further discussion with Vice President Mondale and the Council of Economic Advisors, a full memorandum was sent to the White House on September 2, 1977. It contained an overall description of the program, the state of the economy, and the political situation. This was followed by nine "option papers," covering such subjects as treatment of low incomes, reduced tax rates and a working spouse exclusion, reduction in itemized personal deductions; capital gains and losses; tax shelters and preference income; taxation of transfer payments and treatment of the elderly; employee fringe benefits; the tax treatment of interest, including tax-exempt bonds; international taxation; business tax reductions (here including several alternatives, one of which was partial integration). Each paper had numerous subheads and for each proposal on which the Council of Economic Advisors or other departments had views, these views were fully stated along with the Treasury views. Each item contained at the end three lines—"Agree, Disagree, Want Further Discussion"—which were designed to be checked by the President. It was a formidable document, replete with estimates, lucid explanations, many charts, and was a distinct credit to the Treasury Department's efforts. As a Consultant I had reviewed the entire document, making my suggestions.

It is my understanding that the President did not fill in the lines. Early in October, a person with minor duties in Vice President's Mondale's office disclosed—probably by accident—the entire document to a lawyer who gave it to the press.[19] The BNA Daily Report for Executives of October 7, 1977, included the entire document as a "Special Supplement"—54 pages in small type.[20] This unfortunate September public disclosure of the Treasury's proposals contained in memoranda to the President, with pros and cons fully stated, was also a definite setback to the tax reform efforts.

At this point a period of confusion and uncertainty then prevailed.[g] When the energy bill came to the Senate in 1977, it immediately ran into serious trouble because the tax measures did not meet with the approval of the Senate Finance Committee. The Treasury's efforts on the legislative front therefore had to focus on attempts to rescue the energy program, although as stated earlier Treasury officials had not really been involved in its planning and disapproved of its tax focus. These rescue efforts of the Treasury tax officials in what was really a hopeless task adversely affected their general standing before the Congress and left the Administration in a weakened position when the Treasury later argued for its tax reform program. The travails of the

19. Surrey is a bit off on the details here. In fact, the leak occurred in late September. In a front-page story published on September 30, the *New York Times* reported it had obtained and reviewed all nine Treasury "tax reform option papers" and an "overview" document, all dated September 2; the story also described the highlights of the papers. Edward Cowan, *Treasury Strategy Ties Tax Cuts to Passage of Carter Reform Plan: But Confidential Memorandums Warn a Slump Could Make a '78 Reduction Necessary*, New York Times, Sep. 30, 1977, at A1.

20. BNA Daily Report for Executives, DER No. 196, Special Supplement on Tax Reform Option Papers Prepared by Treasury Department, September 2, 1977, for the White House (October 7, 1977).

energy bill also caused a serious delay in the work on that program and its submission to the Congress. This delay forced a decision whether a tax reform message and bill should be sent to Congress in 1977. If so, should it be a complete package or should the proposals be divided into two parts, a shorter bill for 1977 and the balance in 1978. Time was running short for Hearings and action in 1977, and many thought it was unadvisable to have Hearings in 1977 but postpone further action until 1978. A further complication was the belief by some that a tax cut was needed for macro-economic reasons, to stimulate a lagging economy. Should tax reduction be pushed at once, or separated from reform; for many the latter step was thought to be the end of reform. Also warning signals, some ominous, were being sent by the Congress.

In October when Lubick met with the "liberal" Members of the House Ways and Means Committee they indicated they would find it difficult to support major tax reform in 1978, an election year. The energy fiasco also played its part in this attitude. If the White House signal was to be full steam ahead in 1978, the bill would be clobbered. While there was talk of two bills, one in 1978 and one in 1979, this was not considered helpful. The tone of the meeting was "wait until 1979." Further, Bobby Shapiro, Woodworth's handpicked successor as Chief of Staff for the Joint Taxation Committee, said that Woodworth was not reading the Committee correctly—he was losing touch with it.[21] Senator Kennedy's office also thought that a bill should be postponed until 1978, but then it should be a really major bill and not a "Woodworth compromise." They believed a major bill could pass in 1978.

A conference in October between the Vice President, Eizenstat and Woodworth moved toward a decision to postpone a bill until 1978. It might be advisable to use the two-bill approach for 1978 and 1979, since the 1978 bill could be called the initial step towards fulfilling Carter's promise for tax reform. The drive for reform was losing adherents. Secretary Blumenthal, originally an adherent, was no longer enthusiastic. Eizenstat was shocked and upset by the attitude of the liberals on Ways and Means. The warning signals against tax reform were thus beginning to rise. But the President had called the tax system a "disgrace" and his promise to remedy that disgrace was regularly stressed in the media. Moreover, the President sincerely believed, perhaps more than any top official in his Administration, that there should be major reform. The decision was thus moving toward sending a respectable reform bill in 1978 and to follow that with another bill in 1979.

At Eizenstat's request I summarized my views on the entire situation in a Memorandum of October 21, 1977. Since the memorandum describes the pros and cons of the situation in some detail, and thus gives a picture of the decisions to be made, it is useful to include it in here.[22]

---

21. Bernard M. (Bob) Shapiro served as chief of staff of the Joint Committee on Taxation from 1977 to 1981. He is now retired after a long career with the accounting firm of Pricewaterhouse-Coopers.

22. The editors have shortened the block quotations from the two documents.

October 21, 1977

MEMORANDUM

OPTIONS RE TAX PROGRAM

I. MAJOR PROGRAM

A. Timing

...

In view of the many uncertainties that appear to be springing up regarding the scope of the 1978 tax program, it would seem desirable to postpone any announcement until January. At that time more will presumably be known about the variables involved—which variables we can now turn to.

B. Should There Be a Major Comprehensive Program in 1978?

...

Hence if the President decides to send a major comprehensive program, it is quite likely that the Congress would pare it down. This would then mean that under this approach there would be a Congressional decision as to what should be done in 1978 on tax reform and not a Presidential decision (unless the President is forced in the consideration of the bill to make that decision). The crucial point, however, is that if there is to be any "paring down" it must be done by the President and not the Congress. *The President must choose the battlegrounds.* (The opposite course is to say—"Here is my comprehensive program. The Congress wouldn't take it all. Blame them, not me." I would imagine this is not a desirable framework to proceed upon.)

It is necessary to consider options other than a major comprehensive program. One way of doing this is it to consider what tax action is needed in 1978.

II. NECESSARY TAX ACTION IN 1978

A. Tax Reduction for Economic Purposes

It seems likely that some tax reduction will be required in 1978 for economic purposes. This being so, the nature of the reduction must be decided. One consideration, of course, is what kind of reduction is appropriate to meet the "economic stimulus demands." A second consideration is the relation of the reduction to tax reform. Clearly, tax reform is aided if it can be accompanied by rate reductions.

B. No Tax Reform As Against Splitting Tax Reform

...

It would therefore initially seem unwise to grant tax reductions in 1978 without at the same time seeking some tax reforms. This seems a more limited program in 1978 but with the President making the initial decision on what are to be the "tax reform battlegrounds." This approach means doing some tax reform each year, having in mind a comprehensive goal and seeing what is achievable as we go along—taking into account timing, tax reduction aspects, desirable reforms. It would point to a considerable program in 1979, since there would be two Congressional years to consider the program.

III. LIMITED 1978 PROGRAM

...

As indicated above, the President, not the Congress, should control what the battlegrounds of tax reform will be in 1978. Before one can finally assess the advantages and disadvantages of a major program, no major program, or a limited program, it is necessary to see the appropriate shape of a limited program, so that the President can decide how such a limited program looks. It therefore seems necessary to have the Treasury immediately work on this matter with the White House Staff and develop appropriate alternative packages of tax reduction and tax reform. This course clearly reinforces a decision to postpone any recommendations until January. It is also necessary to have full coordination between tax proposals and the overall Budget proposals.

October 21, 1977

MEMORANDUM

TWO DESIRABLE REINFORCEMENTS FOR 1978 TAX REFORM

I. CONCRETE TREASURY EXAMPLES OF ABUSES

The Treasury must supply the President with concrete and dramatic examples of tax abuses or "tax disgraces." The President should be able to say "Let me point to the return of an individual or corporation with many thousands of dollars who has paid either no tax or a low amount of tax because of this or that aspect of our tax law. This must be ended, and I propose to end it by recommending" etc.

...

II. REDUCTION IN TAX EXPENDITURES

Consideration should be given to the President, stating in his 1978 Budget Message, that there should be a specific overall dollar reduction in tax expenditures accomplished in 1978. This is a way of expressing a target for tax reform to which the Congress can be held....

The White House decision was finally made to proceed with a two-part approach, a tax cut and reform bill in 1978 and a second bill in 1979. The Treasury in the winter of 1977 therefore turned to the task of restructuring the September overall program in an effort to produce a 1978 bill that would, hopefully, be palatable to the Congress while still being a credible compliance with the President's promise. Many thought, however, that this would be an impossible goal. Others though differently, including

Senator Kennedy's office which believed comprehensive programs should be presented. The Senator took this approach in a conference with Carter in December. Maybe this was a tactic to guarantee a strong 1978 bill.

At Ginsburg's request I then turned my activities, in separate discussions with both Ginsburg and the Treasury, to possible alternatives for a limited 1978 program. The press in November almost uniformly said that the tax reform plans were being trimmed; that Chairman Ullman was against a broad-scale package and that it could not pass Congress—he also muddied the waters by urging inclusion of integration, since for him this was a way to make his "mark" on the tax Code. The press gave prominence to testimony by Secretary Blumenthal to the effect that a tax-reform[23] program be dropped—the White House said those were "his personal thoughts" and reiterated reform would be a part of the 1978 program.[24] There was some confusion where Blumenthal stood, since he was the Administration's contact with the business community, which was pressing on him a no-reform of business preferences approach (e.g., DISC, deferral). The Treasury staff in November was unsure whether he was really ready to call off tax reform, or still would stick to it, but Woodworth and the White House were firm on staying with a tax reform course, and the White House was making the decisions.

A series of conferences between the White House, CEA and Treasury ensued in the confused process of making decisions on the contents of a January 1978 Message. Should "deferral" be included, what about capital gains, integration, decrease the corporate rate (Treasury) or raise the investment credit (CEA); to what extent and how should deductions for entertainment expenses be reduced; should withholding on dividends and interest be included (IRS said its data on this had not really been pulled together). Ginsburg thought the conferences were often too hasty and a matter of picking and choosing without a full consideration of the issues. He himself was generally on the side of "let's do more reform," especially as the upper brackets were affected. He complained to me that Treasury sent documents to the White House about 20 minutes before a conference so that there was no time to think about them. Ginsburg also thought that he should see material before they went to Blumenthal and became a Treasury decision. Countering these complaints was the Treasury's request that I keep Ginsburg under control and not press ideas that wouldn't hold in Congress. Ginsburg did add that Eizenstat was the best ally the Treasury had, and that they had a difficult client in the President. I did my best to advise both parties, but saw that Woodworth and Lubick, the latter especially, were keeping reasonably close to the White House thinking, and I conferred constantly with them on their changing plans for the program. But I did explain why Ginsburg desired the proposals and comments he was sending them, all in the direction of a tougher program.

---

23. Surrey has "tax-version" here, but almost certainly he intended either "tax-reform" or "tax-revision."

24. Thomas E. Mullaney, *Administration Fumbling and Uncertainty*, NEW YORK TIMES, Nov. 22, 1977, at 51.

Looking back at 1977 from Woodworth's view, as the year proceeded he felt more and more the obstacles and frustrations that kept arising.[25] The Congress, remembering its past successes in the role of leadership in tax matters, a role to which Larry was the major contributor, was not ready to yield power to the President, even a President of the same party. So Larry, now charged with serving that President, was in part a victim of his prior victories. The energy bill — really a tax bill — was in terrible shape in the Senate and had to be defended, even though Larry and the Treasury staff clearly saw its tax weaknesses. Here also the decision of the President, together with the steady movement of the Tax Committees to use tax measures to meet non-tax issues — a movement which Larry had not strongly resisted in his later years in Congress, or at least had tacitly accepted because of the interest of the Tax Committees in that approach — was now becoming one of his main problems.

The attempt to rescue the energy bill, poor as it was and with all its legislative floundering, became the President's number one goal. Larry thus had to cope with the energy bill — a task whose dimensions in time and detail he apparently underestimated at first — and also had to maintain his strenuous efforts to frame the tax reform program amidst a welter of conflicting advice and inputs from the Congress, the Treasury, other parts of the Administration, and the White House. This combined load was really becoming too heavy for Larry to carry in terms of his own physical energy and time. At this point, the tax reform program, supposed to go to Congress around October 1977 with Hearings in the House in the fall so that there would be ample time for the Congress to handle a large program, was postponed by Presidential decision. The postponement was a political judgment — and the proper one given the President's focus on energy — that presentation and defense of a tax reform program would hamper the rescue efforts on the energy bill. However, that postponement — combined with rising objections in Congress to a lengthy tax reform bill and opposition to the integration-capital gains-rate reduction package — meant that the tax reform program had to be cut back.[h] But at the same time in the President's view the program had to be sufficiently strong to permit him to assert compliance with his campaign statement that he would completely overhaul the income tax system and change it from being "a disgrace to the human race." While some voices in the Administration were even urging no program at all except a tax reduction — because of their feeling that tax reform might be a losing issue in the Congress and hence should be postponed — the President wanted a significant set of proposals.

So in late November 1977, when I last saw Larry, he was in a pessimistic and frustrated mood, so unlike his usual optimistic outlook. He was discouraged by the task of satisfying many conflicting interests, more than he had confronted in Congress, because of the separate positions of strength possessed by the differing interests in

25. In this paragraph and the following five paragraphs, Surrey borrows heavily from Stanley S. Surrey, *Tribute to Dr. Laurence N. Woodworth: Two Decades of Federal Tax History Viewed from this Perspective*, 32 NAT. TAX J. 227, 237–38 (1979).

the Executive Branch. The pattern of operation within the Administration and the relationship of the White House to the Treasury were quite different from the period of the 1960's and presumably Larry in deciding to shift to the Executive Branch had the previous situation in mind. In that period there was much more ready acceptance of the Treasury positions in the tax field and hence fewer conflicting forces within the Executive Branch.

The entire year had thus been a strain. Larry had been a man of the Congress and the Congress had been his world for 33 years, really his entire professional career up to 1977. He knew that world as well as anyone not a legislator can come to know it. But the Executive Branch was a different world, with its own operating processes, its own complex interrelationships, and its own mystique. Even within the Treasury—and also its relationship to the Internal Revenue Service—there was a wholly different set of relationships that had to be learned and understood. In addition, for Larry there was a larger staff to head. Moreover, to be really successful that staff had to be kept operating simultaneously at two levels. One level was the grappling with day-to-day events including the shaping of the tax reform program. The other level was the maintenance somehow of longer range research, for the process of tax legislation and change is never-ending and a Treasury to maintain leadership must always be as ready as foresight can permit.

The year of adjustment had therefore been hard on Larry and had taken its toll. The mood and outlook in November were somber in contrast to the bright and happy days that opened in 1977. More time was needed to work out the manner and style of adjustment that Larry essentially had to solve in the career change he had undertaken. But the time was not to be granted to him.

This stage of Larry's career abruptly closed with his sudden death on December 7, 1977, from a cerebral hemorrhage. Lubick held a meeting with his staff and me after the memorial service. The mood was sad and gloomy. Lubick suddenly had to make more decisions, carry the entire load vis-à-vis the White House and Congress.[i] He was now in charge for the Treasury with developing the altered program for 1978—a program planned to be announced eight weeks later. He had both the task of acquainting himself with issues and compromises that Woodworth had often largely been handling himself and of maintaining the morale of the staff. He, however, surmounted these problems and prepared the restructured program. The staff clearly recognized the new situation and gave their full support to him. Fortunately, Lubick and Eizenstat were close friends outside their official positions, and also Lubick and Blumenthal had a good relationship. By December 17 the program was in shape and the Treasury turned to the necessary documents: a Message from the President on his tax proposals, a short Fact Sheet for the Press and the public giving more data on each proposal, detailed descriptions and supporting analyses of the proposals, and then a briefing book for Secretary Blumenthal covering questions likely to be asked in the Hearings and providing the staff's experienced answers. This meant—I knew from first-hand experience—a really heavy workload compressed in a few weeks, and day and night work for the entire staff.

Lubick sent to me — I was still a Treasury Consultant — the drafts of the President's tax message as it progressed through its various stages. He also sent me the supporting documents. On all of this material I made, necessarily in quick fashion, my specific comments and often phrasing, and these were almost uniformly accepted.

The President sent his Tax Message to Congress on January 21, 1978, containing tax reform proposals and a revenue reduction.[j] The Message cut back on the suggested proposals sent the year before, a cut that was a recognition that the first stage bill (assuming there would be a second stage) could not carry too much freight. There were dropped the earlier proposals for integration; a working spouse deduction; a cutback in the deduction for personal interest, including mortgage interest; the taxation of capital gains in full (instead elimination of a minor aspect, as it then stood, the alternative 25 percent rate); adjusting capital gains for inflation; a reduction to zero of percentage depletion for hard minerals; taxation of scholarships except for the tuition element; revision of the treatment for the elderly; repeal of certain fringe benefit exclusions (e.g., group legal services, group life insurance); withholding on interest. The Carter Tax Reform has thus seen a second retreat. The proposals were now to be a two-stage affair, and some reforms were already being dropped. Yet the Program still contained a significant number of major reforms that could fairly be regarded as compliance, certainly a serious initial compliance step, with the President's promise to end the tax disgrace. Moreover, the Program had been fully discussed with Chairman Ullman, who had indicated its acceptability, and with other legislators.

With the Executive branch having formulated and presented its Program, the scene shifted to the Legislative branch. The subsequent events were dismal indeed for that Program. Senator Kennedy did compliment the President — a position the Senator had to take:[k]

> I am pleased to see that President Carter's Tax Program contains major recommendations for tax reform that will be a solid step toward the goals of equity, efficiency, and simplicity in the tax laws. The earlier reports that the President had abandoned his goal of comprehensive tax reform in favor of tax reduction are now proved untrue, and I welcome this firm restatement by the President of his commitment to tax reform....

But the Senator's release seemed to be the only upbeat note. The Wall Street Journal predicted the Carter Tax Plan would go through a major overhaul in Congress:[l]

> Jimmy Carter isn't going to recognize his tax package when Congress sends it back to him next fall.
>
> The cuts are going to be bigger than the net $24.5 billion the President has proposed. The cuts will look different in form as well as size. And the "reforms" are going to be far fewer than the score of revenue raising changes he is seeking.
>
> That is the burden of opinion among tax experts and politicians here. A minority believes, or hopes, that Mr. Carter can rally the country and Congress behind his complete tax package.

> But the majority, skeptical about the President's ability to lead and the country's willingness to follow, believes that the package will come apart—and soon.

That paper also reported that Chairman Ullman was opposed to some of the changes, and also wanted his "integration" proposal.[m]

The scene now moved to the Hearings before the House Ways and Means Committee.[n] At Hearings on tax reform there is almost a solid phalanx of opposition, especially from business groups faced with a loss of tax preferences, but including any group that is to be "reformed." Supporters of reforms—sometimes the AFL-CIO, but not when *its* preferences are under attack—and an occasional public interest group with few members—are but a handful. Yet this is expected by the Committee members and often rubs off. They are busy testing in their own ways how their affected constituents stand, how strong is the opposition of this and that group, what "reading" do they have on their fellow Committee members and other Congressmen.

Bob Ginsburg, always aggressive himself, was urging the Treasury to be more "aggressive" in building support for the President's program—meet with newspapers; see every Committee member; see if Robert (Bob) Brandon, Public Citizen's Tax Reform Group, a Ralph Nader satellite, who was a real expert on the day-to-day pulse of the Committee and Congress, can help;[26] get the White House—meaning Carter—to fight. Lubick knew all this himself and was doing his best along these lines, but his White House support was really not forthcoming—no major speech, no drum beats at press conferences. A Citizens for Tax Reform Group was formed and many of the names were important but overall it was woefully weak and unfunded.[o] The Treasury Public Affairs office was not very imaginative or working overtime—tax reform was not the Panama Canal. In March Bob Brandon gave Lubick his views on where the Committee stood and what should be done. This was good advice, but Don's staff was small and Don didn't have the time to hold each member's hand, though he did his best.

In this atmosphere of uncertainty and doubt, the House Ways and Means Committee met on April 7, 1978, to commence voting on the President's proposals. The matters first considered were thought to be among those easiest to move through the Committee. The votes, however, were all close and nearly entirely against the Treasury. Repeal of the sales tax deduction was defeated 19–18; an attack on tax shelter annuities lost on a voice vote; a Congressman Fisher[27] proposal, opposed by the Treasury, to allow a charitable deduction outside the standard deduction (i.e., not offset by the zero bracket amount) passed 19–18; the only Treasury position to prevail was the repeal of gasoline tax deduction by a vote of 21–16. The press

26. At the time Robert M. Brandon worked for Public Citizen, a consumer rights advocacy organization. He is now the president and CEO of the Fair Elections Center, a voting rights and election reform organization, the predecessor of which he co-founded in 2006.

27. Joseph L. Fisher (D., Va.) was a member of the House of Representatives from 1975 to 1981.

described these events as a "rout" and a disaster for the President's Program.[28] In the opinion of some observers, this view was too extreme. The votes were close; the members had not yet shaken down to serious work and were not viewing their votes in the same way as the press; the Treasury apparently hadn't "worked the Committee" sufficiently. The Treasury saw the picture in a somewhat different fashion: A number of the Members, including both Democrats and Republicans, each had their non-tax reason to be angry at the White House for its handling of other matters in which they were interested; Congressman Conable,[29] a moderate liberal and supporter of the Treasury, wanted to vote its way but as the ranking minority member he had to follow his fellow Republicans. Congressman Fisher did not expect his amendment to win, but the Republicans voted for it to embarrass the Democrats, and the lobbyists from the charitable organizations for the amendment were sitting right in front of the members — it was an open session. Lubick found the members reasonable, listening to his arguments and agreeing with them, but then voting the other way. The Committee was not taking matters seriously at this stage, and they also saw the White House was not "stroking them." Also, more serious, the Republicans were voting as a bloc so that the adverse votes by the conservative Democrats meant defeat for a proposal.

The press description, however, may have been a correct one. The Treasury had attempted to acquaint as many members as it could with the Program and the issues. But the Committee was a large one — thirty-seven members — and it was difficult to reach each member or always fully to discuss all the proposals. Also, some members were indicating, even before the Committee voting, that they did not want to listen and would not vote for any part of the Program. Brandon was giving very negative readings on various members and already looking ahead to see if the House floor would reverse some of the adverse Committee decisions. In any event, the defeats were serious and the press description had been made. As a consequence the Chairman postponed further consideration to allow the Treasury to regroup its political forces.[p] Indeed, Lubick, somewhat facetiously and yet realistic, said there was a reasonable chance of preventing a worse bill!

The chairman and other senior members told Carter at this point they thought the bill would fail. At the same time, the liberals on the Committee discussed with Carter retreating to a bill that just included a tax cut — this was not the right time for tax reform.[q] But Carter held to his program, keeping the reform proposals but later reducing the amount of tax reduction as economic condition improved.

At this point, however, a wholly new element — the capital gain mania — suddenly came into the open and rapidly overwhelmed all else. This story goes back to 1977.

---

28. *See, e.g.*, Edward Cowan, *Carter is Warned Tax Bill He Wants Won't be Enacted*, New York Times, Apr. 21, 1978, at A1 (reporting that three senior Democratic members of the Ways and Means Committee, including Chairman Ulllman, "outlined to the President the string of defeats his plan had suffered in committee").

29. Barber B. Conable (R., N.Y.) was a member of the House of Representatives from 1965 to 1985.

Many in the business community, and especially in the securities industry, had been seriously worried about the talk of taxing capital gains as ordinary income. They therefore began to organize to defeat that approach. The principal lobbying group that was girding for this battle was the American Council for Capital Formation, advised by Charls E. Walker, a skillful and experienced Washington hand.[r, 30] Allied with the Council was an electronics industry group, American Electronics Association. In 1977 these groups were fully ready to attack the expected change in capital gains treatment; their goal was to defend the status quo. Suddenly, with the abandonment of that change, these groups had no target. With lobbying weapons and plans but no enemy, the groups turned, in a truly brilliant lobbying maneuver, to the target of reducing the existing tax on capital gains. They induced Representative Steiger,[31] a Republican Ways and Means Committee Member, to introduce a bill restoring for all capital gains the maximum twenty-five percent rate that had persisted prior to the 1969 Act. That Act had limited the twenty-five percent rate to the first $50,000 of gain, producing a top rate of thirty-five percent on the balance (fifty percent capital gain exclusion combined with the seventy percent rate on unearned income). With subsequent changes in the minimum tax that top rate could be 39.875 percent, and theoretically, by combining minimum and maximum tax effects, 49.125 percent. The Steiger forces were thus able to point to this forty-nine percent rate and make much of the figure.[s] The Treasury 1968 Proposals had included the elimination of the twenty-five percent alternative rate appendage and a strengthening of the minimum tax, the latter producing a 42.5 percent rate on capital gains and, with the maximum tax, a possible 52.5 percent rate.[t]

At the start apparently no one, not even Representative Steiger, took his proposal seriously. The Treasury and the public interest tax reform groups were still concentrating on the Treasury's proposals. A number of factors, however, were beginning to coalesce; by June they would make capital gains reduction the main issue. Some Congressmen who had recently sold their residences at high prices and with resulting large capital gains found they were liable for the minimum tax. This was unexpected—that tax, they said, was aimed at "tax shelter types" and not people, like Congressmen, who sold residences. Also, many Congressmen had not fully recognized, in 1976, the effect of the minimum tax changes in that Act on the capital gains effective tax rate. As a result, when this effect became apparent in 1978, some may have felt that the earlier descriptions of the 1976 changes had not been as complete as they should have been in underscoring the effect on capital gains, so that the changes just "slipped by." Some well-to-do lawyers also complained about the capital gain "poisoning" of

---

30. Charls E. Walker served first as undersecretary of the Treasury, and then as deputy secretary of the Treasury, in the Nixon administration. (The spelling of the first name is correct; reportedly his mother dropped the "e" so that he would not be known as Charlie.) Following his time at Treasury he became a highly influential tax lobbyist, whose successes included the defense of the deductible three-martini lunch and the capital gains tax cut Surrey describes. Sam Roberts, *Charls Walker, Treasury Official and Business Lobbyist, Is Dead at 91*, NEW YORK TIMES, Jul. 1, 2015, at B14.

31. William A. Steiger (R., Wisc.) was a member of the House of Representatives from 1967 until his death in 1978.

the otherwise applicable fifty percent maximum tax on the income from their legal activities.[u] Here, also, some Congressmen thought the description of the 1976 proposals on the maximum tax had not fully indicated the impact on capital gains.

Business groups, largely representing the securities industry and medium and small business, circulated econometric studies indicating that a reduction in capital gain rates would actually increase revenues. Econometric studies always look convincing—they present endless numbers and tables and carefully omit or disguise their assumptions. The assumptions and models behind the studies are man-made and their construction—or manipulation—is but a reflection of the intellect, judgement, and biases of their makers. The computers simply grind out the numbers according to these human commands. Most of the capital gain studies circulated on this subject merely assumed, or used insupportable equations to demonstrate, that there would be large stock market price rises if the capital gains rate was reduced. Given this command, the computer estimates of revenue gains followed. But faced with this barrage of studies, many Congressmen began to believe that perhaps the results were correct. There was also the steady lobbying rhetoric that capital formation and jobs were needed and that capital gains reduction would make a major contribution to these goals. What went unsaid was that business groups, representing large corporations primarily, in 1977 in urging the President to propose tax changes to aid business—and capital formation—had not even considered capital gains reduction as relevant but had focused instead on corporate rate reduction, more accelerated depreciation, and a stronger investment credit. Nor did a 1977 Joint Committee Staff study on capital formation mention capital gains reduction.[32] The lobbying groups also urged that because of inflation capital gains were not real gains, here glossing over the fact that already fifty percent of a capital gain was excluded from tax.

Belatedly the Treasury saw that it faced a major problem in these multiple attacks on the capital gains rate. Its efforts changed from defending its own proposals to containing the attacks. But its own lobbying efforts and rhetoric were weak in comparison with the tactics and propaganda of the business groups. The President did call the drive for capital gains reduction a "rip-off" but did not do more.[33] The House leadership did not stress the "rip-off line" although that line of attack was fully appropriate, because all of the Steiger reduction went only to the upper brackets. The Steiger proposal provided a maximum rate of twenty-five percent. Thus, to get any benefit, a married couple would have needed a taxable income of around $50,000, which meant a gross income in excess of approximately $70,000.[34] Instead, the leadership allowed the slogans of venture capital, capital formation, jobs, and inflation

---

32. Joint Comm. on Taxation, Tax Policy and Capital Formation, JCS-14-77 (1977).

33. The editors have been unable to find any source for President Carter's use of "rip-off" in this context, but Carter did forcefully oppose the Steiger bill as offering "tax windfalls for millionaires and two bits for the average American." Edward Cowan, *Carter Assails Bills on Capital Gains Tax*, New York Times, Jun. 27, 1978, at A13.

34. Adjusted for inflation, these amounts are equivalent to a bit less than $200,000 and $280,000, respectively, in 2020.

to resound in the ears of the Congress. As a consequence, Chairman Ullman, faced with Committee votes to pass a Republican Steiger bill and desiring to have some bill reported, had to find a Democratic compromise. Hence the Jones bill, named after Democratic Representative James Jones of Oklahoma,[35] a Ways and Means member, was put hastily forth and accepted by Chairman Ullman before the Treasury had the chance to see if it could find support for a stronger bill. This bill removed capital gains from the minimum and maximum taxes and eliminated the alternative twenty-five present tax on $50,000 of gain, thus leaving a top thirty-five percent rate. The bill additionally excluded a one-time $100,000 of gain on the sale of a residence. Also, a weak alternative minimum tax aimed only at capital gains in unusual situations was included to prevent situations in which no tax at all would be paid.

Considering the capital gain storm stirred up by the lobbying forces, the Jones bill was not too great a retreat, and certainly was far better than the Steiger proposal. Suddenly, however, the bill took a new turn. Representative Archer,[36] a conservative Republican, moved to "index" the basis (cost) of a capital asset by increasing that basis in accordance with the extent that the price level had increased since the time the asset was purchased. The revenue cost and further favoritism to the wealthy were obvious. A few liberals, however, without forethought and in an unplanned step, supported the amendment. Their strategy was to make the Jones bill look so bad that it would be defeated by the House. Over the opposition of Chairman Ullman and Representative Jones the indexing proposal was adopted, with a motion to reconsider losing, 19–18. When the bill was debated on the House floor this indexation step was retained by a 249–167 vote. The Treasury in a last minute effort to cut back on the capital gains reduction strongly supported a Corman-Fisher proposal for a stronger minimum tax on capital gains, but this proposal came too late. The entire bill was adopted and the indexation, designed to defeat the bill, was now a major element of the bill.

The House bill was almost bare of reforms: repeal of state and local gasoline taxes; phased-in taxation of unemployment compensation; extension of the tax shelter "at risk" rules, were the major items. New tax expenditures were added: a targeted jobs credit that expanded the existing credit; extension of the investment credit to rehabilitation of commercial and industrial buildings and pollution control facilities. The floor debate did not produce changes in the Committee bill.

The tax show moved now to the Senate, with the customary Hearings and then Senate Finance Committee votes. The Treasury was in a quandary in the Senate. It did not want the Jones bill and it certainly did not want indexation. The scene was thus set for maneuvering by Chairman Long of the Senate Finance Committee, and

35. James R. Jones (D., Okla.) was a member of the House of Representatives from 1973 to 1987.

36. William R. Archer (R., Tex.) was a member of the House of Representatives from 1971 to 2001, and chairman of the Ways and Means Committee from 1995 to 2001. As chairman he was a determined foe of the very idea of an income tax, frequently proclaiming that the income tax should be "torn out by its roots." Clay Chandler, *Archer Calls for End to Income-Based Tax*, The Washington Post, Jun. 6, 1995, at D1.

he as usual moved skillfully to take advantage of the opportunity. In effect, he said he would work to remove the indexation and thus get a "better" capital gains bill than the House had passed, but he had to do something about the capital gains rate because a majority of the Senators were on record as sponsoring the Steiger proposal. Chairman Long's proposal here was a seventy percent exclusion, together with no application, as in the House, of the regular minimum or maximum taxes to capital gains. This seventy percent exclusion was a larger reduction than the Steiger proposal, for it meant a top rate of twenty-one percent and, more important, gave every taxpayer who had a capital gain some reduction. This Finance Committee bill then passed the Senate. Chairman Long's position prevailed, though an "alternative" minimum tax was included, a substitute for the current "add-on" minimum tax, which included the items that had been under the "add-on" tax.

Probably the Treasury felt that Chairman Long's increase in the capital gain exclusion and the elimination of indexation were not tied together. Since the President was strongly opposed to indexation, the Treasury believed it just had to be dropped and hence its elimination was not a quid pro quo. The Treasury may have seen the Senate bargaining as being that of an increased capital gains exclusion or no bill at all. The Treasury also had its sights fixed on trying to obtain as strong an alternative minimum tax applicable to capital gains as it could possibly extract. Other observers, however, saw the situation as one where Chairman Long could obtain some leverage through insuring that indexation would be eliminated in the Senate bill.

The reform proposals received a fate similar to that in the House, with the recommendation on phased-in taxation of unemployment compensation even being dropped. Repeal of the gasoline tax deduction survived only because of an unusual parliamentary situation. Instead, as is its habit, the Senate Committee added a sizable number of new, important tax preferences plus many minor pieces of legislation.

Clearly the President was faced with a dismal prospect in the Conference Committee. The House had less of a capital gains reduction than the Senate bill, but it contained indexation. The Senate bill eliminated indexation but contained a larger capital gains reduction. The "liberal" maneuver in the Ways and Means Committee thus completely backfired and did limit the President's options. Without the indexation, he could at least have said he would accept no reduction beyond the House bill. With indexation, he was more vulnerable to pressure from Senator Long. The President at this point had to decide whether he wanted a tax bill at all, and if so, if he was willing to pay the price of a sixty percent capital gain exclusion, the likely Conference compromise on the level of exclusion. Indeed, even before this a large part of the Treasury maneuvering in the Senate appears to have been based on the belief that the President did want a tax reduction, and hence a tax bill, for fiscal policy reasons, and would pay the sixty percent exclusion price. Perhaps, if he did not want to pay that price, the President could have firmly said no indexation and no more reduction than the House bill and then taken his chances. He might have succeeded, or on the other hand, Chairman Ullman might have retreated from the House position, or Chairman Long might have stalemated the conference. In any event, the

President did not take that position. Instead, as was expected by the Senate, the seventy percent exclusion was reduced to sixty percent and indexation was dropped. The top capital gains rate was thus twenty-eight percent and for brackets below the top the rate was reduced because of the sixty percent exclusion. The capital gain lobby had in a sense done even better than the Steiger proposal.[37]

As to tax reforms that survived, they resembled only the palest reflection of the President's message. The survivors from that message were the repeal of the deduction for gasoline taxes; the phased-in taxation of unemployment compensation (starting at $25,000 of income for married couples); extension of the anti-tax shelter "at-risk" rules; denial of a deduction for entertainment facilities, but not the other entertainment recommendations in the Message.[v] Moreover, a number of the new preferences inserted by the Senate Committee and in floor debate survived: a doubling of the tax credit for political contributions; increased depreciation through adding to the existing ADR method; a targeted jobs credit; the recognition of "cafeteria plans" for fringe benefits; an exclusion from employee income of educational assistance received under an employee plan; plus a number of minor matters. The Treasury was able to persuade the Conference to drop some of the other minor matters.

The President had one decision left—whether to accept the bill or veto it. On the merits it did rate a veto: it adopted hardly any of his own Program. Instead, the taxation of capital gains was in effect moved back to the pre-1969 stage, thus wiping out the 1969 and subsequent reforms. As a consequence, this was the first bill in recent history to provide a very large tax reduction for the wealthiest group of individuals in the country, those with incomes exceeding $200,000—a reduction larger in percentage of present tax than for any other group except taxpayers below $10,000. But the President was probably the only top Administration official really to think in veto terms. He may have been concerned about the absence of tax reform and the capital gains setback. Or, perhaps, he may have shifted his judgment on fiscal policy and thought that fiscal restraint and not revenue loss was the proper macroeconomic policy, although his economic advisors were still holding to the need for a tax reduction. His top advisors, however, all urged signature, focusing on the tax reduction in the bill—which, however, could have in all likelihood been obtained in a quick later measure; on the probably adverse effect, stressed by even some of the liberals in Congress, on some Democrats in the election close at hand—though the action on the bill could have come after the election, an aspect apparently not realized by the President's advisors when they were sounding Congressional sentiment; on the likelihood that Secretary Blumenthal had in various ways signaled that the sixty percent exclusion would be acceptable to the President (as it was acceptable to the Secretary although he thought the change inefficient from the standpoint of encouraging capital formation) and the President had not strongly spoken out against that result; and on the mere fact that a tax bill had been passed. We can only speculate

37. For the capital gains partial exclusion, as enacted, *see* Revenue Act of 1978, Pub. L. No. 95-600, §402, 92 Stat. 2763, 2867.

on what would have been the consequences of a Presidential veto, based on the defects of the bill. There are some close observers of the Congressional scene who believed a veto would have strengthened the President's standing, certainly in the tax committees and also in the Congress itself.[w]

The President signed the bill, quietly and without fanfare, on November 6, 1978 (announced on November 7), later saying it was a better bill than either the House bill (indexation again!) or the Senate bill (sixty percent instead of seventy percent exclusion).[38] The President made the final decision, without advance notice to his staff or the Treasury, saying in an October 26 Florida campaign speech that he would sign the bill.

In sum, the President accepted a major defeat in the capital gain area. It was a defeat that perhaps could have been avoided with more firmness and advocacy on the Administration's part.[x] It was also a defeat that occurred as a result of some bad breaks in the day-to-day legislative processes. Further, it was a defeat that demonstrated the heightened strength and skillfulness of the lobbying efforts conducted by business groups,[y, 39] efforts that not only produced the capital gains result but also defeated other proposals of the President that were serious targets of business lobbying, such as those relating to entertainment deductions, DISC, and deferral of tax on foreign subsidiaries. Some, however, read the 1978 capital gains scene as revealing a serious concern for capital formation, a concern for inflation,[z] a demonstrated sense of overtaxation, a more conservative Congress that reflected a swing to the right in the electorate, and a belief that the tax reduction would really result in more revenue.[aa, 40] Others may have read the 1978 scene more along the lines I suggest, and believed the capital gains defeat was a combination of legislative incidents, inadequate Administration tactics, Congressional weariness from the energy bill—it took their time and energy—and inadequate utilization of the clout that an Administration can exercise.[bb]

Whichever way the capital gain aspect is read, however, there remains the need to explain the defeat of almost the entire tax Program of the President. The year 1978 was not the year for tax reform. Those who had advised this view from the start were the correct prophets. Perhaps a tax bill confined only to rate reduction with no tax reforms would, in retrospect at least, have been the wiser course, and might well have avoided the additional preferences that were in the final measure. While a bill without tax reforms would have meant an unfillment of the Carter promise for tax reform, there was always the choice to say that it would come the next time. On the other hand, the Carter proposals, both those that were in the September 1977 document that became available to the public and in the President's Message, did put on record

38. Terrence Smith, *Bill Cutting Taxes is Signed by Carter*, NEW YORK TIMES, Nov. 8, 1978, at A17.

39. *People and Taxes*, which Surrey cites in his note y, was a monthly periodical published by the Public Citizen's Tax Reform Research Group. The editors have been unable to locate the issue Surrey cites.

40. The editors have been unable to locate the source cited in Surrey's note aa; it does not appear in the complete list of publications of Martin Feldstein at https://scholar.harvard.edu/feldstein/publications.

a rational set of reform measures that could remain as future targets. For the same reason, Senator Kennedy, who fought strongly for reform in the Senate, made a lengthy statement in September 1978 describing the reforms he thought should be made.[cc]

The 1978 push for tax reform ended in the burial of tax reform.[dd] Would the year have been different if Larry Woodworth had lived? We can put the question and only guess at the answer. My own guess is that even Larry's skills would not have changed the turn of events. Perhaps a slight success on this or that proposal, perhaps, even though I doubt it, slightly less of a setback in the capital gains area. But the events of 1978 and the mood of the Congress would, I think, have dragged Larry down along with the others.

Obviously the Congress of 1978 was not the Congress of 1976. The 1976 Congress had an interest in tax reform. The 1978 Congress had no interest in tax reform and readily allowed itself to be pressured by business lobbying. Clearly that lobbying, as noted above, has gained in strength and skill. But the real questions go to whether the individual members of Congress have changed in their perceptions of their job and in their attitudes on policy questions. Some observers say a marked change has occurred: the new members are non-ideological, see their role primarily as ombudsmen, regard themselves as "independent" which can be further translated into first seeing which way the wind is blowing and then acting. But the direction of the wind very often depends on the strength and attention of pressure groups, be they business, labor, local, or environmental. If one pressure group is pushing hard, the careful, watch-out-for-myself course may be to satisfy that group. If several pressure groups are competing, the course then is to see which group is the most threatening. Often it is the group whose financial support may be important, because Congressional campaigns are expensive and well-financed opponents are always a threat. Usually this means that business groups, associated with Political Action Committee financing, can command the most attention.

If this description of Congressional attitudes is to be given credence, then we must ask whether the tax committees are in a position to give guidance and shelter to the general membership. Here, however, one gets the impression on the House side of a closely divided large committee which the Chairman has difficulty in leading to any particular conclusion especially under the procedure of "open" mark-up sessions that is now required. On the Senate side, the Chairman generally is in control but the Committee is probably more conservative than the Senate and may even become more conservative than the Chairman would like. Beyond the Committees are their staffs. In the present confused situation, however, staffs such as the Joint Committee Staff must operate with caution, for there are traps everywhere—a push for this Member's proposal will offend another Member. Moreover, Committee staffs must deal with the staffs of members and this proliferation of people with widely different goals makes orderly central staff activity quite difficult.[ee]

Some informed observers have provided their insights on the defeat of tax reform: thus, they say, once Blumenthal succeeded Burt Lance, who resigned as Director of the Office of Budget and Management, as the Administration's "contact" with the business community, his enthusiasm for tax reform dampened considerably. While many Congressmen thought the capital gains change was a "rip-off," they were worried about the business lobbying talk of "jobs," "venture capital" and "capital formation," all well selected slogans that can cause a Congressman to wonder, "Well, maybe they are right, and I don't want to risk an adverse vote." The President, it was said, sincerely desired tax reform, but he worked by taking an absolute stand at the start, then didn't do much to explain his stand or push for it, and then as reality set in with business and Congressional opposition, he backed off with the urging of a conservative, politically minded White House Staff, excepting Eizenstat and Mondale, who argued for "a bill at any cost." Chairman Ullman, fundamentally a conservative, was not either inclined or strong enough to fight hard against the capital gains proposal in the House, and supported the Jones proposal because he had to have a bill, since not to do so would be a slap at him as Chairman. The indexation feature came at the last minute, with no time for discussion. Also, Ullman sometimes saw himself as a thoughtful person whose role was to think about the "big picture" and push for new matters of importance for tax policy as he saw tax policy, such as a VAT or integration.

Tax reform had not been made a sufficiently serious issue for the public, so that a Congressman did not have the fallback argument to use when business lobbyists pressed hard: "I can see your arguments but the President has taken such a strong public stand on this and my constituents really regard tax reform seriously, so that I must vote for the tax reform." Instead, a vote against tax reform was not seen as a dangerous course; the stakes had not been raised high enough by the Administration. "Fairness" and "equity" in the abstract are considered by the public as desirable goals, but unless education by an Administration desiring tax reform explains the specifics and how they affect reform, the opponents of reform have a much easier task. Also, the wire services do not operate to acquaint local newspapers on how their Congressman or Senator voted on a particular tax reform issue, so that often there was no local accountability and a Senator regarded back home as a "liberal" could vote against a tax reform without their knowing back in his state.

One thus leaves the history of the 1978 Act with the sense that in the tax area—and most likely in other respects—the legislative process was almost out of control by 1978.[ff] The Administration could not control events; the House Tax Committee was too divided to control events and the Senate Tax Committee probably too conservatively inclined to provide full leadership; and the staffs were not sufficiently positioned to present acceptable guidance. There was a sort of "in the doldrums" atmosphere hanging over the tax scene. All of this makes predictions as to the future whatever their source—Congressional, Administration, or outsider—not very reliable.

A look ahead shows this unreliability. The 1981 Act under the Reagan Administration was the most dismal measure in tax history,[41] replete with new tax expenditures, individual rate reductions that favored the upper brackets and went too far in general,

41. Economic Recovery Tax Act of 1981, Pub. L. No. 97-34, 95 Stat. 172.

corporate tax changes that in effect eliminated the income tax on new investment in structures and machines.[gg] However, under the pressure of the need for additional revenue to reduce large deficits, the 1982 Act then swung the other way to both reduce some of the 1981 provisions and also add some positive reforms.[42] But a discussion of these years would take us too far ahead. And I was *not* a Treasury Consultant or a White House consultant in the Reagan Administration!

A large part of my time in 1977 and 1978 was spent on the Carter program and the 1978 legislation. Both Lubick and Ginsburg kept me advised, sometimes almost daily, and I responded by phone calls, memoranda, and meetings. A part of the task was to keep Lubick's morale, and that of his staff, from ebbing away. But Lubick by nature is cheerful and resilient, accepting blows whose origin he readily understands, and looking forward with hope to the next battle.

My work for the Treasury and White House involved other subjects, especially in 1979 and 1980. The nature of the work depended on whatever was a Treasury concern at the moment and the formulation of plans for future activity. The focus of the activity varied, sometimes legislation which the Treasury was pushing and legislation it was opposing; sometimes Regulations; sometimes international tax matters such as tax treaties; sometimes dealing with the White House.

One example of the White House attitude was the Administration's position on proposals of the Department of Energy for a second energy bill. That Department was still pursuing the use of tax solutions rather than direct, non-tax measures. Thus, it was urging acquiescence in the efforts of some Congressmen and its own staff to secure tax credits for such matters as wood-burning stoves, solar energy for houses built to face south, and other similarly picayune activities. Lubick and Ginsburg asked me to see Eizenstat to explain just why the use of tax credits as solutions to problems not in the tax field was undesirable. I did so and at least persuaded Eizenstat to see the merits of my position. Ginsburg later told me that while Eizenstat used my arguments in White House conferences, he ended by following a political path to use tax credits to win over Congressmen not liking the Administration's decontrol policy.[hh] Ginsburg regarded the White House acceptance for the tax credits pushed by the Department of Energy as occurring in a "panic atmosphere" with the President susceptible to Secretary Schlesinger's worries and proposals.

I had sent Eizenstat a memorandum on "The Choice Between Direct Programs and Tax Expenditures" in an effort to strengthen Lubick's opposition to the energy credits. While Eizenstat intellectually accepted the views in that memorandum he too could be swayed by a "political judgement." I then in effect reproduced the memorandum as an article in Tax Notes, without indicating its origin.[ii]

The agendas for the Office of Tax Policy for each year were initially prepared by Lubick and then discussed by me. They show, as would be expected, a large number of issues, some major and some minor, some that did arise and others that did not

42. Tax Equity and Fiscal Responsibility Act of 1982, Pub. L. No. 97-248, 96 Stat. 324.

eventuate. To be added to these agendas were unforeseen matters that arose through Congressional or Administrative actions. It is sufficient here to describe some of the major matters, not in any particular order of importance.

Carryover Basis. Perhaps the most frustrating legislative act, apart from the 1978 provisions, related to "carryover basis." Under early provisions of the Code when a decedent died any appreciated assets received by his estate on his death obtained a basis for future sale equal to their market value on the date of death rather than the original cost of the assets to the decedent—hence the "stepped-up basis." Thus the pre-death appreciation in value escaped the income tax entirely when the assets were sold by the estate or the heirs. The resulting escape from tax was a generous windfall to the family, and the amount of revenue thus lost was quite large. This Code provision was considered by tax reformers as a principal target for reform. The history of their efforts is long and sad.[43]

In a 1959 statement to the Ways and Means Committee on Tax Revision[jj] I said that consideration should be given to taxing unrealized capital gains at death. That matter did not sit well with the Senate Finance Committee when it came up at my confirmation Hearings.[kk, 44] In 1963 the President in his Tax Message did recommend that such unrealized gains be taxed.[ll] Chairman Mills did not favor the proposal but did favor a "carryover" of the decedent's basis, so that on a sale by the estate or the heirs the appreciation would then be taxed. This carryover approach was a second-best solution, but it would have meant an improvement over the existing law. The Committee adopted this carryover proposal on May 28, 1963, and again on August 7, 1963. On August 26, 1963, the Chairman suddenly reversed his position on the carryover approach and the Committee unanimously agreed to drop the entire subject. The Treasury believed that this change in viewpoint was due to considerable opposition expressed by lawyers to various members of the Committee, including a persuasive appeal by a Chicago lawyer to the Assistant Chief Counsel of the Committee. There was also a feeling, undoubtedly correct, that the provision would not survive in the Senate. Secretary Dillon, in a major speech on the tax system made just before he resigned, stressed the importance of the original proposal to tax unrealized gains at death. At this point the matter pretty much dropped from sight.[mm]

In 1976 as a result of a complex legislative situation, a "carryover" provision was adopted in the 1976 Act.[nn, 45] But then came the counterreaction of the bar and an assault on the provision. The bar's first success was in 1978 when Congress deferred the effective date of the provision until 1980.

---

43. For the details of that long sad history, *see* LAWRENCE ZELENAK, FIGURING OUT THE TAX: CONGRESS, TREASURY AND THE DESIGN OF THE EARLY MODERN INCOME TAX 83–99, 110–125 (2018) (describing both the origins of carryover basis at death and the failed reform of 1976).

44. The questioning on this matter from Robert S. Kerr (D. Okla.) goes on for several pages in the transcript of Surrey's confirmation hearing; Kerr is clearly hostile to the idea of taxing capital gains at death.

45. Tax Reform Act of 1976, Pub. L. No. 94-455, § 2005, 90 Stat. 1520, 1872 (codified at former IRC § 1023).

The burden of defending the provision fell on Lubick. His first step was the suggestion of changes to meet the complaint that the provision had been drafted too hastily, and raised record keeping problems and other technical matters. After the 1978 deferral, Lubick reviewed his proposals for a technical clean-up, and at my suggestion included examples of the very large appreciation in value that occurred for some wealthy taxpayers. Typically these situations involved the purchase of stock for a small amount and then a holding of the stock over a period of time in which the corporation whose stock was involved grew and expanded.[oo] These examples should at least have persuaded the Committee that a serious tax preference was involved. But the bar simply sidestepped the equity question and stuck to technical objections often disregarding the clean-up suggestions. Gradually this opposition picked off one Senator after another and in 1980, as a result of Senate action in 1979 followed closely by the House, carryover basis was repealed[pp] in the Crude Oil Windfall Profits Tax of 1980.[46] This resort to a "rider" provision on an unrelated major tax measure prevented a Presidential veto, which would not have been the case if the repeal was contained in a separate bill. However, the groundwork for repeal had been so strongly established that a veto could well have been overridden.[qq]

The record of this assault by the bar is a sad one, illustrating that when the chips were really down, the bar did support a provision — step-up in basis — that surely most lawyers, if they had resorted to objective contemplation, would agree was inequitable. Instead they resorted, often overreacting and exaggerating, to their "expertise as technicians" and as a result forcefully gave a one-sided picture to the Congress. I shared Lubick's hopes and worries during the entire legislative consideration of the issue, feeling as strongly as he did that the carryover basis, even though a second-best approach, should be retained. Together we saw the hopes gradually but steadily become worries and then defeat. I do not think we overlooked any available approach, either in substantive presentation or Congressional contacts, but defeat nevertheless came because the concerted opposition was formidable and was clever enough to bury the tax equity issue under a huge mound of testimony on the technical aspects.

Housing Mortgage Bonds. A successful venture involved housing mortgage bonds. Its history shows the indefatigable efforts of ingenious persons — here investment companies — to search out and then exploit any weakness in tax legislation that they can turn to their advantage. In 1968 Congress greatly restricted the use of "industrial revenue bonds," so styled because they were state and local government bonds where the principal of a bond would be used to benefit a specific industrial concern. For example, in one variant of the mechanics, if a concern desired to obtain a new plant a state would borrow funds through a tax-exempt bond issue, have the plant built according to the needs of the concern, and then the concern would "rent" the plant for the exact amount needed to pay the interest and amortize the principal of the bonds, as would have been the case of a traditional state obligation backed by the general revenues of the state, such as a road project. In these industrial bonds, the

46. Crude Oil Windfall Profits Tax Act of 1980, Pub. L. No. 96-223, § 401, 94 Stat. 229, 299.

state was passing on the benefit of its tax-exempt status to the private company—compared with the rate at which the company would have to borrow if it issued a taxable bond—with the reduced costs reflected in the "rent." The 1968 legislation restricting the use of these bonds provided for certain exceptions, such as airports, certain public utilities and the like. One exception was for "residential real property for family units."[rr] At that time the only bonds issued for that purpose were those issued by state housing finance agencies for multifamily rental housing and these bonds were the intended coverage. In 1978, however, an investment company (__________) sold some municipalities on an interpretation of the 1968 language to include so-called "mortgage subsidy bonds" to finance single-family home mortgage loans.[47] A local government would borrow funds by issuing tax-exempt bonds and then relend the funds, through a private lending institution, to individuals for home mortgages bearing interest rates which, because of the lower interest cost on the tax-exempt bonds, could be fixed below normal mortgage rates. Soon the issuance of these bonds began to sweep across the country. Obviously, the use of these bonds would result in a major—very major—federal housing program to subsidize mortgage rates, completely by-passing an existing modest HUD direct grant program.

The Treasury rapidly perceived the two problems involved: One was the unforeseen development of an unauthorized federal housing program on a vast scale; two, the mechanism to be utilized, that of tax-exempt bonds, would involve a very significant revenue loss for the Treasury and, as a concomitant, a windfall to upper-bracket taxpayers purchasing the bonds, which is always the end result when tax exempt bonds are used.[ss] After Lubick's office studied the matter, the Treasury recommended that the tax exemption for these bonds should be ended. If HUD desired more funds to assist families to borrow through a home mortgage, then HUD should seek a direct grant program, and not acquiesce in the new tax expenditure route. The Congress was itself concerned over the rapidly rising revenue losses these bonds involved, and some states and localities worried over a likely rise in interest rates paid by them on general revenue bonds that could result from a significant increase[48] in tax-exempt bond available to purchasers. The House Ways and Means Committee held hearings in 1979 on the Treasury proposal.[tt] Of course there were many defenders of these bonds: the issuing authorities themselves, the Conference of Mayors, the National League of Cities, the Public Securities Association whose members participated in 90 percent of new municipal securities, the National Association of Home Builders. There were also some defenders of the Treasury: the U.S. League of Savings Associations; the Mortgage Bankers Association of America. In the end an interim temporary compromise, favorable to the Treasury,

47. According to Donald Lubick, a few state agencies began to issue bonds to finance single-family homes in the early 1970s, but the growth of mortgage subsidy bonds "was rather slow until about 1977 and 1978, when it exploded." Lubick does not mention any particular investment company (or anyone else) as the source of the idea. *Tax Treatment of Mortgage Subsidy Bonds, Hearings Before the Comm. on Ways and Means, House of Representatives*, 96th Cong. 1st Sess, Part 1, 6 (1979).

48. Surrey has "interest" here, but presumably "increase" was intended.

resulted: serious limitations were placed on the amount of such bonds that could be issued and the families who could qualify for the lower interest loans. However, all such lending should end after 1983.[uu] The Treasury was the victor, because Congress perceived the revenue stakes were too large to permit the unrestricted use of these bonds. They also recognized the distortion of the 1968 exemption for housing bonds. But the 1983 termination date was seen as a prelude to the next legislative battle over these bonds. [ADD RECENT MATERIAL.][49]

International Tax Matters. I worked with Lubick and his staff on a number of international tax matters. One area was that of the bilateral tax treaties entered into by the United States. As soon as the new Administration arrived I suggested to Lubick that two treaties negotiated by the prior administration and pending in the Senate—those with Egypt and Israel—be withdrawn for further study because they contained "tax sparing" provisions, along with other defects.[vv] This was done, the treaties renegotiated and finally ratified in 1981.[ww, 50] During the course of Lubick's tenure I also periodically discussed with David Rosenbloom,[51] the International Tax Counsel, issues that were arising under the new treaties that he was negotiating.

An important development under Lubick was an effort to write detailed Regulations governing the rules applicable to taxpayer use of the foreign tax credit—a credit against the U.S. tax on foreign source income for the income taxes paid to foreign countries. This simple statement of the provision masks many complex, subtle problems as to what is "income" and what is "a tax" on income. Unfortunately, the Regulations appeared to increase both the complexity and the subtlety. They made it necessary for taxpayers to ask for rulings on what everyone would concede were "income taxes"—the national tax of Canada, France, Germany, etc. Also running a new tax through the many tests under the Regulations was a complex task, as I found in trying to track the new Chinese income tax through the many rules, sometimes apparently conflicting, sometimes uncertain, that were included in the Regulations.[xx] Another main problem under these Regulations was the treatment of special taxes on oil, usually in the Middle East countries. These taxes are at a high rate and under the Proposed Regulations would not have been regarded as creditable income taxes but rather as payment for a special economic benefit, such as the extraction of oil. In going over these Regulations with Lubick I thought he should adopt suggestions being made that the oil tax be split into a creditable portion and a non-creditable portion. The former could, in general, be measured by matching the regular corporate

49. In 1984 Congress extended the mortgage subsidy bond provision through 1987. Deficit Reduction Act of 1984, Pub. L. No. 98-369, §611, 98 Stat. 494, 901. Renamed ("mortgage revenue bonds"), renumbered (IRC §143), and modified in various ways, the provision remains in the Code today.

50. Surrey was correct in his note ww that the tax treaty with Israel had not come into effect as of his writing of his memoirs. The United States and Israel did not exchange instruments of ratification for their income tax treaty until 1994.

51. H. David Rosenbloom served as Treasury's international tax counsel from 1978 to 1981. He is currently a member of the Washington tax law firm of Caplin & Drysdale, as well as director of the international tax program of New York University Law School.

income tax in the country. I believe Lubick agreed in principle but thought this approach required legislation. In any event, because of objections similar to mine and specific difficulties raised by many who had an interest in this area, the Regulations were rewritten in the new Administration and reissued to permit the "dual capacity" treatment of the oil companies, and to moderate other rules, though because of the basic subject matter the new Regulations are still complicated.[52]

There were other international tax developments in this period, such as the Foreign Earned Income Tax Act of 1978 and the Foreign Investment in Real Property Tax Act of 1980.[53] The first measure dealt with the so-called "section 911" treatment of U.S. citizens living abroad, and partially exempted their foreign earnings from U.S. tax. Section 911 has had a checkered history, varying between early tax generosity to such persons and then restrictions on that generosity. Usually the treatment involved an exclusion from U.S. income tax of a specific amount of the earnings and this amount jumped around, becoming lower in the 1960's and 1970's. The 1976 Act would have sharply reduced the amount to $15,000, but objections to this low amount postponed its application. The Foreign Earned Income Tax Act of 1978 revised the formula of exemption of a fixed amount by substituting a series of specific deductions, such as for housing costs, excess living costs, annual home loans, and education of children, but also contained a $20,000 special hardship deduction for location in a "camp," the last item designed to aid construction workers in the Middle East. The U.S. construction companies operating in that area were by no means satisfied with these rules, claiming they made it more difficult to compete with Korean and other companies. This sympathy was not for the employee and his taxes, but rather for the companies since their employment contracts required the companies to absorb U.S. taxes on the foreign earnings of the employees. As a result the 1978 Act did not last for long and was replaced in 1981 by a specific exemption for all foreign earned income up to $95,000, plus a deduction for certain housing costs.[54] As a result of the 1981 legislation, a rational innovation of the Lubick period in the treatment of section 911 became only history.

A more successful legislative venture was the Foreign Investment in Real Property Tax Act of 1980. The venture started with complaints from farmers that foreigners were buying farm land in the United States and then on sale not paying a capital gains tax due to the structure of our tax laws and treaties. With the Congress apparently willing to do something for the farmers, though the complaints as to the overall amount of the purchases may have been exaggerated, Lubick decided to enlarge the project to cover all real property in the United States owned by foreigners. The Con-

52. The Carter administration issued a notice of proposed rulemaking in 1979 (44 Fed. Reg. 36071 (Jun. 20, 1979)), and temporary and proposed regulations in 1980 (45 Fed. Reg. 75647, 75695 (Nov. 17, 1980)). The Reagan administration promulgated final regulations in 1983 (Treas. Dec. 7918, 48 Fed. Reg. 46272 (Oct. 12, 1983)).

53. Foreign Earned Income Act of 1978, Pub. L. No. 95-615, 92 Stat. 3098; Foreign Investment in Real Property Tax Act of 1980, Pub. L. No. 96-499, 94 Stat. 2682.

54. Economic Recovery Tax Act of 1981, Pub. L. No. 97-34, § 111-115, 95 Stat. 172, 190.

gress followed this approach, ending in very complicated legislation. The complications are due to the various forms under which foreigners can own the property, e.g., individually, through a U.S. partnership or corporation, through a foreign entity or combinations of the above. The Congress did reject Lubick's suggestion that withholding of tax by the seller be a method of aiding compliance and relied instead on information returns.[yy] But this legislation was a plus item for Lubick.

Administrative Matters. An important administrative project that received considerable attention in this period was the writing of Regulations dealing with "fringe benefits" received by employees from their employers. Some of these benefits—health insurance, board and lodging on the business premises, legal services, and others—were by statute excluded from an employee's income. But the status of many other benefits—employee discounts, free tuition for children of university faculty members, free athletic facilities, free trips for airline, railroad and bus lines, and many more benefits—depended on court decisions and administrative regulations and rulings. The administration in this area was confused because of an unevenness in the approach of the various IRS offices. In order to provide centralized guidance, the Treasury attempted in 1975 to promulgate Regulations governing the tax treatment of these benefits.[55] However, these Regulations were generally regarded as unsatisfactory and were withdrawn in 1976. The problems persisted as the National Office of IRS was required to respond to particular issues on taxpayer requests for private rulings and District Offices requests for technical advice. At this point Congress intervened through legislation commencing in 1978 and through various extensions of the time limit forbade the Treasury from issuing Regulations until 1984.[56] While this prohibition was in effect, Lubick and Commissioner Kurtz decided to indicate, before they left government, through a Discussion Draft what rules the Treasury would have adopted in Regulations if free to do so. This Draft, announced in January 1981, on which I did considerable work, was a careful application of the principles that should cover the treatment of fringe benefits.[57] Through rules and examples most of the fringe benefits were specifically covered.[zz] The treatment on the whole was to favor taxation of most fringe benefits, since that had been the IRS position and also the position of the courts when cases happened to reach them. But Congress extended the prohibition against Regulations and in 1983 the matter was still stalemated.[58]

---

55. 40 Fed. Reg. 41118.

56. Act of October 7, 1978, Pub. L. No. 95-427, 92 Stat. 996; Act of October 7, 1978, Pub. L. No. 95-427, 92 Stat. 996; Act of December 29, 1979, Pub. L. No. 96-167, 93 Stat. 1275; Economic Recovery Tax Act of 1981, Pub. L. No. 97-34, § 801, 95 Stat. 172, 349.

57. *Miller Sends Rostenkowski Discussion Draft of Regulations on Taxation of Fringe Benefits*, 12 Tax Notes 172 (1981) (noting that the draft was *not* being published in the *Federal Register*).

58. Congress finally brought order to this area in July of 1984 (a month before Surrey's death), by enacting a provision excluding "miscellaneous fringe benefits" from income. Deficit Reduction Act of 1984, Pub. L. No. 98-369, § 531(a), 98 Stat. 494, 877 (codified at IRC § 132). For the most part the statutory exclusions confirmed the de facto exclusions that had developed over the decades.

Another administrative matter in which I was involved was as a member for a year — 1977 — of the Commissioner's Advisory Committee.[59] This Committee is composed of tax lawyers, accountants and executives, chosen annually by the Commissioner. The Committee meets about three (?) times a year on an agenda organized by the Commissioner and his staff, though items can be added at the request of a Committee member. Generally the Commissioner is seeking this outside advice on matters pending at top levels in the IRS. The Committee members, though coming with a varied background, usually were able to give a consensus view that was of help to the Commissioner, or at least to provide him with a foretaste of the reactions he would face in carrying out the new steps he was considering. One matter that particularly interested me related to the activities of the House Ways and Means Subcommittee on Oversight of the IRS. The Counsel for that Subcommittee, Pamela Pecarich,[60] an able person, spoke at one of our meetings on the work schedule being planned for the coming year, involving hearings on various IRS activities. It seemed to me to be unproductive for the Subcommittee to plan its hearings without a sensible coordination with the IRS. I therefore urged Pam to arrange a schedule after talking with the Commissioner. Thus, the Commissioner could suggest matters on which he thought a Subcommittee hearing would be helpful in airing the problems involved. Also, the Commission could, as to a matter Pam was planning to pursue, tell her the IRS had itself understood a change was necessary and was taking the necessary action, so that a hearing would be unproductive and merely take time and effort that could be spent on other matters. Also, the Commissioner could fully cooperate with Pam on the organization of a Hearing to make sure that it would have a focus and the persons called to testify would be helpful to both the Commissioner and the Subcommittee. Pam and Kurtz readily agreed, and this approach proved to be helpful to both.

Tax Expenditures. During this period several matters arose involving tax expenditures. I have mentioned above the adverse results that followed from the White House penchant for using the tax system for solutions to energy problems. Another significant issue arose from so-called "Sunset" legislation in the Congress. This proposed legislation would require the direct programs of the Government to be reviewed periodically under a prescribed schedule by the Committees having jurisdiction over the programs. An obvious issue was whether tax expenditures would be covered under this "Sunset" approach as well as direct programs. The needed inclusion of tax expenditures was clear to the Treasury and me, and we worked together to urge their inclusion through Treasury testimony and discussions with the Committees

---

59. The Commissioner's Advisory Group was established in 1953; in 1998 its name was changed to the Internal Revenue Service Advisory Council. IRSAC, *Mission and Composition*, https://www.irs.gov/tax-professionals/internal-revenue-service-advisory-council-irsac.

60. Pamela J. Pecarich has held several government positions, including chief policy analyst for the Ways and Means Committee; she has also been director of tax policy for the accounting firm of Coopers & Lybrand.

having jurisdiction over the legislation, and with other Congressmen and their staffs. The stakes were high, with both representatives of business and the two Tax Committees forcefully opposed to our position. My guess is that in the end we would have prevailed and that in some way, perhaps under a compromise approach, Sunset would extend to the tax expenditures. But Sunset itself disappeared as an issue, partly because its mechanical problems made the approach unwieldly and partly because one of the chief proponents, Senator Muskie, left to be Secretary of State.[61] So this aspect of tax expenditures did not come to a final decision.[aaa, 62]

There was obvious merit, however, in working toward a combined consideration of direct programs and tax expenditures. I therefore urged Lubick to interest OMB in an approach under which, when OMB was considering the direct programs and budget for a Department, OMB would extend its consideration to those tax expenditures involving that Department. Lubick was in full agreement and undertook to persuade OMB to initiate this dual consideration gradually over a period of time. He made progress with OMB, reaching an understanding that tax expenditures be included in any Sunset legislation and that in principle tax expenditures should be included in the overall budget for an agency. Also, that combined studies of the kind I had suggested would be made, with housing and energy presenting good starting material.[bbb] Later in 1979 and 1980 a start was made with housing, with Treasury, HUD and OMB working together to look at the entire government aid to housing. But apparently this approach and any specific studies were not pursued by the new Administration in 1981 [Check].

The topics discussed above represent a curtailed description of the events in the period I was a consultant. There were other significant matters: the Bankruptcy Tax Act of 1980; legislative disputes on the definition of "independent contractors" not subject to wage and salary withholding; tuition tax credits, defeated in 1978 after considerable legislative activity marked by the Department of Education strongly pushing a direct program of aid to students; the rise and fall of the Administration suggestion of a wage insurance credit as a part of its price-wage program; a revised procedure to audit tax-exempt schools to see if they should lose their exemption because of their activities involving segregation, an IRS program that led to Congressional blocking of the issuance of any revised procedure;[63] increasing IRS activity to

61. Edmund S. Muskie (D. Maine) served in the Senate from 1959 to 1980, and as Secretary of State from 1980 to 1981. R.W. Apple, *Edmund S. Muskie, 81, Dies; Maine Senator and a Power on the National Scene*, New York Times, Mar. 27, 1996, at D21.

62. Unfortunately, there is no known draft of Surrey's planned Chapter Eleven on tax expenditures, to which he refers in his note aaa.

63. This culminated in the Supreme Court's opinion in Bob Jones University v. United States, 461 U.S. 574 (1983), in which the Court ruled that racially discriminatory private schools did not qualify for tax exempt status. The Court reached the merits of the case despite the fact that the Reagan administration, reversing the government's long-standing position, agreed with Bob Jones University that the IRS lacked authority to issue the revenue ruling on which the revocation of exempt status had been based.

combat the use of tax shelters, a high priority item of the Commissioner; preparation of a program for 1981 for President Carter's budget; and on and on.

The work load of an Assistant Secretary for Tax Policy and his staff is heavy, day-by-day. It helps that official in bearing the load if the path is marked by successes, at least by successes outweighing defeats. But the tax history of the Carter Administration was one mainly of frustration and struggle. The Treasury was losing control of tax matters to the White House, the White House was losing control to the Congress, which in turn was losing its control to business lobbyists.[ccc] The difference between my earlier years as an Assistant Secretary and the years as a Consultant to an Assistant Secretary was marked. Writing in 1979 I said:

> The present period thus seems, as far as tax reformers are concerned, a time to regroup and prepare for the swing in public sentiment that it is hoped will occur. It is unfortunately also a time for considerable defensive activity:
>
> —to ward off the diversions of the consumption tax advocates and the corporate integrationists;
>
> —to try to slow down the rush to Congress of every private interest group that does not like a Treasury regulation or ruling, a rush that Congress so far has not shown sufficient strength to resist;
>
> —to keep the slogans of "capital formation", jobs, and "inflation" from fueling further destructive inroads in the tax system;
>
> —to ward off the efforts to solve all our problems through tax credits.
>
> But the necessary defensive tasks should not be permitted to occupy all of the Treasury's energies. There is a need to gather the data and undertake the studies required to support future tax reform efforts when the time for those efforts arrives. The data and studies must also be presented in a more articulate, more attention-getting manner. Thus the annual Treasury reports on the low taxes paid by many individuals with large economic incomes are almost the equivalent of dry economic studies. Instead, they should in a graphic manner really tell the Congress and the public of the serious tax escapes that do exist. The use of specific illustrations—individual A with this high income and little tax, family B with a quarter or perhaps half billion dollars of wealth and no estate tax for several generations, corporation C with huge profits but little or no tax—must be utilized to have the needed impact. Names are not required, the letter designation will do, but the point must be made that the illustrations are real.
>
> The central goal to create support for tax reform is to raise the legislative stakes much higher. It is far too easy for a legislator today to cast a vote against a tax reform proposal. Often his State or District is not even aware of the vote. Many a constituent would be startled at learning that legislators with liberal reputations are casting vote after vote in favor of special tax preferences and against reform. While part of the national press is doing a better job of informing the public, most of the local press is not focusing on the

day-to-day voting patterns of the legislators that add up to constant defeat of tax reform proposals and victories for new tax preferences.

Perhaps public financing of Congressional campaigns will help to raise the stakes. Perhaps a reaction to the heightening lobbying of business groups will also help. In the end, however, an articulate Administration must make the public aware of what is at stake. The President and the Treasury must press the issue as hard as they can and utilize the type of tactics now reserved for Panama Canal matters. Also, an Administration must stand up for its positions and not surrender to lobbying or its own hasty calculations on political tactics. When this approach is taken and the stakes raised higher, a vote against tax reform will no longer be an easy vote in Congress. Tax reformers must then be prepared with plans and data to take advantage of that opportunity.[ddd]

The hope for a better tax system that lay behind those words was not to be realized. The Reagan Administration that followed favored an ill-structured and inequitable program of tax rate-reduction and increased tax depreciation generosity, to be followed by tax preference after tax preference added by a Congress that completely surrendered to the lobbyists. The result was one of the worst revenue measures in tax history—the Revenue Act of 1981.[64]

But by then I was no longer a Treasury or White House Consultant and had passed once more into the ranks of the opposition.

Notes

a. *E.g.*, Robert L. Turner, *Carter Opposed on Mortgage Tax Plan*, Boston Globe, February 26, 1976, at 17; Editorial, *Homeowners and Taxes*, BOSTON GLOBE, February 28, 1976, at 8.

b. Some subjects were: Tax Shelters, Tax Credits for Higher Education, Integration of the Federal Individual and Corporate Income Taxes, Revenue Sharing, Tax Legislation in the U.S. Senate, Federal Tax Reform and the House Ways and Means Committee, Fiscal Policy, Tax Treatment of the Family, Inflation and the Income Tax, and so on.

c. For a history of Woodworth's career up to this point and his possible 1976 plans, see Surrey, *Tribute to Dr. Laurence N. Woodworth: Two Decades of Federal Tax History Viewed from This Perspective* in Laurence N. Woodworth, Memorial Symposium, 32 NAT. TAX J. 227 (1979). Some material in this chapter is taken from that article.

d. *See* Lee Hanson & Michael S. Kaufman, *The National Energy Tax Act of 1978: Taxation Without Rationalization*, 3 HARV. ENV. L. REV.187(1979), for a description of the formulation of the 1977 energy program, based upon interviews with Washington officials. The following from footnote 62 of the article is interesting: "[C}onversations with the Schlesinger group revealed that at the highest levels, Treasury officials were much less concerned with the administrative burden the tax credit would impose than with the appropriateness and the wisdom of the amount of the tax expenditure contemplated. Further Assistant Secretary Laurence Woodworth, who died in 1977 before the Energy Tax Act was passed, was perhaps the one Treasury official most intimately involved with the drafting

---

64. Surrey was so disdainful of the 1981 legislation that he declined to refer to it by its official name, the Economic Recovery Tax Act of 1981.

process. Members of the group stated that while he was critical of the proposed residential energy credit because of its size and scope, he did not oppose the choice of a tax credit on theoretical grounds."

e. The Business Roundtable in July 1977 submitted its proposals for tax reform—which to them meant measures to increase "capital formation" and not to improve equity—and these proposals show distinct ambivalence on the integration issue.

f. See Charles E. McLure, Jr. Must Corporate Income be Taxed Twice? (Brookings Institution, 1979).

g. Surrey, *Reflections on the Revenue Act of 1978 and Future Tax Policy*, 13 Georgia Law Review 687 (1979). Some material in this chapter is taken from this article.

h. *E.g.*, Art Pine, *Trimmed Tax Plan is Urged*, THE WASHINGTON POST, Nov. 15, 1977, at D8; Art Pine, *Tax Proposals Retreat from Tough Talk: Carter's Tax Package May Have Few Reforms*, THE WASHINGTON POST, Nov. 17, 1977, at E10; NAT. J. Nov. 19, 1977, at 1804; BNA DAILY TAX REPORT FOR EXECUTIVES, Nov. 14, 1977, at 10.

i. Lubick was later promoted to the Assistant Secretary. When Secretary Blumenthal called me as to whether this should be done, I strongly supported Lubick. In addition to his ability, I could not see anyone else with his background and familiarity with the program being developed.

j. *The President's 1978 Tax Reduction and Reform Proposals, Hearings Before the Comm. on Ways and Means*, 95th Cong., 2nd Sess., Part 1, 3–27, 160–486 (1978).

k. Statement of Senator Edward M. Kennedy on the President's 1978 Tax Reform Program, January 21, 1978. [A portion of Kennedy's statement included in Surrey's typescript is omitted here.]

l. John Pierson, *Carter Tax Plan, with $24.5 Billion Cuts, Seen Facing Major Overhaul by Congress*, WALL STREET JOURNAL, Jan. 23, 1978, at 3.

m. *Tax Position of House Panel Chief Spells Rough Sailing for Some Carter Proposals*, WALL STREET JOURNAL, Jan. 19, 1978, at 2.

n. Hearings, *supra* note j, Parts 1 through 9.

o. Citizens For Tax Reform in 1978, Inc., membership list as of May 23, 1978.

p. Edward Cowan, *Carter is Warned Tax Bill He Wants Won't be Enacted*, NEW YORK TIMES, Apr. 21, 1978, at A1.

q. Edward Cowan, *President and House Democrats Discuss Tax Cut Without Reform*, NEW YORK TIMES, Apr. 22, 1978, at 1.

r. Elizabeth Drew, *A Reporter at Large: Charlie*, THE NEW YORKER, Jan. 9, 1978, at 32; also, at 124 CONG. REC. 1133 (1978). Walker's own description of the capital gain campaign is in Charls E. Walker & Mark Bloomfield, *How the Capital Gain Tax Fight Was Won*, THE WHARTON MAGAZINE, Winter 1979, at 34.

s. In fact, the 49% rate required an unusual combination of high earned income and high capital gains. The Treasury data showed:

> The average effective tax rate on capital gains in 1976 was 15.9 percent.... For most Americans with capital gains, the effective rate is quite low; for instance, 12.7 percent for those between $20,000 and $30,000 in adjusted gross income, 16.7 percent for those between $30,000 and $50,000. Up to $200,000 a year, the effective rate is below 25 percent. Even for those over $200,000 the average effective rate is only 27.4 percent....
>
> In the current debate, much has been made of the possibility—under the maximum and minimum tax provisions enacted in 1969 and 1976—that individuals may be paying a 50 percent tax or even more on their capital gains. The facts are much less alarming than the rhetoric. Capital gain, at all income levels, is still very much a preference item in our tax system.
>
> More than 60 percent of all capital gains is taxed at 25 percent or less. Of all returns showing capital gains, only about 7 percent is taxed above 25 percent. Though in theory

> the tax rate could exceed 50 percent, this would require a very implausible composition of income, and in fact we have been unable to find even one case where this has happened. We have found fewer than 20 returns — out of 5.4 million returns with capital gains — taxed at more than 45 percent. The capital gains tax very rarely goes above 40 percent. Rates over 40 percent have appeared in less than five hundredths of one percent of returns with capital gains, involving less than four-tenths of one percent of gains.

Statement of Treasury Secretary Blumenthal, in Hearings on Capital Gains Tax Bills, before the Senate Finance Subcommittee on Taxation and Debt Management Generally, 95th Cong, 2d Sess. 118–119 (1978).

t. Woodworth, and also some veteran congressional tax reform personnel, strongly believed that Congress would accept, through minimum tax changes, indirect increases in the capital gains rate as it had in 1976, although they recognized it would not accept a direct increase. They therefore did not expect the minimum tax proposal to trigger any "capital gain response" and thought they could go to that well once more. This was but the first of the Administration's misjudgments of the capital gain issue.

u. The complaint was accompanied by the argument that the lawyers should not be deprived of the 50 percent maximum tax on earned income, a rate they defended as proper, because they also had unrelated capital gains. But the preference offset for the maximum tax can be justified on the ground that a taxpayer who otherwise would have to pay 70 percent rate on earned income is not entitled to relief from the 70 percent rate if the rest of his tax return shows benefits from tax preferences so that his overall effective rate would be lowered.

v. The Act contained complicated "minimum tax" provisions, both the "add-on" tax of present law and an "alternative tax" focusing on a taxpayer with capital gain amounts and large personal deductions which otherwise would offset those gains, and requiring at least some tax payment in this situation.

w. Senator Kennedy recommended a veto, Release of October 18, 1978.

x. When the President did say — firmly — that he would not accept a tuition tax credit and would not accept the large reductions in taxes for future years contained in the Senate bill, the Congress did not present him with those items.

y. Of course, business had to decide whether to trade-off the capital gains reduction against the further reduction in the corporate rate proposed by the President, 45 percent and then 44 percent in 1980, compared with 46 percent in the bill, since the capital gains reduction used up so much of the available revenue loss. When the representatives of large business swung behind the capital gains reduction were the executives thinking of their own pocketbooks, in view of their large holdings of corporate stock (see *People and Taxes*, November 1978, at 4) or were they saying that capital gains reduction is obtainable now and further corporate rate reduction obtainable next time around? Many representatives of large businesses were probably not as interested in the capital gains issue as were the representatives of medium and small businesses and would, instead, have preferred more reduction at the corporate level. But they did not want to be considered renegades by the other business groups and hence backed the capital gains reductions.

z. There is of course a concern regarding inflation. But those who pressed the argument that inflation meant unfair taxation of capital gains did not point out to the Congress that since the capital gains of those above $50,000 and $100,000 were largely real and not inflation-induced gains, the device of a 70 percent or 60 percent exclusion was not the proper response. This failure clearly played a role in the Senate legislative debate, since the testimony could be referred to but its real meaning remained obscured.

aa. Martin Feldstein, *The Tax Revolt and Future Tax Legislation*, in Data Resources, U.S. Rev., December 1978, at 19.

bb. Some observers felt that Bobby Shapiro, Woodworth's successor as Chief of Staff, did not have the authority that Woodworth had in that position. Though his heart was in tax reform, as Larry before him, this was his first appearance as Chief of Staff and he moved cautiously. He was not inclined to "educate" the Committee members as did Woodworth, but stuck more with an "on the one hand, on the other hand" approach without emphasizing subtly as did Woodworth which arguments were more important and relevant and at least led to a compromise. *See A Tax Committee Loses Its Clout*, BUSINESS WEEK, May 7, 1978, at 86.

cc. Remarks of Senator Edward M. Kennedy, Time, Inc., Conference on Taxation, Madison Hotel, Washington, D.C., September 13, 1978 (release of that date). He also made a floor statement in the Senate debate stressing the need for tax reforms, 124 Cong. Rec. 33074–33076 (1978).

dd. Lubick, whose cheerfulness and equanimity survived the 1978 events, in a memorandum evaluated the 1978 performance.

OVERALL EVALUATION IN TERMS OF ORIGINAL TAX PROGRAM GOALS

(HARVARD LAW SCHOOL GRADING SYSTEM)

Revenue loss for 1979 and later years	75
Proper balance of cuts between individuals and businesses	63
Equitable distribution of individual cuts	61*
Incentives for business investment	67
Structural tax reforms for equity	54
Structural tax reforms for simplification	59

* On the capital gains essay question, the grade was 57 for distribution (organization) and 54 for equity (substance).

The energy bill also ended in defeat for Carter's proposal and instead was a bill written in the Congress, especially the Senate Finance Committee.

ee. With 36 members as of 1979 of the Ways and Means Committee, it is difficult for central staff—or the Treasury to have time to acquaint members individually with the background of the various tax issues. The business groups, however, are sufficiently organized to reach all the members.

ff. Obviously, much more can be said about the present legislative process for the consideration of tax, or other, matters. The subject was discussed in a May 1979 Symposium of the National Tax Association-Tax Institute of America on *Federal Tax Policy and the Tax Legislation Process*, 32 NAT. TAX J. (September 1979).

gg. For a description of the history and provisions of the 1981 and 1982 Acts, *see* Robert S. McIntyre and Dean C. Tipps, Inequity and Decline (Center on Budget and Policy Priorities [1983]. *See also* Surrey, Current United States Tax Policy, Skattepolitisk Oversig (4 June 1983, the Alf Ross Memorial Lecture, Copenhagen, Denmark).

hh. The legislation finally emerged as the Crude Oil Windfall Profits Tax Act of 1979, Pub. L. No. 96-223, 94 Stat. 229. It contained a number of special tax credits, such as for coke ovens, intercity buses, production of alternative energy sources, increase in credit for solar, wind and geothermal equipment, certain ocean thermal equipment, and others. The wood stove and solar houses facing south were not accepted by the House Ways and Means Committee.

ii. Stanley S. Surrey, *Government Assistance: The Choice Between Direct Programs and Tax Expenditures*, 8 TAX NOTES 507 (1979).

jj. TAX REVISION COMPENDIUM: COMPENDIUM OF PAPERS ON BROADENING THE TAX BASE, HOUSE COMMITTEE ON WAYS AND MEANS, Vol. 2, 1231 (1959).

kk. Hearings on Nominations Before the Senate Finance Committee, 87th Cong., 1st Sess. (1961) 26.

ll. Message of the President of the United States, January 24, 1963 in Hearings on President's 1963 Tax Messages, House Ways and Means Committee, 89th Cong., 1st Sess. (1963) 24, 128, 365.

mm. The recommendation to tax these unrealized gains was renewed in the Treasury Department's Tax Reform Studies and Proposals, Joint Publication, House Ways and Means Committee, 91st Cong., 1st Sess. (February 5, 1969, original date December 31, 1968), at 28. The matter was not considered in the 1969 Act based on those Studies.

nn. *See* Stanley S. Surrey, Reflections on the Tax Reform Act of 1976, 25 CLEV. ST. L. REV. 986 (1976).

oo. Hearings on Carryover Basis Provisions, House Ways and Means Committee, 96th Cong., 1st Sess. (November 12, 1979) 5, 19. For example, cost $960, value at death $1,029,137 (stock); cost $271,892, value $12,448,135 (business property); cost $755,244, value $21,775,278 (stock).

pp. The history of the carryover provision and the position of the tax bar is discussed in detail in Howard J. Hoffman, *The Role of the Bar in the Tax Legislative Process*, 37 TAX L. REV. 411 (1982).

qq. Some of the principal organizations involved — American Bankers Association, American Bar Association, Section on Real Estate, Probate and Trusts (the Tax Section was also an effective lobbying group), and the American Farm Bureau in 1979 turned down Eizenstat's request that the matter be considered in a separate bill.

rr. Revenue and Expenditure Control Act of 1968, Pub. L. No. 90-364, § 107, 82 Stat. 251, 266 (the exception for "residential real property for family units" was codified at former IRC § 103(c)(4)(A)). In the bargaining in 1968 with a state that was involved in the formulation of the final provision, then Governor Rockefeller of New York asked for exemption both for housing bonds and manpower training bonds. The Congressmen involved said the Governor would have to choose one of the two and he chose the housing bonds.

ss. The Treasury generally states that about two-thirds of the revenue loss on tax-exempt bonds goes to the issuing authority in reduced interest rates compared with taxable bonds and the remaining one-third goes as tax benefits for the upper brackets.

tt. Hearings on Tax Treatment of Mortgage Subsidy Bonds, House Ways and Means Committee, 96th Cong., 1st Sess (1979).

uu. Mortgage Subsidy Bond Tax Act of 1980, Pub. L. No. 96-499, 94 Stat. 2660 (codified at former IRC § 103A).

vv. "Tax Sparing" is discussed in Chapter Five.

ww. The Israel Treaty had not as yet been ratified by Israel [Check].

xx. See Richard D. Pomp, Timothy A. Gelatt & Stanley S. Surrey, "The Evolving Tax System of the People's Republic of China," 16 Texas International Law Journal 11, 66 (1981).

yy. *See* Tax section, New York Bar Association, Proposed Amendments to the FIRPTA Reporting Provisions, 20 TAX NOTES 979 (1983).

zz. A House Ways and Means Committee Task Force on fringe benefits had in 1979 published a discussion draft bill and report which to a considerable extent was similar to the Treasury Discussion Draft, February 15, 1979.

aaa. There is more discussion of "Sunset" in Chapter Eleven on "Tax Expenditures."

bbb. I had given Lubick a memorandum on the point and a suggested list of initial topics for OMB Special Analyses covering direct programs and tax expenditures.

ccc. *See, e.g.*, Ann Crittenden, *Study Finds Corporations in Broader Political Role*, NEW YORK TIMES, May 31, 1979, at D4.

ddd. Surrey, *supra* note g, at 720–21.

Index